This timely and expertly organised compendium is a celebration of the growing understanding on the significance and diverse global practice of female entrepreneurship. An impressive range of contributions from top scholars confirms gender is integral to this understanding, provides valuable insights on strengthening the ecosystem to support women's entrepreneurship and takes into account new demographic contexts and the complexities of female enterprise.

—Anne de Bruin, Professor, Massey University, New Zealand

While the area of women's entrepreneurship is receiving an increased amount of attention over the past few years, the types of questions asked and the way in which answers are pursued has not yet led to a coherent sense of understanding. In *The Routledge Companion to Global Female Entrepreneurship*, Henry, Nelson and Lewis guide us through a collection of works that together provide the necessary bridge between gender theories and entrepreneurship, thereby inviting more of us into the discussion with potential impact for theory, practice and policy.

—Patricia Greene, Professor, Babson College, USA

THE ROUTLEDGE COMPANION TO GLOBAL FEMALE ENTREPRENEURSHIP

The literature in female entrepreneurship has witnessed significant development in the last 30 years, with the research emphasis shifting from purely descriptive explorations towards a clear effort to embed research within highly informed conceptual frameworks.

With contributions from leading and emerging researchers, *The Routledge Companion to Global Female Entrepreneurship* brings together the latest international research, concepts and thinking in the area. With a strong international dimension, this book will facilitate comparative discussion and analysis on all aspects of female entrepreneurship, including start-ups, socio-economic influences, entrepreneurial capital and minority entrepreneurship.

Reflecting the subject's growing importance for researchers, academics and policy makers as well as those involved in supporting women's entrepreneurship through training programmes, networks, consultancy or the provision of venture capital, *The Routledge Companion to Global Female Entrepreneurship* will be an invaluable reference resource.

Colette Henry is a Professor, and Head of School of Business & Humanities at Dundalk Institute of Technology, Ireland, and Editor of the *International Journal of Gender & Entrepreneurship* (IJGE).

Teresa Nelson is a Professor and Director of the Entrepreneurship Program at Simmons College, USA.

Kate V. Lewis is a Reader in Entrepreneurship and Gender Studies in the Department of Management and Sylvia Pankhurst Gender Research Centre at Manchester Metropolitan University, UK.

ROUTLEDGE COMPANIONS IN BUSINESS, MANAGEMENT AND ACCOUNTING

Routledge Companions in Business, Management and Accounting are prestige reference works providing an overview of a whole subject area or sub-discipline. These books survey the state of the discipline including emerging and cutting-edge areas. Providing a comprehensive, up to date, definitive work of reference, Routledge Companions can be cited as an authoritative source on the subject.

A key aspect of these Routledge Companions is their international scope and relevance. Edited by an array of highly regarded scholars, these volumes also benefit from teams of contributors that reflect an international range of perspectives.

Individually, Routledge Companions in Business, Management and Accounting provide an impactful one-stop-shop resource for each theme covered. Collectively, they represent a comprehensive learning and research resource for researchers, postgraduate students and practitioners.

THE ROUTLEDGE COMPANION TO GLOBAL FEMALE ENTREPRENEURSHIP

Edited by
Colette Henry, Teresa Nelson
and Kate V. Lewis

LONDON AND NEW YORK

First published 2017
by Routledge
2 Park Square, Milton Park, Abingdon, Oxon OX14 4RN

and by Routledge
605 Third Avenue, New York, NY 10017

First issued in paperback 2021

Routledge is an imprint of the Taylor & Francis Group, an informa business

British Library Cataloguing-in-Publication Data
A catalogue record for this book is available from the British Library

Library of Congress Cataloging-in-Publication Data
A catalog record for this book has been requested

Typeset in Bembo
by codeMantra

ISBN 13: 978−1−03−224223−1 (pbk)
ISBN 13: 978−1−138−01518−0 (hbk)

DOI: 10.4324/9781315794570

CONTENTS

Contents

LIST OF FIGURES

LIST OF TABLES

LIST OF CONTRIBUTORS

Helene Ahl Professor of Business Administration, School of Education and Communication, Jönköping University, Sweden.

Laurice Alexandre Associate Professor, CEDAG Paris Descartes University, Sorbonne Paris Cité, France.

Wassim J. Aloulou Assistant Professor, Department of Business Administration, College of Economics and Administrative Sciences, Al Imam Mohammad Ibn Saud Islamic University, Saudi Arabia.

Mary Barrett Professor of Management, School of Management, Operations and Marketing, University of Wollongong, Australia.

Karin Berglund Associate Professor in Business Administration and Centre Director of Stockholm School of Entrepreneurship, Stockholm Business School, Sweden.

Nesrine Bouguerra PhD Student, Department of Strategy and Organization, EMLYON Business School, France.

Candida G. Brush Professor of Entrepreneurship and Vice Provost of Global Entrepreneurial Leadership, Babson College, Wellesley, MA, USA.

Janice Byrne Assistant Professor, IESEG School of Management, Paris, France.

Kate Caldwell Postdoctoral Research Fellow, Department of Disability and Human Development, University of Illinois, Chicago, USA.

Stéphanie Chasserio Associate Professor, Department of Management, Law and Organization, SKEMA Business School, Lille, France.

Susan Coleman Professor of Finance, Barney School of Business, University of Hartford, West Hartford, Connecticut, USA.

Thomas Cooney Professor of Entrepreneurship, College of Business, Dublin Institute of Technology; Academic Director of the DIT Institute for Minority Entrepreneurship, Ireland.

Maria Cristina Díaz-García Associate Professor, Department of Business Administration, University of Castilla-La Mancha, Albacete, Spain.

Linda F. Edelman Professor of Management, Bentley University, Waltham, MA, USA.

Henry Etzkowitz Visiting Professor, Birkbeck, University of London, UK and President of the Triple Helix Association, USA.

Alain Fayolle Professor of Entrepreneurship and Director of the Entrepreneurship Research Centre, EM Lyon Business School, France.

Denis Foley Professor of Entrepreneurship, Faculty of Business, Government & Law, University of Canberra, Australia.

Lene Foss Professor of Entrepreneurship and Innovation, School of Business and Economics, UiT – The Arctic University of Norway, Tromsø, Norway.

Richard T. Harrison Professor of Entrepreneurship and Innovation, University of Edinburgh Business School, Edinburgh, UK.

Colette Henry Head of School of Business & Humanities, Dundalk Institute of Technology, Ireland, and Adjunct Professor of Entrepreneurship, UiT-The Arctic University of Norway.

Carin Holmquist Professor Emeritus, Department of Management and Organization, Stockholm School of Economics, Stockholm, Sweden.

Trevor Jones Professor, Centre for Research in Ethnic Minority Entrepreneurship (CREME), Birmingham Business School, University of Birmingham, Birmingham, UK.

Kate Kearins Deputy Dean and Professor of Management, Auckland University of Technology, Auckland, New Zealand.

Helen Lawton Smith Professor of Entrepreneurship and Principal Investigator 'Trigger' Project, Department of Management, Birkbeck, University of London, UK.

Claire Leitch Professor of Entrepreneurial Leadership and Head of Department of Management Learning and Leadership, Lancaster University, Lancaster, UK.

Kate V. Lewis Reader in Entrepreneurship and Gender Studies, Department of Management and Sylvia Gender Research Centre, Manchester Metropolitan University, Manchester, UK.

Patricia Lewis Reader in Management, Kent Business School, University of Kent, UK.

Maura McAdam Professor of Management, DCU Business School, Dublin City University, Dublin, Ireland.

Tatiana S. Manolova Associate Professor of Management, Bentley University, Waltham, MA, USA.

Susan Marlow Professor of Entrepreneurship, Haydn Green Institute, Nottingham University, UK.

Angela Martinez Dy Lecturer in Entrepreneurship, the Glendonbrook Institute for Enterprise Development, Loughborough University London, UK.

Viviana Meschitti Research Fellow, Department of Management, Birkbeck, University of London, UK.

Maria Minniti Professor of Entrepreneurship and Public Policy, Syracuse University, Syracuse, New York, USA.

Ken Moores AM School of Business, Bond University, Queensland, Australia.

Walid A. Nakara Assistant Professor of Entrepreneurship, Department of Management, Montpellier Business School, France.

Helle Neergaard Professor, iCARE, Department of Management, School of Business and Social Sciences, Aarhus University, Denmark.

Teresa Nelson Professor of Strategic Management and Entrepreneurship at Simmons College, Boston, USA.

Barbara J. Orser Professor in the Management of Growth Enterprises, University of Ottawa Telfer School of Management, Ottawa, Ontario, Canada.

Philippe Pailot Associate Professor, Department of Management, Law and Organization, SKEMA Business School, Lille, France.

Sarah Parker Harris Associate Professor and the Director of Graduate and Undergraduate Studies, Department of Disability and Human Development, University of Illinois, Chicago, USA.

Katarina Pettersson Associate Professor in Social and Economic Geography, Department of Urban and Rural Development, Swedish University of Agricultural Sciences, Uppsala, Sweden.

Corinne Poroli Associate Professor of Strategic Management and Entrepreneurship, SKEMA Business School, Lille, France.

Alexandra Poulovassilis Professor of Computer Science, Department of Computer Science and Information Systems, and Deputy Dean for Research Enhancement, Birkbeck, University of London, UK.

Monder Ram Professor and Director of the Centre for Research in Ethnic Minority Entrepreneurship (CREME), Birmingham Business School, University of Birmingham, Birmingham, UK.

Renaud Redien-Collot Professor of Entrepreneurship and Director of International Affairs, Novancia Business School, Paris, France.

Dorthe Refslund Christensen Associate Professor, Department of Aesthetics and Communication, School of Communication and Culture, Aarhus, Denmark.

Maija Renko Associate Professor of Entrepreneurship, University of Illinois, Chicago, USA.

Alicia Robb Senior Fellow, Ewing Marion Kauffman Foundation, University of California at Berkeley, Kansas City, Missouri, USA.

Katrin Schaefer PhD Candidate, Auckland University of Technology, Auckland, New Zealand.

Michael Stuetzer Professor of Economics and Quantitative Methods, DHBW Mannheim, Germany.

Elisabeth Sundin Professor Emeritus in Business Administration, Department of Management and Engineering, Linköping University, Sweden.

María Villares-Varela Lecturer in Sociology, Department of Sociology Social Policy and Criminology, University of Southampton, Southampton, UK.

John Watson Professor in Accounting and Finance, UWA Business School, The University of Western Australia, Crawley, Australia.

Roxanne Zolin Associate Professor, School of Management, QUT Business School, Queensland University of Technology, Brisbane, Australia.

INTRODUCTION

The context and practice of female entrepreneurship

Colette Henry, Teresa Nelson and Kate V. Lewis

Global female entrepreneurship is performed and researched in a variety of contexts that influence its scope, direction and application. The opportunity inherent in the creation of a volume such as this is the chance to bring together a purposive, yet diverse, attentive focus on the phenomenon in question. In so doing, the collective knowledge represented in the volume is a reflection of what we know now, as well as an insight into the potential development pathways for knowledge generation in the future. It is also a textual representation of the current landscape of enquiry with a variety of significant markers embedded within it. For example, contributions from leading scholars, indicators of current foci of interest, and samples that reflect diversity across many spectra, all acknowledge and reveal the significant role of context in relation to practice. In this introductory chapter, we consider some of these contexts and their implications for practice, research and training.

The theoretical context

When one considers a "female entrepreneur", given the existence of a social understanding of the term "entrepreneur", one can assume an embedded gender assumption that to be a "female" entrepreneur is a type of entrepreneur in contrast to something else, something more elemental, i.e. an entrepreneur. For example, we do not talk or write specifically about "male entrepreneurs". This segregation of the female positions what women are, and what they do, as entrepreneurs; it represents our understanding of gender as a positioning of women as "other" (de Beauvoir, 1953). Gender – that which we represent and embed in the word "female" – is then a theoretical construct to be distinguished from sex, which can be taken as a biological classification.

This context of gender has three important implications for work on female entrepreneurship. First, we believe, gender requires that work focusing on women entrepreneurs (academic, policy, business practice) needs to be framed within a gender-female appreciation, e.g. how does gender influence people in their practice, and how do we see, process, evaluate and categorize, entrepreneurial behaviour, policy, programs, capital access, education, training, etc. There are limited studies that identify demographic trends for some simple purpose. That women and men do not share relatively equal experiences of being and

1

doing entrepreneurship begs the questions: Why? And does it matter? Meta-synthesis studies of women and men (Zell, Krizan & Teeter, 2015) – a big-data approach that integrated a population of more than 2 million individuals – confirmed the average, absolute difference between males and females to be small. Yet, dramatic differences in work and life are everywhere when one considers the sex binary. Each of the chapters in this book has taken a particular approach to addressing these issues related to gender.

To develop a more robust articulation of gender as an embedded foundation of female entrepreneurship will require inter-disciplinary research that fully expresses gender theory. Gender as a theoretical domain lives in many intellectual fields, but primarily, in the western tradition, in the social sciences – notably philosophy, psychology and sociology – as well as in the humanities and media studies.

Both critical theory and social construction, and even some post-positivist metaphysical paradigms, conceptualize gender in relation to biological sex within research. Feminist theorists (e.g. Calás, Smircich & Bourne, 2009; Ely & Padavic, 2007; Ahl & Nelson, 2015; Ahl, 2006) have carried this work into management but usually without directly applying particular gender theories developed and discussed outside the business domain.

Research in female entrepreneurship has influenced, and continues to form interstices in, varied entrepreneurship research sub-domains around gender. As Jennings and Brush (2013, p. 679) note, "Perhaps the most fundamental contribution of women's entrepreneurship research lies in acknowledging and documenting that entrepreneurship is not a gender-neutral phenomenon. Rather, entrepreneurial activity occurs within – and is thus impacted by – systems of socially constructed and widely shared beliefs about the characteristics typically associated with women and men and the behaviours and roles deemed appropriate for members of each sex".

Second, if gender is developed in entrepreneurship in relation to women, then it implicitly regards men. We are at a particular historical moment in the West when traditional, patriarchal views of gender (those that advantage men over women in general) have been challenged by a gender-equality paradigm in political, economic, legal and other institutional spheres. Particularly in work situations, the norm continues to move to a gender equality conviction, though this standard is not met in practice. This has interesting implications for how gendered entrepreneurship is studied and described.

We believe it is time for the study of gender and entrepreneurship to expand beyond the study of women, and other "comparative types" to a study of entrepreneurship within a gender context and for researchers to use the gender lens as a consistent point of view, at least some of the time. Historical research and theoretical models could be examined for their relevance to entrepreneurs overall, and new models employing expanded views of male/female and masculinity/femininity, as well as a humanistic viewpoint (i.e. where gender identity is not particularly salient) can be used.

Third, while gender is not *always* salient, it is *often* salient. This has important and complex implications for entrepreneurship research. Sometimes it will make sense to study women/females given the importance of active gender stereotypes; sometimes it may make sense to study men/males. Sometimes other values will be more important.

The academic context

The academy has been impacted by the institutional forces for gender equality. Most teaching institutions and scholarship outlets (journals, books, conferences) are unlikely to endorse or include work that is deemed overtly sexist, though our institutions continue to reflect general societal trends of horizontal and vertical sex segregation. This, too, is a sign of the times in terms of change and transition.

Most entrepreneurship scholars, including those publishing on female entrepreneurship, have not studied gender. Individuals studying entrepreneurship generally may not see gender's relevance to their work. Others may want to integrate more gender ideas but do not know how to begin. This is relevant to scholarship on female entrepreneurship.

Practically, those of us who have explored the gender theory bridge can illuminate the path for others. We can more deeply embrace gender theory in relation to our research, developing arguments and empirical approaches that build cogent arguments around gender in an entrepreneurship context. Well-noted contemporary gender theorists who will give access to theories we consider of particular relevance to entrepreneurship include classics such as: Judith Butler (gender performativity, e.g., 1990), Cecelia Ridgeway (expectation states theory, e.g., 2011), Dorothy Smith (standpoint theory, e.g., 1987), Patricia Collins (black feminist thought, e.g., 2008), Carol Gilligan (psychological theory and women's development, e.g., 1977), Nancy Chodorow (feminist psychoanalysis, e.g., 1999), bell hooks (race, gender and class intersectionality, e.g., 2014), Sandra Bem (gender schema theory, e.g., 1994), and Lawrence Kohlberg (gender cognitive-developmental analysis, e.g., 2011).

The context of change: a world in transition

Another important context we want to explore in terms of female entrepreneurship research and practice relates to our unfolding world. Emerging global shifts across the social landscape related to demographic, economic, technological and social trends will influence how we practice, experience and study women's entrepreneurship.

The world will add .6 billion people by 2025 (to 8 billion), and those 65 years and older represent the fastest growing demographic, though there are regional global variations. For example, the population of Africa will double by 2025, as Europe declines; meanwhile the number of people in Nigeria will come to equal that of the U.S. (PWC, 2016). By 2030, the purchasing power of the "E7" emerging economies – China, India, Russia, Brazil, Mexico, Turkey and Indonesia - will exceed the "G7" – Canada, France, Germany, Italy, Japan, the United Kingdom, the United States (PWC, 2015) – and growth in consumption will rely on the "E7" plus the next emerging wave – Bangladesh, Colombia, Morocco, Nigeria, Peru, Philippines and Vietnam (i.e. the "F7").

The implications for research on female entrepreneurship are many, including the likely growth in the number of businesses and the scale of businesses outside the English-speaking world. There will be a need to teach and research international entrepreneurship from a truly global perspective. We need to start publishing in multiple languages. We need to crack open the topic of growth entrepreneurship beyond Europe and North America while we continue to investigate developmental entrepreneurship and the SME economy run by women worldwide. When are theories and empirical results of women's entrepreneurship developed historically relevant to this new landscape? For example, Ridgeway (2011) reports on findings that African American women do not suffer the same degree of cultural assumption of a secondary gender position as women of other races/ethnicities in the United States. Could this be true in other cultures as well? How does this change our assumptions about gender's influence?

Gender will play a role in industries, government infrastructure, access to capital and education related to entrepreneurship for women. The purchasing power of women is expected to continue to rise globally (EU, 2016), with women now controlling two-thirds of household budgets in the G7 (PWC, 2016). Combined with the rising trend of deeper links through technology in the relationship of companies and customer, women will have more say in what they buy and from whom they buy. This could influence women entrepreneurs if their gendered knowledge is put to use in their companies. Furthermore, women's strength in services, particularly in health care and related services, is a foothold for growth.

Digitization of work and the mobile economy will also likely help women entrepreneurs negotiate gendered household and family responsibilities by delivering more options and flexibility (U.S. Council of Foreign Relations, 2015). This could lead to more training and education for women, thus opening up the entrepreneurial path. Gendering of industries more broadly (tech, life sciences, infrastructure, etc.) will likely evidence trends in entrepreneurship related to women and men. Concerns and opportunities in sustainability, food security, urbanization and energy can be hypothesized to be amenable to a gender lens (EU, 2016).

Technological breakthroughs in digitization through social media, analytics, mobile and the cloud will become available through entrepreneurs with advanced education in STEM fields. While women have made great strides in higher-education degrees on the life sciences side of high technology, progress toward gender equality in educational attainment on the tech/computer side is still very low (NSF, 2016; Eurostat, 2016; Mitchell, 2011). This provides a focus for education, practice and research. How our digital world impacts lives will likely continue to develop with gendered components as consumers develop digital identities and companies integrate digital into their fundamental business designs.

The global context

This book considers various socio-political contexts within which entrepreneurship occurs, with studies from, for example, Saudi Arabia and Sweden, and contributing researchers from Spain, the UK, New Zealand and France. While we begin the global journey, there is much more to be done to study, analyse and synthesize the phenomenon, both historically and futuristically.

The influence of culture on the practice of female entrepreneurship is profound. We see this in the limits and incentives to female entrepreneurship as well as in relation to the institutional structuring of how, where and why venturing is carried out by women. Female entrepreneurship, when viewed as a process, encompasses pre-, active and growth stages of a venture. As such, entrepreneurship engages a woman's life, and those with whom she works, once or through multiple launches, which creates additional complexity for understanding. All levels of analysis – social, organizational, group and individual – are thus relevant.

As conceptualized by Ahl and Nelson (2015), the embedded assumptions that drive the infrastructure creating these limits and incentives have turned in "the West" to a primary vision of female entrepreneurship as a driver of economic growth through innovation and market reach. This discourse has evolved among multiple economic stakeholders including government and beyond (e.g., think tanks, legislative branches, capital providers, non-profit ecosystem members, etc.). The policy discourse of entrepreneurship has identified women as an "untapped resource" to enhance GDP, the fuel that keeps capitalism moving forward (Mitchell, 2011). This discourse runs counter to one of life fulfilment or social equality – or in terms of entrepreneurship most directly – livelihood creation, a priority much more in focus, for example, in India (International Center for Research on Women, 2013).

Beyond recommending more study of these policy implications, this cognitive structuring of the women's entrepreneurship phenomenon draws our attention to the ideas left behind. First, we note the relationship of female entrepreneurship to underlying social patterns around poverty, education, religious practice and health; the role of the female in the household and community, directed by gender norms, positions the entrepreneurship of women. For reference, an estimated 62 million girls globally are not in primary or secondary school, and gender parity is far from the norm in low-income countries and still not achieved in middle- and high-income countries as a group. Further, women are found disproportionately working in the informal sector, doing domestic work for no wage, and they contribute substantially, again unpaid, to family enterprises, including farms. Vertical patterns of industrial engagement place women, as a group, in social work – teaching, services, healthcare – and not in engineering, high technology and science business areas where education levels, profits and wages are higher (World Bank, 2016). Entrepreneurship also steers women in similar ways (Ahl & Nelson, 2015). Examined this way, the drives (by policy and other infrastructures) to "push" women into entrepreneurial practice come into question. Is this the best course? Is this the right track? And if so, for whom? (Ahl & Nelson, 2015; Parker, 2012; Beaver & Jennings, 2005; Kets de Vries, 1985). The nested relationships of female entrepreneurship, entrepreneurship and capitalism, as they play out across a global stage, present interesting and important questions of a philosophical and practical nature, some of which are raised and discussed in this book.

The chapters we have invited are divided into five parts, each representing key strategic themes within the field of female entrepreneurship: context, ecosystems, supports, identity and demography. Part 1 – *The context for female entrepreneurship* – lays the foundation for the subsequent sections and begins with a contribution from Anglea Martinez-Dy and Susan Marlow – *Women entrepreneurs and their ventures: complicating categories and contextualising gender.* Here, the authors offer an overview of critical arguments analysing the influence of gender upon women's propensity and performance in terms of creating and managing entrepreneurial ventures. The chapter evaluates contemporary gendered analyses of entrepreneurial activity advancing this debate when recognising the impact of context and intersectionality upon women's propensity for and experiences of entrepreneurship.

In Chapter 2 – *Experiences of women entrepreneurs in family firms* – Mary Barrett and Ken Moores review the literature on family firms' contribution to regional and national economies, especially their capacity to grow the next generation of entrepreneurs, including women entrepreneurs. The authors then examine 13 cases of women entrepreneurs drawn from various countries and industries (including some traditionally "male" industries). The women's experiences of leadership and entrepreneurship are analysed using three gender-neutral analytical tools: the four stages of learning to lead a family firm, the concept of a community of practice and the theory of women's roles in family firms. The analysis distils common and differing aspects of women entrepreneurs' experiences in family firms.

Kate Kearins and Katrin Schaefer's chapter – *Women, entrepreneurship and sustainability* – reviews the scant research around the nexus of women, entrepreneurship and sustainability. Types of entrepreneurship often associated with sustainability are discussed, namely social, environmental and sustainable entrepreneurship. The literature shows that women interested in entrepreneurial careers appear more inspired by social issues ahead of financial gain than their male counterparts. The integration of eco-feminist ideals is seen potentially to offer a response to the oppression of both women and the environment, and the advancement of nature centric principles in moving towards a greater embrace of sustainability-as-flourishing. An agenda for future research is offered, focusing less on financial performance and investigating more the broader economic, social, environmental and cultural outcomes of entrepreneurship.

In Chapter 4 - *Saudi women's entrepreneurial intentions: the social construction of norms and perceptions* – Renaud Redien-Collot, Laurice Alexandre and Wassim J. Aloulou explore how Saudis – specifically, women - may develop and articulate determinist and agentive approaches in relation to the gendered barriers and opportunities in entrepreneurial processes. As Saudi Arabia is a transitional economy, its population may experience an important set of societal changes that challenge traditional representations of entrepreneurship.

Part 1 concludes with a chapter on *Female academic entrepreneurship and commercialisation: reviewing the evidence and identifying the challenges* by Helen Lawton Smith, Henry Etzkowitz, Viviana Meschitti and Alex Poulovassilis. Here, the authors consider the propensity for women academics to become entrepreneurs and to commercialise their research in comparison to male academics. A review of the academic literature and published reports suggests that women constitute a very small proportion of academic entrepreneurs; this is especially the case in science, technology, engineering and mathematics (STEM) disciplines. The chapter draws on a number of studies to identify commercialisation patterns in the U.S. and Europe.

The contributions in Part 2 deal with *The ecosystem for female entrepreneurs,* and begin with Barbara J. Orser's chapter on *Strategies to redress entrepreneurship gender gaps in Canada.* The study presented in this chapter documents barriers in the development of gender-equality entrepreneurship policies. A case analysis of a national taskforce on women's entrepreneurship identified four barriers in the construction of gender-specific business support. Without advocacy, accountability for gender inclusiveness, clear messaging about construction of gender-appropriate interventions and the integration of women's entrepreneurship in ministries tasked with economic development, significant policy reform is unlikely. The study provides insight into the importance of advocacy and accountability in the development of gender-equality policies to support women's entrepreneurship.

The focus moves to the U.S. in Chapter 7 – *U.S. women entrepreneurs and their access to early-stage financing* – where Linda F. Edelman, Tatiana S. Manolova and Candida G. Brush compare male-led to female-led new ventures. The authors use a "readiness for funding" framework and draw from a proprietary database of 680 firms that over a four-year period sought angel investment from the members of a prominent angel investment group located outside of Boston, MA. Findings indicate that when it comes to angel financing, the gender of the entrepreneur is not critical. Insights from interviews with entrepreneurs provide a window into the entrepreneurial financing decisions.

The final two chapters in this section continue on the theme of finance, first in the context of women's high-growth firms in the U.S., and second in terms of the supply and demand of new venture funding. In Chapter 8 – *Financing high-growth women-owned firms in the United States: challenges, opportunities and implications for public policy* – Susan Coleman and Alicia Robb explore why so few women embark on a path of growth-oriented entrepreneurship. A variety of reasons have been put forth including industry selection; lack of self-confidence combined with a higher degree of risk aversion; lack of access to role models, mentors and networks; cultural and societal factors and the challenges associated with balancing work and family. Using data from the Kauffman Firm Survey, the chapter builds on the increasing number of studies that have examined access to capital as a possible impediment to the growth of women-owned firms.

In Chapter 9 – *Gender differences in new venture funding: supply-side discrimination or demand-side disinclination?* John Watson, Michael Stuetzer and Roxanne Zolin investigate two competing propositions relating to the provision of commercial loans to female-owned new ventures. That is, do banks actively discriminate against women? Or, are women more reluctant to access bank financing than men? The authors draw on data collected from a representative sample of 559 respondents who owned (or partly owned) young firms (less than four years old). Results suggest that female new venture owners are not actively discriminated against by the banking sector but, rather, make a conscious decision to limit their use of commercial loans so as to minimize the risks involved and the potential to lose control of their business.

The chapters in Part 3 focus on *Supporting female entrepreneurs* and begin with Chapter 10 by Walid A. Nakara, Nerine Bouguerra and Alain Fayolle – *Supporting and training female necessity entrepreneurs*. Here, the authors focus on the specific training needs of female necessity entrepreneurs and engage in theory building to explore the most appropriate design of support initiatives. Gathering and analysing data about necessity entrepreneurs in a developed country can help inform policy-makers, since many public policies and measures promoting entrepreneurship are taken up not just by opportunity-driven entrepreneurs, but also by necessity entrepreneurs. Consequently, the main objective of the chapter is to respond to the broad question of how to provide better support and training to female necessity entrepreneurs.

Chapter 11 – *Entrepreneurial role models: an integrated framework from a constructionist perspective*, by Maria Cristina Díaz-García and Janice Byrne – presents a conceptual framework of the dynamic interplay of identity development and role modelling from a social constructionist perspective. The authors synthesize the existing literature on role models, identity formation, gender and entrepreneurship and gender within organizations, providing an integrated way of looking at the gendered nature of role modelling in entrepreneurship. Two prominent approaches have been used to explain role modelling: social learning theories and role identification theories; the authors propose that symbolic interactionism can be used to synergize these two theoretical approaches and help further understanding.

In her chapter – *Female entrepreneurship, role models and network externalities in middle-income countries* – Maria Minniti suggests that sustainable entrepreneurial activity rests significantly with the individuals themselves. By observing and interacting with other individuals, human beings acquire information and skills. The larger the number of role models a person observes with respect to a specific activity, the lower the ambiguity associated to that activity and the higher its legitimacy. In other words, the presence of role models leads to the reinforcement of certain behaviours. However, role models of female entrepreneurs tend to be scarce in middle-income countries. Based on extant theory, Minniti argues that in those cases, personal networks may serve as an effective substitute for role models and, over time, lead organically to the emergence of the latter.

The final chapter in this section – *Revisiting research on gender in entrepreneurial networks*, by Lene Foss – analyses how hegemonic statements are developed and sustained in extant scholarship. Building on her previous analysis of the literature from 1980 to 2008, Foss demonstrates how the same patterns exist: women's networks are measured against men's and are considered less effective, more relationship-based, and consisting of fewer weak ties. Research asks the same question: whether female entrepreneurs differ from their male counterparts and use the same individualist methodological approaches? Foss concludes that future research needs to study the embeddedness of entrepreneurial networks using institutional approaches in order to develop new knowledge of how institutions intersect with entrepreneurship and have different consequences for female and male entrepreneurs' networking.

The chapters in Part 4 deal with the theme of *Identity*, and begin with Chapter 14 – *Identity work, swift trust and gender: the role of women-only leadership development programmes* – by Claire Leitch, Richard Harrison and Maura McAdam. Here, the authors explore the role of women-only leadership development programmes in shaping women entrepreneurial leaders' identity. Given the exploratory nature of their study, Leitch et al. adopt an interpretivist approach to gain understanding of the nuances of how identity is shaped, formed and maintained. Three themes emerge: first, identity and identity work are enacted as a gendered performance; second, leadership development is a specific type of identity work; and finally, enablers of the enactment of identity work included shared safe space, swift trust and self-reflection. The chapter provides insights into how entrepreneurial leadership identity is formed, shaped and maintained and thus advances gender theorising by exploring the role of gender in the design, delivery and impact of leadership development.

In Chapter 15 – *Postfeminism and entrepreneurship: exploring the identity of the mumpreneur* – Patricia Lewis develops the body of research that considers identity as an aspect of business ownership. She examines the emergence and representation of the "mumpreneur" as an entrepreneurial character, understood as a woman who runs a business from home alongside the active parenting of children and the management of a household. Through analysis of media representations of the "mumpreneur", the emergence and representation of this new entrepreneurial identity is explored. Interview data are analysed showing how women perform the new identity of the "mumpreneur" and how this is connected to a postfeminist reconfiguration of contemporary femininity. The analysis demonstrates how being a "mumpreneur" requires that women integrate the feminine ideals of motherhood with the masculine-marked practices of entrepreneurship and as such must occupy a multiplicitous subjectivity.

Female lifestyle entrepreneurs and their business models, by Helle Neergaard and Dorthe Refslund Christensen (Chapter 16), explores female entrepreneurs who have started a thriving business based on the ideals of personal growth and self-transformation. The authors draw on purposefully sampled cases representing successful female entrepreneurs who have become the "rave" in the past 10 to 15 years to demonstrate how these entrepreneurs take their own private disharmonies and turn them into viable businesses. In so doing, they also illustrate the interesting business models adopted by these entrepreneurs. The businesses studied by Neergaard and Christensen make a difference, not only in terms of economic benefit to their owners, but also by impacting socially on others by sharing their experiences. In the past, this particular group of entrepreneurs would have been labelled hobby or lifestyle entrepreneurs, with the term "life-style entrepreneurship" mostly used derogatively to denote businesses with no or poor growth potential. However, research shows that such ventures constitute a new generation of very successful businesses – those that are inspired by one's own lifestyle.

Tales of heroine entrepreneurs – Chapter 17 – by Karin Berglund, Helene Ahl and Katarina Pettersson relates the stories of three celebrated Swedish women entrepreneurs: Amelia Adamo, who built a magazine publishing empire; Anna Carrfors Bråkenhielms, who made history with the reality show "Survivor"; and Clara Lidström, who has made a living blogging about her life as a rural housewife. What they have in common is that they are all part of the media industry and each of their stories was broadcast on Swedish radio in the popular show "Summer". In the stories, they tell openly about their lives and their struggle to gain and defend equal rights for themselves and for other women. By adopting a narrative approach consisting of four readings, the authors analyse the stories and focus on what we can learn as a result of how entrepreneurship and gender are addressed. The chapter contributes to knowledge on how women, despite a male entrepreneurial norm, gain agency through their entrepreneuring and also how feminist rationales are part of their efforts.

Chapter 18 – *Perceived legitimacy of women entrepreneurs in France: between identity legitimacy and entrepreneurial legitimacy*, by Philippe Pailot, Corinne Poroli and Stéphanie Chasserio – concludes Part 4 and explores how women entrepreneurs see themselves as legitimate entrepreneurs ("identity legitimacy") and examines how they are perceived by their different stakeholders ("entrepreneurial legitimacy"). The authors use a qualitative research design based on grounded theory undertaken with 41 French women entrepreneurs operating in different sectors. Findings show how social interactions are strongly imbued with categorical gender judgments. In order to acquire legitimacy, women entrepreneurs must counter these judgments through the development and implementation of interesting strategies.

The final section in this book – Part 5 – focuses on the theme of *Demography*. In their chapter – *Women, disability and entrepreneurship* – Kate Caldwell, Sarah Parker Harris and Maija Renko survey the literature and policy on disability and entrepreneurship, with a focus on women entrepreneurs. In doing so, the authors bridge disability studies with entrepreneurship to provide foundational knowledge, understanding and insights into the state of the field. The chapter offers an overview of current debates, critiques and controversies surrounding entrepreneurship for people with disabilities. Issues covered include barriers and facilitators to labour market participation, and the extent to which this affects decisions to pursue entrepreneurship for people with disabilities; the intersection between disability and business as it relates to opportunity recognition, resources and support and the complexities concerning the effectiveness of entrepreneurship as a tool for empowerment. The chapter positions gender within the broader context of disability and business research.

In Chapter 20 – *Female immigrant global entrepreneurship: from invisibility to empowerment?* – Maria Villares-Varela, Monder Ram and Trevor Jones review key themes in debates on female immigrant entrepreneurship from a global perspective. The authors argue that the main theoretical approaches to immigrant entrepreneurship have overlooked the gendered social structures that constitute migrant entrepreneurial processes. Feminist scholarship has condemned the "gender-blindness" of the field of immigrant entrepreneurship and its failure to explore the implications of patriarchy in the ethnic economy. The chapter discusses (i) the invisibility of gender in the main theoretical approaches to explain ethnic or immigrant entrepreneurship; (ii) the evolution of the female immigrant entrepreneurship sub-field since the mid-'80s up to the present; (iii) how the role of women in the immigrant enterprise has been conceptualised; (iv) approaches to female immigrant entrepreneurship from the global South and (v) new directions for future research.

In *Entrepreneurial activity among Irish Traveller women: an insight into the complexity of survival* (Chapter 21), Thomas M. Cooney and Denis Foley fill a void on research into Irish Traveller women entrepreneurs and establish a foundation for future research. Their primary research methodology consists of face-to-face semi-structured interviews with 35 Traveller women entrepreneurs in Ireland in order to explore the lived-in and lived-through practice of entrepreneurship in the context of the Traveller women's identity and historical legacies. The chapter highlights how Traveller women entrepreneurs build strong maintenance of cultural (kinship) networks with the well-being and care of their families being their primary motivators. However, the lack of racial acceptance within the wider Irish community and the lack of access to start-up capital are critical inhibiting factors for them when starting and growing a business. The authors suggest the need for enhanced political and structural changes to ensure that there are adequate policies and cohesive approaches to capital networks, training and employment opportunities for Traveller women given the discrimination they experience as both Travellers and women.

Chapter 22 – *Entrepreneurship, age and gender: the Swedish case* by Carin Holmquist and Elisabeth Sundin – completes our collection of contributions in this book. Here, the authors argue that age is a dimension of considerable relevance to gender and entrepreneurship. Similar to gender, age is a key identity dimension in society. The chapter discusses how the importance of age varies over time, space and sectors. Sweden is used as an empirical illustration to demonstrate the connection of labour market, entrepreneurship and welfare regimes with regard to genderism and ageism. Data are analysed and compared with the international literature on age and entrepreneurship. Examples from an ongoing project on entrepreneurship and age are provided, from quantitative as well as qualitative studies. The chapter ends with some theoretical conclusions, including that age and entrepreneurship are gendered concepts, and that the age group "older" is not just one group, but a number of sub-groups with diverse characteristics, needs and ambitions.

As the variety of contributors, content and contexts in the book indicates, the field of scholarship oriented to gender and entrepreneurship continues to gain momentum, broaden in scope and diversify in intent. As the title of our edited collection suggests, it is truly global in every sense: for example, in terms of coverage, orientation and relevance. The challenge as the field evolves further, and solidifies its foundations into an even more developed state of maturity, is for those active within its boundaries to continue to push those borders forward both theoretically and empirically. As the chapters taken in their entirety suggest, there is both a willingness and capability to do so. This must be paralleled by scholars and research studies that seek not just to perpetuate individualised lines of enquiry, but attempt to coalesce and integrate what is known with what is not.

References

Ahl, H. (2006). Why research on women entrepreneurs needs new directions. *Entrepreneurship Theory and Practice, 30*(5), 595–621.

Ahl, H., & Nelson, T. (2015). How policy positions women entrepreneurs: A comparative analysis of state discourse in Sweden and the United States. *Journal of Business Venturing, 30*(2), 273–292.

Beaver, G., Jennings, P. (2005). Competitive advantage and entrepreneurial power: The dark side of entrepreneurship. *Journal of Small Business Enterprise & Development, 12*(1), 9–23.

Bem, S.L. (1994). *The Lenses of Gender: Transforming the Debate on Sexual Inequality.* New Haven: Yale University Press.

Butler, J. (1990). *Gender Trouble: Feminism and the Subversion of Identity.* New York: Routledge.

Calás, M.B., Smircich, L., & Bourne, K.A. (2009). Extending the boundaries: Reframing 'entrepreneurship as social change' through feminist perspectives. *Academy of Management Review, 34*(3), 552–569.

Chodorow, N. (1999). *The Reproduction of Mothering: Psychoanalysis and the Sociology of Gender, 2nd Edition.* Oakland, CA: University of California Press.

Collins, P.H. (2008). *Black Feminist Thought: Knowledge, Consciousness, and the Politics of Empowerment.* New York: Routledge.

de Beauvoir, S. (1953). *The Second Sex.* New York: Knopf.

Ely, R., & Padavic, I. (2007). A feminist analysis of organizational research on sex differences. *Academy of Management Review, 32*(4), 1121–1143.

EU (European Union). (2016). Assessment of Global Megatrends. Available 6/18/16 at: http://www.eea.europa.eu/themes/scenarios/global-megatends.

Eurostat. (2016). Tertiary Education Statistics. Available 6/18/16 at: http://ec.europa.eu/eurostat/statistics-explained/index.php/Tertiary_education_statistics.

Gilligan, C. (1977). *In a Different Voice: Psychological Theory and Women's Development.* Boston: Harvard University Press.

hooks, b. (2014). *Feminism Is for Everybody: Passionate Politics.* New York: Routledge.

International Center for Research on Women. (2013). *Addressing Comprehensive Needs of Adolescent Girls in India a Potential for Creating Livelihoods*, available 6/18/16 at: http://www.icrw.org/files/publications/Adolescent%20Girls_22ndmar13.pdf.

Jennings, J.E. and Brush, C.G. (2013). Research on women entrepreneurs: Challenges to (and from) the broader entrepreneurship literature. *The Academy of Management Annals*, 663–715.

Kets de Vries, M.F.R. (1985). The dark side of entrepreneurship. *Harvard Business Review, 63*(6), 60–67.

Kohlberg, L. (2011). *The Measurement of Moral Judgment*. Cambridge, UK: Cambridge University Press.

Mitchell, L. (2011). Overcoming the Gender Gap: Women Entrepreneurs as Economic Drivers. Available 6/18/16 at: http://www.kauffman.org/~/media/kauffman_org/research%20reports%20and%20covers/2011/09/growing_the_economy_women_entrepreneurs.pdf.

NSF (National Science Foundation). (2016). Women, Minorities and People with Disabilities in Science and Technology. Available 6/18/16 at: http://www.nsf.gov/statistics/2015/nsf15311/digest/theme2.cfm.

Parker, S.C. (2012). The costs of entrepreneurship. *International Journal of Entrepreneurial Venturing, 4*(4), 121–131.

PWC (PriceWaterhouseCoopers). (2016). Five Global Megatrends. Available 6/18/16 at: http://www.pwc.com/gx/en/issues/megatrends.html.

Ridgeway, C. (2011). *Framed by Gender: How Gender Inequality Persists in the Modern World*. Oxford: Oxford University Press.

Smith, D.E. (1987). *The Everyday World as Problematic: A Feminist Sociology*. Lebanon, NH: Northeastern University Press.

U.S. Council on Foreign Relations. (2015). Global Future Trends. Available 6/18/16 at: http://www.cfr.org/global-future-trends/global-future-trends/p33893.

World Bank (2016), available 6/18/16 at: http://www.worldbank.org/en/topic/gender/overview#1.

Zell, E., Krizan, Z., & Teeter, S.R. (2015). Evaluating gender similarities and differences using metasynthesis. *American Psychologist, 70*(1), 10–20.

PART I

The context for female entrepreneurship

1

WOMEN ENTREPRENEURS AND THEIR VENTURES

Complicating categories and contextualising gender

Angela Martinez Dy and Susan Marlow

Introduction

Within this chapter we offer an overview of critical arguments that analyse the influence of gender upon women's propensity and performance in terms of creating and managing entrepreneurial ventures. Whilst it is now recognised that gendered ascriptions critically influence the entrepreneurial activity of women, the literature has largely focused upon women as a homogeneous category to explain this thesis (Marlow, 2014). Developing a critical discourse exposing the inherent gender bias within the ontological foundations of entrepreneurship theory and practice has been essential to recognising how discriminatory assumptions fundamentally shape understandings of 'who or what' is an entrepreneur (Gartner, 1989). Such debate (Ahl and Marlow, 2012; Henry, Fosse and Ahl, 2015) has exposed the normative stereotype of the entrepreneur to be a white, middle-class, middle-aged male, which conceptually and empirically narrows understanding of entrepreneurship and entrepreneurial behaviour. Thus, the critical analysis of the influence of gender upon women's propensity for, and experiences of, business venturing has been of fundamental and far-reaching importance in challenging the prevailing axioms that have informed contemporary understanding of the phenomenon of entrepreneurship. In addition, this academic focus of enquiry has spilled over into policy debate and development worldwide. Encouraging more women to engage with business venturing is deemed highly desirable to address issues ranging from poverty alleviation in developing nations (Scott, Dolan, Johnston-Louis, Sugden and Wu, 2012), post-conflict empowerment (Tobias, Mair and Barbosa-Leiker, 2013), refugee poverty (Al Dajani and Marlow, 2010) unemployment and flexible working in developed economies (Jayawarna, Rouse and Kitching, 2013), and impediments to advancement faced by women in the corporate context (Patterson and Mavin, 2009; Weyer, 2007). Consequently, the analytical exposure of gendered bias within assumptions underpinning entrepreneurial activities has fuelled an academic debate that has grown in scope and complexity (Calás et al., 2007; Carter et al., 2015; De Bruin et al., 2007; Klyver et al., 2013; Marlow and McAdam, 2013; Mavin and Grandy, 2012) and also prompted a wide-scale policy response: for example, recent UK government initiatives to fund and support women entrepreneurs through mentoring programmes and facilitating access to broadband Internet (Government Equalities Office, 2014a and 2014b).

As such, this gender turn in entrepreneurship has challenged the existing paradigm of the normative entrepreneur, which is predicated upon traditional conceptions of masculinity. As this debate matures, however, new questions arise regarding a number of assumptions that have shaped its emergence and potentially limit its contribution. Accordingly, within the field of entrepreneurship, the construct of gender 'sticks' to women (Kelan, 2009: 460) whilst men, as ciphers of masculinity, are still assumed to be representative of the ideal entrepreneurial type. Thus, the signifier of the *female* entrepreneur creates a metonymy – a special category that captures and homogenises those who share just one aspect of their identity – that of their sex (Marlow, 2014). As Hogberg, Scholin, Ram and Jones (2014: 10) argue in their review of ethnic minority entrepreneurship, using narrow identity denominators 'encompasses the creation of etiquettes and labels that as soon as they are directed against an individual, makes the person synonymous with the category as well as with its associated values no matter how unique he or she may be'. Assuming gender only applies to women who, in turn, experience and reproduce gendered ascriptions as a universal group, has two detrimental effects – it reinforces the subordination of women within the gender binary whilst simultaneously homogenising them on the basis of an assumed shared biological identity. Accordingly, for debate to progress, such assumptions must be challenged.

Within this chapter we contribute to this debate by critically evaluating contemporary analyses of gender, women and entrepreneurship. In addition, we acknowledge the impact of context upon women as gendered entrepreneurial actors and, relatedly, explore notions of intersectionality and positionality, constructs drawn from black feminism that, by contextualising gender amongst other categories of difference, bring to light widespread heterogeneity and nuanced experiences of privilege and oppression within the generic category of 'woman'. In so doing, we challenge the generic homogenisation of women and indicate how diverse socially constructed ascriptions intersect to situate women in differing positions in the socio-economic strata, which in turn impacts upon their entrepreneurial activities. Drawing from such debates, we suggest future avenues for theoretical and empirical enquiry to advance understanding of the relationship among gender, women and entrepreneurship. To achieve these ambitions, the chapter is structured as follows: first, there is an overview of contemporary theorising regarding gender and entrepreneurship and how this influences women's venturing. This is followed by our second section, which further explores the notion of social context and how this influences the enactment of gender and women's entrepreneurial activity. The third section explores notions of intersectionality and positionality and concludes by considering the implications of these arguments for developing a future research agenda in the realm of female global entrepreneurship.

Contemporary overview – gender, women and entrepreneurship[1]

Theoretical trends

The association among gender, women, entrepreneurial propensity, new venture creation and business ownership has been recognised in mainstream theorising since the latter part of the twentieth century (Henry, Foss and Ahl, 2015). On one hand, it emerged in conjunction with an increased interest in entrepreneurial behaviour and activity as an individualised socio-economic approach reflecting the growth of contemporary neo-liberalism (du Gay, 2004; Goss, 2005; Jones and Spicer, 2009). On the other hand, it should be recognised that entrepreneurial women were not suddenly produced by this research 'gaze', which increasingly illuminated their experiences beginning in the late 1980s. On the contrary, women have been active entrepreneurs throughout history; for example, in the British context they dominated the brewing trade of the fourteenth century, were renowned speculators during the emergence of capital markets in the seventeenth century and have undertaken a critical role in family enterprises over history (Kay, 2012; Herbert and Link, 2012; Marlow and Swail, 2014). Thus, entrepreneurial women are not a new phenomenon; however, the manner in which gender influences and constrains such activities is of more recent interest for the reasons described above.

When reviewing this field, there has been a notable shift in the sophistication of prevailing debate as the emphasis has moved from *women* as deficient entrepreneurs to critical feminist analyses of the influence of gender upon perceptions and practices of entrepreneurship (Henry et al., 2015). As such, we can see change in the unit of analysis within extant research over time; so, prior to the mid-2000s, the overwhelming focus was almost exclusively upon an individual woman's experiences of business ownership, generally articulated as explorations of female entrepreneurship (see Mirchandani, 1999, and Marlow, 2002, as exceptions). As the unit of analysis within the debate was the woman herself, her perception of entrepreneurship as a career option and her approach to managing her business were of critical interest. The field of entrepreneurship – how it was represented, researched and interpreted – was tacitly presumed to be a neutral activity or, in other words, a meritocratic site of agentic activity available and accessible to all. The hegemonic masculinity of the phenomenon was rendered invisible (Ahl, 2006). In taking this ontological stance, structural issues such as gender-related disadvantages constraining access to entrepreneurial resources, labour market segmentation (channelling women towards lower-order service-sector start-ups) and domestic responsibilities (resulting in a greater propensity for part-time home-based firms) were confused with agentic deficiencies. This confusion was exacerbated by the tendency to use sex as a variable such that the entrepreneurial activities of men and women were compared across a range of performance indicators, with women inevitably positioned in deficit such that their enterprises were condemned as *smaller* than, *weaker* than, *lacking* growth orientation or pejoratively dismissed as home-based, part-time, or life-style businesses (Ahl, 2006; Ahl and Marlow, 2012; Marlow and McAdam, 2013). It is a maxim well observed that almost every detrimental business term has been visited upon the hapless female entrepreneur to explain her alleged deficiencies as a business owner/manager (Marlow, Carter and Shaw, 2009). To treat female entrepreneurs as deficient in this way was problematic as it confused sex (a biological category) with gender (a social construction that devalues femininity and, ergo, women) and reproduced gendered stereotypes when associating typical small-firm performance profiles (marginal, volatile and growth averse) with female deficiency.

The assumption that arose from this body of research, reflecting the epistemological presumption of female deficiency, was that women needed 'fixing'. As Taylor and Marlow (2009: 1) conclude, the underpinning subtext rests upon the notion of 'why can't a woman be more like a man?' and relatedly, 'what can be done to make this happen'. This liberal feminist agenda assumed a male template to which women should aspire, and this argument was replicated in emerging policy directives. Thus, reports such as that published by the United Kingdom Small Business Service (2003) advocated addressing female deficiencies such as risk aversion, lack of confidence and poor entrepreneurial orientation through dedicated support and advice to enable more women to create new ventures and so contribute to national and personal socio-economic growth. This debate encompassed almost an evangelical moral tone inciting women to develop an entrepreneurial spirit in order to exploit their potential and so create new ventures that in turn would generate employment and economic growth and offer a social welfare contribution to society (Small Business Service, 2003).

The prevailing focus upon the agentic essence of entrepreneurship was subject to increasing scrutiny in the early 2000s; thus, critical work by Ogbor (2000) and Ahl (2006) raised a number of challenges to orthodox theorising. Analysing institutional and discourse biases, each author drew attention to the socially constructed processual nature of entrepreneurship and in particular how this privileged certain subjects as idealised normative entrepreneurs. As such, Ogbor raised a broad critique of the entrepreneurial field and particularly the failure of prevailing literature to recognise the institutional biases embedded within the discourse in that ascribed characteristics such as race, class and gender inherently shape how entrepreneurship is accessed, understood and enacted. Ahl (2006) developed a post-structural feminist critique that questioned the alleged gender-neutrality of the entrepreneurial discourse. She argued that entrepreneurship is embedded in masculinity; the textual representation of the entrepreneur is inevitably male, which, in turn, positions women as outsiders or intruders to this field. However, as Ahl points out', much of the extant literature drawn from the 'gender as a variable' approach actually failed to find many significant differences between men and women firm owners. Yet, given embedded gendered assumptions, the quest for difference persisted (and persists) with small variations exaggerated to satisfy social expectations of male dominance and female deficit (see Kepler and Shane, 2007; Klapper and Parker, 2011).

A more theoretically informed debate has since emerged to challenge notions of entrepreneurship as a gender-neutral meritocracy and women as deficit actors (de Bruin et al., 2007; Calás et al., 2007; Marlow and Patton, 2005). This analytical shift to *gendering entrepreneurship* (Gherardi, 2015) rather than separating and categorising women as problematic entrepreneurs marked greater engagement with theoretical criticism rather than the previous focus upon descriptive comment. The theoretical debate and repository of empirical evidence pertaining to gender, women and entrepreneurship has clearly grown in terms of complexity and substance over a relatively short period of time (McAdam, 2012). We have moved from a focus upon the individual woman and her supposed entrepreneurial deficiencies with research defined by small samples and atheoretical description (Carter and Shaw, 2006) to more sophisticated analyses centred upon gender and how this generates broader socio-economic disadvantages for women – including entrepreneurial activity (Henry et al., 2015). In turn, this debate has been increasingly informed by feminist theory to analyse and explain how women fit into the contemporary entrepreneurial turn whilst challenging the ontological and epistemological assumptions underpinning entrepreneurship discourse (Ahl and Marlow, 2012).

However, denotations of gender remain a proxy for femininity (Kelan, 2009). As such, within the mainstream entrepreneurship field, only women are afforded a gender, which is used as a categorising device and until recently has positioned women in deficit (Marlow, 2014). Given the negative values associated with femininity, women are generically disadvantaged as gendered subject beings given that as humans we become visible and comprehensible through our ascribed gender (Butler, 1993). In addition, the epistemological privilege afforded to masculinity establishes what constitutes knowledge and who can be a legitimate 'knower' (Harding, 1986). Harding argues that the authorisation process is embedded in masculinity, as 'the voice of science is male, history is written from a male stance, [and] the subject of the authoritative sentence is assumed to be male' (1986: iv). Offering uncritical authorisation to a dominant form of knowledge generation and analysis decides what may be defined as normative (Harding, 1986; Allcoff and Potter, 1993; Kelan, 2009). This process of valorisation and subordination is largely hidden by assumptions of gender-neutral scientific enquiry, buttressed by logic and rationality. Only by rebalancing the current gender agenda to fully and separately acknowledge the assumptions fuelling masculinity as a default setting can we challenge these presumptions and, in so doing, analytically expose how both women and men 'do' gender and 'do' entrepreneurship.

The issue of causality has also been considered regarding to what extent gender as a variable can be effectively identified as a definitive influence upon entrepreneuring (Gill, 2011). This debate introduces notions of intersectionality and context, which serve to usefully complicate simplistic gender categories and so will be discussed in more detail later. Adopting such perspectives illustrates that previous work has been embedded in generic racist and heteronormative assumptions that uncritically position gender subordination as universal; moreover, it presumes the mature, developed, Western economy to be the normative entrepreneurial site (Bruton, Ahlstrom and Obloj, 2008; Imas, Wilson and Weston, 2012). Consequently, unless gender theorising within entrepreneurship adopts a critical feminist perspective, refutes universality and explores contextual influences, it is in danger of producing, at best, a blunt instrument that assumes that gender only applies to women and homogenises disadvantage, whilst at worst, in making such assumptions, reproducing the subordination it purports to critique.

Empirical evidence

In substantive terms, there exists an increasing evidence base describing women's entrepreneurial behaviour that, in turn, offers empirical illustration of theoretical arguments. Thus, based upon the Global Entrepreneurship Monitor (Kelley, Brush, Greene and Litovsky, 2013) we know that in almost every economy, women-owned firms are in a minority (Marlow, Hart, Levie and Shushal, 2013). Within developed Western economies, the 2008 global economic recession and related cuts to public sector spending have prompted a rise in women's business ownership (McKay, Cambell, Thompson and Ross, 2013). In the case of the United Kingdom, for example, the coalition government (2010–2015) has focused spending cuts on welfare benefits and lower-paid public sector employment redundancies disproportionately affecting women and so pushing increasing numbers into self-employment (ONS, 2014). Effectively, previous patterns of churn have been disrupted as those who would normally select back into employment from poorly performing self-employment or seek employment due to benefit cuts no longer have such options (ibid).

It has been suggested that the minority status of women as entrepreneurs reflects a lack of entrepreneurial orientation and competency (HM Treasury, 2008). Yet, a more nuanced analysis suggests that within developed economies this differential reflects the articulation of a range of gendered disadvantages (Marlow, 2002). So for example, women's lower participation in the labour market per se, labour market segmentation constraining the accrual of knowledge, resources and networks necessary for new venture creation, and a lower presence in sectors conducive to self-employment (for example, construction) combine to constrain women's entrepreneurial activity. Domestic responsibilities and related time constraints are additional limitations upon the development of viable ventures (see McAdam, 2012 for an overview). Similarly, such gendered constraints also act to channel sectoral choices and operating profiles; thus, women are over-represented in lower-order service sectors and as owners of home-based part-time ventures – characteristics that affect sustainability, growth and returns (Jayawarna et al., 2013). However, caution is required; whilst it may be accurate to describe women-owned firms as small, service-sector marginal operators, the majority of ventures operated by the self-employed and small firm owners reflect this profile. Very few firm owners desire to grow their firms and indeed, very few do so (Anyadike-Danes, Hart and Du, 2015). Women are, however, under-represented in growth-oriented sectors; at the same time, negative gendered stereotypes militate against the accrual of the resources necessary for growth should this be sought (Carter, Ram, Jones, Trehan... 2015). The propensity for constrained performance profiles should not, however, be confused with female deficit. Analyses by Robb and Watson (2012) indicate that when sector and resources are matched, there are no significant performance differentials that can be attributed to the sex of the owner, whilst Saridakis, Marlow and Storey (2014) find women to be as motivated by economic returns from venture ownership as their male counterparts. Thus, in this analysis, gendered ascriptions disadvantage women – but biological sex is not the source of such deficit.

Turning to developing economies, we have less evidence regarding the experience of women entrepreneurs. Given the greater scarcity of formal employment and higher incidences of patriarchal cultures constraining education, access to employment and domestic responsibilities, there are higher levels of self-employment amongst women (Kelley et al., 2013). However, their ventures – reflecting the normative profile in such contexts – are likely to be on a micro scale, extremely vulnerable and volatile (Scott et al., 2012); they are disproportionately concentrated in low value-added sectors, particularly agriculture, catering and small-scale market trading. For example, recent political volatility in the Middle East and related geographical movement of refugees has also prompted more women to turn to self-employment as traditional family forms are disrupted and men find it difficult to attain employment (Al Dajani and Marlow, 2010). Simultaneously, in wealthier nations, such as the UAE, entrepreneurship is increasingly encouraged as an economic activity for educated women who are prevented by patriarchal cultural norms from entering mainstream employment (Danish and Lawton-Smith, 2012). There is some evidence that more women are entering self-employment in transitional economies (Welter and Smallbone, 2008), but again, they are concentrated in traditional feminised sectors and struggle to negotiate patriarchal and overtly corrupt local bureaucracies given their lack of status and resources.

Thus, we know that on a global scale, more women are entering self-employment as a result of both push and pull factors. It is also evident that gendered influences critically influence their entrepreneurial experiences regardless of context, but the socio-economic and cultural-political environment will critically shape women's entrepreneurial propensity and experience. It is to this issue, context, we now turn to explore in a little more detail.

Context

As Wright (2012: 8) notes, 'although context has received relatively little attention in the entrepreneurial literature, studying entrepreneurs in the context which they find themselves is central to understanding the entrepreneurial process'. As such, we cannot view entrepreneurial activities as separated from context; reflecting work by Welter (2011) and Wright (2012) there are four broad dimensions of context:

- Spatial – place, location, geography
- Institutional – rules, regulations, policies, status of entrepreneurial activity
- Social – culture, norms, media representation, networks
- Time – attitudes to entrepreneurial activity, life cycle of the firm.

To this list we would also add:

- Finance – availability of formal and informal funding to finance new and growth-oriented ventures.
- Economic – market volatility and competition.

This list captures both substantive and tacit environmental influences that shape social attitudes towards entrepreneurs, such as whether they are good or bad for society, physical aspects such as the availability of affordable premises and economic issues such as funding and market viability. Drawing upon the discussion above regarding developed, developing and transitional economies, quite clearly these aspects will differ sharply in terms of their influence and so in turn will constrain or enable entrepreneurial activity. Thus, as Bruton et al. (2008) have pointed out, presuming the advanced Western economy to be the natural template or idealised context for entrepreneurship is a myopic view; this approach excludes the majority of the global population whilst encouraging a narrowed and patronising attitude. In many ways, just as ignoring the influence of gender upon entrepreneurship ensured an ontological and epistemological bias, so does a US/UK/developed economy contextual bias. Thus, acknowledging and accommodating contextual factors is essential to advance debate; in terms of how context shapes the influence of gender upon entrepreneurship, this relationship remains under-researched. This is problematic in terms of theoretical advancement and empirical activity as it assumes a universal construction of gender experienced by a homogeneous population of women, and this, in turn, prompts normative conceptual frameworks to analyse diverse entrepreneurial experiences. In addition, existing contextual issues, such as those noted above, rarely acknowledge whether gender is a discrete contextual influence in and of itself or the extent to which these broad contextual aspects should be considered through a gendered lens.

In exploring this debate, Brush, de Bruin and Welter (2009) recognise that how women engage with their context is gendered. Thus, in addition to key contextual aspects such as market, money and management – the three M framework – they suggest this should be extended to include motherhood and meso/macro environment, resulting in a five M framework. By so doing, they acknowledge that gender positions women in different spaces and places in the broader socio-economic context that will critically impact upon their entrepreneurial propensity and experiences. As such, any identification and analysis of context is always already biased if it in fact presumes that entrepreneurship *is* a gender-neutral activity. There is a growing body of literature that explores household dynamics in terms of how women access time, space and resources to create and manage new firms (Jayawarna et al., 2013); this offers insight into notions of how household context and gender intersect to facilitate or constrain women's self-employment. This relationship requires greater exploration and acknowledgement. So, for example, Klyver, Neilson and Evald (2013) focus upon the strong collective welfare context in Sweden, which offers very good quality public sector employment for women with opportunities for flexible working, childcare breaks et cetera, arguing that in such a context it is counter-intuitive for women to select into uncertain self-employment. Clearly, some will – but far fewer than in neo-liberal or developing economies – where such employment opportunities are less available.

Developing this theme, Al Dajani and Marlow (2013) focus upon the entrepreneurial activities of displaced Palestinian women creating home-based enterprises in Amman, Jordan. One very particular gendered aspect of context in this instance is the patriarchal culture that dominates; this restricts women's freedom of movement and socio-economic participation.

This aspect, combined with the displaced status of their families and communities positions women in very specific circumstances – experiencing poverty and few opportunities for economic engagement. Exploiting traditional craft skills, however, enables them to produce heritage goods within the home that are then sold to intermediary contractors. This entrepreneurial process, shaped and constrained as it is by economic, social and cultural contextual influences, has nevertheless enabled women to generate independent incomes and gain increased status within their communities. Quite evidently, civil war, displacement and wide-scale social fragmentation such as is occurring in countries such as Syria and Iraq is generating considerable numbers of refugees for whom self-employment is the only available option. Thus, exploring new contextual influences reflecting volatility, poverty and status is essential.

From these very brief vignettes, we argue that the influence of context requires greater recognition and exploration. It is critical to understand how entrepreneurial activity unfolds per se (Zahra, Wright and Abdelgawad, 2014) but less recognised is how gendered influences are embedded within context, which in turn produces and reproduces gendered assumptions and stereotypes. Recognising and exploring this issue is essential to moving beyond notions of gender as universal and women as homogeneous. To develop this theme, we now explore notions of intersectionality and positionality.

Intersectionality and positionality

Intersectionality is a theoretical paradigm, originating in black feminism, that has refined monolithic conceptions of gender and come to be accepted as a cornerstone of contemporary feminist scholarship (Hancock, 2007; Kelan, 2014). It theorises the interplay of social categories of difference, such as race/ethnicity, gender, class and socio-economic status, as they relate to social hierarchies, and analyses their impacts upon lived experience. The theory was developed to highlight the experiences of people at particular neglected intersections of categories (originally, black American women) as unique and yet unaccounted for in either mainstream feminism or critical race studies (Crenshaw, 1989; McCall, 2005). Crucially, these early accounts of intersectionality posited the categories of race, gender and class as co-constructed and central to accounts of the social (e.g. Combahee River Collective, 1977; Hill Collins, 1990/2000). The paradigm has now been expanded and analytically applied to a variety of additional categories of difference, including sexual orientation, disability, body size, age and geographic location, implemented across a number of disciplines (Bowleg, 2008; Kelan, 2014; Oleksy, 2011). It is today generally regarded as a foundational feminist concept used in both academic and popular discourse to theorise and explain oppression on multiple bases, heterogeneity within groups of women and variability across populations.

With regard to entrepreneurship, intersectionality has been used to study various combinations of intersections, such as race, class and gender (Harvey, 2005), gender, ethnicity and religion (Essers and Benschop, 2009; Essers, Benschop, and Dooreward, 2010), and gender, ethnicity, national origin and national context (Verduijn and Essers, 2013). In a similar manner to early intersectional work, these scholars point out that separate analyses of, for instance, women's entrepreneurship and immigrant/ethnic minority entrepreneurship, fail to highlight significant phenomena that are the result of intersectional issues, such as the unique challenges experienced by immigrant Muslim women entrepreneurs in the Netherlands (Essers et al., 2010). Thus, they introduce an intersectional perspective to investigations of entrepreneurial activity in order to bring these issues to light, while also illustrating the ways in which the politics of entrepreneurship are simultaneously affected by considerations of both gender and ethnicity.

Although early debates on marginality tended to attempt to prioritise the effects of one category over others, or utilise an additive approach that assumed step-wise increases in inequality with each additional stigmatised identity (see Anthias, 2008; Bowleg, 2008), contemporary intersectionality has returned to its roots, explicitly conceiving of exclusionary categories, and the social inequalities they precipitate, as interdependent and mutually constitutive (Bowleg, 2008), such that "classes are always gendered and racialised and gender is always classed and racialised and so on" (Anthias, 2008: 13). As the processes of their co-production are complex, it is commonly acknowledged that the effects of the categories may be mutually reinforcing or contradicting (Acker, 2006: 442; Anthias, 2013).

This leads us to the following predominant set of critiques of the intersectional approach, which, despite its popularity, has been the subject of significant debate across the disciplines in which it has been applied (Davis, 2008). Scholars have pointed out that a key limitation of intersectionality is that it has overwhelmingly been used to theorise experiences of oppression and structural constraints, to the detriment of an analysis of privilege and agency (Geerts and van der Tuin, 2013; Nash, 2008). This is despite the fact that, as discussed, the effects of various aspects of social belonging could lead to nuanced experiences of privilege and disadvantage that differ from context to context, rather than simply multiplying or amplifying oppression in every case. Another significant limitation arises from the challenges inherent in operationalising such a complex construct, which has resulted in a lack of methodological consensus (Bowleg, 2008; Martinez Dy, Martin and Marlow, 2014; McCall, 2005) as well as the concern of some scholars that extending the concept to include ever-growing numbers of categories of difference could possibly draw attention away from the 'most salient' differences (see Davis, 2008) or prevent general analytical claims from being made.

In response to such valid concerns, the concept of translocational positionality as developed by Anthias (2001a, 2001b, 2006, 2007, 2008) may be a means by which to take the concept of intersectionality beyond the methodological challenges it currently presents. Anthias argues that intersectionality is a 'social process related to practices and arrangements' that gives rise to particular forms of positionality (2006: 27). The construct of positionality is two-fold: it combines social position, as outcome, with social positioning, a processual set of practices, actions and meanings (2001b: 634). It is conceptualised as comprising the space at the intersection of structure and agency (2001a: 635). Importantly, positionality is said to be translocational, or, in other words, 'in terms of locations which are not fixed but are context, meaning and time related and which therefore involve shifts and contradiction' (2008: 5). As such, it moves away from the idea of given groups or categories and towards broader social locations and processes (2008), of which the most salient for a particular investigation can be brought to the analytical fore. Thus, it addresses and rectifies some of the most prominent conceptual limitations of intersectionality, namely its tendency to lend itself to conceptions of categorical belonging as fixed, a general inattention to agency and privilege, and the challenges of attempting to consider the impacts of all possible categories of difference.

A further strength of the positionality construct is its explicit linkages to resource allocation, which has obvious benefits for the study of entrepreneurship. The body of work by Anthias elaborates upon the notion of social hierarchies from which intersectionality emerged, noting that social positions are characterised first by a hierarchical 'pecking order' and second, by unequal resource allocation. Resources are here conceived of broadly to include both tangible and intangible resources, among them economic, political, symbolic and cultural; thus, resource allocation includes the unequal allocation of power, authority and legitimacy, which are then naturalised and made to seem invisible (2001a: 635). Whilst entrepreneurship scholarship generally acknowledges the heterogeneity of resources to be highly relevant to entrepreneurial activity, it focuses primarily on differences in belief about the value of resources (Schumpeter, 1934; Kirzner, 1979; Shane and Venkataraman, 2000, as cited by Alvarez and Busenitz, 2001: 756) rather than unequal distribution of, and access to, the resources themselves. Hence, in a number of relevant ways, positionality directly answers the calls for context made by contemporary entrepreneurship scholars. It can be used to articulate how particular spatial, social, economic, political and cultural conditions affect individuals and groups within and outside of certain social positions and boundaries in different ways. With the understanding of social hierarchies and the unequal resource distribution it advances, it can be used to coherently explain such phenomena as why women entrepreneurs are perpetually seen in deficit as compared to men, whilst also complicating universal notions of gender that have too frequently been generic and prescriptive.

The notions of intersectionality and positionality reveal important differences across the social ascriptions and lived experiences of people who are generally considered to belong to a wider categorical group, as well as highlight those people whose experiences are marginalised within a group itself. In addition to their widespread application, the theories are continually being critiqued, developed, and expanded, for example, to include the notion of privilege (Nash, 2008; Martinez Dy et al., 2014). For the study of entrepreneurship, this opens up a number of interesting research possibilities, such as exploring how the privilege conveyed by normative identities can function as an entrepreneurial resource. The question thus arises: can intersectionality be used for critical gender investigations of men and male subjects? In a sense, by virtue of its focus on women as marginalised subjects, it is already used to critique the unearned privilege that men receive in patriarchal societies. However, it has predominantly been used for explicit analysis of women's experiences and not frequently for those of men, although it has informed some investigations of black men (e.g. doyal, 2009; hooks, 2004). The concepts are also arguably broad enough to transcend binary conceptions of gender and can therefore be used as such to explain the experiences of not only women and men, but also transgendered, genderqueer and non-binary individuals from a variety of demographic backgrounds. What seems essential to using intersectionality and positionality in a way that preserves their roots is that their use must be politicised; in other words, that intersecting social hierarchies and the power dynamics implicit to them must be taken into account. Although not necessarily limited to analyses of marginalised subjects, an intersectional or positional analysis implies an inherent awareness of issues of social hierarchy, marginality and inequality, as well as an intention to challenge and rectify those inequalities. Thus, as black feminist theoretical tools, they should be regarded as non-neutral, historically embedded as they are in a politics of liberation and an intellectual tradition based upon the principles of social justice.

Thus, interesting research questions abound when adopting an intersectional or positional approach as a means by which to address the notion of context in entrepreneurship studies. Aspects of intersectionality could be used to frame variability in entrepreneurial activity and experiences among groups of women, or the particular social conditions and challenges faced by women facing particular obstacles to employment and/or self-employment as a result of their marginalised positionalities (e.g. transgender identity, lower socio-economic status, disability, etc.). Conversely, including an awareness of privilege as well as disadvantage enables the exploration of questions regarding whether women from certain social positions are able (or not) to mobilise certain resources, such as, for example, labour market privilege (Jayawarna et al., 2013) when they enter into entrepreneurship. Translocational positionality could be used to explore immigrant or transnational entrepreneurship (Drori, Honig and Wright, 2009), as well as the entrepreneurship of refugee women as outlined above. It may also be useful in the development of alternative contextual frameworks with which to analyse the entrepreneurial activity of the most marginalised, for whom Imas, Wilson and Weston (2012) explain that traditional conceptions of entrepreneurship and the entrepreneur simply do not apply. From these limited examples, it is clear that intersectional and positional perspectives are able to contextualise and give conceptual shape to the variety of social conditions in which entrepreneurial activity is embedded, thereby intervening in and advancing existing theories of entrepreneurial context and offering significant explanatory power.

Conclusions

This chapter has critically evaluated the existing academic literature on women, gender and entrepreneurship. It has highlighted how, although women have long been engaged in entrepreneurial activity, their efforts were not recognised in mainstream theorising until the growth of contemporary neo-liberalism and its attendant individualised approach to promoting social and economic progress interpellated them into entrepreneurial discourse. Whilst early debates focused on women as deficient entrepreneurs in comparison to men, critical feminist analyses have moved the conversation to the influence of gender upon entrepreneurial practices and how they are perceived by individuals and wider societies. In particular, women are found to encounter structural obstacles to entrepreneurship as a result of their feminine gender ascription, due to its systemic effects upon gender role expectations as well as upon access to material, cultural and political resources. This is complicated further by women's wider social positionalities in intersecting hierarchies of race, ethnicity and class or socio-economic status, as well as other characteristics and positions, such as sexual orientation, disability and geographic location, that result in nuanced and complex experiences of marginality as well as, in some cases, privilege. Additionally, attention has been called to the ways in which the concept of gender should not be limited to analyses of women, as the social meaning it carries has significant implications for the lives of men as well as those who transverse or defy the gender binary. This theoretical development of the relationship between gender and entrepreneurship complements the recent contextual turn of the field, in which spatial, temporal, institutional, social and economic concerns are acknowledged as not only relevant, but essential to understanding the nature of entrepreneurial activity in its wide variety of forms. Taken together, a contextual approach with a well-developed critical understanding of the effects of gender can help to advance an ambitious but necessary future research agenda that strives to accurately represent and comprehend the diversity of experiences of entrepreneurial women around the world.

Note

1 A longer version of the arguments presented in this section can be found in Marlow (2014).

References

Acker, J. (2006) Inequality Regimes: Gender, Class, and Race in Organizations, *Gender & Society*, 20(4): 441–464.

Ahl, H. (2006), Why Research on Women Entrepreneurs Needs New Directions, *Entrepreneurship Theory and Practice*, 30(5): 595–623.

Ahl, H. and Marlow, S. (2012) Gender and Entrepreneurship Research: Employing Feminist Theory to Escape the Dead End, *Organization*, 19(5): 543–562.

Al Dajani, H. and Marlow, S. (2010), The Impact of Women's Home Based Enterprise on Marriage Dynamics: Evidence from Jordan, *International Small Business Journal*, 28(5): 360–378.

Al Dajani, H. and Marlow, S. (2013) Empowerment and Entrepreneurship: A Theoretical Framework, *International Journal of Entrepreneurial Behaviour & Research*, 19(5): 503–524.

Allcoff, L. and Potter, E. (1993) *Feminist Epistemologies*. New York: Routledge.

Alvarez, S. and Busenitz, L. (2001) The Entrepreneurship of Resource-Based Theory, *Journal of Management*, 27(6): 755–775.

Anthias, F. (2001a) New Hybridities, Old Concepts: The Limits of 'Culture', *Ethnic and Racial Studies*, 24(4): 619–641.

Anthias, F. (2001b) The Material and the Symbolic in Theorizing Social Stratification: Issues of Gender, Ethnicity and Class, *British Journal of Sociology*, 52(3): 367–390.

Anthias, F. (2006) Belongings in a Globalising and Unequal World: Rethinking Translocations. In N. Yuval-Davis, K. Kannabiran, and U. Vieten. *The Situated Politics of Belonging*. London: Sage.

Anthias, F. (2007) Ethnic Ties: Social Capital and the Question of Mobilisability, *The Sociological Review*, 55(4): 788–805.

Anthias, F. (2008) Thinking through the Lens of Translocational Positionality: An Intersectionality Frame for Understanding Identity and Belonging, *Translocations: Migration and Social Change*, 4(1): 5–20. [online] http://www.dcu.ie/imrstr/volume_4_issue_1/Vol_4_Issue_1_Floya_Anthias.pdf [Accessed 19 Jan 2013].

Anthias, F. (2013) Hierarchies of Social Location, Class and Intersectionality: Towards A Translocational Frame, *International Sociology*, 28(1): 121–137.

Anyadike-Danes, M., Hart, M. and Du, J. (2015) Firm Dynamics and Job Creation in the United Kingdom: 1998–2013, *International Small Business Journal*, 33(1): 26–40.

Bowleg, L. (2008) When Black + Lesbian + Woman ≠ Black Lesbian Woman: The Methodological Challenges of Qualitative and Quantitative Intersectionality Research, *Sex Roles*, 59(5–6): 312–325.

Bruton, G.D., Ahlstrom, D. and Obloj, K. (2008) Entrepreneurship in Emerging Economies: What Are We Today and Where Should the Research Go in the Future, *Entrepreneurship Theory and Practice*, January (2008): pp. 1–15.

Butler, J. (1993). *Bodies that Matter: On the Discursive Limits of Sex*. New York: Routledge.

Calás, M., Smircich, L. and Bourne, K. (2007) Knowing Lisa? Feminist Analyses of 'Gender and Entrepreneurship'. In: Eds D. Bilimoria and S. K. Piderit. *Handbook on Women in Business and Management*. Cheltenham: Edward Elgar, pp. 78–105.

Carter, S., Ram, M., Trehan, K. and Jones, T. (2015) Barriers to Ethnic Minority and Women's Enterprise: Existing Evidence, Policy Tensions and Unsettled Questions, *International Small Business Journal*, 33(1): 54–78.

Carter, S.L. and Shaw, E. (2006) Women's Business Ownership: Recent Research and Policy Developments. Report to the UK Small Business Service: http://strathprints.strath.ac.uk/8962/1/SBS_2006_Report_for_BIS.pdf.

Combahee River Collective (1977) A Black Feminist Statement from The Combahee River Collective. [online] Available at: <http://www.feministezine.com/feminist/modern/Black-Feminist-Statement.html> [Accessed 22 Jan 2013].

Crenshaw, K. (1989) Demarginalizing the Intersection of Race and Sex: A Black Feminist Critique of Antidiscrimination Doctrine, Feminist Theory and Antiracist Politics, *University of Chicago Legal Forum*: 139–167.

Danish, A. and Lawton-Smith, H. (2012) Female Entrepreneurship in Saudi Arabia: Opportunities and Challenges, *International Journal of Gender and Entrepreneurship*, 4(3): 216–236.

Datta, P.B. and Gailey, R. (2012) Empowering Women through Social Entrepreneurship: Case Study of a Women's Co-operative in India, *Entrepreneurship, Theory & Practice*, 36(3): 569–587.

Davis, K. (2008) Intersectionality as Buzzword: A Sociology of Science Perspective on What Makes a Feminist Theory Successful, *Feminist Theory*, 9(1): 67–85.

De Bruin, A., Brush, C.G., and Welter, F. (2007) Advancing a Framework for Coherent Research on Women's Entrepreneurship, *Entrepreneurship Theory and Practice*, 31(3): 323–339.

De Vita, L., Mari, M. and Poggesi, S. (2014). Women Entrepreneurs in and from Developing Countries: Evidences from the Literature, *European Management Journal*, 32(3), 451–460.

Doyal, L. (2009) Challenges in Researching Life with HIV/AIDS: An Intersectional Analysis of Black African Migrants in London, *Culture, Health & Sexuality*, 11(2): 173–188.

Drori, I., Honig, B. and Wright, M. (2009) Transnational Entrepreneurship: An Emergent Field of Study, *Entrepreneurship Theory and Practice*, 33(5): 1001–1022.

du Gay, P. (2004) Against 'Enterprise' (but not against 'enterprise', for that would make no sense), *Organization*, 11(1): 37–57.

Essers, C. and Benschop, Y. (2009) Muslim Businesswomen Doing Boundary Work: The Negotiation of Islam, Gender and Ethnicity within Entrepreneurial Contexts, *Human Relations*, 62(3): 403–423.

Essers, C., Benschop, Y., and Dooreward, H. (2010) Female Ethnicity: Understanding Muslim Immigrant Businesswomen in the Netherlands, *Gender, Work and Organization*, 17(3): 320–339.

Gartner, W.B. (1990) What Are We Talking about When We Talk about Entrepreneurship? *Journal of Business Venturing*, 5(1): 15–28.

Geerts, E. and Van der Tuin, I. (2013) From Intersectionality to Interference: FEMINIST Onto-epistemological Reflections on the Politics of Representation, *Women's Studies International Forum*, (41): 171–178.

Gherardi, S. (2015), Authoring the Female Entrepreneur While Talking the Discourse of Work–Family Life Balance, *International Small Business Journal*, DOI: 10.1177/0266242614549780.

Gill, R. (2011). Sexism Reloaded, or, It's Time to Get Angry Again! *Feminist Media Studies*, 11(1): 61–71.

Goss, D. (2005) Schumpeter's Legacy? Interaction and Emotions in the Sociology of Entrepreneurship, *Entrepreneurship Theory and Practice*, 29(2): 205–218.

Government Equalities Office. (2014a) Vital Mentoring Support for Female Entrepreneurs. [online] Available at: <https://www.gov.uk/government/news/vital-mentoring-support-for-female-entrepreneurs> [Accessed 30 June 2015].

Government Equalities Office. (2014b) Female Entrepreneurs Set to Benefit from Superfast Broadband. [online] Available at: <https://www.gov.uk/government/news/female-entrepreneurs-set-to-benefit-from-superfast-broadband> [Accessed 24 Feb 2015].

Hancock, A. (2007) When Multiplication Doesn't Equal Quick Addition: Examining Intersectionality as a Research Paradigm, *Perspectives on Politics*, 5(1): 63–79.

Harding, S. (1986) *Feminism and Methodology*. Bloomington: Indiana University Press.

Harding, S. (1993) Rethinking Standpoint Epistemology: What Is Strong Objectivity?. In: Eds L. Alcoff and E. Potter, *Feminist Epistemologies*. New York: Routledge.

Hartsock, N. (1983) The Feminist Standpoint: Developing the Ground for a Specifically Feminist Historical Materialism. In: Eds S. Harding and M. Hintikka, *Discovering Reality*. Dordrecht: Reidel.

Henry, C., Foss, L. and Ahl, H. (2015) Gender and Entrepreneurship Approaches: A Methodological Review, *International Small Business Journal*, DOI: 10.1177/0266242614549779.

Herbert, R. and Link, A. (2012) *A History of Entrepreneurship*. London: Routledge.

Hill Collins, P. (1990/2000) *Black Feminist Thought*. 2nd Edition. New York: Routledge. (Harvey, 2005).

Högberg, L., Schölin, T., Ram, M. and Jones, T. (2016) Categorising and Labelling Entrepreneurs: Business Support Organisations Constructing the Other through Prefixes of Ethnicity and Immigrantship, *International Small Business Journal*, (34)3: 242–260.

Högberg, L., Scholin, T., Ram, M. and Jones, T. (2014) Entrepreneurs: Business Support Organisations Constructing the Other through Prefixes of Ethnicity and Immigrantship, *International Small Business Journal*, doi:10.1177/0266242614555877.

hooks, b. (2004) *We Real Cool: Black Men and Masculinity*. London: Routledge.

Imas, J.M., Wilson, N. and Weston, A. (2012) Barefoot Entrepreneurs, *Organization*, 19(5): 563–585.

Jayawarna, D., Rouse, J. & Kitching, J. (2013) Entrepreneur Motivations and Life Course, *International Small Business Journal*, 31(1): 34–56.

Jones, C. and Spicer, A. (2009) *Unmasking the Entrepreneur*. Cheltenham: Edward Elgar.

Kay, A. (2012) *The Foundations of Female Entrepreneurship*. London: Routledge.

Kelan, E. (2009) *Performing Gender at Work*. New York: Springer.

Kelan, E. (2014) From Biological Clocks to Unspeakable Inequalities: The Intersectional Positioning of Young Professionals, *British Journal of Management*, 25(4): 790–804.

Kelley, D., Brush, C., Greene, P. and Litovsky, Y. (2013) Global Entrepreneurship Monitor: Women's Report, Global Entrepreneurship Monitor Foundation: Accessed January 21st, 2015. http://www.gemconsortium.org/docs/2825/gem-2012-womens-report.

Kepler, E. and Shane, S. (2007) Are Male and Female Entrepreneurs Really That Different? Working Paper for the Small Business Association, Office of Advocacy, under Contract Number SBAHQ-06-M-0480.

Kirzner, I. (1979) *Perception, Opportunity, and Profit*. Chicago: University of Chicago Press.

Klapper, L. and Parker, S. (2011) Gender and the Business Environment for New Firm Creation, *The World Bank Research Observer*, 26(2): 237–257.

Klyver, K., Neilsen, S. and Evald, M. (2013) Women's Self-Employment: An Act of Institutional (Dis) Integration? A Multilevel, Cross-Country Study, *Journal of Business Venturing*, 28(4): 474–488.

Marlow, S. (2002) Female Entrepreneurs: A Part of or Apart from Feminist Theory? *International Journal of Entrepreneurship and* Innovation, 3(2): 83–91.

Marlow, S. (2014) Exploring Future Research Agendas in the Field of Gender and Entrepreneurship, *International Journal of Gender and Entrepreneurship*, 6(2): 102–120.

Marlow, S., Hart, M., Levie, J. and Shamsul, K. (2013) *Women in Enterprise: A Different Perspective*. Report to the Royal Bank of Scotland. [online] Available at: <http://www.inspiringenterprise.rbs.com/resources/research-publications>.

Marlow, S. and McAdam, M. (2013) Gender and Entrepreneurship: Advancing Debate and Challenging Myths; Exploring the Mystery of the Under-Performing Female Entrepreneur, *International Journal of Entrepreneurial Behaviour & Research*, 19(1): 114–124.

Marlow, S. and Patton, D. (2005) All Credit to Men? Entrepreneurship, Finance, and Gender, *Entrepreneurship Theory and Practice*, 29(6): 717–735.

Marlow, S. and Swail, J. (2014) Gender, Risk and Finance: Why Can't a Woman Be More Like a Man?, *Entrepreneurship and Regional Development*, 26(1–2): 80–96.

Marlow, S., Shaw, E. and Carter, S. (2008) Constructing Female Entrepreneurship Policy in the UK: Is the USA a Relevant Role Model?, *Environmental Planning C*, 26(1): 335–351.

Martinez Dy, A., Martin, L. and Marlow, S. (2014) Developing a Critical Realist Positional Approach to Intersectionality, *Journal of Critical Realism*, 13(5): 447–466.

Mavin, S. and Grandy, G. (2012) Doing Gender Well and Differently in Management, *Gender in Management: An International Journal*, 27(4): 218–231.

McAdam, M. (2012) *Female Entrepreneurship*. London: Routledge.

McCall, L. (2005) The Complexity of Intersectionality, *Signs: Journal of Women in Culture and Society*, 30(3): 1771–1800.

McKay, A., Cambell, J., Thompson, E. and Ross, S. (2013) Economic Recession and Recovery in the UK: What's Gender Got to Do with It, *Feminist Economics*, doi/full/10.1080/13545701.2013.808762.

Mirchandani, K. (1999), Feminist Insight on Gendered Work: New Directions in Research on Women and Entrepreneurship, *Gender, Work & Organization*, 6(4): 224–235.

Nash, J. (2008) Re-Thinking Intersectionality, *Feminist Review*, 89: 1–15.

Office for National Statistics: 'Self Employed Workers in the UK – 2014', accessed January 21st 2015. http://www.ons.gov.uk/ons/rel/lmac/self-employed-workers-in-the-uk/2014/rep-self-employed-workers-in-the-uk-2014.html.

Ogbor, J.O. (2000) Mythicizing and Reification in Entrepreneurial Discourse: Ideology-Critique of Entrepreneurial Studies, *Journal of Management Studies*, 37(5): 605–635.

Oleksy, E. (2011) Intersectionality at the Cross-Roads. *Women's Studies International Forum*, 34(4): 263–270.

Patterson, N. and Mavin, S. (2009) Women Entrepreneurs: Jumping the Corporate Ship and Gaining New Wings, *International Small Business Journal*, 27(2): 173–192.

Rindova, V., Barry, D. and Ketchen, D. Jr. (2009) Introduction to Special Topic Forum: Entrepreneuring as Emancipation, *Academy of Management Review*, 34: 477–491.

Robb, A.M. and Watson, J. (2012) Gender Differences in Firm Performance: Evidence from New Ventures in the United States, *Journal of Business Venturing*, 27(5): 544–558.

Saridakis, G., Marlow, S. and Storey, D. (2014) Do Different Factors Explain Male and Female Self-Employment Rates? *Journal of Business Venturing*, 2(3): 345–362.

Schumpeter, J.A. (1934) *Change and the Entrepreneur*. Cambridge, MA: Harvard University Press.

Scott, L., Dolan, P., Johnstone-Louis, M., Sugden, M. and Wu, M. (2012) Enterprise and Inequality: A Study of Avon in South Africa, *Entrepreneurship, Theory and Practice*, 36(3): 543–566.

Small Business Service (2003) A Strategic Framework for Women's Enterprise, Small Business Service, London, http://webarchive.nationalarchives.gov.uk/+/http://www.berr.gov.uk/files/file38358.pdf.

Taylor, S. and Marlow, S. (2009) Why Can't a Woman Be More Like a Man? Paper to the 25th EGOS conference, Naples, July.

Tobias, J.M., Mair, J. and Barbosa-Leiker, C. (2013) Toward a Theory of Transformative Entrepreneuring: Poverty Reduction and Conflict Resolution in Rwanda's Entrepreneurial Coffee Sector, *Journal of Business Venturing*, 28(6): 728–742.

Verduijn, K. and Essers, C. (2013) Questioning Dominant Entrepreneurship Assumptions: The Case of Female Ethnic Minority Entrepreneurs, *Entrepreneurship & Regional Development*, 25(7–8): 612–630.

Welter, F. (2011) Contextualising Entrepreneurship – Conceptual Challenges and Ways Forward, *Entrepreneurship Theory and Practice*, 35(1): 165–178.

Welter, F. and Smallbone, D. (2008) Women's Entrepreneurship from an Institutional Perspective: The Case of Uzbekistan, *International Entrepreneurship and Management Journal*, 5 March.

Weyer, B. (2007) Twenty Years Later: Explaining the Persistence of the Glass Ceiling for Women Leaders, *Women in Management Review*, 22(6): 482–496.

Wright, M. (2012) Entrepreneurial Mobility, Resource Orchestration and Context. In: Eds F. Welter, D. Smallbone, and A. Van Gils, *Entrepreneurial Processes in a Changing Economy*. London: Edward Elgar, pp. 6–24.

Zahra, S., Wright, M. and Abdelgawad, S. (2014) Contextualisation and the Advancement of Entrepreneurship Research, *International Small Business Journal*, 32(5): 479–501.

2

EXPERIENCES OF WOMEN ENTREPRENEURS IN FAMILY FIRMS

Mary Barrett and Ken Moores

Introduction

Family enterprises are often said to be the most common type of business in the world: they make a substantial contribution to virtually every economic sector. The family business research and advocacy organisation European Family Businesses (EFB) argued in 2012 that, depending on the definition of family business, on a world-wide basis family businesses contribute between 60 and 90 percent of non-government GDP, 50 to 80 percent of all private sector jobs, and represent 70 to 95 percent of all business entities. EFB further argues that family money funds 85 percent of all start-ups and that family firms are responsible for 75 percent of new job growth in the U.S. (2012). Yet assessing the size of family firms' contribution is complicated because family firms are defined in many different ways. The U.S.-based Family Firm Institute (FFI) uses the broad definition of Miller et al. (2007), namely, that "family firms are those in which multiple members of the same family are involved as major owners or managers, either contemporaneously or over time." Figures 2.1 and 2.2 were compiled using this definition. Figure 2.1 shows that many countries whose economies are infrequently discussed in the Western economic literature but are growing rapidly, such as Brazil, have an even larger percentage of family firms than countries in which the contribution of family firms is regularly discussed and debated, such as Europe and the U.S.

Figure 2.2 suggests that it is important to understand the complexity of family firms because they account for large percentages of the workforce in some of the world's fastest growing economies.

Family firms are also widely acknowledged for their role in incubating and financing new businesses and so researchers are seeking to understand entrepreneurship as practised by families in business (Roberts and Davis, 2015). Research thus far shows that entrepreneurial action in the family firm context has a specific 'flavour'. Zahra (2005), for example, argues that aspects of the family business structure ensure an effective alignment between the goals of the firm and its owners. It also leads to continuity by maintaining enduring relationships

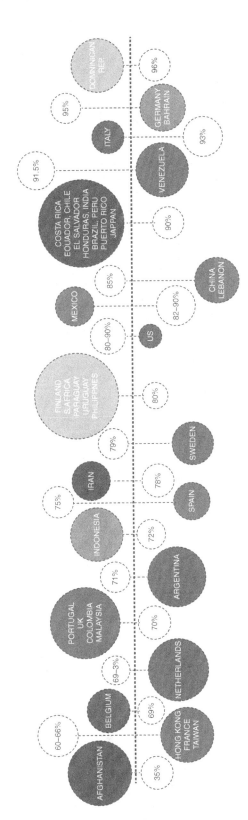

Figure 2.1 Percentage of family businesses in the private sector

Source: Family Firm Institute (2015a).

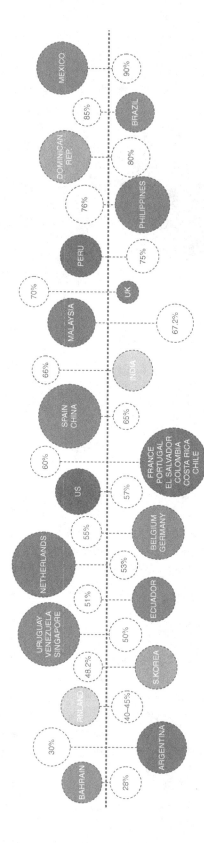

Figure 2.2 Percentage of workforce employed by family businesses
Source: Family Firm Institute (2015b).

with key stakeholders and encouraging patient investment in developing radically new businesses and technologies. These enduring relationships expedite family firms' recognition of entrepreneurial opportunities as well as ways of exploiting them (Aldrich and Cliff, 2003; Rogoff and Heck, 2003).

Women as entrepreneurial leaders in family firms

These same characteristics of longevity, patient capital and a propensity for innovation mean that family businesses also grow the next generation of entrepreneurs, including women entrepreneurs. Yet family firms have a chequered history in terms of how easy it is (or is not) for women to act entrepreneurially inside family firms. Because of the variety of definitions of family firms, and due to the lack of formal data, which would enable cross-country comparisons, it is difficult to gauge how many women are active in family firms, formally and at senior levels. However, recent literature on the topic (e.g. Dugan et al., 2011; Crutzen et al., 2012), echoes much previous literature (e.g. Lyman, Salganicoff and Hollander, 1985; Cole, 1997; Iannarelli, 1993; Salganicoff, 1990; Frishkoff and Brown, 1993; Danes and Olson, 2003; Vera and Dean, 2005) in pointing to the social norms about the roles of men and women that make it more difficult for women to reach positions of entrepreneurial leadership in the family firm. Family and business roles are often seen as 'conflictual' (Philbrick and Fitzgerald, 2007), with women traditionally seen as 'household managers' and men as 'business managers' (Danes and Olson, 2003). Female spouses and other female family members are often just paid employees or, almost as often, unpaid employees in family firms: Danes and Olson (2003) found 57 percent of working spouses even in family firms owned by their husbands, with 47% being paid. However this belies female spouses' importance as decision-makers; for example, Danes and Olson (2003) found 42 percent of wives were major decision-makers in family firms owned and managed by men.

Crutzen et al. (2012), looking at the position of women in Franco-Belgian family firms, argue that while there has been a shift in thinking about women as entrepreneurs within the family business, as evidenced by studies such as MassMutual (2007), this shift is not yet reflected in reality. Women still tend to remain invisible though important. This is shown by the many commentators: academics (e.g. Salganicoff, 1990; Cole, 1997; Jimenez, 2009; Dugan et al., 2011), as well as family business groups, which consistently refer to the ways women act as the 'glue' that holds the family and the business together; women's skill in reducing conflict; their sensitivity to others' needs; their preference for cooperation and interaction especially compared to men; their capacity for an empathetic, listening management style; and their often indirect financial contribution to the family business.

Looking at the literature more widely, Crutzen et al. (2012) also say there has not been much scholarly attention afforded to the question of how family businesses develop women's entrepreneurial behaviours *when this entrepreneurship is exercised outside the context of the 'original' family business*, that is, one started earlier by someone in the same family. The study we report on in this chapter attends to both issues: the role of family firms in fostering – and sometimes hindering – women's entrepreneurship within the family firm and the influence of family firms on women who start their own firms separately from an 'original' family firm. To answer these questions we carried out a series of case studies of entrepreneurial women in various countries who came from family firm backgrounds, examining their experience of reaching – or sometimes not quite reaching – positions of leadership in the family firm, and how their family firm experience influenced their experience of starting a firm themselves.

From this point, the chapter is organised as follows. We first review a number of frameworks used to analyse our cases of entrepreneurial women, then briefly explain how we gathered the sample and carried out the analysis. The findings are presented as a set of ten principles for and about entrepreneurial women in and beyond family firms.

Analytical framework

To avoid considering stereotypical conceptions of women's contributions that have dogged women entrepreneurship research (Ahl, 2004; Bruni, Gherardi and Poggio, 2004), we analysed these experiences using three gender-neutral analytical models. The first was Moores and Barrett's (2002) four phases of learning family business. Phase 1, 'learn business', involves leaving the family firm to gain business experience and personal discipline elsewhere. Phase 2, 'learn our business', means returning to the family firm and learning its special qualities as a family firm. In phase 3, 'learning to lead our business', leaders acquire a strategic view of the firm's future and how to achieve it while still maintaining its family qualities. Finally, in phase 4, leaders plan for and manage succession; they 'learn to leave' the family firm.

The second tool was the idea of a community of practice (Lave and Wenger, 1991). Family firms resemble communities of practice by virtue of their informal, free-flowing, often invisible, yet highly effective ways of transmitting important knowledge. This capacity to transmit knowledge tacitly and efficiently is one aspect of 'familiness', defined as the unique bundle of resources capable of producing sustainable competitive advantages for family firms (Habbershon and Williams, 1999; Habbershon et al., 2003). Family/familiness ties bind family firms together by shared expertise and passion for a shared enterprise, just as communities of practice do (Wenger and Snyder, 2000). In our analysis we focused on four ways a community of practice strengthens the individuals within it and within the community as a whole:

- *Belongingness*: finding and creating an identity through the CoP;
- *Engagement*: working on joint projects and solving problems together;
- *Imagination*: envisaging a shared future; and
- *Alignment*: producing routines and documents that increase the firm's acceptance in the outside world.

Our third analytical tool was Curimbaba's (2002) typology of women's roles in non-CEO positions in family businesses. Curimbaba discerned three roles for family business heiresses: 'Invisibles', 'Professionals' and 'Anchors'. The Invisible family business woman is typically a middle child who has older brothers. As a result, daughters in the family are not regarded as necessary to include in the ranks of managerial staff from whom a successor will be drawn. 'Invisibles' have not been prepared for a professional career in the business and tend to care more about the job itself than the business. Anchors come from families with predominantly female offspring, with few men. With great visibility inside the family business, they become essential for its continuity, despite passing through phases that tend to reduce their significance. Professionals work in mature family companies with complex ownership structures, where a reasonable number of men, but not an overwhelming majority, also work. They typically join the family company when they can make a particular contribution to it, often to resolve conflict in the family part of the system, but after that no one intervenes to push their careers further. As a result of our analysis, we added a further role, that of 'Entrepreneur', which was omitted from Curimbaba's framework since she, like others who have compiled typologies of women's roles in family firms (e.g. Poza and Messer, 2001; Dumas, 1998) do not include women who contribute as CEOs and entrepreneurs.

The cases

We examined the case histories of 16 entrepreneurial women from a range of countries who occupied a range of roles inside or outside the original family business, and who were at different stages in their occupancy of them. These 16 cases were subsequently reduced to 13, when we determined that data saturation had been reached. Following Sharma and Chrisman (1999) we defined entrepreneurship broadly as including both 'independent' entrepreneurship, that is, where new organisations are created independently of any association with an existing organisation, and 'corporate' entrepreneurship, namely, as "the process whereby an individual or a group of individuals, in association with an existing organization, create a new organization or instigate renewal of innovation within that organization" (Sharma and Chrisman, 1999, p. 18). This approach helped manage the notorious inconsistencies in definitions of entrepreneurship (Sharma and Chrisman, 1999) and, just as importantly, helped us not to miss aspects of women's entrepreneurship that are easily overlooked (cf. Brush, 2006; de Bruin et al., 2007; Hurley, 1999) particularly given "the more silent feminine personal end" of much female entrepreneurial activity (Bird and Brush, 2002, p. 57).

Method

We followed the series of steps for developing a case study presented in Eisenhardt (1989). Our research question was a broad one: we wanted to know what it was like for women with a family business background to attain leadership and entrepreneurial roles in and beyond the family firms in which they grew up. Keeping the question broad in this way avoided an assumption that women's ways of leading and acting as entrepreneurs would be either the same as or different from men's. It also permitted a fresh view of women's experiences, the ways they contribute to the special strengths of family firms, and how family firms help (or not) to 'incubate' women entrepreneurs. In line with Eisenhardt's recommendations (1989, pp. 536–37), we selected cases for their theoretical usefulness, analysing both cases where we expected to find entrepreneurial behaviour and, later, cases that would fill theoretical gaps as they emerged in the analysis. The cases where we expected to find entrepreneurial behaviour were women who were acknowledged by their peers or others to be established leaders in family firms or had subsequently started their own firms, who appeared to have completed the four stages of learning in Moores and Barrett (2002) or held the title of CEO and so on. To fill theoretical gaps, we examined cases of 'less obvious' leaders, such as women who clearly undertook leadership roles but had not achieved one or more of these stages. Other cases selected to fill theoretical gaps were women who in their own view had not achieved leadership roles in the family firm despite having wanted to do so and despite having some of the necessary attributes. We used multiple data collection techniques: structured and unstructured interviews, on-site observations, archival data about the firm's history, the firm's place in its industry and so on. Interviews were held over the course of one or more visits to the interviewee's workplace.

We began analysing our material as soon as we had a fair-sized body of data, although gathering an international sample meant we could not undertake a step-by-step, overlapping process of data collection and analysis. Nevertheless we were able to take advantage of emergent themes such as the varying ways women dealt with visibility or its opposite, 'deliberate invisibility', which is not a common theme in the traditionally 'heroic' view of entrepreneurship espoused by much of the literature. This in turn led to important new links such as between visibility and flexibility and between visibility and legitimacy.

As noted earlier, we reached data saturation – the point when analysing more cases yields no new insights – after 13 interviews, so we analysed these 13. Note that two interviewees, Deborah and Robyn who were mother and daughter, belonged to the same firm. Robyn had succeeded Deborah in the CEO role a few years earlier. Participants and their firms came from Canada, the United States, Hong Kong, Saudi Arabia, Lebanon, the United Kingdom, New Zealand and Australia. They included business founders and non-founders (the latter including instances of father-daughter and mother-son succession), CEOs and non-CEOs. There was also considerable variety in the size, age and industry of the participants' firms. A snapshot of our sample of interviewees appears in Table 2.1. The range of industries represented in the sample appears in Table 2.2.

Table 2.1 Participants by CEO/non-CEO and founder status

	Non-CEOs	CEOs
Founders	Brenda, Deborah	Jane, Ellen, Miriam, Nancy, Hannah
Non-founders	Felicity, Sue, Gloria, Cass	Robyn, Ingrid

Table 2.2 Industries of participants' family firms

Name	Industry sector
Brenda	Motor vehicle retailing
Cass	Wholesale/retail (fruit and vegetables)
Deborah/Robyn	Personal services (home care)
Ellen	Clothing manufacturing
Felicity	Personal services (funeral directing)
Gloria	Machinery manufacturing
Hannah	Food retailing (supermarkets)
Ingrid	Machinery manufacturing/Real estate
Jane	Publishing
Miriam	Business services (marketing consulting)
Nancy	Business services (management consulting)
Sue	Roof manufacturing

Note: Names of the interviewees have been disguised.

Findings

The results of the study yield ten vital principles for family firms seeking to turn the idea of having women in entrepreneurship and leadership into a reality.

Principle 1: give promising women early external learning opportunities and a clear route back to the family firm

According to Moores and Barrett (2002), a study that focused mainly on male family business leaders, people who want to get to the top of a family firm first have to 'go outside' to learn business. For men, this usually means working in a firm in the same or a similar industry to the family firm. Some may even develop a new division of the family firm, a subsidiary, or a new firm in a related industry. Leaving the family firm is vital for learning the technical aspects of business and the personal discipline needed for a business career. But it is also a threat to the continuity of the family firm, because the potential leader may create a career elsewhere and never return to the family firm.

This finding was not reflected in the present study of the experiences of family business women. While almost all the women in our study moved outside the family firm in their early careers, none gained experience in a firm in the same industry as the one in which she eventually led or founded a firm. The hotel business, academic studies in history and politics, a psychology practice, the police service and working as a sewing demonstrator in a department store, are among the places our interviewees gained 'outside' experience. This suggests that women in family firms still have less access to business learning opportunities in organisations similar to the family firm than men. They were seriously considered as potential successors even less often, learning outside the family firm as a preliminary to returning to it. Finally, women were less likely to find that the outside learning environment was a forgiving context where they could experiment and make mistakes and be well equipped to manage the family firm. Several interviewees who started their own firms did so because they had been discouraged from envisaging a long-term future as a leader in their original family firms. Others had absorbed a general message that business was not suitable for women or had been put off returning to the family firm by its high level of conflict. Women, like men, need early learning experiences in an outside, but related, business environment and a clear route back to the family firm.

Principle 2: be wary of stereotypical ideas about women's management style

The second learning phase in Moores and Barrett's (2002) model requires the potential leader to come back to the family firm to learn what makes it special, even unique. This entails the paradox of 'continuing the family firm differently': developing it in new directions while respecting and reinforcing its fundamental values. Some women in our sample took the task of 'continuing differently' much further than men had done in the 2002 study. Rather than simply reinforcing the firm's fundamental philosophies with some variations in its practices, they tried to establish a contrasting set of values in a separate firm, or sought to change the existing family firm's values and practices radically. This sometimes meant new ventures run on 'softer' lines compared to the interviewees' original family firms, such as the CEO taking a close personal interest in staff's needs.

This reflects conventional views of female management styles, but other, less stereotypically feminine approaches were also represented. Two participants tried to create more transparent and systematic approaches to managing their firms by introducing computer systems or more-professional approaches to staff recruitment – whether family or non-family (cf. Kotey, 2005). This resulted in considerable conflict. Another interviewee, also against considerable opposition, had radically changed the traditional cash-only basis of the firm's retail operations. Yet another sought to lift the performance of her father's firm by removing people she regarded as failing to meet reasonable targets. In their view, the family firms they had joined suffered from 'constrictive familiness' (Habbershon and Williams, 1999): that is, the darker side of familiness that manifests itself as insularity, lack of transparency and nepotism. In some cases it appeared that our interviewees' concerns were justified; in others the women eventually modified their views and reached a compromise solution with the current leaders. In all cases, however, members of the firm were initially taken aback or confused by what they saw as the interviewee's unfeminine or 'unfamily-like' approach to management.

Principle 3: women's unconventional experience requires creating legitimacy for their leadership

Our analysis showed that women often contributed to the family firm using skills learned in unrelated industries or even in the domestic context. In terms of a community of practice (Lave and Wenger, 1991), these are the skills of experience rather than the skills of acknowledged competence. This is potentially a problem because in a community of practice one is only as skilled as the other members deem one to be. Other members' acknowledgement transforms mere experience into recognised competence. For women's skills to be acknowledged as sufficient for leadership of the family firm requires their experience be backed with some form of legitimacy. The same was true for the firms women established away from the original family firm. Zimmerman and Zeitz (2002, p. 414) define firm legitimacy as a "social judgment of acceptance, appropriateness, and desirability." It is a vital resource for new ventures, as important as capital, technology, personnel, customer goodwill and networks because it helps overcome the 'liability of newness' (Stinchcombe, 1965), which sinks so many not-yet-profitable ventures. Furthermore, Zimmerman and Zeitz (2002) point out that formal qualifications, accreditations, testimonials and so on are important in new firms so they can present themselves as legitimate players in the market; later, profitability supplies natural legitimacy.

The women in our sample often lacked legitimacy in terms of their positions as family firm leaders. They were less likely than men to have gained adequate outside experience, or they had been subtly or not so subtly removed from the list of possible successors. One had left the firm to get a formal qualification in business, and others had never gained formal qualifications in business or in a field directly related to the firm's industry. Even women with the 'right' qualifications – as seen from the outside – might be denied personal legitimacy inside the firm. Cass, for example, found her senior corporate experience clashed with the family firm's culture of informality. Some interviewees tried to achieve institutional and personal legitimacy at the same time. Jane developed a business plan for her new publishing firm to remind herself she was a businessperson and to give herself confidence. Simultaneously, her mentor introduced her to important industry players and firms outside the firm. This and her association with the mentor – himself a prominent businessperson – helped her gain legitimacy in the publishing industry.

The principle for family businesswomen is that they need to know where the 'front door' to leadership is located – the skills that serve as indicators of competence – and whether less formal skills might be substituted for it. Intending women leaders of family firms need to ascertain whether the firm's current norms value informal or formal learning and how the women can acquire skills that will be acknowledged within the firm. Even now, women should not be surprised to find that membership and leadership criteria vary for women as compared to men and be prepared to tackle those differences. Finally, to achieve legitimacy, women leaders in family firms should pay attention to the community of practice principle of *Alignment*, for themselves as well as the firm. Alignment means making sure the community's business practices, such as how it recruits staff and how it acknowledges and rewards competence, are commensurate with those of the wider world. Focusing on Alignment early in the entrepreneurial process helps both new ventures and existing corporate entities undergoing renewal achieve greater external legitimacy.

Principle 4: choose mentors who are 'in' but not 'of' the family firm

Research has established the value of mentorship for women with corporate leadership aspirations (Donaldson et al., 2000; Ensher et al., 2000; Ensher and Murphy, 2005; Noe, 1988), but there is very little written about the role of mentors for women in family firms, with Barrett and Moores (2009) and Dugan et al. (2011) among the few exceptions. Principle 2 showed the value of a mentor for helping a woman establish her legitimacy as a businessperson. Because family businesswomen may have less opportunity than men to gain experience outside the family firm, mentors inside the firm may be even more important; however, mentors may present dangers. The academic and popular business literature point out both advantages and disadvantages to women of having a mentor of the same or the other sex, who works in the same or a different firm. The mentor's own corporate fortunes may decline, so associating with them becomes a political hazard, and other problems may arise (Berfield, 2007; Ensher and Murphy, 2005). Dugan et al. (2011, p. 44) talk about the scarcity of suitable mentors for family businesswomen with strong business qualifications, and the value senior women in family firms are finding in mentoring the younger female generation. We found that a good mentor for a female entrepreneur needs adequate distance from her protégée and protégée's firm, yet an understanding of the detail of her situation.

Our cases suggest that the best mentors for women in family business are 'in' but not 'of' the family firm. Two excellent mentors we encountered were firmly entrenched inside the family firm yet had no personal career stake in it to interfere with the protégée's personal ambitions. Both had already achieved prominence over long careers and had no need to compete with the people they were mentoring. Oddly, their mentorship worked because they were not family members. Only two family members, Robyn's mother and Gloria's father, were senior enough in the firm and close enough to their protégées to know what learning experiences their daughters needed and to give them the necessary leeway to try new things. Gloria's father let her learn how to manage risk: the large sums she spent on marketing in a firm that had never paid attention to this must have caused him some concern. However, in refusing to sack a person Gloria believed was an under-performer, he also gave her a short, sharp lesson in familiness. Robyn's mother Deborah mentored her over a period of 17 years, during which time the issue of Robyn's future as leader was never discussed. Robyn had the patience to leave the decision to her mother, and the mentoring process meant both of them were confident in Robyn's abilities when Deborah finally handed over leadership.

Less helpful founders presented as many dangers to women in family firms as did some mentors in non-family business settings. Ingrid's father was capricious and created rivalries among his children. Felicity's father set her up as head of a division but rapidly shifted his attention to new projects, leaving her in a largely figurehead role. This is not unusual. Vadnjal and Zupan (2009), in their study of family businesswomen in Slovenia, found it was common for family business women to have high-sounding titles that disguised their relatively low-level functions. Outside advisors or consultants sometimes mentored family businesswomen, but the mentoring only lasted a short time: the outsider's position in the firm was not secure enough for his or her advice to be available for long. Strike (2013) examines the most trusted advisor and the subtle advice that this person offers to family firms. Her findings suggest that the value of such a person to a woman in a family firm is matched only by its rarity.

Principle 5: visibility and invisibility are potential leadership strategies for women

Phase 3 of learning a family business, according to the Moores and Barrett (2002) model, means learning to lead it. Women leaders in our sample often made important issues visible to everyone in the firm: opening up issues, pointing to problems, and producing, measuring, and sharing results. Some combined this approach with a participative style of problem-solving or a nurturing approach to managing staff. Such leaders usually placed themselves in the leadership spotlight, inviting scrutiny of themselves as well as of the firm's performance. However, this does not work or is extremely difficult if the culture of the family firm is not receptive to such openness. If people in the firm prefer not to hear the evidence the would-be leader is putting forward, then she is unlikely to succeed. Two participants had spent years disentangling the firm's structure from the dysfunctional effect of family conflicts, and one remained heavily engaged with this task when she was interviewed for this study.

An alternative approach is 'strategic invisibility': working behind the scenes using stories, ideas, and even invoking family history to bring about change. At least two interviewees in the sample had quietly worked themselves into positions of leadership before being recognised as such. One never allowed herself to be described as a leader, even when she was being interviewed, let alone by members of the firm. Others worked with both visible and invisible approaches. Inside the family firm, Gloria needed to get her father to notice her performance and she did this through daring, high-risk and high-expenditure projects that could bring a major increase in revenues. The strategy worked: she created record-breaking sales and neglected no possible avenue to bring the firm to public notice. In turn she was promoted and given more staff to help her keep producing results. However, in other respects and especially to the external world she remained deliberately invisible, promoting her father as a self-made man through the romance of his escape from China after the Long March. Where the firm founder was a close relative such as a father or a husband, aspiring family firm leaders preferred not to stress their achievements or their leadership roles.

Principle 6: invisibility must be a strategic choice

While Principle 5 says that women may lead through visible means, invisible means, or a combination of both, there is an important qualification if invisibility is to be a means of exercising power in the firm. Women need to make a tactical choice of invisibility: unsought invisibility leads away from leadership and entrepreneurship. Brenda was pushed into the limelight of firm leadership after her husband died suddenly; she nevertheless made a success of the firm. The same does not occur when women are *pushed* into invisibility. Hannah, Sue, and Felicity found that, despite working hard for the firm, they disappeared into others' glory. The dominant strategies for learning in their firms had been put into place by someone else: their father, the CEO. Hannah's father maintained the boundaries of his firm to resist possible incursions from in-laws. In Sue's family firm, knowledge was defined by the firm's identity with its engineering history and its reputation for product quality. The overriding strength of this identity, which focused on the current CEO's skillset, scuppered Sue's plans to focus the firm's attention on better marketing and more transparent decision-making. Felicity's family firm was well known in the funeral business, and the family name was an important part of its marketing strategies. Felicity, a third-generation member, found herself heading a new division, which was prominently advertised using her first name and family name. This was a search for legitimacy as well as a competitive strategy: 'the woman's touch' was becoming a source of competitive advantage in the funeral business. However, Felicity was not consulted about having her name used, and the contrast between the prominence of her name and the reality of her comparatively minor role in the family firm added to her lack of confidence about pursuing her earlier leadership ambitions.

Principle 7: women and men manage succession in similar ways

Phase 4 of learning family business leadership means dealing with family business's classic dilemma: succession. Family business leaders must manage the paradox of leading in anticipation of the time when they will no longer be leaders and work out how to manage their relationship with the family firm after they retire. Few of our interviewees had to deal with this stage: only Brenda and Deborah had truly moved through it. They had long since overcome their early internal legitimacy problems and did not hesitate to determine how firm ownership would be transferred to the next generation. These women's experience of succession – good and bad – closely resembled the learning experience of men in Moores and Barrett (2002): they experienced similar problems and reached for similar solutions. Brenda, for example, adopted an ambassadorial role in the business soon after her son took over from her. She was a well-known figure in the business community when she retired, in part because she was a prominent female figure in the male-dominated car industry. An ambassadorial role was typical of the strategies male leaders used to manage the post-retirement phase of their relationship with the family firm.

Principle 8: women use the full range of learning strategies to develop the family firm

We compared how participants learned and developed as individuals with the learning strategies that predominated in their family firms. The results suggested that women did not lean on any one way of managing their firm as a learning community to the exclusion of others: they used the full range. *Belongingness* strategies were important for many. Belongingness strategies include *Engagement*, or working on projects together. Brenda, the CEO of an automobile distributorship and Robyn, the eventual CEO of the personal care firm started by her mother, Deborah, both involved their staff in problem solving. Deborah and Nancy preferred *Imagination*: projecting their idea of how their firms might be in the future and using this to unite the firm's members. Gloria imagined a new vision of the past: packaging her father's romantic life-story of escape from the Chinese mainland soon after the Long March and the Communist rise to power and using the story to enhance perceptions of the firm in its home city of Hong Kong. *Alignment* approaches were also prominent. Jane, Cass, Nancy, and Ingrid tried to create an internal sense of shared purpose and a professional approach to management to bring their firms into line with the wider corporate world.

The family firm community's *Boundaries* and its *Identity* (Lave and Wenger, 1991) also mattered. Miriam led less by creating Belongingness than by managing her firm's Boundaries, keeping them closed enough to maintain the firm's separate identity, but permeable enough to allow members to come and go as the firm's skill requirements demanded. In contrast, Cass's attempt to align the firm with standard business practices played havoc with other members' sense of *Belongingness*. She needed to work through her husband, the focus of the firm's identity.

Principle 9: women need a home base, a reminder about where they have been, and support for their multiple identities

Our study showed three things needed by women developing their own firms. First, they need a home base in a physical sense. Lave and Wenger (1991) point out that learning communities need a clearly defined home base for members to experience knowing as a form of social competence. Our results suggest this also applies to women aspiring to family firm leadership or who establish their own business separately from the family firm. Several of our interviewees had established a home base for their firm – separate premises and no client referrals through the family firm – to separate it from the original family business. This proved that their business, with its different values, style, and knowledge, had a viable separate existence. For some it countered their disappointment at being excluded from a senior role in the original family firm.

Second, women need a reminder of where they have been and how they have come to their present position to feel sure of their competence. They need a sense of their 'learning trajectory' (Lave and Wenger, 1991). Rather than being something static, a community of practice with a healthy identity allows its members to bring the past and the future into the experience of the present. Jane kept an early, rather naïve business plan in a desk drawer and looked at it from time to time to remind herself of how far she had come and how much she and her firm had learned together. Women in family business often lack this evidence due to their more haphazard path to leadership and the uncertainties about their competence being recognised.

Third, the original family firm or the firm a woman has started herself need to support her multiple identities (Lave and Wenger, 1991). Many commentators have reflected on the 'double burden' of women's domestic responsibilities, the tasks they do in addition to their professional roles. However, something even more complex and difficult happens for some family businesswomen. The meaning of their roles in the family business – that is, the way others perceive their family business identities – may change when they have children. As Felicity found out and as others in the sample feared, women are sometimes perceived as important primarily because they have produced the firm's next generation rather than because they contribute to the family business in their own right. Healthy family firms allow women to sustain their roles in the firm independently of their roles as mothers. Vadnjal and Zupan (2009) point out that this is difficult for women in family firms if the firms stay small. However, real flexibility in a family firm can allow women to comfortably manage their multiple identities.

Principle 10: Anchors and Professionals, but not unwilling Invisibles, may become Entrepreneurs

Our case studies showed how Curimbaba's (2002) typology of women's roles in family firms helped predict which women may become entrepreneurs. First, our findings showed that Anchors are as likely as Professionals to become Entrepreneurs. Brenda and Robyn – neither of them founders – spent a long period as Anchors, doing unexciting jobs that were nevertheless indispensable to their family firm's operations. Gloria, Cass, and Ingrid – also non-founders – took a professional view of their roles in the family firm when they entered it. They remained highly aware of their market value, maintained an exit strategy, and avoided merging their personal goals with those of the firm. All five eventually took on entrepreneurial roles in the firm. This is surprising: we would expect Professionals, who are more knowledgeable about and connected to the real world of business (Curimbaba, 2002), to be more likely to become Entrepreneurs. Professionals enter the family firm to pursue a particular agenda or personal opportunity and, having entered it, keep a close eye on their value in the marketplace. Finally, they are always concerned to find the 'right' solutions to problems, without regard to family politics. In contrast, Anchors are less alert to their personal value to the family firm. They tend to 'just be there', never completely overlooked but sometimes taken for granted. But they are more likely than Professionals to adopt a solution to a problem that suits the culture and political realities of the family firm even if it is not the most meritorious in conventional corporate terms.

Perhaps this finding is less surprising when we consider why some Professionals in our sample originally entered the family firm. Ingrid, an obvious Professional, entered the family firm primarily to solve a problem within its family system. As a result, her business leadership agenda – to create a smoothly functioning firm with a strategic plan and a viable vision for the future – was repeatedly postponed. Robyn, by contrast, entered her mother's firm to work out her life direction and found it by working out solutions to the firm's operational problems. As a typical Anchor, she quietly worked on this and developed a comprehensive and strategic understanding of the firm while her sisters were being assessed for their leadership potential and found wanting.

Conclusions

Putting all ten principles together shows that understanding how women learn entrepreneurial leadership in family firms helps us understand entrepreneurial leadership in general. First, the principles implicitly argue that there are more useful and valid research tasks than trying to identify inherently 'male' or 'female' approaches to leadership and entrepreneurship. Some family businesswomen in our sample used 'female' management styles to deal with their firm's issues; others tackled similar problems using more conventional, apparently 'male' approaches. Women and men in family firms manage succession in similar ways. Other studies of entrepreneurial women and men are making similar findings.

Some women's experiences were consistent with trying to overcome well-known structural barriers to career advancement. Many of these resonate with current literature about the difficulties women experience in getting to senior positions in their firms and the solution many adopt: avoid the glass ceiling by starting their own firms. Some of their stories seem akin to Weber's 'heroic' narratives of entrepreneurship (cf. Weber, 1904), which have been criticized by authors such as Ogbor (2000), Smith and Anderson (2004), and Bruni et al. (2004). However, getting to leadership just as often entailed devising a personal, nurturing, approach to management, which brought the participant and her firm into a closer, more communal relationship. Hence, we need to continue investigating how leadership and entrepreneurship play out within organisational communities – not just how these roles present themselves as the dramas of individual women and men.

Finally, the principles show that constrictive familiness may present some special problems for women, but many women in our sample had developed solutions to this, which may be generalisable. Several theorists (e.g. Nicholson, 2008) have suggested that non-family firms should try to emulate family firms' qualities of familiness as a source of competitive advantage. Hence, the solutions women in our sample devised to achieve their leadership and entrepreneurship roles may present new insights for entrepreneurs of both genders.

Avenues for future research

Future research into women as leaders and entrepreneurs in family firms should include monitoring the presence of women in these roles to see whether the frequent predictions that women are reaching senior positions in family firms are being realised. To do this, however, better quantitative data about family firms in general will need to be gathered by government bodies or financial institutions in various countries. In both cases, it will be important that the data is comprehensive enough to form the basis of further investigations.

Even without this research, which will give us information about the 'who', 'what', and 'where' of women in family business leadership, there are many avenues of future research that could probe the 'how' of women's leadership and entrepreneurship in family firms. To take one example, which we are pursuing ourselves, professionalizing the family firm involves creating suitable governance mechanisms for keeping the wider family in touch with the firm's prospects and needs, and for recruiting future employees for the firm. Typical mechanisms for this include annual family retreats, family councils, and their more complex counterparts, boards of directors. So far, however, there is little or no research into how these governance mechanisms work at a detailed level and whether the presence of women on them affects their functioning, whether positively or negatively. Again, the results could be instructive for future research related to achieving a more equal balance of women and men on boards of directors.

Further, our findings about the need for women in family businesses to gain appropriate early learning experiences, establish legitimacy, and find an appropriate mentor resonate with the research agenda for women entrepreneurs in general. The findings in this study could serve as a jumping-off point for more research into these issues for all women who aspire to business ownership and leadership.

Note

Please note that the artwork in this chapter has been used with permission from The Family Firm Institute, Inc. Artwork by Tharawat Magazine

References

Ahl, H. (2004) *The Scientific Reproduction of Gender Inequality: A Discourse Analysis of Research Texts of Women's Entrepreneurship*. Liber: Copenhagen Business School Press.

Aldrich, H. E. and Cliff, J. E. (2003) 'The Pervasive Effects of Family on Entrepreneurship: Toward a Family Embeddedness Perspective', *Journal of Business Venturing*, 18, 573–596.

Allen, I. E. and Langowitz, N. (2003) *Women in Family-Owned Businesses*. Wellesley, MA: Center for Women's Leadership, Babson College/MassMutual Financial Group.

Astrachan, J. H. and Shanker, M. C. (2003) 'Family Businesses' Contribution to the U.S. Economy: A Closer Look', *Family Business Review*, 16, 211–219.

Barrett, M. A. and Moores, K. (2009) *Women in Family Business Leadership Roles: Daughters on the Stage*. Cheltenham: Edward Elgar.

Berfield, S. (2007) 'Mentoring Can Be Messy: Companies love it, but what if that colleague just wants your job?' *Business Week*, 29 January, p. 80.

Bird, B. and Brush, C. G. (2002), 'A Gendered Perspective on Organizational Creation', *Entrepreneurship Theory and Practice*, 26(3), 41–65.

Bruni, A., Gherardi, S. and Poggio, B. (2004), 'Doing Gender, Doing Entrepreneurship: An ethnographic account of intertwined practices', *Gender, Work & Organization*, 11, 406–429.

Brush, C. G. (2006) 'Women Entrepreneurs: A research overview', in M. Casson, B. Yeung, A. Basu and N. Wadeson (eds), *The Oxford Handbook of Entrepreneurship*, Oxford: Oxford University Press, pp. 611–628.

Cole, P. (1997) 'Women in Family Business', *Family Business Review*, 10(4), 353–371.

Crutzen, N., Pirnay, F. and Aouni, Z. (2012) *La place des femmes dans les entreprises familiales belges francophones en 2012*. Ecole de Gestion de l'Université de Liège. June.

Curimbaba, F. (2002) 'The Dynamics of Women's Roles as Family Business Managers', *Family Business Review*, 15(3), 239–252.

Danes, S. M. and Olson, P. D. (2003) 'Women's Role Involvement in Family Businesses: Business tensions and business success', *Family Business Review* 16(1), 53–68.

De Bruin, A., Brush, C. G. and Welter, F. (2007) 'Advancing a Framework for Coherent Research on Women's Entrepreneurship', *Entrepreneurship Theory and Practice*, 31(3), 323–339.

Donaldson, S. I., Ensher, E. A. and Grant-Vallone, E. J. (2000) 'A Longitudinal Examination of Mentoring Relationships on Organizational Commitment and Citizenship Behaviour', *Journal of Career Development*, 26, 233–249.

Dugan, A. M., Krone, S. P., Le Couvie, K., Pendergast, J. M., Kenyon-Rouvinez, D. H. and Schuman, A. M. (2011) *A Woman's Place: The Crucial Roles of Women in Family Business*. London: Palgrave Macmillan.

Dumas, C. A. (1992) 'Integrating the Daughter into Family Business Management', *Entrepreneurship: Theory and Practice*, 16(4), 41–55.

Dumas, C. A. (1998) 'Women's Pathways to Participation and Leadership in the Family-Owned Firm', *Family Business Review*, 11(3), 219–228.

Eisenhardt, K. (1989) 'Building Theories from Case Study Research', *Academy of Management Journal*, 14(4), 532–550.

Ensher, E. A. and Murphy, S. E. (2005) *Power Mentoring: How Successful Mentors and Protégés Get the Most Out of Their Relationships*. San Francisco: Jossey-Bass.

Ensher, E. A., Murphy, S. E., and Vance, C. M. (2000) 'The Application of Career Strategies from Mentoring, Self-Management, and Self-Leadership for Entrepreneurs', *International Journal of Entrepreneurship*, 1(2), 99–108.

European Family Businesses (EFB) (2012) *EFB Position Paper: Family Business Statistics*. Available at http://www.europeanfamilybusinesses.eu/uploads/Modules/Publications/pp---family-business-statisticsv2.pdf, accessed 13 November 2015.

Family Firm Institute, Inc. (FFI) (2015a, b) *Global Data Points*. Available at http://www.ffi.org/?page=globaldatapoints, accessed 13 November 2015.

Frishkoff, P. and Brown, B. (1993) 'Women on the Move in Family Business', *Business Horizons*, 36(2), 66–70.

Habbershon, T. G. and Williams, M. L. (1999) 'A Resource-Based Framework for Assessing the Strategic Advantages of Family Firms', *Family Business Review*, 12(1), 1–25.

Habbershon, T. G., Williams, M. L., and MacMillan, I. C. (2003) 'A Unified Systems Perspective of Family Firm Performance', *Journal of Business Venturing*, 18, 451–465.

Hurley, A. (1999) 'Incorporating Feminist Theories into Sociological Theories of Entrepreneurship', *Women in Management Review*, 14(2), 54–62.

Hytti, U. (2005) 'New Meanings for Entrepreneurs: From Risk-Taking Heroes to Safe-Seeking Professionals', *Journal of Organizational Change Management*, 18(6), 594–611.

Iannarelli, C. L. (1993) 'The Socialization of Leaders: A Study of Gender in Family Business', *Dissertation Abstracts International*, 53(9-A), 3283–284.

Jimenez, R. M. (2009) 'Research on Women in Family Firms: Current Status and Future Directions', *Family Business Review*, 22(1), 53–64.

Kotey, B. (2005) 'Goals, Management Practices, and Performance of Family SMEs', *International Journal of Entrepreneurial Behavior and Research*, 11(1), 3–24.

Lansberg, I., Perrow, E., and Rogolsky, S. (1988) 'Family Business as an Emerging Field', *Family Business Review*, 1(1), 1–8.

Lave, J. and Wenger, E. (1991) *Situated Learning: Legitimate Peripheral Participation*. Cambridge: University of Cambridge Press.

Lyman A., Salganicoff, M. and Hollander, B. (1985) 'Women in Family Business: An Untapped Resource', in C. E. Aronoff and J. L. Ward (eds), *Family Business Sourcebook*. Detroit: Omnigraphics, pp. 46–49.

MassMutual (2007) *American Family Business Survey*. Available at https://www.massmutual.com/mmfg/pdf/afbs.pdf retrieved 27 March 2015.

Miller, D., Le-Breton Miller, I., Lester, R. H., and Canella Jr., D. (2007) 'Are Family Firms Really Superior Performers?' *Journal of Corporate Finance*, 13(5), 829–858.

Moores, K. and Barrett, M. A. (2002) *Learning Family Business: Paradoxes and Pathways*. Aldershot: Ashgate Publishing.

Nicholson, N. (2008) 'Evolutionary Psychology, Organizational Culture, and the Family Firm', *Academy of Management Perspectives*, 22(2), 73–84.

Noe, R. A. (1988) 'Women and Mentoring: A Review and Research Agenda', *Academy of Management Review*, 13(1), 65–78.

Ogbor, J. O. (2000) 'Mythicizing and Reification in Entrepreneurial Discourse: Ideology-Critique of Entrepreneurial Studies', *Journal of Management Studies*, 37(5), 605–635.

Philbrick, C. A. and Fitzgerald, M. A. (2007) 'Women in Business Owning Families: A Comparison of Roles, Responsibilities and Predictors of Family Functionality', *Journal of Family and Economic Issues*, 28, 618–634.

Poza, E. J. and Messer, T. (2001) 'Spousal Leadership and Continuity in the Family Firm', *Family Business Review*, 14(1), 25–36.

Roberts, M. J. and Davis, J. A. (2015) 'Managing the Family Business: Entrepreneurs Needed for Long-Run Success', *Working Knowledge*, Harvard Business School, 13 August. Available at http://hbswk.hbs.edu/item/managing-the-family-business-entrepreneurs-needed-for-long-run-success. Accessed 13 November 2015.

Rogoff, E. G. and Heck, R. K. Z. (2003) 'Evolving Research in Entrepreneurship and Family Business: Recognizing Family as the Oxygen that Feeds the Fire of Entrepreneurship', *Journal of Business Venturing*, 18(5), 559–566.

Salganicoff, M. (1990) 'Women in Family Business: Challenges and Opportunities', *Family Business Review*, 3(2), 125–137.

Sharma, P. and Chrisman, J. L. (1999) 'Toward a Reconciliation of the Definitional Issues in the Field of Corporate Entrepreneurship', *Entrepreneurship Theory and Practice*, Spring, 11–27.

Smith, R. and Anderson, A. R. (2004) 'The Devil Is in the E-Tale: Form and Structure in the Entrepreneurial Narrative', in Daniel Hjorth and Chris Steyaert (eds), *Narrative and Discursive Approaches in Entrepreneurship: A Second Movements in Entrepreneurship Book*. Cheltenham: Edward Elgar, pp. 125–143.

Stinchcombe, A. L. (1965) 'Social Structure and Organizations', in March, J. G. (ed.), *Handbook of Organizations*. Chicago: Rand McNally, pp. 142–193.

Strike, V. M. (2013) 'The Most Trusted Advisor and the Subtle Advice Process in Family Firms', *Family Business Review*, 26(3), 293–313.

Vadnjal, J. and Zupan, B. (2009) 'Women's Roles in Family Business', *Economic and Business Review*, 11(2), 159–177.

Vera, C. F. and Dean, M. A. (2005) 'An Examination of the Challenges Daughters Face in Family Business Succession', *Family Business Review*, 18(4), 321–345.

Weber, M. (1904/1905, English translation of 1976) *The Protestant Ethic and the Spirit of Capitalism*. London: George Allen and Unwin.

Wenger, E. C. and Snyder, W. M. (2000) 'Communities of Practice: The Organizational Frontier', *Harvard Business Review*. Available at https://hbr.org/2000/01/communities-of-practice-the-organizational-frontier retrieved 27 March 2015.

Zahra, S. A. (2005) 'Entrepreneurial Risk Taking in Family Firms', *Family Business Review*, 18(1), 23–40.

Zimmerman, M. and Zeitz, G. (2002) 'Beyond Survival: Achieving New Venture Growth by Building Legitimacy', *Academy of Management Review*, 27(3), 414–431.

3

WOMEN, ENTREPRENEURSHIP AND SUSTAINABILITY

Kate Kearins and Katrin Schaefer

Introduction

In presenting this chapter, we should have liked to be able to say definitively that women are out there contributing to social and environmental sustainability through entrepreneurial businesses and that researchers have captured this as fact. The nexus of women, entrepreneurship and sustainability is, however, relatively rare in research to date (for an exception see Gray, Duncan, Kirkwood, & Walton, 2014), as it is also specifically for men, entrepreneurship, and sustainability.[1]

It is often more gender-neutral studies that begin to explore entrepreneurship and sustainability (e.g. Cohen & Winn, 2007; Kearins & Collins, 2012; Parrish & Foxon, 2009). This nascent field of women, entrepreneurship, and sustainability is ripe for attention. The question is what sort of attention should we rightfully give it as we attempt to move the agenda forward?

Entrepreneurship research in general focuses on the actors themselves (Walter & Heinrichs, 2015), the entrepreneurial context (Zahra, Wright, & Abdelgawad, 2014), and the ways they work to create value (Leyden & Link, 2015; Shane, 2012; Steyaert, 2007). Over time, there has been particular emphasis on outcomes. Outcomes, as in much business research, have often focused on performance. In the case of entrepreneurship, economic (e.g. Carton & Hofer, 2006; Luke, Verreynne, & Kearins, 2007; Zahra, 1991) and social outcomes have both been of interest, whether at individual business, community, or broader economy level (Ward & Aronoff, 1993). A more explicit focus on social and environmental outcomes, as well as economic ones, is hinted at in the fields of social, environmental, and sustainability entrepreneurship. But even there, we are missing an explicit analysis of whether the achievements of these forms of entrepreneurship are consistent with what is required for sustainability broadly writ – that is, beyond just sustainability of the enterprise and the direct and obvious effects of its activities.

Admitting complexity while offering what we see as a worthy ideal, we take the view that sustainability is a construct based on biophysically and socially interconnected systems (Bradbury, 2003; Stead & Stead, 1994). We suggest that sustainability may be contributed to by entrepreneurial businesses. We premise the chapter on the view that we should question the existence – and our support of – dirty, damaging, and dangerous businesses that put people and other life forms, including nature, at risk. We are thus far less interested in entrepreneurial businesses sustaining themselves – *unless* they are contributing to the possibility of all life on Earth flourishing. We advocate the ideal of sustainability-as-flourishing put forward by John Ehrenfeld (2008) as a positive aspirational goal for entrepreneurial and other business activity. We acknowledge that business and entrepreneurial activity are part of the current problems of unsustainability, which we document below, and that they are commonly also seen as part of the solution (Gibbs, 2009; Mackey & Sisodia, 2013; Tilley & Young, 2009). Other arenas of human endeavour beyond business and entrepreneurship as it is traditionally conceived – such as education, regulation, ethical consumerism, community engagement, and lifestyle adjustments – are also essential to achieve sustainability-as-flourishing. These arenas may also be seen as places where entrepreneurial activity can take place, or from which to derive new opportunities and innovations.

We conceive of 'business' as an overarching umbrella term, and the term 'entrepreneurship' as a subset of what can occur when those in business act in particular ways. Established 'incumbent' organisations in a managerial phase are often distinguished from where entrepreneurship more typically occurs. Entrepreneurship is referred to as the process of establishing a new organisation or continuing to change an existing one, with the potential to evoke disruptive sustainability innovation (Hockerts & Wüstenhagen, 2010). Current businesses are criticised for adopting environmental and social sustainability strategies that at best lead to business-almost-as-usual and incremental change towards less unsustainability (Ehrenfeld & Hoffman, 2013; Welford, 1998). They often neglect sustainability strategies that integrate social and environmental goals at the core of the business and would likely lead to a fundamental organisational change towards sustainability. This being said, we acknowledge the fact that entrepreneurship has also been rebuked for being unequal and exploitative in line with market economics (Tedmanson et al., 2012). In that way, commercial entrepreneurship, in particular, may be seen to contribute to current levels of unsustainability. But equally it has the potential to provoke radical changes in behaviour towards sustainability.

Our intention in this chapter is to lay some groundwork for future research on women, entrepreneurship, and sustainability by summarising extant research, identifying gaps and possible research questions. We do so as sustainability scholars with an interest in the potential of entrepreneurship and faith in humanity if working concertedly – women and men, older and younger, and through them their children – to contribute to a better future. First, however, and somewhat counter-intuitively, we provide a rationale for our focus on sustainability by sounding some alarm bells before elaborating on the ideal of sustainability-as-flourishing.

Social inequalities, environmental degradation and economic instability

In describing the current state of unsustainability, we admit a certain reluctance. It is depressing – and focusing on it is generally not empowering for people. The problems we describe seem bigger than any individual working alone can solve. Yet we, and others, see hope for entrepreneurs in this space (Tilley & Young, 2009; Zahra et al., 2009).

Currently, humanity is facing severe and unprecedented levels of unsustainability, across at least three domains – social, environmental, and economic. These three domains are those most commonly recognised in the business and sustainability literature and in business discourse inspired by Elkington's (1997) triple bottom line heuristic (sometimes also referred to as people, planet, and profit[2]). They are used in an inclusive and not exclusive sense.

In the social domain, there are increasing levels of social disintegration and social inequalities, with the latter even in high-income nations (OECD, 2011). Extreme human deprivation, social exclusion, and vulnerability remain acute for one-third of the population worldwide (The Worldbank, 2013). Across various dimensions, humanity does not achieve the social foundations required for a socially just space, including undernourishment, lack of access to drinking water, and extreme income poverty (Raworth, 2013). Also, social and gender inequality are still significant (Raworth, 2013, p. 32). In addition to material deprivations mostly in the developing world, an "impoverishment of human life" (Balakrishnan, Duvall, & Primeaux, 2003, p. 299), pathological and psychological distress is witnessed, despite rapidly rising material standards (Ehrenfeld & Hoffman, 2013; Scharmer & Kaufer, 2013).

In the environmental domain, there is increasing consensus among scientists that environmental degradation has reached an unsustainable level. Climate change, rate of biodiversity loss, and human interference with the nitrogen cycle (Folke, 2013; Rockström et al., 2009) are at unprecedented levels. Forecasts predict no reversal of these trends, but rather further environmental degradation (Engelman, 2013; IPCC, 2013).

The economic domain is the scene of global economic instability, as the financial system, seemingly stable two decades ago, has not recovered from a crisis that almost created financial collapse (Jackson, 2011; Morgan, 2013). The sovereign-debt crisis at record level, in particular in Europe and the United States, is not only regarded as a sign of instability, but as a sign of failure of our economic model (Lietaer et al., 2012; Morgan, 2013). Moreover, "the prevailing financial system"—which is at the core of our economic system—"is incompatible with sustainability", among other reasons due to its short-term orientation, assumption of unlimited growth, and destruction of social capital (Lietaer et al., 2012, p. 14).

These examples that span the social, environmental, and economic domains highlight the considerable extent of our current level of unsustainability, if not yet – according to Hoffman – amounting to "systemic breakdowns in mainstream institutions of society" (Ehrenfeld & Hoffman, 2013, p. 4). Korten (2006) refers to this unravelling requiring a 'Great Turning' on the part of humanity towards a much more nurturing, life-centred, sustainable, and democratic 'Earth Community'. Fundamental changes in our economic, social, and political systems are advocated to address unsustainability (Alvord, Brown, & Letts, 2004; Ehrenfeld & Hoffman, 2013; Hall, Daneke, & Lenox, 2010; Jackson, 2011). Arguably these problems and the changes they inspire provide opportunities for entrepreneurs – and a worthy focus for entrepreneurship scholars.

Sustainability-as-flourishing

On a more positive note – and in response to the seemingly intractable problems we have described, Ehrenfeld (2008) offers sustainability-as-flourishing as an ideal that is attracting growing interest (Cooperrider & Fry, 2012; Ehrenfeld & Hoffman, 2013; Laszlo et al., 2014). Sustainability-as-flourishing is defined as "the possibility that humans and other life will flourish on the Earth forever" (Ehrenfeld, 2008, p. 6). It encompasses a meaningful vision, a "nurturing possibility" of a positive thriving future for all (Ehrenfeld & Hoffman, 2013, p. 16).

Moving towards such a positive possibility as a society requires a change in cultural beliefs (Ehrenfeld & Hoffman, 2013; Kurucz, Colbert, & Wheeler, 2013). According to Ehrenfeld (2012, p. 615), we need to embrace two basic beliefs underlying sustainability. First, he sees the true nature of human beings as "based on care, not need". He advocates our changing the focus from our insatiable needs to caring. Caring involves the authentic expression of wider compassion for our fellow human beings. Second, Ehrenfeld (2012) advocates acknowledging that large living systems like the Earth are extremely complex and can only be understood via holistic and organic approaches. Taking atomistic and individualistic approaches, such as efforts to develop a single 'good' business, are worthless if the planetary ecosystems on which it relies are rendered defunct. Equally, if problems incurred by the business' activities are merely passed along the supply chain, or onto consumers, we are failing to take the holistic approach required for sustainability-as-flourishing. Organic approaches, such as Ehrenfeld (2012) suggests, see us tune into the environment, feel what the impacts of our activities are, and make adjustments. These beliefs, though fundamental to a better world, are pretty much against the grain of much of what we have traditionally focused on in business and business education – and in the domain of entrepreneurship.

Sustainability-as-flourishing is opposed to a more enterprise-centric view of sustaining firm performance and profit as the overarching priority. It goes well beyond the contested concept of sustainable development – popularised by the World Commission on Environment and Development (WCED) in the 'Our Common Future (or Brundtland) Report' (1987). The report offers the most widely cited definition characterising sustainable development as a "development that meets the needs of the present generation without compromising the ability of future generations to meet their own needs" (WCED, 1987, p. 43).[3] Although the Brundtland conception of sustainable development has people's well-being at heart and holds potential to reduce unsustainability, it is substantially flawed. The conception is deeply in dispute with sustainability since it retains economic growth "as the operative concept" (Ehrenfeld, 2005, p. 23) and, thus, ignores bio-physical boundaries including resource limits. Current practices following this definition are not actually helping us to achieve sustainability (Ehrenfeld & Hoffman, 2013). They invoke trade-offs, often in favour of economic performance at individual firm level (Hahn et al., 2010) and invariably result in what has been termed 'weak' sustainability.

A partial view is inadequate to the challenges we face. What is required is a more systemic view, one that is a challenge for all sectors, not least for the business sector, which is often predicated on: competition rather than co-operation, privatised profits, and potentially socialised losses and growth often of a kind that is depleting non-renewable resources, degrading the environment, and heightening social inequality. Some hope does lie in new forms of entrepreneurship – social, environmental and sustainable, which we discuss next.

Social, environmental and sustainable entrepreneurship

There has been recent interest in various forms of entrepreneurship – social, environmental and sustainable – in the spirit of new or substantially altered organisational forms and behaviours being needed to address the pressing sustainability challenges (Gibbs, 2009; Hall et al., 2010; Tilley & Young, 2009). With slightly different but overlapping foci, these forms of entrepreneurship privilege the generation of social and/or environmental value alongside, or ahead of, economic value (Dacin, Dacin, & Matear, 2010; Short, Moss, & Lumpkin, 2009; Zahra et al., 2009). In this sense, these new forms are redolent of the optimism inherent in the win-win hypothesis (achieving a win for the environment/society at the same time as a financial win for business). They do so, however, less in the sense of these new opportunities providing for secondary or added value, but generally with environmental or social value creation as their primary purpose. We see all three types as potentially contributing to sustainability-as-flourishing and the distinctions between them as more of an academic than practical interest, as the social, environmental, and economic dimensions are inextricably linked.

Within social entrepreneurship there is often a focus on empowering and uplifting marginalised and poor people (Alvord et al., 2004; Mair & Martí, 2006; Martin & Osberg, 2007), with profit being considered as a means of addressing social outcomes (Thompson, Kiefer, & York, 2011). Social enterprises are on a continuum of for-profit and non-profit organisations, including newly emerging forms like community-based enterprises and intrapreneurial efforts (those of individual social entrepreneurs in existing corporations) (Thompson et al., 2011).

Environmental entrepreneurship looks to simultaneously create environmental and economic value "by addressing environmentally relevant market failures" (Lenox & York, 2012; Thompson et al., 2011, p. 218). As well as seeking to solve environmental problems, this form of entrepreneurship tends to ascribe equal importance to the creation of economic growth (Thompson et al., 2011). Another, similar variant sometimes mentioned is ecopreneurship (Isaak, 2002; Schaper, 2002). Again the focus is on environmental and economic value creation but with greater primacy given to environmental outcomes.

Sustainable entrepreneurship centres on "a 'triple-bottom-line' of *people, planet, profit*" (Thompson et al., 2011, p. 204). In other words, the focus is on simultaneous creation of social, environmental, and economic value (Hall et al., 2010; Parrish, 2010). These enterprises seek to create products and services that help shift towards a socially and environmentally more sustainable society (Parrish & Foxon, 2009; Thompson et al., 2011).

Notably much of this literature is gender-neutral in its approach. We turn now to the wider field of entrepreneurship research and what we know specifically about women and entrepreneurship.

Women and entrepreneurship – relevant research contributions to date

The rate of female participation in entrepreneurship varies across countries and over time. Generally, however, it is clear that women play a less than proportionate role in entrepreneurship (Acs et al., 2011), in both developed and less developed countries (Bönte & Piegeler, 2013). Various factors have been identified as contributing to the lower rate of female participation. DeBruin, Brush, and Welter (2007) see financing, networking and social capital, and growth and performances as recurrent topics and possible areas of growth potential in research on women and entrepreneurship. Griffiths, Gundry, and Kickul (2013) also point to the importance of training programmes and local networks. Bönte and Piegeler (2013) found women were less competitively inclined than men in almost all countries they sampled – and less willing to take risks than their male counterparts. Acs et al. (2011) suggest that some of the roles women tend to play such as taking primary responsibility for childrearing and care giving might dissuade them from becoming entrepreneurs. Al Kaylani (2013) points to Arab women in Middle Eastern and North African countries struggling to access capital and technology, as well as needing networking and other skills to be able to identify and exploit opportunities. "Cultural attitudes about the value of women's work and gender equality affect women's participation in every part of the world" but in the Arab region arguably more so (p. 7).

Female entrepreneurship has been seen to be traditionally concentrated on personal service and small-scale retailing, often serving a household clientele (Bates, 2002). Brush (1992) saw women's businesses as smaller, service-oriented, and generating less revenue than those of men. More recently, DeTienne and Chandler (2007, p. 365) claim, "women and men utilise their unique stocks of human capital to identify [entrepreneurial] opportunities and that they use fundamentally different processes of identifying opportunities". In their sample, they encountered different experiential backgrounds and different ways of thinking between women and men. Other studies point to women entrepreneurs having less years of industry experience than men entrepreneurs at the time of start-up (see DeTienne & Chandler, 2007). The work of these authors also points to the women reporting lower levels of technical expertise than the men they surveyed and drawing from different stores of knowledge. They allude less to a deficit perspective in respect of gender difference than to uniqueness and potential complementarity. DeTienne and Chandler (2007) find women were more likely to be involved in a learn/innovate approach than men, who were more likely to use a learn/acquire or learn/replicate sequence, possibly explained by the latter having a stronger motivation towards financial success and faster growth of their enterprises.

Griffiths et al. (2013) quote Wilson and Kickul's (2006) finding that women who are interested in entrepreneurial careers appear "more likely than males to be motivated by social aspects than by economic motives" (p. 346), whereas males are reportedly more motivated by the prospect of financial success than they are by social aspects. However, the different social and economic motives are not mutually exclusive. These authors see younger women wanting to succeed financially but unwilling to compromise on "also making a positive difference, making them a powerful source of future entrepreneurship that will have both social and economic value at its core" (Wilson & Kickul, 2006 in Griffiths et al., 2013, p. 346). We see here a familiar theme about the *potential* for women entrepreneurs to contribute.

There has been a strong historical focus on performance in research on entrepreneurship, which has carried on into research on women and entrepreneurship (Hughes et al., 2012). The story here is no less rosy. Bates (2002) pointed to abundant research done on opportunities and constraints faced by women entrepreneurs but a gap existing in terms of the performance of women-owned businesses.[4] Where the performance of women's businesses has been measured, it has tended to be less in financial terms when compared to those of men across several studies (Robb, 2002; Coleman, 2007). Ownership gender, of course, is not necessarily the only relevant variable.

In much of this discussion, there is a rather unfortunate sense of the 'female resource base' being underutilised, where it appears eminently possible that it is undervalued (see Waring, 1988). Datta and Gailey (2012, p. 569) claim, "too often entrepreneurial efforts by women have gone unnoticed, and their contributions have been underappreciated". This leads us to consider what women entrepreneurs are seen to be able to contribute towards sustainability.

Conundrums as to what women entrepreneurs can contribute towards sustainability

The potential for women to contribute to sustainability is a frequent topic – both in a direct and in a more nuanced sense. The combination of productive and reproductive roles (Acs et al., 2011), while advocated in research on women and entrepreneurship, is not unproblematic. Ang (2004) and many other commentators see women as agents of change within their households, instilling values conducive to long-term growth and development of community. Levie and Hart (2011, p. 214) find evidence that "women are more likely than men to make deep commitments to address local needs by engaging in social entrepreneurial activities".

Psychological research suggests women's 'reality' is more typically characterised by connectedness and relationships as opposed to autonomy and logic as for men (Brush, 1992).

Interpersonal relationships are seen as important with women tending to "view their businesses as a cooperative network of relationships rather than a separate economic entity" (p. 24). Ang (2004) points to the importance of trust and social capital for women's success in creating and growing sustainable micro-enterprises.

Surveys demonstrate fairly consistent differences between men and women in relation to environmental concern, with no real consensus on reasons (Bord & O'Connor, 1997). Women appear more environmentally concerned than men (Hunter, Hatch, & Johnson, 2004). One possibility Bord and O'Connor allude to is that women may perceive themselves to be more vulnerable rather than necessarily having higher ecological sensibilities. Women are shown to value altruism, which is also associated with environmental behaviours (Hunter et al., 2004). Gender socialisation theory asserts that women have a stronger ethic of care but that it is seen to be slower to manifest in environmentalism (and even slower in environmental activism) (Braun, 2010). Somewhat counter to the previous assertion, this author also suggests female entrepreneurs may be more engaged in 'green issues' than male entrepreneurs. However, little systematic or wide-scale research has been done on these topics. One of the confounding issues for women and men is whether attitudes actually translate into behaviour.

Much of the research on women and entrepreneurship that tilts at sustainability is situated in developing country contexts where more entrepreneurial engagement in the community is commonly seen as an avenue for poverty alleviation. Micro-finance strategies are one purported solution (Ang, 2004; Halkias et al., 2011). Sigalla and Carney (2012) caution against seeing microcredit as a panacea and are more ambivalent about women's lived experience. Such schemes, they say, "can have widely heterogeneous impacts that can affect women in very different ways", with changes in social dynamics and potentially an individualistic approach to poverty reduction being taken. We earlier mentioned the importance of a more systemic view in the understanding and achievement of sustainability.

Taking a positive view on adversity, Gray et al. (2014) draw on the case of a non-governmental organisation that supports women and their families in setting up sustainable enterprises. The authors claim extreme situations (such as severe environmental events) "may spark the emergence of institutional entrepreneurs who acquire, develop and leverage resources to create new organisational forms and processes" (p. 401). They see such prompting moving potential entrepreneurs from an internal, organisational focus to an external orientation towards empowering others. Here the focus can be on addressing wider systems' problems, with these becoming more evident in extreme situations. These authors are not alone in seeing social or environmental catastrophe as prompting necessary changes.

Less concerning, perhaps, are some interesting findings from a study of women entrepreneurs participating alongside men entrepreneurs in a green entrepreneurship programme in Victoria, Australia. This research conducted by Braun (2010) found six men dropping out of the programme because they were reportedly too busy or purportedly already doing much of what the programme covered and all the women in the programme completing. The women were found to be more eager participants and keener to gather and contribute information, as well as to network, "seeing networking as both a learning experience and business opportunity" (p. 251). Women participants saw themselves as agents for more profound change in their businesses, while men on exiting the programme saw it as contributing more by way of eco-efficiency – leaner business practices and operational savings. The total sample of 30 in this research limits the generalisability of its findings, but again women's potential to contribute meaningfully and profoundly to sustainability is hinted at here.

Our review points to possible gender attributes and how they might play out in achieving the wider system objectives of sustainability-as-flourishing. Next, we introduce a range of ideas under the umbrella of eco-feminism. Of a more political nature, the discourses in the eco-feminist space, we believe, prompt us to think differently about the kind of research we need going forward.

Where might an eco-feminist perspective take us?

Returning to Ehrenfeld and Hoffmann's (2013) call for fundamental cultural change to achieve sustainability-as-flourishing, we look at some of the underpinning aspects of eco-feminist analysis. Eco-feminism calls for a "different, non-dualistic relationship between human groups and between humans and nature" (Bullis & Glaser, 1992, p. 51). Specifically, it calls for a non-hierarchical (or non-competitive) relationship between men and women and for any perceived hierarchy of men and women over nature to be abolished. Domination, objectification, and disassociation are seen as problematic, as are dualisms such as man/woman, human/nature, rationality/emotion (Crittenden, 2000). They are seen as separating the self from emotional connections with others. More radical forms of eco-feminism see patriarchy and hierarchy as ultimately destructive of all life (Bullis & Glaser, 1992) and thus in complete disharmony with the achievement of sustainability-as-flourishing.

Eco-feminist analysis, more positively construed, focuses "on the relationship between women and the environment as central to human survival and environmental integrity" (Hessing, 1993, p. 15). This author suggests "that only when the analysis of society and environment starts with women will the challenge of sustaining development be met" (p. 15). This view postulates that "women's reproductive capabilities, emotional qualities and nurturing activities are the foundations of women's alliance with nature" (p. 15) and that our understanding of the Earth as mother is reflected in women's/mother's own ethic of care for the Earth and all life, now and into the future.

This eco-feminist analysis therefore extends the ethic of care towards valuing the work more often performed by women in looking after children and the elderly, the sick and their families – working within the system (Hessing, 1993) and contributing to overall flourishing. Whereas these domains might not be so obviously construed as places in which entrepreneurial activity takes place, we need only to look at the rise of institutionalised aged-care and child-care arrangements to see women's contributions as important in the way we design and operate enterprises that offer opportunities for clients, their families, and the workers themselves to flourish. While rejecting patriarchal, large-scale, centralised and mechanistic forms of organising, eco-feminists support co-operation, non-hierarchy, and organic forms (Hessing, 1993).

Depending on who one reads within the field of eco-feminism and which of the many variants one follows, the approach is either entirely pro-women and anti-men or more united. In the latter case, unqualified or unhelpful dualisms become inappropriate within the discourse. The approach we advocate in support of sustainability-as-flourishing, in support of all life, is more united, cognisant of the need for diversity and simultaneous solidarity (Bullis & Glaser, 1992). More and more, while understanding the differences that tend to persist between genders and the potential for working together, a partnership culture is called for by Gaard (2001; see also Korten, 2006).

A future research agenda

We start this discussion with what, in our opinion, having reviewed the extant literature, we probably need to do *less* of to support sustainability-as-flourishing.

Focusing *less* on the financial performance and growth of entrepreneurial businesses[5] – or at least not evaluating these aspects as reducible to male or female owner-managers seems in order as we begin to build a future research agenda that is more united and representative of the work the genders do and could more optimally do together. This does not mean researchers should ignore unwarranted hierarchies (male entrepreneurs, owners, and managers and lower paid female workers etc.). Note, we are not making a case for non-gender specific and non-politicised research – we need and invite change!

Focusing *less* on the minutiae of processes that are employed in traditional entrepreneurial businesses and linking these to traditional gender stereotypes may also be in order. Allowing for different approaches to emerge and studying what does emerge is important.

Focusing *less* on the individual in an atomised and decontextualised sense also seems to be important in entrepreneurship research going forward (Ahl, 2006). In feminist studies there are increasing acknowledgements of the futility of a 'blame the women' mentality; equally, a 'blame the men' one might only take us so far. What is missing is situated context and historical explanation (Ahl, 2006).

We juxtapose the above statements with what we think we might need to do *more* of. While focusing less on financial performance and growth outcomes of entrepreneurial businesses themselves, we need to focus *more* on broader economic, social, environmental, and cultural outcomes of entrepreneurial business activities. We need to ask: What negative outcomes or externalities are being incurred and how might these be avoided or mitigated if possible? Considering gender in this equation becomes important. Do the outcomes change traditional gender power structures – in good ways or in less than optimal ways – and, for whom? For sustainability-as-flourishing, we need to ask what additional or new positive outcomes might we jointly realise? Outcomes not just for the entrepreneur and the business, but systemically and for all.

Rindova, Barry, and Ketchen (2009) nudge researchers towards a broader view of entrepreneurship as an emancipatory act of change creation, rather than just an economic outcome-focused enactment towards wealth creation. With change needed from our current more enterprise-centric focus towards a more systems-centric one for sustainability-as-flourishing, such broadening of the research agenda appears appropriate. How do entrepreneurial businesses work together to produce more synergistic outcomes of greater/wider benefit, would be an interesting question for researchers to answer.

While focusing less on the minutiae of processes employed in traditional entrepreneurial businesses, it might be of *more* utility to look at what works in new hybrid forms of business including social and environmental enterprises and partnership organisations, including along supply chains. What lessons can be learned that might be transferrable and that might lead to expansion and growth in numbers of enterprises and supply chains with positive sustainability outcomes?

While focusing less on the individual we need to focus *more* on the situated context and institutionalised power structures in which people are embedded. At the same time, we need not to move from simply blaming the women to a discourse of needing to change the women in a bid to develop what researchers have identified as female entrepreneurial potential. Sensitive research questions as to where women entrepreneurs' interests and talents lie, and how and if these might be different from men's, would be useful. Exploring the nature and expression of eco-feminist thinking among women entrepreneurs, we think, might be new territory that could yield interesting answers. A number of researchers have called for acknowledgement and recognition of the remarkable heterogeneity among female entrepreneurs (de Bruin, Brush, & Welter, 2007; Hughes & Jennings 2012; Hughes et al.,

2012). Following Ahl (2006), we consider deeper attention to how gender is interpreted and experienced with and through others might also be useful.

In terms of new arenas for a research focus on women, entrepreneurship, and sustainability, we should seek out and investigate the existence of and roadblocks to entrepreneurial activity in arenas where an ethic of care is to the fore, or could/should be – such as hospitals, child-care facilities, educational institutions, and aged-care facilities. Many of these arenas boast a preponderance of women staff, if not always senior managers. To what extent does entrepreneurial activity flourish in these arenas? From where do the ideas and opportunities for enhanced practice come? What are the outcomes beyond a focus on the financial? And what trade-offs occur?

What other arenas, more traditionally devoid of a caring ethic, can be seen as frontiers for change? What role does the union entrepreneur have in enhancing working conditions, and in changing institutionalised practices? What role might imaginative regulators have – when private gain is set aside? What is the role of the academic entrepreneur in changing our own institutions? More explicitly in the business context, we could look at what opportunities exist for businesses to promote ethical consumerism – selling goods that are more socially and environmentally responsible, selling materially less, promoting shared ownership arrangements, cutting out unwarranted links in the supply chain so as to ensure returns are greatest to those who deserve them, encouraging community engagement and lifestyle adjustments such as greater spiritual connectedness. All are, in essence, entrepreneurial opportunities that on various levels can be complicated by the adoption of a sustainability ethic but can also be inspired by one.

Much hope seems to lie in local studies by local researchers who can understand the setting and context, the cultural norms and challenges, as indeed much hope lies in the entrepreneurs themselves making change at the local level. Sustainability-as-flourishing is as we have said a global if not planetary systems construct. An argument is sometimes made that it can be harder for entrepreneurs to tackle big sustainability challenges when they are starting out or when the business is small. A counter-argument is that smart set-ups with strong localist orientations may be able to make positive contributions to sustainability, precisely by not incurring environmental impacts associated with the tyranny of distance or size.

We do see hope in these new forms of social, environmental, and sustainability entrepreneurship. However, research that focuses solely on either the social or the environmental dimensions of sustainability and/or the economic dimension may be missing the point. Sustainability as we currently understand it comprises at least three dimensions – social, environmental and economic – and all three are simultaneously challenging and important. How entrepreneurs rationalise what they see as inevitable trade-offs among the dimensions may well tell us more about them and the kind of entrepreneurship they practice than we previously have known. This would take us beyond the predominant focus on the economic or the labels of social, environmental or sustainability entrepreneurship that many of these entrepreneurs, in our experience, seem themselves to eschew. Again, we need to focus on whether the outcomes – social, environmental, and economic – are ones that lead to a flourishing life for all. How we might know or be able to evaluate or judge that achievement, or lack of it, is a key question for researchers to consider.

There exists potential for a rich terrain for future research on women, entrepreneurship, and sustainability. Whether one takes a more gender-specific or broader focus, nuanced understandings of how gender is constructed and what is required for sustainability are needed in the pursuit of entrepreneurship research that is of positive consequence in securing our common future.

Notes

1 There were more search results for gender, entrepreneurship, and sustainability, but the articles often refer to sustainability in terms of business continuity (e.g. Ang, 2004; Kumar, 2013), rather than the wider systems focus we invoke in this paper.

2 Entrepreneurship literature has also focused on these three domains. More recently the focus on social and environmental (also sustainable entrepreneurship) has extended the more traditional focus on economic or what has been termed commercial entrepreneurship research (Corner & Ho, 2010).

3 Hessing (1993, p. 15) points out the obvious gender neutrality of the Brundtland definition, suggesting that like other contemporary discourses in the field, it "reduces women to just another user group seeking to maximize their own interests in the ongoing struggle to redistribute global wealth and resources". We take less issue with this aspect than with the overall flaws in the definition and associated philosophy that appears to be a pragmatic compromise towards taking us down the same development path we are currently on, albeit more knowingly and more efficiently, perhaps.

4 We would extend this to include a gap on social and environmental performance of both men- and women-owned businesses, important dimensions of sustainability where research relies heavily on self-reports of performance.

5 Financial performance and growth outcomes of women's businesses have been a major research focus (Ahl, 2006; Hughes et al., 2012).

References

Acs, Z., Bardasi, E., Estrin, S., & Svejnar, J. (2011). Introduction to special issue of Small Business Economics on female entrepreneurship in developed and developing economies. *Small Business Economics*, *37*(4), 393–396.

Ahl, H. (2006). Why research on women entrepreneurs needs new directions. *Entrepreneurship: Theory & Practice*, *30*(5), 595–623.

Al Kaylani, H. (2013). Employment, entrepreneurship and young women leaders. *International Trade Forum*, (1), 6–8.

Alvord, S. H., Brown, L. D., & Letts, C. W. (2004). Social entrepreneurship and societal transformation: An exploratory study. *Journal of Applied Behavioral Science*, *40*(3), 260–282.

Ang, M. H. (2004). Empowering the poor through microcredit. *International Journal of Entrepreneurship & Innovation Management*, *4*(5), 485–494.

Balakrishnan, U., Duvall, T., & Primeaux, P. (2003). Rewriting the bases of capitalism: Reflexive modernity and ecological sustainability as the foundations of a new normative framework. *Journal of Business Ethics*, *47*(4), 299–314.

Bates, T. (2002). Restricted access to markets characterizes women-owned businesses. *Journal of Business Venturing*, *17*(4), 313–324.

Bönte, W., & Piegeler, M. (2013). Gender gap in latent and nascent entrepreneurship: Driven by competitiveness. *Small Business Economics*, *41*(4), 961–987.

Bord, R., & O'Connor, R. (1997). The gender gap in environmental attitudes: The case of perceived vulnerability to risk. *Social Science Quarterly*, *78*(4), 830–840.

Bradbury, H. (2003). Sustaining inner and outer worlds: A whole-systems approach to developing sustainable business practices in management. *Journal of Management Education*, *27*(2), 172–187.

Braun, P. (2010). Going green: Women entrepreneurs and the environment. *International Journal of Gender and Entrepreneurship*, *2*(3), 245–259.

Brush, C. (1992). Research on women business owners: Past trends, a new perspective and future directions. *Entrepreneurship: Theory & Practice*, *16*(4), 5–31.

Bullis, C., & Glaser, H. (1992) Bureaucratic discourse and the goddess: Towards an ecofeminist critique and rearticulation. *Journal of Organizational Change Management*, *5*(2), 50–60.

Carton, R. B., & Hofer, C. W. (2006). *Measuring organizational performance: Metrics for entrepreneurship and strategic management research*. Northampton, MA: Edward Elgar.

Cohen, B., & Winn, M. I. (2007). Market imperfections, opportunity and sustainable entrepreneurship. *Journal of Business Venturing*, *22*(1), 29–29.

Coleman, S. (2007). The role of human and financial capital in the profitability and growth of women-owned small firms. *Journal of Small Business Management, 45*(3), 303–319.

Cooperrider, D., & Fry, R. (2012). Mirror flourishing and the positive psychology of sustainability. *Journal of Corporate Citizenship, 46*, 3–12.

Corner, P. D., & Ho, M. (2010). How opportunities develop in social entrepreneurship. *Entrepreneurship: Theory & Practice, 34*(4), 635–659.

Crittenden, C. (2000). Ecofeminism meets business: A comparison of ecofeminist, corporate, and free market ideologies. *Journal of Business Ethics, 24*(1), 51–63.

Dacin, P. A., Dacin, M. T., & Matear, M. (2010). Social entrepreneurship: Why we don't need a new theory and how we move forward from here. *Academy of Management Perspectives, 24*(3), 37–57.

Datta, P. B., & Gailey, R. (2012). Empowering women through social entrepreneurship: Case study of a women's cooperative in India. *Entrepreneurship: Theory & Practice, 36*(3), 569–587.

de Bruin, A., Brush, C. G., & Welter, F. (2007). Advancing a framework for coherent research on women's entrepreneurship. *Entrepreneurship: Theory & Practice, 31*(3), 323–339.

De Tienne, D. R., & Chandler, G. N. (2007). The role of gender in opportunity identification. *Entrepreneurship: Theory & Practice, 31*(3), 365–386.

Ehrenfeld, J. R. (2005). The roots of sustainability. *MIT Sloan Management Review, 46*(2), 23–25.

Ehrenfeld, J. R. (2008). *Sustainability by design: A subversive strategy for transforming our consumer culture.* New Haven, CT: Yale University Press.

Ehrenfeld, J. R. (2012). Beyond the brave new world: Business for sustainability. In P. Bansal & A. J. Hoffman (Eds), *The Oxford handbook of business and the natural environment* (pp. 611–619). Oxford: Oxford University Press.

Ehrenfeld, J. R., & Hoffman, A. J. (2013). *Flourishing: A frank conversation about sustainability.* Stanford, CA: Stanford University Press.

Elkington, J. (1997). *Cannibals with forks: The triple bottom line of twenty-first century business.* Oxford: Capstone.

Engelman, R. (2013). Beyond sustainababble. In L. Starke, E. Assadourian, & T. Prugh (Eds), *State of the world 2013: Is sustainability still possible?* (pp. 3–16). Washington, DC: Island Press/Worldwatch Institute.

Folke, C. (2013). Respecting planetary boundaries and reconnecting to the biosphere. In L. Starke, E. Assadourian, & T. Prugh (Eds), *State of the world 2013: Is sustainability still possible?* (pp. 19–27). Washington, DC: Island Press/Worldwatch Institute.

Gaard, G. (2001). Women, water, energy: An ecofeminist approach. *Organization & Environment, 14*(2), 157–172.

Gibbs, D. (2009). Sustainability entrepreneurs, ecopreneurs and the development of a sustainable economy. *Greener Management International, 55*, 63–78.

Gray, B. J., Duncan, S., Kirkwood, J., & Walton, S. (2014). Encouraging sustainable entrepreneurship in climate-threatened communities: A Samoan case study. *Entrepreneurship & Regional Development, 26*(5), 401–430.

Griffiths, M. D., Gundry, L. K., & Kickul, J. R. (2013). The socio-political, economic, and cultural determinants of social entrepreneurship activity. *Journal of Small Business and Enterprise Development, 20*(2), 341–357.

Hahn, T., Figge, F., Pinkse, J., & Preuss, L. (2010). Editorial: Trade-offs in corporate sustainability: You can't have your cake and eat it. *Business Strategy and the Environment, 19*, 217–229.

Halkias, D., Nwajiuba, C., Harkiolakis, N., & Caracatsanis, S. M. (2011). Challenges facing women entrepreneurs in Nigeria. *Management Research Review, 34*(2), 221–235.

Hall, J. K., Daneke, G. A., & Lenox, M. J. (2010). Sustainable development and entrepreneurship: Past contributions and future directions. *Journal of Business Venturing, 25*(5), 439–448.

Hessing, M. (1993). Women and sustainability: Ecofeminist perspectives. *Alternatives, 19*(4), 14–21.

Hockerts, K., & Wüstenhagen, R. (2010). Greening Goliaths versus emerging Davids: Theorizing about the role of incumbents and new entrants in sustainable entrepreneurship. *Journal of Business Venturing, 25*(5), 481–492.

Hughes, K. D., & Jennings, J. E. (2012). *Global women's entrepreneurship research: Diverse settings, questions and approaches.* Cheltenham/Northampton: Edward Elgar.

Hughes, K. D., Jennings, J. E., Brush, C., Carter, S., & Welter, F. (2012). Extending Women's Entrepreneurship Research in New Directions. *Entrepreneurship: Theory & Practice, 36*(3), 429–442.

Hunter, L., Hatch, A., & Johnson, A. (2004). Cross-national gender variation in environmental behaviours. *Social Science Quarterly, 85*(3), 677–694.

IPCC. (2013). *Climate change 2013: The physical science basis - Summary for policymakers*. Geneva, Switzerland. Retrieved from http://www.ipcc.ch/report/ar5/wg1/.

Isaak, R. (2002). The making of the ecopreneur. *Greener Management International, 38*, 81–91.

Jackson, T. (2011). Societal transformations for a sustainable economy. *Natural Resources Forum, 35*(3), 155–164.

Kearins, K., & Collins, E. (2012). Making sense of ecopreneurs' decisions to sell up. *Business Strategy and the Environment, 21*(2), 71–85.

Korten, D. C. (2006). The great turning: From empire to earth community. San Francisco CA: Berrett-Koehler & Bloomfield CT: Kumarian Press.

Kumar, A. (2013). Women entrepreneurs in a masculine society: Inclusive strategy for sustainable outcomes. *International Journal of Organizational Analysis, 21*(3), 373–384.

Kurucz, E. C., Colbert, B. A., & Wheeler, D. (2013). *Reconstructing value: Leadership skills for a sustainable world*. Toronto: University of Toronto Press.

Laszlo, C., Brown, J. S., Ehrenfeld, J., Gorham, M., Pose, I. B., Robson, L., ... Werder, P. (2014). *Flourishing enterprise: The new spirit of business*. Stanford, CA: Stanford Business Books.

Lenox, M., & York, J. G. (2012). Environmental entrepreneurship. In P. Bansal & A. J. Hoffman (Eds), *The Oxford handbook of business and the natural environment* (pp. 70–82). Oxford: Oxford University Press.

Levie, J., & Hart, M. (2011). Business and social entrepreneurs in the UK: Gender, context and commitment. *International Journal of Gender and Entrepreneurship, 3*(3), 200–217.

Leyden, D., & Link, A. (2015). Toward a theory of the entrepreneurial process. *Small Business Economics, 44*(3), 475–484.

Lietaer, B., Arnsperger, C., Goerner, S., & Brunnhuber, S. (2012). *Money and sustainability: The missing link, The Club of Rome EU Chapter to Finance Watch and the World Business Academy - Summary*. Retrieved from http://www.clubofrome.org/cms/wp-content/uploads/2012/05/Money-and-Sustainability-the-missing-link-Executive-Summary.pdf.

Luke, B., Verreynne, M.-L., & Kearins, K. (2007). Measuring the benefits of entrepreneurship at different levels of analysis. *Journal of Management & Organization, 13*, 312–330.

Mackey, J., & Sisodia, R. (2013). *Conscious capitalism: Liberating the heroic spirit of business*. Boston, MA: Harvard Business School Publishing Corporation.

Mair, J., & Martí, I. (2006). Social entrepreneurship research: A source of explanation, prediction, and delight. *Journal of World Business, 41*(1), 36–44.

Martin, R. L., & Osberg, S. (2007). Social entrepreneurship: The case for definition. *Stanford Social Innovation Review, 5*(2), 28–39.

Morgan, T. (2013). Perfect storm: Energy, finance and the end of growth. *Strategy Insights* (9).

OECD. (2011). *Divided we stand: Why inequality keeps rising*. Retrieved 23 September 2013, from http://www.oecd.org/els/soc/dividedwestandwhyinequalitykeepsrising.htm.

Parrish, B. D. (2010). Sustainability-driven entrepreneurship: Principles of organization design. *Journal of Business Venturing, 25*(5), 510–523.

Parrish, B. D., & Foxon, T. J. (2009). Sustainability entrepreneurship and equitable transitions to a low-carbon economy. *Greener Management International, 55*, 47–62.

Raworth, K. (2013). Defining a safe and just space for humanity. In L. Starke, E. Assadourian, & T. Prugh (Eds), *State of the world 2013: Is sustainability still possible?* (pp. 28–38). Washington, DC: Island Press/Worldwatch Institute.

Rindova, V., Barry, D., & Ketchn, D. J. (2009). Entrepreneuring as emancipation. *Academy of Management Review, 34*(3), 477–491.

Robb, A. M. (2002). Entrepreneurial performance by women and minorities: The case of new firms. *Journal of Developmental Entrepreneurship 7*(4), 383–397.

Rockström, J., Steffen, W., Noone, K., Persson, Å., F. Stuart Chapin, I., Lambin, E. F., Foley, J. A. (2009). A safe operating space for humanity. *Nature, 461*(7263), 472–475.

Schaper, M. (2002). The essence of ecopreneurship. *Greener Management International 38*, 26–30.

Scharmer, C. O., & Kaufer, K. (2013). *Leading from the emerging future: From ego-system to eco-system economies*. San Francisco: Berrett-Koehler.

Shane, S. (2012). Reflections on the 2010 AMR Decade Award: Delivering on the promise of entrepreneurship as a field of research. *Academy of Management Review, 37*(1), 10–20.

Short, J. C., Moss, T. W., & Lumpkin, G. T. (2009). Research in social entrepreneurship: Past contributions and future opportunities. *Strategic Entrepreneurship Journal, 3*(2), 161–194.

Sigalla, R. J., & Carney, S. (2012). Poverty reduction through entrepreneurship: Microcredit, learning and ambivalence amongst women in urban Tanzania. *International Journal of Educational Development, 32*, 546–554.

Stead, W. E., & Stead, J. G. (1994). Can humankind change the economic myth? Paradigm shifts necessary for ecological sustainable business. *Journal of Organizational Change Management, 7*, 15–31.

Steyaert, C. (2007). 'Entrepreneuring' as a conceptual attractor? A review of process theories in 20 years of entrepreneurship studies. *Entrepreneurship and Regional Development, 19*(6), 453–477.

Tedmanson, D., Verduyn, K., Essers, C., & Gartner, W. B. (2012). Critical perspectives in entrepreneurship research. *Organization, 19*(5), 531–541.

The Worldbank. (2013). *Poverty*. Retrieved 25 September 2013, from http://web.worldbank.org/WBSITE/EXTERNAL/TOPICS/EXTPOVERTY/EXTPA/0,,contentMDK:20040961~menuPK:435040~pagePK:148956~piPK:216618~theSitePK:430367~isCURL:Y,00.html.

Thompson, N., Kiefer, K., & York, J. G. (2011). Distinctions not dichotomies: Exploring social, sustainable, and environmental entrepreneurship. In G. T. Lumpkin & J. A. Katz (Eds), *Social and sustainable entrepreneurship* (pp. 201–230). Bingley, UK: Emerald.

Tilley, F., & Young, W. (2009). Sustainability entrepreneurs: Could they be the true wealth generators of the future? *Greener Management International, 55*, 79–92.

Walter, S. G., & Heinrichs, S. (2015). Who becomes an entrepreneur? A 30-years-review of individual-level research. *Journal of Small Business and Enterprise Development, 22*(2), 225–248.

Ward, J., & Aronoff, C. (1993). Will it stand the light of day? *Nation's Business, 81*(1), 61–62.

Waring, M. (1988). *Counting for nothing: What men value and what women are worth.* Wellington: Allen & Unwin / Port Nicholson Press.

WCED. (1987). *Our common future (The Brundtland Report).* Oxford: Oxford University Press.

Welford, R. J. (1998). Editorial: Corporate environmental management, technology and sustainable development: Postmodern perspectives and the need for a critical research agenda. *Business Strategy and the Environment, 7*(1), 1–12.

Zahra, S. A. (1991). Predictors and financial outcomes of corporate entrepreneurship: An exploratory study. *Journal of Business Venturing, 6*(4), 259–285.

Zahra, S. A., Gedajlovic, E., Neubaum, D. O., & Shulman, J. M. (2009). A typology of social entrepreneurs: Motives, search processes and ethical challenges. *Journal of Business Venturing, 24*(5), 519–532.

Zahra, S. A., Wright, M., & Abdelgawad, S. G. (2014). Contextualization and the advancement of entrepreneurship research. *International Small Business Journal, 32*(5), 479–500.

4

SAUDI WOMEN'S ENTREPRENEURIAL INTENTIONS

The social construction of norms and perceptions

Renaud Redien-Collot, Laurice Alexandre and Wassim J. Aloulou

Introduction

As various reports published by the International Labor Office over the course of the last 30 years have demonstrated, the participation of women in regional economic development is a source of growth and innovation in both developed and developing countries (ILO, 2010). The dynamic impact of working women on national economies is related to their level of qualifications and the skills that they acquire over the course of their careers. Female entrepreneurship constitutes a key stage in women's economic empowerment, since it takes into account the possibility for women to exploit sources of capital and business networks in order to develop new activities or acquire production tools and thus play an important role in the creation of value (Orhan, 2005).

Institutional theory (North, 1990) points to two types of macro-level factors that may either encourage or inhibit women's entrepreneurship. The regulatory dimension provides a set of laws and support systems that may nurture women's entrepreneurial initiatives. The normative dimension reveals a set of tacit social and cultural rules that offer women a basic framework when they develop entrepreneurial intentions and projects. In the context of female entrepreneurship in Mid-Eastern transitional economies, Jamali (2009) points out that it is worth studying normative dimensions before imposing new laws. As Erogul (2011) stresses in her study of women entrepreneurs in the United Emirates: family and work conceptions may resist regulations; therefore, it is important that present academic research in female entrepreneurship focuses on the current norms in order to inform future regulations. In a national culture, gender norms provide a framework defining what is possible for women in terms of organizational and entrepreneurial action (Brush, 1992). In our view, study of the entrepreneurial intentions of Saudi women would make it possible to understand how the values either hindering or stimulating the passage to the entrepreneurial act are crystalized.

In fact, figures on women in Saudi Arabia are highly contrasting. These contrasts are the fruit of a rapidly evolving economy. According to Auty (2001) and Simmons (2005), Saudi

Arabia's economy experienced a turning point in its development in the early 2000s and has become a transitional economy. Saudi Arabia's rulers have been engaged in several reforms in order to accelerate the economic maturity of their country. As female education and professional qualification are levers of development, they have introduced policies over the course of the last ten years or so focusing on promoting the role of women in the economy. According to the study carried out by the ILO in 2007 on global trends in female employment, Middle Eastern countries have the lowest female employment rates in the world (37%). In comparison, female employment rates are 75% in Sub-Saharan Africa and 80% in the European Union. According to the same source, the Middle East also has the highest female unemployment rate in the world, especially in the 15–24 age groups. And yet, a substantial number of colleges and universities catering to women have been opened in Saudi Arabia since 2002. Nevertheless, while Saudi women account for 58% of the college student body, only 14% of the workforce is female, a rate much lower than that of neighboring Islamic countries; 85% of Saudi women work in the education sector, and 6% in the health sector. In total, 95% of Saudi women in employment work in the public sector (World Bank, 2009).

Furthermore, among the factor-driven economies in the region, Saudi Arabia had the lowest total entrepreneurial activity (TEA) rate, only 4.7% of the adult population (18–64 years old) were actively involved in the start-up of a new business or owned a business less than three and half years old (GEM, 2009). However, according to a United Nations report '*Where Do Arab Women Stand in the Development Process*' (2004), 72% of registered Saudi female-owned businesses operate outside the home—making them one of the largest groups in the Middle East and North African regions according to a recent study undertaken by JCCI and the Monitor Group (Hampole, 2010). According to the same study, these results, while encouraging, may obscure a number of challenges that remain in fostering female entrepreneurship in the Kingdom:

- **Male guardianship:** Current Saudi law requires women to seek permission from men to register their businesses under the man's name, travel and perform other business and everyday-life duties. This contributes to legal and regulatory barriers in creating business, employing workers, registering property, getting credit and growing their businesses.
- **Limited government assistance**: The Saudi government has initiated only a limited number of programs targeting women's development. Most of the current initiatives receive support from the business and academic communities.
- **Lack of business experience**: The majority of Saudi women do not work outside the home (only 14% are employees), so they often lack business experience and exposure to vital skills that contribute to fueling entrepreneurship.

In a quickly transforming era, the Saudi government has started pushing for reforms to bring more women into the workforce—a push that is part of a larger campaign to increase the number of Saudi nationals employed in the private sector. (The current 8% employment rate of nationals is much lower than the government's 30% target.) The Saudi government has already taken a small number of steps to address these challenges:

- The Labor Ministry has modified the Labor Law (2008) to make it easier for men and women to interact in a professional and business environment.
- Likewise, women no longer have to get approval from their male guardians to accept or leave jobs.

Furthermore, Saudi Arabia has made a considerable effort to encourage entrepreneurship in all its facets since the "Doing Business, 2011" report ranked the country 13th out of 185 in terms of how easy it was to set up a business.

In order to interpret these contrasting results on the participation of women in the economic life of Saudi Arabia, we must get to the heart of what female entrepreneurship will be tomorrow and take an interest in the question of the entrepreneurial intentions of female students. In this regard, Hayton et al. (2002), Jamali (2009) and Naser et al. (2009) argue that cultural norms—the values, beliefs and models of a group or territory—play a key role in the emergence of entrepreneurial intentions and in the launching of entrepreneurial ventures. Mueller (2004) reminds us that, within the framework of international studies, the entrepreneurial behaviors of established male and female entrepreneurs are relatively similar (Arenius and Minitti, 2005). However, the entrepreneurial intentions of men and women vary widely from country to country. Mueller (2004) and Langowitz and Minitti (2007) point out that while these contrasts are pronounced in developed countries they are less pronounced in underdeveloped countries. What, then, is the situation in Saudi Arabia, a rapidly developing country in which the government has launched a series of important initiatives in favor of female education and employment?

Using data from a wide range of international reports, Gundry et al. (2002) highlight the fact that relations between men and women have a very substantial impact on the ambiance of business and the success of entrepreneurial initiatives in all economies. A positive male attitude to female economic initiatives is a source of innovation (Gherardi, 2000). Similarly, the capacity of women to get to know and become involved in "male" sectors is a vector of economic and social dynamism (Crompton and Lefeuvre, 2000). But social and cultural structures need to encourage shared attitudes and practices that make it possible to deconstruct overly defined gendered functions and role models and to develop new needs and markets, or, in other words, new opportunities for a larger entrepreneurial population (Gundry et al. 2002).

Beyond considering these ideas theoretically and contextually from a Saudi perspective, this study integrates exploratory results on a study of the entrepreneurial intentions and perspectives of Saudi young men and women to inform our thinking and provide direction for future empirical work. In our discussion we consider how Saudi women may act as major agents of change and how the entrepreneurial environment that surrounds them may encourage or inhibit such transformation.

Literature

In the field of research into entrepreneurial intention, we focus more on the emergence of that intention than on the transition between initial intention and the emergence of opportunity (Eckhardt and Shane, 2003). Nevertheless, these two aspects are dialectically linked. In this context, we point out that values are normative constructs that are embedded in the entrepreneurial motivational architecture. It seems that, in most countries, values may inhibit women in terms of the emergence of entrepreneurial intention and its subsequent development (GEM, 2009). Many studies explore how values stimulate entrepreneurial intentions. We think that it is also important to pinpoint how values may restrain entrepreneurial motivations. Therefore, we will, initially, examine the construct of entrepreneurial intention, before focusing on the two major ways in which it is inhibited.

1. Entrepreneurial intention

Most studies in the field present entrepreneurship as the result of planned action guided by a certain degree of intentionality (Shapero and Sokol, 1982; Bouchikhi, 1993). Intentionality feeds into both the rational and personal aspects of the entrepreneur's decision-making process with regard to the emerging opportunity that he or she has created or discovered (Eckhardt and Shane, 2003). Entrepreneurial intention is the dynamic that enables individuals to design their projects by encouraging them simultaneously to externalize their desire to become entrepreneurs and internalize a certain number of environmental constraints (Arenius and Minitti, 2005). More generally, intention makes it possible for entrepreneurs to develop a strong, dialogical relationship with their projects, which enables them to incorporate a large number of changes and perspectives in order to render them viable (Fayolle 2004).

As suggested in the model proposed by Ajzen (1985), for the individual, intention marks the moment when beliefs concerning desirability and feasibility converge. Desirability is what prompts the individual to perceive a certain number of desirable and positive (entrepreneurial) behaviors (Krueger and Brazeal, 1994). Feasibility is what prompts the individual to consider (entrepreneurial) behaviors as belonging to his or her field of competence (Bandura, 1977). Desirability and feasibility are both the object of a learning process (Fishbein and Ajzen, 1975) and strongly determined by cultural and social factors.

Desirability and feasibility are perceptions that, when combined, give rise to entrepreneurial intention (Fayolle, 2002). It is important to situate the normative anchoring of these perceptions: they inform us about how they are linked to affects (subjective norms) and cultural rules (collective norms). According to Bandura (1977), collective representations constitute the cultural matrix of a group or nation. This makes it possible to measure the direct and indirect impacts of culture on the motivational and intentional schema. To a substantial degree, perceptions of desirability are defined by subjective norms, while perceptions of feasibility are defined by an (actionable) synthesis of subjective and collective norms (Ajzen, 1985). Nevertheless, Bandura (1977) observes that some perceptions are largely influenced by collective norms: perceptions of legitimacy or appropriateness (Radu and Redien-Collot, 2008).

In our view, in order to understand the role of the cultural dimension in the formation of entrepreneurial intention, we need to take into account not only beliefs concerning desirability and feasibility, which traditionally structure the theory of planned behavior, but also beliefs in the appropriateness of the actions to be undertaken. Consequently, we propose a ternary structure of the theory of planned behavior, as follows:

- **Desirability**, or a perception that triggers a favorable attitude to entrepreneurship backed up by an acceptance of personally selected (and thus subjective) social norms that create a sense of legitimacy.
- **Appropriateness**, or a perception that emphasizes the normative (and thus central) character of entrepreneurship. The perception of appropriateness is based on an acceptance of collective norms; a belief in appropriateness gives rise to a capacity to take risks by seeing shared rules as opportunities rather than constraints.
- **Feasibility**, or a perception that designates entrepreneurship as a possibility; this perception derives from a sentiment of self-efficacy, which generates confidence in one's own abilities (locus of control) in both individual and collective contexts. It pre-supposes that the individual is capable of exploiting his or her competencies in regard to subjective and collective norms in a given situation.

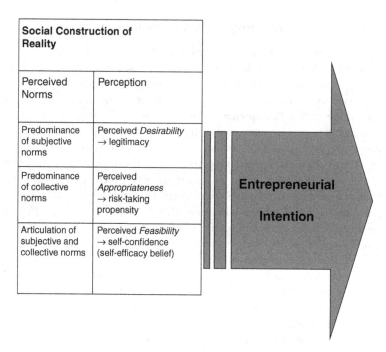

Social Construction of Reality	
Perceived Norms	Perception
Predominance of subjective norms	Perceived *Desirability* → legitimacy
Predominance of collective norms	Perceived *Appropriateness* → risk-taking propensity
Articulation of subjective and collective norms	Perceived *Feasibility* → self-confidence (self-efficacy belief)

Entrepreneurial Intention

Figure 4.1 The norms and perceptions underlying entrepreneurial intentions
Source: (Radu and Redien-Collot, 2008).

Of course, the cultural issue, or, in other words, the influence of collective norms, is central to perceptions of appropriateness, but it is also operative in perceptions of feasibility and, *in fine*, in perceptions of desirability. In effect, even if the perception of desirability is largely based on subjective norms, in order to affirm them, the individual has to detach them from collective norms without creating a rupture. A synoptic representation of the three types of perceptions underlying entrepreneurial intention is provided in Figure 4.1.

In a study on entrepreneurial intention, we can identify entrepreneurial perceptions, namely, the intensity of perceptions of desirability, appropriateness and feasibility of given subjects. Nevertheless, in order to accurately gauge the influence of culture, our measurement of perception must focus on cultural representations in a given field, that of the press, for example (Radu and Redien-Collot, 2008). As Brush (2002) observes, the question of the difference between male and female perceptions of a particular issue, be it public (professional) or private, presupposes that the cultural context be taken into account. In effect, the difference between male and female entrepreneurial perceptions is at the origin of all regional and national cultural specificities (Dodd and Patra, 2002; Wennekers et al., 2001). By focusing on male and female Saudi students' perception of the entrepreneurial approach, we intend to consider what, culturally, structures the relation of a given population to entrepreneurship. Because women's perceptions reveal what otherwise remains unsaid within a culture (Guionnet and Neveu, 2005), we accord more importance to women than to men in this study.

2. *The entrepreneurial intention of women*

We should first summarize what has been said to date about women's entrepreneurial intention. In fact, after initially being characterized by a comparative approach between men and women, research on female entrepreneurship has, for the last 20 years, assumed a gynocentric focus, or, in other words, an exclusive emphasis on the perceptions of women. According to Brush (1992), the role of sex in the construction of the individual and of the entrepreneurial process is relatively easy to track. All the specificities characterizing women's access to the field of entrepreneurship are to be found here. In most cases, these specificities are associated with socio-cultural constructs that often have deep roots in education and childhood, even when the educational system proclaims perfect gender equality or a soon-to-be-successful assault on gender equality. Furthermore, according to Du Rietz and Henrekson (2000), in many entrepreneurial configurations researchers observe, amongst other things, that men feel more easily able to question their coaches and consequently make more rapid progress, while women generally feel excluded, in mixed groups, from the right to ask questions, which holds them back from starting up businesses.

Meanwhile, the environment is characterized by the presence of substantial barriers that women entrepreneurs have to confront, namely, the hostility of banks, suppliers and networks of entrepreneurs. Fisher et al. (1993) and Watson and Newby (2005) provide an overall vision of the studies carried out on obstacles to female entrepreneurship. They underline that, since the late 1980s, entrepreneurial studies have been characterized by two feminist currents:

- **Social feminism**, which identifies differences in approaches to entrepreneurship located in early processes of socialization taking recurrent explicit and implicit forms and
- **Liberal feminism**, which defends the idea of equal opportunities for men and women in terms of access to entrepreneurship and underlines the fact that women have more problems than men in developing their enterprises and, consequently, structure their firms differently because they find it hard to access certain kinds of resources and are victims of various kinds of discrimination.

When applied to entrepreneurship, social and liberal feminism postulate that, historically, inequalities exist and that a reformist approach applying egalitarian policies would make it possible to eradicate them (Baughn et al., 2006).

Nevertheless, in terms of entrepreneurial intention, there are still pronounced contrasts between men and women. Taking inspiration from the theory of planned behavior (Ajzen, 1985), Mueller (2004) carried out a comparative international study in which he highlighted that women's entrepreneurial intentions were less ambitious than men's. He explained this phenomenon in reference to a minor locus of control and a propensity to take fewer risks in the female populations studied. Nevertheless, as Hayton et al. (2002) observe, these two factors do not entirely explain why women are less involved in entrepreneurship than men. Studying the gender bias from a cultural point of view implies taking into account men's and women's attitudes to female entrepreneurship and the reflexive viewpoint of women concerning the issue (Butler, 2004). Our study therefore addresses the question of the entrepreneurial intention of Saudi women not only from the point of view of various perceptions of the problematic (Mueller, 2004), but also of its representations defined as subjective and collective beliefs. This will enrich the traditional approach to the research issue of female entrepreneurial intention and open new analytical perspectives.

Gundry et al. (2002) underline the degree to which the success of female entrepreneurs is conditioned by the economic context. Nevertheless, as Smith et al. (1997) point out, the economic context is organized in function of male and female role models in which, in the majority of cultures, stereotypes continue to attribute a wider range of legitimate professions, functions and sectors to men than to women. These stereotypes have a deci-sive influence on professional life and business culture (Gundry et al., 2002). According to Mueller (2004), the emergence of female entrepreneurial intention is, of necessity, affected by such stereotypes.

3. The cultural context, the Saudi context

As Mueller (2004) observes, all countries are characterized by cultural factors that either inhibit or encourage female entrepreneurial intention. According to the results of the com-parative study by Langowitz and Minitti (2007), female entrepreneurial intention is always less pronounced than its male equivalent due to issues associated with women's internal locus of control and their lesser propensity to take risks (Mueller, 2004). Nevertheless, the authors underline the fact that the contrast between men and women in terms of entrepreneurial intention is stronger in developed countries and less pronounced in developing countries. The Saudi Arabia of 2012 presents a particular case of an economy in transition, which calls Mueller's results into question. Our initial objective is, then, to advance our understanding of the role of the cultural context—linked to the question of gender and, more specifically, to that of relations between men and women—in the development of female entrepreneurial intention.

We refer to the analyses of Mueller (2004) and Langowitz and Minitti (2007) of the contrast between men and women with regard to entrepreneurial intention. Initially, re-searchers focused on a highly comparative approach to relations between women and men in different countries. Indeed, they concluded that there were gender-based differences in perception in terms of risk-taking and the internal locus of control. This comparative approach can produce reductive results by defining male and female samples in reference to their apparent specificities, thereby reinforcing stereotypes. As Butler (2004) observes, the notion of gender is eminently interactive and, as such, is fully consonant with inter-actionist theory. Since, in all cultures, the masculine "makes" the feminine, and vice-versa, to study gender is not merely to make comparisons, but also to take into account the intersecting and reflexive views of men and women about given behaviors and atti-tudes—in this instance, women's choice of entrepreneurial trajectory. In their critique of gender studies in the field of entrepreneurship, most of which were limited to an analysis of differences in stereotypical sex roles, Watson and Newby (2005) recall the importance of integrating an interactionist vision into the research design. Therefore, we support the articulation of a sex-based comparison with a gender-based approach in order to better understand the role of the cultural context in the development of female entrepreneurial intention in Saudi Arabia.

In the field that interests us, culture—values, beliefs, models—can have three types of major impacts on perceptions at the origin of entrepreneurial intention in both men and women: due to collective norms, it can impact on the desirability, feasibility and meaning of appropriateness. In order to measure that impact, it is therefore necessary to evaluate the perceptions of young Saudi women and compare them with those of young women in other countries. More precisely, the following factors need to be measured:

- The desire to become involved in entrepreneurship (desirability) nourished by the per-ceived attractiveness of entrepreneurship.
- The capacity to take risks, or, in other words, not to (entirely) respect certain subjective and collective norms in order to achieve their goals; in other words, their perception

of appropriateness, which could prompt them to run the risk of, on occasion, seeming improper.

- The confidence in themselves (internal locus of control) and their feeling of self-efficacy when confronted by a new object (entrepreneurial project), nourished by a capacity to compare subjective and collective norms; in other words, their perception of feasibility.

We take up these topics in an exploratory fashion with description in the next section.

Exploratory empirical work

To explore these ideas in relation to our understanding of the cultural context of entrepreneurial behavior, we conducted a simple survey of male and female students in Saudi Arabia, most particularly students likely to have a more open attitude to the outside world, or, in other words, students in international disciplines. Indeed, Kabasakal and Bodur (2002) observe that in these disciplines, young people have a greater propensity to become involved in entrepreneurship, whether it involves taking over the family firm, setting up a business, or focusing on innovation. Consequently, our sample does not reflect the young Saudi population as a whole, but the population likely to express the most advanced, and, at the same time, the most diversified desires in the field of entrepreneurship. These results are not intend to be generalized, but rather illuminative of cultural context.

We consider entrepreneurial intentions and perceptions of the entire group, comparisons of females and males, and then particular gender-based considerations of women around their confidence and their attitude to risk-taking as it relates to entrepreneurial potential. We note that male and female points of view on entrepreneurship in general and on the potential for women to become entrepreneurs in particular exert, at a very early stage and to a very large degree, different forms of direct and indirect pressure on choices of professional trajectory (Morgan et al., 2001; Francis, 2002).

The questionnaire was distributed to 163 students in the university in which one of the co-authors teaches. The sample included 75 women and 88 men. The questionnaire, translated into Arabic, was distributed to students in the first year through the sixth year of university; 80% of them in the third and fourth year, aged between 18 and 25 with a median age of 20, and studying different disciplines: 90% economics and management and the rest concerned technical and human sciences. The questionnaire was divided into three sections including a general section for all participants, a second where sex of respondent was noted and a third offered exclusively to female subjects. Please see our data analysis in Tables 4.1, 4.2 and 4.3.

Discussion: gender and mainstream entrepreneurial intentions

An analysis of the responses of our sample highlights the fact that gender has a relative impact on perception of entrepreneurial desirability as perceived by individuals, and a more notable impact on their perceptions of entrepreneurial feasibility. In effect, male and female students have the same rate of entrepreneurial motivation, but female students tend to envision launching their entrepreneurial projects later than their male counterparts. Additionally, in terms of conveying the objectives that guide them in an entrepreneurial project, male students have a more idealized vision ("making my dreams come true" for 55% of them), while female students express more fundamental motivations ("working in an area that they like" for 33% of them). Furthermore, 80% of male and female students recognize

Table 4.1 Perceptions of entrepreneurship practice

Difficulty level of launching a venture (N=163)

Easy	26 (16%)
Difficult	113 (69%)
Don't know	23 (14%)
Missing	1 (1%)

Is it easier for a man than for a woman to create a venture? (N=163)

Yes	130 (80%)
No	13 (8%)
Don't know	18 (11%)
Missing	2 (1%)

What do you believe are the chances of success of your venture given the national environment?

Yes	45 (28%)
No	90 (55%)
Don't know	27 (17%)
Missing	1 (1%)

Table 4.2 Entrepreneurial intentions, by sex

	Men	Women	Total
Entrepreneurial intention (N=163)			
Intend to launch	62 (38%)	53 (33%)	115 (71%)
Not sure	20 (12%)	17 (10%)	37 (23%)
No intent to launch	6 (4%)	5 (3%)	11 (7%)
Of those who intend to launch (N=115), what is your time frame for entrepreneurship?			
After completing studies	14 (22%)	6 (11%)	20 (17%)
After acquiring some experience	30 (26%)	26 (23%)	56 (49%)
When father decides to pass on enterprise to son/daughter	0	1 (0%)	1 (0%)
Don't know when	6 (5%)	11 (10%)	17 (15%)
Other	11 (10%)	10 (9%)	21 (18%)
Motivations for setting up an enterprise. Multiple answers accepted.			
Be autonomous	32	25	
Make my dreams come true	48	30	
Do as my parents do	4	0	
Don't have a boss to answer to	10	7	
Enjoy a high social status	24	19	

	Men	Women	Total
Work in an area that we like	32	26	
Other	1	1	
No response	2	3	

**Is aid from government expected in setting up
an enterprise? (N=163)★**

	Men	Women	Total
Yes	29 (18%)	16 (10%)	45 (28%)
No	42 (26%)	48 (29%)	90 (55%)
Don't know	17 (10%)	10 (6%)	27 (17%)
Missing	0	1 (0%)	1 (0%)

Table 4.3 Perceptions of women

Do you have sufficient skills to start a business? (N=75)

Yes	45 (59%)
No	29 (40%)
Missing	1 (1%)

**For those who do not believe they have sufficient skills to start a
business: what doubts do you have about your entrepreneurial capacity?
(N=29)**

This is not a job for a woman	1 (3%)
I do not have enough skills (I need to be better prepared)	14 (48%)
Nobody would find me credible	3 (10%)
This is frowned upon in my country	2 (7%)
Other	9 (31%)

**What are your sectorial preferences for your entrepreneurship project?
(N=75)**

Tourism/trips	6 (4%)
Sewing/handicraft	6 (4%)
Shops	33 (20%)
Services	19 (12%)
Other	8 (5%)
Missing	3 (2%)

**What do you perceive as external barriers to your entrepreneurial
project? Multiple answers accepted.**

This is frowned upon by society	26
Parents did not permit it	14
It is very difficult for her administratively	60
It all depends on religion	17
Other	5

that it is more difficult for a woman than for a man to become involved in entrepreneurship. Behind this affirmation there is, on the one hand, an observation—concerning a socio-economic situation in which men and women do not enjoy the same level of opportunity—and, on the other, prescriptive implications that can dissuade young women from becoming involved in entrepreneurship from displaying a degree of ambition in terms of their entrepreneurial projects.

If we focus on the perceptions of entrepreneurial feasibility of Saudi female students, we observe that they are more pessimistic than their male counterparts about external barriers (68%, as against 45%), or, in other words, about the kind of aid and support available in Saudi Arabia for entrepreneurial initiatives. Clearly, this attitude is a source of inhibitions (Orhan, 2005). More specifically linked to regional or national values, feminine awareness of certain cultural obstacles can reveal areas of progress that are just as valid for male entrepreneurs as for female ones.

In their entrepreneurial future, when female respondents do not see obstacles, they see restrictions. The vast majority of the respondents (96%) located their first venture in fairly traditional sectors. They thus projected themselves into a conventionally feminine world in which taking too many economic or social risks is frowned upon. To judge by the data, 35% are worried about what people might say, while 41% (18.7% + 22.6%) are concerned about running up against familial and religious norms. For a fairly large proportion of female respondents, respecting norms of appropriateness is central to underpinning the feasibility of the entrepreneurial project. However, as the Saudi government plans to see women playing a more important economic role in the next years, Saudi policies may also influence respondents' answers.

We note that this inquiry was carried out at a time of pronounced economic and educational transition for Saudi female students (Simmons, 2005). Emphasis should be placed on the way in which the quest for entrepreneurial feasibility provokes different states of awareness—for which a typology encompassing states ranging from simple awareness to political involvement (Redien-Collot, 2012) should be established, which, by defining new approaches to entrepreneurial feasibility, aim to displace—and effectively manage really to displace—existing norms and systems of appropriateness.

Overall, we see that an analysis of factors underpinning the entrepreneurial intention of Saudi students reveals the impact of gender and values, particularly regarding the question of appropriateness. On the other hand, if, as can be observed in the case of Saudi female students, individual motivation reveals a tension between desirability and feasibility, then values can provide counterweights, or, in other words, elements of rebalancing, that should not be neglected if our aim is to intensify the entrepreneurial commitment of individuals.

Saudi female students have thus made some progress in their quest for the kind of entrepreneurial legitimacy that provides the basis of the desire to become involved in entrepreneurship. Seventy percent of them claim to share that desire. The stage concerning feasibility and norms of appropriateness is more problematic: many Saudi female students envision lateral entrepreneurial strategies that make it possible to avoid certain social pressures that might have the effect of discouraging or destabilizing them. In such cases, entrepreneurial feasibility conforms to current norms of appropriateness. Nevertheless, the silence of some female respondents with regard to this question perhaps reveals that they are seeking to reverse/transgress certain professional gender norms with a view to finding other approaches to entrepreneurial feasibility, and, therefore, accomplishment.

A world economic area with several challenges

Similar to other Gulf nations, Saudi Arabia has a higher female labor force than other nations of the MENA region (Mc Loughlin, 2013). This is due to lower unemployment rates overall, a better level of female education, and different recent government policies that attempt to reduce dependence on foreign labor. However, Saudi women empowerment is a key issue in the context of a major turning point of the national economic model. Several reports have stressed that Gulf nations and nations of the MENA region have to valorize their best talents in order to rely less on oil revenues and growth generated by large public companies and more on the development of SMEs and skillful entrepreneurial teams (Devlin, 2010). The economy has to diversify its activities and respond to the internal demand of the countries of the region.

The economies will have to rely on men and women of the rising generation to address the needs of the national markets and their different segments and should facilitate access to a range of resources to allow individual entrepreneurs of this generation to elaborate a consistent offer and meet the market. If female students demonstrate strong perception of desirability for entrepreneurship, policy makers could increase their self-confidence and their chance to launch their venture if they set up initiatives that would decrease the respondents' negative perception of the feasibility of their entrepreneurial projects. They could provide aid for and facilitate access to entrepreneurship, thus mirroring the situation in the United Arab Emirates or in Bahrain and Oman as analyzed respectively by Erogul (2011) and Dechant and Lamky (2005). In these countries, educational structures and entrepreneur clubs make it possible to make women aware of obstacles to entrepreneurship that have encouraged not only the emergence of new initiatives, but also of new entrepreneurial perceptions and values.

Dechant and Lamky (2005) suggest that a new generation of Mid-Eastern women feel responsible for highlighting the importance of coaching and relational aspects in incubators that, initially, were little more than hotels for start-up companies. Similarly, in her focus on MENA countries Jamali (2009) underlines the role played by women in drawing attention to the importance of "modeling" in the field of entrepreneurship. In our study, of the 40% of female respondents who have concerns about their lack of entrepreneurial skills, 59% have identified their problems and will very probably ask for or even set up structures providing education and advice in the field of entrepreneurship.

In the MENA region, Mc Loughlin (2013) observes the emergence of formalized support systems for women entrepreneurs. Whereas the Goldman Sachs 10,000 Women initiatives target high-potential female entrepreneurs who launch ventures in high-tech industries and social innovation, other associations are focused on more-modest entrepreneurial projects. In encouraging basic entrepreneurial initiatives, the organizers of the Women's Business Development Center in Egypt have two goals. They plan to fuel the entrepreneurial spirit in a population that is frequently facing unemployment.

At the same time, they do not discourage young female students from using their projects in a traditionally feminine industry as a first step to gain self-confidence and develop further projects with the financial support of their families and friends. Moreover, as Casa Pionnières in Morocco and the Palestinian Business Women's Association (ASALA) mention on their websites, the promotion of women's cooperation and transfer of skills and know-how allow women to appreciate and explore the economic chain of value that they can deploy together. In order to surmount their fears in terms of entrepreneurial feasibility, Saudi policy makers could encourage these types of networks. However, in doing so, they have to face a very challenging issue: Saudi women will gain true business expertise and leadership that may be undermined by other national business actors. The Saudi government must have a clear agenda concerning these types of tensions that will be reflected in business women's difficulty in raising funds for ambitious projects. In other words, we are not sure whether the Saudi government measures the different implications embedded in the promotion of female entrepreneurial initiatives.

Saudi women as major agents of change

The rising generation of Saudi women identifies entrepreneurship as a professional option. At the same time, they are conscious that they will face several obstacles. Generational consciousness of these types of obstacles may help them to relativize objective and subjective challenges. Social media may help them to see that they are all experiencing the syndrome of the first-timer that will change the perceptions of young professional women in Saudi Arabia and their social representations. At the same time, they have to deploy an important effort of communication in order to relate this change with the emergence of the new national economic model. Given a relative legitimacy in the perception of their entrepreneurial future, females can establish a dialog with their siblings and the different stakeholders of their entrepreneurial projects in order to obtain moral and practical support, assert their leadership and attract resources (Krueger et al., 2000). In parallel, the consciousness of their lack of skills and resources will help them:

- To connect their entrepreneurial desirability with the broad expectations of policy makers and co-construct with them and their local representatives appropriate support; for example, Erogul (2011) points out how a set of Emirati women's single voices has helped to better integrate women entrepreneurship in the agenda of the Ministry of Economy.
- To articulate the expected outcomes of the future SMEs with the inputs that government will provide; for example, Jamali (2009) stresses how Lebanese women who have struggled for the development of their entrepreneurial skills seem to run more growth-oriented firms than their male and female counterparts who belong to business milieus.
- To identify situations and institutions that can help them to develop skills and access resources in several types of entrepreneurial situations; for example, Dechant and Lamki (2005) show how women entrepreneurs have convinced academic partners to launch workshops for female entrepreneurs. A few years later, this type of initiative has inspired The Goldman Sachs 10,000 Women to develop a partnership with UK and USA universities and launch several entrepreneurial programs for women in the MENA region.

In developing self-reflectiveness on the social and cultural challenges in achieving female entrepreneurial projects, Saudi women may:

- Develop their male counterparts' awareness in order to support female entrepreneurs' initiatives; similar to another study that we conducted in Egypt (Alexandre-Leclaire and Redien-Collot, 2013), the male respondents of our sample seemed to be keen on encouraging their female counterparts. However, within a couple of years, men and women may have to negotiate several aspects of work/life balance so that women can achieve their entrepreneurial projects.

- Connect more well-off and under-privileged women who face the same challenges in the exploration and concretization of their entrepreneurial projects. During the last ten years, the Women's Business Development Center in Egypt has stimulated these types of interactions that accelerate transfer of knowledge, practices and social capital and can help women to find associates and design more-robust business models.

Conclusions

Our study questions the conclusions reached by Mueller (2004) and Langowitz and Minitti (2007) who pointed out that, in developing countries, women present weaker entrepreneurial intentions than men. It can be argued that, in countries whose economies are developing rapidly, there are no differences between men and women in terms of the degree of entrepreneurial desirability but significant differences in terms of feasibility. Nevertheless, due to certain contradictions in the results of studies that have already been carried out and the not generalizable character of our study, we believe that it is important to develop new international research projects on the entrepreneurial intention of women especially in developing countries.

In view of the fact that results produced by Mueller (2004) indicate that women in developing countries present a weaker degree of entrepreneurial intention than women in developed countries do, the comparison in the perception of the entrepreneurial desirability of French female students (13%) and Saudi female students (70%) is problematic. As Manolova et al. (2007) suggest, for the population as a whole, it is possible that economic transition brutally accelerates the desire of female populations to become involved in entrepreneurship but that, once the economy has attained a certain stage of development in which a greater number of salaried jobs have become available, entrepreneurial intentions are tempered. This is an area that would be worthwhile exploring.

We recommend to the political and educational actors in today's Saudi Arabia that training programs more specifically aimed at women attempting to develop entrepreneurial projects be introduced in order to not only improve their skills, but also work on the values and norms of appropriateness associated with the entrepreneurial approach. In terms of how values and norms are integrated into choices about what kind of entrepreneurial projects to develop, we suggest the importance of the role played by perceived norms of appropriateness. Further studies should be undertaken with a view to defining, for a given culture, the situations and conditions in which certain norms of this kind act as hindrances or levers. This type of study could later be extended to various national and/or regional samples, thereby making comparisons possible.

In order to develop the observations made by Bandura (1977) concerning the fact that the impact of norms of appropriateness makes it possible, or otherwise, to take risks, it will be necessary to ascertain in which social and socio-educative groups these norms have the most impact. Furthermore, emphasis should be placed on the way in which the influence of norms of appropriateness encourages individuals to use camouflage or diversionary tactics (i.e., use of social media) in the field of entrepreneurship, tactics that, perhaps, characterize a substantial percentage of entrepreneurial initiatives. We should also ask ourselves whether the authors of these "camouflaged" initiatives should be offered aid and advice with a view to restoring their confidence by helping them free themselves from the shackles of norms of appropriateness or to making individuals aware of their relationship with certain norms of appropriateness in order to help them become involved in "lifestyle"-type entrepreneurship corresponding to a certain socio-cultural configuration and to economic needs that are not always explored.

References

Ajzen, I. (1985). From intentions to actions: A theory of planned behaviour, in J. Kuhl and J. Beckman (eds), *Action-Control: From cognition to behaviour* 11–39, Heidelberg, Germany: Springer.

Alexandre-Leclair, L. and Redien-Collot, R. (2013). L'influence de la culture sur l'intention entrepreneuriale des femmes; le cas de l'Egypte. *Revue Internationale PME* 26 (1): 93–117.

Arenius, P. and Minitti, M. (2005). Perceptual variables and nascent entrepreneurship. *Small Business Economics* 24: 233–247.

Auty, R.M. (ed.) (2001). *Resource Abundance and Economic Development.* Oxford, UK: Oxford U.P.

Bandura, A. (1977). Self-Efficacy: Toward a unifying theory of behavioral change. *Psychological Review* 84: 191–215.

Baughn, C., Chua, B.L. and Neupert, K. (2006). The normative context for women's participation in entrepreneurship: a multicountry study. *Entrepreneurship Theory & Practice* 30 (5): 687–708.

Binks, M., Starkey, K. and Mahon, C. (2006). Entrepreneurship education and the business school. *Technology Analysis & Strategic Management* 18 (1): 1–18.

Boissin, J.P., Chollet B. and Emin, S. (2007). Les croyances des étudiants envers la création d'entreprise. *Revue Française de Gestion* 180: 25–43.

Bouchikhi, H. (1993). A constructivist framework for understanding entrepreneurship performance. *Organization Studies* 14 (4): 549–570.

Brush, C. (1992). Research on women business owners: past trends, a new perspective and future directions. *Entrepreneurship Theory & Practice* 16 (4): 5–30.

Brush, C. (2002). A gendered perspective on organisational creation. *Entrepreneurship Theory and Practice*, 26 (3): 41–66.

Butler, J. (2004). *Undoing Gender.* Abington, Oxfordshire, UK: Routledge.

Crompton, R. and Lefeuvre, N. (2000). Gender, family and employment in comparative perspective: The realities and representations of equal opportunities in Britain and France. *Journal of European Policy,* 10 (4): 334–348.

Dechant, K. and Lamky, A. (2005). Toward an understanding of Arab women entrepreneurs in Bahrain and Oman. *Journal of Developmental Entrepreneurship* 10 (2): 123–140.

Devlin, J. (2010). Challenges of economic development in the Middle East and North Africa region, in *World Scientific Studies in International Economics* (8), Washington, DC: World Scientific Publishing Company.

Dodd, D.S. and Patra, E. (2002). National differences in entrepreneurial networking. *Entrepreneurship and Regional Development,* 14: 117–134.

Du Rietz, A. and Henrekson, M. (2000). Testing the female underperformance hypothesis. *Small Business Economics* 14 (1): 1–10.

Eckhardt, J. and Shane, S. (2003). Opportunities and entrepreneurship. *Journal of Management,* 29 (3): 333–349.

Economic and Social Commission for Western Asia (2004). *Where Do Arab Women Stand in the Development Process: A Gender-Based Statistical Analysis.* New York, NY: United Nations.

Erogul, M.S. (2011). Social capital impediments in the United Arab Emirates: A case of Emirati Female entrepreneurs. *Journal of Enterprising Culture,* 19 (3): 315–339.

Fayolle, A. (2002). Insights to research on the entrepreneurial process from a study of perceptions of entrepreneurship and entrepreneurs. *Journal of Enterprising Culture,* 10 (4): 257–285.

Fayolle, A. (2004). *Entrepreneuriat: Apprendre à entreprendre.* Paris: Dunod.

Fishbein, M. and Ajzen, I. (1975). *Belief Attitudes, Intention and Behavior: An Introduction to Theory and Research.* Reading, MA: Addison-Wesley.

Fischer, E.M., Reuber, A.R. and L.S. Dyke, L.S. (1993). A theoretical overview and extension of research on sex, gender and entrepreneurship. *Journal of Business Venturing,* 8 (2), 151–168.

Francis, B. (2002). Is the future really female? The impact of gender for 14–16 year olds' career choices. *Journal of Education and Work,* 15 (1): 75–88.

GEM (2008). Report on Women Entrepreneurship, A. Allen, N. Ellam, M. Langowitz, and M. Dean (eds).

GEM (2009). Global Entrepreneurship Monitor, Global Report. N. Bosma and J. Levie (eds).

Gherardi, S. (2000). Practice-based theorizing on learning and knowing in organizations. *Organization,* 7 (2): 211–223.

Guionnet, C. and Neveu, E. (2005). *Féminin/Masculin. Sociologie du genre.* Paris: Armand Colin.

Gundry, L., Ben Yoseph, M. and Posig, M (2002). Contemporary perspectives on women's entrepreneurship: A review and strategic recommendations. *Journal of Enterprising Culture*, 10 (1): 67–86.

Hampole, N., (2010), *Advancing Entrepreneurship with Women in Saudi Arabia*, http://www.bsr.org/en/our-insights/blog-view/advancing-entrepreneurship-with-women-in-saudi-arabia.

Hayton, J.C. George, G. and Zahra, S.A. (2002). National culture and entrepreneurship: A review of behavioral research. *Entrepreneurship Theory and Practice*, 26 (4): 33–53.

ILO (2010). Women in Labour Markets: Measuring Progress, Identifying Challenges. http://www.ilo.org/wcmsp5/groups/public/---ed_emp/---emp_elm/---trends/documents/publication/wcms_123835.pdf. accessed 21 December 2013.

Jamali, D. (2009). Constraints and opportunities facing women entrepreneurs in developing countries: A relational perspective. *Gender in Management: An International Journal*, 24 (4): 232–251.

Kabasakal, H. and Bodur, M. (2002). Arabic cluster: A bridge between East and West. *Journal of World Business*, 37 (1): 40–54.

Krueger, N.F. and Brazeal, D. (1994). Entrepreneurial potential and potential entrepreneurs. *Entrepreneurship Theory & Practice*, 18: 91–104.

Krueger, N., Reilly, M., and Carsrud, A. (2000), Competing models of entrepreneurial intentions. *Journal of Business Venturing*, 15: 411–432.

Langowitz, N. and Minitti, M. (2007). The entrepreneurial propensity of women. *Entrepreneurship Theory and Practice*, 31 (3): 341–364.

Mc Loughlin, C. (2013), Women's economic role in the Middle East and North Africa, *GSDRC Helpdesk Research Report*.

Manolova, T., Carter, N., Manev, I. and Gyoshev, B. (2007). The differential effect of men and women entrepreneurs' human capital and networking on growth expectancies in Bulgaria. Entrepreneurship Theory and Practice 31(3): 407–426.

Morgan, C.L., Isaac, J.D. and Sansone, C. (2001). The role of interest in understanding the career choices of female and male college students. *Sex Roles*, 44 (5–6): 295–320.

Mueller, S. (2004). Gender gaps in potential for entrepreneurship across countries and cultures. *Journal of Developmental Entrepreneurship*, 9 (3): 199–220.

Naser, K. Mohamed, W.R. and Nuseibeh, R. (2009). Factors that affect women entrepreneurs: Evidence from an emerging economy. *International Journal of Organization Analysis*, 17 (3): 225–247.

North, D. (1990). A transactional cost theory of politics. *Journal of Theoretical Policy*, 2 (4): 355–367.

Orhan, M. (2005). Why Women Enter into Small Business Ownership, in S. Fielden and M. Davidson (eds), *International Handbook of Women and Small Business Entrepreneurship*, 3–17, Cheltenham, UK: Edward Elgar.

Radu, M. and Redien-Collot, R. (2008). The social representation of entrepreneurs in the French press: Desirable and feasible models. *International Small Business Journal*, 26 (3): 259–298.

Redien-Collot, R. (2012). Motivations of gay entrepreneurs: A focus on the construct of appropriateness. *International Journal of Entrepreneurship and Innovation*, 13 (2): 89–100.

Shapero, A. and Sokol, L. (1982). The social dimensions of entrepreneurship, in C.A. Kent, D.L. Sexton and K.H. Vesper (eds), *Encyclopedia of Entrepreneurship*, 72–90, Englewood Cliffs, NJ, USA: Prentice Hall.

Simmons, M. (2005). *Twilight in the Desert: The Coming Saudi Oil Shock and the World Economy*. Hoboken, NJ, USA: Wiley.

Smith, P.B., Dugan, S. and Trompenaars, F. (1997). Locus of control and affectivity by gender and occupational status: A 14 nation study. *Sex Roles*, 36: 51–77.

Watson, J. and Newby, R. (2005). Biological sex, stereotypical sex-roles, and SME owner characteristics. *International Journal of Entrepreneurship Behaviour and Research*, 11 (2): 129–43.

Wennekers, S., Noorderhaven, N., Hofstede, G. and Thurik, R. (2001). *Cultural and Economic Determinants of Business Ownership across Countries*, Babson College: http://www.babson.edu/entrep/fer/Babson2001/V/VA/VA/v-a.htm.

World Bank (2009). The Status of Progress of Women in the Middle East and North Africa, Washington D.C.

5

FEMALE ACADEMIC ENTREPRENEURSHIP AND COMMERCIALISATION

Reviewing the evidence and identifying the challenges

Helen Lawton Smith, Henry Etzkowitz,
Viviana Meschitti and Alex Poulovassilis

Introduction

The commercialisation of academic science is acknowledged as economically desirable for institutions, individual researchers and the public (de Melo-Martin, 2013). In this chapter, the relative propensity for women in academic science, technology, engineering and mathematics (STEM) disciplines to commercialise their research by, for example, becoming entrepreneurs and patenting is explored through a review of the available academic literature and published reports. The overall evidence suggests that women – as in knowledge-based sectors generally (Arenius and Minniti, 2005; Micozzi et al., 2014) – comprise very few academic entrepreneurs[1] and commercialise their research less frequently than their male counterparts.

Rosser (2012) found that although in the US women are the dominant sex in small business start-ups, they lag behind their male peers in the STEM disciplines (see also Schiebinger, 2008). Women file proportionately fewer invention disclosures and patents, launch fewer start-up companies and are less successful in attracting venture capital and angel funds than their male counterparts. This pattern arguably represents an under-used resource because unexploited technology with the potential to benefit society is not developed and diffused. It is also a problem for universities, as new technologies can support expanded experimental learning for students and provide funding streams for researchers and their institutions (Howe et al., 2014).

This chapter addresses the question: under what circumstances do women academics try and, subsequently, either fail or succeed in commercialising their research? Additional questions, such as: are these circumstances related to the women themselves, the external environment (Polkowska, 2013) or other factors are also explored. We perceive the context for our discussion to be twofold. First, there is a general drive to commercialise university research. In the UK, for example, the Higher Education Business and Community Interaction

Survey records information on Knowledge Exchange. In North America, the Association of University Technology Managers (AUTM)[2] collects similar data. Such monitoring highlights the significance attributed to commercialisation endeavours. Second, the relationship among career objectives, seniority and commercialisation is deemed important. Within this narrative are assumptions about the priorities given to commercialisation by women scientists, and whether, as Polkowska (2013) suggests, such assumptions represent the crowning achievement of a scientific career. In many countries, the association between seniority and commercialisation activity means that the actual number of women who might commercialise their research is small. There are also differences within STEM subjects (see, for example, Micozzi et al., 2014, with regard to the Italian context). Moreover, gender plays a part in the choices women make in the form of commercialisation. It has been found that women opt for soft choices such as consultancy, while men are more likely to form spin-off companies (Klofsten and Jones-Evans, 2000; Polkowska, 2013). Such tendencies are not, however, related to the quality of women's research but are more to do with the lesser rate at which their research is commercialised. There is also a measurement issue, i.e. what exactly is being measured, and whether quality versus quantity is being accounted for (see Colyvas et al., 2012).

Reviewing patterns of commercialisation

General patterns

Commercialisation covers a variety of activities. Extant literature has mainly focused on the formation of academic spin-off companies, pre-commercialisation activity such as academic publishing and patents and licensing. Other forms include consultancy, commercial research collaborations and media contents, e.g. educational videos and industrial scholarships.

Patenting performance is often linked to assessments of men's and women's publishing activity. These are taken as an indication of a scientist's research capabilities and important determinants of career outcomes (Smith-Doerr, 2004; Whittington and Smith-Doerr, 2005). Many studies have found women to be less productive on this measure as they publish less often than male counterparts. However, Long (1992) found that although women publish less often, their publications had a greater impact than men's across career years and have consistently higher citations than those written by their male counterparts.

Studies to date also show that not all science disciplines can be equally commercialised to the same extent or in the same way, i.e. they do not affect men and women equally (Polkowska, 2013). While most commercialisation is in biotechnology, mathematics, physics and chemistry, there are differences in terms of gender balance. For example, there are more women in biology, but fewer in computer science. The context is a rise in the number of PhD candidates amongst female students in the US. However, women still lag behind men in pay and promotion. There has also been a gradual increase in the presence of women in science, technology and engineering. For example, in the US by 2010 women held half of all medical (MD) degrees and 52% of all PhDs in the life sciences (Ceci and Williams, 2011, as cited in de Melo-Martin, 2013). However, with regard to maths, statistics and physical sciences, women's share of doctorates was lower (Schintler and McNeeley, 2014).

The main findings from extant literature on female academic entrepreneurship and commercialisation (patents and disclosure of inventions, i.e. licensing) are summarised in Table 5.1. While these highlight a gender gap between men and women in the quantity of activity, they also reveal more positive findings relating to the quality of women's commercialisation activity.

Table 5.1 Some patterns evident in the literature

Indicator	General patterns	Location	Authors
Entrepreneurship – academic spin-offs	Gender gap is significant but spatially heterogeneous – possibly reflecting cultural and environmental differences between Italian provinces (more in the North and Central regions); a disadvantage to females at the start-up funding stage, which reduces their chances of success and forces them into the service sector. Social relationships between females may compensate and reduce barriers to entrepreneurship.	Italy	Micozzi et al., 2014.
	Female students are less likely to start their own businesses than males. There are significant gender differences in perceived feasibility and desirability. Females are less confident, more tense, reluctant and concerned about entrepreneurship, but fewer differences exist in entrepreneurial intention. Mentoring and tutoring structures rated as more important by females than males. Incubators.	10+ countries	Dabic et al., 2012.
Patents	Women yield fewer patents than male counterparts.	Sweden	Lindholm Dahlstrand and Politis, 2013. Whittington and Smith-Doerr, 2004; Murray and Graham, 2007.
	Quality and impact of women's patents are equal or superior to those of male scientists.	US	Bunker Whittington and Smith-Doerr, 2005; Ding et al., 2006; Stephan and El-Ganainy, 2007; McMillan, 2009.
	Women produce less commercial work than male counterparts.	US	
Disclosure of inventions (licensing)	Women are less likely to disclose invention than men although no significant differences in publications.	US	Thursby and Thursby, 2005.
		US	Colyvas et al., 2012.

Entrepreneurship

The underlying context to patterns of female academic entrepreneurship in STEM subjects is that of female entrepreneurship in general. Female entrepreneurship as a discrete research area has expanded significantly since the 1980s, attracting concerted academic attention in recent years (Henry, Foss and Ahl, 2015). Extant literatures suggest that entrepreneurship is gendered and that women face considerably more challenges in their entrepreneurial endeavours than their male counterparts. There are also marked differences in the level, type and scope of new ventures established by men and women. Explanations for gender differences in business start-ups include context (country, sector, etc.), human capital, entrepreneurial intention and motivation and gender and entrepreneurial networks (Hanson and Blake, 2009; Etkzowitz et al., 2000). Overall, regardless of country, men are more likely to be involved in entrepreneurial activity than women at all stages from start-up through growth. National and regional differences are also shown to be important. For example, in the US the majority of small businesses are started by women (Howe et al., 2014). Overall, the number of women entrepreneurs per se is increasing in the UK and elsewhere (Mayer, 2008). It is, however, greatest in the highest income countries (Ranga and Etzkowitz, 2010). Significantly, women's commercialisation activities are found to be greater in industry than in academia (Whittington and Smith-Doerr, 2004), which may be an indication of the importance of organisational type in women's propensity to be entrepreneurial. This is borne out by a lack of examples – either in academic literature or the media – of women academics who have founded successful businesses or who have commercialised their research in other ways. One report that does address successful women entrepreneurs is by Weston-Smith (2015). She gives examples of not only women academic entrepreneurs in biotechnology but also of female leaders who are playing a key role in driving the growth of UK bioscience.[3] The implication of this broader range of women leaders is, potentially, both a variety of successful role models and more senior women with whom to network. An example of a woman academic turned business woman from a different discipline is Sarah Wood, Co-founder and co-CEO of video advertising technology (adtech) business *Unruly*. Wood has been voted UK Female Entrepreneur of the Year, named one of the 10 London-based 'Entrepreneurs to Watch' by Forbes and awarded the title of Digital Woman of the Year by *Red Magazine* in 2015. Her academic field – rather than being a STEM subject – was revolutionary literature and visual culture.[4]

One possible explanation for the low level of female academic entrepreneurship found in the literature could be that universities as organisational types present particular inhibitors to female academic entrepreneurship. However, such suggestions need to be treated with some caution. There is a difference between the number of academic women who start a company and the number of academic women who are shareholders and, therefore, part of the entrepreneurship and commercialisation process. In this regard, Hewitt-Dundas (2015) emphasises two key points in relation to women's involvement in founding UK USOs (university spin-outs). First, as the number of founders in a UK USO increases, so too does the probability of a female being involved in the founding team. Second, where a female is the main founder, then the founding team tends to be smaller.[5] Where a male is the main founder then the founding team has on average 3.0 members (sd=1.44) as compared to female-led UK USOs where the founding team is comprised of 2.0 members (sd=1.02).

Similarly, Micozzi et al. (2014) analysed a database of all academic spin-offs set up in Italy in 2002–2007. They found that females were the majority shareholders in less than 20% of Italian academic spin-offs. They also found that the number of female shareholders at start-ups is higher when the majority shareholder is a female and is lower for firms with a higher average shareholder share. This finding extends to the number of female shareholders post-incubation. Firm size has a negative relationship with the number of females only at start-up and not in the post-incubation stage. Micozzi et al. (2014) found weak evidence of a positive relationship between the share of the majority shareholder and number of female shareholders at start-up, when province, industry and year are not controlled for.

Moreover, the number of female shareholders as companies mature – for example in the post-incubation period – is strongly affected by the number of female shareholders at start-up, showing a degree of persistence in the number of female shareholders over time. Micozzi et al. (2014) also found that those spin-offs where the number of female shareholders is particularly high belonged to service sectors, which in turn may be related to lower levels of capital invested at start-up (cf. Dautzenberg, 2012). This might also explain why academic spin-offs formed by females produce fewer patents or licenses and/or are more failure-prone than those formed by men.

Patenting and licensing

While women academics in STEM subjects yield fewer patents than their male counterparts, there is evidence that the quality and impact of women's patents is either equal or superior to those of male scientists. Furthermore, there is strong evidence that women produce less commercial work than their male counterparts. Colyvas et al. (2012) examined the period 1991 to 1998 when patenting had become more prevalent in academic medicine. They captured the first step in the commercialisation process (efforts to inventions), as well as subsequent successful licensing of faculty inventions to a company using invention disclosures and licenses (an estimate of transfer to firms). Thus, they were able to compare behaviour in engaging in commercialisation to that of outcomes of engagement. Their findings revealed that women disclosed fewer inventions than their male counterparts. However, women's inventions were just as likely to secure licenses to firms as those of men. This suggests that women could be an untapped resource of entrepreneurial talent in academia.

In their study, Link et al. (2007) used a Research Value Mapping Program (Georgia Tech) Survey of Academic Researchers. Survey data were collected from a sample of university scientists and engineers with a PhD at the 150 Carnegie Extensive Doctoral/Research Universities during the time period spring 2004 to spring 2005. The sample was proportional to the number of academic researchers in the various fields of science and engineering and balanced between randomly selected men and women. They found that Probit estimates reveal that male faculty members are more likely than female faculty members to engage in informal commercial knowledge transfer and consulting. Overall, very few academics engage in licensing (Thursby and Thursby, 2005). Their findings also revealed that only 2 in 10 academics in 11 US research universities disclosed or had disclosed once in 17 years. There was some increase over time but only in a minority of faculty members over the 17-year period from 1983 to 1999.

De Melo-Martin (2013) argues that commercial activity, particularly that resulting from patenting, appears to be producing changes in the standards used to evaluate scientists' performance and contributions. In this context, concerns about a gender gap in patenting activity have arisen and some have argued for the need to encourage women to seek more patents. The author argues that because academic advancement is mainly dependent on productivity (Stuart and Ding, 2006; Azoulay et al., 2009), differences in research output have the power to negatively impact women's careers. Furthermore, De Melo-Martin (2013, 495) argues that, on the basis of the evidence in relation to the quality of women's academic outputs and citations, 'there is no evidence that women do less important work than men'. However, women generally produce less commercial work than men throughout their careers (see also Whittington and Smith-Doerr, 2005). Similarly, Thursby and Thursby (2005) in their sample of US Science and Engineering Faculty at 11 major US research institutions found that women were less likely than men to disclose inventions despite the lack of significant differences in publication patterns. Disclosure patterns converged over time, but a gap remained.

Nevertheless, calls to encourage women to patent on the grounds that such activity is likely to play a significant role in the betterment of both women's careers and society seem to be based on two problematic assumptions: (1) that the methods to determine women's productivity in patenting activities are an appropriate way to measure their research efforts and the impact of their work and (2) that patenting, particularly in academia, benefits society (De Melo-Martin, 2013).

Patents, moreover – as an indicator of the respective value of men's and women's measure of productivity – have at least two problems. The first is that not all patents are of a similar quality and importance, for example, through commercial impact and technological influence (Whittington and Smith-Doer, 2005). The second is that propensity to patent varies by sector. Colyvas et al. (2012) caution against the use of patent data as an empirical measure of innovation, suggesting that the nature of the sample limits tend to impact the ability to capture institutional differences; faculty entry and exit rates would address selection effects. Furthermore, commercial efforts might be conditioned by teaching loads and forms of research support. Finally, patent data only reflect one form of technology transfer, especially in the life sciences.

Explanations and effectiveness

The regional context

Explanations of why the regional context matters can have several different but associated dimensions. For example, networks are embedded in place-based social, economic, cultural and political structures (Hanson and Blake, 2009). Some networks may be linked to different status positions that are inherent in gender relations, reflecting inequality of opportunity, for example, in access to business development resources such as venture capital (Mayer, 2008). Mayer suggests that more research is needed on how networks are embedded in broader cultural discourses and structures and how this affects potential agency for change. Brush et al. (2014) found that in the US, many fundable women entrepreneurs had the requisite skills and experience to lead high-growth ventures. In spite of this, women were consistently left out of the networks of growth capital finance and appeared to lack the contacts needed to break through.

Human capital arguments suggest that levels of entrepreneurial activity are associated with education. High levels of formal education have been found to be associated with a propensity for entrepreneurship (Reynolds et al., 2001). In academia, this relationship does not hold true for women scientists. The explanation might be found in studies by Unger et al. (2011) and Marvel et al. (2013) who suggest that the relationship between education and entrepreneurship is more complex. For example, one individual can invest in education and experience, but one's outputs depend partly on the rate of return on the human capital one possesses. Specific human capital refers to skills or knowledge that is useful to a particular setting or industry. In this regard, Unger et al. (2011) suggest that human capital is most important if it is task-related and consists of outcomes of human capital investments rather than human capital investments themselves. It should be understood as processes of learning, knowledge acquisition and the transfer of knowledge to entrepreneurial tasks. In this context, it is not the level of education that matters – as it is a given that women academics have high levels of human capital – rather, it is the skills and knowledge required for entrepreneurship and commercialisation that matter, and these are often founded to be lacking in women (Ahl, 2006). This is necessarily interdependent with entrepreneurial motivation and intention (Micozzi et al., 2014).

Gender and the technology transfer process

The process of commercialisation has been explained as a social process, for example in networking and human capital (see, for example, Polkowska, 2013). Women have been found to have less access to important networks and R&D, which affects the likelihood of commercialising their research. Both affect an academic's position in relation to external funding and being published, i.e. key precursors to entrepreneurial activity. This has been explained in relation to opportunity recognition as social networks and prior work/life experiences influencing the process of opportunity recognition (DeTienne and Chandler, 2007; Micozzi et al., 2014).

Men typically have larger social networks and more extensive previous work/life experience – as well as different types of networks – than women. These types of networks are particularly important when raising finance. Networks have been shown to be important in the university context in the broader technology transfer process. For example, Ding et al. (2006) found that females were less likely to know people who could first help them recognise the commercial potential of their research and second help them commercialise it effectively.

Furthermore, females are more likely to obtain start-up funds through strong tie networks (family and friends) (Granovetter, 1973) and obtain less than men, which again ties them into starting businesses with lower capital intensity (see also Dautzenberg, 2012). Friendship in the research world is gender-based, and women have a lower capacity for associating with colleagues who are patenting, commercialising or have contacts with industry (Murray and Graham, 2007).

Networks are also important in the formation of scientific advisory boards (which are usually male; see, for example, Murray and Graham, 2007), and in access to venture capitalists. Women are, therefore, possibly excluded from academic entrepreneurial networks (Fältholm et al., 2010; Stephan et al., 2007). Scientific advisory board membership is one of the selection criteria that businesses take into account when prospecting for partners (Polkowska, 2013). This raises the question of why women may be less successful in selling research results to others, being selected for honours, or being invited to participate in start-up activity (Babcock and Laschevr, 2003; Murray and Graham, 2007).

Institutional analysis

It has already been suggested that the organisation context (industry and academia) seems to have an impact on the propensity of women in STEM to form companies or commercialise their research; one possible explanation for this may be found in institutional analysis. Within the domain of social sciences, institutional analysis examines how institutions – i.e. structures and mechanisms of social order, as well as the cooperation governing the behaviour of individuals – behave and function according to both empirical rules (informal rules-in-use and norms) and also theoretical rules (formal rules and law). It concerns how individuals and groups construct institutions, how institutions function in practice and the effects of institutions on individuals, societies and the community at large. Institutional analysis helps identify constraints within an organisation that might undermine policy implementation. Such constraints may exist at the level of internal processes, as well as relationships among organisations or they may be system-wide. Institutional analysis evaluates formal institutions, such as rules, resource allocation and authorisation procedures, as well as "soft" institutions, such as informal rules of the game, power relations and incentive structures that underlie current practices. In the latter sense, institutional analysis identifies organisational stakeholders that are likely to support or obstruct a given reform.[6]

Studies have identified that women often lack institutional support for patenting (Etzkowitz et al., 2000; Fox, 2001). Whittington and Smith-Doerr (2008), for example, found that women are more likely to patent in more flexible network-based organisational structures than in hierarchical organisations in both academia and industry. These authors analysed detailed data from a sample of academic and industrial life scientists working in the United States. They found that controlling for education and career-history variables, women were less likely to patent than men. However, in biotechnology firms, industrial settings characterised by flatter, more flexible, network-based organisational structures, women scientists were more likely to become patent-holding inventors than in more hierarchically arranged organisational settings in industry or academia. Moreover, discipline as an institutional factor is important. For example, Morgan et al. (2001) compared the patenting and inventing activity of US scientists and engineers in industry and academia. They found that women in the US who patent are five times more likely to be life scientists than engineers, with the tilt being more pronounced for academia over industry. Overall, in academia women constituted 25% of doctorate holders but only 11% of patenting activity.

Other research such as that by Corley and Gaughan (2005) has suggested that gender findings may be attenuated by the institutional setting. This is supported by Link et al. (2007) who found that women who are affiliated with interdisciplinary university research centres have commercial activity profiles that more closely resemble male centre affiliates than females affiliated only with traditional academic departments. They also found that tenured faculty members and those who are actively involved in research grants are more likely to engage in informal technology transfer than non-tenured faculty members.

In patenting, commercial involvement may also be a new fault-line: i.e., between those who patent and those who do not. Owen-Smith and Powell (2001) argue that an understanding of gender inequality in commercial activity requires a conceptualisation of the multiple ways in which men and women may be involved and explore whether a commercial 'pipeline' of involvement is present for women in science. Thus, Whittington and Smith-Doerr (2005) suggest that female life scientists must overcome two kinds of gender disparity in commercial activity – in both involvement and their decisions to patent – and in productivity. They note that in the US at least, scientists have to make decisions about the level of involvement they will have in commercial work. Those who are involved are institutionally and personally rewarded: increases in research funding, access to better equipment, personal wealth and the UK status in the Research Excellence Framework in which 'Impact' such as through patenting in STEM subjects is assessed.[7]

The policy implication of all this is that universities would benefit from devoting resources to enable women scientists to commercialise (Whittington and Smith-Doerr, 2005).

However, de Melo-Martin (2013) argues that encouraging women to patent more may harm their careers. Rather, it would be better to be clear about the goals of such activity and assess the overall impact rather than counting the number of patents. She also challenges the notion that patents per se are of value to society, as they increase secrecy and may delay access to new knowledge; she also highlights other limitations about the assumptions relating to the value of patents.

Colyvas et al. (2012) found that gender differences in commercialising research in three US medical schools are highly conditioned by the employment context and resources. In their study, gender differences are attributed to the use of outcome measures that capture both behaviour and performance.

Howe et al. (2014) found that developing solutions to low levels of women academic entrepreneurs at Ohio State University in the form of a curriculum for an entrepreneurship workshop series was problematic. This was due to cultural differences in what women would need to know to become motivated to engage in commercialisation. This is when activity is framed in terms of societal impact. In practice, this required getting women to envision themselves as entrepreneurs, with activities and learning tailored to their own work. This involved one-to-one analysis of research potential of the market place. This also meant that women needed to learn the landscape – that forming a start-up was not the only way forward; to realise that commercialisation partners will take on tasks that women would prefer not to do and identifying resources. The NSF-funded REACH programme has supported nearly 100 women (faculty and post-docs) at nearly 15 institutions. Post-docs were keen as were individuals who had experience in commercialisation. Cultivating a community of women entrepreneurs is essential: women have different experiences to men; hence, sharing experiences is beneficial. Networks expand one's circle of colleagues. Similarly, Nilsson (2015) argued that attracting more women to engineering would occur if the content was made more socially meaningful by reframing the goals of the engineering research and curriculum to be more relevant to societal needs. Moreover, in the US, universities' commercialisation is not part of the reward structure. Therefore, explicit value must be placed on entrepreneurialism for promotion and tenure, annual salary reviews and contributing to career development.

The 'impact' agenda in the UK is focusing more attention on commercialisation per se, which may in turn bring about a reassessment of internal reward structures. Evidence from the US (see, for example, Howe et al., 2014, and Nilsson, 2015) suggests that universities should adopt a gender-sensitive approach to supporting academic entrepreneurship and commercialisation. This might take the form of a 'talent scout' who can offer a "one-to-one analysis of research potential of the market place" (Howe et al., 2014) and role models of successful women academic entrepreneurs across the career spectrum profiled in events and on dedicated websites. Where there are examples of discussions in the media of science professors as entrepreneurs, these are often male dominated. In an article by Levine (2012),[8] all of the examples of successful academic entrepreneurs were men.

Other institutional measures to promote entrepreneurship include incubators, and these also need to be made more effective in order to address gender differences in propensity to commercially exploit university research. In their study, Lindholm Dahlstrad and Politis (2013) focused on university incubators for women's academic entrepreneurship and examined the significance of university incubators for the promotion and development of women's academic business start-ups. They concluded that the Swedish incubators in their study did not show any evidence of being able to decrease the gender gap in the commercialisation of university science.

Conclusions

This chapter considered the propensity for women academics in STEM subjects to be academic entrepreneurs or to commercialise their research through patents and licenses. Drawing on relevant and contemporary scholarship, as well as extant reports, in the areas of entrepreneurship and gender, patenting and licensing, technology transfer and institutional analysis, the authors sought to uncover the particular circumstances under which women attempt to commercialise their research.

In quantitative terms, the evidence reveals significantly less commercialisation activity among female academics than among their male counterparts. However, the quality of women's commercialisation activity appears to be superior to men's, suggesting that counting alone does not offer a full and accurate picture.

The evidence we reviewed also suggests that the explanations for women's lower commercialisation levels are multi-faceted. Notwithstanding the many definitional issues associated with commercialising academic research, and the fact that not all science disciplines may be commercialised to the same extent, academic publishing activity was found to have a positive impact on women's careers as it is seen as an indication of esteem. The level of patenting and licensing; access to networks and venture capital; propensity toward and involvement in entrepreneurship and the specific and typically limited institutional support environment were all highlighted as other key influencing factors impacting the level of commercialisation amongst women. In parallel to general entrepreneurial activity, it is clear that women academics seeking to commercialise their research do experience different and often more complex challenges than their male counterparts.

Given the above, the evidence shows that women academics attempt to commercialise their research under extremely challenging conditions, many of which relate to inherent gender biases in the academic system, the majority of which reflect trends in entrepreneurship globally. In light of this, the question then becomes: what, if anything, can be done to change the situation so as to increase women's level of commercialisation activity? Finding appropriate solutions by way of addressing this question, however, can be problematic, with some commentators observing that solutions can often make things worse (Melo-Martin, 2013). Practical suggestions offered to date include providing executive coaching and network coaching to overcome gender stereotypes (Brighetti and Lucarelli, 2015). Incubation facilities seem a logical approach to establishing a commercialisation-friendly environment, but evidence to date shows them to have little or no impact on decreasing the gender gap in the commercialisation of university science (Lindholm Dahlstrad and Politis, 2013).

We conclude that universities would be best served investing efforts in two main areas: first, developing women's confidence levels and increasing their self-efficacy with regard to their commercialisation abilities. Second, consistent with Colyvas et al. (2012), academic researchers' employment context and resources should be reviewed and improved so that gender differences are overcome. After all, women need to be able to first see themselves as valued employees, commercial actors and potential entrepreneurs before they can expect others to see them as such (Howe et al., 2014).

Avenues for future research

As the commercialisation process is both lengthy and complicated, varies from discipline to discipline and feels the effects of the particular environment in which the academic researcher resides, future studies would benefit from adopting both longitudinal and comparative research designs. Such studies could explore the impact of different academic support environments, examine reward structures in specific institutions and in particular countries, account for the gender balance in academic research staff cohorts and consider the impact on career trajectories. Further work is also required to evidence the effectiveness of existing support measures, especially those that claim to encourage women academics' commercialisation activity. It would be especially interesting to note whether scientific disciplines that were traditionally male-dominated and are now experiencing a considerable gender shift toward the predominately female – for example, human and veterinary medicine – offer new and valuable insights for the study of women academics' commercialisation activity. Moreover, technology-based entrepreneurship by academics is not necessarily confined to STEM subjects. Studies that examine the broader scope of academic women's commercialisation activity would contribute to theory, but could also yield considerable practical value in terms of appropriate support mechanisms to develop women's commercialisation potential.

Notes

1 Academic entrepreneurs are members of the academic staff of universities who choose to set up their own businesses. They may or may not continue to work in the university after setting up a company.
2 https://www.autm.net/Home.htm [accessed June 1st 2015].
3 http://www.mws-consulting.co.uk/wordpress/wp-content/uploads/2015/02/50-Movers-and-Shakers-in-BioBusiness-2015-final.pdf [accessed February 19 2016).
4 http://startups.co.uk/how-to-succeed-as-a-technology-start-up/ [accessed February 18 2015].
5 Where males are the main founder then the founding team has on average 3.0 members (sd=1.44) as compared to female-led UK USOs where the founding team is comprised of 2.0 members (sd=1.02).
6 http://siteresources.worldbank.org/INTPSIA/Resources/490023-1121114603600/12996_workshop_instanalysis.pdf [accessed April 8 2015].
7 http://www.ref.ac.uk/ [accessed April 8 2015].
8 http://www.sciencemag.org/careers/features/2012/09/finding-balance-professorentrepreneur [accessed February 18 2015].

References

Achatz, J., Beblo, M. and Wolf, E. (2009) 'Berufliche Segregation', in *Geschlechterungleichheiten im Betrieb. Arbeit, Entlohnung und Gleichstellung in der Privatwirtschaft*, edited by Projektgruppe GiB, Berlin, pp. 89–139.

Ahl, H. (2006) 'Why Research on Women Entrepreneurs Needs New Directions', *Entrepreneurship Theory and Practice*, 30.5, 595–621.

Arenius, P. and Minniti, M. (2005) 'Perceptual Variables and Nascent Entrepreneurship', *Small Business Economics*, 24.3, 233–47.

Azjen, I. (1991) 'The Theory of Planned Behavior', *Organizational Behavior and Human Decision Processes*, 50 (1991), 179–211.

Azoulay, P., Ding, W. and Stuart, T. (2009) 'The Impact of Academic Patenting on the Rate, Quality, and Direction of (Public) Research Output', *The Journal of Industrial Economics*, 57.4, 637–76.

Babcock, L. and Laschevr, S. (2003) *Women Don't Ask*. Princeton: Princeton University Press.

Bozeman, B., Dietz, J. and Gaughan, M. (2001) 'Models of Scientific Careers: Using Network Theory to Explain Transmission of Scientific and Technical Human Capital', *International Journal of Technology Management*, 22.7, 716–40.

Brighetti, G. and Lucarelli, C. (2015) 'Gender Differences in Attitudes towards Risk and Ambiguity: When Psycho-Physiological Measurements Contradict Sex-Based Stereotypes', *International Journal of Entrepreneurship and Small Business*, 24.1, 62–82.

Brockhaus, R. H. (1980) 'Risk Taking Propensity of Entrepreneurs', *Journal of Academic Management*, 23.3, 509–20.

Brush, C. G., Greene, P. G., Balachandra, L. and Davis, A. E. (2014) *Diana Report Women Entrepreneurs 2014: Bridging the Gender Gap in Venture Capital* http://www.babson.edu/Academics/centers/blank-center/global-research/diana/Documents/diana-project-executive-summary-2014.pdf [accessed January 18, 2016].

Ceci, S. J. and Williams, W. M. (2011) 'Understanding Current Causes of Women's Underrepresentation in Science', *Proceedings of National Academy of Science of the United States*, 22, 8 <http://www.pnas.org/content/108/8/3157.full> [accessed June, 1, 2015].

Colyvas, J. A., Snellman, K., Bercovitz, J. and Feldman, M. (2012) 'Disentangling Effort and Performance: A Renewed Look at Gender Differences in Commercialising Medical School Research', *Journal of Technology Transfer*, 1–12.

Corley, E. and Gaughan, M. (2005) 'Scientists' Participation in University Research Centres: What Are the Gender Differences?', *Journal of Technology Transfer*, 30.4, 371–81.

Dabic, M., Daim, T., Bayraktaroglu, E., Novak, I. and Basic, M. (2012) 'Exploring Gender Differences in Attitudes of University Students towards Entrepreneurship: An International Survey', *International Journal of Gender and Entrepreneurship*, 4.3, 316–36.

Dautzenberg, K. (2012) 'Gender Differences of Business Owners in Technology-Based Firms', *International Journal of Gender and Entrepreneurship*, 4.1, 79–98.

Delmar, F., Davidsson, P. and Gartner, W. B. (2003) 'Arriving at the High-Growth Firm', *Journal of Business Venturing*, 18.2, 189–216.

De Melo-Martín, I. (2013) 'Patenting and the Gender Gap: Should Women Be Encouraged to Patent More?', *Science and Engineering Ethics*, 19.2, 491–504.

DeTienne, D. R. and Chandler, G. (2007) 'The Role of Gender in Opportunity Identification', *Entrepreneurship Theory and Practice*, 31.3, 365–86.

Ding, W. W., Murray, F. and Stuart, T. (2006) 'Gender Differences in Patenting in the Academic Life Sciences', *Science*, 313, 665–67.

Etzkowitz, H., Kemelgor, C. and Uzzi, B. (2000) *Athena Unbound: The Advancement of Women in Science and Technology*. Cambridge: Cambridge University Press.

Fältholm, I., Abrahamsson, L. and Källhammer, E. (2010) 'Academic Entrepreneurship – Gendered Discourses and Ghettos', *Journal of Technology Management and Innovation*, 5.1, 5–163.

Fox, M. F. (2001) 'Women, Science and Academia: Graduate Education and Careers', *Gender and Society*, 15.5, 654–66.

GEM Women's Report (2012) <http://www.babson.edu/Academics/centers/blank-center/global-research/gem/Documents/GEM%202012%20Womens%20Report.pdf> [accessed June 1 2015].

Granovetter, M. S. (1973) 'The Strength of Weak Ties', *The American Journal of Sociology*, 78 (6): 1360–80.

Hanson, S. and Blake, M. (2009) 'Gender and Entrepreneurial Networks', *Regional Studies*, 43.1, 135–49.

Henry, C., Foss, L. and Ahl, H. (2015) 'Gender and Entrepreneurship Research: A Review of Methodological Approaches', *International Small Business Journal*, on-line first.

Henry, C. and Marlow, S. (Forthcoming) 'Exploring the Intersection of Gender, Feminism and Entrepreneurship', in the *Handbook of Research in Entrepreneurship*, ed. by Alain Fayolle. Cheltenham: Elgar.

Hewitt-Dundas, N. (2015) 'UK University Spin-Outs', *ERC Research Paper No. 35*, mimeo Queens University Belfast.

Howe, S. A., Juhas, M. C. and Herbers, J. M. (2014) 'Academic Women: Overlooked Entrepreneurs', *Peer Review*, 16.2, available from: <https://www.aacu.org/peerreview/2014/spring/howe> [accessed January 29 2015].

Hunter, L. A. and Leahey, E. (2010) 'Parenting and Research Productivity: New Evidence and Methods', *Social Studies of Science*, 40.3, 433–51.

Jennings, J. E. and McDougald, M. S. (2007) 'Work-Family Interface Experiences and Coping Strategies: Implications for Entrepreneurship Research and Practice', *Academy of Management Review*, 32.3, 747–60.

Klofsten, M. and Jones-Evans, D. (2000) 'Comparing Academic Entrepreneurship in Europe – The Case of Sweden and Ireland', *Small Business Economics*, 14, 299–309.

Laznjak, J., Šporer, Z. and Švarc, J. (2011) 'Women in Science Commercialization: Looking for Gender Differences', *Gender, Technology and Development*, 15, 175–200.

Leahey, E. (2006) 'Gender Differences in Productivity: Research Specialization as a Missing Link', *Gender & Society*, 20.6, 754–80.

Linan, F. and Santos, F. J. (2007) 'Does Social Capital Affect Entrepreneurial Intentions?', *International Advances in Economic Research*, 13.4, 443–53.

Lindholm Dahstrand, A. and Politis, D. (2013) 'Women Business Ventures in Swedish University Incubators', *International Journal of Gender and Entrepreneurship*, 5.1, 78–96.

Link, A. N., Siegel, D. S. and Bozeman, B. (2007) 'An Empirical Analysis of the Propensity of Academics to Engage in Informal Technology Transfer', *Industrial and Corporate Change*, 16.4, 641–55.

Long, S. (1992) *From Scarcity to Visibility: Gender Differences in the Careers of Doctoral Scientists and Engineers*, Washington, D.C: National Academy Press.

McMillan, G. S. (2009) 'Gender Differences in Patenting Activity: An Examination of the US Biotechnology Industry', *Scienometrics*, DOI: <10.1007/s11192-008-2101-0>.

Marvel, M. R. (2013) 'Human Capital and Search-Based Discovery: A Study of High-Tech Entrepreneurship', *Entrepreneurship: Theory & Practice*, 37.2, 403–19.

Mayer, H. (2008) 'Segmentation and Segregation Patterns of Women-Owned High-Tech Firms in Four Metropolitan Regions in the United States', *Regional Studies*, 42.10, 1–27.

Micozzi, A., Micozzi, F. and Pattitoni, P. (2014) 'Fostering Female Entrepreneurship in Academic Spin-Offs', in *University Evolution, Entrepreneurial Activity and Regional Competitiveness*, ed. by D. Audretsch, E. Lehmann, M. Meoli, and S. Vismara, London: Springer, pp. 49–70.

Morgan, R. P., Kruytbosch, C. and Kannankutty, N. (2001) 'Patenting and Invention Activity of U.S. Scientists and Engineers in the Academic Sector: Comparisons with Industry', *Journal of Technology Transfer*, 26, 173–83.

Murray, F. and Graham, L. (2007) 'Buying Science and Selling Science: Gender Differences in the Market for Commercial Science', *Industrial and Corporate Change*, 16, 657–89.

Nilsson, L. (2015) How to Attract Female Engineers http://www.nytimes.com/2015/04/27/opinion/how-to-attract-female-engineers.html?_r=0 (accessed December 25 2016).

Owen-Smith, J. and Powell, W.W. (2001) 'To Patent or Not: Faculty Decisions and Institutional Success at Technology Transfer', *Journal of Technology Transfer*, 26.1, 99–114.

Polkowska, D. (2013) 'Women Scientists in the Leaking Pipeline: Barriers to the Commercialisation of Scientific Knowledge by Women', *Journal of Technology Management and Innovation*, 8.2, 156–65.

Ranga, M., and Etzkowitz, H. (2010) 'Athena in the World of Techne: The Gender Dimension of Technology, Innovation and Entrepreneurship', *Journal of Technology Management and Innovation*, 5.1, 1–12.

Reynolds, P., Camp, S. M., Bygrave, W. D., Autio, E., and Hay, M. (2001) Global Entrepreneurship Monitor: 2001, Executive Report, Kauffman Center for Entrepreneurial Leadership, Kansas City, MO.

Robb, A. and Coleman, S. (2010) 'Financing Strategies of New Technology-Based Firms: A Comparison by Gender', *Journal of Technology Management & Innovation*, 5.1, 30–50.

Rosser, S. V. (2012) *Breaking into the Lab: Engineering Progress for Women in Science*, New York: New York University Press.

Schiebinger, L. L. (2008) *Gendered Innovations in Science and Engineering*, Stanford: Stanford University Press.

Schintler, L. A. and McNeeley, C. (2014) 'Gendered Science in the 21st Century: Productivity Puzzle 2.0?' <http://genderandset.open.ac.uk/index.php/genderandset/article/view/219/389> [accessed June 1 2015].

Shapero A. and Sokol, L. (1982) 'Social Dimensions of Entrepreneurship', in *The Encyclopedia of Entrepreneurship*, ed. by C. Kent, D. Sexton, K. Vesper. Englewood Cliffs: Prentice-Hall, pp. 72–90.

Smith-Doerr, L. (2004) *Women's Work: Gender Equality vs. Hierarchy in the Life Sciences*, London: Lynne Rienner Publishers.

Stephan, P., Black, G. and Chaing, T. (2007). 'The Small Size of the Small Scale Market: The Early-Stage Labor Market for Highly Skilled Nanotechnology Workers', *Research Policy*, 36.6, 887–92.

Stephan, P. E. and El Ganainy, A. A. (2007) 'The Entrepreneurial Puzzle: Explaining the Gender Gap', Andrew Young School of Policy Studies Research Paper Series, No. 07–09.

Stuart, T. and Ding, W. (2006) 'When Do Scientists Become Entrepreneurs? The Social Structural Antecedents of Commercial Activity in the Academic Life Sciences', *American Journal of Sociology*, 112.1, 97–144.

Thursby, J. G. and Thursby, M. C. (2005) 'Gender Patterns of Research and Licensing Activity of Science and Engineering Faculty', *Journal of Technology Transfer*, 30, 343–53.

Unger, J. M., Rauch, A., Frese, M. and Rosenbusch, N. (2011) 'Human Capital and Entrepreneurial Success: A Meta-Analytical Review', *Journal of Business Venturing*, 26, 341–58.

Whittington, K. B. and Smith-Doerr, L. (2005) 'Gender and Commercial Science: Women's Patenting in the Life Sciences', *Journal of Technology Transfer*, 30, 355–70.

Whittington, K. B. and Smith-Doerr, L. (2008) 'Women Inventors in Context Disparities in Patenting across Academia and Industry', *Gender & Society*, 22.2, 194–218.

PART II

The ecosystem for female entrepreneurs

6

STRATEGIES TO REDRESS ENTREPRENEURSHIP GENDER GAPS IN CANADA

Barbara J. Orser

Introduction

In Canada, women have been starting new businesses at faster rates than men for several decades; however, female-owned firms remain smaller than those owned by males even after allowing for such systemic factors as sector, firm age, etc. (Jung, 2010; Orser, Riding and Jung, 2013). In spite of higher rates of business start-up, the overall proportion of self-employed females is significantly lower than the proportion of females in the labor force (Jung, 2010; GEM Canada Report, 2013).

To investigate this 'entrepreneurship growth gap', the 2011 *Canadian Taskforce for Women's Business Growth* was assembled to consult widely with women business owners and other stakeholders to identify barriers and advance recommendations for entrepreneurship policy reform. The taskforce was a national and non-partisan consortium of prominent women business owners, service agencies, academics, and industry associations. Founded in 2009, the mandate was to grow women's enterprises through the creation of public policy, advocacy, applied research, collaboration, and sharing of best practices. By 2015, none of the taskforce recommendations had been implemented. Failure to achieve Canadian policy reform is an outcome similar to other large-scale consultations.

The purpose of the study presented in this chapter is to report on the taskforce recommendations and to reflect on the inability of the taskforce to influence national entrepreneurship policy. The work is motivated by several observations. First, among developed economies, there appears to be an inverse relationship between the level of gender equality legislation and the proportion of women (relative to men) who choose self-employment (Klyver et al., 2013). Whereas gender equality legislation confers rights and benefits for female employees, self-employed women are not generally covered. Entrepreneurship scholars have called for research to understand how *institutions*, at different levels, influence the construction of gender and policy (GEM, 2013; Ahl, 2004). This study addresses this through a country-level case study (Canada) that examines processes that stymie gender-specific entrepreneurship policy and programming reform.

Second, Canada is among leading nations with respect to gender equality as it pertains to employed females (Gender Inequity Index, 2013; Gender Empowerment Measure, 2012; Women's Economic Opportunity Index, 2012). This is not the case for policies to support female entrepreneurs. This infers a policy gap in supporting employed and self-employed females. This is despite numerous studies that have reported on the status of female entrepreneurs and the need for entrepreneurship policy reform. Examination of the *consultative processes* may help to close the gap by informing future initiatives that seek to redress gender differences in engagement and enterprise performance.

Third, the Organization for Economic Development and Coordination has called for 'deeper analysis' of the entrepreneurship gender gap (OECD, 2013). The costs of not doing so are only now being recognized through studies that report on outcomes of entrepreneurship training. For example, The World Bank Group (2014, p. 15) has reported:

> Three main themes emerge from the evaluations of these [entrepreneurship, innovation and technology] programs. First, these programs appear to be successful in improving the management skills of beneficiaries—both men and women. Second, there appears to be little to no impact on firm growth among female entrepreneurs. Third, there is a gender differential in attrition rates, business outcomes, and overall program efficacy. Two reasons may account for the lack of effectiveness of entrepreneurship programs for women. First, beneficiaries of such programs may be primarily necessity entrepreneurs, who are less likely to grow their businesses or be motivated to do so. There is some evidence that impact is enhanced when larger enterprises are targeted. Second, the programs evaluated may not be designed to address the main binding constraints to female enterprise growth.

The World Bank study attributes gender differences in outcome to curriculum, reporting that most programs focus on the initial resourcing of firms rather than on strategies to address: "...*binding constraints to female enterprise growth, such as concentration in low-productivity and low-growth activities, intra-household choices, and the role of institutions and legal frameworks in shaping the overall business environment for women entrepreneurs.*" The report also calls for a gender-sensitive curriculum that incorporates soft skills such as negotiation, leadership, communication; mobility strategies; peer learning from other female (or male) peers; relatable and inspirational role models; female-centered case studies; and instructors/trainers who are qualified to address gender constraints. These are recommendations advanced by the 2011 taskforce.

Finally, the outcome of the Canadian taskforce suggests consultation processes to inform entrepreneurship policy should also examine *mechanisms* to effect policy reform. Identification of best in class policy and advisory processes is required. The literature review found no studies that have examined the efficacy of 'women in enterprise' advisory initiatives (e.g., resultant provisions of gender-specific policy support) such as those undertaken by the Scottish Government (2013), Enterprise Ireland (2014), Invest Northern Ireland (2007), and United Kingdom (2003, 2009). Sample multi-lateral consultation initiatives include Asia Pacific Economic Co-operation (APEC, 2010), Organization for Economic Development (Piacentini, 2013), and Quantum Leaps (2010). This study seeks to inform future consultations about the challenges of entrepreneurship policy reform.

The chapter is structured as follows. The next section provides an overview of Canadian entrepreneurial activity, including secondary analysis of Statistics Canada data. Global indices are also used to profile the status of gender equality. Canadian policies are compared to the United States, the country ranked first among 120 economies for entrepreneurial gender equity (Gender-Global Entrepreneurship Development Index, Gender-GEDI, 2014). Participant observations and summary recommendations of the 2011 Canadian Taskforce on Women's Business Growth are then presented. The discussion of findings describes the evolution of policies and practices in two of the world's most geographical, cultural, and linguistically similar countries. Rationales for gender differences in entrepreneurial engagement and equality entrepreneurship policies are considered. The implications for research and country-level consultations about women's entrepreneurship are then presented. The study in this chapter will be of interest to women in enterprise agencies, sector associations, policymakers, and entrepreneurship policy scholars.

The Canadian entrepreneurship gender gap

Country-level data are important given that scholars, who have examined entrepreneurial engagement and institutional contexts, suggest policymakers employ targeted approaches to stimulate and sustain new business activity (De Clercq, Lim, and Oh, 2013). This includes customized training (e.g., financial and educational systems, promotion of trust-based relationships). To do so requires gender-disaggregated, country-level data to inform the design of appropriate program interventions.

Assessments of Canadian legislation and policy support for women vary considerably. Canada ranks among the top 10 economies for 'overall gender equality' by the Gender Empowerment Measure (2012) and Women's Economic Opportunity Index (2012), but 23rd by the United Nations' Gender Inequality Index (GII, 2013), which captures three aspects of human development—reproductive health, 'empowerment' (parliamentary seats occupied by females; level of education) and 'economic status' (e.g., labor force participation rates). The 2015 *Global Women Entrepreneur Leaders Scorecard* ranks Canada (and Australia) second only to the US in terms of 'support of high-impact women's entrepreneurship', among 31 countries surveyed. And while gender equity legislation has contributed to narrowing the gender wage gaps and to the advancement of women in corporate jobs, the impact of such legislation does not necessarily extend to women's entrepreneurial engagement (Golla et al., 2011; Kabeer, 2012). The following analysis of secondary data illustrates that policymakers cannot assume that 'overall gender equality' translates into economic and social benefits for female entrepreneurs.

Total early stage entrepreneurship activity

In 2013, 'total early stage entrepreneurship activity' (TEA) in Canada was second to the US and leads all other 'innovation-driven' economies. In the US and Canada, TEA among males was significantly higher than among females in the working population (15 percent versus 10 percent, respectively) (GEM, 2013). Motives for entrepreneurial engagement also differ by gender. In Canada, males are more likely than females to be opportunity driven (GEM, 2013, p. 83).

The Business Development Bank of Canada (BDC, 2012) reports that the intensity of entrepreneurial activity in Canada has decreased for both men and women since the 2008 recession, but that it is substantially lower among females than among males. This is primarily because self-employed women fail to achieve scale in their firms. The BDC *Index of New Entrepreneurial Activity* is calculated by expressing, as a proportion of the overall labor force, the number of Canadians who became independent workers and also hired employees during the past year. In 2011, the BDC Index was 0.31 percent for males, double that of females (0.14 percent), mainly because self-employed females were less likely than males to hire paid help.

Self-employment

Self-employment continues to increase among both males and females, with the rate of increase among females exceeding that of males. Analysis of *Canadian Labour Force Survey* data shows that in the decade from January 2004 to December 2013 the number of self-employed Canadians increased by 245,200, the majority of whom (150,100) were female. This reflects an annual *growth rate* in self-employment of 1.9 percent for females (compared to 0.6 percent for males). However, even though women are entering self-employment at a higher rate than men, their businesses are less substantive: almost 62 percent of self-employed females are unincorporated sole proprietorships that do not use paid help. By comparison, only 41.8 percent of males are unincorporated sole proprietorships without paid help; self-employed males incorporate or use paid help much more frequently than do females. Self-employment, without paid help, is especially problematic during periods when owners exit the market due to personal or family commitments (e.g., maternity leave, eldercare responsibilities).

Owner and firm profile

Like other nations, Canadian female business owners tend to be younger and less experienced (yet more likely to hold a post-graduate degree) compared to male business owners. Analysis of data from the *Survey on Financing and Growth of Small and Medium Enterprises* (Industry Canada, 2010) found that compared to male-owned firms, female-owned businesses tend to be concentrated in sectors in which barriers to entry are low, competitiveness is high, and dramatic growth is less likely. As noted above, The World Bank (2014) calls for gender-specific interventions to address the concentration of female-owned enterprises in low-productivity and low-growth activities. This is timely given that Canadian female business owners are at least as likely to voice growth aspirations as male business owners (Jung, 2010) but are less likely to achieve growth outcomes, particularly in the services sectors. Table 6.1 presents a profile of Canadian SMEs by gender of ownership.

Collectively, these data comprise *prima facie* evidence supportive of an entrepreneurship gender gap. Specifically, while women are entering more rapidly than men into self-employment—the formation of embryonic firms—female-owned enterprises remain smaller, even after accounting for systemic differences such as sector and age of firm (Orser, Riding and Jung, 2010). The finding of an entrepreneurship gender gap prompts a review of the Canadian entrepreneurship ecosystem.

Entrepreneurship ecosystems

In Canada, entrepreneurship policies are delivered through a wide array of business programs, training centers, loans, websites, portals, webinars, incubators, sector associations, training materials, newsletters, and other resources. There is overlap at the federal, provincial, and regional-levels. Like other OECD (Piacentini, 2013) and APEC member economies, the backbone of Canadian entrepreneurship policy comprises mainstream programs (that is, generic programs that do not take gender into account), complemented by regional, occasionally gender-specific small business support services. Female-focused small business centers are funded in Western and Eastern Canada and Northern Ontario. There are no federally funded women in enterprise training centers in Southern Ontario or Quebec, Canada's largest economic regions.

Table 6.1 Demographic profile of Canadian SMEs by gender of ownership

Proportion of firms reporting....	Share of female ownership				
	None	*1%–49%*	*50%*	*51%–99%*	*100%*
All SMEs	**53.9**	**12.5**	**18.1**	**2.1**	**13.4**
Size (Employment)					
1 to 4 employees	53.2	11.1	18.3	1.4	16.0
5 to 19 employees	52.4	13.1	19.7	2.7	12.0
20 to 99 employees	61.0	16.4	12.6	3.7	6.4
100 to 499 employees	66.0	16.6	9.9	3.5	4.0
Industry sectors					
Agriculture, Forestry, Mining, etc. (NAICS 11, 21)	47.4	23.9	23.9	1.6	3.3
Construction (NAICS 23)	66.7	11.5	16.8	2.2	2.9
Manufacturing (NAICS 31–33)	59.3	14.1	20.1	1.9	4.6
Wholesale Trade (NAICS 41)	61.1	13.5	18.7	1.4	5.4
Retail Trade (NAICS 44–45)	44.7	12.2	18.7	1.6	22.8
Transportation and Warehousing (NAICS 48–49)	61.8	12.2	17.1	1.8	7.1
Professional, Scientific, and Technical Services (NAICS 54)	55.7	12.4	17.6	2.5	11.8
Accommodation and Food Services (NAICS 72)	50.8	7.7	16.2	3.1	22.3
Other Services (NAICS 81)	47.5	10.4	18.5	2.5	21.2
Health Care etc. (NAICS 62), Information etc. (NAICS 51), Arts, etc. (NAICS 71)	48.9	11.6	17.1	2.3	20.1
Knowledge-Based Industries (KBI)	54.5	12.5	20.4	2.8	9.7
Location					
Rural	49.0	14.0	21.4	2.4	13.3
Urban	55.2	12.1	17.2	2.0	13.5
Age of firm					
2009–2011 (2 years or younger)	56.6	9.3	15.0	2.9	16.2
2001–2008 (3 to 10 years old)	53.1	11.4	18.4	2.3	14.8
1991–2000 (11 to 20 years old)	53.6	11.4	18.3	1.2	15.6
Prior to 1991 (more than 20 years old)	54.2	14.1	18.2	2.4	11.1
Owner age					
• <30 years old	64.4	12.0	X	X	17.9
• 30 to 39 years old	60.8	10.7	X	X	14.7
• 40 to 49 years old	55.4	10.0	19.1	1.2	14.3
• 50 to 64 years old	51.5	14.4	19.0	2.6	12.6
• 65+ years old	52.5	12.3	19.3	2.9	12.9
Proportion of owners with at least 10 years of experience	77.2	84.4	80.7	76.8	66.1
Highest level of education attained by owner					
Less than high school	54.8	14.0	19.1	1.7	10.4
High school	55.0	11.4	16.7	2.8	14.1

(Continued)

99

Table 6.1 (Continued)

Proportion of firms reporting....	Share of female ownership				
	None	1%–49%	50%	51%–99%	100%
College/CEGEP/trade school	51.7	11.6	21.7	1.8	13.3
Bachelor's degree	58.0	13.5	15.9	1.8	10.8
Master's degree or above	49.5	13.7	14.8	2.5	19.5
Financial profile ($)					
Annual revenues	2,080,199	2,327,991	1,238,835	1,593,688	736,192
Net income before tax	235,186	284,772	140,010	161,978	85,565
Assets	1,559,459	2,060,406	1,373,998	992,441	950,281
Liabilities	708,186	748,713	1,168,897	420,304	317,432

Source: 2011 Survey of Financing and Growth of SMEs, various tables.

While Canada has historically led the world in gender (employment) equality legislation, reform has not extended to gender-based procurement or entrepreneurship policy. For example, Canadian legislation introduced in 1986 requires all large employer firms (defined as firms that employ 100 persons or more) wishing to bid on Canadian federal contracts or supply goods and services to the federal government to commit to implementing and demonstrating gender employment equity. While federal agencies are expected to report on gender equality, the government does not report on client gender in federally funded entrepreneurship programs or SME procurement. While the Canadian government has not made broad use of small business set-asides, as permitted by trade agreements (Industry Canada, 2014), there are exceptions. These include procurement policies for Aboriginal businesses and the Canadian Innovation Commercialization Program (CICP). However, female Aboriginal business leaders have complained that the Aboriginal set-aside program lacks gender-disaggregated reporting. Anecdotal evidence suggests that female business owners are under-represented in supplier contacting (Roundtable on Aboriginal Women and Economic Development, Ottawa, 2009).

Employing an online search of Canadian websites, Orser (2004) concludes:

> Federal policy and programs targeted specifically at women business owners are limited. The majority (10 of 16 agencies [examined]) were defined as inactive or passive in their commitment to support women business owners. Furthermore, most federal decision makers appear to assume, without evidence, that existing services meet the needs of both male and female business owners.

In Canada, the lack of federal policy response is not attributable to lack of knowledge about the challenges facing female entrepreneurs. Studies about gender-related barriers to enterprise growth date to the early 1990s (Baird, 1992). The literature identified 15 Canadian studies about the status of women's entrepreneurship. Table 6.3 suggests consistencies in recommendations across studies. The most frequently cited recommendations (in descending order) include: increased access to start-up and growth capital; provision for mentoring and networking opportunities among women; and more efficient coordination of federal support and related services (e.g., horizontal communication across agencies, private/public service partnerships targeted at women entrepreneurs). Seven studies called for increasing awareness of the economic and social contributions of female entrepreneurs and provision of gender-specific business support.

Such realizations were the genesis of the Canadian Taskforce on Women's Business Growth. The objective was to inform the federal government about gender-specific entrepreneurship policies and programming.

Canadian Taskforce for Women's Business Growth

The taskforce emerged from informal discussion about an absence of reform following numerous calls for policy development, including a 2003 [Canadian] *Prime Minister's Taskforce on Women Entrepreneurs.* The grassroots initiative was formalized in 2009 through monthly conference calls, invitations to experts on regional, language, and sector issues, drafting of working papers on women's entrepreneurship, and development of project website funded in-kind contributions. Data collection was collaborative. The project was housed in the management faculty of a Canadian university.

In 2010, the taskforce hosted four roundtables comprising a total of 250 participants in Vancouver, Toronto, Halifax, and Ottawa. Participants were identified through national and regional women business-owner organizations; invitations were sent under the signature of prominent community leaders. Roundtable meetings were four to five hours in length. Participants were asked to discuss a series of pre-determined topics that were identified by taskforce members. Table conversations were recorded. Drawing on participant discussions, taskforce members drafted a series of federal policy and program recommendations. Figure 6.1 depicts the framework of the 2011 Taskforce for Women's Business Growth (Women's Enterprise Centre of Manitoba, 2010).

In 2011, the taskforce released *Canadian Taskforce Roundtable Report. Action Strategies to Support Canadian Women-owned Enterprises.* Summary recommendations included: (a) a national strategy to facilitate women's enterprise growth; (b) female-focused programs on financial and technology literacy; (c) increasing access to growth capital, grants, and related resources; and (d) reporting on the economic contributions of women to the Canadian economy (see Table 6.2: Canadian taskforce for women's business growth summary recommendations). Following the release of the taskforce report, ad hoc regional and federal political and bureaucratic briefings were initiated, including presentations to politicians, senior bureaucrats, and the Standing Senate Committee on Banking, Trade and Commerce. Taskforce conference communications ended six months following the release of the 2011 report. Committee member feedback indicated that the taskforce report was a useful communications tool about women's entrepreneurship to share with sponsors and other stakeholders. To date, none of the recommendations has been implemented.

This study advances four propositions to explain what appears to be government indifference to the 2011 taskforce recommendations. Participant observations of taskforce meetings, roundtable discussions, ad hoc political and bureaucratic briefings, and the policy frameworks of other countries (in particular the US) provide windows through which to discern barriers to advancing gender-specific entrepreneurship policy.

Participant observations

This section employs retrospective analysis of the 2011 Canadian taskforce. Participant-observer responses call for engaged scholarship to advance the entrepreneurship literature (Stratigea and Papadopoulou, 2013) and a need to assess women's enterprise strategies (Piacentini,

Table 6.2 Canadian taskforce for women's business growth summary recommendations (2011)

Priorities	Recommendations
National strategy	A national strategy to facilitate women's enterprise growth, increased funding to gender-specific business support and program expansion in regions that do not support programs. The two largest Canadian provinces (Ontario and Quebec) offered few gender-specific business support services. Program delivery through public/private partnerships as no one organization retains the expertise to launch a comprehensive, women-focused economic development strategy.
Coordination of policies and programs	There have been at least 4 ad hoc federal interdepartmental committees in the last 15 years. To ensure policies address the needs of females, the Taskforce called for a permanent, interdepartmental federal committee. The committee would be tasked with coordinating gender-specific entrepreneurship policies. An Office for Women's Enterprise is needed to support the interdepartmental committee (e.g., work across the federal government to coordinate programs, policies, research, knowledge sharing), and should be granted sufficient funding and power to reach into all federal agencies.
Access to growth capital	Participants voiced concern that small business clients are left without adequate support following start-up training. Higher loan amounts and working capital are required for expansion (e.g., some agencies provide less than $20,000 in start-up funding). The government was asked to establish a business development credit to offset costs to obtain professional financial advice ($2,000 to $5,000).
Technology adoption	Participants sought information about how to identify, select, and adopt technology across stages of firm evolution (e.g., social media, cloud-based software, on-line procurement, communication systems). Information sharing could be accomplished through a portal. The portal would support an interactive database with search/matching functionality and facilitate matching of qualified experts. Federal program eligibility criteria should be reviewed given reported differences in women's engagement in the advanced technology sectors.
Develop new markets	More sophisticated, timely and consolidated information to assist female business owners who intend to do business in foreign markets. Web-site proliferation and duplication across agencies erode awareness and limit program usage. A 'go-to' portal would showcase case studies about female business owners who have internationalized and include 'how to' tools and checklists grounded in practice and research. Maps would provide users with strategies to efficiently link import/export/investment information with industry associations and regional programs. Participants sought gender-sensitive information such as cultural and gender norms in different countries. The portal would employ matchmaking, knowledge-sharing technology and a hot line.

Gender-specific procurement policy	Participants reported that it is difficult to find companies that have supplier diversity policies and that procurement was not on the 'diversity agenda' of most firms. Many did not know about supplier diversity agencies such as WEConnect International and Canadian Aboriginal and Minority Supplier Council. These entities were deemed catalysts to accessing foreign (primarily American) contracts. Public Works and Government Services Canada, in collaboration with other ministries, was encouraged to create public relations opportunities to recognize federal buyers and private corporations that support supplier diversity. Participants recommended that government proactively support certified female-owned enterprises that seek to leverage US diversity-supplier procurement opportunities and fund trade missions, training, workshops, and grants to offset costs of prospecting, travel, and certification.
Financial literacy	Participants sought learning opportunities to increase understanding about SME financing. Need for training was also evidenced in studies that report females are less likely to seek equity capital compared to males. Concerns included lack confidence, limited access to angel networks and other sources of equity, confusion about terms and jargon, limited understanding about types of equity and debt capital, and need to better understand best practices in structuring deals and utilizing financial information. Participants sought an on-line financing curriculum. The envisioned program would support an e-based learning network.
Reporting and accountability	There are no provisions to ensure equitable access to, or use of, federally funded business support programs.[1] There are no mechanisms to identify the gender composition of firm ownership. The Taskforce recommended mandating all federally funded economic development, small business, science, technology and innovation programs to report on client profiles and program usage using sex-disaggregated data. Federal agencies should be held accountable for ensuring that economic stimulation programs include female applicants and users. To do so, agencies need to be more proactive in outreach and in undertaking internal reviews to examine potential gender differences in program usage, impacts, and outcomes.

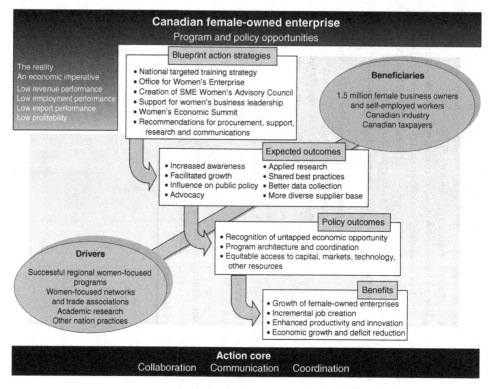

Figure 6.1 Framework of the 2011 Taskforce for Women's Business Growth

Source: Women's Enterprise Centre of Manitoba (2010)

2013). Stratigea and Papadopoulou (2013) maintain that engaged scholarship can facilitate stakeholder consultations and coproduce recommendations to inform policy and program design, build consensus, and enhance social learning. As the Founding Chair of the 2011 taskforce, the author is in a unique position to observe the interactions among taskforce members and decision-makers responsible for producing, maintaining, and modifying entrepreneurship policies. Retrospective analysis suggests that (at least) four factors impeded implementation of the 2011 taskforce recommendations:

- absence of advocacy;
- lack of oversight and accountability;
- conflicting perspectives about women's enterprise and policy priorities; and
- ghettoization of women's entrepreneurship policy development.

Collectively, such barriers to policy reform help to sustain a male-centric entrepreneurship ecosystem. The propositions are now explained.

Proposition 1: lack of advocacy

In Canada, there are no national women's entrepreneurship advocacy organizations or forums to advance gender-sensitive entrepreneurship policies and programming. Over the past 20 years, several organizations have positioned themselves as representing policy interests of

Table 6.3 Canadian gender-focused entrepreneurship policy reports, taskforces, and forums (1986–2011)

Author(s)	Increased access to SME financing	Networking, mentoring, training, advisory support	Better coordination of services (e.g., horizontal, private/public) partnerships, reduce red tape)	Increased awareness of economic contributions of women ENTs address, credibility gaps	Female-focused SME programs and services	Promotion of entrepreneurship as a career option	Female-friendly training, advisory services, curriculum	Access to federal programs, services, grants, contributions	One-stop access hub for information	Income protection, self-employment training benefits, insurance)	Increase access to federal procurement (e.g., contracts)	Gender-disaggregated program reviews and data	Internationalization support (e.g., export training, missions)	Reporting best practices to facilitate enterprise growth
Millar, A. (1986)[2] *A Study of Women Entrepreneurs in Canada*, Ottawa, Small Business Secretariat.	✓			✓	✓	✓						✓		
Stevenson, L. (1988)[4]		✓	✓	✓							✓			
Baird, B. (1992)[2]		✓	✓	✓										
Belcourt, Burke, Lee-Gosselin, (1991)[4]	✓	✓	✓				✓	✓	✓			✓		
Bérard and Brown (1994)[2,4]	✓	✓	✓		✓	✓	✓							
Thompson, P. (1994)[3]	✓					✓								

(Continued)

Table 6.3 (Continued)

Policy and program recommendations

Author(s)	Increased access to SME financing	Networking, mentoring, training, advisory support	Better coordination of services (e.g., horizontal, private/public) partnerships, reduce red tape)	Increased awareness of economic contributions of women ENTs address, credibility gaps	Female-focused SME programs and services	Promotion of entrepreneurship as a career option	Female-friendly training, advisory services, curriculum	Access to federal programs, services, grants, contributions	One-stop access hub for information	Income protection, self-employment training benefits, insurance)	Increase access to federal procurement (e.g., contracts)	Gender-disaggregated program reviews and data	Internationalization support (e.g., export training, missions)	Reporting best practices to facilitate enterprise growth
Hughes, K. (1999)[2,4]	✓	✓		✓	✓	✓	✓	✓		✓			✓	✓
Lever, A. (2004)[1]	✓	✓	✓	✓	✓			✓						
St. Onge, A. and Stevenson, L. (2001)[1]	✓	✓			✓	✓	✓	✓	✓	✓			✓	
Bates, J. (2002)[2,4]	✓									✓				
Prime Minister's Taskforce (2003)[2]	✓	✓	✓	✓	✓	✓		✓	✓	✓	✓			
Rooney et al., (2003)[4]	✓	✓	✓	✓	✓			✓		✓		✓		
Industry Canada (2004)[2,4]	✓	✓	✓	✓	✓	✓	✓			✓	✓			
Aboriginal Women & Economic Development (2009)[2]	✓	✓	✓	✓	✓	✓	✓	✓		✓	✓	✓		
Canadian Taskforce for Women's Business Growth (2011)[4]	✓				✓			✓	✓		✓	✓	✓	✓

Source: 1=private sector; 2=government or government sponsored, 3=not-for-profit/non-governmental, 4=academic.

Canadian female entrepreneurs (e.g., Women Entrepreneurs of Canada (WEC), Canadian Association of Executives and Entrepreneurs (CAWEE), Foundation of Canadian Women Entrepreneurs, Start-up Canada). Compared to the US, impact on policy reform has been restricted due to limited funding and organizational capacity and lack of solidarity among regional and national women in enterprise organizations. Canadian legislation also prohibits organizations that receive federal funding from advocacy work, including women's enterprise centers and female-focused sector associations. This is problematic for several reasons.

First, women in enterprise and related organizations retain expert knowledge about the business support needs of female entrepreneurs. Advocacy is left to female business owners. Second, the profile of SMEs suggests female business owners are more likely than males to operate micro-enterprises. Characteristically, such firms are less likely to have employees to delegate to when owners engage in advocacy or retain excess capital to help fund advocacy. This advantages male-dominated sectors (e.g., sectors such as construction, extraction, and technology).

With no national advocacy organization to monitor and report on policies and programs associated with women's entrepreneurship, reform is left to political will and/or individual champions. By comparison, American female entrepreneurs benefit from professional lobbying from organizations such as Women Influencing Public Policy (WIPP) and Quantum Leaps. The impact of organized advocacy is, in part, evidenced in the US advisory framework (a description follows).

Proposition 2: lack of accountability

Anecdotal information suggests significant gender differences in applicability and utilization of federal SME, technology and innovations programs (Bulte et al., 2003; Canadian Taskforce of Women's Business Growth, 2011). For example, innovation is deemed instrumental in sustaining Canadian competitive advantage and is a means of enabling enterprise growth. MaRS—a flagship Canadian enterprise incubator—is among the very few agencies that report on the engagement of women, but less than 10 percent of MaRS clients are female (Treurnicht, 2012). While the federal government is mandated to provide equitable access to business support programs and services, few (if any) systematic, gender-based evaluations are undertaken. Within federal agencies, there are no mechanisms to identify (hence, report on) gender of program users. The federal agency tasked with undertaking gender-based analysis (Status of Women Canada) no longer funds or annually reports on the state of women's entrepreneurship.

In contrast, an example of 'good practice' is the US advisory framework, a framework that is the product of advocacy (Littlejohn, as cited in Orser and Elliott, 2015). A 1978 Interagency Task Force on Women's Business Ownership led to the establishment in 1979 of The Office of Women's Business Ownership (OWBO) within the Small Business Administration and Interagency Committee on Women's Business Enterprise. Passage in 1988 of the US Women's Business Ownership Act (Public Law 100–533) established the National Women's Business Council (NWBC). Reporting to the White House, Congress, and US Small Business Administration, the National Women's Business Council provides a formal voice for the women's enterprise sector, through annual reporting, briefings, outreach, and online resources training tools. The bill also requires the Census Bureau to include women-owned firms in the business census.

The World Bank Group *Doing Business Report* (2015) suggests Canada/US differences in entrepreneurship policy are not a product of variations in small business regulations, tax regimes, or employment standards. In 2015, the US outranked Canada with respect to the ease of doing business (7th versus 16th among 189 economies). Canada leads the world in 'starting a business' (criteria such as 'number of procedures' and cost) and ranked 7th with respect to 'protecting minority investors'. In all other criteria the US outranked Canada, including dealing with construction permits, getting electricity, registering property, securing credit, paying taxes, across-border trade, and enforcing contracts. The report does not measure gender equality or monitor security, state of the financial system, and level of training and skills of the labor force (World Bank Group, 2015). Without formalized accounting and reporting to Parliament, the Senate and key federal ministries tasked with small business (e.g., Industry Canada), history suggests that gender-specific entrepreneurship policy reform is unlikely.

Proposition 3: conflicting perspectives about women's enterprise and policy priorities

Differing views about appropriate interventions were evidenced in internal committee and roundtable discussions. Differences focused primarily on: (a) how gender influences the venture creation process (e.g., rationale for gender differences in engagement and enterprise performance); (b) perceived value of mainstream versus gender-specific business support; (c) merit of private versus public service providers (e.g., Why should government finance gender-focused business support? What is the role of the private sector in advising small businesses?); and (d) rationales for government investment in women's enterprise. Debate reflects the complexity of women's entrepreneurship; need to engage multiple players in policy development; and the perceived value of mainstream and gender-specific business supports. Such debate also suggests that a 'one size fits all' entrepreneurship policy is not appropriate (Thompson, Scott, and Downing, 2012).

How one views women's entrepreneurship is seen to influence one's perceptions about appropriate market interventions. With respect to *how* gender influences entrepreneurial engagement and enterprise performance, several schools of thought are advanced. Table 6.4 presents two rationales and the associated policy interventions. Readers who adhere to the liberal feminist rationale tended to favor mainstream intervention; those who support the social feminist rationale tended to favor gender-specific policy and program interventions. As the taskforce conversations suggested, the two rationales are not mutually exclusive.

Taskforce discussions also reflected differences in perception about why government should invest in women entrepreneurs. At least three rationales are advanced in the literature. The *business case* suggests female-owned enterprises comprise an under-utilized and/ or under-performing resource, one to be supported for employment creation and economic growth. Attracting and retaining women and increasing access to resources lead to enterprise performance and hence, national competitiveness (McKinsey & Company, 2008; EY, 2009; Caranci and Preston, 2012; Canadian Imperial Bank of Commerce, 2004). *Operational outcomes* of gender-specific market interventions are also described. Client perceptions include opportunities to work and network with other women, sensitivity and knowledge about gender-related challenges of business ownership, inviting and supportive learning environment and culture, and being taken seriously (Orser, Elliott, and Findlay-Thompson, 2012). Within an *international development paradigm*, gender-specific interventions are viewed as a means to alleviate poverty, by increasing women's per capita income.

Differing perspectives are further evidenced in communications about women's entrepreneurship programs. For example, employing content analysis of a French government

Table 6.4 Feminist rationales for entrepreneurial gender gaps and associated policy responses

Theoretical rationale	Associated entrepreneurship policies
Liberal feminism women entrepreneurs must circumvent systemic barriers to grow their firms (Fischer, Reuber, and Dyke, 1993). To the extent that females can do so, entrepreneurial engagement and enterprise performance are equivalent to that of male counterparts. Hence, liberal feminists argue that "…men and women are essentially similar" and that "…[m]en and women are seen as equally able and any subordination of women must depend on discrimination or on structural barriers" (Ahl, 2006, p. 596). Liberal feminist theory (Bardasi et al., 2011) identifies 'constraint-driven' differences that build on the tenets of resource-based theory (Delmar, Davidsson and Gartner, 2003) as a rationale for gender differences in enterprise performance. Constraints reflect professional and personal barriers that women may face in acquiring resources requisite to start-up and growth (e.g., overt discrimination can deprive female entrepreneurs of resources needed throughout the venture creation processes).	• Equitable access to resources requisite to start-up and growth: networks, financial capital, loan guarantee schemes, advisory boards, trade missions, crowd funding • Proactive program outreach, recruitment targets or quotas for small business training, innovation, and economic development agencies • Legislation reporting on the status of women on public boards or quotas
Social feminism: gender is embedded within the antecedents of entrepreneurial engagement (e.g., intentions, sector choice, management, strategy). According to Ahl (2006, p. 597) "…men and women are seen to be, or have become, essentially different." One can expect differences in entrepreneurial engagement given gender influences in the underlying nature, construction, and operational practices of enterprises. Entrepreneurship policy should adhere more closely to women's lived experiences rather than the interests of third-party (e.g., government) suppliers of financial capital. Program evaluation criteria should reflect priorities of clients rather than suppliers (Byrne and Fayolle, 2010). For example, Aboriginal Canadians have called for federal entrepreneurship policy and program assessment criteria such as reduction of Aboriginal children in government care, increased number of Aboriginal women homeowners, and diversification of occupations among Aboriginal women (Roundtable on Aboriginal Women and Economic Development, 2009).	• Federal spending commensurate with needs of all citizens, including women • Universal provision of female-focused entrepreneurship training/curriculum • Gender-specific entrepreneurship or small business centers, programs, curricula, procurement policies • Program assessment criteria that reflect client rather than funder (and other intermediary's) needs • Mandated monitoring and reporting about the status of women's entrepreneurship • Reconceptualization of economic policy, in order to include non-market contributions and social policy (Mayoux, 2001) • Program assessment criteria should capture cultural, economic and social impacts, as defined by communities of women.

campaign to promote women's entrepreneurship, Bryne and Fatoum (2013) describe themes of *dependence* ("In order to be successful, women-led small businesses and entrepreneurs need to be helped by the government and the numerous women-specific network and support organizations which exist."); *motherhood*-communications predicated on unquestioned presumptions that women make professional and career-based decisions based on childcare options; and the position that *women are different.* Similarly, Perren and Jennings (2005) examined government texts that promote women's entrepreneurship programs. Most emphasized the *business case* as a rationale for market intervention. Perren and Jennings labeled a second theme *legitimization*, in which governments report that: "...small businesses account for job creation and economic growth and emphasize the role of government departments in enabling this growth/job creation." A third theme observed was again a presupposition of *dependency.*

The above observations suggest that differing perspectives, including dated narratives about women's entrepreneurship, reinforce gender stereotypes, inaccurately reflect client motives to utilize female-focused business support, and negate the fact that women operate firms across all sectors and size categories. The need to challenge narratives about female entrepreneurs is further evidenced in personal observation. When briefing bureaucrats about the taskforce recommendations, discussions were populated with references to family (daughters and/or wives who own firms), status of women in the work force (particularly females in executive roles within the federal government), and need for women in the trades, science, technology, and math (STEM). For example, the author participated in a briefing with a Deputy Minister of an agency tasked with economic development. Discussion was deflected with numerous references to a daughter's roommate's home-based dog washing business. Speaking on behalf of women, denial, and lip service are also recognized behaviors to stifle advocacy (Schalkwyk, 2000). While these topics are important to the wellbeing of women, raising such issues deflects constructive dialogue about targeted strategies to empower female entrepreneurs.

The above observations are consistent with The World Bank (2014) report that calls for a change in the public discourse about women's entrepreneurship. Gender-sensitive policy infers examination of potential biases across all components of the entrepreneurship ecosystem, including communiqués.

Proposition 4: ghettoization of gender-focused entrepreneurship policies

Canadian policy studies have called for the establishment of an office of women's enterprise within a key ministry tasked with economic development. Women's entrepreneurship policy currently resides within Status of Women Canada. The small agency is mandated to address social and economic policy yet demonstrates limited expertise in the venture creation process (e.g., expertise with respect to enterprise start-up, growth, internationalization, financing, and other aspects of development such as commercialization of innovation and adoption of digital technologies). In 2015, Status of Women Canada priorities included women on corporate boards, domestic violence, workplace harassment, poverty reduction, income security, women in the trades, and leadership. The agency's convening power is weak relative to key economic federal ministries. By design, the agency is obliged to 'push' policy recommendations through various ministries rather than respond to mandated gender-focused policy priorities of lead economic ministries. It is not realistic to expect a small federal agency to be able to effectively design and administer the breadth of policy characteristic of federal entrepreneurship ecosystem (Ahmad and Hoffman, 2007).

Conclusions

Monitoring agencies report that the integration of women's issues within entrepreneurship policy is weak and that gender-specific initiatives remain selective, one-off, pilot projects and are generally poorly funded (UNIFEM, 2006). As such, multilateral forums and studies have called for policies and programs to better support women entrepreneurs, including monitoring the implementation of national plans for women's entrepreneurship (Piacenini, 2013). For example, within the European Union (EU), Central, and Eastern Europe, the provision of female-focused entrepreneurship initiatives is limited. A regional study that examined the availability of female-focused initiatives reported that over 70 percent of small business member organizations made no provision for women entrepreneurs (Smallbone et al., 2000).

The evidence reported in this retrospective case analysis presents several reasons policy and program reform can be elusive. The study described four barriers within the interface between industry recommendations and policy. To create an inclusive ethos for enterprise and business, policy reform requires advocacy, formalized accountability, bureaucratic and political leadership, clear and multiple policy priorities, and gender-disaggregated evaluations to report biases in federal funding, policies, and programming. These findings also suggest the need for research to examine: (a) impacts of country-level 'women in enterprise' consultations; (b) efficacy of advisory processes on policy reform (e.g., grassroots initiatives, industry-driven taskforces, federally appointed expert panels, internal interdepartmental committees, and public workshops); and (c) federal discourses about gender-specific business support. Sample initiatives include those undertaken by the Government of Scotland (2013), Enterprise Ireland (2014), Invest Northern Ireland (2007), and United Kingdom (2003, 2009). The efficacy of entrepreneurship policies that reside within economic development agencies (such as the US Small Business Administration) versus women's agencies (for example, Status of Women Canada) is also worthy of examination. Criteria might include incremental job creation, women's participation in mainstream versus female-focused SME programming and access to capital, including federally funded loan guarantee schemes. This is because this Canadian case study presents evidence that discourses, even at the most senior levels of government, can be informed by anecdotes and assumptions about the status of women in the paid workplace.

Limitations

The taskforce reported on here was not designed to conform to scientific methodology. Rather, the objective of the grassroots initiative was to inform federal policy. Hence, this Canadian retrospective study is exploratory. The propositions require further study across different modes of consultation and country-contexts. The study also reflects limitations inherent in engaged scholarship, including observer bias (Van de Ven and Johnson, 2006) given the author's role as the Founding Chair of the taskforce. This report does not seek to represent the views or experiences of other taskforce members and contributors. Finally, scholars argue that academic research often has little impact on entrepreneurship policy (Curran and Storey, 2002; Blackburn and Smallbone, 2008; Thompson, Scott and Downing, 2012). This may be for a number of reasons, including lack of political sensitivity.

This case supports concerns of other feminist scholars who argue that entrepreneurship policies continue to be framed through the experiences and expectations of male entrepreneurs (Walker and Joyner, 1999; Ljunggren and Alsos, 2012). The study raises questions about how entrepreneurship policymakers, program delivery agencies, sector associations, and academics might more effectively communicate. For example, it is not yet clear how decision-makers (such as politicians and policymakers) weigh industry versus political interests. Without examination, the impact of consultations on entrepreneurship policy reform is questionable. Ironically, one next step is collaborative research to consider this question.

References

Ács, A., Szerb, L. and Autio, E. (2014). *Gender Global Development Index.* Accessed at: http://thegedi.org/global-entrepreneurship-and-development-index/.

Ahl, H. (2006). Why Research on Women Needs New Directions, *Entrepreneurship Theory and Practice,* 30 (5): 595–621.

Ahl, H. (2004). *The Scientific Reproduction of Gender Inequality,* CBS Press, Copenhagen.

Ahmad, N. and Hoffman, A. (2007). *A Framework for Addressing and Measuring Entrepreneurship.* Paris: OECD Entrepreneurship Indicators Steering Group, November 20, 2007), 4, accessed at http://www.oecd.org/industry/business-stats/39629644.pdf.

Asia Pacific Economic Cooperation (APEC, 2010). APEC Women's Entrepreneurship Summit, October 1, 2010, Gifu, Japan. Also see High Level Policy Dialogue on Women and the Economy, San Francisco, 2011.

Baird, B. (1982). *Canadian Women Owner/Managers.* Toronto: Small Business Secretariat Queen's Park.

Bardasi, E., Sabarwal, S., and Terrell, K. (2011). How Do Female Entrepreneurs Perform? Evidence from Three Developing Regions. *Small Business Economics,* 37(4): 417–441.

Bates, J. (2002). *Women in Own-Account Self-Employment: A Policy Perspective.* Ottawa: Commissioned by Status of Women Canada Research Directorate.

Belcourt, M., Burke, R. J., and Lee-Gosselin, H. (1991). *The Glass Box: Women Business Owners in Canada.* Ottawa: Canadian Advisory Council on the Status of Women.

Berard, J. and Brown, D. (1994). *Services to Women Entrepreneurs: The Western Canadian Case.* Manitoba, Canada: Western Economic Diversification Canada.

Biosca, A.B. (2010). *Growth Dynamics, Exploring Business Growth and Contraction in Europe, U.S.* National Endowment for Science, Technology and the Arts.

Blackburn, R.A. and Smallbone, D. (2008). Researching Small Firms and Entrepreneurship in the UK: Developments and Distinctiveness. *Entrepreneurship, Theory & Practice,* 32(2): 267–288.

Bulte, S. Callbeck, C. Duplain, R., Fitzpatrick, K., Redman, and Lever, A. (2003). *The Prime Minister's Task Force on Women Entrepreneurs.* Ottawa: National Liberal Caucus Research Bureau, Information Management.

Business Development Bank of Canada (BDC, 2012). *BDC Index of New Entrepreneurial Activity.* http://www.bdc.ca/en/Documents/other/BDC_INDEX_ENT_ACTIVITY_EN.pdf.

Byrne, J. and Fattoum, S. (2013). Government Support for Women Entrepreneurs: A Helping Hand or Poisoned Chalice? *Proceedings, RENT XXVII Conference,* ISM University of Management and Economics, Vilnius Campus, Arkliųstr 18.

Canadian Imperial Bank of Commerce (CIBC, 2004). *Women Entrepreneurs: Leading the Charge.* Accessed at: https://www.cibc.com/ca/pdf/women-entrepreneurs-en.pdf.

Canadian Labour Force Survey (various years) Ottawa: Statistics Canada.

Canadian Taskforce for Women's Business Growth. Strategies to Growth. Accessed on September 24, 2015 at Accessed at http://sites.telfer.uottawa.ca/womensenterprise.

Caranci, B. and Preston, L. (TD Economics, 2012). The Venus vs. Mars Approach to Entrepreneurial Success in Canada. *Observation,* January 31, 2012. Accessed at: http://www.td.com/document/PDF/economics/special/lp0112_women_ent.pdf.

Castillo, S. (2007). *The Business Case: Women-Owned Businesses in the Supply Chain,* 8. May 17, 2007. Access at: http://www.wbecanada.org/uploads/Image/Connextions/WomenOwnedBusinesses_in_the_SupplyChainWBENC.pdf.

Curran, J., and Storey, D.J. (2002). Small Business Policy in the United Kingdom: The Inheritance of the Small Business Service and Implications for Its Future Effectiveness. *Environment and Planning C: Government and Policy,* 20(2): 163–177.

De Clercq, D., Lim, D., and Oh, C.H., (2013). Individual-Level Resources and New Business Activity: The Contingent Role of Institutional Context. *Entrepreneurship Theory and Practice*, 37(2): 303–330. ISSN (print) 1042–2587.

Delmar, F., Davidsson, P., and Gartner, W. (2003). Arriving at the High-Growth Firm, *Journal of Business Venturing*, 18(2): 189–216.

Diana Project (2015). See http://www.babson.edu/Academics/centers/blank-center/global-research/diana/Pages/home.aspx.

Economist Intelligence Unit (2012). Women's Economic Opportunity, 2012. A Global Index and Ranking from The Economist Intelligence Unit. Findings and Methodology, London: Economist Intelligence Unit.

Enterprise Ireland (2014). Presentation to the International Council for Small Business and Entrepreneurship, Women Entrepreneurship Forum (Dublin, June 11, 2014) based on *Investing in Women. Report on Strategy Development and Implementation*.

EY (2009). *Groundbreakers. Using the Strength of Women to Rebuild the World Economy.*

EY (2009). *Scaling Up. Why Women-Owned Businesses Can Recharge the Global Economy.* Accessed January 7, 2017 at http://www.ey.com/Publication/vwLUAssets/Scaling_up_-_Why_women-owned_businesses_can_recharge_the_global_economy_-_new/$FILE/Scaling_up_why_women_owned_businesses_can_recharge_the_global_economy.pdf.

Fischer, E., Reuber, R., and Dyke, L. (1993). A Theoretical Overview and Extension of Research on Sex, Gender, and Entrepreneurship. *Journal of Business Venturing*, 8(2): 151–160.

Gender Empowerment Measure (2012). *United Nations Development Programme, Human Development Reports*. Accessed January 7, 2016 at http://hdr.undp.org/en/content/gender-inequality-index-gii.

Gender Inequality Index (2013). *United Nations Development Programme, Human Development Reports*. Accessed on December 26, 2016 at hdr.undp.org/en/content/gender-inequality-index.

Global Entrepreneurship Monitor (GEM) Canada Report (2013). Accessed January 7, 2017 at http://www.thecis.ca/.

Global Entrepreneurship Monitor (GEM) Report on Women and Entrepreneurship (2007). Accessed at: http://www.gemconsortium.org/docs/281/gem-2007-report-on-women-and-entrepreneurship.

Global Entrepreneurship Monitor Global Report (GEM, 2013). Accessed at: http://www.gemconsortium.org/docs/3106/gem-2013-global-report.

Global Women Entrepreneur Leaders Scorecard (2015). Sponsored by Dell and produced by ACG Inc. Accessed September 30, 2015 at https://www.dell.com/learn/us/en/uscorp1/corporate~secure~en/documents~2015-gwel-country-category-scores.pdf.

Golla, M., Malhotra, A., Nanda, P., and Mehra, R. (2011). *Understanding and Measuring Women's Economic Empowerment: Definition, Frameworks, Indicators*. Washington, DC: International Centre for Research on Women.

Hughes, K. (1999). *Gender and Self-Employment in Canada: Assessing Trends and Policy Implications*. Ottawa: Canadian Policy Research Networks, Inc.

Industry Canada (2005). *Summary Report from Sustaining the Momentum. An Economic Forum on Women Entrepreneurs*. Ottawa, Canada.

Industry Canada (2014). Innovation Canada: A Call to Action Special Report on Procurement. The Scope for Using Procurement to Enhance Innovation. Accessed at http://rd-review.ca/eic/site/033.nsf/eng/00320.html.

Invest Northern Ireland (2007). *Investing in Women Strategy*. Accessed at: http://www.investni.com/news/invest-ni-pathclearing-initiative-8211-opening-pathways-through-the-business-support-network-for-women.html.

Jung, O. (2010). *Small Business Financing Profiles. SME Financing Initiative Women Entrepreneurs*, Industry Canada, Ottawa, available at: www.sme-fdi.gc.ca/eic/site/sme_fdi-prf_pme.nsf/eng/h_02215.html.

Kabeer, N. (2012). Women's Economic Empowerment and Inclusive Growth: Labour Markets and Enterprise Growth, SIG Working Paper 2012/1. Ottawa: Department for International Development and the International Development Research Centre.

Klyver, K., Nielson, S.L., Evald, M.R., (2013). Women's Self-Employment: An Act of Institutional (Dis)Integration? A Multilevel, Cross-Country Study. *Journal of Business Venturing*, 28(4): 474–488.

Lever, A. (2004). *Best Practices to Support Women Entrepreneurs*. Toronto: Foundation of Canadian Women Entrepreneurs.

Ljunggren, E. and Alsos, G.A. (2012). *Gender and Innovation- Towards a Research Framework*. Working paper, Nordland Research Institute, Norway.

McKinsey & Company (1997). *Women Matter. Gender Diversity, a Corporate Performance Driver*, McKinsey & Company, Inc. Also see McKinsey & Company, *Women Matter 2* (2008). *Female Leadership, a Competitive Edge for the Future*, McKinsey & Company, Inc.

Morissette, R., Picot, G. and Lu, Y. (2013). *The Evolution of Canadian Wages over the Last Three Decades*. Ottawa: Statistics Canada. Analytical Studies Branch Research Paper Series, Catalogue no. 11F0019M—No. 347.

Organization for Economic Co-operation and Development (OECD, 2013). Entrepreneurship Statistics by Gender: A Review of Existing Sources and Options for Data Development. Accessed at: http://unstats.un.org/unsd/gender/Events/5-6%20Dec%202013/Background%20Paper.pdf.

Orser, B. (2004). *A Pilot Study on Federal SME Policies to Support Women Business Owners and Trade*. Ottawa: Status of Women Canada and Department of Foreign Affairs and International Trade.

Orser, B. and Elliott, C. (2015) *Feminine Capital. Unlocking the Power of Women Entrepreneurs*. Stanford: Stanford University Press.

Orser, B., Elliott, C., Findlay-Thompson, S. (2012). Women–Focused Small Business Programming: Client Motives and Perspectives. *International Journal of Gender and Entrepreneurship*, 4(3): 236–265.

Orser, B., Riding, A., and Jung, O. (2013). Gender of Ownership and the Growth of Young Enterprises, Paper presentation, 2013 Babson College Entrepreneurship Research Conference, EMLYON Business School, Écully, France, June 5–8, 2013.

Orser, B.J. and Weeks, J. (2009). *Procurement Strategies to Support Women-Owned Enterprise*. Written and prepared on Behalf of WEConnect Canada, Ottawa, available at: www.weconnectcanada. org/links_research.html.

Perren, L. and Jennings, P. L. (2005). Government Discourses on Entrepreneurship: Issues of Legitimization, Subjugation, and Power. *Entrepreneurship Theory & Practice*, 29: 173–184.

Piacentini, M. (2013). *Women Entrepreneurs in the OECD: Key Evidence and Policy Challenges*, OECD Social, Employment and Migration Working Papers, No. 147, OECD Publishing Paris, https://dx.doi.org/10.1787/5k43bvtkmb8v-en.

PROWESS (2014). Women in Business. *A Manifesto for Women in Business An Environment Where Women in Business Can Flourish*. Accessed at: http://www.prowess.org.uk/wp-content/uploads/2014/05/A-Manifesto-for-Women-in-Business-May-14.pdf.

Quantum Leaps (2010). *The Roadmap to 2020-Fueling the Growth of Women's Enterprise Development*. Washington, DC. Ed. V. Littlejohn.

Rooney, J., Lero, D., Korabik, K., Whitehead, D.L., Abbondanza, M., Tougas, J., Boyd, J. and Bourque, L. (2003). *Self-Employment for Women: Policy Options that Promote Equality and Economic Opportunities Centre for Families, Work and Well-Being*. Accessed at: http://www.rwmc.uoguelph.ca/cms/documents/87/Rooney_1-138.pdf.

Roundtable on Aboriginal Women and Economic Development, Ottawa (2009). Co-Chairs: Dawn Madahbee, Executive Member of National Aboriginal Economic Development Board (NAEDB) and Clare Beckton, Deputy Head of Status of Women Canada, Ottawa, April 29, 2009.

Schalkwyk, J., (2000). Culture, Gender Equity and Development Cooperation. Ottawa: Canadian International Development Agency, Prepared on behalf of the OECD, 2000, 6, accessed at http://www.oecd.org/social/gender-development/1896320.pdf.

The Scottish Government (2013). *Women in Enterprise. A Framework and Action Plan to Increase the Contribution of Women's Enterprise to the Scottish Economy*. Accessed at:http://www.inspiringenterprise.rbs.com/sites/default/files/resources/wes-action-framework.pdf.

The Shiver Report, Reporting from the front lines of our changing lives. Accessed at: http://shriverreport.org/.

Smallbone, D., Johnson, S., Virk, B., and Hotchkiss, G. (2000). *Young Entrepreneurs, Women Entrepreneurs, Ethnic Minority Entrepreneurs and Co-Entrepreneurs in the European Union and Central and Eastern Europe*. London, U.K.: Middlesex University Business School, Centre for Enterprise and Economic Development Research.

St. Onge and Stevenson (2001). *Creating an Entrepreneurial Environment to Foster the Start-up and Growth of Women-owned Entrepreneurs: Best Practices from Atlantic Canada*. Unpublished paper, previously presented at Durham University, UK, 2001.

Statistics Canada (various years). *Labour Force Survey*, Ottawa: Statistics Canada. Accessed at: http://www.statcan.gc.ca/eng/survey/household/3701.

Stevenson, L. (1984). *An Investigation of the Entrepreneurial Experience of Women: Implications for Small Business Policy in Canada.* Acadia University, Wolfville, Nova Scotia.

Stevenson, L. (1988). Some Methodological Problems Associated with Researching Women Entrepreneurs. Proceedings: Women in Management Research Symposium. Halifax, NS: Mount Saint Vincent University, 1988.

Stratigea, A. and Papadopoulou, C.-A. (2013). Foresight Analysis at the Regional Level-A Participatory Methodological Framework. *Journal of Management and Strategy*, 4(1): 802–821.

Taskforce for Women's Business Growth (2011). *Taskforce Roundtable Report: Action Strategies to Support Canadian Women-Owned Enterprises*, University of Ottawa, Telfer School of Management. Accessed at http://sites.telfer.uottawa.ca/womensenterprise.

Thompson, J., Scott, J., and Downing, R. (2012). Enterprise Policy, Delivery, Practice and Research: Largely Rhetoric or Under-Valued Achievement? *International Journal of Public Sector Management*, 10/2012; 25(5): 332–345. DOI: 10.1108/09513551211252369.

Thompson Lightstone & Company Ltd. (1997, 1998). *Small and Medium-Sized Businesses in Canada: Their Perspective of Financial Institutions and Access to Financing.* Toronto: Prepared for the Canadian Bankers Association.

Treurnicht, I., (2012). We Must Draw More Women into Ambitious Entrepreneurship, MaRS, March 8, 2012. For a list of female-owned firms supported by MaRS, see http://www.marsdd.com/2012/03/08/draw-women-ambitious-entrepreneurship.

UNIFEM (2006). OECD Gender Equality, accessed at http://www.oecd.org/gender; The World Bank & The International Bank for Reconstruction and Development, Women, Business and the Law: Removing Barriers to Economic Inclusion. Washington, DC: The International Bank for Reconstruction and Development/The World Bank, 2012, accessed at http://wbl.worldbank.org/~/media/FPDKM/WBL/Documents/Reports/2012/Women-Business-and-the-Law-2012.pdf.

United Kingdom (2003). *A Strategic Framework for Women's Enterprise.* Sharing a Vision: A Collaborative Approach to Increasing Female Entrepreneurship. London: Department of Trade and Industry.

United Kingdom (2009). *Women's Enterprise Task Force. Greater Return on Women's Enterprise.* Also see United Kingdom (2009). *Women's Enterprise Task Force's Final Report and Recommendations.*

Van De Ven, A.H. and Johnson, P. (2006). Knowledge for Theory and Practice. *Academy of Management Review*, 31(4): 802–821.

Walker, D. and Joyner, B. (1999). Female Entrepreneurship and the Market Process: Gender-Based Public Policy Considerations. *Journal of Developmental Entrepreneurship*, 2(4): 21–31.

Women's Economic Opportunity Index (2012). *The Economist.* Accessed January 7, 2017 at https://www.eiu.com/public/topical_report.aspx?campaignid=weoindex2012.

Women's Enterprise Centre of Manitoba (2010). Archived documents submitted to the Canadian Taskforce for Women's Enterprise Growth, 2010.

World Bank Group (2014). *Technology, Innovation and Entrepreneurship Policy Note. Supporting Growth-Oriented Women Entrepreneurs: A Review of the Evidence and Key Challenges.* Accessed at: http://wlsme.org/sites/default/files/resource/files/Supporting%20Growth-Oriented%20Women%20Entrepreneurs%2010-2-14web%20(2).pd.

World Bank Group (2015). *Doing Business.* Accessed at: http://www.doingbusiness.org/reports.

World Economic Forum's Global Competitiveness Report (2014). Accessed at: http://www.weforum.org/reports/global-competitiveness-report-2014-2015.

7

U.S. WOMEN ENTREPRENEURS AND THEIR ACCESS TO EARLY-STAGE FINANCING

Linda F. Edelman, Tatiana S. Manolova and Candida G. Brush

Introduction

Angel financing is defined as "[i]nformal venture capital-equity investments and non-collateral forms of lending made by private individuals ... using their own money, directly in unquoted [private] companies in which they have no family connection" (Harrison & Mason, 1999). It plays a crucial role in financing growth-oriented ventures by filling the gap between informal family and friends and more formal institutional (venture capital) investment (Harrison & Mason, 1999; Van Osnabrugge & Robinson, 2000). However, comparatively little is known about the angel market, due in large part to its private nature (Mason & Harrison, 2008).

Given the private nature of angel investment data, getting exact investment numbers is difficult. Recent research in the U.S. estimates the amount of capital provided by angels is nearly equal to the money provided by venture capital firms (Sohl, 2005). Worldwide, researchers estimate that angel investors provide up to 11 times the amount of funding provided by venture capitalists (Reynolds, Bygrave, & Autio, 2003). Specifically, the Center for Venture Research estimates that U.S. angels invested $22.9 billion in 67,030 companies in 2012 (http://wsbe.unh.edu/cvr), while the National Venture Capital Association (NVCA) reports that in 2012, venture capitalists invested $27.4 billion in 3,877 companies (http://www.nvca.org). Further, the NVCA suggests that the impact of angel financing from groups and individuals overall is approximately $100 billion in the United States.

In this study, we are interested in women's ability to obtain critical early-stage, angel funding. Statistics indicate that women receive a small proportion of the total angel capital awarded (Center for Venture Research, 2005). However, women also participate in the angel investment market at much lower rates than men do. When women do apply for funding, the yield rate, which is the ratio of the number of deals funded to the number of proposals submitted, for men- and women-led ventures is about the same (13.33% for women as compared to 14.79% for men) (Becker-Blease & Sohl, 2006).

Despite recent successes, only 4.2 percent of all revenues in the U.S. economy are generated by women-owned businesses, and only 3% of all women-owned firms have revenues of $1 million or more compared with 6% of men-owned firms (CWBR, 2009). Women typically start their firms with fewer resources and have slower and less reliable delivery of orders from suppliers (Weiler & Bernasek, 2001) and more restricted access to business clients (Bates, 2002). Women also have fewer financial resources, in that they receive less debt financing (Coleman, 2000) and fewer women-led businesses receive equity funding (Brush, Carter, Gatewood, Greene, & Hart, 2004; CWBR, 2009).

In this paper we use the concept of "readiness for funding" to explore the level of readiness of women entrepreneurs to obtain early-stage investments. Readiness is defined as "the venture's state of willingness or preparedness to take a new investor" (Mason & Harrison, 2003), coupled with the investor's perception of management skills, business model, market, and growth perspectives (Mason & Harrison, 2004; Douglas & Shepherd, 2002). Previous research has examined three aspects of readiness (Brush, Edelman, & Manolova, 2013): organizational readiness—the capability and experience of the management team (Van Osnabrugge & Robinson, 2000); strategic readiness—the extent to which the organization's structure and systems are ready for strategic change, growth, or movement into new product/market arenas (Wong, 2002; Freear et al., 2002); and technological readiness—the proof of concept and acceptance of an innovation by a particular group. In the angel-investing context, the perceptions of readiness for funding could be influenced by gender stereotypes held by investors and the entrepreneurs themselves.

We use a mixed-methods approach to explore women's readiness for angel funding. First, drawing on data from 680 entrepreneurial ventures applying for angel financing over a four-year period, we looked at firms led by women, which comprised 12.96% of the sample, to determine which aspects of readiness were most likely to influence women moving through the angel investment decision-making process. To further investigate the concept of readiness for funding, we then interviewed the founders of five New England-based, entrepreneurial ventures (both men led and women led), each at a different stage of the start-up process. Our objective was to learn more about their attitudes towards obtaining early-stage financing.

Our paper proceeds as follows: After a review of the theoretical perspectives that guide our study, we formulate and test two hypotheses on the readiness for funding of women-led new ventures. We report the results from the statistical analysis and augment our discussion with findings from our qualitative data to present a more complete picture of readiness. We conclude by presenting future research suggestions and theoretical and practitioner implications.

Theory and hypotheses

Readiness

Readiness is "the state of being fully prepared for something" (Dictionary.com, 2011). It is a concept that has been explored in several different literatures, including organizational behavior, strategic management, and management of technology. In organizational behavior, readiness is typically about change. Readiness for change generally begins with an organization member's perception of the benefits of change, perception of the risks of failing to change and perceived external demands of the change (Armenakis et al., 1993; Prochaska et al., 1994). Self-efficacy and confidence in coping with change as well as job characteristics also influence an individual organization member's perceived readiness (Prochaska et al., 1997; Armenakis et al., 1993). In all, organizational readiness for change has to do with the extent to which organization members have the attitudes, experience, perceptions, and confidence to move forward with a change.

Strategic readiness assesses how well prepared a company's people, systems, and organizational culture are to carry out its strategy. It is defined as the human, information, and organizational capital of the firm, or the intangible assets that are the foundation for strategic change (Kaplan & Norton, 2004). These assets typically involve new markets, products, or corporate transformation. In sum, strategic readiness considers the extent to which the organization's structure and systems are ready for strategic change, growth, or movement into new product/market arenas.

Technology readiness is different from organizational and strategic readiness. It is a measurement system that allows for comparison of maturity among different types of technologies (Mankins, 1995), the readiness of a technology for commercialization (Heslop et al., 2001), or an individual's readiness to use new technology in general (Parasuraman, 2000). In sum, technology readiness has to do with the proof of concept and acceptance of the innovation by a particular group.

We believe that an investigation of the concept of readiness from the perspective of the female entrepreneur can enhance our understanding of the process of obtaining angel financing. When an entrepreneur submits a proposal to an angel investment group, s/he has made a determination that the venture is fully prepared, or ready to grow. In terms of organizational readiness, this would mean that the new venture is ready for change; in that it has a capable team with previous experience and that the key management roles are filled (Van Osnabrugge & Robinson, 2000; Wong, 2002). Woman's new businesses showing strategic readiness would already have an investment in the business and hence a stronger resource base (Freear et al., 2002). Technology readiness is characterized by those businesses that have intellectual property (IP) that is protectable in some way (Harrison & Mason, 1999).

Research about angel investor decision-making suggests that all three aspects of readiness are important to pass the screening stage (Sudek, 2006). Hall and Hofer (1993) showed that venture capitalists (VCs) put more weight on aspects of the opportunity during the screening stage, while Haar et al. (1988) found that angels were interested in management's ability and market potential. Mason and Harrison (1999) found that the most common reasons for deal rejection were the state of the entrepreneurial team, marketing, and finance, resulting in the new ventures' not being "investment ready" (2003). Having a management team or a revenue stream is an indication to potential investors that the new venture has completed the initial research and development phases (Wong, 2002).

Readiness and gender stereotypes

Drawing from role congruity and gender stereotype schema theory, we argue that impressions of readiness may be influenced by the widely shared beliefs about characteristics attributed to men and women and the appropriateness of their behavior in the investment setting (Fiske, 2000; Heilman, 2001). Stereotyped characteristics influence classification of different occupations and jobs as masculine or feminine (Cejka & Eagly, 1999). Role Congruity theory suggests that in non-traditional situations, women may be perceived in a less positive manner than men (Eagly & Karau, 2002) and that this perception is even more pronounced in situations where there is a large disparity between the activity in which the women are engaged and traditional female gender roles. Entrepreneurship is traditionally seen as a male preserve; the image of the entrepreneur is more often male, and men tend to own investor-preferred businesses that are larger, more profitable, and faster growing (Brush et al., 2006; Ahl, 2006; Bruni et al., 2004; Bird & Brush, 2002). Similarly, women's managerial qualities and skills are perceived as inferior to men's (Greene et al., 2001; Marlow, 2002). The bias may be derived from deep-seated beliefs that ascribe entrepreneurial leadership characteristics such as dominance, forcefulness, self-confidence, and ambition more strongly to men and less so to women. Recent research on gender effects in private equity financing has documented that investors overwhelmingly prefer pitches presented by male entrepreneurs, even when the content of the pitch is the same (Brooks, Huang, Kearney, & Murray, 2014; Balachandra, Briggs, Eddleston, & Brush, 2013; Eddleston, Ladge, Mitteness, & Balachandra, 2016).

In addition, gender stereotype schema theory (Bem, 1981) argues that there are gender-based networks of information that allow for some types of information to be more easily integrated than others and that these strong sex-based networks make it easier to absorb information that is stereotype congruent, which further solidifies gender stereotypes. This suggests that women-owned businesses would be less likely to be perceived as "ready for investment" because of conflict with the male stereotype, whereas men-owned businesses would be more likely to be perceived as "ready for investment" because of their fit to the male stereotype. However, in this paper we argue that women are aware of this perception, and as our interview data suggest, over prepare in order to countervail the gender stereotype and demonstrate readiness for angel investment. In essence, we suggest that a self-selection mechanism may be in place through which women abstain from applying for growth financing until such time as they feel they are more than ready for investment. Hence, we suggest:

H1: Compared to men-led new ventures applying for angel financing, women-led new ventures have a higher degree of (H1a) organizational; (H1b) strategic, and (H1c) technological readiness for investment.

We further expect that this self-selection mechanism resulting in a higher degree of readiness along the three dimensions (organizational, strategic, and technological) will increase the likelihood of women-led businesses successfully passing through the administrative review stage of the angel investment process. Formally:

H2: Women-led businesses are more likely to pass the administrative review phase (stage one, desk reject) of the angel investment decision-making process.

Methods

Interview Data

This study employed a mixed-methods approach (e.g., Mingers, 2001). We chose this approach, which allows greater accuracy by collecting different types of data on the same phenomenon, as a way to provide for a more holistic and contextual portrayal of gender differences in early-stage financing. In particular, we chose to augment our larger, quantitative data collection effort with qualitative interviews. We felt that interviews were a particularly salient choice of method as interview data can uncover hidden conclusions to which other methods would be blind (Jick, 1979). Therefore, by using more than one method, we can not only examine gender differences in early-stage angel financing from multiple perspectives, but we can also develop a deeper overall understanding of the reasons men and women make different early-stage financing choices and hence are more or less "ready."

We drew our sample of firms in our qualitative study from the larger, overall sample of angel financing proposals (N = 680) reported in our quantitative study below. All of the firms in our qualitative sample were over two years old to help to ensure a sample of firms that were of the size in which angel investors would be interested in funding. In addition, to control for unwanted differences that could possibly confound our findings, each of the entrepreneurs we interviewed was in a firm that sold to consumers (Business to Consumers/ B to C) and was in some way focused on food or sustainability. Specifically, we interviewed five early-stage firms, three led by women entrepreneurs, and two led by men. We looked for firms that had different experiences with early-stage financing, so we interviewed two firms that never tried to obtain funding, two firms that tried for funding and were desk rejected and one firm that tried for funding and made it to due diligence. For each interview, at least two principal investigators were present and involved in the process, and all interviews were recorded and subsequently transcribed. The average length of the interviews was 55 minutes with the shortest interview lasting for 30 minutes and the longest interview lasting for 90 minutes. For this round of data collection, given the manageable number of transcripts, data were hand coded by one principal investigator and then the conclusions drawn from that data were discussed and then validated among the co-authors. Table 7.3 provides information about the interview process. While the names of the individual firms and corresponding entrepreneurs are confidential, Table 7.4 provides descriptive information about the firms in our sample, focusing specifically on the differences between women-led and men-led businesses.

In qualitative research, validity and generalizability are gained by insuring high credibility and transferability (Erlandson, Harris, Skipper, & Allen, 1993). To ensure credibility, the interviews were coded and categories were created by one principal investigator and then validated by another principal investigator. While the strength of qualitative research is its ability to provide fine-grained details about particular phenomena, and not to generalize across large populations of firms, we ensured data transferability to other contexts by providing detailed descriptions of each firm (see Table 7.4). In sum, our analytical process initially involved developing categories around reasons for using different types of financing (friends and family, debt and equity), issues around growing the new venture and factors that impede growth, and women's access to early-stage finance. As such, our qualitative interview data serves to inform our quantitative findings.

Statistical data

The data for the study come from a portion of the investment proposals (N = 680) submitted to a large angel financing group located in the Northeast over a four-year period (2007–2010). In this paper, we were specifically interested in the differences between women-led new ventures and those new ventures that were led by men. We defined women-led as a new venture that had a female founder or CEO. These new and small ventures applying for angel funding were on average less than five years old (mean = 4.45 years) and had fewer than 10 employees (mean = 7.09). Almost ¾ of them operated in either the technology (54.40%) or the medical sector (19.9%), and close to 60% (58.33%) came from New England. The ventures in this sample are generally representative of those funded by angel investors in that biotechnology, medical devices, and software are the most popular for angel investment (http://www.angelcapitaleducation.org).

The angel group had a four-step decision-making process. The investment proposal was reviewed by an administrative committee that made a decision to "desk reject" the proposal or to move it on to a screening committee presentation. Ventures successful in passing the screening presentation were invited to present to the larger group of investors. Those successful at the large group presentation were in turn able to enter the due diligence process. The angel group provided us with the pool of investment proposals submitted over the period, the desk reject decisions, screening committee decisions, and outcome of the formal presentations. The investment proposals were between one and five pages in length and offered detailed information about the qualifications of the founding team, the nature of the business, the amount of capital sought, cash flow, and the intended use of the funds, as well as a variety of additional product, intellectual property, market, and financial projections. For this study, we chose to focus on the initial administrative review or stage-one, desk reject decisions. The administrative review or stage-one, desk reject decision is closest to the submission of the investment proposal and hence there is the least amount of intervening and uncontrollable variance between the investment proposal and the desk-reject decision.

To generate the initial dataset, two trained research assistants independently coded the investment proposals, following a specific coding scheme developed by the principal investigators, which consisted of 64 categories. We then calculated inter-rater reliability, implementing the kappa procedure in STATA, and utilized the linear weighted Cohen's Kappa statistics for the ordinal categories. The percent agreement across the coding categories ranged between 75.91% and 98.51%, well above the recommended .70 threshold (Stemler, 2004). One of the study's coauthors resolved coding inconsistencies, which occurred infrequently.

The dependent variable for this study was an ordinal variable, which captured whether the angel group decision was to "desk reject" the proposal. More specifically, if the new venture was *desk rejected*, the outcome of the angel investment process was coded as "0"; if the new venture *passed the "desk rejection" stage*, the outcome was coded as "1." *Organizational readiness* was captured by three variables: the *number of employees* of the new venture (self-reported), the *number of people on the top management team* (calculated as the tally of managers listed in the proposal), and the top management team's *industry experience* (extracted from the "Management" section of the proposal and coded as "1" if the team had industry experience and "0" otherwise). *Strategic readiness* was captured by four self-reported variables: a binary measure of whether or not the company had *current customers*, an ordinal measure of the level of *new product development* ("concept" coded as "1"; "prototype" coded as "2"; "product in development" coded as "3"; "product ready" coded as "4"; and "revenue generated from sale of product" coded as "5"), *expected revenues in third year following the proposal*, and the *new venture's pre-money valuation*. Finally, *technological readiness* was captured by a binary measure that reflected whether or not the new venture had *intellectual property* in the form of a patent or patent-pending technology, trademark, or proprietary technology. The variable was extracted from the "Competitive Advantage" section of the investment proposal.

The ultimate explanatory variable of interest to the study is whether or not the top management team of the new venture is led by a man or a woman. To this end, we coded whether the new venture had a woman founder or CEO (coded as "0") or all of these roles were held by men (coded as "1"). Seventy-eight of the new ventures in our sample (11%) were led by a woman.

In the regression specifications, we controlled for company age, industrial sector (two dummies for the technology and medical sector, respectively, estimating the effects relative to the baseline category of the consumer goods sector), the amount of financing the new venture had already secured, and the amount of financing sought.

Results

Statistical test results

To test for the effect of gender on the different dimensions of organizational, strategic, and technological readiness, we performed analysis of variance (independent samples t-tests or cross-tabulations). Results are reported in Table 7.1. There were no significant differences in any of the dimensions of readiness for investment between men-led and women-led ventures. Thus, H1a, H1b, and H1c were not supported.

To test for the effect of factors that determine the progress of the new venture in the initial stage one, desk reject stage of the angel investment decision-making process, we used the *logit* procedure in Stata. To remedy for potential over-dispersion, we log-transformed the variables "expected revenues," "pre-money valuation," "amount of capital raised," and "amount of capital sought" prior to entering them in the regression function. The regression coefficients are exponentiated and reported as odds ratios. Thus, they can be directly

Table 7.1 Analysis of variance (n=680)

	Mean (continuous variables) or Percentage (categorical variables)		
Variable	*Men-led ventures*	*Women-led ventures*	*t-test or chi-squared*
	(n=602)	*(n=78)*	
Readiness			
Organizational			
Number of employees	7.09	7.12	−0.013
Size of TMT	3.06	3.01	0.340
Industry experience (% Yes)	85.69%	79.73%	1.830
Strategic			
Current customers (% Yes)	46.06%	48.65%	0.177
Expected revenues (Year 3, $)	204,247	46,815	0.339
Premoney valuation ($)	3,874,302	5,296,120	−1.044
Stage of product development (1-5 scale)	3.59	3.58	0.103
Technological			
IP (% Yes)	44.94%	41.33%	0.350
Demographics			
Company age (years)	4.42	4.60	−0.412
Industrial sector:			
Consumer goods (% Yes)	26.29%	20.78%	1.086
Technology (% Yes)	54.24%	55.84%	0.071
Medical (% Yes)	19.47%	23.38%	0.654
Amount of capital raised ($)	1,126,363	1,067,471	0.108
Amount of capital sought ($)	1,562,757	14,075,792	−0.977

Table 7.2 Logit estimates (n=477)

Variable	Pass desk rejection	
	Odds Ratio	S.E.
Gender	0.99	0.34
Readiness		
Organizational		
Number of employees	**0.96†**	0.02
Size of TMT	1.17	0.13
Industry experience (% Yes)	1.37	0.51
Strategic		
Current customers (% Yes)	**3.05★★★**	0.77
Expected revenues (Year 3, $)	0.99	0.51
Premoney valuation (In $)	1.02	0.07
Stage of product development (1-5 scale)	1.01	0.09
Technological		
IP (% Yes)	**1.89★★**	0.45
Demographics		
Company age (years)	0.94	0.04
Industrial sector:		
Technology (% Yes)	1.56	0.46
Medical (% Yes)	**1.90†**	0.68
Amount of capital raised (In $)	**1.19★**	0.09
Amount of capital sought (In $)	**0.74★★**	0.08
Regression Function		
Log likelihood = –245.011		
Likelihood Ratio chi^2(df = 14)= 58.71★★★		

†significant at p<0.1; *significant at p<0.05; **significant at p<0.01; ***significant at p<0.001.

Table 7.3 Qualitative methodology

Firm	Person interviewed	Length of interview
Artisanal food delivery service	Founder/CEO	35 minutes (phone)
Organic garden beds	Founder/CEO	90 minutes
High-end wooden iPhone cases and ear buds	Entrepreneur brought in for her expertise in obtaining external financing	65 minutes
Organic chocolate producer and distributor	Founder/CEO	45 minutes
Compressed wood logs for home heating	Founder/CEO	40 minutes

Table 7.4 Interview firm description: women- versus men-led businesses

Investment Categories	Never tried for funding	Tried for funding and were desk rejected	Tried for funding, made it to due diligence
Women-Led Businesses			
Type of business	Artisanal food delivery service	Maintains organic garden beds for residential and commercial applications	High end wooden iPhone cases and ear buds
Location of firm	Rural	Urban	Suburban
Number of founders on founding team	Founded firm with a partner 2	Two	Two
Number of employees	Six full time, six part time	12 full and part time	At least three
Current stage of business	Growth: Experimenting with new product that would sell in grocery stores.	Trying to grow but experiencing severe cash restraints; selling receivables to make payroll. Stated growth rate is 55% per year	Unclear, they are still selling products.
How plan on financing growth?	Organically (friends and family)	Is interested in applying for external funding but currently is not ready to give up any control.	Only applies for funding when absolutely necessary, so not externally.
What influenced decision to apply/not apply for funding	Does not want to grow too fast; does not want to lose control.	Applied early on, entrepreneur stated that she was too early.	Needed the money to grow: poor timing, applied as financial markets crashed, scaled back growth expectations.
Men-Led Businesses			
Type of business	Organic chocolate producer and distributor	Compressed wood logs for home heating	No interviews in this category
Location of firm	Urban	Rural	Not Applicable
Number of founders on founding team	Three	Founded with wife: Two	Not Applicable
Number of employees	60 full and part time	Three	Not Applicable
Current stage of business	Growth (8% growth this year)	Stagnant, little growth	Not Applicable
Future growth expectations (5 years)	Expects to continue to grow, wants to keep running the business not interested in cashing out	Entrepreneur was unclear, the business is more like a hobby	Not Applicable
What influenced decision to apply/not apply for funding	Does not want to cash out, niche business and unclear that others would be interested, did not want to lose control	He thought initially that growth was possible, but product pricing issues have made growth problematic	Not Applicable

interpreted as the increase/decrease in the odds of the event's happening (in our case, passing the desk-reject stage of the angel investment process) compared either to the baseline category (in the case of binary variables) or with one unit increase in the independent variable (in the case of continuous variables). Results are presented in Table 7.2. After controlling for the degree of readiness and other industry and firm-level variables, top management team diversity had no significant marginal effect on the likelihood of the new venture to be rejected at the administrative review stage. Thus, Hypothesis 2 was not supported.

Discussion

Small gender gap in early-stage financing

Research suggests the presence of significant structural barriers for women trying to obtain equity financing. The historically male composition of the equity capital community implies the presence of network gaps that may present serious challenges for women trying to grow their ventures (Aldrich et al., 1989). For at least one of the women in our sample, all of the financing for the new venture came from friends and family.

> All of our initial funding came from, ninety percent of it came from my family … we put the money in and then we've had sort of friends and family who have put a little money in here and there.
>
> *(Artisanal food delivery service)*

Pursuing additional outside debt or equity financing for a new project that would grow the business was perceived as intimidating.

> We're at the point where we are looking for funding and I wouldn't even go for funding at this point because I've been intimidated by it. I mean [my female business partner] and I have talked about going to banks to look and right now I wouldn't dare because I'm just not…I don't feel comfortable in that world and they they you know you look at all of it and it's very intimidating.
>
> *(Artisanal food delivery service)*

However, despite the reticence to look for outside investment, the goal in this firm remained to grow the business.

> In five years we'd like to be a five to seven million dollar business. Right now we run about a million.
>
> *(Artisanal food delivery service)*

Despite the obvious lack of women decision makers in the equity capital community, neither the men nor women we interviewed in our inquiry perceived a gender gap when it came to women receiving equity financing. Instead, lack of business experience was most often cited as the reason women might be treated differently when it came to obtaining financing.

> Most of the women I interact with who have small businesses feel the same way that we don't talk the talk and we were not in finance previously or we're not bankers or money

[managers]. Certainly the way that this guy who's come on recently who works with me gets treated and the way I get treated is like night and day, but I'd be … it would be rude of me to imply it's entirely because of my gender.

(Artisanal food delivery service)

Women who did have more experience in obtaining early-stage equity financing were also skeptical of a gender gap when it came to obtaining financing. Here, the feeling was that the stronger the resume, the more likely that a woman could prove her worth in the male-dominated equity-capital world. This implies however, that women have to prove their abilities with a strong history of successes, before private equity investors are likely to take them seriously.

You've got your resume, you can prove what you've been able to do in the past and so that tends to speak volumes and that opens things up.

(High-end wooden iPhone cases and ear buds)

In sum, despite the lack of women in the private-equity world, women entrepreneurs do not perceive a gender gap when it comes to obtaining early-stage financing, and if they do think that sex is an issue in receiving funding, they are convinced that a winning record of accomplishment will overcome any lingering gender biases.

Readiness in all new ventures

When we look at our entire sample, we do find some significant "readiness" criteria. Specifically, at stage one, desk-rejection level, one of our measures of organizational readiness, number of employees, was significant as well as one of our measures of strategic readiness, current customers.

The number of employees is negatively associated with the likelihood of getting through the desk-reject stage of the angel investment process. This surprised us as we thought that a critical number of employees would suggest that the new venture is legitimate and is not merely a manifestation of the intentions of the founder and hence ready for funding. Given the negative relationship, we surmised that angel investors perceived these ventures as "too large" and hence more suitable for later-stage venture capital funding.

While number of employees was negatively associated with the likelihood of getting through the desk-reject stage of the angel investment process, it was a sense of pride for early-stage firms.

I have six full-time employees including my cousin there's six full-time and then we have about, about six part-time
Interviewer: *Six full-time and six part-time?*
Interviewee: *Yeah!*

(Artisanal food delivery service)

We did find that new ventures that had a customer were more likely to make it through the administrative review phase of the angel investment decision-making process. Having customers indicates that the new venture is no longer in the startup phase and that the new firm has the potential to grow and become sustainable (Reynolds & Miller, 1992). This is a form of legitimacy and so indicates the overall readiness of the new venture to move through the angel investment decision-making process. More specifically, new ventures with current customers had three times the odds of passing through the administrative review stage of the angel investment process compared to new ventures without customers.

> There was huge demand for the product, like they couldn't keep up with the demand, that's why they wanted an [angel] investment.
>
> *(High-end wooden iPhone cases and ear buds)*

Our measure of technological readiness, intellectual property, was also significant at the stage one, desk-rejection level. New ventures reporting some form of protectable intellectual property had almost two times the odds of passing through the administrative review stage of the angel investment process compared with new ventures without intellectual property. Having intellectual property protection suggests that the new venture has developed its technology (Haeussler, Harhoff & Müller, 2009). In addition, the independent evaluation by the patent or other IP office may lend credibility to the intellectual property (Heil & Robertson, 1991). Previous literature has discussed the importance of patents in particular for young firms attempting to gain early-stage financing (Lemley, 2000, Ueda, 2004). In the venture capital literature, researchers have found that an important selection criterion is proprietary products or products that can be otherwise protected (Hambrick & MacMillan 1985). Therefore, the existence of intellectual property protection provides early-stage angel investors with the confidence that they are investing in something that is protectable and so helps the new venture move through the angel investment decision-making process.

In addition to our readiness indicators, a number of our control variables were also significant. Specifically, amount of capital sought from the angel investors, the capital raised prior to applying for angel funding, and the industry sector were significant in initially determining whether new ventures would move through the angel investment decision-making process. The importance of prior investment in early-stage firms is well documented in the entrepreneurship literature (Shane & Cable, 2002; Wong, 2002). Even with a reputable entrepreneur, the illiquid nature of early-stage financing makes it inherently risky. Therefore, the significance of the amount of both the capital sought from the angel investors and the capital raised prior to applying for angel funding is not surprising in the angel investment decision-making process.

Our findings also indicate that industry sector, and specifically the medical sector, is significant. Research suggests that entire industries can have legitimacy and that this legitimacy is conferred upon the firms operating within them (Aldrich & Fiol, 1994; Suchman, 1995; Zucker, 1988; Zimmerman & Zeitz, 2002). New ventures can use the past actions of the industry members, in conjunction with the industry's norms and practices, to acquire legitimacy (Aldrich & Fiol, 1994; Suchman, 1995; Zucker, 1988; Zimmerman & Zeitz, 2002). The new ventures in the medical sector are known for their long product lead times, which present investors with few returns in the short run in exchange for the promise of significant payoffs later on. Firms operating in this sector are more likely to pass through the initial stage of the angel investment decision-making process.

Losing control of the business: a universal concern

One of the benefits of a mixed-methods approach is that the interview data uncover issues that are opaque in the larger data set. In the larger data set, we focused on the entrepreneur's readiness for funding, and in doing so, we made an implicit assumption that the entrepreneur wanted to receive outside investment and in exchange was willing to accept losing a certain amount of control over the venture. However, the interview data painted a different picture. Our conversations with entrepreneurs indicated that the control over the venture, and in particular the fear of losing control, was of significant concern. This concern was universal across both sexes and at all stages of new venture development.

> [We received a]major investment, it was giving up a lot of ownership pieces so I looked at it as difficult investment just because of the control piece, it certainly wasn't ideal, but given the time that it was occurring and it was an angel investment, I think it was probably one of the best things that happened.
>
> *(High-end wooden iPhone cases and ear buds)*

While expressing concerns about continuing to fund his current operation with money from the current operations augmented with debt, another entrepreneur clearly stated that equity financing, with the inevitable long-term issues around exit, was not an option for his firm, and instead he wanted to build the company for the long term.

> Interviewer: So then what about infusions of money for faster growth?
>
> We have not built this company to be a buyout target. We have not done anything that could be viewed as like a short-term value decision. You know, everything that we're doing is long-term, for the long haul.
>
> We want to build a company we can be incredibly proud of. We want to build a brand that's incredibly strong, that people have positive feelings about. And we want a great place to come to work every day. And everyone here is behind that, and working towards doing it.
>
> There's certain types of venture capital that would [invest in a food company]. They're generally more interested in exit opportunities, like selling to Kraft Foods, or something. And I don't see how selling the business would really do that [create pride] ... maybe it would create a big chunk of money, but then, you know, I would have to just do it again.
>
> *(Organic chocolate producer and distributor)*

Conclusions and future research

The objective of this paper was to examine the differences between men-led and women-led new ventures with respect to their readiness for angel investment. Drawing from literatures of organizational, strategic, and technological readiness, we studied the extent to which the readiness of the top management team changes based on the leadership of that team. We then looked at how the readiness in all the new ventures in our sample, regardless of their top management team composition, affects the new venture's ability to make it through the angel investment decision-making process.

Our findings indicate that there are no statistical differences between men-led and women-led top management teams with respect to the degree of readiness for angel investment. Our limited qualitative data anecdotally supports this finding as well. When we interviewed women business owners about their access to early-stage finance, they did not feel that their sex was a barrier to funding. We did find however that there were issues around readiness that were highlighted in the interviews and that other issues around control were present but not evident in the larger dataset.

When we looked at the entire sample, we did find that number of employees, current customers, intellectual property protection, and a number of control variables were significant predictors of all firms making it past the stage-one, desk-rejection stage. However, given the nature of our data, we only analyzed them up to the point where the new venture passed or failed the administrative review, or stage one, desk reject. While we can postulate that other, softer factors, such as persuasiveness and ability to speak, reason and answer questions in front of an audience may outweigh the measureable factors we examined when we examine later stages of the angel investment decision-making process, this line of inquiry remains an open question for future research.

Other limitations of our study include that our data are collected from one angel investment group located in the greater Boston, MA, area. While we are confident that our findings would be replicable to other groups located on the East Coast of the United States, research has indicated possible differences in investment patterns between angel groups based on their location. In addition, our data were drawn from the information provided to the angel group by the entrepreneur and are limited to only one stage in the decision-making process. Therefore, the dataset does not include information that would be uncovered in the later stages of the investment decision-making process. In addition, for our variable operationalizations, we were dependent on the information provided to the angel group by the entrepreneur.

Limitations notwithstanding, this paper offers a glimpse at the factors necessary for new ventures to move through the angel investment decision-making process. For practitioners, our results indicate that while the literature suggests that there are stereotypes against women in business, these are less important when it comes to obtaining early-stage angel funding. In terms of readiness in general, however, there are a few things that new ventures can do to enhance their readiness for funding, such as protecting their IP and getting customers. In sum, our inquiry adds to the burgeoning literature on angel investment in general and in particular to the smaller but growing literature on women's entrepreneurial finance.

References

Ahl, H. (2006). A Foucauldian framework for discourse analysis, in H. Neergard & J.P. Ulhoj (Eds), *Handbook of qualitative research methods in entrepreneurship*. Camberley: Edward Elgar.

Aldrich, H., Fiol, M. (1994). Fools rush in? The institutional context of industry creation, *The Academy of Management Review*, 19(4), 645–670.

Aldrich, H.E., Reese, P.R., & Dubini, P. (1989). Women on the verge of a breakthrough? Networking among entrepreneurs in the United States and Italy, *Entrepreneurship and Regional Development*, 1, 339–356.

Armenakis, A.A., Harris, S.G. & Mossholder, K.W. (1993). Creating readiness for organizational change, *Human Relations*, 46, 681–703.

Balachandra, L., Briggs, A.R., Eddleston, K., & Brush, C. (2013). Pitch like a man: gender stereotypes and entrepreneur pitch success, *Frontiers of Entrepreneurship Research*, 33(8), 2.

Bates, T. (2002). Restricted access to markets characterizes women-owned businesses, *Journal of Business Venturing*, 17, 313–324.

Becker-Blease, J.R., & Sohl, J. (2007). Do women-owned businesses have equal access to angel capital? *Journal of Business Venturing*, 22, 503–521.

Bem, S.L. (1981). Gender schema theory: A cognitive account of sex typing, *Psychological Review*, 88(4), 354.

Bird, B., & Brush, C. (2002). A gendered perspective on organizational creation, *Entrepreneurship Theory & Practice*, 26(3), 41–65.

Brooks, A.W., Huang, L., Kearney, S.W., & Murray, F.E. (2014). Investors prefer entrepreneurial ventures pitched by attractive men. *Proceedings of the National Academy of Sciences*, 111(12), 4427–4431.

Bruni, A., Gherardi, S., Poggio, B. (2004). Entrepreneur-mentality, gender and the study of women entrepreneurs, *Journal of Organizational Change Management*, 17(3), 256–268.

Brush, C.G., Carter, N.M., Gatewood, E.J., Greene, P.G. & Hart, M. (2004). Gatekeepers of Venture Growth: A Diana Project Report on the Role and Participation of Women in the Venture Capital Industry, *http://sites.kauffman.org/pdf/diana_2004.pdf*.

Brush, C., Carter, N.M., Gatewood, E.J., Greene, P.G. and Hart, M.M. (2006). *Growth Oriented Women Entrepreneurs and Their Businesses*, Cheltenham: Edward Elgar.

Brush, C.G., Edelman, L.F., & Manolova T.S. (2013). Ready for funding? Growth-oriented ventures and the pursuit of angel financing. *Venture Capital: An International Journal of Entrepreneurial Finance*, 14(12), 111–129.

Cejka, M. A., & Eagly, A. H. (1999). Gender-stereotypic images of occupations correspond to the sex segregation of employment. *Personality and Social Psychology Bulletin*, 25, 413–423.

Center for Venture Research (2005). *The Angel Investor Market in 2005: The Angel Market Exhibits Modest Growth*. Durham, NH: Center for Venture Research at the University of New Hampshire.

Center for Women's Business Research (CWBR) (2009). *The Economic Impact of Women-Owned Businesses in the United States*. McLean, VA: CWBR. Available at: http://www.nwbc.gov/sites/default/files/economicimpactstu.pdf (Accessed April 15, 2014).

Coleman, S. (2000). Access to capital and terms of credit: A comparison of men and women owned businesses. *Journal of Small Business Management*, 38, 37–52.

Douglas, E. & Shepherd, D. (2002). Exploring investor readiness: Assessments by entrepreneurs and investors in Australia. *Venture Capital*, 4(3), 219–236.

Eagly, A.H., & Karau, S.J. (2002). Role congruity theory of prejudice toward female leaders. *Psychological Review*, 109(3), 573.

Eddleston, K.A., Ladge, J.J., Mitteness, C., & Balachandra, L. (2016). Do you see what I see? Signaling effects of gender and firm characteristics on financing entrepreneurial ventures. *Entrepreneurship Theory and Practice*, 40(3), 489–514.

Erlandson, D.A., Harris, E.L., Skipper, B.L., & Allen, S.D. (1993). *Doing Naturalistic Inquiry: A Guide to Methods*, Newbury Park, CA: Sage Publications.

Faircloth, K. Roy, J. & Jefferies, A. (2012). The depressing gender gap at the nation's top 71 venture capital firms, *Betabeat, The Lowdown on High Tech*. May.

Fiske, S.T. (2000). Stereotyping, prejudice, and discrimination at the seam between the centuries: Evolution, culture, mind, and brain. *European Journal of Social Psychology*, 30, 299–322.

Freear, J., Sohl, J.E. & Wetzel, W. (2002). Angels on angels: Financing technology-based ventures: A historical perspective. *Venture Capital: An International Journal of Entrepreneurial Finance*, 4(2), 275–287.

Greene, P.G., Brush, C.G., Hart, M.M. and Saparito, P. (2001). Patterns of venture capital funding: Is gender a factor? *Venture Capital: An International Journal of Entrepreneurial Finance*, 3(1), 63–83.

Haar, N.E., Starr, J., & MacMillan, I.C. (1988). Informal risk capital investors: Investment patterns on the east coast of the USA. *Journal of Business Venturing*, (3), 11–29.

Haeussler, C., Harhoff, D. and Mueller, E. (2009). *To Be Financed or Not... - The Role of Patents for Venture Capital Financing. London, Centre for Economic Policy*. Available 12/31/2016 at: Research. http://www.cepr.org/active/publications/discussion_papers/dp.php?dpno=7115.

Hall J. & Hofer, C.W. (1993). Venture capitalists' decision criteria in new venture evaluation, *Journal of Business Venturing*, 8(1), 25–42.

Harrison, R.T. & Mason, C.M. (1999). Editorial: An overview of informal venture capital research, *Venture Capital: An International Journal of Entrepreneurial Finance*, 1, 1–1.

Heil, O., Robertson, T. (1991). Toward a theory of competitive market signaling: A research agenda, *Strategic Management Journal*, 12(6), 403–418.

Heilman, M.E. (2001). Description and prescription: How gender stereotypes prevent women's ascent up the organizational ladder. *Journal of Social Issues*, 57, 657–674.

Heslop, L.A. McGregor E. & Griffith, M. (2001). Development of a technology readiness assessment measure: The cloverleaf model of technology transfer, *Journal of Technology Transfer*, 26(4), 369–384.

Jick, T.D. (1979). Mixing qualitative and quantitative methods: Triangulation in action, *Administrative Science Quarterly*, 24(4), 602–611.

Kaplan R.S. & Norton, D.P. (2004). Measuring the strategic readiness of intangible assets, *Harvard Business Review*, February.

Lemley, M.A. 2000. Reconceiving patents in the age of venture capital, *Journal of Small and Emerging Business Law*, 4(1), 137–148.

Mankins, J.C. (1995). Technology Readiness Levels. White paper prepared for the Advanced Concepts office, Office of Space Access and Technology, NASA.

Marlow, S. (2002). Self-employed women: Apart of, or apart from, feminist theory? *Entrepreneurship and Innovation*, 2(2), 83–91.

Mason, C.M. & Harrison, R.T. (2003). Auditioning for money: What do technology investors look for at the initial screening stage? *Journal of Private Equity*, 6(2), 29–42.

Mason, C.M. & Harrison, R.T. (2004). Improving access to early stage venture capital in regional economies: A new approach to investment readiness, *Local Economy*, 19(2), 159–173.

Mason, C.M. & Harrison, R.T. (2008). Measuring business angel investment activity in the United Kingdom: A review of potential data sources, *Venture Capital: An International Journal of Entrepreneurial Finance*, 10(4), 309–330.

Mingers, J. (2001). Combining IS research methods: Towards a pluralist methodology, *Information Systems Research*, 12(3), 240–259.

Parasuraman, A. (2000). Technology readiness index (Tri), *Journal of Service Research*, 2(4), 307–320.

Prochaska, J.O., Velicer, W.F., Rossi, J.S., Goldstein, M.G., Marcus, B.H., Rakowski, W., Fiore, C., Harlow, L.L., Redding, C.A., Rosenbloom, D., & Rossi, S.R. (1994). Stages of change and decisional balance for 12 problem behaviors, *Health Psychology*, 13(1), 39–46.

Reynolds, P., Bygrave, W. & Autio, E. (2003). Global Entrepreneurship Monitor, Executive Report, from http://www.gemconsortium.org/download/1311280723111/ReplacementFINAL ExecutiveReport.pdf.

Reynolds, P. & Miller, B. (1992). New firm gestation: Conception, birth, and implications for research, *Journal of Business Venturing*, 7(5), 405–417.

Shane, S., & Cable, D. (2002). Network ties, reputation, and financing of new ventures, *Management Science*, 48(3), 364–381.

Sohl, J. (2005). *The Angel Investor Market in 2004*. University of New Hampshire: *Centre for Venture Research*. http://www.unh.edu/news/docs/cvr2004.pdf.

Stemler, S.E. (2004). A comparison of consensus, consistency, and measurement approaches to estimating interrater reliability. *Practical Assessment, Research and Evaluation*, 9, 66–78.

Suchman, M. (1995). Managing legitimacy: Strategic and institutional approaches, *The Academy of Management Review*, 20(3), 571–610.

Sudek, R. (2006). Angel investment criteria. *Journal of Small Business Strategy*, 17(2), 89–103.

Ueda, M. (2004). Banks versus venture capital: Project evaluation, screening, and expropriation. *Journal of Finance*, 59(2), 601–621.

Van Osnabrugge, M. & Robinson, R.J. (2000). *Angel Investing*. San Francisco: Jossey Bass.

Weiler, S. & Bernasek, A. (2001). Dodging the glass ceiling? Networks and the new wave of women entrepreneurs, *Social Science Journal*, 38, 85–110.

Wiltbank, R. (2005). Investment practices and outcomes of informal venture investors, *Venture Capital: International Journal of Entrepreneurial Finance*, 7(4).

Wong, A. (2002). Angel Finance: The Other Venture Capital (unpublished Ph.D. dissertation, University of Chicago) (available at http://papers.ssrn.com/sol3/papers.cfm?abstract_id=941228).

Zimmerman, M. A. & Zeitz, G. J. (2002). Beyond survival: Achieving new venture growth by building legitimacy, *The Academy of Management Review*, 27(3), 414–431.

Zucker, L.G. (1988). Where do institutional patterns come from? Organizations as actors in social systems, *Institutional Patterns and Organizations: Culture and Environment*, 23–49.

8

FINANCING HIGH-GROWTH WOMEN-OWNED FIRMS IN THE UNITED STATES

Challenges, opportunities and implications for public policy

Susan Coleman and Alicia Robb

Introduction

Women-owned firms represent an important segment of the business sector. The data reveal that there were nearly 10 million women-owned firms generating $1.6 trillion in revenues in 2012 (*2012 Survey of Business Owners*). In spite of their impressive gains over the course of the last decade, however, women-owned firms continue to comprise a minority of all firms (36%). Further, they generate a relatively small percentage of total revenues (4.8%), employment (7.8%), and payroll (4.6%) (ibid).

Why do we care that so few women embark on a path of growth-oriented entrepreneurship? There are two primary reasons. The first is the potential for high-growth firms to contribute to the economic growth of a city, state, or nation (Audretsch, 2007; Tracy, 2011; Wennekers & Thurik, 1999). Second, growth-oriented firms are more likely to create a significant number of new jobs. Prior research reveals that young, growth-oriented entrepreneurial ventures are the primary source of job creation and employment growth in the United States (Haltiwanger et al., 2012; Haltiwanger, Jarmin, & Miranda, 2010). Although established and mature firms employ large numbers of individuals, they are not the predominant job creators. Women entrepreneurs are an important component within this economic development/job creation mix, because they represent an economic resource that has yet to be fully tapped. Although women represent roughly 50 percent of the population, they represent less than one-third of entrepreneurs (Minitti, 2010). The "gender gap" in high-growth entrepreneurship is even wider. A recent report from the Kauffman Foundation points out:

> With nearly half of the workforce and more than half of our college students now being women, their lag in building high-growth firms has become a major economic deficit. The nation has fewer jobs—and less strength in emerging industries—than it could if women's entrepreneurship were on a par with men's. Women capable of starting growth companies may well be our greatest under-utilized economic resource.
>
> *(Mitchell, 2011, p. 2)*

Why do so few women embark on a path of growth-oriented entrepreneurship? A variety of reasons have been put forth, including industry selection; lack of self-confidence combined with a higher degree of risk aversion; lack of access to role models, mentors, and networks; cultural and societal factors; and the challenges associated with balancing work and family. In addition to these factors, an increasing number of studies have examined access to capital as a possible impediment to the growth of women-owned firms (Brush et al., 2001; Brush et al., 2004; Coleman & Robb, 2009). This study seeks to extend this line of inquiry by using data from the Kauffman Firm Survey. To our knowledge, this is the first study to explore issues relating to access to capital with a specific focus on growth-oriented women-owned firms using a large, longitudinal data set of U.S. firms.

In exploring the theme of access to capital for growth-oriented women entrepreneurs, we will incorporate two themes that we feel provide significant value. The first of these is a discussion of the public policy implications of our research findings. Previous research reveals that women entrepreneurs, in general, raise dramatically lower amounts of capital than men. Further, women entrepreneurs confront continued challenges in raising both debt and equity. In light of that, we will discuss measures that can help close the financing gap and address some of the challenges.

Our second theme will be to explore the limitations of research based upon large data sets such as the KFS. Although the KFS provides a wealth of information on U.S. entrepreneurs and their firms, it is less effective in providing insights into more qualitative issues such as motivations, attitudes, beliefs, and the effects of cultural and societal factors. In this article, we will discuss the strengths and weaknesses of the KFS for conducting research on growth-oriented women entrepreneurs. We will also explore alternative methods for reaching out to this small but growing segment of the entrepreneurial population.

Women and growth

Prior research has fairly consistently indicated that women-owned small businesses underperform businesses owned by men in measures of size and growth. Coleman (1999) used data on U.S. firms from the 1993 National Survey of Small Business Finances to find that women-owned firms were smaller than men-owned firms, were more likely to be organized as sole proprietorships, and were more likely to be in service lines of business. Bitler et al. (2001) had similar findings using data from the 1998 Survey of Small Business Finances. Using data from the Census Bureau's Characteristics of Business Owners Survey, Fairlie and Robb (2009) found that women-owned firms were substantially smaller and less likely to hire employees than those owned by men. Coleman and Robb (2009) had similar findings using four years of data from the Kauffman Firm Survey.

Previous studies linking gender and growth support both social and liberal feminist perspectives. Social feminism contends that women and men are, in fact, different in terms of characteristics, values, and motivations due to differences in the ways in which each gender is socialized (Black, 1989; Fisher et al., 1993). Consistent with this theme, previous researchers have addressed gender differences in attitudes and motivations that may affect the entrepreneur's willingness to grow her firm. As an example, qualities typically associated with growth-oriented entrepreneurship include self-confidence and a willingness to assume risks that may accompany failure. Previous studies suggest gender differences in both of these dimensions (Kirkwood, 2009; Koellinger et al., 2008; Minniti, 2010). In terms of self-confidence, women are often seen, or even describe themselves, as less confident in their own abilities than men (Allen et al., 2008; Catalyst, 2000). Similarly, prior research has often found that women lag behind men in the area of *self-efficacy* or "the self-confidence that one has the necessary skills to succeed in creating a business" (Wilson et al. 2007, p. 388).

From the standpoint of risk aversion, a number of studies have similarly identified the fear of failure as a major impediment to the launch and growth of women-owned firms (Allen et al., 2008; Canizares & Garcia, 2010; Cliff, 1998; Sexton & Bowman-Upton, 1990; Watson & Newby, 2005). Other studies suggest that women are less motivated by economic goals such as firm size and wealth creation, preferring to focus on more personal goals such as flexibility, being my own boss, and work/life balance (Anna et al., 1999; Buttner & Moore, 1997; Coleman & Robb, 2012b; Morris et al., 2006).

In contrast to the social feminist view, liberal feminism contends that women and men are not different, but rather that women are disadvantaged relative to men by structural, social, and cultural barriers (Marlow, 2002; Marlow & Patton, 2005). Consistent with this theme, previous studies point to the lower representation of women in many of the STEM fields (science, technology, engineering, and math) that serve as a birthplace for many growth-oriented firms (*National Center for Education Statistics, Fast Facts*, 2013).[1] Prior research also notes that the vast majority of high-profile growth-oriented entrepreneurs in these fields are men (Menzies et al., 2004). Think Bill Gates, Steve Jobs, Mark Zuckerberg, Jack Ma. Conversely, less attention is devoted to industries such as health care, retail, and personal services where women are more heavily represented. Thus, women entrepreneurs have fewer role models with whom they can identify. Although there are an increasing number of growth-oriented women entrepreneurs in a broad range of industries, they have not yet gained the stature or visibility of their male counterparts (*National Business Council 2012 Annual Report*).

Previous research also highlights both structural and attitudinal factors that prevent women from gaining the type of senior management or Board experience that would equip them for growth-oriented entrepreneurship (Ding et al., 2013; Nelson & Levesque, 2007; Piacentini, 2013). Although the majority of working-age women, including those with children, are in the workforce, women have been slow to reach the upper echelons of corporations where they would gain strategic planning and senior level decision-making experience (*Women in the Labor Force*, 2013). Studies conducted by Catalyst, an organization devoted to expanding opportunities for women, found that women held only 4.2 percent of the CEO positions in Fortune 500 firms in 2013 (http://www.catalyst.org). Similarly, women held only 16.6 percent of the Board seats for these firms (*Missing Pieces*, 2013). In a study on the development of "high potentials" capable of serving on Boards for both public and private companies, the authors noted that:

> Men are more likely than women to have career experiences managing people, being responsible for profit functions, and attaining executive status in their current jobs.
>
> *(Carter et al., 2013, p. 6)*

Prior research has also revealed that women entrepreneurs are often excluded from networks that could provide access to key resources. As an example, women are less likely to have previous experience with launching an entrepreneurial firm than men (Coleman & Robb, 2016). Experience of this type develops knowledge about the entrepreneurial process and its inevitable ups and downs, but it also provides contacts with individuals and groups capable of providing financial capital. Similarly, studies have shown that angel and venture capital networks tend to be male-dominated and relatively closed, thus posing a challenge for growth-oriented women entrepreneurs who seek external financing (Brush et al., 2001; Brush et al., 2004; Harrison & Mason, 2007).

Women and financial capital

Many of the factors we have cited impinge upon women's willingness and ability to launch growth-oriented firms as well as upon their ability to secure the financing needed to do so. Previous studies consistently reveal that women start their businesses with smaller amounts of financial capital than men and are less likely to raise capital from external sources (Coleman, 2000; Coleman & Robb, 2009; Constantinidis et al., 2006; Hadary, 2010; Orser et al., 2006; Fairlie & Robb, 2009; Robb & Wolken, 2002).

As noted above, women are less likely to reach the senior ranks of corporations. Similarly, women are more likely to experience career interruptions associated with the birth and care of children (Maani & Cruickshank, 2010; OECD, 2012). Thus, women have lower levels of earnings and accumulated wealth that could be used to launch a growth-oriented venture. In the area of bank lending, research done in recent years suggests that women-owned firms are just as likely to be approved for loans as are men-owned firms (Coleman, 2002; Haynes & Haynes, 1999; Orser et al., 2006). Nevertheless, women borrow smaller amounts, and a higher percentage of women than men avoid bank debt because they assume they will be denied (Cole & Mehran, 2009; Coleman & Robb, 2009; Robb & Wolken, 2002; Treichel & Scott, 2006).

In particular, women employ a much lower percentage of external equity capital to finance their firms (Coleman & Robb, 2009; Ibid., 2012a). Some researchers attribute this discrepancy to lower levels of demand prompted by women entrepreneurs' preference for less, or at least slower, rates of growth (Cliff, 1998; Morris et al., 2006; Orser & Hogarth-Scott, 2002). Others, however, find evidence of supply problems, pointing out that networks providing access to external equity tend to be closely knit and male dominated (Brush et al., 2004; Becker-Blease & Sohl, 2007). Taken together, these results from prior research suggest that gender differences in financial strategies and structures persist, resulting in a lower predilection for growth among women entrepreneurs. Our research, as detailed in this chapter, confirms these results but adds value by identifying those financial strategies that are specific to growth-oriented women-owned firms as well as public policy recommendations designed to increase the number of growth-oriented women entrepreneurs.

Data and research methodology

The sample for this study is the pooled cross-sectional time series of more than 4,000 businesses in the Kauffman Firm Survey (KFS), a nationally representative survey of the cohort of businesses that started operations in 2004, followed over the 2004 to 2011 period. Detailed information on the sample and its construction is available at http://sites. kauffman.org/kfs/. The KFS provides us with a valuable source of information on new firms including data on owner and firm characteristics, financing sources and amounts, firm performance, and motivations. Further, the years covered by the KFS spanned the financial shocks of 2008–2010, which began in the fourth year of operations for the firms included in the survey. This allowed us to examine access to capital, financial strategies, and structures in women-owned firms in a relatively benign economy as well as in one that was much more challenging.

We first provide an overview of the firms in the KFS at the baseline year of 2004, comparing firms owned by men and women, and then examining the differences between those and just those that have high growth potential. In this analysis, high growth potential firms are those that have at least five employees by the end of the period of observation (2011). While five employees may seem relatively small, remember that out of around 25 million tax returns filed each year, only about 6 million businesses have any employees other than the owners themselves. A very small percentage of firms have more than five employees. As such, this was used to proxy for high growth potential (HGP). As a part of this exercise, we also created a subset of the largest HGP firms owned by women and by men as measured by employment in 2011, the end year of the survey. This group is called the "Top 25." See Table 8.1 for the baseline characteristics (2004) of each of these subsets of firms.

In terms of similarities, Table 8.1 reveals that both women- and men-owned HGPs and Top 25 firms are less likely to be home-based than all firms. Conversely, they are more likely to be organized as corporations versus sole proprietorships or partnerships, and they are also

Table 8.1 Baseline characteristics (2004)

Firm Characteristics	All	All		High Growth Potential		Top 25	
		Female	Male	Female	Male	Female	Male
Employment	1.74	1.13	2.06	3.76	6.28	5.29	19.96
High Tech	5.5%	2.6%	6.9%	5.1%	9.0%	4.9%	8.6%
Any Intellectual Property	19.5%	18.2%	19.9%	17.3%	27.1%	9.2%	44.5%
Product Offered	51.8%	54.8%	50.5%	37.1%	60.0%	46.6%	44.3%
Home Based	49.8%	50.9%	49.4%	32.7%	16.8%	16.0%	10.6%
Incorporated	57.8%	48.5%	62.0%	83.5%	87.1%	88.0%	97.0%
Team Ownership	30.1%	28.5%	30.8%	52.9%	57.8%	56.4%	58.5%
High Credit Score	8.5%	7.8%	8.8%	12.9%	20.1%	17.0%	7.0%
Medium Credit Score	49.0%	47.1%	50.0%	47.9%	57.0%	42.0%	76.0%
Low Credit Score	42.5%	45.2%	41.2%	39.3%	23.0%	41.0%	16.9%
Primary Owner Characteristics							
Hours Worked	42.2	40.2	43.1	42.3	56.1	39.8	48.1
Owner Age	44.9	44.8	44.9	42.7	44.1	45.7	46.3
Prev. Industry Exp.	11.7	8.9	12.9	10.4	14.5	11.9	16.8
Prev. Startup Exp.	42.7%	35.7%	45.9%	33.0%	48.2%	53.3%	63.5%
Some High School	2.0%	0.8%	2.6%	0.0%	0.5%	0.0%	0.0%
High School Grad or Less	13.6%	10.6%	15.3%	5.0%	7.6%	5.1%	0.7%
Some College	36.6%	42.7%	34.8%	30.3%	25.6%	31.8%	33.4%
College Grad	30.2%	28.1%	31.8%	45.1%	42.1%	53.8%	28.0%
Graduate Degree+	17.5%	18.1%	17.7%	19.7%	24.8%	9.3%	37.9%

Source: KFS microdata.

more likely to be founded by teams. In terms of gender differences, Table 8.1 shows that high growth potential and Top 25 men had more years of prior industry experience than their female counterparts. Similarly, a higher percentage of HGP and Top 25 men had previous startup experience. Finally, from an educational standpoint, HGP and Top 25 men were more likely to have graduate degrees than women. This gap was particularly pronounced in the case of Top 25 women versus Top 25 men (9.3% vs. 37.9%).

As a second step, we examined growth expectations versus actual growth by gender using KFS survey questions that were added in 2009 (see Table 8.2). In that year, respondents were asked how fast they expected their firms to grow over the 2008–2011 period. In 2012, the growth over that same period of time could actually be measured from the employment numbers provided for 2008 through 2011. Although we only have growth expectations for firms that survived 2008, we can still see some striking gender differences in terms of expectations of growth. While nearly one-quarter of males said they expected their firms to grow by at least 30% from 2008 to 2011, only 16% of women expected this rate of growth. Conversely, 38% of females expected to grow by less than 5% at most or even decrease for that timeframe compared to 35% of men. More than 46% of women expected their firms to grow by 5% to 29% over the period, compared with 41% of men.

When we compare actual employment growth rates over the 2008–2011 timeframe, however, we found that more than 58% of women-owned firms grew by 30% or more compared to 53% of firms owned by men. Roughly 23% of males and 22% of females experienced a decrease in employment over the 2008–2011 period, while about 24% of men and 20% of women saw an increase in employment of 30% or less. Thus, although both women and men exceeded their growth expectations, the gap between expected and actual growth was more pronounced for women.

Sources of financial capital by gender

We next examine the types of startup financial capital, both internal and external, that are employed by women-owned firms and how their amounts and sources of capital differ from those of firms owned by men. In addition, we examine how the sources of capital used by growth-oriented firms compare to those that are smaller, lifestyle businesses. For purposes of this analysis, we follow Robb and Robinson (2013) and group financial capital into six main categories: 1) Owner Equity: Equity invested by the owner(s) of the firm; 2) Insider Equity: Equity invested by spouse(s) or parent(s) of the owner(s); 3) External Equity: Equity invested by informal investors, venture capitalists, other businesses, government, or other

Table 8.2 Growth expectations and actual growth (2008–2011)

	2008–2011 growth expectations		actual growth for 2008–2011	
	Male	*Female*	*Male*	*Female*
Decrease	15.8%	13.5%	23.3%	22.4%
No change or increase of less than 5%	19.4%	24.4%	22.1%	18.5%
Increase between 5–29%	40.7%	46.2%	1.8%	0.9%
Increase by 30% or more	24.1%	16.0%	52.9%	58.2%
	100%	100%	100%	100%

Source: KFS microdata.

individuals, such as angel investors; 4) Owner Debt: Owner loans to the business, personal credit cards in the name of the owner(s) used for business financing; 5) Insider Debt: Personal credit for the business provided to the owner from family, employees, and others and business credit provided by family of the owners, employees of the businesses; 6) External Debt: Business credit cards, personal bank loans, business bank loans, business credit lines, other business loans, business loans from the government, business loans from non-bank sources, other business loans from individuals and others. Thus, Total Financial Capital is the sum of all financing from the six categories: owner debt, owner equity, insider debt, insider equity, external debt, and external equity.

As Table 8.3 reveals, women started their firms with roughly $75,000 on average, compared to nearly $135,000 for men. Women were slightly more reliant on owner equity and insider and outsider debt. Nevertheless, women-owned firms in the HGP and Top 25 category raised considerably smaller amounts of outside debt than men-owned firms did. Further, the gender gap in the amount of outside debt raised widened considerably for the Top 25 firms. This finding is consistent with earlier studies suggesting that women raise smaller amounts of financial capital and are more reluctant to apply for loans because they believe they will be denied.

Consistent with prior research, the largest gender gap occurred in the category of outside equity. Only 2 percent of the funding came from outside equity for women-owned firms, compared with 18 percent for men-owned firms. This gap was also evident in both HGP firms (6% vs. 9%) and Top 25 firms (18% and 48%). Table 8.3 shows that, on average, high growth potential firms started their businesses with approximately twice as much capital as non-growth businesses. HGPs were also more likely to rely on outsider financing, both debt and equity. Firms owned by men, growth or non-growth, used far more capital than their female-owned business counterparts. While male-owned firms used nearly twice the amount of capital used by female-owned firms in the non-growth category, they used more than twice the amount of capital that females did in the high growth potential category. In the case of Top 25 firms, men used more than six times as much financial capital as women on average in their first year of observation. This finding helps to explain our earlier results indicating that the male-owned Top 25 employer firms were much larger than the women-owned Top 25 employer firms.

Table 8.3 Start-up capital (2004)

	All	All		High growth potential		Top 25	
		Female	*Male*	*Female*	*Male*	*Female*	*Male*
Owner Equity	$33,153	$24,087	$37,087	$46,764	$79,356	$47,076	$170,472
Insider Equity	$2,106	$1,901	$2,022	$930	$4,808	$1,835	$–
Outsider Equity	$16,619	$1,450	$23,794	$8,868	$56,037	$19,664	$611,814
Owner Debt	$4,810	$3,750	$5,327	$6,152	$18,188	$7,282	$45,058
Insider Debt	$6,699	$5,994	$7,160	$12,169	$16,199	$19,130	$45,408
Outsider Debt	$51,847	$37,871	$59,010	$73,379	$144,731	$116,077	$407,121
Total Fin. Cap.	$115,233	$75,053	$134,399	$148,262	$319,320	$211,064	$1,279,873
Outside Debt Ratio	19%	18%	19%	21%	28%	23%	16%

Source: KFS microdata.

Multivariate analysis

Our descriptive results from the previous tables show that women entrepreneurs raised smaller amounts of external financial capital than men entrepreneurs did in their first year of observation. In the case of external debt, this gap occurred at the HGP level and actually widened at the Top 25 level. In the case of external equity, the gap occurred at all levels of growth and was particularly dramatic at the Top 25 level. These findings persisted in subsequent years as well, which prompted us to examine the external debt and equity experiences of our sample of startups that began operations in 2004 in a multivariate setting that would allow us to control for differences in factors that might influence those experiences. In particular, we employed a series of multivariate regressions to examine the determinants of financing patterns (outside debt ratio, outside equity) as well as credit market experiences (not applying for fear of denial, loan application outcomes) that could influence those patterns by gender. For example, the model for outside debt ratio can be expressed as a function of the following characteristics:

$$Outside\ Debt\ Ratio\ (t)_i = \alpha + \beta_1 Gender_i + \beta_2 Firm_i + \beta_3 Owner_i + CredRisk(t)_i + e_i$$

Firm is the vector of firm characteristics such as baseline employment, legal form, industry, product offering, and industry (2 digit NAICS level controls);

Owner is the vector of the entrepreneur's personal characteristics such as age, education, industry experience, startup experience, and team ownership;

Gender is a dummy variable equal to 1 if the primary owner is female; and

CreditRisk is a measure of the firm's creditworthiness, which also provides an indication of the firm's ability to raise external capital.

The dependent variables we examined include: the ratio of outside debt to total financial capital, the log of outsider equity, not applying for a loan when credit was needed due to a fear of having the loan application denied, and loan application(s) always approved. We ran the multivariate regressions pooled with a gender dummy for each of these models for the whole sample and ran the regressions separately by year over the period of observation: 2004–2011. Our results are presented in Tables 8.4 and 8.5.

External debt

Our first regression model examined the ratio of outside debt to total financial capital raised for each year (Table 8.4). Controlling for other variables, we found that the coefficient for female ownership was consistently negative in all of the years of observation and statistically significant in the early years after startup (2005, 2006, and 2007). Thus, women raised smaller amounts of external debt during the very years that one would expect their firms to start growing. In contrast, firms with high growth potential (HGP) were more likely to rely on outsider debt. The coefficient for the HGP variable was consistently positive and statistically significant in six of the eight years observed. Taken together, the results pertaining to these two variables suggest that growth-oriented firms need higher levels of external debt to grow, and women entrepreneurs were either not raising it or not getting it.

Table 8.4 also shows that owner age, the number of hours worked, good credit scores, incorporation, level of employment, and product offerings were all positively related to greater reliance on outsider debt. Conversely, industry experience, intellectual property, and being home-based were negatively related to the use of external debt. At first glance, our findings

Table 8.4 Regressions by year of outside debt ratio

	2004	2005	2006	2007	2008	2009	2010	2011
Female	-0.000426	-0.0343**	-0.0447**	-0.0459**	-0.00379	-0.0311	-0.0188	-0.0120
	(0.0131)	(0.0171)	(0.0201)	(0.0225)	(0.0223)	(0.0235)	(0.0254)	(0.0249)
Some College	-0.0167	0.00826	0.00660	0.0534*	0.0638**	0.0359	0.0151	0.0531
	(0.0184)	(0.0234)	(0.0289)	(0.0311)	(0.0315)	(0.0357)	(0.0370)	(0.0369)
Coll. Degree	-0.0365*	0.00646	-0.00239	0.0205	0.0707**	0.0246	-0.00922	0.0235
	(0.0196)	(0.0255)	(0.0304)	(0.0325)	(0.0327)	(0.0367)	(0.0385)	(0.0379)
Grad Degree	-0.0147	-0.00571	-0.0247	0.00717	-0.00610	0.0211	-0.0368	-0.00115
	(0.0221)	(0.0277)	(0.0328)	(0.0361)	(0.0361)	(0.0401)	(0.0418)	(0.0408)
Startup Exp.	-0.00324	0.00158	-0.00291	0.0243	0.00552	0.00448	0.0237	-0.0107
	(0.0117)	(0.0158)	(0.0182)	(0.0202)	(0.0208)	(0.0218)	(0.0223)	(0.0221)
Ind. Experience	-0.00147**	-0.00178**	-0.00190**	-0.00230**	0.000544	-0.00128	-0.000762	0.000246
	(0.000604)	(0.00076)	(0.00092)	(0.00100)	(0.00103)	(0.00107)	(0.00109)	(0.00112)
Owner Age	0.00831***	0.00885**	0.00977**	0.00105	-0.000122	0.0175***	0.0120*	0.0167***
	(0.00301)	(0.00434)	(0.00493)	(0.00560)	(0.00598)	(0.00575)	(0.00663)	(0.00604)
Hours Worked	0.000600**	0.00156***	0.00181***	0.00155***	0.00169***	0.00129***	0.000904*	0.00153***
	(0.000235)	(0.00033)	(0.00036)	(0.00041)	(0.00042)	(0.00044)	(0.00046)	(0.000462)
High Credit Score	0.0809***	0.0972***	0.0103	0.105***	0.121***	0.0839**	0.0672	0.0703
	(0.0242)	(0.0310)	(0.0331)	(0.0393)	(0.0413)	(0.0410)	(0.0455)	(0.0434)
Med Credit Score	0.0460***	0.0436***	0.0156	0.0248	0.00923	0.0248	0.00693	0.0370
	(0.0120)	(0.0161)	(0.0188)	(0.0210)	(0.0216)	(0.0220)	(0.0231)	(0.0230)
Incorporated	0.0340***	0.0783***	0.0671***	0.0799***	0.0782***	0.0867***	0.0781***	0.0791***
	(0.0127)	(0.0167)	(0.0195)	(0.0222)	(0.0225)	(0.0230)	(0.0244)	(0.0250)
Intel. Property	-0.0243*	-0.0205	-0.0363*	-0.0424*	-0.0168	-0.0361	0.00341	-0.0241
	(0.0136)	(0.0187)	(0.0215)	(0.0243)	(0.0252)	(0.0265)	(0.0278)	(0.0267)

Product	0.0226*	0.0218	0.0279	0.00633	−0.00134	0.0638***	−0.0298	0.0132
	(0.0128)	(0.0172)	(0.0195)	(0.0218)	(0.0227)	(0.0237)	(0.0242)	(0.0243)
Home Based	−0.0256**	0.00359	−0.0360*	−0.0195	−0.0282	−0.0280	−0.0134	0.00873
	(0.0121)	(0.0169)	(0.0194)	(0.0214)	(0.0218)	(0.0230)	(0.0238)	(0.0245)
Employment	0.00631***	0.00441**	0.00535***	0.00282	0.00324	0.00165	−0.000682	−0.000956
	(0.00137)	(0.00210)	(0.00199)	(0.00258)	(0.00220)	(0.00222)	(0.00231)	(0.00236)
Team Ownership	0.0114	0.0241	−0.00363	−0.00541	0.0196	0.0412	0.0178	−0.0224
	(0.0136)	(0.0183)	(0.0208)	(0.0237)	(0.0248)	(0.0258)	(0.0271)	(0.0263)
High Growth Pot.	0.0321	0.0778**	0.0390	0.0633*	0.0966***	0.127***	0.201***	0.207***
	(0.0235)	(0.0307)	(0.0322)	(0.0350)	(0.0368)	(0.0364)	(0.0370)	(0.0355)
Constant	−0.0613	−0.0167	0.0933	0.235*	0.218	−0.195	−0.0595	−0.255*
	(0.0715)	(0.106)	(0.121)	(0.142)	(0.147)	(0.144)	(0.165)	(0.150)
Observations	3,971	3,458	3,031	2,540	2,415	2,209	2,034	1,893
R-squared	0.067	0.076	0.066	0.070	0.086	0.092	0.086	0.109

Standard errors in parentheses.
*** p<0.01, ** p<0.05, * p<0.1.

regarding the industry experience and intellectual property may be a bit puzzling, because one would anticipate that these attributes would make the firm more attractive to lenders. It is possible, however, that industry experience and intellectual property open doors to alternative sources of financing in the form of angel and venture capital. We explore this possibility in our next regression model.

External equity

Our descriptive statistics from the earlier tables revealed that women entrepreneurs use dramatically smaller amounts of external equity to launch their firms than men. Our findings as presented in Table 8.5 confirm that women-owned firms were less likely to rely on external equity than were men-owned firms in four of the first five years of observation, even after controlling for industry, high growth potential, and a myriad of other factors. Overall, the coefficient for female ownership was negative and statistically significant in five of the eight years. Conversely, those variables that were positively associated with the use of outside equity included higher education, previous startup experience, being organized as a corporation, higher levels of employment, and team ownership. Similarly, intellectual property, which was not positively associated with the use of external debt, was positively associated with the use of external equity. This suggests that firms with intellectual property, an intangible asset, are more attractive to equity investors than they are to lenders who may focus more heavily on firms with tangible assets that can be used as collateral.

Our results as presented in Tables 8.4 and 8.5 confirm that women entrepreneurs raised smaller amounts of external debt and external equity than their male counterparts in many of the years of observation. Our analysis also identifies factors that are, in fact, associated with greater reliance on outside debt and equity. As noted in our introduction, however, the KFS is less effective when it comes to determining the impact of attitudinal factors and beliefs on women's experiences in the debt and equity markets. One way to approach this is to examine the extent to which women altered their behaviors based on their beliefs about the extent to which they would succeed or fail in raising particular types of external financial capital. Consistent with this approach, our next multivariate model examined entrepreneurs' beliefs and experiences in the credit market.

Debt and equity market experiences

In order to address some of these attitudinal factors, the KFS added questions on respondents' demand for external credit as well as their ability to secure it in 2007. This modification allowed us to use data from 2007 through 2011 to construct a series of logistic regression models using the dependent variable "did not apply for credit when needed due to fear of denial." Independent variables included those used in the previously reported multivariate models. Our findings for this added layer of analysis revealed that the women in the KFS sample were more likely to refrain from applying for loans when they needed them because they anticipated that they would be turned down. The coefficient for female ownership was positive in all five years, but the difference was statistically significant only in two of the five years (2009 and 2011).[2]

Our final set of logistic regression models for the years 2007 through 2011 used actual loan application outcomes as the dependent variable together with the independent variables used in earlier models. Results of this analysis revealed that the coefficient for female ownership was negative in four of the five years but only statistically significant in 2008.[3] This

Table 8.5 Regressions by year of log of outsider equity

	2004	2005	2006	2007	2008	2009	2010	2011
Female	-0.230***	-0.192**	-0.0798	-0.140***	-0.122**	0.0879	-0.0979*	0.00994
	(0.0817)	(0.0776)	(0.0788)	(0.0530)	(0.0502)	(0.0806)	(0.0569)	(0.0897)
Some College	0.194*	0.173**	0.171*	-0.0253	0.0898	0.0623	-0.000299	0.0768
	(0.102)	(0.0725)	(0.0972)	(0.0671)	(0.0606)	(0.0596)	(0.0690)	(0.0513)
Coll. Degree	0.0539	0.221**	0.150	0.127	0.0316	0.0892	0.0347	0.151**
	(0.115)	(0.0933)	(0.103)	(0.0785)	(0.0593)	(0.0675)	(0.0946)	(0.0765)
Grad Degree	0.280*	0.344***	0.418***	0.403***	0.231**	0.0382	0.0432	-0.0260
	(0.154)	(0.123)	(0.153)	(0.144)	(0.108)	(0.0777)	(0.122)	(0.0476)
Startup Exp.	0.125	0.112	0.0942	0.0157	0.132**	0.0956	0.116*	0.183***
	(0.0870)	(0.0783)	(0.0804)	(0.0713)	(0.0596)	(0.0745)	(0.0649)	(0.0697)
Ind. Experience	-0.00877*	0.00303	0.000715	-0.000444	-0.00118	-0.00125	-0.00555	-0.00874**
	(0.00459)	(0.00443)	(0.00438)	(0.00412)	(0.00383)	(0.00427)	(0.00345)	(0.00444)
Owner Age	0.0567***	-0.00713	-0.00393	-0.0137	0.00244	0.0171	0.00622	0.000320
	(0.0207)	(0.0253)	(0.0202)	(0.0283)	(0.0196)	(0.0180)	(0.0173)	(0.0133)
Age Squared	-0.00534**	8.30e-05	6.93e-05	0.000200	-1.86e-05	-0.000158	-1.24e-05	8.07e-05
	(0.000214)	(0.000267)	(0.000219)	(0.000322)	(0.000202)	(0.000204)	(0.000168)	(0.000156)
Hours Worked	0.00145	0.00455***	0.000410	0.00483**	-0.000994	0.00167	0.000777	0.00250
	(0.00178)	(0.00175)	(0.00174)	(0.00221)	(0.00136)	(0.00252)	(0.00135)	(0.00236)
High Credit Score	-0.00116	-0.0197	0.0606	-0.273**	-0.0363	-0.270***	-0.264**	-0.0945
	(0.184)	(0.182)	(0.181)	(0.118)	(0.143)	(0.0794)	(0.126)	(0.106)
Med Credit Score	0.00857	-0.0196	0.0284	-0.0754	-0.0210	-0.0153	-0.112	0.0259
	(0.0867)	(0.0800)	(0.0819)	(0.0687)	(0.0606)	(0.0714)	(0.0699)	(0.0684)
Incorporated	0.450***	0.200***	0.219***	0.0784	0.0419	0.0884	0.0474	0.0992
	(0.0816)	(0.0704)	(0.0802)	(0.0556)	(0.0408)	(0.0744)	(0.0669)	(0.0644)
Intel. Property	0.277**	0.411***	0.283**	0.173*	0.365***	0.184	0.123	0.00255
	(0.118)	(0.123)	(0.120)	(0.0997)	(0.123)	(0.113)	(0.133)	(0.0931)

(Continued)

	2004	2005	2006	2007	2008	2009	2010	2011
Product	0.0195	-0.0178	0.0831	0.146*	0.142*	-0.0306	-0.0195	-0.00360
	(0.0971)	(0.0858)	(0.0985)	(0.0853)	(0.0854)	(0.0723)	(0.0891)	(0.0824)
Home Based	-0.192**	-0.148*	-0.0468	0.00600	-0.0519	-0.0673	-0.173***	-0.0105
	(0.0853)	(0.0865)	(0.0784)	(0.0787)	(0.0648)	(0.103)	(0.0592)	(0.0929)
Employment	0.0610***	0.0428**	0.0293*	0.0180**	0.0271	0.0449*	0.00288	0.0120
	(0.0167)	(0.0214)	(0.0171)	(0.00917)	(0.0202)	(0.0237)	(0.00848)	(0.0109)
Team Ownership	0.226*	0.236**	0.242**	0.222**	0.162*	-0.0840	-0.0248	-0.0440
	(0.117)	(0.111)	(0.115)	(0.0960)	(0.0956)	(0.0935)	(0.0981)	(0.0916)
High Growth Pot.	0.345	-0.0635	-0.305*	-0.0478	0.0894	-0.0573	0.505**	0.193
	(0.246)	(0.225)	(0.169)	(0.153)	(0.183)	(0.182)	(0.198)	(0.150)
Constant	-1.558***	-0.358	-0.167	-0.247	-0.104	-0.550	-0.129	-0.197
	(0.486)	(0.593)	(0.469)	(0.555)	(0.447)	(0.489)	(0.417)	(0.356)
Observations	3,971	3,458	3,031	2,540	2,415	2,209	2,034	1,893
R-squared	0.074	0.059	0.039	0.055	0.056	0.051	0.053	0.037

Standard errors in parentheses.
***p<0.01, **p<0.05, *p<0.1.

finding indicates that these women were less likely to have their loans approved in only one of the years observed, after controlling for firm and owner characteristics, as well as for credit quality. These results suggest that it may be a good idea for women to reexamine their beliefs about their perceived higher likelihood of rejection of loan applications.

In terms of equity market experiences, the KFS only includes questions on applications for outside equity for the years of 2009 through 2011. During that period of time, survey respondents were asked if they refrained from applying for outside equity because they felt that they would be turned down. Roughly 4 to 5% of both women and men indicated that was the case each year. However, a relatively small percentage of women, in particular, actually applied for outside equity, so we did not feel that multivariate results would yield meaningful results.

Conclusions

Prior research suggests that access to financial capital is a key resource input for growth-oriented firms. Further, previous studies have shown that raising financial capital is more of a challenge for women entrepreneurs than for men. Our findings, using data from the Kauffman Firm Survey confirm these results, revealing large gender gaps in the amounts of financing across time (2004–2011) for all firms, high growth potential firms, and even in a subset of the Top 25 firms ranked by end of period employment. Overall, men started firms with nearly twice the capital women had. Similarly, for HGP firms, men raised twice as much capital as women. For the Top 25 firms, as measured by employment and gender, men used six times the amount of financing that women did in the first year of observation. These discrepancies, which actually widened at the higher end of the firm size spectrum, have implications for the growth trajectories of firms and appear to be one driver of the relatively smaller sizes of women-owned firms.

In terms of the mix of startup sources, women were more reliant on owner equity and insider financing than men. A very small fraction of funds came from outsider equity for firms owned by women, regardless of where they were on the size spectrum. Multivariate analysis confirmed that women used lower levels of both outside debt and outside equity in many of the years observed, even after controlling for owner education and experience, credit scores, and firm characteristics such as industry, incorporation status, and size. In terms of credit market experiences, our results suggest a greater unmet credit need among women, because women were more likely than men to refrain from applying for credit when they needed it for fear of having their loan applications denied. Our multivariate findings on actual loan approvals revealed that women were, in fact, less likely to have their loans approved in only one of the years observed. From the standpoint of growth-oriented firms, our findings show that both Top 25 and HGP women-owned firms started with much more capital than women-owned firms overall. Nevertheless, growth-oriented firms launched by women started with dramatically lower levels of financial capital than their male-owned Top 25 and HGP counterparts.

Although we want to be sure not to over-state our results, taken as a whole they would seem to support the liberal feminist perspective. Our research shows that both women and men share growth aspirations and are capable of growing their firms. Nevertheless, women raise dramatically lower amounts of financial capital and use a much smaller percentage of external equity in particular. In the case of external equity, our results do not allow us to determine whether this is by choice, implying differences in demand, or due to barriers that effectively exclude women and create a supply problem. In the case of external debt, however, we did find women were more likely to fear denial, even controlling for a variety of firm and owner characteristics. This finding provides support for the existence of attitudinal factors that disadvantage women relative to men. The following section addresses ways in which we can remove barriers, change attitudes and perceptions, and give women tools that will help level the playing field for growth-oriented entrepreneurship.

Recommendations for public policy

Our findings highlight a substantial financing gap between high growth potential firms owned by women and those owned by men. Given financial capital's key role in helping entrepreneurs grow their firms, we conclude with several recommendations that will help close the funding and size gaps for growth-oriented women entrepreneurs. Some of these measures target initiatives that can help women entrepreneurs develop their resources in the areas of human, social, and financial capital. Others are measures directed toward addressing structural and attitudinal barriers that may hamper the ability of women to grow their firms.

1   Continue to develop initiatives that increase the number of women in the STEM fields. Many of these are already underway at the K-12 and college levels, but select fields including computer science and engineering remain heavily male-dominated. As noted earlier, the STEM fields serve as a veritable "hotbed" for growth-oriented entrepreneurship, so increasing the number of women in these disciplines will simultaneously increase their opportunities.
2   Develop programs to increase women's competence and confidence in the area of finance. Currently, many girls and women continue to shy away from quantitative skills and careers because they lack confidence in their ability to succeed. Programs that target girls early can help to overcome these barriers, thereby enhancing women's financial skills and self-efficacy. Both of these qualities are essential for growth-oriented entrepreneurs who need to raise external financial capital.
3   Provide opportunities for women to learn how to launch and grow their businesses. The majority of growth-oriented entrepreneurs featured in the media are male, and it is important for women entrepreneurs to understand that these same opportunities are available to them. Programs that connect aspiring growth-oriented women entrepreneurs with those women who have successfully grown their firms can provide inspiration as well as insights into financial strategies that work.
4   Encourage and facilitate team startups. Our findings highlight the importance of team ownership in securing financial capital, particularly during the critical early years of the firm. There are an increasing number of organizations and events such as Startup Weekend Women's Edition, Startup Grind, Founder Fridays, and Co-Founder speed dating that can facilitate this goal.
5   Programs that specifically target HGP women-owned firms have also shown considerable success. Astia and Springboard Enterprises are two programs that have built successful track records in helping scale women-owned companies by providing access to equity financing, as well as business mentorship and training. The success of these programs attests to the benefits of approaches that focus on the strengths, capabilities, and opportunities of growth-oriented women entrepreneurs.
6   Increase the number of women in decision-making roles in venture capital firms. A recent study conducted by the Diana Project team revealed that only 6% of VC firms had women partners (Brush et al., 2014). This finding is significant because firms with

women partners were twice as likely to invest in companies with a woman on the management team and three times as likely to invest in companies with women CEOs.

7   Similarly, increase the number of women investors. Prior research documents the low level of representation of women as investors in angel investing and venture capital funds (Sohl, 2014; Harrison & Mason, 2007). A growing number of angel groups, such as Golden Seeds, Astia Angels, Pipeline Angels, and the Rising Tide Fund are preparing women to become investors in this space, but there is ample room for further measures to correct the gender imbalance on the funding side.

8   Promote and recognize the importance of women's entrepreneurship and the role of context in shaping women's entrepreneurial ventures. As noted above, the current stereotype of an entrepreneur is someone who is male, typically white, launching a technology-based venture. As Brush and her colleagues (Brush et al., 2009) point out, this stereotype creates an environment that is dismissive of and often hostile toward women and the types of firms they start. In light of that, a broader and more inclusive view of entrepreneurship would benefit not only women entrepreneurs but also the economy as a whole. Growth-oriented women-owned firms that have the potential to create jobs, pay taxes, develop innovative products and services, and contribute to their communities in a variety of ways emerge in many different industries. The contributions of these firms and the entrepreneurs who found them should be recognized and valued.

Opportunities for further research

As noted earlier, the Kauffman Firm Survey provides a wealth of information on over 4,000 new firms launched in the United States in 2004 and tracked over an 8-year period. The advantage of large data sets like the KFS is that they provide vast amounts of information on entrepreneurial firms. This, in turn, allows for descriptive and predictive analyses as well as comparisons between firm types on dimensions such as gender and growth orientation. A potential disadvantage of large data sets, however, lies in their relatively standardized methods for collecting data through surveys or computer-assisted telephone interviews. This type of uniformity is necessary when soliciting data from a large number of subjects, often using multiple interviewers or computer-assisted means. Uniformity in data collection also has the benefit of increasing the legitimacy of comparisons between various sub-populations within the data. In spite of these benefits, however, large data sets are less effective in providing insights into variables that may be more challenging to measure and standardize such as processes, motivations, and attitudes. This suggests the need for alternative means for data collection such as interviews, observations, case studies, focus groups, and surveys that include open-ended questions. Consistent with this theme, a recent paper authored by Swartz et al. (2014) calls for the use of multi-method and mixed-mode approaches. Thus, entrepreneur interviews could be used to supplement findings based on the Kauffman Firm Survey data (mixed method), thereby providing further insights into key issues such as attitudes toward growth, self-efficacy, and perceived barriers to securing financial capital. Swartz et al. also note that different "modes" such as telephone, email, web-based, computer-assisted, or in-person surveys and even the use of social media can yield different types of information.

Another potential shortcoming of the KFS lies in its very inclusiveness. Although the KFS firms are similar in that they are all U.S. firms launched in 2004, they are different in many regards including industry, size, and growth rates. Thus, the KFS does not focus specifically on the experience of growth-oriented entrepreneurs, and the majority of firms included in the survey are quite small, even after 8 years of operation. This highlights the importance of further research targeting the experience of high growth entrepreneurs and their firms in particular. From the standpoint of financial capital, these are the types of firms most likely to pursue external sources of capital. Further data on these types of firms could be gathered through the development of smaller but more focused groups of survey participants. Alternatively, some of the methods we noted above including personal interviews and case studies could be designed to zero in on the experience of growth-oriented women entrepreneurs in their attempts to raise external capital. As an example, within the context of the KFS, those women-owned firms that we have categorized as being in the Top 25 could be candidates for in-depth interviews on the types of questions we have raised in this chapter. These suggestions are not meant to diminish the value of the KFS, but rather to point out that we are still in the process of learning why and how women entrepreneurs grow their firms. To achieve this end, high-quality data sets like the KFS can benefit from other more qualitative approaches capable of providing new insights and directions for further study.

Notes

1　In spite of women's lower overall participation in STEM, it should be noted that women have high levels of participation at the PhD level in the biological sciences, also a birthplace for many entrepreneurial and high-growth firms (*National Center for Education Statistics, Fast Facts*, 2013).
2　Results are not shown but are available from the authors upon request.
3　Results are not shown but are available from the authors upon request.

References

Allen, I. Elaine, Amanda Elam, Nan Langowitz, and Monica Dean (2008). *Global Entrepreneurship Monitor 2007 Report on Women and Entrepreneurship*. Wellesley, MA: Babson College.

Anna, Alexandra L., Gaylen N. Chandler, Erik Jansen, and Neal P. Mero (1999). Women Business Owners in Traditional and Non-Traditional Industries. *Journal of Business Venturing* 15, 279–303.

Audretsch, David B. (2007). Entrepreneurship Capital and Economic Growth. *Oxford Review of Economic Policy* 23 (1), 63–78.

Becker-Blease, J.R. and J.E. Sohl (2007). Do Women-Owned Businesses Have Equal Access to Angel Capital? *Journal of Business Venturing* 22 (4), 503–521.

Bitler, Marianne, Alicia M. Robb and John D. Wolken (2001, April). Financial Services Used by Small Businesses: Evidence from the 1998 Survey of Small Business Finances. *Federal Reserve Bulletin*, 183–204.

Black, N. (1989). *Social Feminism*. New York: Cornell University Press.

Brush, Candida G., Anne de Bruin, and Friederike Welter (2009). A Gender-Aware Framework for Women's Entrepreneurship. *International Journal of Gender and Entrepreneurship* 1 (1), 8–24.

Brush, Candida, Nancy Carter, Elizabeth Gatewood, Patricia Greene, and Myra Hart (2001). *The Diana Project: Women Business Owners and Equity Capital: The Myths Dispelled*. Kansas City, MO: Kauffman Center for Entrepreneurial Leadership.

Ibid. (2004). *Gatekeepers of Venture Growth: A Diana Project Report on the Role and Participation of Women in the Venture Capital Industry*. Kansas City, MO: Kauffman Center for Entrepreneurial Leadership.

Brush, Candida G., Patricia G. Greene, Lakshmi Balachandra, and Amy E. Davis (2014, September). *Women Entrepreneurs 2014: Bridging the Gender Gap in Venture Capital*. Wellesley, MA: Arthur M. Blank Center for Entrepreneurship, Babson College.

Buttner, E.H. and D.P. Moore (1997). Women's Organizational Exodus to Entrepreneurship: Self-Reported Motivations and Correlates with Success. *Journal of Small Business Management* 35 (1), 34–46.

Carnizares, Sandra, Ma Sanchez, and Fernando J. Fuentes Garcia (2010). Gender Differences in Entrepreneurial Attitudes. *Equality, Diversity and Inclusion: An International Journal* 29 (8), 766–786.

Carter, Nancy M., Heather Foust-Cummings, Liz Mulligan-Ferry, and Rachel Soares (2013). *High Potentials in the Pipeline: On Their Way to the Boardroom*. Retrieved at http://www.catalyst.org on 10/31/13.

Catalyst (2000). *Women and the MBA: Gateway to Opportunity.* Center for Education of Women at the University of Michigan and University of Michigan Business School. Retrieved at: http://www. catalystwomen.org on 4/27/15.

Cliff, Jennifer E. (1998). Does One Size Fit All? Exploring the Relationship between Attitudes toward Growth, Gender, and Business Size. *Journal of Business Venturing* 13, 523–542.

Cole, Rebel A. and Hamid Mehran (2009). Gender and the Availability of Credit to Privately Held Firms: Evidence from the Surveys of Small Business Finances. Federal Reserve Bank of New York Staff Report No. 383.

Coleman, Susan (1999). Sources of Small Business Capital: A Comparison of Men- and Women-Owned Small Businesses. *Journal of Applied Management and Entrepreneurship* 4 (2), 138–151.

Ibid. (2000). Access to Capital and Terms of Credit: A Comparison of Men- and Women-Owned Businesses. *Journal of Small Business Management* 38 (3), 37–52.

Ibid. (2002). Characteristics and Borrowing Behavior of Small Women-Owned Firms. Evidence from the 1998 Survey of Small Business Finances. *Journal of Business and Entrepreneurship* 14 (2), 151–166.

Ibid. (2007). The Role of Human and Financial Capital in the Profitability and Growth of Women-Owned Small Firms. *Journal of Small Business Management* 45 (3), 303–319.

Coleman, Susan and Alicia Robb (2009). A Comparison of New Firm Financing by Gender: Evidence from the Kauffman Firm Survey. *Small Business Economics* 33, 397–411.

Ibid. (2010). Financing Strategies of New Technology-based Firms: A Comparison of Women- and Men-Owned Firms. *Journal of Technology Management and Innovation* 5 (1), 30–50.

Ibid. (2012a). Gender-based Performance Differences in the United States: Examining the Roles of Financial Capital and Motivations. In K.D. Hughes and J.E. Jenning (Eds) *Showcasing the Diversity of Women's Entrepreneurship Research.* New York: Edward Elgar, pp. 75–92.

Ibid. (2012b). *A Rising Tide: Financing Strategies for Women-Owned Firms.* Stanford, California: Stanford University Press.

Ibid (2016). *The Next Wave: Financing Women's Growth-Oriented Firms.* Stanford, California: Stanford University Press.

Constantinidis, Christina, Annie Cornet and Simona Asandei (2006). Financing of Women-Owned Ventures: The Impact of Gender and Other Owner- and Firm-Related Variables. *Venture Capital* 8 (2), 133–157.

Ding, Waverly W., Fiona Murray, and Toby E. Stuart (2013). From Bench to Board: Gender Differences in University Scientists' Participation in Corporate Scientific Advisory Boards. *Academy of Management Journal* 56 (5), 1443–1464.

Fairlie, Robert, and Alicia Robb (2009). Gender Differences in Business Performance: Evidence from the Characteristics of Business Owners Survey. *Small Business Economics* 33 (375–395).

Hadary, Sharon (2010, October). *Launching Women-Owned Businesses on to a High Growth Trajectory.* Retrieved at http://www.nwbc.gov on 8/29/13.

Haltiwanger, John, Henry Hyatt, Erika McEntarfer, and Liliana Soufa (2012). *Business Dynamics Statistics Briefing: Job Creation, Worker Churning, and Wages and Young Businesses.* Kauffman Foundation.

Haltiwanger, John, Ron Jarmin, and Javier Miranda. 2010. *Who Creates Jobs? Small vs. Large vs. Young.* NBER Working Paper No. 16300.

Harrison, Richard T. and Colin M. Mason (2007). Does Gender Matter? Women Business Angels and the Supply of Entrepreneurial Finance. *Entrepreneurship Theory and Practice* 31 (3), 445–472.

Haynes, George W. and Deborah C. Haynes (1999). The Debt Structure of Small Businesses Owned by Women in 1987 and 1993. *Journal of Small Business Management* 37 (2), 1–19.

Kirkwood, J. (2009). Is a Lack of Self-Confidence Hindering Women Entrepreneurs? *International Journal of Gender and Entrepreneurship* 1 (2), 118–133.

Koellinger, P., M. Minniti and C. Schade (2008). *Seeing the World with Different Eyes: Gender Differences in Perceptions and the Propensity to Start a Business.* Tinbergen Institute Discussion Paper, TI 2008–035/3. Available at http://www.tinbergen.nl.

Maani, Sholeh A. and Amy A. Cruickshank (2010). What Is the Effect of Housework on the Market Wage, and Can It Explain the Gender Wage Gap? *Journal of Economic Surveys* 24 (3), 402–427.

Marlow, Susan (2002). Self-Employed Women: A Part Of, or Apart From, Feminist Theory? *Entrepreneurship and Innovation* 2 (2), 83–91.

Marlow, Susan and Dean Patton (2005). All Credit to Men? Entrepreneurship, Finance, and Gender. *Entrepreneurship Theory and Practice*, 717–735.

Menzies, Teresa V., Monica Diochon, and Yvon Gasse (2004). Examining Venture-related Myths concerning Women Entrepreneurs. *Journal of Developmental Entrepreneurship* 9 (2), 89–107.

Minniti, Maria (2010). Female Entrepreneurship and Economic Activity. *European Journal of Development Research* 23 (3), 294–312.

Missing Pieces: Women and Minorities on Fortune 500 Boards (2013). Retrieved at http://www.catalyst. org on 10/31/13.

Mitchell, Lesa (2011, September). *Overcoming the Gender Gap: Women Entrepreneurs as Economic Drivers.* Kansas City, MO: Ewing Marion Kauffman Foundation. Retrieved at http://www. kauffman.org on 10/27/13.

Morris, Michael, H., Nola N. Miyasaki, Craig E. Watters, and Susan M. Coombes (2006). The Dilemma of Growth: Understanding Venture Size Choices of Women Entrepreneurs. *Journal of Small Business Management* 44 (2), 221–244.

National Center for Education Statistics Fast Facts (2012). Retrieved at http://www.nces.edu.gov on 12/4/2013.

National Women's Business Council 2012 Annual Report. Retrieved at http://www.nwbc.gov on 8/29/13.

Nelson, Teresa and Laurie L. Levesque (2007). The Status of Women in Corporate Governance in High-Growth, High-Potential Firms. *Entrepreneurship Theory and Practice*, 209–232.

OECD (2012). Closing the Gender Gap: Act Now. OECD Publishing. Retrieved at http://dx.doi. org/10.1787/9789264179370-en on 12/1/13.

Orser, Barbara and Sandra Hogarth-Scott (2002). Opting for Growth: Gender Dimensions of Choosing Enterprise Development. *Canadian Journal of Administrative Sciences* 19 (3), 284–300.

Orser, Barbara J., A.L. Riding, and K. Manley (2006, September). Women Entrepreneurs and Financial Capital. *Entrepreneurship Theory and Practice*, 643–665.

Pettersson, Katarina and Malin Lindberg (2013). Paradoxical Spaces of Feminist Resistance: Mapping the Margin to the Masculinist Innovation Discourse. *International Journal of Gender and Entrepreneurship* 5 (3), 323–341.

Piacentini, Mario (2013). Women Entrepreneurs in the OECD: Key Evidence and Policy Challenges. *OECD Social Employment and Migration Working Papers*, No. 147, OECD Publishing. Retrieved at http://dx.doi.org/10.1787/5k43bvtkmb8v-edn on 1/7/14.

Robb, Alicia and David Robinson (2014). The Capital Structure Decisions of New Firms. *Review of Financial Studies* 27 (1), 153–179.

Robb, Alicia M. and John Wolken (2002). Firm, Owner, and Financing Characteristics: Differences between Female- and Male-Owned Small Businesses. Federal Reserve Working Paper Series: 2002–18.

Robb, A., J. Ballou, T. Barton, D. DesRoches, F. Potter, E. J. Reedy, and Z. Zhao (2009). *An Overview of the Kauffman Firm Survey: Results from the 2004–2007 Data*. Kauffman Foundation.

Sexton, Donald L. and Nancy Bowman-Upton (1990). Female and Male Entrepreneurs: Psychological Characteristics and Their Role in Gender-Related Discrimination. *Journal of Business Venturing* 5 (1), 29–36.

Sohl, Jeffrey (2014). *The Angel Investor Market in 2013: A Return to Seed Investing*. University of New Hampshire: Center for Venture Research.

Swartz, Ethne, Frances Amatucci, and Susan Coleman (2014, August). Using Digital Social Networks to Explore Term Sheet Negotiation Styles of Women Entrepreneurs. Paper presented at the Annual Meeting of the Academy of Management, Philadelphia, Pennsylvania.

Tracy, Spencer L. Jr. (2011, July). *Accelerating Job Creation in America: The Promise of High-Impact Companies*. Retrieved from http://www.sba.gov/advo on 8/29/13.

Treichel, Monica Zimmerman and Jonathan A. Scott (2006). Women-Owned Businesses and Access to Bank Credit: Evidence from Three Surveys Since 1987. *Venture Capital* 8 (1), 51–67.

Watson, J. and R. Newby (2005) Biological Sex, Stereotypical Sex-roles, and SME Owner Characteristics. *International Journal of Entrepreneurial Behavior and Research* 11 (2), 129–143.

Wennekers, Sander and Roy Thurik (1999). Linking Entrepreneurship and Economic Growth. *Small Business Economics* 13, 27–55.

Wilson, Fiona, J. Kickul and D. Marlino (2007). Gender, Entrepreneurial Self-Efficacy, and Entrepreneurial Career Intentions: Implications for Entrepreneurship Education. *Entrepreneurship Theory and Practice* 31 (3), 387–406. *2012 Survey of Business Owners.* http://www.census.gov/csd/sbo.

Appendix: variable definitions

Firm characteristics

Employment—# of employees in the firm

High Tech: We use a two-part strategy to define technology-based firms. The first part identified a set of occupations that are science and engineering intensive as well as industries whose shares of employment in those occupations were three times the national average. For purposes of this research, we used this refined list of industries at the six-digit NAICS level provided by the Carnegie Mellon University Center for Economic Development (CED). Firms included in these industries are referred to as "technology employers." The second part is based on a definition that uses industry data from the NSF's Survey of Industrial Research and Development, which classifies firms as primary technology generators if they exceeded the U.S. average for both research and development expenditures per employee and for the proportion of full-time-equivalent R&D scientists and engineers in the industry workforce. These are called "technology generators." There is some overlap between firms defined as "technology employers" and those defined as "technology generators." For our purposes, technology employers and technology generators are referred to as "High Tech Firms."

Any Intellectual Property—Firm has any patents, trademarks, or copyrights
Product Offered—Firm offers a product for sale (as opposed to a service)
Home Based—Firm is operated out of owner's home
Incorporated—Firm is incorporated as a C-corp, an S-corp, or a Limited Liability Corporation (LLC)
Team Ownership—Firm owned by two or more owners
Credit Score, Dun & Bradstreet Credit Score put into high, medium, and low categories based on continuous score, with high having the lowest probability of default.

Primary Owner Characteristics: For firms with multiple owners (35 percent of the sample), the primary owner was designated by the largest equity share. In cases where two or more owners had equal shares, hours worked and a series of other variables were used to create a rank ordering of owners to define a primary owner. (For more information on this methodology, see Robb et al., 2009). Firms with a female primary owner are classified as women-owned firms.

Hours Worked—Average hours worked in a given week
Owner Age—Owner age in years
Prev. Industry Exp.—Number of years of working in the industry
Prev. Startup Exp.=1 if owner has previously started a company or multiple companies
High School Grad or Less =1 if owner's highest level of education is high school degree or less
Some College=1 if highest level of education is some college
College Grad =1 if highest level of education is a college degree
Graduate Degree+ =1 if highest level of education is a graduate degree

Financial Capital Variables: We follow Robb and Robinson (2014) to separate out the financial capital into six buckets. First, we can distinguish whether the source of capital is the owner, insiders, or outsiders. Although owners may use personal assets as collateral to obtain bank loans, we classify loans from banks as originating from outsiders—the fact that personal collateral may have secured the loan highlights the fact that the entrepreneur may be holding an equity claim in the firm. Second, for each of these sources of capital, we can further distinguish whether the capital is provided in the form of debt or equity. We use this classification scheme to provide a detailed look at the capital structure choices that nascent firms make. The 30 different sources of capital for startup businesses from the KFS are grouped into the six categories described above: owner debt, owner equity, insider debt, insider equity, outsider debt, and outside equity.

9

GENDER DIFFERENCES IN NEW VENTURE FUNDING

Supply-side discrimination or demand-side disinclination?

John Watson, Michael Stuetzer and Roxanne Zolin

Introduction

Prior research consistently reports that female-owned ventures typically have lower overall capitalization rates than male-owned ventures (Carter, Shaw, Lam and Wilson, 2007), and this applies to both external (bank) debt and the equity contributed by venture owners. However, the reasons for the observed capitalization differences between male- and female-owned ventures are not clear. Some authors have suggested that the observed capitalization differences are the result of discrimination against women by the banking sector; indeed, Fay and Williams (1993, p. 363) note that "there is a widely held view that women are subject to discrimination by financial institutions." Further, Carter, Mwaura, Ram, Trehan and Jones (2015, p. 57) suggest that being able to access external (bank) finance "has long been regarded as the major obstacle preventing women from starting and growing a successful enterprise." Should this be true, it raises major concerns for both the banking sector and governments focused on trying to stimulate their economies by promoting the establishment and growth of new female-owned ventures. However, there is another school of thought that suggests that the observed capitalization differences between male- and female-owned ventures are largely (if not entirely) driven by demand-side factors; namely, the characteristics of venture owners (for example, their risk aversion and growth aspirations) and their businesses (in particular, the industry sector in which the business operates). The purpose of the study in this chapter, therefore, is to determine whether supply-side discrimination or demand-side disinclination best explains observed capitalization differences between male- and female-owned new ventures.

To help shed further light on these two competing points of view we draw on Myers' (1984) pecking order theory (POT). According to POT, firms with information asymmetries (which is typically the case with small new ventures) should first draw on internally available funds (i.e., owner equity/retained earnings), followed by low risk (bank) debt, and finally (as a last resort) external equity (Eriksson, Katila and Niskanen, 2009). As few new ventures are able to access external equity, the focus of this study is limited to an examination of the capital provided to new male- and female-owned ventures by both their owners and the banking sector. In particular, our focus is on the proportion of funding provided to new ventures by the banking sector relative to that contributed by the owner(s); that is, the venture's debt to equity ratio (debt/equity ratio). Based on POT, we would expect the debt/equity ratio of a new venture to be relatively high in the early years and then to reduce as the business generates revenues that can be used to replace the need for bank funding. However, if female-owned ventures do indeed experience bank discrimination we would expect this discrimination to reduce over time (as the female-owned ventures establish a track record), and, as a result, the debt/equity ratios of female-owned ventures could be expected to increase sharply in the early years before reducing in later years. That is, once the optimal size of a female-owned venture has been achieved (and the same applies to male-owned ventures) the owners will use revenues generated from their ventures to repay bank debt; thereby reducing their venture's debt/equity ratio. In summary, based on POT, we propose (as explained in more detail below) that the mean debt/equity ratio for both male- and female-owned new ventures will vary systematically over time and, further, we would expect there to be predictable differences in the debt/equity ratios of male- and female-owned ventures in the presence of bank discrimination and/or other demand-side differences. In the following section of this chapter, we review the available literature on this topic in more detail to provide support for the two competing propositions we propose, and subsequently test.

Theoretical context

Asiedu, Kalonda-Kanyama, Ndikumana and Nti-Addae (2013, p. 293) note that the "existing empirical evidence specifically suggests that the lack of access to financing is one of the most important constraints to firm growth" and that the existing literature has paid little attention to the relationship between gender and access to finance. Similarly, Alsos, Isaksen and Ljunggren (2006) suggest there is limited available research concerning the funding of start-up and early-stage ventures, particularly with a gender focus. Further, Alsos et al. (2006) note that while the evidence indicates that female entrepreneurs start their ventures with less funding than male entrepreneurs, the available research fails to explain the reasons for such differences. It has been suggested that one potential reason female entrepreneurs start their ventures with less funding than male entrepreneurs could be bank discrimination. Indeed, Arenius and Autio (2006, p. 93) argue that there exists a "pervasive belief" that female business owners face more supply-side difficulties than male business owners when it comes to obtaining bank financing for their new ventures.

However, it has also been suggested that this "pervasive belief" concerning bank discrimination against females is largely based on anecdotal evidence and/or studies that have failed to adequately control for demand-side factors other than gender; namely, various owner and firm characteristics (Constantinidis, Cornet and Asandei, 2006). In support of this proposition, the findings reported by Fabowale, Orser and Riding (1995, p. 58) indicate that "after accounting for structural differences between male and female business owners, no difference remained in the rate of loan rejections; nor did any differences persist in other objective measures of terms of credit." In the following sections we explore these two competing theories (beliefs) in more detail.

Supply-side: bank discrimination

Carter et al. (2007, p. 427) argue that extant literature "provides unequivocal evidence" that female-owned new ventures are associated not only with lower overall levels of capitalization but, more importantly, with lower ratios of debt/equity financing. Further, the authors note that differences in firm characteristics explain most, but by no means all, of the variations in the capitalization profiles of male- and female-owned ventures. Carter et al. (2007, p. 427) suggest that any explanation of residual differences, "viewed in terms of supply-side discrimination or demand-side debt and risk aversion, remain controversial." More recently, research findings presented by Bellucci, Borisov and Zazzaro (2010) and Presbitero, Rabellotti and Piras (2014) support the perception that gender-based discrimination exists within the banking sector, and the findings they present are robust to the inclusion of various owner and firm characteristics. Similarly, Roper and Scott (2009) find that U.K. women are more likely than U.K. men to perceive financial barriers to new venture start-up. The authors argue that because perceived financial barriers are inextricably linked to actual start-up rates this is likely to disproportionately affect the rate of female-owned new venture start-ups. The findings of female discouragement (Kon and Storey, 2003) reported by Roper and Scott (2009) were confirmed in a subsequent U.K. study by Kwong, Jones-Evans and Thompson (2012) and in a U.S. study by Mijid (2014).

However, while "it is relatively easy, and not uncommon, to paint banks as the villains" (Freel, Carter, Tagg and Mason, 2012, p. 401), Fay and Williams (1993, p. 363) suggest that any "discriminatory behavior by loan officers may not be, and probably is not, intentional." Instead, the authors argue that it is more likely that any observed discrimination, rather than being deliberate, is unconscious and, as a consequence, is likely to be difficult to change. Further, Leitch and Hill (2006) suggest that any differences between male and female business owners in terms of access to finance could well be the result of 'business' discrimination rather than 'gender' discrimination.

It seems, therefore, that while some research suggests that, compared to their male counterparts, women entrepreneurs are (or at least they perceive they are) treated differently by bank lending officers, there appears to be limited empirical evidence of systematic gender discrimination by the banking sector (Fabowale et al., 1995). Indeed, given the recent growth in female entrepreneurship, this emerging sector constitutes an expanding and important new market for the banking sector and, therefore, it is difficult to see how it would be in the best interests of banks to deliberately exclude this growing market segment (Carter et al., 2007). Indeed, Carter et al. (2007, p. 428) suggest that a key reason for the ongoing debate concerning the presence of bank discrimination against female new venture owners is largely due to "dissatisfaction with existing explanations, coupled with the methodological difficulties facing researchers in providing clear and unequivocal evidence" to either support or refute this proposition.

As noted by Freel et al. (2012, p. 401), banks are not the providers of risk capital and, therefore, loan officers will necessarily consider "the perceived characteristics of the business (including those of the owner)" when assessing the probability of loan default. In an attempt to provide more clarity about how lending decisions are made, Blake (2006) and Fabowale et al. (1995) explain the 5 Cs of commercial lending and how this process might, unwittingly, negatively impact female loan applicants. The 5 Cs represent the key factors used by the banking sector to assess the risks involved with commercial loan applications.

The 5 Cs of commercial bank lending

The 5 Cs of commercial bank lending include: capacity, capital, collateral, character and conditions. Capacity relates to the owner's ability to meet all financial obligations as they fall due. Capital is the amount invested in a venture by the owner, also referred to as the owner's equity in the business. The more capital invested in a new venture by the owner, other things being equal, the more a bank is likely to be prepared to lend to help establish and grow the venture. Collateral relates to the assets that can be pledged as security in the event that the owner defaults on his/her loan repayments. Again, the more collateral available to support a commercial loan, the more banks are likely to be prepared to lend to a new venture owner. Character encompasses a range of factors including the track record of the business and its owners; the age of the business; and the owner's human capital (in terms of his/her prior management experience, for example). Finally, conditions "refers to the market demand for the product or service offered by the business and can be a pivotal element in the loan decision" (Blake, 2006, p. 195).

Blake (2006) argues that although the 5 Cs are gender blind they are not necessarily gender neutral. For example, given the recent rapid growth in the number of female-owned businesses, the average age of female-owned businesses is almost certainly going to be significantly less than the average age of male-owned businesses. Given that businesses are most at risk of failure in their first five years, and particularly in their first two to three years (Watson and Everett, 1993), banks are understandably reluctant to lend to this cohort, and this will, therefore, inevitably impact female-owned businesses to a greater extent than male-owned businesses in any cross-sectional study that does not control for firm age. Similarly, given that female-owned ventures tend to be over-represented in the retail and services sectors, which typically have fewer tangible assets available for collateral purposes than, for example, the manufacturing sector (where male-owned ventures are typically over-represented) female new venture owners are at greater risk (than male new venture owners) of having their commercial loan applications rejected.

Demand-side: female disinclination

Constantinidis et al. (2006, p. 133) argue that observed barriers to financing experienced by new venture owners are "mainly dependent on factors other than gender" and include various owner- and firm-related attributes (demand-side factors). Indeed, Haynes and Haynes (1999, p. 3) suggest that female owners may "simply prefer to hold less debt because they prefer less risk," a view supported by Orser, Riding and Manley (2006, p. 659) who refer to previous studies in experimental economics indicating that "women exhibit lower levels of risk tolerance than men." Similarly, Treichel and Scott (2006) find that (compared to males) females are less likely to apply for bank loans and, where they do apply for a loan, the size of their loan application will be smaller. Treichel and Scott (2006, p. 51) suggest that this finding "may be due to an omitted variable that could capture women's concerns about maintaining control over their business." Treichel and Scott (2006) note, however, that females are no more likely to have their applications denied.

Interestingly, Watson, Newby and Mahuka (2006) report that for male- and female-controlled firms less than five years old there is no significant difference in terms of either their total bank debt or leverage (the ratio of bank debt to total assets). The authors suggest that this finding indicates that any funding constraints that exist within the SME sector must apply equally to both men and women. However, for firms greater than five years old Watson et al. (2006) find that the female owners are noticeably more inclined (than the male owners) to repay their bank debt than to extend their level of borrowing. The authors suggest that while the "reasons for this contrasting behavior are not known, it might reflect attitudes to risk (leverage) and control" (p. 210).

Pecking Order Theory (POT)

Fatoki and Asah (2011) note that a firm's capital structure is represented by the mix of debt and equity that an owner uses to finance the start-up and ongoing operations of a new venture. In a study of listed and unlisted small firms, Chittenden, Hall and Hutchinson (1996) find that POT provides a good explanation for the capital structures of small unlisted firms, which, typically, rely heavily on internally generated funds. Similarly, Eriksson et al. (2009) argue that, because information asymmetries are more pronounced for small firms, Myers' (1984) pecking order framework should be more relevant to small than to large firms. In support of this proposition, Eriksson et al. (2009, p. 182) note that a "number of studies have concluded that this framework holds particularly well for SMEs." Further, because females are typically perceived as more risk averse than males and have a greater desire to maintain control over their ventures (Treichel and Scott, 2006; Watson et al., 2006; Eriksson et al., 2009), it is reasonable to expect that POT will apply more strongly to female- than to male-owned businesses (Watson, 2006).

Competing propositions

Proposition 1: banks do not actively discriminate against female new venture owners

Assuming banks do not actively discriminate against female new venture owners we would expect to find no difference in the mean debt/equity ratio of female- and male-owned new ventures at start-up. Once established, we would then expect the capital structures of new ventures to vary systematically over time in a manner consistent with POT. That is, we would expect the debt/equity ratios of new ventures to decline once the venture has reached an operating size with which the owner is comfortable. However, it is conceivable that a new venture's debt/equity ratio could rise in the early years before subsequently reducing in later years. The reasoning behind this expectation is that a bank will necessarily be cautious when lending to a new venture (based on the 5Cs). However, as the venture develops a track record the bank is likely to be more inclined to extend further financing to the venture without necessarily requiring the owner(s) to provide the same level of equity as was required for the initial loan. That is, the ratio of new debt provided by banks to new equity provided by owners is likely to be higher once the venture has established a track record and while the venture is still growing. As the growth of the new venture plateaus, we can expect (due to POT) that any subsequent funding of the venture will rely to a greater extent on internally generated funds (owners' equity) than on bank funding. This expected relationship in the debt/equity ratios of new ventures is depicted in Figure 9.1.

As depicted in Figure 9.1, we would expect (in the absence of bank discrimination) the debt/equity ratios for male- and female-owned new ventures to be similar at the outset but, over time, the debt/equity ratio for female-owned new ventures is expected to reduce more quickly than that for male-owned new ventures. We base this expectation on the evidence provided in the literature (as discussed above) indicating that women typically appear to have a greater level of risk aversion and a stronger desire to maintain control over their ventures and, therefore, we expect POT to apply more strongly to female-owned businesses.

Proposition 2: banks do actively discriminate against female new venture owners.

Assuming banks do indeed actively discriminate against female-owned new ventures we would expect (as depicted in Figure 9.2) the initial debt/equity ratio for female-owned new ventures to be significantly lower than that for male-owned new ventures. Subsequently, as they establish a track record, discrimination against female-owned ventures should diminish

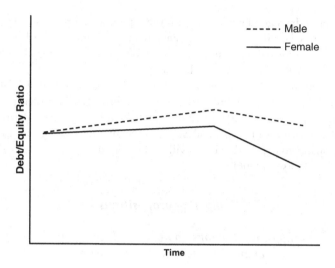

Figure 9.1 Theoretical debt/equity ratios assuming 'no' bank discrimination against female new venture owners

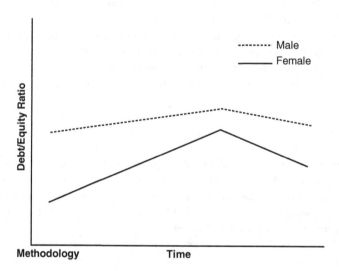

Figure 9.2 Theoretical debt/equity ratios assuming bank discrimination against female new venture owners

and, therefore, their debt/equity ratios should rise at a faster rate than that for male-owned ventures. As was the case in Figure 9.1, once the new ventures have reached their optimal size we would expect the ratio for female-owned new ventures to reduce more quickly than that for male-owned new ventures.

To test the propositions developed above, we use CAUSEE (Comprehensive Australian Study of Entrepreneurial Emergence) data collected from a representative sample of 559 respondents who owned (or partly owned) young firms (less than four years old). CAUSEE is a panel study that followed nascent and young firms over time. The firms were identified via random digit dialing phone interviews of over 30,000 Australian households. Young firms are defined as businesses that were: four years or younger at the time of the screening interview; had already experienced a 12-month period with revenues exceeding costs for at least half of the time; and were sole or co-owned. Applying this procedure, 1,058 young firms were identified with the owners of 559 firms completing the first round interview in 2007 (Wave 1). Subsequent interviews were scheduled at 12-month intervals. With respect to gender and firm ownership, we classified firms as female-owned if all the owners were female. Similarly, firms were classified as male-owned if all the owners were male. Note, therefore, that the female- and male-owned firms include both single-owner and multiple-owner firms (provided all owners are of the same gender). All firms with a mixed gender ownership structure were excluded from the analysis because this procedure allowed for a cleaner test of gender differences. This reduced the sample from 559 firms to 377 firms, of which 148 were female owned and 229 were male owned. By Wave 2 the number of responding firms had fallen to 255 (of which 106 were female owned and 150 were male owned), and by Wave 3 the number had reduced to 200 (of which 80 were female owned and 120 were male owned).

In the Wave 1 interviews, the owners were asked to indicate (approximately) how much money (financial resources of any kind) had been invested in the business up to that point in time. In the subsequent interviews (Waves 2 and 3), the owners were asked to indicate (approximately) how much additional money (financial resources of any kind) had been invested in the business over the past 12 months. In each of the three interviews the owners were also asked to estimate how much of the investment in the business had been in the form of bank loans. We assume that the difference between the total investment in the business and the amount provided by external bank loans represents the owners' equity in the new venture. It is possible, however, that family and friends (or even Angel investors) could have provided some of the funding for the new ventures, and we acknowledge this as a limitation.

Results

Table 9.1 provides the descriptive statistics for the level of debt, the owners' equity, and the debt/equity ratios for our sample of male- and female-controlled new ventures over the three waves. The results provided in Table 9.1 indicate no statistical difference in either the mean debt levels or the debt-to-equity ratios of the male- and female-owned new ventures in Wave 1; however, the male new venture owners had contributed significantly more equity. The results for Waves 2 and 3 indicate no statistical difference in terms of the subsequent equity investment by the male and female new venture owners; however, the male new venture owners raised significantly more bank financing during the 12-month period prior to the Wave 2 and Wave 3 interviews, and this resulted in the male-owned new ventures having a significantly higher debt/equity ratio than their female counterparts. Interestingly, the standard deviations in the three key measures examined (debt, equity and debt/equity) are very large, suggesting that the differences among individual businesses whose owners are of the same sex are likely to be much larger than the average difference, if any, between male- and female-owned businesses (supporting the observation by Ahl, 2006, with respect to the individual characteristics of business owners).

The results presented in Table 9.1 with respect to the debt/equity ratios for the male- and female-owned new ventures are graphically depicted in Figure 9.3 to more clearly illustrate the changes that were observed over the period of this longitudinal study. As can be seen in Figure 9.3, the debt/equity ratios for the male-owned new ventures continued to rise over the period of this study, while the debt/equity ratios for the female-owned new ventures declined steadily. This finding suggests that the male-owned new ventures might

Table 9.1 Debt, equity and debt/equity ratio

| | *Wave 1* | | *Wave 2* | | *Wave 3* | |
	Male n=90	Female n=73	Male n=141	Female n=103	Male n=113	Female n=77
Debt						
Mean	8,211	1,939	54,779	17,146 ★★★	46,988	2,533★★
Std. Dev.	31,587	11,833	262,732	120,793	204,710	12,242
Equity						
Mean	157,242	40,913 ★★★	15,809	7,343	50,132	10,174
Std. Dev.	535,457	118,438	50,137	22,371	336,983	29,475
Debt/Equity	n=75	n=52	n=79	n=61	n=56	n=38
Mean	0.21	0.14	0.37	0.10★★	0.50	0.03★
Std. Dev.	0.72	0.59	0.91	0.41	1.46	0.13

Significance: ★★★1%, ★★5%, ★10%.

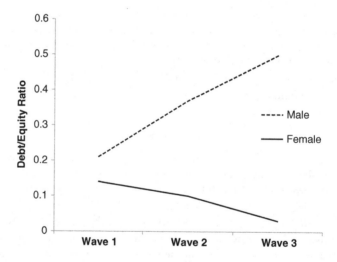

Figure 9.3 Actual debt/equity ratios

have been more debt constrained than the female-owned new ventures. It is difficult to argue that bank discrimination against the female new venture owners only commenced after their businesses had been established and initial funding had been provided to them by the banking sector. Indeed, the findings presented in Figure 9.3 (and Table 9.1) suggest that the initial limits placed on commercial loans (by the 5 Cs) are more likely to restrict the growth of male-owned new ventures than their female counterparts. This finding suggests that the lower levels of bank financing observed in female-owned businesses are more likely the result of the personal preferences of female owners (for less risk and more control) than bank discrimination.

The findings presented in Figure 9.3 (and Table 9.1) are consistent with those of Carter and Rosa (1998, p. 238) who found that men rather than women "were more likely to be refused institutional finance." Similarly, in a study of micro enterprises in Trinidad and Tobago, Storey's (2004, p. 401) findings "suggest there is discrimination against males. They are more likely than females to want loans and to apply, but are more likely to be denied."

Discussion

In summary, and consistent with the findings presented by Watson (2006), our analysis suggests that POT provides a better explanation for observed differences in the capital structures of female- and male-owned new ventures than does bank discrimination. This finding advances our understanding of the factors associated with observed differences in the capitalization rates of male- and female-owned businesses. In particular, it would appear that POT applies more strongly to female- than to male-owned ventures.

As noted by Eriksson et al. (2009, p. 179), while female-owned businesses may have lower debt levels, "researchers have failed to confirm that they are clearly discriminated against by banks." Indeed, the results from our study suggest that the lower levels of debt observed in our sample of female-owned new ventures (compared to their male counterparts) is most likely the result of individual preferences and not bank discrimination. This finding is consistent with Arenius and Autio (2006) who found that female business owners were equally as likely as their male counterparts to have used external financing, primarily in the form of bank credit. Indeed, Arenius and Autio (2006) found no evidence of gender bias (discrimination) when it came to accessing bank finance. Similarly, Bardasi, Sabarwal and Terrell (2011), in a study of three developing regions, found no evidence of gender discrimination in terms of access to formal sources of finance. The findings presented by Bardasi et al. (2011, p. 436) indicate that "(conditional on a firm's creditworthiness characteristics) banks are as likely to lend to a female-owned firm as to a male-owned firm." Similar evidence has been found in Australia by Watson (2006), Watson et al. (2006), Watson, Newby and Mahuka (2009) and van Hulten (2012); in Barbados, Jamaica and Trinidad and Tobago by Presbitero et al. (2014); in Canada by Fabowale et al. (1995), Orser et al. (2006) and Riding and Swift (1990); in Finland by Arenius and Autio (2006) and Eriksson et al. (2009); in Norway by Alsos et al. (2006); and in the U.S. by Asiedu, Freeman and Nti-Addae (2012), Coleman (2000), Haynes and Haynes (1999) and Treichel and Scott (2006).

It seems, therefore, that the prior literature suggesting female new venture owners face bank discrimination is likely to have been based on either anecdotal evidence or poorly designed studies that failed to adequately control for key differences between new venture owners (for example, their experience, risk preferences and desire to maintain control) and their ventures (for example, the age of the business, the industry involved and the collateral available). However, despite the numerous studies concluding that female business owners do not appear to be actively discriminated against by the banking sector, there appears to be some evidence that female business owners are more likely than male business owners to be discouraged from applying for commercial loans, presumably because they believe they will face discrimination (see, for example, Roper and Scott, 2009; Freel et al., 2012; Kwong et al., 2012; Mijid, 2014; Singh, 2014). Again, however, when appropriate controls are introduced into the analysis, female ownership (in whole or in part) typically "fails to distinguish discouraged firms from applicant firms" (Freel et al., 2012, p. 414) and, indeed, van Hulten (2012) concludes that gender is unrelated to the probability of an owner being discouraged from applying for a commercial loan. Similarly, Orser et al. (2006, p. 659) found "no evidence of discrimination in terms of lending or approval, either perceived or actual."

In summary, the majority of previous research (including the current study) suggests that women are neither actively discriminated against by the banking sector nor discouraged from applying for commercial loans (once they have embarked on a new venture). What is not so clear from the available evidence, however, is whether the pervasive belief (even if it is a false belief) that females are actively discriminated against by banks has resulted in a significant number of potential female business owners' being discouraged from ever launching a new venture. This is clearly an area that warrants further investigation.

Conclusions

The aim of the study presented in this chapter was to use POT to investigate two competing propositions relating to the provision of bank financing for female-owned new ventures. That is, do banks discriminate against women? Or, are women more reluctant (because of the risks involved and the potential to lose control of their ventures) to access bank financing than men? As noted by Roper and Scott (2009, p. 150) this is a complex issue, and it is difficult to "isolate and characterise any specific gender effects." Riding and Swift (1990, p. 327) suggest that while the extant literature "reveals a pervasive perception that there is discrimination by bankers against women business owners" there appears to be a serious lack of any real statistical evidence to support this widespread, but largely subjective, perception.

Indeed, Treichel and Scott (2006, p. 56) argue that much of the available evidence concerning the perceived disadvantage faced by women with respect to accessing commercial loans is contradictory. While some studies report having found evidence of bank discrimination against women, there have been a number of studies suggesting that any differences in the provision of commercial loans to female- and male-owned ventures can be explained by the characteristics of both the owner(s) and their business(es), rather than by the gender of the business owner(s). It seems that much of the conflicting evidence emanating from prior research could, potentially, be due to the samples and methodologies used.

Our results suggest that female new venture owners are not actively discriminated against by the banking sector but, rather, that female owners typically make a conscious decison to limit their use of commercial loans (particularly once their new venture is up and running) so as to minimize the risks involved and the potential to lose control. Indeed, it seems that POT applies more strongly to female- than to male-owned ventures.

However, "despite widespread empirical evidence that a relatively small proportion of small firms have their loan applications rejected" (Freel et al., 2012, p. 399), it appears that "[c]oncerns that small firms encounter credit constraints are well entrenched in the literature" (Haynes and Haynes, 1999, p. 1). Further, Haynes and Haynes (1999, p. 1) note that while research provides no evidence of comercial loan discrimination against females "advocacy groups still claim that female business owners face discrimination." To the extent that this (false) message espoused by such advocacy groups is believed by women contemplating a new venture start-up it could potentially negatively impact the rate of female-owned new venture start-ups. This should be of concern not only to the banking sector but to policy makers focused on encouraging women-owned new venture start-ups to help boost economic development.

In conclusion, we trust our findings will help to eradicate the (ill-informed) view that banks actively discriminate against women in making commercial loan decisions. It would be very unfortunate if potential female-owned new ventures were not pursued because of such an eroneous belief. Given the relatively small sample size available for this research study and the fact that it only relates to one country, it would be particularly helpful if similar studies could be undertaken in other countries. It would also be useful if future studies could try to estimate the extent to which women might have been 'discouraged' from launching a new venture because they believed they would be discriminated against by the banking sector. Further, following the lead of Kim (2006), it would also be useful if future research could examine how capitalization rates differ between new ventures with a mixed gender ownership structure and those that are solely male owned or solely female owned. Interestingly, van Hulten (2012, p. 278) finds a significant positive association between using/having an accountant and securing a bank loan. This suggests that business owners (male or female) who find applying for a commercial loan challenging should consider enlisting the services of an accountant who can act on their behalf in negotiations with the banking sector.

References

Ahl, H. (2006). Why Research on Women Entrepreneurs Needs New Directions. *Entrepreneurship: Theory & Practice*, 30(5), 595–621.

Alsos, G. A., Isaksen, E. J. & Ljunggren, E. (2006). New Venture Financing and Subsequent Business Growth in Men- and Women-Led Businesses. *Entrepreneurship Theory and Practice*, 30(5), 667–686.

Arenius, P. & Autio, E. (2006). Financing of Small Businesses: Are Mars and Venus More Alike Than Different? *Venture Capital*, 8(2), 93–107.

Asiedu, E., Freeman, J. A. & Nti-Addae, A. (2012). Access to Credit by Small Businesses: How Relevant Are Race, Ethnicity, and Gender? *American Economic Review*, 102(3), 532–537.

Asiedu, E., Kalonda-Kanyama, I., Ndikumana, L. & Nti-Addae, A. (2013). Access to Credit by Firms in Sub-Saharan Africa: How Relevant is Gender? *American Economic Review*, 103(3), 293–297.

Bardasi, E., Sabarwal, S. & Terrell, K. (2011). How Do Female Entrepreneurs Perform? Evidence from Three Developing Regions. *Small Business Economics*, 37(4), 417–441.

Bellucci, A., Borisov, A. & Zazzaro, A. (2010). Does Gender Matter in Bank–Firm Relationships? Evidence from Small Business Lending. *Journal of Banking & Finance*, 34(12), 2968–2984.

Blake, M. K. (2006). Gendered Lending: Gender, Context and the Rules of Business Lending. *Venture Capital*, 8(2), 183–201.

Carter, S., Mwaura, S., Ram, M., Trehan, K. & Jones, T. (2015). Barriers to Ethnic Minority and Women's Enterprise: Existing Evidence, Policy Tensions and Unsettled Questions. *International Small Business Journal* 33(1), 49–69.

Carter, S. & Rosa, P. (1998). The Financing of Male- and Female-Owned Businesses. *Entrepreneurship & Regional Development*, 10(3), 225–241.

Carter, S., Shaw, E., Lam, W. & Wilson, F. (2007). Gender, Entrepreneurship, and Bank Lending: The Criteria and Processes Used by Bank Loan Officers in Assessing Applications. *Entrepreneurship Theory and Practice*, 31(3), 427–444.

Chittenden, F., Hall, G. & Hutchinson, P. (1996). Small Firm Growth, Access to Capital Markets and Financial Structure: Review of Issues and an Empirical Investigation. *Small Business Economics*, 8(1), 59–67.

Coleman, S. (2000). Access to Capital and Terms of Credit: A Comparison of Men- and Women-Owned Small Businesses. *Journal of Small Business Management*, 38(3), 37–52.

Constantinidis, C., Cornet, A. & Asandei, S. (2006). Financing of Women-Owned Ventures: The Impact of Gender and Other Owner- and Firm-Related Variables. *Venture Capital*, 8(2), 133–157.

Eriksson, P., Katila, S. & Niskanen, M. (2009). Gender and Sources of Finance in Finnish SMEs: A Contextual View. *International Journal of Gender and Entrepreneurship*, 1(3), 176–191.

Fabowale, L., Orser, B. & Riding, A. (1995). Gender, Structural Factors, and Credit Terms between Canadian Small Businesses and Financial Institutions. *Entrepreneurship Theory and Practice*, 19(4), 41–65.

Fatoki, O. & Asah, F. (2011). The Impact of Firm and Entrepreneurial Characteristics on Access to Debt Finance by SMEs in King Williams' Town, South Africa. *International Journal of Business and Management*, 6(8), 170–179.

Fay, M. & Williams, L. (1993). Gender Bias and the Availability of Business Loans. *Journal of Business Venturing*, 8(4), 363–376.

Freel, M., Carter, S., Tagg, S. & Mason, C. (2012). The Latent Demand for Bank Debt: Characterizing "Discouraged Borrowers". *Small Business Economics*, 38(4), 399–418.

Haynes, G. W. & Haynes, D. C. (1999). The Debt Structure of Small Businesses Owned by Women in 1987 and 1993. *Journal of Small Business Management*, 37(2), 1–19.

Kim, G., O. (2006). Do Equally Owned Small Businesses Have Equal Access to Credit? *Small Business Economics*, 27(4–5), 369–386.

Kon, Y. & Storey, D. J. (2003). A Theory of Discouraged Borrowers. *Small Business Economics*, 21(1), 37–49.

Kwong, C., Jones-Evans, D. & Thompson, P. (2012). Differences in Perceptions of Access to Finance between Potential Male and Female Entrepreneurs: Evidence from the UK. *International Journal of Entrepreneurial Behavior & Research*, 18(1), 75–97.

Leitch, C. M. & Hill, F. M. (2006). Guest Editorial: Women and the Financing of Entrepreneurial Ventures: More Pieces for the Jigsaw. *Venture Capital*, 8(1), 1–14.

Mijid, N. (2014). Why Are Female Small Business Owners in the United States Less Likely to Apply for Bank Loans than Their Male Counterparts? *Journal of Small Business & Entrepreneurship*, 27(2), 229–249.

Myers, S. C. (1984). The Capital Structure Puzzle. *Journal of Finance*, 39(3), 575–592.

Orser, B. J., Riding, A. L. & Manley, K. (2006). Women Entrepreneurs and Financial Capital. *Entrepreneurship Theory and Practice*, 30(5), 643–665.

Presbitero, A. F., Rabellotti, R. & Piras, C. (2014). Barking up the Wrong Tree? Measuring Gender Gaps in Firm's Access to Finance. *Journal of Development Studies*, 50(10), 1430–1444.

Riding, A. & Swift, C. S. (1990). Women Business Owners and Terms of Credit: Some Empirical Findings of the Canadian Experience. *Journal of Business Venturing*, 5(5), 327–340.

Roper, S. & Scott, J. M. (2009). Perceived Financial Barriers and the Start-up Decision: An Econometric Analysis of Gender Differences Using GEM Data. *International Small Business Journal*, 27(2), 149–171.

Singh, R. (2014), *Gender Based Financing Preferences of SMEs: Discouraged Borrowers*, MSc. Degree in Management, University of Ottawa, Ottawa, Canada.

Storey, D. J. (2004). Racial and Gender Discrimination in the Micro Firms Credit Market?: Evidence from Trinidad and Tobago. *Small Business Economics*, 23(5), 401–422.

Treichel, M. & Scott, J. (2006). Women-Owned Businesses and Access to Bank Credit: Evidence from Three Surveys Since 1987. *Venture Capital: An International Journal of Entrepreneurial Finance*, 8(1), 51–67.

van Hulten, A. (2012). Women's Access to SME Finance in Australia. *International Journal of Gender and Entrepreneurship*, 4(3), 266–288.

Watson, J. (2006). External Funding and Firm Growth: Comparing Female- and Male-Controlled SMEs. *Venture Capital: An International Journal of Entrepreneurial Finance*, 8(1), 33–49.

Watson, J. & Everett, J. E. (1993). Defining Small Business Failure. *International Small Business Journal*, 11(3), 35–48.

Watson, J., Newby, R. & Mahuka, A. (2006). Comparing the Growth and External Funding of Male- and Female-Controlled SMEs in Australia, in *Growth-Oriented Women Entrepreneurs and Their Businesses: A Global Research Perspective*. Ed. Candida G. Brush, Nancy M. Carter, Elizabeth J. Gatewood, Patrica G. Greene and Myra M. Hart. Cheltenham: Edward Elgar, 205–231.

Watson, J., Newby, R. & Mahuka, A. (2009). Gender and the SME 'Finance Gap'. *International Journal of Gender and Entrepreneurship*, 1(1), 42–56.

PART III

Supporting female entrepreneurs

10

SUPPORTING AND TRAINING FEMALE NECESSITY ENTREPRENEURS

Walid A. Nakara, Nesrine Bouguerra and Alain Fayolle

Introduction

Necessity entrepreneurs are defined as individuals who see entrepreneurship as their last resort and start a business because all other work options are either non-existent or unsatisfactory (Minniti et al., 2005; Acs, 2006). Necessity entrepreneurs make up a sizeable proportion of the total entrepreneurial population, particularly in countries characterized by high entrepreneurship rates (Poschke, 2012). 'Push' factors such as long-term unemployment, redundancy or the threat of losing one's job lead to individuals' engagement in necessity entrepreneurship (Thurik et al., 2008). The opportunities they exploit are generally less profitable and their businesses are said to be less successful financially than those built by opportunity-based entrepreneurs (Amit & Mueller, 1995; Poschke, 2012). While necessity-based entrepreneurship is more dominant in less-developed and developing economies (Kelley et al., 2013), it is not just a developing-world phenomenon. Entrepreneurs in precarious, socially isolated and poverty-stricken situations also exist in developed 'rich' countries (Fayolle, 2011; Lambrecht & Beens, 2005; Levratto & Serverin, 2011). Far from constituting the successful enterprises of tomorrow, an overwhelming number of independent entrepreneurs are the 'working poor' of today (Levratto & Serverin, 2011).

Several Western economies have implemented programs to encourage small-firm formation (Evans & Leighton, 1989; Fairlie, 2005; Caliendo & Kritikos, 2010), and many assistance schemes disproportionately encourage necessity-based entrepreneurship (Fayolle, 2010; Block & Wagner, 2010). A large proportion of the socially marginalized individuals choose self-employment as an alternative route to economic and societal integration. Indeed, society's marginalized and disadvantaged groups are more likely to be engaged in necessity entrepreneurship and are also more likely to be women (Allen et al., 2006, 2007; Reynolds et al., 2004; Bosma et al., 2009; Pines et al., 2010). Today we are bombarded with media images of 'male entrepreneurs' as 'dynamic wolfish charmers, supernatural gurus, successful skyrockets or community saviors and corrupters' (Nicholson & Anderson, 2005). In the picture of the struggling rich world, the female entrepreneur is rarely rendered visible. A more complete account of the inclusion—or lack of inclusion—of disadvantaged groups in the entrepreneurship domain is needed (Chell, 2007). Many necessity-based entrepreneurs simply do not have the necessary resources (human, financial, physical, psychological, social or relational) to 'make it' as entrepreneurs (Lambrecht & Beens, 2005; Fayolle, 2011). Gathering more information about necessity entrepreneurs helps provide a more complete perspective on entrepreneurship. It also informs policy design, since many policies and support measures promoting entrepreneurship are taken up not just by 'opportunity entrepreneurs', but also, and maybe even more so, by 'necessity entrepreneurs' (Poschke, 2012).

In this chapter, we respond to the broad research question of how to provide support and training to the female necessity entrepreneur. Gender streamed training and assistance programs remain under-researched, and little is known about the design, delivery and outcome of such programs (Byrne & Fayolle, 2010). We begin by defining the necessity entrepreneur and demonstrating the gendered nature of this phenomenon. We then outline an exploratory study we undertook, which collected the narratives of 15 female necessity entrepreneurs and 10 business-support consultants. Based on these narratives, we recommend the need for training programs tailored to their needs.

Theoretical grounding

Necessity entrepreneurship and the necessity entrepreneur

Since 2001, the Global Entrepreneurship Monitor (GEM) annually assesses the entrepreneurial activity, aspirations and attitudes of individuals across a wide range of countries. GEM differentiates between two types of entrepreneurs: necessity based and opportunity based. The difference depends on the motivation of the entrepreneur to start his or her venture (Block & Sandner, 2009). Necessity entrepreneurship is about having to become an entrepreneur because you have no other choice, while opportunity entrepreneurship is an active choice to start a business based on the perception that an unexploited (or underexploited) opportunity exists (Acs, 2006). Opportunity entrepreneurship arises from positive 'pull' factors, such as the desire for greater autonomy, independence, freedom, financial gain, social status or even recognition (Carter et al., 2003; Kolvereid, 1996; Wilson et al., 2004) and perhaps resonates most strongly with the wider public image of entrepreneurship. By contrast, necessity entrepreneurship results from 'push' factors that are more negative in nature, such as long-term unemployment (Thurik et al., 2008). Socio-economic factors in the broader environment, such as insufficient job opportunities, low income and social marginalization, often force people to enter self-employment (Serviere, 2010). The decision to become self-employed is not always made for positive reasons; rather, it is sometimes the lesser of labor-market evils (Dennis, 1996). The opportunities exploited by necessity entrepreneurs are generally less profitable. Businesses started by entrepreneurs who experienced push factors are said to be less successful (financially) than those built upon pull factors (Amit & Mueller, 1995). Necessity entrepreneurs have been found to be less satisfied with their occupational situation than opportunity entrepreneurs (Block & Wagner, 2010).

In particular, necessity entrepreneurship has been observed among society's marginalized and disadvantaged groups and is more prevalent among women (Allen et al., 2006, 2007; Reynolds et al., 2004; Bosma et al., 2009; Pines et al., 2010). Disadvantaged people in entrepreneurship may be defined as "those individuals who have difficulty integrating into the marketplace, and typically are located outside the mainstream of social and institutional support for entrepreneurship" (De Clercq & Honig, 2011, p. 354). These may constitute disabled persons (e.g., Pavey, 2006; Maher, 1999), young adults from disadvantaged families (Fairlie, 2005), immigrants or ethnic minorities (Mata & Pendakur, 1999; Collins, 2003), long-term unemployed (Goldsmith et al., 1997, 1996) or women (Boyd, 2000; Hytti, 2010;

Pines et al., 2010). Prior research acknowledge the role of financial, human and social capital as critical elements for success in entrepreneurial endeavors (i.e., Davidsson & Honig, 2003). Opportunity-based entrepreneurs are said to be in a better position to acquire the specific human and social capital necessary to discover profitable opportunities (Block & Wagner, 2010), whereas necessity entrepreneurs tend to have lower educational attainment (Poschke, 2012). Members of disadvantaged groups may experience constricted access to all types of capital, with particularly limited access to symbolic and cultural capital (DeClercq & Honig, 2011). Some individuals may, of course, belong to more than one marginalized group, and thus 'accumulate' disadvantage, which leads to their social marginalization and deprives them of access to opportunities—even the more pronounced ones.

Regardless of their ascribed source of disadvantage, necessity-based entrepreneurs share an often multi-faceted problem: financial, psychological, physical and relational (Lambrecht & Beens, 2005). Once the decision to become self-employed has been made, individuals are often socially isolated, deprived of access to support networks and cut-off from the broader social welfare system (Fayolle, 2010; Lambrecht & Beens, 2005; Serviere, 2010). Independent entrepreneurs often work long hours and earn below-average salaries. The failure rate is high because of competition, poor sales, restricted capital and lack of managerial ability (Hisrich et al., 2005).

How is necessity entrepreneurship gendered?

Scholars introduced the term gender to distinguish between biological sex (human bodies with male or female reproductive organs) and socially constructed sex, i.e., the social practices and representations associated with femininity or masculinity (Acker, 1992). In fact, a great deal of studies did not analyze the notion of gender; it was viewed as an individual characteristic rather than a social construct. Gender, as a social construct, subordinates the feminine and presents gender-related challenges (Carter et al., 2012). It has also been shown to have an impact on people's opportunities, social roles and interactions; in this respect, women's perceptions of opportunities and their entrepreneurial activities are impacted by their societal and institutional environments (Delmar & Holmquist, 2004). Most of the works studying female entrepreneurship focused on comparing men and women entrepreneurs, referring to 'bridging the gap' between the genders. It is, nevertheless, contradictory as 'entrepreneurship' itself is seen as a gendered phenomenon (Ahl, 2006). Entrepreneurship behavior has been associated with terms such as individualism, pro-activeness, competitive orientation, innovativeness and risk taking (Autio et al., 2013). These are similar to the terms individualistic, ambitious, independent and aggressive, used to characterize both masculinity and individual entrepreneurs (Ahl, 2006). This gender culture is acquired at an early stage; individuals' gendered identities shape gendered institutions in a particular context (Bird & Brush, 2002), which in turn reproduce the inequalities that compose the gender identity (Kimmel, 2008).

Globally, females still represent "a minority of those who are self-employed, start new firms, or are small business owner-managers" (Delmar & Holmquist, 2003, p. 46). Necessity entrepreneurship was observed prevalently among women (Allen et al., 2006, 2007; Reynolds et al., 2004; Bosma et al., 2009; Pines et al., 2010). Contemporary entrepreneurship researchers have largely ceased to ask 'whether' gender makes a difference; rather they seek to explore 'how' it makes a difference (Shaw & Carter, 2006). Studies investigating the respective human, social and financial capital of men and women entrepreneurs deliver conflicting findings (de Bruin et al., 2007). However, women have often been found to have lower financial capital (Hisrich & Peters, 1989), which also limits their access to social networks (Marlow & Patton, 2005). Women may be deprived of essential opportunities such as education (Fischer et al., 1993), excluded from key financial networks or come from lower paying jobs. Some researchers attribute societal incidents of women's subordination to discrimination or structural barriers (Fischer et al., 1993; Ahl, 2006). Structural factors in the economy prevent women from gaining experience, accessing markets and generating resources or networks necessary for entrepreneurship (Brush et al., 2004).

The very factors that discriminate against women in wage employment also work against them in entrepreneurship (Pines et al., 2010). These problems may be exacerbated for society's poor and under-privileged groups. While many women are poor for some of the same reasons as men—they live in poor areas, they lack the necessary skills or education—much of women's poverty is due to two causes that are basically unique to females. First, women must often provide all or most of the support for their children, and they are disadvantaged in the labor market (Pearce, 1985). Second, some may have no other means to earn a living (Orhan & Scott, 2001). They choose self-employment as they have 'no other choice' when they find themselves jobless. While Western society exhibits a growing number of single fathers taking care of young children when couples separate or divorce, it is still largely women who are responsible for their primary care (Bradley, 2007). Child care is often deemed to be the woman's responsibility (Pearce, 1985). Thus, some women choose self-employment as a means of income generation, which is more compatible with child care (Orhan & Scott, 2001). Others may choose self-employment as a result of the lack of promotional prospects in their jobs or because they returned to work after several years of childrearing and could not find suitable employment (Orhan & Scott, 2001). Whether as widows, divorcees or unmarried mothers, women have always experienced more poverty than men (Pearce, 1985). The 'feminization of poverty' is not a new phenomenon, but not all female necessity entrepreneurs are single, divorced or widowed. For example, some find themselves unemployed after having moved with a spouse to a new location (Orhan & Scott, 2001).

In sum, women entrepreneurs suffer as a result of various manifestations related to the operation of inequality and exclusion (Pines et al., 2010). Just as arguments have been made that gender discrimination is a key element behind the feminization of poverty (Pearce, 1985), we argue that the phenomenon of necessity entrepreneurship both shapes and is shaped by the gender regime.

Several Western economies have adopted programs to foster and support small firm formation by unemployed workers (Evans & Leighton, 1989; Fairlie, 2005; Caliendo & Kritikos, 2010). Legislative and administrative changes in France, Germany, Poland and Portugal have been introduced to make becoming self-employed an easier process (Fayolle, 2010; Levratto & Serverin, 2011; Oberschachtsiek & Scioch, 2011). The increase in such measures promotes the view that start-ups by individuals from disadvantaged groups can really succeed and are worth working for (Bergmann & Sternberg, 2007). Gathering more information about necessity entrepreneurs can help provide a more complete perspective on entrepreneurship and inform policy design (Poschke, 2012). We further posit that recognizing the heterogeneity of entrepreneurs is key to providing appropriate entrepreneurship training and support (Byrne et al., 2014). Hence, we believe there is a need to more closely investigate the profile and needs of women necessity entrepreneurs in order to design appropriate training and educational support. As such, we present our broad research question as the following:

How can we best provide support and training to female necessity entrepreneurs?

Methodology

Context and sample

This chapter draws on a large research project that addressed necessity entrepreneurship among unemployed individuals in France. The project collected narratives of 15 necessity entrepreneurs and 10 business consultants. The project did not have a specific gender focus, which we feel adds to the value of this research in that we were not purposefully looking for gender effects when collecting narratives from necessity entrepreneurs and their business coaches; there was no preconceived 'gender agenda' in mind. Case selection was purposive. Purposeful sampling can be used as a research strategy "when one wants to learn something and come to understand something about certain select cases without needing to generalize to all such cases" (Patton, 1980, p. 100).

In all cases, the interviews were carried out with one individual at a time. All interviews were recorded and transcribed. They were the subject of manual thematic coding and content analysis (Demazière & Dubar, 1997; Bardin, 2001). The varying steps of coding and analysis were carried out in French with relevant quotations later translated into English for presentation purposes. We chose not to use content analysis software because of the volume of data that appeared compatible with manual treatment; we also wanted to engage with our material through multiple readings and re-readings of our transcripts.

The meetings' content was very rich; the storytelling method allowed us to listen to the necessity entrepreneurs' 'stories.' Entrepreneurs consider these oral interviews a way to 'shift the responsibility of finding solutions on the interlocutor and waiting for outside help.'

Data analysis

We employed a narrative analysis to explore our participants' 'storied talks' of being entrepreneurs. We position our participants' accounts of entrepreneurship in these interviews as personal narratives, in that they involve "large sections of talk and interview exchanges—extended accounts of lives that develop over the course of interviews" (Reissman, 2000). Personal narratives are, at their core, "meaning-making units of discourse" (Reissman, 2000). It is best to present detailed transcripts of speech where possible so that readers can see the stories apart from their analysis (Reissman, 2000).

Female necessity entrepreneurs unanimously expressed their 'relief' after these interviews by repeated thanks and usually the request to keep in touch and extend the study, in order to investigate the continuation of their entrepreneurial experience. While some consultants considered this research an evaluation or a question mark over their methods of work, the majority expressed interest in the results and acknowledged the need for support.

Support for female necessity entrepreneurs

The female necessity entrepreneurs we met share a common trait: they suffered from unemployment, and the entrepreneurial adventure for them is, somehow, a phenomenon that they underwent because it was the best available solution. We find among them immigrants and sometimes young people with a personally and socially chaotic life (integration difficulties, divorce, housing problems, etc.).

Most concerns we have identified from our sample of women necessity entrepreneurs relate to the lack of training and support (i.e., lack of support, lack of finance, isolation, lack

Table 10.1 The sample of female entrepreneurs

Entrepreneur	Age	Profile of entrepreneur	Type of business	Nationality	Age of business
Female necessity Entrepreneur 1	56	– Divorced woman – No children to support – She has been unemployed for 1 year before becoming an entrepreneur	Beauty salon	French	10 years
Female necessity Entrepreneur 2	50	– Divorced woman – No children to support – She has been unemployed for 2 years before becoming an entrepreneur	Restaurant	French	13 years
Female necessity Entrepreneur 3	44	– Divorced woman – Two children to support – She has been unemployed for 4 years before becoming an entrepreneur	Mini-market	French	2 years
Female necessity Entrepreneur 4	35	– Divorced woman – No children to support – She has been unemployed for 7 months before becoming an entrepreneur	Culturel animation center	Polish	1 year
Female necessity Entrepreneur 5	41	– Divorced woman – One child to support – She has been unemployed for 3 years before becoming an entrepreneur	Beauty salon	Spanish	2 years
Female necessity Entrepreneur 6	47	– Divorced woman – One child to support – She has been unemployed for approximatively 2 years before becoming an entrepreneur	Artisanal jewelry store	French	5 years
Female necessity Entrepreneur 7	50	– Divorced woman – Three children to support – She has been unemployed for 1 year before becoming an entrepreneur	Freelancer in consulting (organization)	French	3 years
Female necessity Entrepreneur 8	57	– Divorced woman – One child to support – She has been unemployed for 3 years before becoming an entrepreneur	Real estate agency	French	4 years
Female necessity Entrepreneur 9	48	– Divorced woman – Two children to support – She has been unemployed for 18 months before becoming an entrepreneur	Freelancer in consulting (environment)	French	2 years

	Age	Description	Business	Origin	Duration
Female necessity Entrepreneur 10	35	– Divorced woman – One child to support – She has been unemployed for 3 years before becoming an entrepreneur	e-commerce (toys)	French	4 years
Female necessity Entrepreneur 11	33	– Divorced woman – One child to support – She has been unemployed for 2 years before becoming an entrepreneur	Tea room and tea shop	Russian	6 mouths
Female necessity Entrepreneur 12	28	– Single woman – No children to support – She has been unemployed for 15 months before becoming an entrepreneur	Fruit and vegetables store	Moroccan	3 years
Female necessity Entrepreneur 13	39	– Divorced woman – Three children to support – She has been unemployed for more than 2 years before becoming an entrepreneur	Clothing store	Tunisian	2 years
Female necessity Entrepreneur 14	40	– Single woman – One child to support – She has been unemployed for 3 year before becoming an entrepreneur	Babysitting		1 year
Female necessity Entrepreneur 15	55	– Divorced woman – Two children to support – She has been unemployed for 4 years before becoming an entrepreneur	Jewelry and ornamentation store	Portuguese	3 years

Table 10.2 The sample of business consultants

Consultants	Age	Experience (in support)	Organization	Nationality
Business consultant 1	43	– Master degree – Experience of 10 years in support	Private	French
Business consultant 2	39	– Bachelor degree – Experience of 5 years in support – Experience of 10 years in bank & finance	Public	French
Business consultant 3	37	– Master degree in management – Experience of 10 years in support & marketing	Private	French
Business consultant 4	35	– Master degree in finance – Experience of 7 years in support	Public	French
Business consultant 5	71	– Bachelor degree – Experience of 8 years in Finance – CEO during 30 years – Experience of 5 years in support	Volunteer	French
Business consultant 6	40	– Master degree in foreign language – Experience of 10 years in secretary – 2 years in support	Public	French
Business consultant 7	32	– Master degree in Management – Experience of 6 years in support	Public	French
Business consultant 8	51	– Master degree in history – Experience of 15 years in human resource – Experience of 10 years in support	Public	French
Business consultant 9	65	– No diploma – Entrepreneur since 42 years	Volunteer	French
Business consultant 10	48	– Master degree in accounting – Accountant for 12 years – Experience in teaching – Experience of 8 years in support	Private	French

of experience, lack of listeners). Moreover, women necessity entrepreneurs, due to their long and stressful unemployment period, express a lack of confidence and, in some cases, impose the negative impact of related personal problems on the development of their entrepreneurial project. As a result, there is a frequent feeling of disillusionment and a lack of conviction in going further.

Supporting female necessity entrepreneurs requires special skills. Thus, active listening, empathy, psychological support, hermeneutic techniques and psychotherapy can solve the complexity of the phenomenon. "… (Our work) requires a lot of listening and other competencies that go much further than making projections or putting together a business plan" (Consultant 3). This need has been observed in both the consultants and the female necessity entrepreneurs. The psychological and human dimension is central for them. These types of entrepreneurs are in precarious situations where they have a psychological need; they are distressed and have a strong need for reassurance (Consultant 2).

However, the profile and the skills of consultants (traditional entrepreneurs, senior managers, CEOs, prestigious high school graduates) did not match the expectations of this particular category of entrepreneur. The consultants have to adapt their advice to the female necessity entrepreneur's profile. Consistent with findings from the few studies on this category of entrepreneur, the people we met lacked some of the key skills required for the entrepreneur's 'job.' "From the very first meeting we realized that people are not really capable… they are not ready for the business creation dynamic" (Business consultant 5).

The 'history' of some entrepreneurs also explains their 'present' and their entrepreneurial experiences. To better understand female necessity entrepreneurs, consultants had to take this into consideration in order to avoid breaching the psychological contract with the female necessity entrepreneurs. "My task is to help people structure their project, by helping them consider all the various parameters that may challenge it. We discuss their personal and financial situation, their professional background, their training and qualifications, etc." (Business consultant 1).

Our narratives of female necessity entrepreneurs revealed how business counselors often engage in entrepreneurship coaching with single mothers who are struggling to make ends meet. The consultants talked of isolated and vulnerable 'clients' who had nobody to rely on. The potential entrepreneurs who were the most precarious were generally people who had been made redundant, single women who were divorced and had children to look after (Consultant 10). Women who have children are, indeed, more disadvantageous but have a 'phenomenal motivation' to start a business (Business consultants 4 and 7).

Both the female necessity entrepreneurs and the consultants felt the misunderstanding, the lack of motivation and the uncertainty. They were skeptical about the usefulness and effectiveness of business support. This is mainly due to the mismatch between the consultants' competence and the entrepreneurs' needs and expectations. The consultant was often restricted to a single transfer of technical skills and thus did not meet the psychological needs of entrepreneurs. Female necessity entrepreneurs need comfort rather than pure advice for solving problems. The consultants' competence transformed 'the sufferance' of necessity entrepreneurs into 'knowledge.' The consultants we met pointed out the difficulties they encountered with these entrepreneurs. Many of them complained about being obliged to listen to the female necessity entrepreneurs' personal difficulties in every appointment: "We find ourselves dealing with people who have social problems, personal problems, some who have been made redundant, so we have to look at the problem more closely to verify that business creation is not a denial or rebound from a difficult situation" (Consultant 8). Some of them believed that this was a waste of resources; their current skills did not allow them to help this category of entrepreneur, and they would have preferred to work with other entrepreneurs on technical issues in which they were more competent. There is an urgent need for start-up business support programs with an educational component designed specifically for female necessity entrepreneurs.

The importance of family network and human support of female necessity entrepreneurs

The importance of the network concept in the entrepreneurial environment is central. In fact, networks have an impact on entrepreneurial intention, opportunity recognition and the decision to become an entrepreneur, especially if closely surrounded by a circle of entrepreneurs (Aldrich & Zimmer, 1986). Networks can also help sustain and grow the business through facilitating access to the tangible and intangible resources needed for the business, namely capital (human, financial and social), training and support (Aldrich & Zimmer, 1986). Entrepreneurs need to make greater use of their networks when they start their businesses or when they experience difficulties. This was the case with the female necessity entrepreneurs in our sample.

Consistent with Kotha and George (2012) and Khayesi and George (2011), our findings indicate that those who manage to survive are able to mobilize their own networks of friends and family members. Also, they are more prepared to access associations, specialized websites or discussion forums on the web. Indeed, we noted the female entrepreneurs' extensive use of the Internet to facilitate the support process. As some of the consultants admitted, due to a lack of time, they often guided entrepreneurs to specialized websites to finish up the support process. However, in the case of female necessity entrepreneurs, this 'virtual' support reduces human contact and, thus, may isolate them further, aggravating their 'exclusion' from society and not helping them regain their self-confidence.

Some consultants were aware of the isolation of female necessity entrepreneurs and felt sympathy because the entrepreneurs experienced chaotic pathways on personal and professional levels. This category of consultants, attaching great importance to the human dimension, tried to understand the 'past' and the psychological constraint of female necessity entrepreneurs and took into account, even informally, the psychological dimension of those necessity entrepreneurs who were often very fragile. Another category of consultants preferred to focus only on their core business rather than 'wasting' their time dealing with the principle needs of female necessity entrepreneurs, namely, self-esteem, integration and self-confidence. Due to the increasing number of entrepreneurs, some necessity entrepreneurs' organizations operate in a quantitative way without taking the human and social aspects into consideration.

Discussion

The findings of our study suggest that supporting female necessity entrepreneurs requires special skills, namely: active listening, empathy, psychological support, hermeneutic techniques and psychotherapy, which are likely to ease the challenges faced by such entrepreneurs. Nevertheless, there is an apparent mismatch between consultants and their assigned clients or entrepreneurs. In other words, the profile and the skills of consultants do not meet the expectations of this particular category of entrepreneur. As a result, both the female necessity entrepreneurs and the consultants experienced misunderstanding, a lack of motivation and uncertainty, which raises serious questions about the usefulness and effectiveness of business support.

To better understand female necessity entrepreneurs, consultants must take into account the 'past' of these entrepreneurs in order to understand the present; try to avoid the breach of the psychological contract between them and provide better and more customized support. Support can also be gained from the female entrepreneurs' close network of family and friends. The centrality of their networks is crucial, as entrepreneurs—including female necessity entrepreneurs—need networks for both business creation and growth. The Internet has been used—either spontaneously or at the advice of the consultants—in order to exploit other sources of support and complete the process. Nevertheless, this virtual support eliminates human contact and is likely to isolate and further marginalize female necessity entrepreneurs from society. While some consultants focus on business related issues only, others recognize this isolation and sympathize with those entrepreneurs struggling at the personal and professional levels.

Recent policies in the world's rich countries have tended towards encouraging self-employment among the unemployed (Block & Wagner, 2010; Fayolle & Nakara, 2012; Fairlie, 2005). From a psychological standpoint, employment is important to people because it gives status, structure, contact with others and purpose (Goldsmith et al., 1997). The long-term unemployed are more 'desperate' than their short-term unemployed counterparts are and are thus more likely to seek relief through risky entrepreneurial ventures (Light & Rosenstein, 1995; Boyd, 2005). Necessity entrepreneurs who have been unemployed long term exhibit an extreme need for reassurance and confidence building. Indeed, entrepreneurship is no 'easy ride' (Jones & Spicer, 2009). Many individuals who take on this new status of entrepreneur are ill equipped for what it entails. Female necessity entrepreneurs are perhaps even less prepared. Not all disadvantaged, unemployed or marginalized individuals are intrinsically motivated to 'be' entrepreneurs. Thus, it is necessary to strengthen the mutual listening between the two stakeholder groups and to give more legitimacy to consultants and support to female necessity entrepreneurs. Female necessity entrepreneurs are demanding this 'listening' from both consultants and policy makers. Sometimes, their efforts to seek support for business creation are a concealed form of an urgent request for help because they are simply confused.

The successful integration of disadvantaged people into the field of entrepreneurship depends on the extent to which they can negotiate the tensions between "dominant field arrangements about entrepreneurship on the one hand and potentially contradictory facets of their activities stemming from their very membership in a disadvantaged group on the other" (de Clercq & Honig, 2011). This creates further tension between the necessity-based entrepreneurs and other socially disadvantaged groups. It also calls for policy makers to rethink their strategy of integrating the socially disadvantaged into the entrepreneurship domain. The findings from this study point to the need for start-up business support: effective policy with an educational component designed specifically for female necessity entrepreneurs (Block & Sandner, 2009). It is often feared that the formerly unemployed lack the basic qualifications to become entrepreneurs (Caliendo & Kritikos, 2010); they also often lack the necessary resources (financial, physical, psychological, social or relational) to succeed (Lambrecht & Beens, 2005; Fayolle & Nakara, 2012).

Conclusions

The economic and social conditions that have developed in recent years have led to a rise in long-term unemployment and an increase in the number of necessity entrepreneurs, which deteriorates the quality of the available support. The increasing number of self-employed files results in a veritable policy of 'industrialization' of support for necessity entrepreneurs, which reduces the time devoted to such individuals. More resources are required: a longer support process for the entrepreneurs as well as additional training for the consultants. This is a real dilemma for policy makers: should they fund new resources to support necessity entrepreneurs or abandon the idea of supporting this type of 'entrepreneur' altogether?

Public policies need to be redefined or even reinvented. Recent years have witnessed a series of measures to encourage business creation by emphasizing the ease of the process without referring to its risks and difficulties. Policy makers voluntarily highlighted entrepreneurship as a solution to unemployment. However, neither necessity entrepreneurs nor their counselors share this point of view.

This chapter contributes to the field of entrepreneurship by shedding light on the challenges female necessity entrepreneurs face and the nature of their relationship with their business counselors. It also provides policy makers with clear guidance on how to best provide support and training to the female necessity entrepreneur, in light of the challenges they face throughout their entrepreneurial process, using customized support skills and programs unique to this very special type of entrepreneur. The study points to a number of avenues for future research; for instance, to investigate whether policy makers are providing any support and training to female necessity entrepreneurs; the effectiveness of such programs and what their implications are for the entrepreneur and the economy. An analysis of why policy makers seem to avoid providing female necessity entrepreneurs with support and training may also be necessary. Finally, a study of business counselors is needed in order to understand how—by supporting them as key actors—they can provide the female necessity entrepreneur with the most effective support.

References

Acker, J. (1992). "Gendering Organisational Theory". In A. Mills & P. Tancred (Eds), *Gendering Organisational Analysis.* pp. 248–260. London: Sage.

Acs, Z. J. (2006). "How Is Entrepreneurship Good for Economic Growth?" *Innovations*, 1(1): 97–107.

Ahl, H. (2006). "Why Research on Women Entrepreneurs Needs New Directions". *Entrepreneurship Theory and Practice*, 30(5): 595–621.

Aldrich, H. & Zimmer, C. (1986). "Entrepreneurship through Social Networks". In D. Sexton & R. Smiler (eds), *The Art and Science of Entrepreneurship*, pp. 3–23. New York: Ballinger.

Allen, I., Elam, A., Langowitz, N. & Dean, M. (2006). *Global Entrepreneurship Monitor 2007 Report on Women and Entrepreneurship.* Babson College and London Business School.

Allen, I., Langowitz, N. & Minniti, M. (2007). *Global Entrepreneurship Monitor 2006 Report on Women and Entrepreneurship.* Babson College and London Business School.

Amit, R. & Mueller, E. (1995). "Push" and "Pull" Entrepreneurship. *Journal of Small Business and Entrepreneurship*, 12(4): 64–80.

Autio, E., Pathak, S. & Wennberg, K. (2013). "Consequences for Cultural Practices for Entrepreneurial Behaviours". *Journal of International Business Studies*, 44(4): 334–362.

Bardin, L. (2001). "*L'analyse de contenu, Presses Universitaires de France.*" Paris, 2001.

Bergmann, H. & Sternberg, R. (2007). "The Changing Face of Entrepreneurship in Germany". *Small Business Economics*, 28: 205–221.

Bird, B. & Brush, C. (2002). "A Gendered Perspective on Organizational Creation. Entrepreneurship". *Theory and Practice*, 26: 41–65.

Block, J. & Sandner, P. (2009). "Necessity and Opportunity Entrepreneurs and their Duration in Self-Employment". *Journal IndCompet Trade*, 9: 117–137.

Block, J. & Wagner, M. (2010). "Necessity and Opportunity Entrepreneurship in Germany: Characteristics and Earning Differentials". *Schinalenbach Business Review*, 62(2): 150–179.

Bosma, N., Acs, Z.J., Autio, E., Coduras, A. & Levie, J. (2009). *Global Entrepreneurship Monitor 2008 Executive Report. Babson College, Universidad del Desarrollo.* London Business School, Global Entrepreneurship Research Consortium.

Boyd, R. (2005). "Race, Gender, and Survivalist Entrepreneurship in Large Northern Cities during the Great Depression". *The Journal of Socio-Economics*, 34: 331–339.

Boyd, R. L. (2000). "Race, Labor Market Disadvantage, and Survivalist Entrepreneurship: Black Women in the Urban North during the Great Depression". *Sociological Forum*, 15: 647–670.

Bradley, H. (2007). "*Gender: Key Concepts*". Malden, MA: Polity Press.

Brush, C., Carter, N., Gatewood, E., Greene, P. & Hart, M. (2004). "*Clearing the Hurdles: Women Building High Growth Businesses*". New Jersey: Financial Times Prentice Hall.

Byrne, J. & Fayolle, A. (2010). "A Feminist Inquiry into Entrepreneurship Training". In D. Smallbone, J. Leitao, M. Raposo & F. Welter (Eds), *The Theory and Practice of Entrepreneurship. Frontiers in European Entrepreneurship Research.* pp. 76–100. Cheltenham, UK: Edward Elgar.

Byrne, J., Fayolle, A. & Toutain, O. (2014). "Entrepreneurship Education: What We Know and What We Need To Know". In E. Chell and M. Karatas Ozkan (Eds), *Handbook of Research on Small Business and Entrepreneurship.* Cheltenham, UK: Edward Elgar Publishing Limited.

Caliendo, M. & Kritikos, A.S. (2010). "Start-Ups by the Unemployed: Characteristics, Survival and Direct Employment Effects". *Small Business Economics*, 35(1): 71–92.

Carter, N.M., Gartner, W.B., Shaver, K.G. & Gatewood, E.J. (2003). "The Career Reasons of Nascent Entrepreneurs". *Journal of Business Venturing*, 18(1): 13–39.

Carter, S., Marlow, S. & Bennett, D. (2012). "Gender and Entrepreneurship". In: S. Carter, J. Dylan (Eds), *Enterprise and Small Business: Principles, Practice and Policy*, pp. 218–230. London: Pearson Education Ltd.

Chell, E. (2007). "Social Enterprise and Entrepreneurship: Towards a Convergent Theory of the Entrepreneurial Process". *International Small Business Journal*, 25: 5–26.

Collins, J. (2003). *"Ethnic Entrepreneurship in Australia"*. Willy Brandt Series of Working Papers in International Migration and Ethnic Relations 1/02.

Davidsson, P. & Honig, B. (2003). "The Role of Human and Social Capital among Nascent Entrepreneurs". *Journal of Business Venturing*, 18(3): 301–331.

De Bruin, A., Brush, C.G. & Welter, F. (2007). "Advancing a Framework for Coherent Research on Female's Entrepreneurship". *Entrepreneurship Theory and Practice*, 31(3): 323–339.

De Clercq, D. & Honig, B. (2011). "Entrepreneurship as an Integrating Mechanism for Disadvantaged Persons". *Entrepreneurship & Regional Development*, 23(5/6): 353–372.

Delmar, F. & Holmquist, C. (2003). *"Female Entrepreneurship: Issue and Policies"*. OECD Report, presented at the 21st session of the Working Party on Small and Medium-Sized Enterprises and Entrepreneurship, Paris, 1–3 December 2003.

Delmar, F. & Holmquist, C. (2004). *"Women's Entrepreneurship: Issues and Policies"* 2nd OECD Conference of Ministers Responsible for Small and Medium-Sized Enterprises (SMEs) Istanbul, Turkey 3–5 June 2004.

Demazière, D. & Dubar, C. (1997). *"Analyser les entretiens biographiques: l'exemple des récits d'insertion"*. Nathan, collection Essais & Recherches, 1997.

Dennis, J. (1996). "Self-Employment: When Nothing Else Is Available?". *Journal of Labour Research*, 17(4): 645–661.

Evans, D.S. & Leighton, L.S. (1989). "Some Empirical Aspects of Entrepreneurship". *American Economic Review*, 79: 519–535.

Fairlie, R. (2005). "Entrepreneurship and Earnings among Young Adults from Disadvantaged Families." *Small Business Economics*, 25: 223–236.

Fayolle, A. (2010). *"Nécessité et opportunité: les 'attracteurs étranges de l'entrepreneuriat"*. Revue Pour, 204: 33–38.

Fayolle, A. (2011). "Necessity Entrepreneurship and Job Insecurity: The Hidden Face of Entrepreneurship". *International Journal of E-Entrepreneurship and Innovation*, 2(3): 1–10.

Fayolle, A. & Nakara W.A. (2012). "Création par nécessité et précarité: la face cachée de l'entrepreneuriat". *Revue Économies et Sociétés. Études critiques en management.*

Fischer, E.M., Reuber, A.R. & Dyke, L.S. (1993). "A Theoretical Overview and Extension of Research on Sex, Gender and Entrepreneurship". *Journal of Business Venturing*, 8(2): 151–168.

Goldsmith, A.H., Veum, J.R. & Darity, W. (1996). "The Psychological Impact of Unemployment on Joblessness". *Journal of Socio-Economics*, 25: 333–358.

Goldsmith, A.H., Veum, J.R. & Darity, W. (1997). "Unemployment, Joblessness, Psychological Well-Being and Self-Esteem: Theory and Evidence". *Journal of Socio-Economics*, 26(2): 133–158.

Hisrich, R.D. & Peters, M.P. (1989). *"Entrepreneurship: Starting, Developing, and Managing a New Enterprise"*. Homewood: B.P.I./Irwin.

Hisrich, R.D., Peters, M.P. & Shepherd, D.A. (2005). *"Entrepreneurship, (6th Ed.)"*. New York: McGraw Hill / Irwin.

Hytti, U. (2010). "Contextualizing Entrepreneurship in The Boundary Less Career". *Gender in Management: An International Journal*, 25(1): 64–81.

Jones, C. & Spicer, A. (2009). *Unmasking the Entrepreneur*. Cheltenham (UK): Edward Elgar.

Kelley, D.J., Brush, C.G., Greene, P.G. & Litovsky, Y. (2013). *Global Entrepreneurship Monitor: 2012 Women's Report*. Boston: The Center for Women's Leadership at Babson College and London Business School.

Khayesi, J.N.O. & George, G. (2011). "When Does the Socio-Cultural Context Matter? Communal Orientation and Entrepreneurs Resource Accumulation Efforts in Africa". *Journal of Occupational and Organizational Psychology*, 84(3): 471–492.

Kimmel, M. (2008). *"The Gendered Society"*. 3rd Ed. New York: Oxford University Press, Inc.

Kolvereid, L. (1996). "Organizational Employment versus Self-Employment: Reasons for Career Choice Intentions", *Entrepreneurship Theory and Practice*, 20(3): 23–31.

Kotha, R. & George, G. (2012). "Friends, Family, or Fools: Entrepreneur Experience and Its Implications for Equity Distribution and Resource Mobilization". *Journal of Business Venturing*, 27(5): 525–543.

Lambrecht, J. & Beens, E. (2005). "Poverty among Self-Employed Businesspeople in a Rich Country: A Misunderstood and Distinct Reality". *Journal of Developmental Entrepreneurship*, 10(3): 205–222.

Levratto, N. & Serverin, E. (2011). *Become Independent! The Paradoxical Constraints of France' Auto-Entrepreneur Regime*. EconomiX working paper 6. University of Paris West, Nanterre La Défense, EconomiX.

Light, I.H. & Rosenstein, C.N. (1995). *Race, Ethnicity and Entrepreneurship in Urban America*. New York: Aldine de Gruyter.

Maher, K. (1999). "Net Interest: Internet Offers New Freedom to the Disabled. *The Wall Street Journal*, June 24, 11.

Marlow, S. & Patton, D. (2005). "All Credit to Men? Entrepreneurship, Finance and Gender". *Entrepreneurship Theory and Practice*, 29(6): 699–716.

Mata, R. & Pendakur, R. (1999). "Immigration, Labor Force Integration and the Pursuit of Self-Employment". *International Migration Review*, 33(2): 378–402.

Minniti, M., Bygrave, W.D. & Autio, E. (2005). *Global Entrepreneurship Monitor, Executive Report*. Babson College: MA.

Nicholson, L. & Anderson, A.R. (2005). "News and Nuances of the Entrepreneurial Myth and Metaphor: Linguistic Games in Entrepreneurial Sense-Making and Sense-Giving". *Entrepreneurship Theory & Practice*, 29: 153–172.

Oberschachtsiek, D. & Scioch, P. (2011). *The Outcome of Coaching and Training for Self-Employment: A Statistical Evaluation of Non-Financial Support Schemes for Unemployed Business Founders in Germany*. IAB Discussion Paper, 16. Institute for Employment Research, German Federal Employment Agency.

Orhan, M., & Scott, D. (2001). "Why Women Enter into Entrepreneurship: An Explanatory Model". *Women in Management Review*, 15 (5/6): 232–243.

Patton, M.Q. (1980). *Qualitative Evaluation Methods*. Beverly Hills, CA: Sage.

Pavey, B., (2006). "Human Capital, Social Capital, Entrepreneurship and Disability: An Examination of Some Current Educational Trends in The UK". *Disability and Society*, 21 (3): 217–229.

Pearce, D. (1985). "Welfare Is Not for Women: Toward a Model of Advocacy to Meet the Needs of Women in Poverty". *Clearinghouse Review*, 19: 412–418.

Pines, A.M., Lerner, M., & Schwartz, D. (2010). "Gender Differences in Entrepreneurship: Equality, Diversity and Inclusion in Times of Global Crisis". *Equality, Diversity and Inclusion: An International Journal*, 29 (2): 186–198.

Poschke, M. (2012). *Who Becomes an Entrepreneur? Labor Market Prospects and Occupational Choice*. CIREQ Working Paper 12.

Reissman, C.K. (2000). "Analysis of Personal Narratives". *Handbook of Interviewing*, edited by J.F. Gubrium and J.A. Holstein, Sage Publications.

Reynolds, P.D., Carter, N.M., Gartner, W.B., & Greene, P.G. (2004). "The prevalence of nascent entrepreneurs in the United States: Evidence from the panel study of entrepreneurial dynamics". *Small Business Economics*, 23(4): 263–284.

Serviere, L. (2010). "Forced to Entrepreneurship: Modeling the Factors behind Necessity Entrepreneurship". *Journal of Business and Entrepreneurship*, 22: 37–43.

Shaw, E. & Carter, S. (2006). "Social Entrepreneurship: Theoretical Antecedents and Empirical Analysis of Entrepreneurial Processes and Outcomes". *Journal of Small Business and Enterprise Development*, 14(3): 418–434.

Thurik, A.R., Carree, M.A., Van Stel, A.J. & Audretsch, D.B. (2008). "Does Self-Employment Reduce Unemployment?". *Journal of Business Venturing*, 23(6): 673–686.

Wilson, F., Marlino, D. & Kickul, J. (2004). "Our Entrepreneurial Future: Examining the Diverse Attitudes and Motivations of Teens across Gender and Ethnic Identity". *Journal of Developmental Entrepreneurship*, 9(3): 177–197.

11

ENTREPRENEURIAL ROLE MODELS

An integrated framework from a constructionist perspective

Maria Cristina Díaz-García and Janice Byrne

Introduction

Entrepreneurship is widely perceived by national governments as an appropriate vehicle for increasing economic and societal value. As such, attempts are made to nurture and foster individuals' engagement in entrepreneurship. One way to do so is by the use of role models. Entrepreneurial role models play a vital role in stimulating individuals to 'elaborate anticipatory scenarios of their own future career and identity' (Radu and Loué, 2008, p. 445). Thus far, two prominent approaches have been used to explain role modelling: social learning theories and role identification theories (Gibson, 2006).

Despite an upsurge in the interest of role models as an important developmental relationship, the extant literature is limited (Bosma, Hessels, Schutjens, van Praag and Verheul, 2012), especially regarding the process of role modelling – how the mental construction of role models works – (Eriksson-Zetterquist, 2008; Ibarra, 1999) which is imbued with symbolic values (Sealy and Singh, 2010) and gendered identification patterns (Kelan and Mah, 2014), which are also understudied. Besides this, within the entrepreneurship field there is an emphasis on male-related constructs, and this is reflected in a gender-biased concept of entrepreneurial activity, supporting a hierarchical valuation in which the masculine is prioritised over the feminine (Ogbor, 2000; Hamilton, 2013). In this context, it is worth further examining how gender influences the dynamics of role modelling in entrepreneurship. Following the call for further research on role modelling and observing the impact that the social construction of gender and entrepreneurship can have in this process, we consider that there is a gap in understanding the process of role modelling, its antecedents (how it is affected by gender and business context) and its outcomes (how it is interconnected with self-efficacy and identity development). We consider it important to observe the process of role modelling in order to understand the forces that prompt individuals to behave as they do, considering how this process is affected by gender and context. How does the macro-level context affect the process of social interaction in the entrepreneurship field (meso-level) and micro-level mental processes of identification and identity construction? We contend that there is a need to achieve better knowledge of how and why (certain) role models impact (potential) entrepreneurs or whether there is real value in promoting certain women role models for fostering women's entrepreneurial intentions. This understanding leads us to illuminate how institutions and individuals identify and promote certain female entrepreneurial role models.

We aim to provide an integrated way of looking at the research problem and open up a broader understanding of role modelling in entrepreneurship. Following Ahl (2006), who advocated a social constructionist approach to research on entrepreneurship, we focus on the importance of examining how societal institutions and norms position the woman entrepreneur. Besides this, and in line with Radu and Loué (2008), we consider that there should be a move towards a more context-related and individual-centred role-modelling approach, which deals with the potential cognitive, emotional and behavioural impact of role models. That is, we choose a constructionist perspective in contrast with the current initiatives in role-modelling promotion, which are normally based on liberal feminist ideals. In this perspective, the focus is on the agent and her actions and choices: if some successful individual women have made it, it is feasible to overcome the obstacles and barriers. The focus on role models in these initiatives seems to be "a psychological version of the American dream: if women merely follow the lead of so-called role models, we all, every one of us, can succeed" (Fisher, 1988, p. 212). This reflects the overtly individualist focus that pervades entrepreneurship research and leaves 'the system' devoid of blame (Ahl, 2006). On the contrary, social constructionism implies greater regard for context, since it assumes that reality is socially constructed, that is, created in interaction with others (persons, artefacts, symbols and images). In line with this, a symbolic interactionist perspective considers the 'embedded agent' and considers institutional forces.

Role models: different perspectives on their importance for entrepreneurship

Role models are defined as "individuals who provide an example of the kind of success that one might achieve, and often also provide a template, of the behaviours that are needed to achieve success" (Lockwood, 2006, p. 36). They are individuals whose "behaviours, personal styles and specific attributes are emulated by others" (Shapiro et al., 1978, p. 52). Role models play an important role in identity construction (Sealy and Singh, 2010) and are vital for the successful development of young professionals (Ibarra, 1999; Gibson, 2004).

The basis of the role-model relationship is the identification and social comparison process: an individual makes another a role model by identifying with them or looking up to them (Gibson, 2006). The role model acts as a reference for other individuals, setting examples and inspiring them to take certain (career) decisions and achieve certain goals (Shapiro et al., 1978). Individuals actively select which models they want to compare to depending on their goals and motivations, their capacity for processing information and the personal and situational involvement of that person (Buunk and Gibbons, 2007; Gibson, 2004).

A number of studies have identified the importance of role models in the backgrounds of practising entrepreneurs (Brockhaus and Horwitz, 1986; Hisrich and Brush, 1984; Scherer et al., 1989). Observing, identifying with and appreciating the behaviour of others make certain career choices more obvious than others (Bandura, 1977; Scherer et al., 1989). Entrepreneurial role models are invaluable sources of information and also play a motivational role, inspiring confidence and enabling self-projection (Radu and Loué, 2008) by stimulating observers to "elaborate anticipatory scenarios of their own future career and identity" (Radu and Loué, 2008, p. 445). Indeed, individual behaviour is very often influenced by others' behaviours, opinions and examples (Akerlof and Kranton, 2000).

Social learning theory vs. role identification theory:
Symbolic interactionism as the link

A social learning theoretical approach emphasises learning and suggests that individuals refer to models because they can be helpful in acquiring new tasks, skills and norms. In entrepreneurship, role models have been found to impact on entrepreneurial self-efficacy and career choice (Scherer et al., 1989). In social cognitive theory, Bandura (1977) postulates a triadic relationship among individual, context and behaviour. If the individual in his/her interaction with the context perceives that he/she has abilities and capacities to develop with success a specific task (high self-efficacy), then it will be more probable that he/she will carry it out and persevere with it (Bandura, 1997). If the individual has a role model, he/she can learn from him/her, increasing his/her self-efficacy in that activity and, therefore, his/her intention to pursue that behaviour.

On the other hand, researchers evoking role identification theories place more emphasis on the motivational and self-definitional aspects of role models, underlining the importance of perceived similarity between the individual and the chosen role model (Gibson, 2006). Role models have been found to play an important role in the construction of a professional identity (Shapiro et al., 1978; Ibarra, 1999; Gibson, 2003). An individual's identity refers to the self-conceptions attached to the individual by him-/herself or by others, since identity is socially and symbolically constructed (Haslam, 2004). Hence, one's self-concept is composed of three dimensions: the 'actual self', the 'ideal self' and the 'ought self' (traits one should possess because of a moral obligation or duty) (Higgins, 1984). This is the reason individuals have multiple and sometimes conflicting images of one-self impacting on cognitions, emotions and behaviours. Furthermore, the way in which individuals engage in the role-modelling process, using 'ideal' or 'ought' selves appears to be gendered, where the 'ought' self is more extensively evoked by females than males (Kelan and Mah, 2014; Eriksson-Zetterquist, 2008).

In this paper, we adopt a symbolic interactionist approach (Mead, 1934) as a way to combine and synergise these two theoretical approaches to role modelling. When doing identity work an individual works on his/her 'external' identity and at the same time shapes the 'internal' aspects of his/her personal identity (Watson, 2008). The *symbolic interactionism* (dialectic) between the two – internal self-identity and external social identity – is especially important in terms of furthering understanding of entrepreneurship (Lewis, 2015) and, we propose, is particularly crucial to our understanding of role modelling in entrepreneurship. Individuals build their identity constructing both the 'me' that represents the external, socially directed part who takes socially gendered discourses of reality into consideration and the 'I', which represents the creative-destructive part who can go against the grain (Klyver et al., 2013). When engaging with established social groups, individuals who aim to take on the role of entrepreneur are often challenged with how this role fits with existing identities and roles (Ollila, Middleton and Donnellon, 2012).

From a symbolic interactionist standpoint (Mead, 1934), employment choices (and the selection of inspirational role models) are derived from an interactive conversation between individual and social institutional processes. Roles are the link between self and social structure and culture (Turner, 2013). Symbolic interactionist theories of identity stress the role played in identity formation by the exchange with the other – individuals, groups, organisations or institutions (Turner, 2013). Individuals adapt to new roles by experimenting with 'provisional selves' that serve as trials for possible but not yet fully elaborated professional identities (Ibarra, 1999). Potential entrepreneurs aim for identity verification, and to achieve it they engage in interactions with others in a continual 'gestalt' dynamic of experimentation, feedback and behavioural adaptation (Turner, 2013). Consequently, the process of projecting oneself in the image of a role model is not a one-way process, but a socially embedded one. In this way, an interactionist perspective on role modelling pushes us beyond the liberal feminist focus on the individual.

How gender and context influence the role-modelling process

Observing the role-modelling process from a symbolic interactionism standpoint requires understanding it in terms of socially situated cognition (Mitchell et al., 2014). It implies adopting an approach that combines consideration of cognition, affect and action and is a process that involves cognitive evaluations/appraisals, affective/emotional arousal and behavioural responses.

According to Roselli et al. (1995), when people process messages of persuasion, two mechanisms mediate the process: a cognitive and an emotional one. The first implies that social appeals influence the *cognitive elaborations* of a persuasive message by influencing the quantity and valence of cognitive responses to the persuasive message. The other mechanism argues that social appeals trigger *affective responses*, which disrupt the cognitive elaborations, accounting for some of the variances in persuasion outcomes (Petty et al., 2003).

We propose that individuals, after a cognitive appraisal, will selectively observe and copy what appears to be effective for career and life success, and if female role models provided do not fit, they will not generate emotional arousal and motivate entrepreneurial intention. But if an appropriate image of women entrepreneurs is projected, they can act as positive role models, leading other women to improve their symbolic value outcomes (obtain higher self-efficacy) and to reaffirm their identity construction as entrepreneurs with the acceptation by others. But what is 'a successful entrepreneur' and an 'appropriate' image of a woman entrepreneur? How do those seeking role models identify, define and gauge this?

Role modelling: a cognitive (and gender sensitive) appraisal

Role models can be cognitively evaluated as positive or negative. Successful entrepreneurial role models have been found to reinforce role model identification and generate favourable attitudes, enhancing the self-efficacy and entrepreneurial intention of students (Laviolette, Lefebvre and Brunel, 2012; Krueger, 1996; Krueger and Brazeal, 1993). Interestingly, Mungai and Velamuri (2011) observe that a parent's failure in entrepreneurial activity negatively affects their children's entrepreneurial intentions. This is because negative role models motivate individuals to avoid undesirable outcomes while positive role models facilitate the motivation to reach desirable outcomes (Lockwood, Marshall and Sadler, 2005).

Hancock et al. (2014) provide evidence that individuals largely associate an entrepreneur's characteristics with those stereotypically considered male or androgynous, with a notable absence of female characteristics. That is, a socially constructed gender stereotyping persists in contemporary culture, influencing the continued predominance of the perception that entrepreneurial activity is a masculine activity. Masculine traits are predominantly used to describe entrepreneurs – the entrepreneur is a hero and pioneer (Ogbor, 2000) – while feminine traits are often in opposition to entrepreneurial characteristics (Ahl, 2006), leading to the fact that entrepreneurial identity remains a strongly male-gendered one (Hamilton, 2013). Since individuals' behaviours are assessed based on socially accepted conceptions of gender (West and Zimmerman, 1977) and unfortunately, prejudiced social constructions still pervade in social interactions, women endeavouring to take on the role of entrepreneur may face a challenge when matching this role with existing identities and roles (Ollila, Middleton and Donnellon, 2012).

We propose that if female entrepreneurs are projected as producing lower business returns, because they assume the role of primary family carer and/or because they are crammed into a few low-value sectors with few entry barriers and cut-throat competition, the effect of these role models is the inverse of what might be hoped. Women will choose not to engage in imitation – anticipating the business survival difficulties in this type of behaviour – or they will imitate these role models, reinforcing this disadvantaged position within the business realm. Ambitious, growth-oriented women entrepreneurs may be left with no available 'similar' women role models.

Maybe because of this, women report being less likely to find role models who share their concerns of finding a life-work balance, being less likely to have specific individuals as role models and more likely to identify with 'negative' role models – finding things to avoid (Gibson and Cordova, 1999). This fact appears to be particularly apparent in scientific and technological industries (Martin et al., 2015). Because entrepreneurship is still largely construed in masculine terms (Ogbor, 2000; Ahl, 2002), engaging with the phenomenon may represent a significant challenge to women as they experience the 'double bind' of incongruity between their gender role and entrepreneurial stereotypes. This tendency at an individual level is compounded by institutional and societal-level factors. Indeed, the contemporary construction of entrepreneurship is inextricably related to how a particular society values parental roles, especially motherhood, and to what extent parents are judged as equally agentic and career-committed compared to non-parents (Fuegen et al., 2004; Ridgeway and Correll, 2004). Women with children are perceived either to be less committed to their firms because of their caretaker roles or to have difficulty performing both roles well. Indeed there is a lack of fit between the woman entrepreneur and the idealised image of an entrepreneur, which is entwined in masculine stereotypes (full commitment to the firm with no distractions from a separated private sphere, focus on economic performance when developing the activity in an attractive sector with a technological base). The representation of women entrepreneurs in the media, for example, is thought to "restrict the propensity for women to seriously consider entrepreneurship as a career option" (Achtenhagen and Welter, 2011).

However, despite this apparent lack of fit, researchers advise policy makers that entrepreneurship support programs should encourage the use of other women as role models, due to the utility/importance of same-sex role models (Lockwood and Kunda, 1997; Lockwood, 2006; Sealy, 2007). The premise of such recommendations is that exposing women to positive female entrepreneurial role models can close the entrepreneurial self-efficacy gender gap thereby encouraging women to follow example. The rationale under this affirmation was that in organisational life, the fact that women have a lack of female role models makes women's experience more difficult than men's, as they have to perform more sophisticated cognitive operations to identify with cross-sex role models. From our point of view, the reasoning under this recommendation is biased: it springs from a liberal feminist tradition and departs from a very narrow understanding of the role-modelling process. First, it seems to sustain, according to liberal feminist theorising, that if some individual women have been successful, then opportunities have been made available to womanhood, and other women can overcome barriers if they try hard enough. However, such a vision places the responsibility on women to use role models successfully to correct their 'deficits in attributes and behaviours' and leaves the 'system' – including formal institutions and informal ones such as the society's culture – devoid of criticism (Ahl, 2002).

Second, the individual's role model does not have to take the form of one (or more) 'actual' persons. Eriksson-Zetterquist (2008) argues that role modelling also alludes to the creation of an idealised image and that acknowledging the distinction of an actual person and an idealised image can be helpful to understand the complexities of the process. She argues that individuals may proceed by reconstructing the image of an actual person into an image that will serve as role model. This will happen through operations of idealisation (selection of positive traits) and composition (assembling such traits in a role model). Role modelling is a process of conscious and unconscious identification and imitation of desires, but also a process of negotiation with oneself and others (Eriksson-Zetterquist, 2008). People do not evoke actual persons but rather an image composed of impressions of various actual persons in their role modelling (Eriksson-Zetterquist, 2008; Gibson, 2004). That is, the role-modelling process is a complex one, in which individuals use compartmentalised identification processes, drawing on a myriad of different personal profiles to form their ideal entrepreneurs (Eriksson-Zetterquist, 2008). Individuals tend to use a selection of role models from a variety of domains (workplace, family, peers and sport activities) to help them build appropriate identities (Singh, Vinnicombe and Turnbull, 2006). Therefore, different role models in concert shape an entrepreneur's identity within the multiple identities possible for an individual (Akerlof and Kranton, 2000).

Considering the possibility of using several 'actual' persons as role models and the existence of a male-gendered discourse of entrepreneurship, women are more likely to construct cross-sex role models (Gibson and Cordova, 1999), and they need to engage more frequently in complex cognitive processes in their role-modelling behaviour (combining both same-sex and cross-sex proto-models). Whereas men, who have many same-sex role models within the organisation, will be more likely to form composite role models – combining idealised traits from different men, choosing a female role model only in gender-balanced settings (Gibson and Cordova, 1999).

Along this line of reasoning, Kelan and Mah (2014) analysed the identification patterns of MBA students. They found that most male and female MBA students 'idealised' the self-made authentic CEO or founder of an organisation, which embodies the hegemonic masculinity that a business owner is supposed to display. Only women MBA students engaged in a social-psychological identification pattern of other women, which the authors labelled 'admiration', which means discussing positive as well as negative and neutral characteristics of a person. This demonstrates how when engaging in role-model processing, women act to 'smooth out' potential inconsistencies between the characteristics of their female role model and those of the idealised business owner (Kelan and Mah, 2014). This reflects the struggle women face in reconciling their 'ideal' and 'ought' selves. Gibson and Cordova (1999) find that female role models were less likely than male role models to be described as organisationally effective, but were often recognised for their ability to manage personal and professional lives at the same time.

Eriksson-Zetterquist (2008) focuses on how young career-oriented men and women sought both male and female 'proto-models', that is, actual persons from whom they could construct their role models. Whereas men were often mentioned as proto-models, women were seldom mentioned and only by female trainees. Women were chosen (or not) as proto-models because of how they acted at the interface of work and family, because they managed to have both family and career. Being 'successful' (for women) meant being simultaneously successful in work and family. Male trainees assembled positive/negative traits in composite role models based on same-sex observations (other men): no matter how heterogeneous a composite is, gender identification is a must. This is the reason gender identification is not present in male narratives, since they have plenty of men to use as proto-models and, therefore, the focus is on traits/actions, "how would I like to act?" However, women did not construct same-sex composite role models: gender identification is a basis, but they do not have enough proto-models, since the few women who work close to them were not chosen, and this left only a few women that they admire at a distance. This led the author to conclude that "modelling requires closeness in order to see that people are worthy of admiration but it demands distance in order to keep admiring them" (Eriksson-Zetterquist, 2008, p. 268). Therefore, women perform cross-sex idealisations with same-sex idealisations of women who are not close to them.

Finally, it seems that the construction of role models might change in the course of socialisation. Eriksson-Zetterquist (2008) points out that the female trainees did not appear to appreciate the gender aspects of role models initially, but organisational experience led them to understand the relevance of gender identification in role modelling. Therefore, it turns out that women are more sensitive than men to the presence of same-gender role models, particularly within masculine professional occupations, notwithstanding the foregoing warning about avoiding a liberal feminist perspective or a narrow understanding of the role-modelling process.

Role modelling and emotional arousal

Emotional arousal implies positive or negative judgements about one's own personal psychological state when confronting a situation (Bandura et al., 1961). Recent theorising on identity processes has emphasised the importance of considering emotions, as people put 'their identities on the line' when they interact with others (Turner, 2013). Whether an 'ideal' or 'ought' self is used as a 'standard' against which to compare also determines the different degree of emotion that may arise (Radu and Loué, 2008). Role models who embody an 'ideal self' have been found to more strongly impact self-efficacy and entrepreneurial intention than an 'ought self' (Radu and Loué, 2008).

Emotions and affect also explain what leads people to discard or retain 'provisional selves' (Ibarra, 1999). They serve as 'markers of inadequacy' in role performances, telling individuals whether their performances are acceptable (Turner, 2013). If an individual experiences negative emotions as a result of a discrepancy between behaviour and self-conceptions when engaging in the role-modelling process, he or she may subsequently decide to abandon the pursuit of this particular identity. On the other hand, if positive feedback is provided, the role modelling may confirm a 'provisional self' with which the individual is experimenting, allowing an entrepreneurial identity to be seized and assumed.

Women who have entrepreneurial mothers might experience positive emotional arousal when considering this career path. Indeed, children of successful women entrepreneurs have a higher preference for entrepreneurship than those who have not had this role-model effect (Brennan, Morris and Schindehutte, 2003). In the same line, Greene, Han and Marlow (2013) showed how self-employed mothers disconfirm masculinised stereotypes (having a counter-stereotypical effect) and so act as positive role models for their daughters to become self-employed. The overall evidence suggests that the stereotypical views of the cohort member's mother affect the cohort member as she grows up and, indirectly, go on to influence her self-employed status, which is far more common when growing up with non-stereotypical views promoting equal opportunities.

Role modelling outcomes: self-efficacy and identity

Individuals are constantly exposed to discourses, for example, about what it takes to be a successful leader, and this might produce in them the idea/image of what it is to be a successful leader. Only if the person consciously or unconsciously models his/her behaviour on such an image, desiring to be perceived similarly to the model, can it be said that the process of role modelling has taken place (Eriksson-Zetterquist, 2008). Behaviour modelling is attained through an increase of self-efficacy and reaffirming an identity once constructed.

Self-efficacy

Entrepreneurial self-efficacy (ESE) is a construct that measures a person's belief in his or her ability to successfully launch an entrepreneurial venture (McGee et al., 2009) and is considered a particularly important antecedent to new venture intentions (Barbosa et al., 2007; Boyd and Vozikis, 1994; Zhao, Seiber and Hills, 2005). According to Bandura et al. (1961), modelling helps individuals increase their self-efficacy through observational learning, but it can also increase through mastery experiences, social persuasion and emotional arousal.

Bosma et al. (2012) affirm the importance of role models for entrepreneurship since half of their study respondents had a role model in the pre-start up and post-start-up stage, with the majority relying on the same role model in these two stages. This was particularly the case for those who were creating their first venture. Students should be exposed to role models as part of entrepreneurship program participation, whether 'real', in-class personal visits or 'fictional' case study protagonists. Entrepreneurship students highly value role models who involve them in professional activities, employ them in the business or discuss business issues with them (Van Auken, Fry and Stephens, 2006). Consistent with both social learning and role-identification theory, the most important function of role models is 'learning by example', although 'learning by support', 'increasing entrepreneurial self-efficacy' and 'inspiration/motivation' are also perceived as important functions. As mentioned, individuals learn in a social context by observing those with whom they can identify and who perform well in an area in which they wish to be involved. Therefore, the identification of role models helps individuals define their sense of self and enhance their self-efficacy in order to engage in entrepreneurship.

Previous literature has signalled that ESE represents a key stumbling block for women, limiting their ultimate career choices and leading them to shun entrepreneurial endeavours because of their lack of confidence in their abilities and skills (Chen, Greene & Crick, 1998). Even among women who have chosen a management career path and are actively pursuing an MBA, gender differences in entrepreneurial self-efficacy persist. Women exhibit lower entrepreneurial self-efficacy (ESE) than men and report stronger effects of entrepreneurship education on their ESE (Wilson, Kickul and Marlino, 2007). After being exposed to role-model profiles, one's identification with the model and the success of the respective role model influence the pre-founding process distinctively, with these effects found to be more significant for women (Geissler and Zanger, 2013).

Identity

Individuals experiment by acting out different behaviours, effectively 'trying on provisional selves' to see which behaviours best fit and match with their self-conception and desired possible self (Ibarra, 1999). They engage in a process of observing role models, experimenting by imitating certain behaviours and attributes of their selected models and then assessing the outcomes of their experimental acts. Their 'provisional selves' are validated and verified (or not), and this feedback determines the continuation (or discontinuation) of the target behaviour. Individuals verify their sense of self in the eyes of others (Turner, 2013).

Biological sex is culturally linked to a stereotypical construction of gender, with "gender role prescribed behaviour" being very important for final expressed behaviours. In considering socially prescribed attributes for men and women, androgynous individuals (those punctuating high in both masculinity and femininity scales) must also be accounted for (Bem, 1974, 1981). Androgyny is a balanced psychological behaviour that combines the social behaviour of both genders; the androgynous individual can access both behaviour patterns depending on the situational necessity without being constrained by socially dictated gender-stereotypical behaviour. Gartzia et al. (2012) observe that androgynous persons, in comparison with those with stereotyped identities (instrumental masculine and expressive feminine), have higher levels of emotional intelligence. Emotional intelligence can be defined as the ability of individuals to understand and regulate their own emotions, perceive the emotions of others and use them to achieve their goals. This ability has been found to create value in business by developing win-win situations (Foo, Elfenbein, Tan and Aik, 2004). These individuals are flexible in order to adapt to changing environments that present continuous challenges. This can explain why women in their construction of role models go beyond sex differences, looking for less-stereotyped referents of gender identity. They refer to women who have the ability to manage personal and professional lives simultaneously *and* use cross-sex trait idealisation in composing their models (Gibson and Cordova, 1999; Eriksson-Zetterquist, 2008; Kelan and Mah, 2014).

Along this line, Martin, Wright, Beaven and Matlay (2015) observe that due to their 'unusual' status, female entrepreneurs in scientific, engineering and technology (SET) sectors engage in a continual process of adjustment to cope with the perceptual tendencies of 'visibility, contrast and assimilation' (Kanter, 1993). In order to overcome the limited opportunities for women in traditional SET roles, participants perceived assimilation in terms of becoming an 'honorary man', occasionally in attitude, but primarily via hard-earned proof of personal expertise. Similarly Kelan and Mah (2014) find that women MBA students believe that allowing emotion to enter the business realm is not necessarily a good business practice. Therefore, when engaging in role-model processing, women act to 'smooth out' potential inconsistencies between the characteristics of their female role model and those of the idealised business owner, despite provided evidence of their benefit. Subsequently, the development of a non-stereotyped identity can be encouraged in younger women, especially by male mentors (Ely, 1995).

Discussion: the construction of gender in the business realm – how it is and how it should be

We believe that researchers and policy makers alike need to be wary of focusing only on promoting more role models as best practice. Using more examples of individual successful women, without focusing on the message transmitted, conveys the idea that the system is not at fault, that opportunities are available, that boundaries are permeable, that the perception of barriers is overstated. At the same time, it places the responsibility on women's shoulders to try 'hard enough' to overcome their 'deficits' in attributes and behaviour to emulate those women. For example, many women entrepreneurial role models in the media raise the issue of successfully juggling work and life, promoting the 'mompreneur' label as a liberating force. Not only does this reinforce the (unobtainable) 'superwoman' image, it also fails to question the status quo of responsibilities for domestic labour. Rather than empowering women, this serves to reinforce the unequal division of labour and 'double shift' burden of home and child care that women disproportionately bear (Calas, Smircich and Bourne, 2009; Ahl, 2002). On the contrary, women role models should be individuals undertaking the entrepreneurship journey for the benefit of those who follow, removing any perceived ceilings with regards to their ability to achieve co-responsibility at home and their competence to compete in specific sectors and with a certain business dimension.

It is interesting to study the role-model figure, since it conveys a link among the macro-level discourse, the meso-level relational context and the micro-level cognitive processes of identity formation. At the macro level, Budgeon (2015) claims that 'choice feminism' is the new trend in feminism that reorients feminist politics towards assuming that feminism's role is to validate women's choices without passing judgement. Women's choices are located within a modern gender order associated with a form of femininity characterised as self-determining and 'empowered'. More recently, this 'empowerment' slogan has been associated with the freedom of (high profile, popular culture) women such as Kim Kardashian or Beyoncé Knowles to use and show their bodies as they see fit, thus blurring the lines between empowerment and sexual objectification by choice. Indeed this empowerment perspective fails to take into account how the relationship between femininity and choice has been complicated by changing social conditions, that is, how certain processes impact on the social organisation of gender. This macro-trend translates at the micro-level, where the individuated feminist subject contributes by reproducing the neoliberal mentality with a certain level of gender denial operating in today's post-feminist climate. In the work context, one clear example is how women managers have been found to rationalise disadvantage as the outcome of personal decisions, purposefully avoiding reference to gendered organisational practices that work against them (Simpson, Ross-Smith and Lewis, 2010). Some women business owners seek to conceal the gendered nature of entrepreneurship, actively avoiding being identified as different from the masculine norm (Lewis, 2006). In turn, this gender denial complicates doing research on role models, identification and entrepreneurship and uncovering the behavioural, cognitive and emotional aspects of the role-modelling process.

The social construction of gender in entrepreneurship permeates the cultural and social realms (informal institutions) but also institutions, policies, programs and laws (formal institutions). This influence is circular given that the actions carried out in the political realm, while they may explicitly be geared towards achieving equality, actually contribute to maintaining the status quo in the social construction of gender. While there seems to be a common goal among developed countries to advance an egalitarian position for women in business generally, there appear to be a few different approaches for improving gender-effective equality through the discourse of those women promoted as role models. First, some messages seem geared towards maintaining the social construction of gender; in these instances, women gain success by using feminised appeals from a position of submission. Another approach is engaging in a 'passive' disruption of the social construction of gender, that is, diminishing sex and gender as a factor in search of an egalitarian performance. Such an approach denies gender-related differences and promotes an illusion of a level playing field, which is just as damaging. Finally, a 'far-reaching' disruption of the social construction of gender "showing how many women have characteristics that are useful, though not valued, in business: emotion, empathy, resilience, intuition" has to be fostered within women entrepreneurs (Díaz-García and Welter, 2013).

Therefore, to achieve gender equality using role models, it is important to distil the gendered assessment of what is regarded as success, since this gendered message is crucial in the construction of role models. When men engage in cross-sex role modelling with more frequency, a higher level of equality can be achieved. The idea of a need for same-sex unique role models has to be changed for the idea that the composite character of role models is possible, even with cross-sex traits idealisation. Policy makers should concern themselves more with promoting a diverse and sufficient number of role models, with some closeness to the individuals. The 'what' traits/actions I would like to imitate are more important than the 'who' I would like to imitate, since rarely one person has all the traits that can be idealised.

In reaction to the biased (and dichotomised) construction of entrepreneurship, some researchers have called for recognition of the importance of a feminine approach to business. Business-owners need a mix of feminine and masculine attributes to engage successfully in entrepreneurship (Bird and Brush, 2002). Thus, one could argue for the importance of role models exhibiting both feminine and masculine approaches, that is, an androgynous identity. However, in practice, the male (or masculine) entrepreneurial norm seems to stubbornly linger. For example, we argue that emotion, which traditionally has been considered a female attribute within the private sphere, has to be taken into account in the business realm (Cardon, Foo, Shepherd, Wiklund, 2012). Some researchers recognise the importance of emotions at work (Hochschild, 1983) and the fact that entrepreneurship is an emotional journey, establishing the importance of affect in all stages of this process (Baron, 2008). Baron and Markman (2003) show that social competence – an entrepreneur's ability to use social skills to interact effectively with others – predicted firm performance. Emotional labour, efforts taken to achieve organisationally desired emotional expressions, has been found to be related to customer satisfaction (Tan, Foo, Chong and Ng, 2003) and positively influence venture capitalists' intentions to fund a business, although preparedness was more important (Chen, Yao and Kotha, 2009), controlling for the business idea and investors' characteristics (Cardon, Sudek and Miteness, 2009). Despite all of this evidence that emotions are positive when doing business, women have traditionally been criticised for being 'too emotional' to do business efficiently. Nevertheless, changing societal norms and the gendered practice of keeping business 'emotion free' appear to be ingrained in the business realm and in the literature.

In entrepreneurship, stereotypes have been found to influence aspirations and behaviours in achievement-oriented activities like evaluating new business opportunities, with women evaluating fewer opportunities than men do (Gupta, Goktan and Gunay, 2014). The theory of stereotype threat (Steele, 1997; Steele and Aronsson, 1995), proposes that a person can have a concern about confirming a negative stereotype of his/her social group, leading him or her to perform worse than abilities would suggest in the challenging situation and, thereby, confirming the entrenched stereotype. How can we invert this stereotype threat? By offering in-group models with counter-stereotypic behaviours that are capable of buffering stereotyped individuals from the adverse effect of stereotype threat (Marx and Goff, 2005). By emphasising the role of feminine attributes in entrepreneurship it is possible to alter the gender gap in opportunity evaluation (Gupta et al., 2014). Indeed, it is not the mere fact of genetic make-up that determines an individual's propensity to achieve as an entrepreneur, but the values attached to gendered characterisations of feminine and masculine stereotypes (Marlow and Patton, 2005). As suggested by Sealy and Singh (2010), both men and women have to change their stereotypical cognitive schema of gender in entrepreneurship, and this might be the key contribution of role models, but not in the current form.

Table 11.1 Suggested research questions on gender and role models

---

- Under what circumstances do women (and men) engage in cross-sex trait idealisation?
- When do women recognise the importance of same-gender identification?
- When are direct role models favoured over fictional ones?
- Which behavioural and symbolic outcomes do women obtain depending on the type of role model selected?
- Which traits and behaviours do women idealise from other women (i.e. strategies to find balance between family and work)? And which traits do they strive to avoid in their identity construction (negative role models)?
- How do fictional role models produce emotional arousal in young women leading to entrepreneurial intention?
- How do women benefit from role models to manage and negotiate the perceptual tendencies of 'visibility, contrast and assimilation' in male-dominated fields?

We thus call on researchers to address the important topic of role models. We propose that there is enough evidence to confirm that gender affects the role-modelling process and, therefore, research questions should centre on when and how this takes place. In Table 11.1, we offer some potential research questions that build on our theorising and above discussion.

Conclusions

Given the importance of role models in fostering young professionals' career aspirations, it is unsurprising that policy makers mobilise role-model participation in entrepreneurship training and support initiatives. An individual's exposure to role models is not produced in a vacuum but rather takes place in a cognitive and cultural context that, in turn, influences the dimension of his or her self-concept that is activated when observing these role models. We posit that our understanding of role models and their gendered nature in entrepreneurship is broadened by simultaneously considering both social learning theory (and entrepreneurial self-efficacy) and role identification theories (influencing the identity-formation processes). Using symbolic interactionism as the dialectic between the two – internal self-identity and external social identity – is especially important in terms of furthering understanding.

Individuals have been found to be inspired by leaders of their gender in their professions, and role models are particularly important for under-represented groups in the labour market. Women's presence in positions of power positively affects the social construction of gender and the processes that create gender identity at work. However, we need to pay more attention to the role models available and the role-modelling process. In sum, it is not enough to expose cases of 'successful women' if what they say and how they participate in the entrepreneurial realm does not help to challenge the gender stereotypes that still pervade in the business realm. It is important to offer role models exhibiting both feminine and masculine approaches to counteract stereotypical cognitive schema of gender in entrepreneurship. Besides this, role modelling has to be understood as a process (which traits would I would like to have?) rather than focusing on the specific actual persons who are selected as role models. Both men and women are capable of doing cognitive operations of cross-sex idealisation of certain traits and construct a composite role model, although it still seems to be a must that this model is based on gender identification.

We conclude by sounding a call to entrepreneurship researchers, and particularly those interested in gendered aspects of entrepreneurship, to pursue this promising line of research.

We also invite policy makers to examine and address the complexity of role models in entrepreneurship and to appreciate that promoting women's entrepreneurship is more than just a numbers game.

References

Achtenhagen, L. and Welter, F. (2011). "'Surfing on the ironing board' the representation of women's entrepreneurship in German newspapers", *Entrepreneurship and Regional Development*, 23 (9), 763–786.

Ahl, H. (2002). *The Making of the Female Entrepreneur: A Discourse Analysis of Research Texts on Women's Entrepreneurship*. Sweden: Jönköping International Business School.

Ahl, H. (2006). "Why Research on Women Entrepreneurs Needs New Directions", *Entrepreneurship Theory and Practice*, 30 (5), 595–621.

Akerlof, G.A. and Kranton, R.E. (2000). "Economics and identity". *The Quarterly Journal of Economics*, 115 (3), 715–753.

Bandura, A. (1997). *Self-Efficacy: The Exercise of Control*. New York: Freeman.

Bandura, A. (1977). *Social Learning Theory*. Englewood Cliffs, NJ: Prentice-Hall.

Bandura, A., Ross, D. and Ross, S. A. (1961). "Transmissions of Aggressions through Imitation of Aggressive Models", *Journal of Abnormal and Social Psychology*, 63 (1), 575–582.

Barbosa, S., Gerhardt, M. and Kickul, J. (2007): "The Role of Cognitive Style and Risk Preference on Entrepreneurial Self-Efficacy and Entrepreneurship Intentions", *Journal of Leadership and Organizational Studies*, 13 (4), 86–104.

Baron, R. and Markman G., (2003). "Beyond Social Capital: The Role of Entrepreneurs' Social Competence in Their Financial Success", *Journal of Business Venturing*, 18 (1).

Baron, R.A. (2008). "The Role Of Affect In The Entrepreneurial Process". *Academy of Management Review*, 33 (2), 328 – 340.

Bem, S. (1974). "The Measurement of Psychological Androgyny", *Journal of Consulting and Clinical Psychology*, 42 (2), 155–162.

Bem, S. (1981). *Bem Sex Role Inventory. Professional Manual*. 1st ed. Palo Alto, CA: Consulting Psychologist Press, Inc.

Bird, B. and Brush, C.G. (2002). "A Gendered Perspective on Organizational Creation". *Entrepreneurship Theory and Practice*, 26 (3), 41–65.

Bosma, N., Hessels, J., Schutjens, V., van Praag, M. and Verheul, I. (2012). "Entrepreneurship and Role Models", *Journal of Economic Psychology*, 33 (2), 410–424.

Boyd, N. and Vozidis, G. (1994). "The Influence of Self-Efficacy on the Development of Entrepreneurial Intentions and Actions", *Entrepreneurship Theory and Practice*, 18 (4), 63–67.

Brennan, C., Morris, M. and Schindehutte, M. (2003). "Entrepreneurs and Motherhood: Impacts on Their Children in South Africa and the United States", *Journal of Small Business Management*, 41 (1).

Brockhaus, R. H., Sr.. & Horwitz. P. S. (1986). "The Psychology of the Entrepreneur". In D. L. Sexton & R. W. Smilor (Eds), *The Art and Science of Entrepreneurship*, pp. 25–48. Cambridge, MA: Ballinger.

Budgeon, S. (2015). "Individualized Femininity and Feminist Politics of Choice", *European Journal of Women's Studies*, 1–16.

Buunk, A. P. and Gibbons, F. X. (2007). "Social Comparison: The End of a Theory and the Emergence of a Field", *Organizational Behaviour and Human Decision Processes*, 102 (1), 3–21.

Calas, M., Smircich L. and Bourne K. (2009), "Extending the Boundaries: Reframing 'Entrepreneurship as Social Change' through Feminist Perspectives", *Academy of Management Review*, 34 (3), 552–569.

Cardon, M.S., Foo, M.D., Shepherd, D., & Wiklund, J. (2012). "Exploring the Heart: Entrepreneurial Emotion Is a Hot Topic", *Entrepreneurship Theory and Practice*, 36 (1), 1–10.

Cardon, M. S., Sudek, R. and Mitteness, C. (2009). "The Impact of Perceived Entrepreneurial Passion on Angel Investing", *Frontiers of Entrepreneurship Research*, 29 (2), Article 1.

Chen, C. C., Greene, P. G., Crick, A. (1998). "Does Self-Efficacy Distinguish Entrepreneurs from Managers?" *Journal of Business Venturing*, 13, 295–316.

Chen, X., Yao, X., & Kotha, S.B. (2009). "Passion and Preparedness in Entrepreneurs' Business Plan Presentations: A Persuasion Analysis of Venture Capitalists' Funding Decisions", *Academy of Management Journal*, 52 (1).

Díaz-García, C. and Welter, F. (2013). "Gender Identities and Practices: Interpreting Women Entrepreneurs' Narratives", *International Small Business Journal*, 31 (4), 384–403.

Ely, R. (1994). "The Effects of Organizational Demographics and Social Identity on Relationships among Professional Women", *Administrative Science Quarterly*, 39 (2), 203–238.

Ely, R. J. (1995). "The Power in Demography: Women's Social Constructions of Gender Identity at Work", *Academy of Management Journal*, 38 (3), 589–634.

Eriksson-Zetterquist, U. (2008). "Gendered Role Modelling. A Paradoxical Construction Process", *Scandinavian Journal of Management*, 24 (3), 259–270.

Fisher, B. (1988). "Wandering in the Wilderness: The Search for Women Role Models Signs". *Journal of Women in Culture and Society*, 13 (2), 211–233.

Foo, M. D., Elfenbein, H. A., Tan, H. H. and Aik, V. C. (2004). "Emotional Intelligence and Negotiation: The tension between creating and claiming value", *International Journal of Conflict Management*, 15 (4), 411 – 429.

Fuegen, K., Biernat, M., Haines, I., & Deaux, K. (2004). "Mothers And Fathers in the Workplace: How Gender and Parental Status Influence Judgments of Job-Related Competence", *Journal of Social Issues*, 60 (4), 737–754.

Gartzia, L., Aritzeta, A., Balluerka, N. and Barberá, E. (2012). "Inteligencia emocional y género: más allá de las diferencias sexuales", *Anales de Psicología*, 28 (2), 567–575.

Geissler, M. and Zanger (2013). "Factors on the Perception of Entrepreneurial Opportunities and Their Influence on Entrepreneurial Intention - An Empirical Study", ICSB World Conference.

Gibson, D. E. (2004): "Role Models in Career Development: New Directions for Theory and Research", *Journal of Vocational Behaviour*, 65 (1), 134–156.

Gibson, D. E. (2006). Editors' Introduction, in Jeffrey H. Greenhaus & Gerard A. Callanan (Eds), *Encyclopedia of Career Development*. Thousand Oaks, CA: Sage Publications.

Gibson, D. E. and Cordova, D. (1999). "Women's and Men's Role Models: The Importance of Exemplars". In A. J. Murrel, F. J. Crosby and R. J. Ely (eds), *Mentoring Dilemmas: Developmental Relationships within Multicultural Organizations*.Mahwah, NJ: Erlbaum, pp. 121–142.

Greene, F. J., Han, L, and Marlow, S. (2013). "Like Mother, Like Daughter? Analyzing Maternal Influences upon Women's Entrepreneurial Propensity", *Entrepreneurship Theory and Practice*, 37 (4), 687–711.

Gupta, V, Goktan, A. and Gunay, G. (2014). "Gender Differences in Evaluation of New Business Opportunity: A Stereotype Threat Perspective", *Journal of Business Venturing*, 29 (2), 273–288.

Hamilton, E. (2013). "The Discourse of Entrepreneurial Masculinities (and Femininities)", *Entrepreneurship and Regional Development*, 25, 1–2, 90–99.

Hancock, C., Pérez-Quintana, A. & Hormiga, E. (2014). "Stereotypical Notions of the Entrepreneur: An Analysis from a Perspective of Gender", *Journal of Promotion Management*, 20 (1), 82–94.

Haslam, S. A. (2004). "Leadership". In A. Kuper and J. Kuper (eds), *The Social Science Encyclopedia* (3rd ed., 566–568), New York: Routledge.

Higgins, E. T. (1984). "Self-Discrepancy: A Theory Relating Self and Affect", *Psychological Review*, 94, 319–340.

Hisrich, R. D. & Brush, C. (1984). "The Woman Entrepreneur: Management Skills and Business Problems". *Journal of Small Business Management*, 22, 1, 30–37.

Hochschild, A. R., (1983). *The Managed Heart: Commercialization Of Human Feeling*. Berkeley: University of California Press.

Hochschild, A. and Machung, A. (1990). *The Second Shift*. New York: Avon Books.

Ibarra, H. (1999). "Provisional Selves: Experimenting with Image and Identity in Professional Adaptation", *Administrative Science Quarterly*, 44 (4), 764–791.

Kanter, R. M. (1993). *Men and Women of the Corporation*. New York: Basic Books.

Kelan, E. K. and Mah, A. (2014). "Gendered Identification: Between Idealization and Admiration", *British Journal of Management*, 25 (1), 91–101.

Klyver, K., Nielsen, S. L. & Evald, M. R. (2013). "Women's Self-Employment: An Act of Institutional (Dis)integration? A Multilevel, Cross-Country Study". *Journal of Business Venturing*, 28 (4), 474–488.

Krueger, N. F. (1996). "The Cognitive Infrastructure of Opportunity Emergence", *Entrepreneurship Theory and Practice*, 24 (3), 5–24.

Krueger, N. F. and Brazeal, A. (1993). "Entrepreneurial Intentions: Applying the Theory of Planned Behaviour", *Entrepreneurship and Regional Development*, 5, 316–330.

Laviolette, E. M., Lefebvre, M. R. and Brunel, O. (2012). "The Impact of Story Bound Entrepreneurial Role Models on Self-Efficacy and Entrepreneurial Intention", *International Journal of Entrepreneurial Behaviour and Research*, 18 (6), 720–742.

Lewis, K. V. (2015). "Enacting Entrepreneurship and Leadership: A Longitudinal Exploration of Gendered Identity Work". *Journal of Small Business Management*, 53, 662–68.

Lockwood, P. (2006). "Someone Like Me Can Be Successful: Do College Students Need Same-Gender Role Models?", *Psychology of Women Quarterly*, 30 (1), 36–46.

Lockwood, P. and Kunda, Z. (1997). "Superstars and Me: Predicting the Impact of Role Models on the Self". *Journal of Personality and Social Psychology*, 73 (1), 91–103.

Lockwood, P., Marshall, T. and Sadler, P. (2005). "Promoting Success or Preventing Failure: Cultural Differences in Motivation by Positive and Negative Role Models", *Personality and Social Psychology Bulletin*, 31, 379.

Marlow, S. and Patton, D. (2005). "All Credit to Men? Entrepreneurship, Finance and Gender", *Entrepreneurship Theory and Practice*, 29 (6), 717–735.

Martin, L., Wright, L., Beaven, Z., & Matlay, H. (2015). "An Unusual Job for a Woman? Female Entrepreneurs in Scientific, Engineering and Technology Sectors". *International Journal of Entrepreneurial Behavior & Research*, 21 (4), 539–556.

Marx, D. M. & Goff, P. A. (2005). "Clearing the Air: The Effect of Experimenter Race on Target's Test Performance and Subjective Experience". *British Journal of Social Psychology*, 44, 645–657.

McGee, J. E., Peterson, M., Mueller, S. L. and Sequeira, J. M. (2009). "Entrepreneurial Self-Efficacy: Refining the Measure". *Entrepreneurship Theory and Practice*, 33, 965–988.

Mead, G. H. (1934). *Mind, Self and Society: From the Standpoint of a Social Behaviourist*. In Morris, C. W. (Ed.), University of Chicago Press, Chicago.

Mitchell, J. R., Mitchell, R. K., Randolph-Seng, B. (2014). *Handbook of Entrepreneurial Cognition*. London, UK: Edward Elgar.

Mungai, E. and Velamuri, S. R. (2011). "Parental Entrepreneurial Role Model Influence on Male Offspring: Is It Always Positive and When Does It Occur?", *Entrepreneurship Theory and Practice*, 35 (2), 337–357.

Ogbor, J. O. (2000). "Mythicizing and Reification in Entrepreneurial Discourse: Ideology Critique of Entrepreneurial Studies", *Journal of Management Studies*, 37 (5), 605–635.

Ollila, S., Middleton, K. and Donnellon, A. (2012). "Entrepreneurial Identity Construction – What Does Existing Literature Tell Us?", Institute of Small Business and Entrepreneurship Conference 2012.

Petty, R. E., Fabrigar, L. R. and Wegener, D.T. (2003). "Emotional Factors in Attitudes and Persuasion", in R. J. Davidson, K. R. Scherer, H. H. Goldsmith (Eds), *Handbook of Affective Sciences*. New York: Oxford University Press, 752–772.

Radu, M. and Loué, C. (2008). "Motivational Impact of Role Models as Moderated by "Ideal" vs "Ought Self-Guides" Identifications", *Journal of Enterprising Culture*, 16 (4), 441–465.

Ridgeway, C. L., & Correll, S. J. (2004). "Motherhood as a Status Characteristic". *Journal of Social Issues*, 60 (4), 683–700. doi:10.1111/j.0022-4537.2004.00380.x.

Rosselli, F., Skelly, J. J. and Mackie, D. M. (1995). "Processing Rational and Emotional Messages: The Cognitive and Affective Mediation of Persuasion", *Journal of Experimental Social Psychology*, 31 (2), 163–190.

Scherer, R. F., Adams, J. S., Carley, S. S. & Wiebe, F. A. (1989). "Role Model Performance Effects on Development of Entrepreneurial Career Preference", *Entrepreneurship Theory & Practice*, Spring, 53–71.

Sealy, R. (2007). "Relational Identity and Identification: The Importance of Senior Female Role Models", *British Academy of Management Conference*, Warwick, September.

Sealy, R. and Singh, V. (2010). "The Importance of Role-Models and Demographic Context for Senior Women's Work Identity Development", *International Journal of Management Reviews*, 12 (3), 284–300.

Shapiro, E., Haseltine, F. and Row, M. (1978). "Moving Up: Role Models, Mentors and the "Patron System"", *Sloan Management Review*, 6 (1), 19–47.

Simpson, R., Ross-Smith, A., and Lewis, P. (2010). "Merit, Special Contribution and Choice: How Women Negotiate between Sameness and Difference in Their Organizational Lives", *Gender in Management: An International Journal*, 25 (3), 198 – 207.

Singh, V., Vinnicombe, S. & Turnbull, J. K. (2006). "Constructing a Professional Identity: How Young Female Managers Use Role Models", *Women in Management Review*, 21 (1), 67–81.

Steele, C.M. (1997). "A Threat in the Air: How Stereotypes Shape Intellectual Identity and Performance", *American Psychologist*, 56 (6), 613–629.

Steele, C. M., & Aronson, J. (1995). "Stereotype Threat and the Intellectual Test Performance of African-Americans". *Journal of Personality and Social Psychology*, 69, 797–811.

Tan, H. H., Foo, M. D., Chong, C. L. and Ng, R. (2003). "Situational and Dispositional Predictors of Displays of Positive Emotions", *Journal of Organizational Behaviour*, 24, 961–978.

Turner, J, (2013). *Contemporary Sociological Theory*, Sage Publications, University of California, Riverside, US.

Van Auken, H., Fry, F. L. and Stephens, P. (2006). "The Influence of Role Models on Entrepreneurial Intentions", *Journal of Developmental Entrepreneurship*, 11 (2), 157–167.

Watson, T. J. (2008). "Managing Identity: Identity Work, Personal Predicaments and Structural Circumstances", *Organization*, 15 (1), 121–143.

West, C. and Zimmerman, D. H. (1987). "Doing Gender", *Gender and Society*, 1 (2), 125–151.

Wilson, F., Kickul, J. and Marlino, D. (2007). "Gender, Entrepreneurial Self-Efficacy, and Entrepreneurial Career Intentions: Implications for Entrepreneurship Education", *Entrepreneurship Theory and Practice*, 31 (3), 387–406.

Zhao, H.; Seibert, S. E.; Hills, G. E. (2005). "The Mediating Role of Self-Efficacy in the Development of Entrepreneurial Intentions", *Journal of Applied Psychology*, 90 (6), 1265–1272.

12

FEMALE ENTREPRENEURSHIP, ROLE MODELS AND NETWORK EXTERNALITIES IN MIDDLE-INCOME COUNTRIES

Maria Minniti

Introduction[1]

Across the world, the last two decades have witnessed a remarkable improvement in the educational accomplishments of women, even in economies where the gender gap is still widest and women face significant institutional constraints (Bae et al., 2014). Considering the phenomenal rise in women's education, and the dramatic fall in fertility, one would expect female participation in public life to be increasing. And yet, across all countries (albeit to different degrees), the participation of women in all aspects of economic life is still lagging behind that of men and, more importantly, it does not match their educational achievements (for example, see Majbouri, 2015).

In recent years, women around the world have made substantial progress in health, education and participation in the labor force. Women have made significant progress also in the context of new business creation where they are participating in startup activities in increasing numbers. For example, using the most recent wave of GEM data for more than 80 countries, Kelley et al. (2015) have found that although substantial differences exist in women's early-stage entrepreneurial activity, participation rates are highest in Nigeria and Zambia with 41%, and that in Brazil, El Salvador, Ghana, Indonesia, Malaysia, Nigeria, the Philippines, Vietnam, Uganda and Zambia no significant difference exists between the participation rates of men and women. Furthermore, Kelley et al. (2015) found that in Latin America and the Caribbean, Africa and many Asian countries in the study, no significant differences in entrepreneurial intentions seem to emerge across gender.

A significant amount of evidence exists that role models and networks play a significant role in fostering female entrepreneurship in middle-income economies (Kelley et al., 2015). Following the widely accepted definition of the World Bank, middle-income (or developing) countries are defined as economies exhibiting a per capita Gross National Income of more than $1,045 but less than $12,736. Importantly, no sufficient evidence exists that role models and networks play a similarly important role in the poorest countries or in situations characterized by conflict or socio-political unrest. While intuition suggests that this is likely to be even more true in such cases, more work is necessary to determine the characteristics, roles and challenges of role models and networks in such situations. As a result, the argument presented in this paper will focus on middle-income countries only.[2]

In spite of significant improvement in early nascent female entrepreneurship, middle-income countries still show rates of established female business activity (businesses that have survived for at least three and a half years) that are about half of their nascent activity counterparts. This suggests that, unfortunately, in spite of very positive signs with respect to entrepreneurial intentions and gestation activities, comparatively fewer women-led enterprises make it to the mature stage. Importantly, and somewhat surprisingly, Kelley et al. (2015) also find that starting a business with a team is particularly rare among women in middle-income countries, on average, only 7% in Asia, and 11% in Africa and the Middle East. As a result, while very important for their communities, women entrepreneurs still face serious challenges in growing and sustaining their businesses.

Formal and informal institutions are a big part of the problem. In many countries, women do not have the same rights enjoyed by men, and even when some relevant institutional constraints are relaxed, the visible participation of women in economic life is neither easy nor quick to develop (Bekele and Worku, 2008; Field et al., 2010). Within this context, a sizable amount of literature has pointed out the relationship between the presence of appropriate social capital and the emergence of female entrepreneurship (Poon et al., 2012). Indeed, all human action is embedded in social relationships that determine and legitimize what is acceptable or desirable (Zukin and DiMaggio, 1990). By observing and interacting with other individuals, human beings acquire information and skills. This web of interactions is usually referred to as a person's social capital and provides cues and resources for action, influences decisions and legitimizes activities (Coleman, 1990; Walker et al., 1997).

Importantly, while all individuals are affected by the available social capital, women are particularly influenced by it because of their tendency to be less mobile and more reliant on localized information and networks (Allen et al., 2006). In certain regions, for example, women may lack knowledge about the activities necessary to enter and succeed in the labor force. Also, because of institutional constraints, women more than men may lack the skills and tools necessary to cope with ambiguity, particularly in middle-income contexts (Majbouri, 2015). As a result of women's tendency to exhibit limited mobility, and human beings' heavy reliance on social cues, I argue that the emergence of social capital conducive to women's participation in entrepreneurship (in all its forms) is particularly dependent on the presence of strong role models.

At the aggregate level, the effect of role models may be thought of as being produced by network externalities. A network externality exists when the action of one person influences (positively or negatively) the actions of others. Because of network externalities, the perceived returns to any particular action increase with respect to adoption (Minniti, 2005). In other words, the more people have already performed an action, the lower the opportunity costs (both tangible and intangible) become for any additional person who decides to repeat it. Thus, everything else being the same, the larger the number of role models a woman observes, the lower the ambiguity she experiences with respect to entrepreneurship. Notwithstanding the institutional constraints that may be imposed on women in any country or community, the participation of women in entrepreneurship is a grass-roots phenomenon in which women themselves create a "culture" of their own influence and position in society to be embraced and followed by other women.

Importantly, while the availability of male role models has a positive influence, studies on homophily and the relationship between role models and self-efficacy support the thesis that gender homophily is an important aspect of a role model's effectiveness. In fact, empirical evidence shows that individuals and their role models tend to be similar in terms of gender and race (Ruef et al., 2003). In particular, gender homophily has been found in various contexts, such as large organizations (Kalleberg et al., 1996), networks (Ibarra, 1992) and voluntary organizations (McPherson and Smith-Lovin, 1987). Within the context of entrepreneurship, homophily has been shown to play a role also in entrepreneurial teams and networks (Ruef et al., 2003).

Female role models, however, may not exist or may be hard to identify. Also, as mentioned earlier, their paucity may be especially pronounced in middle-income countries or in socio-political contexts characterized by high instability. I argue that in these situations, personal networks may substitute for role models and provide the ambiguity-reducing environment and higher legitimacy leading to increased entrepreneurial activity. Unlike role models, who need to emerge organically and be legitimized by a community, personal networks can be developed in a shorter period of time and more easily from a policy perspective. Thus, the creation of networks is a necessary, though not sufficient, condition for the emergence of female entrepreneurship. Indeed, the existence, depth and size of women's networks have been identified as important in explaining the gender gap in entrepreneurship since, over time, they lead organically to the emergence of role models. While personal networks influence decisions in a way that is distinctly different from that of role models, their effectiveness also hinges on the creation of a network externality that, by providing emotional and practical support to individuals, lowers the opportunity costs of specific actions.

In the remainder of the chapter, section 2 describes the emergence of sustainable entrepreneurial intentions and, I hope, startup activity as a bottom-up phenomenon relying on the presence of appropriate social capital. Section 3 highlights the function played by role models and discusses why they are important for women's entrepreneurial intentions and the mechanism by which role models influence decisions and provide incentives for others to become entrepreneurs. Section 4 reviews our understanding of female networks and discusses how and why networks may serve as substitutes for role models. Section 5 concludes and suggests avenues for further research.

Social capital and female entrepreneurial intentions

Entrepreneurship is a bottom-up phenomenon, meaning that it emerges at the intersection of the individual-opportunity nexus (Shane and Venkataraman, 2000; Shane, 2003). The ability of individuals to act upon perceived opportunities rests on the presence of a context that enables them to do so. Appropriate forms of social capital contribute to the creation of an environment conducive to entrepreneurship and even determine what type of entrepreneurship will emerge (Baumol, 1990).

Recent empirical studies of individual behavior have shown the particular importance of social capital for women and the existence of remarkably consistent differences in accessing it across genders. For example, using a large representative sample of men and women from a variety of countries, Allen et al. (2006) have shown that men (who have more role models and social connections than women do) tend to have a more optimistic perception of their abilities. To be distinctively conducive to women's participation, social capital needs to include equality of rights across genders and allow women to discover and exploit the opportunities they perceive. Indeed, it is now well known that some of the most effective programs aimed at increasing women's participation in public life emphasize the need for social capital that is specifically valuable for women and capable of providing resources leading to the emergence of role models (Allen et al., 2006). In other words, role models are a key component of the social capital available to individuals.

The concept of social capital has its roots in classical sociology. Early studies stressed the importance of developing the individual in social organizations (Burt, 1992). Later conceptualizations included not only social relationships among individuals, but also the shared norms and values associated with them (Walker et al., 1997). As a result, some critics have defined social capital as a concept that means too many things to too many people (For a critical discussion of the concept see Durlauf (2002)). To eliminate some of the confusion generated by such a variety, Adler and Kown (2002) summarized many of the definitions used in the literature by classifying them and distinguishing them on the basis of where social capital is assumed to reside. According to their classification, two main approaches can be identified.

The first approach considers social capital to be a resource lying in the interactions between individuals. Within the context of this first approach, Bourdieu (1986) defines social capital as the sum of the actual or potential resources necessary for the existence of a network of formal or informal relationships. That is, the first approach considers social capital to be an attribute of the individual rather than of the social structure and adopts an individual-based view in which individuals access social capital through their connections.

The second approach views social capital as the social structure of a group of individuals and the specific linkages that provide cohesiveness among them, thereby facilitating the achievement of shared goals. Within this context, Coleman (1990) describes social capital as consisting of the links between the human nodes of interactions in a group or between groups. In other words, according to Coleman, social capital exhibits four main characteristics. First, it has, at least in part, the characteristic of a public good in that it is not excludable (it is not a private property). Second, it is specific to a given society or group. Third, it has value only when individuals of a particular group or society actually use it for their activities. Fourth, it emerges from, and changes with, existing social structures (such as, for example, memberships or families). Thus, according to Coleman, social capital is an attribute of the social structure in which a person is embedded. It is not provided to individuals through the links in their social networks; rather, it is the links of such networks and it facilitates certain actions of the individuals who are within the structure.

Economists conceptualized social capital in a way consistent with Coleman's characterization. According to Becker (1996), for example, social capital takes the form of preferences developed through past experiences. In general, however, economists treat social capital as a resource capable of creating untraded interdependencies and of producing trust, thereby reducing transaction costs and encouraging sustainable cooperative behavior (Brüderl and Preisendörfer, 1988). Thus, social capital is viewed as a mixed-public good that provides simultaneously private and public benefits.

In this chapter, I view social capital as a resource and, within this context, Bordieu's and Coleman's approaches are clearly related and somewhat complementary. Specifically, Coleman's view seems more appropriate to describe a context where well-established social structures exist and are clearly defined. In fact, when such a context exists, social capital provides role models who are embedded in these social structures and are, as a result, perceived as relevant. Bordieu's view, on the other hand, seems to provide a good starting point to describe how social capital may emerge in contexts where social structures are changing or emerging as is the case for the women in the labor force in developing economies. In those situations, social structures are not clearly identifiable and, as a result, embedded and relevant role models may be harder to find. When individuals access social capital by leveraging their connections, they create networks that, at least to some extent, compensate for the absence of role models.

Role models and women's entrepreneurial behavior

The effect of role models on entrepreneurial intentions

Entrepreneurial orientation is not congenital; entrepreneurs are made. In fact, entrepreneurship is a cognitive category learned most effectively when role models are present. A significant amount of research in the social sciences has established the importance of role models for the development of entrepreneurship. In psychology, for example, Baron (2000) and Begley and Boyd (1987) have discussed the importance of role models because of their ability to enhance self-efficacy.

An important distinction must be made, however, between different types of role models, specifically between those who share the entrepreneur's context and those who do not. For example, while renowned entrepreneurs such as Oprah Winfrey may be influential in a developed context, they are unlikely to resonate as models of action in a developing country where their circumstances may be perceived as inapplicable. Role models are important because by reducing ambiguity, they increase the perceived returns to, and incentives for, a specific activity, entrepreneurship in our case. Nguyen (2008), for example, provides experimental evidence from Madagascar showing that exposing subjects to a role model (an actual person sharing his/her success story) makes a much more significant difference in convincing someone of the importance of education than providing even very compelling and credible statistics.

Indeed, since role models increase self-efficacy, it is not surprising that some degree of similarity should be present between the entrepreneur and the role model (at least in the perception of the entrepreneur) (Bosma et al., 2012). Without such similarity, it is difficult for the entrepreneur to perceive the behavior of the role model as compatible with its own perceived behavioral opportunities. As Bosma et al. (2012) note, there should be opportunities to learn from a role model, and this is more likely to happen when the role model is more highly qualified than its "user." Indeed, Kram and Isabella (1985) and Shapiro et al. (1978) have shown that role models often have higher hierarchical positions. In other words, women potentially interested in entrepreneurship are likely to respond to role models they can identify with but who have achieved what is perceived as a desirable position. This is also consistent with the homophily argument (Ruef et al., 2003; Ibarra, 1992) discussed in the Introduction, which states that potential female entrepreneurs are more likely to react positively to female role models.

Within this context, GEM data, for example, show that *personally* knowing other individuals who have started businesses is a very strong indicator of the likelihood that a person will also start a business. In fact, personally knowing other entrepreneurs has been shown to be highly correlated to entrepreneurial orientation (Langowitz and Minniti, 2007). However, as Figure 12.1 shows, across a large number of countries, fewer women than men know other people who have started a business or were in the process of starting one.

Specifically, Figure 12.1 shows the number of women compared to men who personally know someone who started a business in the two years preceding the GEM survey. Regardless of their country of origin, there are significantly fewer women than men who personally know someone who started a business although, as discussed in the Introduction, the trend is showing an improvement, especially in middle-income countries. These gender differences are statistically significant. The magnitude of these differences and their significance, however, is strongly reduced (and in some countries eliminated) when only women who are starting or have recently started a business are compared to their male counterparts. In

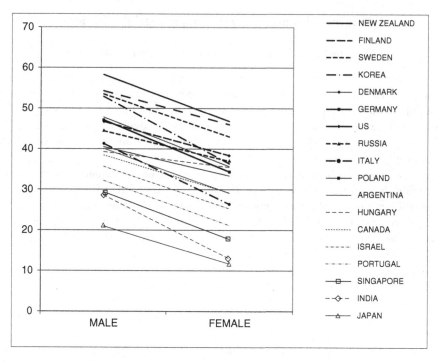

Figure 12.1 Percentage of surveyed individuals who personally know someone who started a business in the 2 years preceding the GEM survey by gender

Source: Global Entrepreneurship Monitor (GEM) data 2006.

other words, the GEM data used to construct Figure 12.1 suggest that the rates of early-stage entrepreneurial activity for men and women who know a comparable number of role models converge. Albeit merely descriptive, this evidence is consistent with the literature cited earlier and supports the suggestion that role models may be crucial factors in the decision to start a new venture.

As mentioned earlier, people learn by identifying with role models, experimenting with new identities, and assessing the results of such experiments against their own self-imposed standards and the acceptance they receive externally (Ibarra, 1999). Women, however, encounter few role models whose styles are feasible or congruent with their self-images (Ely, 1994; Ibarra, 1999). Compared to men, women who may aspire to becoming entrepreneurs face lower social support for learning how to credibly claim such a role. In addition, institutional constraints (sometimes as strong as laws and regulations, religious beliefs and family structures) often expose women to stronger stigmas than men and give them less latitude for experimentation (Bell and Nkomo, 2001). In turn, this increases women's opportunity costs (both tangible and intangible) of becoming visible and makes them more averse to failure (Kanter, 1977). Following a vicious cycle, the presence of few female entrepreneurs signals that being female disqualifies a person from such a role, perhaps because of inability to succeed. This, of course, further dampens the entrepreneurial intentions of women who may be interested in trying. The presence of role models counteracts these negative effects in at least two significant ways. First, the presence of role models reduces ambiguity by providing action paths that can be replicated. Second, the presence of role models increases the legitimacy of entrepreneurship, thereby reducing the social costs associated with it.

The mechanism by which role models influence decisions

How role models influence the behavior of individuals and, specifically, women, may be grasped by thinking about them as the source of externalities. We may call them perceptual externalities or, more commonly, network externalities. Fads and fashion, for example, are significantly influenced by network externalities. Similarly, in regions, countries or industries where many women are already involved, the concentration of women makes that environment more suitable for other women to follow.

The self-reinforcing nature of network externalities is at the root of the important effect exercised by role models in favoring the emergence of high female participation in entrepreneurship. This argument rests on the observation that when the number of women entrepreneurs is relatively large, more information about the characteristics, requirements, needs and rewards of women in a particular context is available and, usually, solutions are already available and have become almost a routine. The strength of the network externality is also a measure of the degree of interdependence among people. The relative strength of this interdependence, in turn, can be thought of as a bandwagon effect (Granovetter, 1978; Granovetter and Soong, 1983). In a bandwagon model, a community is defined as a set of individuals in which one agent's decision to adopt a certain behavior generates a positive feedback mechanism. The feedback mechanism provides information to new agents and encourages further adoptions. In this context, thresholds are used to account for the fact that individuals have different participation propensities and that each member will join in only if the bandwagon pressure exceeds the member's threshold. As a result, the extent of bandwagon diffusion depends on the distribution of thresholds across members as well as on the network of relations existing among members (see also Minniti, 2005).

Traditionally, bandwagon effects and network externalities have been studied using the mathematics of non-linear path-dependent processes. Also known as Polya processes, non-linear path-dependent processes have been used in social sciences since the early 1980s (Arthur, 1989; Kindleberger, 1983). In these dynamic systems, positive feedback causes certain patterns to be self-reinforcing. Of course there is a multiplicity of such patterns, and since these systems tend to be sensitive to early dynamic fluctuations, they are very well suited for describing how local externalities matter in determining the social make-up of a region. These models support also empirical findings showing the existence of non-linearities in social interdependence related to phenomena such as crime, youth drop-out rates, viral diseases, etc. (Crane, 1991; Gleaser et al., 1999). In general, non-linear path-dependent processes allow researchers to understand how the accumulation of decisions made by different individuals may push the dynamics of individuals' behavior into a pattern and, eventually, lock in the structure (Arthur, 1989). Although applicable to a variety of phenomena, this dynamic's pushing people into pre-established patterns implicitly illustrates why role models are conducive to increased rates of female participation in entrepreneurship.

Finally, it should be noted that network externalities can be both positive and negative in the sense that they can facilitate women's participation or inhibit it by creating a low-involvement trap. Positive externalities reduce transaction costs, information search costs and contract costs. This has a positive effect on women's choices because it reduces the risks of and need for experimentation. Negative externalities, on the other hand, can have a negative effect if they contribute to reinforcing routines and practices that prevent women from increasing their participation in entrepreneurship.

In the context of this chapter, positive network externalities are triggered by the presence of role models because the latter facilitate other women's exposure to opportunities that would not be easily available otherwise. In addition, role models reduce ambiguity and uncertainty and legitimize women's participation in entrepreneurship. Those effects, in turn, reduce the opportunity costs of choosing entrepreneurship above other behaviors. With their actions, role models create, develop, renovate and protect social capital. Thus, they are, at the same time, creators and users of social capital.

Women's networks as substitutes for role models

Women's networks and personal social capital

Under certain environmental conditions, namely in developing countries, role models are often hard to come by. It is possible, however, for other social structures (both formal and informal) to emerge and generate externalities that, to some extent, produce a reduction in ambiguity and an increase in legitimacy similar to those produced by role models. Indeed, when the appropriate social capital is lacking, the creation of networks may be a necessary, though not sufficient, alternative used to promote the participation of women in entrepreneurship—a phenomenon that, in turn, increases the amount of distinctively female social capital. Thus, as noted already in Section 2, role models fit organically in Coleman's (1990) and Becker's (1996) views of social capital as a semi-public good independent from any specific individual. Personal networks, instead, influence individuals' decisions via a process akin to Bourdieu's (1986) view where social capital is an attribute of the individual rather than the social structure, and individuals access it through their connections. Still, while the vehicle is different, the mechanism is in both cases a network externality. Because of the externality, the network provides the potential entrepreneur with emotional support and practical help and advice that, in turn, reduce the opportunity cost of starting a new venture. Importantly, this reduction in opportunity costs may be intangible (consisting of an improved perception of entrepreneurship) or tangible (consisting of practical help to defray startup costs).

Harper (2008) and Parker (2008) have discussed the importance of teams and formal networks, respectively, using an economics lens. In sociology, Aldrich (1999), among others, has discussed the role of personal networks and their ability to enhance confidence by providing advice, support and examples. Indeed, well-established literature exists on the importance of networks in general and among women in particular (see Aldrich, 1999, and Aldrich and Zimmer, 1986, among others). Also, general agreement exists that women, on average, have more limited access to networks than men and, in some cultures, have access to fewer social resources (Rosenthal and Strange, 2012).

From a historical perspective, the importance of women's networks has been established by the analysis of cornerstones focusing specifically on women that resulted in a significant increase in the number of women participating in organizations and entering the labor force (Goldin, 1990). For example, even in the context of developed countries such as the United States, the emergence of powerful networking groups of women entrepreneurs developed beginning with the Equal Credit Opportunity Act of 1975, the Affirmative Action Act of 1978 and the Glass Ceiling Commission of 1991. Similar trajectories are observed in the context of middle-income economies. For example, using the case of Pakistan, Azam-Roomi and Harrison (2008) found that women-only training programs helped significantly in overcoming the dichotomy between female entrepreneurial intentions and patriarchal societies. Specifically, their empirical findings show that training programs based on women's specific needs play an important role in improving the performance of women's ventures and also provide an opportunity to build self-esteem and confidence.

A related, albeit negative, example, comes from Jamali (2009) who found that in Lebanon, in addition to the serious economic recession and stagnation, the lack of access to distinct networks and specific government support was perceived by women entrepreneurs as one of the main causes of the gender gap in economic life. This is particularly significant considering that Lebanon is among the Arab countries that have allowed women to increasingly assume functions outside traditional family roles. Due to heavy male migration to oil-producing countries in the '80s and '90s, and the civil war in 1990, women were called to participate actively in the country's labor force. And yet, Lebanese women entrepreneurs felt disadvantaged by the lack of gender-specific business networks that would allow them to overcome their underrepresentation in network memberships and on the boards of almost all syndicates and chambers of commerce.

In general, the success of women-only programs can be attributed to shared practices targeted specifically to women's situational needs, a relationship-oriented approach, but, in particular, to the personal networking activities that created a bridge between local social capital and individual women. In fact, the networks women rely on tend to operate quite differently from the networks men rely on, and often, when talking about the paucity or narrowness of women's networks, discrimination is mentioned as a cause of the observed gender differences. Even within the labor market, for example, a division of labor exists that distributes men and women differently across different professions and, even within professions, assigns them different tasks. Unfortunately, however, discrimination is very difficult to document, and even harder to measure, especially in the context of middle-income economies where data are scarcer.

While institutional discrimination is a contributing factor (in some countries more than in others), Neumark and McLennan (1995) and Kanazawa (2005) have shown that a significant portion of gender differences in networking stems also from different family commitments, as well as gender segregation across work fields (fields that tend to employ women also tend to pay less). This argument is supported by the observation that women, as well as men, earn less in workplaces that predominantly employ women (Devine 1994a, 1994b). Along similar lines, Madichie (2009) provides some evidence that the relevance of the age-long glass ceiling may become questionable as women's career progression prospects in the corporate world are improving significantly, even in some African economies. Empirically, evidence about the root causes of differences between female and male networks is, unfortunately, much more difficult to document.

Using data from a large number of countries, Allen et al. (2006), for example, found important distinctions between the content and relevance of men's and women's networks and noted that women's networks were organized around spheres of work, family and social life. Their work showed that women's networks were largely similar to men's in terms of activity and density but that men's networks included very few women, whereas women's networks were more likely to include men. Women and men also use their networks differently. Whereas men's networks are homophilous (i.e., mostly men) and multipurpose, women tend to build functionally differentiated networks, obtaining instrumental access from men and friendship and social support from women (Ibarra, 1992). Men are better resourced, and women are easier to relate to on a personal level (Ragins and Kram, 2007).

Along similar lines, Lerner et al. (1995) showed that network affiliation, human capital and motivation were more effective at explaining women's performance than social learning or environmental theories. This is consistent with Greve and Salaff (2003), who found that women use their kin to a larger extent than men. In this area, of particular relevance are studies distinguishing between the influence of formal and informal networks (Aldrich,

1999). Unfortunately, although the importance of women's personal networks was studied already in the second half of the 1980s, few studies on the topic existed outside the United States. Women in middle-income countries, for example, often have significantly smaller networks and less geographic mobility (Kelley et al., 2015; Allen et al., 2006). As a result, as Chamlee-Wright (1997) showed for the case of Ghana, they construct relatively personal but strong social ties that allow them to substitute these personal network relationships for some of the formal legal contracts used to govern most business transactions.

Women's networks and the perception of self-efficacy

In general, women seem to forge egalitarian coalitions and long-term relationships based on affective ties, whereas men tend to form hierarchical coalitions and short-term relationships based on mutual interest and weak ties. Abell et al. (2001), for example, examined the link between social capital and the propensity of women to get involved in employment activity and noted that women seem to rely significantly on three types of networks. First, legitimizing networks, which consist of strong ties between a woman and others and confer legitimacy upon the individual's decision to become self-employed; second, opportunity networks, which consist of ties between the women and others who operate in industries offering entry opportunities; third, resource networks, which consist of relations between the individual and others who have the resources and appropriate human capital for entry. In line with the literature stressing the importance of role models emerging from networks, their work confirms that having self-employed friends has an impact on one's decision to become self-employed and highlights the externality that belonging to a network produces. Specifically, the externality produced by personal networks takes the form of an increase in self-efficacy generated by the emotional support and practical help provided by the other members.

Entrepreneurship is expressed in the way individuals address challenges and opportunities, and it is strongly associated with the perception of having control of one's actions and with self-efficacy. Self-efficacy refers to the subjective belief that one is capable of performing in a certain manner to attain certain goals (Bandura, 1997). Clearly, people will be more inclined to take on a task if they believe they can succeed. The stronger the self-efficacy, the more active the efforts, since people generally avoid tasks where their self-efficacy is low but will engage in tasks where their self-efficacy is high (Bandura, 1997; Zhao et al., 2005). Boyd and Vozikis (1994) too have shown that individual self-confidence, defined as a person's belief in her capability to perform a task, influences the development of both intentions and actions.

Batjargal et al. (2009) found the positive effect of networks on the revenue growth of new ventures to be stronger for male-owned than female-owned ventures and stronger in highly relationship-oriented economies such as China and most developing countries in South-East Asia. Along similar lines, Koellinger et al. (2013) found that, across all countries in their sample, a very strong positive and significant correlation exists between confidence in one's own skills and a woman's likelihood of starting a business, regardless of per capita GDP. A similar result holds for men as well. However, Koellinger et al. (2013) also found that the confidence in one's own skills was much higher in men than in women with otherwise similar characteristics.

Overall, this argument contributes to the body of literature on social network theory suggesting that the effects of networks are contingent upon social and cultural contexts. Social networks, as sources of business resources, advice and emotional support, are important in contexts where relationships are valued highly, and, as argued earlier in the chapter, this is more important in contexts where personal relationships (providing support) substitute for role models (who normally, by reducing ambiguity and increasing legitimacy) recue the opportunity costs of action. Indeed, research suggests that entrepreneurs not only discuss their ideas about starting new ventures with their family members, close friends and colleagues, but also receive emotional support in return (Reynolds and White, 1997). Such emotional support enhances the motivation and determination of entrepreneurs to build successful firms. Finally, emotional support networks are likely to generate greater psychic resources, i.e., ability to withstand stress created by sharp fluctuations in new venture performance and increased personal perseverance (Bayjargal et al., 2009).

GEM data are again useful as they can be used to highlight a basic difference between the self-efficacy attitudes of women and men when looking at patterns of business creation.

In Figure 12.2, perceptual differences between men and women appear systematically across all countries in the sample, with men exhibiting significantly higher confidence in their own skills, knowledge and ability to start a business. Clearly, Figure 12.2 provides again only descriptive evidence. Still, such evidence is consistent with additional empirical evidence showing that, everything else being the same, women tend to participate in fewer and narrower networks, to have fewer role models and to exhibit lower levels of self-efficacy. These three factors are highly correlated and, in turn, influence women's opportunity costs of participating in entrepreneurship.

Because of a preference to interact with individuals of the same sex, the composition and structure of men's and women's networks differ (Aldrich, 1999; Ibarra, 1992; McPherson et al., 2001). This, in turn, often influences women's ability to establish a credible identity. In general, the more prominent one's position, the less likely formally established routines apply

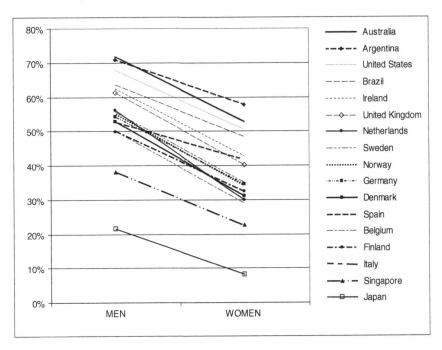

Figure 12.2 Percentage of surveyed individuals who thought of having the skills, knowledge and ability necessary to start a business by gender

and the more critical one's personal network becomes (Kanter, 1977). As a result, expanding the range of relational efforts and increasing their depth is a fundamental component of one's ability to start a business. Since women have access, on average, to fewer role models, it is more difficult for them to start a business. Personal networks, however, replicate many features of the social service provided by role models. Thus, personal networks are important because, by increasing the likelihood and speed of creating reputation and ultimately influence (Granovetter, 1985; Podolny and Baron, 1997), they too shape entrepreneurial trajectories.

Conclusions

The development of entrepreneurial intensions and capabilities is, at least to some extent, the result of a relational effort. In fact, entrepreneurship is an embedded phenomenon where embeddedness is defined as the contextualization of economic exchange in patterns of ongoing interpersonal relations that include cognitive, cultural and political embeddedness (Zukin and DiMaggio, 1990). In other words, entrepreneurs emerge in the context of a set of relationships with and among other individuals, and role models and networks (both formal and informal) play a key role in the process of becoming an entrepreneur.

Extant literature has identified the presence of role models as a key ingredient for the emergence of female entrepreneurship. Unfortunately, however, female role models may be lacking especially in middle-income countries since the latter are characterized by evolving social institutions and may lack the interpretive stability necessary for role models to emerge clearly and achieve sufficient visibility. This institutional fluidity makes networks a possible substitute for role models in middle-income countries. Like any other form of capital, social capital can be appropriated and converted into other forms. After appropriating capital, an individual (or group of individuals) can transform it into opportunities for advancement and change. From the individual's perspective, social capital is a resource only as far as one is able to actually use it and extract value from it. Within its context, social capital necessary to act entrepreneurially has a real positive value to women only if they have access to it and are able to use it to pursue their own goals. This, of course, does not happen overnight. In many cases, however, the initial development of social capital takes place within an exclusive network. Thus, women must first connect to a network.

In light of gender differences and the need to interact with both genders in a variety of contexts, women need to learn how to expand and deepen their networks by finding more occasions to interact with key players both internal and external to the networks themselves. Interestingly, as Ely et al. (2011) point out, women tend to be more reluctant to engage in networking activities because the latter are perceived as being analogous to "using people" (which has a negative connotation), as opposed to a way to convey a vision or exchange information (which has a positive connotation). Entrepreneurs, however, are required to communicate and negotiate on a routine basis. Thus, increased participation in networks helps women to understand that going beyond one's comfort zone is personally desirable and also necessary if one wants to succeed.

An increased perception of self-efficacy, defined as the perception of being able to determine one's destiny, tends to be associated with heightened entrepreneurial intentions (Minniti, 2005). Once the process of self-discovery and the perception of self-efficacy are triggered, history has shown us that women tend to be creative and resourceful in balancing work and life demands and are well able to integrate networking into daily activities (Minniti, 2009).

Because of the reinforcing effects of their externalities, networks help in various phases of the creation and development of skills necessary to create a virtuous cycle, which over time reinforces formal and informal institutions and creates additional social capital (as a form of public good). Each woman has a decisional threshold, namely the point at which her personal returns become positive, and she may decide to become involved in entrepreneurship. At any point in time, the sequence of individuals' decisions made on the basis of these thresholds determines the local amount of entrepreneurship. For any region, the involvement of a critical number of women represents the regional threshold, so that their involvement in public life becomes visible and causes more to become active and visible themselves.

Throughout this process, becoming an entrepreneur entails not only figuring out what to do and how to do it, but also positioning oneself to feel able to execute one's plan while understanding the potential sources of others' opposition. Women must come to see their own value and find ways to make it visible, learn how others have fared in similar circumstances and explore possible alternatives. Figure 12.1 and Figure 12.2 show that men have more access to role models and are more confident in their own skills than women across all countries in the sample. Those differences are significantly more pronounced in some countries than in others (the slopes of some country bars are steeper). These cross-country differences suggest that cultural, economic and social factors (that vary across countries) influence both the average prevalence rate of self-confidence with respect to starting a business and also the extent to which men and women exhibit differences in their self-perceptions (Koellinger et al., 2013).

Importantly, however, Kelley et al. (2015) found that, across all countries in the GEM sample, 46% of women believe they have the skills and knowledge necessary to start a business, compared to 59% of men. They found also that more than 50% of women in almost all economies in Africa and Latin America believe they have the skills and knowledge necessary to start a business, with Nigeria and Ghana showing almost equal self-reported rates for women and men. Finally, they found a number of Latin American and Caribbean economies, and Belize and El Salvador in particular, to exhibit low gender differentials, as well as the Philippines, Vietnam and Indonesia in Southeast Asia. These findings show a significant reduction in the gender gap over time.

A further important (and somewhat underappreciated) point, is that the phenomenon leading to the emergence of entrepreneurship shares significant commonalities with that leading to the emergence of leadership. In fact, akin to entrepreneurs, individuals who become visible in public life are also able to influence and change it (Ibarra, 1999). Of course, the criteria by which a community grants leadership status are shaped by culturally available ideologies about what it means to be a leader (Cohen and Bradford, 2005). In most cultures, this is associated with features such as one's ability to be decisive, assertive and independent, characteristics that are usually associated with men (Bailyn, 2006; Dennis and Kunkel, 2004). By contrast, women are thought of as being better suited to dealing with children or other situations in which patience and nurturing are seen as being relatively more important (Fletcher, 2004; Giscombe and Mattis, 2002). While these are certainly important tasks, they are often perceived as somewhat inconsistent with leadership roles in public life. Networks, on the other hand, provide scope and support for the development of leadership characteristics.

To sum up, developing women's capacity to become entrepreneurs is critical, as women often find themselves in highly uncertain environments where radical changes may be required. However, there is strength in numbers. This is why networks and the positive externalities they create matter. The involvement of women in entrepreneurship and as agents of change matters. It makes a difference for individuals, for communities, for international relations and, ultimately, for the sustainable growth of the economy.

Of course, an appealing trait of the argument presented in this chapter is the claim that, even in developing contexts, the establishment of personal networks may be a faster and more feasible way to foster female entrepreneurship than any government attempt to pick winners by setting up targeted subsidies or programs. Within this context, as discussed in the Introduction, some positive signs are already emerging. Kelley et al. (2015), for example, provide robust evidence based on GEM data showing that in many factor- and efficiency-driven economies in Africa, Asia and Oceania, more than half of the women in the populations already personally know someone who started a business. Albeit descriptive, these indicators signal that female entrepreneurial intentions in developing contexts are significantly on the rise. Similarly, some authors have argued that, by definition, entrepreneurial opportunities require specific and localized knowledge and that, as a result, government programs are unsuitable for identifying effective means to support entrepreneurs (Koppl, 2008). Clearly, finding out how women's personal networks can be fostered in a sustainable and unbiased way is beyond the scope of this chapter. Unfortunately, it is also far from easy.

This chapter argues that under these circumstances, the creation of local networks may provide a viable alternative, one that is less costly and more feasible from a policy point of view. Importantly, some evidence exists (and has been included in this chapter) that public programs targeting women specifically seem to contribute to the emergence of female entrepreneurship; the importance of network as a substitute for visible role models points toward the desirability of looking at the problem from bottom-up solutions that leverage local knowledge and long-term relationships. Thus, I argue in favor, of the "complexity frame" for policy, in which "policy makers have to continually think how to work with evolutionary pressures, and try to guide those pressures toward desirable ends. Within the complexity frame, top-down control actions are a last resort" (Colander & Kupers, 2014, p. 8). I believe this is one of the most promising and important venues for future research in this area, one that will identify which institutional structures and policy environments better enable women to discover opportunities for themselves. The specific structure of these options and their welfare profile fall outside the scope of any one chapter, but they are, of course, very important and provide additional venues for further research. I hope this work will provide an initial seed for further investigations.

Notes

1 The content of this chapter relies on previous and ongoing work by the author, in particular Minniti (2009, 2005) and Allen, Langowitz, and Minniti (2006).
2 The grouping of countries by Gross National Income (GNI) follows the World Bank Atlas method. Thus, for 2016, low-income economies are defined as those with a per capita Gross National Income of $1,045 or less in 2014, whereas middle-income economies are those with a per capita Gross National Income of more than $1,045 but less than $12,736. In turn, middle-income economies can be divided into lower-middle-income and upper-middle-income economies separated at a per capita Gross National Income of $4,125. Some examples of these countries are Albania, El Salvador, Ghana, Nigeria, Pakistan, the Philippines, and Vietnam. All examples mentioned explicitly in the text are drawn from middle-income economies.

References

Abell, P., R. Crouchley, and C. Mills, 2001. "Social Capital and Entrepreneurship in Great Britain," *Enterprise and Innovation Management Studies* 2(2): 119–144.
Adler, P. S., and S. W. Kwon, 2002. "Social Capital: Prospects for a New Concept," *Academy of Management Review* 27: 17–40.

Aldrich, H., 1999. *Organizations Evolving*. London: Sage Publications.

Aldrich, H., and C. Zimmer, 1986. "Entrepreneurship through Social Networks." In: D. Sexton and R. Smilor (Eds). *The Art and Science of Entrepreneurship*. Cambridge: Ballinger.

Allen, E., N. Langowitz, and M. Minniti, 2006. *2005 Global Entrepreneurship Monitor Special Report: Women in Entrepreneurship*. Center for Women Leadership, Babson College. Babson Park, MA.

Arthur, W. B., 1989. "Competing Technologies, Increasing Returns, and Lock-in by Historical Events." *Economic Journal* 99, 116–131.

Azam-Roomi, M., and P. Harrison, 2008. "Impact of Women-Only Entrepreneurship Training in Islamic Societies." Ch. 10 In P. Kyro, E. Sundin, & I. Aaltio (Eds), *Women Entrepreneurship and Social Capital: A Dialogue and Construction*. Copenhagen: Copenhagen Business School Press, pp. 225–254.

Bae, T. J., S. Qian, C. Miao, and J. Fiet, 2014. "The Relationship between Entrepreneurship Education and Entrepreneurial Intentions: A Meta-Analytic Review." *Entrepreneurship Theory and Practice*: 217–254.

Bailyn, L., 2006. *Breaking the Mold: Redesigning Work for Productive and Satisfying Lives*. Ithaca, NY: Cornell University Press.

Bandura, A., 1997. *Self-Efficacy: The Exercise of Control*, New York: Freeman.

Baron, R. A., 2000. "Psychological Perspectives on Entrepreneurship: Cognitive and Social Factors in Entrepreneurs' Success." *Current Directions in Psychological Science* 9: 15–18.

Batjargal, B., M. Hitt, J. Webb, J. L. Arregle, and T. Miller, 2009. "Women and Men Entrepreneurs' Social Networks and New Venture Performance across Cultures." In G. Solomon, (Ed.) *Best Paper Proceedings of the Annual Meeting of the Academy of Management*. Chicago, IL.

Baumol, W., 1990. "Entrepreneurship: Productive, Unproductive, and Destructive." *Journal of Political Economy* 98: 893–921.

Becker, G. S., 1996. *Accounting for Tastes*. Cambridge, MA: Harvard University Press.

Begley, T. M., and D. P. Boyd, 1987. "Psychological Characteristics Associated with Performance in Entrepreneurial Firms and Smaller Businesses." *Journal of Business Venturing* 2(1): 79–84.

Bekele, Eshetu, and Zeleke Worku, 2008. "Women Entrepreneurship in Micro, Small and Medium Enterprises: The Case of Ethiopia." *Journal of International Women's Studies* 10(2): 3–19.

Bell, E., and S. Nkomo, 2001. *Our Separate Ways*. Cambridge, MA: Harvard Business School Press.

Bosma, N., J. Hessels, V. Schutjens, M. van Praag, and I. Verheul, 2012. "Entrepreneurship and Role Models." *Journal of Economic Psychology* 33(2): 410–424.

Bourdieu, P. 1986. "The Forms of Capital." In: J. C. Richardson (Ed.) *Handbook of Theory and Research for the Sociology of Education*. New York: Greenwood Press, pp. 241–258.

Boyd, N. G., and G. S. Vozikis, 1994. "The Influence of Self-Efficacy on the Development of Entrepreneurs." *Entrepreneurship Theory and Practice* 18(4): 63–77.

Brüderl, J., and P. Preisendörfer, 1988. "Network Support and the Success of Newly Founded Businesses," *Small Business Economics* 10: 213–225.

Burt, R. S., 1992. *Structural Holes: The Social Structure of Competition*. Cambridge, MA: Harvard University Press, 1992.

Chamlee-Wright, E., 1997. *The Cultural Foundations of Economic Development*. London and New York: Routledge.

Cohen, A., and D. L. Bradford, 2005. *Influence without Authority* 2nd edition. Hoboken, NJ: Wiley.

Colander, D., and R. Kupers, 2014. *Complexity and the Art of Public Policy: Solving Society's Problems from the Bottom Up*. Princeton and Oxford: Princeton University Press.

Coleman, J., 1990. *Foundation of Social Theory*. Cambridge: Belknap Press of Harvard University.

Crane, J., 1991. "The Epidemic Theory of Ghettos and Neighborhood Effects on Dropping Out and Teenage Childbearing." *American Journal of Sociology* 96, 1226–1259.

Dennis, M. R., and A. D. Kunkel, 2004. "Perceptions of Men, Women, and CEOs: The Effects of Gender Identity." *Social Behavior and Personality: An International Journal*, 32: 155–172.

Devine, T. J., 1994a. "Changes In Wage-and-Salary Returns to Skill and the Recent Rise in Female Self-Employment." *American Economic Review* 84(2): 108–112.

Devine, T. J., 1994b. "Characteristics of Self-Employed Women in the United States." *Monthly Labor Review* 117(3): 20–34.

Durlauf, S. N., 2002. "Bowling Alone: A Review Essay." *Journal of Economic Behavior and Organization* 47: 259–273.

Ely, R. J., 1994. "The Effects of Organizational Demographics and Social Identity on Relationships among Professional Women." *Administrative Science Quarterly*, 39: 203–238.

Ely, R. J., H. Ibarra, and D. Kolb, 2011. "Taking Gender into Account: Theory and Design for Women's Leadership Development Programs." *Academy of Management Learning & Education* 10(3): 474–493.

Field, E., S. Jayachandran, and R. Pande, 2010. "Do Traditional Institutions Constrain Female Entrepreneurship? A Field Experiment on Business Training in India." *American Economic Review* 100(2): 125–129.

Fletcher, J. K., 2004. "The Paradox of Post Heroic Leadership: An Essay on Gender, Power and Transformational Change. *Leadership Quarterly* 15: 647–661.

Giscombe, K., and Mattis, M. C., 2002. "Leveling the Playing Field for Women of Color in Corporate Management: Is the Business Case Enough?" *Journal of Business Ethics* 37: 103–119.

Gleaser, E., D. Laibson, J. Scheinkman, and C. Soutter, 1999. "What Is Social Capital? The Determinants of Trust and Trustworthiness." NBER Working Paper 7216.

Goldin, C., 1990. *Understanding the Gender Gap: An Economic History of American Women*. New York: Oxford University Press.

Granovetter, M., 1985. "Economic Action and Social Structure: The Problem of Embeddedness." *American Journal of Sociology* 91: 480–510.

Granovetter, M., 1978. "Threshold Models of Collective Behavior." *American Journal of Sociology* 83: 1420–1443.

Granovetter, M., and R. Soong, 1983. "Threshold Models of Diffusion and Collective Behavior." *Journal of Mathematical Sociology* 9, 165–179.

Greve, A., and J. Salaff, 2003. "Social Networks and Entrepreneurship." *Entrepreneurship, Theory & Practice* 28(1): 1–22.

Harper, D., 2008. "Toward a Theory of Entrepreneurial Teams." *Journal of Business Venturing* 23: 613–626.

Ibarra, H., 1992. "Homophily and Differential Returns: Sex Differences in Network Structure and Access in an Advertising Firm." *Administrative Science Quarterly* 37: 422–447.

Ibarra, H., 1999. "Provisional Selves: Experimenting with Image and Identity in Professional Adaptation." *Administrative Science Quarterly* 44: 764–791.

Jamali, D., 2009. "Constraints and Opportunities Facing Women Entrepreneurs in Developing Countries: A Relational Perspective." *Gender in Management: An International Journal* 24(4): 232–251.

Kalleberg, A. L., D. Knoke, P. V. Marsden, and J. L. Spaeth, 1996. *Organizations in America: Analyzing Their Structures and Human Resource Practices*. Thousand Oaks, CA: Sage.

Kanazawa, S., 2005. "Is 'Discrimination' Necessary to Explain the Sex Gap in Earnings?" *Journal of Economic Psychology* 26(2): 269–287.

Kanter, R., 1977. *Men and Women of the Corporation*. New York: Basics Press.

Kelley, D., C. Brush, P. Greene, M. Herrington, A. Ali, and Y. Kew, 2015. *Women's Entrepreneurship: 2015 GEM Special Report*. GERA.

Kindleberger, C., 1983. "Standards as Public, Collective and Private Goods." *Kyklos* 36: 377–396.

Koellinger, P., M. Minniti, and C. Schade, 2013 "Gender Differences in Entrepreneurial Propensity." *Oxford Bulletin of Economics and Statistics* 75(2): 213–234.

Koppl, R., 2008. "Computable Entrepreneurship." *Entrepreneurship Theory and Practice* 32(5): 919–926.

Kram, K. E., and L. Isabella, 1985. "Mentoring Alternatives: The Role of Peer Relationships in Career Development." *Academy of Management Journal* 28(1): 110–132.

Langowitz, N., and M. Minniti, 2007. "The Entrepreneurial Propensity of Women." *Entrepreneurship Theory and Practice* 31(3): 341–364.

Lerner, M., C. G. Brush, and R. D. Hisrich, 1995. "Factors Affecting Performance of Israeli Women Entrepreneurs: An Examination of Alternative Perspectives." In: D. Bygrave et al. (Eds), *Frontiers of Entrepreneurial Research*. Boston, MA: Babson College, pp. 308–322.

Madichie, N. O., 2009. "Breaking the Glass Ceiling in Nigeria: A Review of Women's Entrepreneurship." *Journal of African Business* 10(1): 51.

Majbouri, M., 2015. "Female Labor Force Participation in Iran: A Structural Analysis." *Review of Middle East Economics and Finance* 11(1): 1–24.

McPherson, M., and L. Smith-Lovin, 1987. "Homophily in Voluntary Organizations: Status Distance and the Composition of Face-to-Face Groups." *American Sociological Review* 52: 370–379.

McPherson, M., L. Smith-Lovin, and J. Cook, 2001. "Birds of a Feather: Homophily in Social Networks." *Annual Review of Sociology* 27: 415–444.

Minniti, M., 2005. "Entrepreneurship and Network Externalities." *Journal of Economic Behavior and Organizations* 57(1): 1–27.

Minniti, M., 2009. "Gender Issues in Entrepreneurship." *Foundations and Trends in Entrepreneurship* 5(7–8): 497–621.

Neumark, D., and M. McLennan, 1995. "Sex Discrimination and Women's Labor Market Outcomes." *The Journal of Human Resources* 30, 713–740.

Nguyen, T., 2008. "Information, Role Models and Perceived Returns to Education: Experimental Evidence from Madagascar." MIT Working Paper.

Parker, S. C., 2008. "The Economics of Formal Business Networks." *Journal of Business Venturing* 23(6).

Podolny, J., and J. Baron, 1997. "Resources and Relationships: Social Networks and Mobility in the Workplace." *American Sociological Review* 62: 673–693.

Poon, P. H., D. T. Thai, and D. Naybor, 2012. "Social Capital and Female Entrepreneurship in Rural Regions: Evidence from Vietnam." *Applied Geography* 35(1–2): 308–315.

Ragins, B. R., and K. E. Kram (Eds), 2007. *The Handbook of Mentoring at Work: Theory, Research and Practice.* Thousand Oaks, CA: Sage Publications.

Reynolds, P., and S. White, 1997. *The Entrepreneurial Process: Economic Growth, Men, Women, and Minorities.* Westport, CT: Quorum Books.

Rosenthal, S., and W. C. Strange, 2012. "Female Entrepreneurship and a New Agglomeration Spatial Mismatch." *Review of Economics and Statistics* 94(3): 764–788.

Ruef, M., H. Aldrich, and N. Carter, 2003. "The Structure of Founding Teams: Homophily, Strong Ties, and Isolation among US Entrepreneurs." *American Sociological Review* 68(2): 195–222.

Shane, S. A., 2003. *A General Theory of Entrepreneurship: The Individual-opportunity Nexus.* Cheltenham: E Elgar Press.

Shane, S. A., and S. Venkataraman, 2000. "The Promise of Entrepreneurship as a Field of Research." *The Academy of Management Review* 25(1): 217–226.

Shapiro, E., F. Haseltine, and M. Rowe, 1978. "Moving Up: Role Models, Mentors, and the Patron System." *Sloan Management Review* 6(1): 19–47.

Walker, G., B. Kogut, and W. Shan, 1997. "Social Capital, Structural Holes and the Formation of an Industry Network," *Organization Science* 8: 109–125.

Zhao, H., S. E. Seibert, and G. E. Hills, 2005. "The Mediating Role of Self-Efficacy in the Development of Entrepreneurial Intentions." *Journal of Applied Psychology* 90(6), 1265–1272.

Zukin, S., and P. DiMaggio, 1990. *Structures of Capital: The Social Organization of the Economy.* New York: Cambridge University Press.

13

REVISITING RESEARCH ON GENDER IN ENTREPRENEURIAL NETWORKS

Lene Foss

Introduction

Women's entrepreneurship as a growing global phenomenon has attracted considerable research attention in recent decades (Jennings and Brush, 2013; Marlow and McAdam, 2012; Henry, Foss and Ahl, 2015). Alongside this development, the importance of social networks for business creation and development constitutes a significant proportion of work in terms of entrepreneurship research (Aldrich, Rosen and Woodward, 1987; Foss, 1994; Johannisson, 2000; Greve and Salaff, 2003; Hoang and Antoncic, 2003; Jack, Dodd and Anderson, 2004; Renzulli and Aldrich, 2005; Witt, 2004). The premise of this chapter is that empirical research practice constitutes a discursive field (Foucault, 1972) that influences how researchers write and talk about entrepreneurship. Therefore, how women's entrepreneurship is portrayed within research on entrepreneurial networks is an important area to study. Discourse analysis of empirical research articles from 1980 to 2008 revealed that almost 30 years of research have produced hegemonic statements that female entrepreneurs are not good networkers compared to their male counterparts (Foss, 2010). This is mainly due to lack of a gendered perspective, implying that treating gender as a binary category (sex) and performing quantitative analysis highlight differences instead of similarities (cf. Henry et al., 2015). Recognising that such hegemonic statements imply that female networks are only measured against male networks, this chapter builds on that previous work by analysing scholarly publications from 2008. The core research question addressed is: *Which hegemonic statements characterise the discourse in published scholarly work, and is there a change in the use of gender perspectives from 2008 to 2015?* In comparing the various discourses, this study contributes to future scholarship by describing the value of using institutional approaches in order to create new knowledge related to the embeddedness of gendered entrepreneurial networks. The remainder of the chapter is organised as follows: the first section describes the selection of articles from 2008 to 2015, examines how networks are defined, and describes commonalities in the research. This is followed by the identification of the relevant hegemonic statements. The final section discusses how institutional perspectives can provide scholars with new angles on how to research gendered entrepreneurial networks.

Current research

Selecting and evaluating new articles

A discourse is defined as "practices which form the object of which they speak" (Foucault, 1972, p. 49). Thus, how we interpret this relationship in our analyses creates truth effects, which in turn influence what is considered valid knowledge in a field (Alvesson and Due Billing, 1999; Ahl, 2007). The purpose of the analysis in this chapter is to reveal whether the scholarly discourse in the literature from 2008 to 2015 has changed or whether the hegemonic statements from the author's 2010 analysis remain pertinent. This focus is important because researchers seldom go beyond the written text and seek to understand how the discourse of research evolves over time and the role of the researchers themselves in that evolution.

A thorough discourse analysis of the research field of gender and networks in entrepreneurship research from 2008 to 2015 is not feasible in a single chapter. Rather, a sampling of research texts is used in an exploratory fashion to identify the dominant discourses. The criteria used for sampling included empirical studies published over time in mainstream entrepreneurship journals with a significant impact, as confirmed by citation counts. Two main databases were used: the ProQuest Research Library and the Scopus Bibliographic Database. ProQuest covers scholarly journals that fall into 38 database categories. The search criteria used were entrepreneurship AND network AND gender OR women to search the abstracts of English language articles in scholarly journals published between 2008 and 2015. This search resulted in 57 articles, of which 13 were selected for analysis. The Scopus Database includes journals in the scientific, technical, medical and social science arenas; here the search criteria used were entrepreneurship AND network AND gender OR women OR female, across papers published between 2008 and 2015 in the Life Sciences, Health Sciences, Physical Sciences, Social Sciences and Humanities sections. This resulted in 77 articles, of which 11 were selected for analysis.[1]

In a closer evaluation of the 24 articles, some articles in journals such as *Clothing & Textiles Research Journal* and *Journal of International Women's Studies* were omitted as they were too far removed from the area of entrepreneurship. Another article dealing with women entrepreneurs' use of the virtual network Facebook was excluded. Furthermore, three articles in the journals *International Journal of Business and Globalisation* and *International Journal of Entrepreneurship and Small Business* were excluded, as they were not accessible through the normal university library system. Of the remaining 18 articles, several were review or conceptual articles (Hanson, 2009; Hanson and Blake, 2009; Brush, de Bruin and Welter, 2009); as the focus of this study was purely on empirical studies, these were excluded. A selection of the 15 remaining articles is presented below.

As illustrated in Table 13.1, citations of the selected texts varied from 0 to 41 (Web of Science), from 0 to 56 (Scopus) and from 1 to 127 (Google). Articles from *Journal of Management* (JM) and *Journal of Business Venturing* (JBV) held the highest journal rankings in Scopus and Web of Science metrics, and the article in JBV had the highest citation level in the whole sample. The articles in the *International Small Business Journal* (ISBJ) had the second highest citation levels in both Google Scholar and Web of Science. ISBJ is a relatively highly ranked journal and had the third highest journal ranking among the selected articles in both Scopus and Web of Science metrics. The article from *International Journal of Entrepreneurship* (JEL) holds a low journal ranking but had a relatively high number of citations. The *International*

Table 13.1 Sample of articles

Author	Journal	Web of science citations	Scopus citations	Google scholar citations	Five year impact factor	Article influence score	IPP	SJR	SNIP
Grossman, Yli-Renko & Janakiraman (2012)	Journal Management	7	8	20	8,027	4,138	7,451	7,728	4,676
Kwon & Arenius (2010)	Journal of Business Venturing	41	56	127	4,571	2,041	5,837	5,561	3,894
Maas et al. (2014)	International Entrepreneurship and Management Journal	1	1	1	-	-	1,115	0,614	1,156
Tsuchiya (2010)	International Entrepreneurship and Management Journal	5	5	8	-	-	1,115	0,614	1,156
Hampton, Cooper & McGowan (2009)	International Small Business Journal	10	16	46	2,375	0,535	2,143	1,444	1,296
Watson (2012)	International Small Business Journal	9	16	41	2,375	0,535	2,143	1,444	1,296
Fernández-Pérez et al. (2014)	Industrial Management & Data Systems	0	0	4	1,544	0,351	1,928	0,846	1,477
Hampton, McGowan & Cooper (2011)	International Journal of Entrepreneurial Behavior & Research	-	5	17	-	-	1,117	0,515	1,072
Klyver (2011)	Gender in Management: An International Journal	-	6	13	-	-	0,899	0,437	0,742
Robinson & Stubberud (2009)	International Journal of Entrepreneurship	-	18	37	-	-	0,0,83	0,107	0,041
Klyver & Grant (2010)	International Journal of Gender and Entrepreneurship	-	32	41	-	-	-	-	-

Note: *About IPP (Scopus)*: The Impact per Publication measures the ratio of citations per article published in the journal. *About SNIP (Scopus)*: Source Normalized Impact per Paper measures contextual citation impact by weighting citations based on the total number of citations in a subject field. *About SJR (Scopus)*: is a measure of scientific influence of scholarly journals that accounts for both the number of citations received by a journal and the importance or prestige of the journals where such citations come from. See http://www.journalmetrics.com/sjr.php.

Journal of Gender and Entrepreneurship (IJGE) is a relatively new journal in the journal ranking system; however, the IJGE article had the second highest number of Scopus citations in the sample.

In comparing the sample selected here (2008–2015) with the sample (1980–2008) in Foss (2010), a striking difference is that no articles from highly ranked journals such as *Entrepreneurship Theory and Practice* (ETP) and *Entrepreneurship & Regional Development* appeared. Closer investigation reveals that since 2008 there are several publications in higher ranked journals relating to networks and entrepreneurship, and gender and entrepreneurship, but few articles on gender, networks *and* entrepreneurship. The reasons for this absence are difficult to explain and may be due to editorial decisions, as well as changes in the usage of key vocabulary words, which can influence search results. Social capital theory has become more popular with time, and researchers may have moved away from structurally oriented network research.

Another difference from Foss (2010) is that other highly ranked journals were represented, such as ISBJ, IJEBR and JM. At the other end of the scale, publications in lower ranked journals are also present, such as the *International Entrepreneurship and Management Journal* (IEMJ) and the *International Journal of Entrepreneurship* (IJE). This could indicate two issues: 1) gender and networks in entrepreneurship has become more widely recognised as an important research topic in more journals, but 2) this work is not being published in the higher-ranked journals. A description of the research problem, theoretical perspective, method, data and findings is provided for each of the articles in Table 13.2.

With regard to the focal research problem, many of the articles in the review did not explicitly formulate a research question to guide the research. With regard to theoretical perspectives the articles varied in their focus on networks, ranging from a structural perspective (Fernandez et al., 2014; Klyver, 2011; Robinson and Stubberud, 2009; Watson, 2011) to the dynamics of networks (Grossman et al., 2012; Hampton et al., 2009; Hampton et al., 2011; Kwon and Arenius, 2010; Maas et al., 2014; Tsuchiya, 2010) to how networks could be related to stages in the entrepreneurship process (Klyver and Grant, 2010).

How are networks defined?

Mass (2014, p. 59) found that Bourdieu and Wacquant's definition of social capital provided the most appropriate focus for exploring social networks: "Social capital is the sum of the resources, actual or virtual, that accrue to an individual or group by virtue of possessing a durable network of more or less institutionalised relationships of mutual acquaintance or recognition". Similarly, Fernandez et al. (2014, p. 293) drew on Hoang and Antoncic's (2003) statement that social networks are defined by a set of actors (individuals or organisations) and by the linkages between these actors and provide crucial channels for the acquisition of information and resources. In their more strategy-oriented article, Grossman et al. (2012, p. 1763) defined networks in the following way: "In aggregate, for our current purposes, the work suggests that a firm's instrumental resource requirements are likely to manifest in strategic network-building efforts—with actors establishing ties to secure those resources that they view as most critical to firm success". Hampton et al. (2009, p. 195) wrote: "A network is defined by the interactive relationships or alliances that individuals have, or may seek to develop between them and others, in pursuit of some enterprise in which they have a particular interest". In their 2011 article, the same authors defined a network as providing "access to key resources necessary to exploit opportunities and improve entrepreneurial effectiveness, particularly in circumstances of limited resources. A network is any interactive relationship or

Table 13.2 Articles chart

Article	Research problem	Theoretical perspective	Method and data	Findings
Maas 2014	How are entrepreneurial networks developed and used by female entrepreneurs in Bangladesh, and how can a third party stimulate network development?	Network and social capital theory. No gender theory.	Longitudinal Monitoring Programme, in-depth interviews, questionnaires and Photo Voice Methodology.	Four strategies in building networks: modifying/building on existing bonding networks, transferring linking ties, teaching to build bridging networks, creation of a network of entrepreneurial peers. Third party can stimulate network development for poorest in Bangladesh. Patterns of network development different from corporate studies.
Fernandez Perez et al. 2014	How do business networks and social networks influence academics' intentions to start a business venture based on their research knowledge from an academic cognitive perspective?	Entrepreneurial intentions, opportunity recognitions, networks. No gender theory	Structural Equation Modelling Analysis, Path Model Analysis performed on LISREL 8.71 software on 500 Spanish academics (telephone surveys and a web-based survey) in commercially oriented fields of research. Likert-type seven point scales used.	Positive roles played by business (industrial and financial) networks, directly via promoting academics' entrepreneurial intentions and indirectly via entrepreneurial attitudes and self-efficacy on opportunity recognition. Male and female academics differ in perceptions of support from business/ financial networks and in use of resources.
Grossman et al. 2012	What are some of the instrumental and interpersonal mechanisms driving nascent entrepreneurs' value attributions about contacts met in establishing initial networking ties?	Resource based theory, networks, interpersonal similarity (psychology)	Semi-structured interviews of 32 entrepreneurs, information on 1,407 network dyads, periodic surveys of entrepreneurs over the next six months, Harman's one-factor test.	Content benefits of entrepreneurial networks form a clear basis for entrepreneurs' assessments of value. Process benefits of interpersonal age and gender similarity play an amplifying role. No direct interpersonal similarity effects.

	Research question	Theory	Method	Findings
Hampton et al. 2011	Does the quality of the networks of female entrepreneurs in the science, engineering and technology (SET) sectors change through time as the venture becomes more mature and the entrepreneur gains more experience?	Networks. No gender theory	Qualitative, in-depth, interview-based study of 18 female entrepreneurs in SET-based ventures in Northern Ireland. Nvivo used in data analysis.	Results focus on implication of findings for issues of quality in networks and impact on the value of female networks.
Klyver 2011	How is the outside involvement of family members and the exchange of emotional support associated with the gender of an entrepreneur or the gender of entrepreneurs' alters?	Homophily theory, relational theory and social support theory. No gender theory	Builds on homophily theory, relational theory and social support theory. Three hypotheses tested on sample of Danish entrepreneurs and alters. Hierarchical logistic regression approach.	Female entrepreneurs involve other females and family members who are not partners. Female focal entrepreneurs involve female family members; male focal entrepreneurs involve male family members. Female and males equally likely to receive emotional support. Females more likely to provide it.
Watson 2011	Are there any systematic differences between male and female SME owners and is there an association between networking and firm performance for male- or female-controlled SMEs?	Networks. No gender theory	Networking model proposed; Categorical Regression used. Firm performance model proposed;-Logistic Regression used. Large Longitudinal Database used obtained from Stratified Random Sampling Framework. Data collection through Self-administered Questionnaires.	Little difference in the networks of male and female SME owners after controlling for education, experience, industry, age and size. Only formal networks associated with growth. Formal and informal networks both associated with survival. External accountant important for survival/growth of both male- and female- controlled SMEs.

(Continued)

Article	Research problem	Theoretical perspective	Method and data	Findings
Klyver & Grant 2010	What is the nature of an individual's personal acquaintance with an entrepreneur as it related to his/her participation in entrepreneurial activity through three distinct new venture stages: discovery, start-up and young?	Networks. No gender theory	Global Entrepreneurship Monitor data used from 35 countries across three years. Multinomial Logistic Regression used.	People who know an entrepreneur more likely to participate in entrepreneurial activities at any stage. Females less likely to know an entrepreneur in general. Women lack entrepreneurial resource providers/role models in social networks.
Kwon 2010	What are the effects of social capital on entrepreneurial opportunity perception and weak tie investment on a societal level?	Social capital, weak ties, opportunity perception	Multi-level models applied to data from Global Entrepreneurship Monitor and World Values Survey. Individual level data from Global Entrepreneurial Monitor. Control variables applied. Probit Regression Models, Two-Stage Least Squares, ordered logit model, and 'cluster' option in Stata's estimation command used.	People from a country with higher generalised trust and breadth of formal organisational memberships more likely to perceive entrepreneurial opportunities. Higher generalised trust also associated with willingness to invest in a weak personal tie.
Tsuchiya 2010	Does past participation in cooperative networks with adjacent neighbours and voluntary contributions to community organizational activities enhance or diminish the performance of female self-employment activities?	Neighbourhood social networks	Taiwan Women and Family Survey (1989) and Income and Expenditure Survey (1988) used for data. 134 observations analysed. Ordinary Least Squares model and Endogenous Treatment Effect model used for multivariate analysis. Variance Inflation Factor tests conducted for Linear Regression Models.	Past provision of personalised assistance to adjacent neighbours increases current self-employment earnings. Past voluntary contributions to community organisational activities increase current earnings. Female self-employed workers with high earnings capacity less likely to participate in these types of social networks.

Hampton et al. 2009	How are the networks of female entrepreneurs in technology-based firms developed and managed as opposed to those of men in the same field, and what are the reasons for such differences?	Networks and Networking	18 semi-structured, in-depth interviews performed. Research exploratory and qualitative. Inductive analysis, followed by second-stage interviews. Data collected and analysed concurrently. NUDIST used for further analysis.	Networking important to how female entrepreneurs do business through business life cycle. Network types vary depending on firms' stage of development. Pre-start up stage with largely male-dominated network. Established entrepreneurs are more inclusive regarding gender. Female entrepreneurs of established firms sophisticated networkers; face many challenges.
Robinson & Stubberud 2009	What are the gender differences in the networks of women and men, and how do these differences affect the quality of those networks?	Social networks. No gender theory	Data from Eurostat's Metadata Database (2005–2006). 287,837 business-owners across 9 countries. Chi-square analyses.	Women more likely to name friends and family as source of advice. Men more likely to name professional acquaintances and consultants as sources of advice. Informal sources may be less useful; women at a disadvantage.

alliance that an individual has or seeks to develop between themselves and others" (Hampton et al., 2011, p. 589).

Klyver and Grant (2010, p. 213) wrote: "Entrepreneurs are embedded in social networks which include advisors, business partners, buyers, customers, employees, friends/relatives, investors, mentors, shareholders, and suppliers. Through their social networks, entrepreneurs may be able to acquire financial capital, advice, credibility/reputation, funding, information, knowledge/skills, social legitimacy, and social support".

In 2011, Klyver (p. 334) gave this definition: "In diverse ways, social networks provide focal entrepreneurs with a wide range of valuable resources not already in their possession and help them achieve their goals, the resources that focal entrepreneurs obtain from networks involve a wide range of variations. Among the most important resources that networks can provide are information, access to finance, access to skills, knowledge and advice, emotional support, and social legitimacy".

Kwon (2010) wrote: "We define national social capital as a resource reflecting the character of social relations within the nation, expressed in residents' levels of generalized trust and breadth of formal organisation memberships, (...) social capital is concerned with a much more narrowly defined realm of social life, namely one's relationship network" (pp. 316–317). Robinson and Stubberud (2009) did not define networks but referred to other research: "Social networks are becoming increasingly important as they provide firms with access to markets, ideas, information, advice, business opportunities, and other resources" (Birley, 1985; Farr-Wharton and Brunetto, 2007; Gulati, Nohria and Zaheer, 2000; Hoang and Antoncic, 2003). One result of networking is the development of social capital, which essentially consists of the "resources individuals obtain from knowing others, being part of a network with them, or merely being known to them and having a good reputation" (Nahapiet and Ghoshal, 1998, p. 107). The result is that networks relate to the survival and growth of new firms (Brüderl and Preisendörfer, 1998, p. 84).

Tsuchiya (2010, p. 145) also referred to prior research: "Although entrepreneurial networks are typically construed as the fundamental factor of the process of new firm formation, (Brüderl and Preisendörfer, 1998; Bosma et al., 2004), the reliance on networks is not restricted to the startup stage. Entrepreneurs continue to rely on networks for business information, advice, and problem solving (Johannisson et al., 1994). (...) For female self-employed workers, their perceived reputation in the community is a specific asset that affects their businesses performance".

Watson (2011, p. 537) used definitions in an oppositional way: "Coleman (1988) notes that while information is important to decision-making, it is costly to obtain, hence networks provide a means by which important information can be potentially acquired in a cost-effective manner. Similarly, Hanson and Blake argue that networking can help SME owners 'reduce transaction costs' and 'provide access to resources' (2009, p. 144). Therefore, networking can enhance an SME owner's social capital by providing access to information and just as physical capital and human capital facilitate productive activity, social capital does as well" (Coleman, 1988, p. 101).

An increased awareness of gender perspectives?

In evaluating whether gender perspectives have been more explicitly applied in the reviewed literature on networks and entrepreneurship, this chapter distinguishes between the commonly accepted categorisations in feminist theory (Harding, 1987; Cálas and Smircich, 1996; Neergaard et al., 2011): gender-as-variable (GAV), feminist standpoint theory (FST) and post-structural feminism (PSF). A recent systematic literature review of gender in entrepreneurship research from 1983 to 2012 revealed that the GAV approach is dominant throughout the 30-year review period; FST gained momentum from the 1990s, and PSF emerged from 2003 to 2012. However, the latter period is characterised by a trend of research using no feminist perspective and is also overshadowed by a continuous trend towards the GAV approach (Henry et al., 2015, pp. 9–10).

Maas (2014) did not use any theoretical perspective regarding gender; rather, female entrepreneurs were considered representative of how marginalised communities build their entrepreneurial networks. Fernandez et al. (2014, p. 298) did not define gender in their study of differences between male and female academics' perceptions of business start-up. Their theoretical starting point was studies that found that gender influenced the development of entrepreneurial intentions and cognitive factors (suggesting that gender may affect the predisposition towards entrepreneurial intentions). Furthermore, they referred to studies of women not only viewing themselves as being less capable of becoming entrepreneurs, but also perceiving their environment as more difficult and less appropriate for entrepreneurial initiatives. Finally, they referred to studies suggesting that gender differences may exist in networking, with women being more likely to turn to family and friends for advice than men are.

In their study of gender similarity, Grossman et al. (2012, p. 1767) use an implicit FST perspective, referring to prior research: "Underlying this tendency toward gender similarity are the gender based values, beliefs, and communication patterns that individuals develop through socialization. Abundant evidence has shown that women, for example, are socialized to show their emotions, to be caring toward others, and to be listeners".

Hampton et al. (2009, p. 197) were explicit on gender theory but referenced research that highlighted the differences between men and women stating: "Some research suggests that, unlike men who espouse more formal approaches to networking women may receive similar support through the development of informal networks. Men and women, it appears, have different priorities when establishing networks; women tend to seek social relationships while men tend to seek personal advantages". This supports the use of FST. Similarly, Hampton et al. (2011, p. 591) referred to prior research showing the differences between men and women in networking. "According to existing literature, some key differences exist in the way in which men and women network, particularly in the early stages of business development. Women look to develop many, collaborative, inclusive relationships and seem not to identify greatly with existing business associations, clubs, or networks, suggesting that females choose not to enter into male networks, due to low self-confidence, while others indicate that because women are relatively new to business ownership they are only just developing their networks".

Klyver and Grant (2010, pp. 215–216) built on social network theory and emphasised the differences between men and women in networking, making a GAV approach visible. They stated: "Consistent with research on social networks among men and women in traditional organisations, research on entrepreneurs' social networks reveals that men and women develop social networks that are structurally different. Female entrepreneurs' social networks typically include a larger proportion of women and a smaller proportion of men than do male entrepreneurs' social networks". Furthermore, they wrote: "In addition, the importance of entrepreneurial networking for entrepreneurial participation may vary by gender. Relational theory is a model of how women's development and sense of self and personal worth is shaped by a sense of connection to others, including family members, and has been identified as salient to the experiences and approaches used by female entrepreneurs". This, however, seems to be an implicit use of a FST perspective.

Klyver (2011, p. 336) also emphasised the differences between men and women (GAV), but focused on alters' gender differences and developed hypotheses based on homophily theory, relational theory, and social support theory, "Supporting the homophily theory, a growing body of research investigates the presence of gender differences in focal entrepreneurs' social networks, consistently finding that the networks of female focal entrepreneurs are characterised by higher proportions of female alters. According to relational theory (Miller, 1976), females' development and sense of self and personal worth are shaped by a sense of connection to others, including family members. Most females spend a large proportion of their lives helping to develop others, and through these activities they develop important skills such as authenticity, openness, care and compassion". Again, this indicates an implicit FST perspective.

Robinson and Stubberud (2010, p. 85) focused on gender differences, referring to research stating that women have customarily been at a disadvantage in terms of formal and informal networks as men and women tend to develop different networks. "Both men and women tend to interact with people of the similar gender, and women tend to be especially adept at building informal networks with other women". Although an implicit GAV approach, the argument seems to build on the notion that women are disadvantaged, making FST the underlying rationale.

Tsuchiya (2010) used a gender-as-variable approach and focused on gender differences regarding performance and social networking. She referred to studies that "found that the business discussion networks of potential female startup founders included a higher proportion of kin and less heterogeneous contacts than in the case of male potential startup founders. Finally, for female self-employed workers, their perceived reputation in the community is a specific asset that affects their businesses performance" (p. 144).

Watson (2011, p. 538) used no explicit gender-based theory, as his focus was on gender differences in networks, which implies gender-as-variable. He referred to social network research on possible differences between the networks of male and female SME owners, where it was argued that because the majority of women enter self-employment from a domestic and/or non-managerial background it is likely that their personal network contacts will not be as extensive, or as well developed, as their male counterparts. Furthermore, housework and child rearing are extremely lonely forms of work, and this isolation results in many women having limited network contacts compared to men. Thus, this study seems to have an implicit FST perspective.

In conclusion, this sample of articles seems to have little grounding in gender theories, as the articles did not refer explicitly to any gender perspectives. As most of the studies aimed to analyse differences between male and female entrepreneurs, GAV seems to be implicitly used. Furthermore, some articles seemed to use FST implicitly, as they argued that women are caregivers, inherently relational by nature and are drawn towards kinship and strong ties in their networks. Consequently, an increased awareness of feminist perspectives could be detected in the sample. The articles cited previous network research in a descriptive way and did not apparently aim to move beyond researching differences between male and female entrepreneurs.

Commonalities across the articles

A commonality amongst the articles is that they all appeared to focus on the *effects of gender as a binary variable* on networks. In other words, they continued to reproduce the essentialism that lies in using biological sex instead of gender as a construction. Very few articles defined gender at all, and none used an explicit gender perspective with references to literature on gender-as-variable, FST or PSF.

A second common characteristic is that a majority of the papers were *mainstream quantitative papers,* with men and women as a binary independent variable and different ego or alter network characteristics as the dependent variable (Fernandez et al., 2014; Klyver and Grant, 2010; Klyver, 2011; Kwon and Arenius, 2010; Robinson and Stubberud, 2009; Tsuchiya, 2010; Watson, 2011). This indicates that the methodological variety has not expanded since 2008. Some exceptions were the qualitative papers by Hampton et al. (2009), Hampton et al. (2011), Maas et al. (2014) and a mixed-method paper by Grossman et al. (2012).

A third characteristic is that *the larger social and structural system in which gender is embedded is not a part of the framework.* The only articles that did discuss this were Klyver and Grant (2010) and Klyver (2011). It is interesting that many of the papers referred to the embeddedness statement of Granovetter, but none of them, apart from Klyver, actually used this argument to study gendered networks within a larger embedded system. This is critical, as the reader then misses the very concept of embeddedness. If network research loses the wider institutional, cultural and political structure of embeddedness, we have lost the very meaning of the entrepreneurship social phenomenon in respect of it (cf. Davidsson, 2003; Steyaert and Katz, 2004).

The discourse in research on gender and networks does not go beyond asking entrepreneurs who they relate to. This does not allow for taking the larger system shaping opportunities and directions for networking into consideration. Interestingly, the sample in this chapter showed that we have more network studies from entrepreneurs in non-Western countries than in Western societies. Paradoxically this has not led us to theorise how the cultural context for entrepreneurship may affect how entrepreneurial networks develop.

The reason for the lack of theoretical development may lie in that available databases, such as GEM, etc., provide researchers with easy access to data and facilitate quantitative studies, which are easier to publish. This choice of methodology, and using the gender-as-variable approach, limits our understanding of how gender is socially constructed and how this affects networks. More ethnographic studies of entrepreneurial networks and journals that invite more cross-disciplinary network research are needed.

Hegemonic statements from discourse

Surprisingly, many of the hegemonic statements detected in Foss (2010) still seem to persist. Three of the hegemonic statements are still richly embedded in the discourse: 1) Female entrepreneurs have inadequate networks, 2) Weak ties (the universal key to economic performance) and 3) female entrepreneurs are primarily family oriented in their networking.

Female entrepreneurs have inadequate networks

This is a semantic issue, as it indicates how researchers continue to subordinate females in their writing. Below, quotes from the articles are provided to support this statement.

> Like their male counterparts, female entrepreneurs need to be effective networkers (Brush, 1997). Evidence suggests, however, that female networks suffer from problems of size, density, diversity and tie strength (Ibarra, 1993) which impact directly on network quality, which in turn may impact on the potential for enterprise development and growth.
>
> *(Hampton and McGowan, 2011 p. 591)*

Our study reveals that the main gender difference affecting female academics involves their relation with industrial and financial social networks; there are no significant differences in psychological variables or in the indirect effects of social networks. Thus, we find that male and female academics differ in their perceptions of the direct support received and in their use of business and financial social networks to undertake an entrepreneurial initiative.

(Fernández-Pérez et al., 2014, p. 310)

The findings indicate that individuals who personally know an entrepreneur are more likely to participate in entrepreneurial activity at any venture stage but that female entrepreneurs, compared with their male counterparts, are less likely to be acquainted with an entrepreneur. Taken together, these findings suggest that one of the reasons why women are less likely to become entrepreneurs is that they lack entrepreneurial resource providers or role models in their social networks.

(Klyver and Grant, 2010, p. 213)

In summary, it would seem past research suggests that, compared to men, women are likely to have fewer networks, less time available for networking, and networks that favour family and friends (strong ties with few structural holes) over professional advisers (weak ties with many structural holes). This gives rise to the first four hypotheses examined in this study.

(Watson, 2011, p. 538)

Consistent with a large body of research on entrepreneurship, we found that gender was one of the strongest predictors of entrepreneurial opportunity perception and weak tie investment, with females significantly less likely to report that they perceived entrepreneurial opportunities or invested in a stranger's good idea. Although there may be multiple reasons for this, females in many societies may have a lower level of social capital at the individual level, which in turn may contribute both to their lack of opportunity perception and to their reliance on strong ties.

(Kwon and Arenius, 2010, p. 327)

The manner in which scholars appear to reinforce the subordination of women to men has consequences for how our research is interpreted by others in the research community and also by those audiences interested in developing policy implications. The hegemonic statement that women network poorly compared to men seems to be reinforced in that research tends to replicate prior findings, rather than defining new research questions where more nuanced gender perspectives and empirical methods are used and can create new knowledge.

Weak ties (the universal key to success)

An underlying assumption in many articles was that gender differences in networks explain differences in business performance, as illustrated by the following quotes:

As shown in this study of successful new business owners in the European Union, women are more likely than men to use friends and family as advisers, whereas men are more likely to use professional acquaintances. These results may, in future work, be used to help further explain differences in business performance.

(Robinson and Stubberud, 2009, p. 98)

Further findings derived from studying the new ventures emphasized the challenges expressed in other studies as to why women have not entered into quasi-formal "male" – dominated networks, highlighting issues such as personal self-confidence and a perceived lack of competence relative to male members.

(Hampton, Cooper and McGowan, 2009, p. 205)

Women tend to involve a higher proportion of family members in their networks and thus a lower proportion of arms-length business contacts.

(Klyver and Grant, 2010, p. 215)

Although research has documented that weak ties have proved most efficient for access to new information, there seems to be an unexplained link between the share of weak ties and entrepreneurial success in the network literature. Further, researchers seem to fall into the essentialist trap by assuming that women are all relation oriented and thus less able to develop weak ties.

Women are inherently relational

Several of the articles continued the theme that women are oriented towards family relations (kinship), which is considered a drawback for business.

Women spend a large proportion of their lives helping to develop others, and through these activities often build important skills such as authenticity, openness, care, and compassion. This relational model is in contrast to mainstream male-dominated models, and may emerge from girls' relationships with their mothers, in contrast to boys' desired autonomy. The relational aspects are reflected in gender differences in choices about involvement of kin in entrepreneurial networks.

(Klyver and Grant, 2010, p. 215)

It is found that female focal entrepreneurs are more likely to involve female and family members who are not partners. Furthermore, it was found that female focal entrepreneurs would more likely involve female family members while male focal entrepreneurs would more likely involve male family members. And finally, it was found that females and males are equally likely to receive emotional support while females are more likely to provide it.

(Klyver, 2011, p. 332)

While the findings of this study did not confirm that family responsibilities reduced significantly the amount of time available to female entrepreneurs for networking, most of the women acknowledged the societal pressure on them to undertake domestic and caring roles.

(Hampton, Cooper and McGowan, 2009, p. 206)

From these results, a more sophisticated perspective is gained regarding different gender roles in entrepreneurship. Females are more often providing emotional support to the focal actor. These results follow the stereotype of females as the sympathetic, understanding and supporting person behind the focal actor. Males on the other hand, seem to be less likely to provide emotional support.

(Klyver, 2011, p. 346)

These quotes reinforce essentialism, i.e. the idea that women entrepreneurs are inherently different from men, characterising *FST* approaches and taking little account of within-sex variation. Since quantitative methodological approaches using gender as a binary variable do not capture the within-group variance; research reinforces the hegemonic statement that women are more relation oriented in their networks than are men. As none of the reviewed articles took an explicit gender perspective, and very few referred to any gender theory, it appears that feminist theories are still not popular in the field of gender and networks. Using an individualist focus (every actor develops his/her network in a vacuum) reifies female subordination. Women network less than men do. As networking is inherently a social and structural phenomenon, conditioned by other actors, systems and structures in work life, it seems that research on gender in entrepreneurial networks needs to adopt novel approaches, both theoretically and methodologically, and support new articles on gender and entrepreneurship in this domain (Brush, de Bruin and Welter, 2009; Ahl and Nelson, 2010; Henry et al., 2015). This is the focus of the next section.

Towards studying gender and networks as embedded in larger institutional structures

In this section a new agenda for studying gendered networks within a larger embedded system is suggested. The rationale for this builds on Hanson and Blake's conclusion (2009) that gender differences in the composition and functioning of people's networks is part of a larger system:

> Most of these differences are attributable to the different status positions that are inherent in gender relations, suggesting that unless and until women and men have equal access to opportunities, gender differences in network patterns will endure and will of course thereby continue to under-grid unequal access to opportunity.

Echoing this are the recent calls for institutional entrepreneurship, such as by Ahl and Nelson (2010) who argued that gender connotes the institutionalised understandings and practices of masculinity and femininity: "The nation, the state, religion, welfare and other regulatory systems, language, data and statistics as means of research, are all examples of institutions that intersect with entrepreneurship so as to have consequences for men and women entrepreneurs, and thus society" (p. 6). Thus, the most promising article in this sample was the paper by Kwon and Arenius (2010) as they used multi-level methods and data from the *Global Entrepreneurship Monitor* combined with the World Values Survey. Their finding that countries' higher generalised trust and breadth of formal organisational membership affected people's perception of entrepreneurial opportunities positively and their willingness to invest in a weak personal tie is an example how the normative institutional pillar works. Welter (2010, p. 68) also suggested that context at a higher level of analysis (the political and economic system) impacts on the phenomenon on lower levels (opportunities identified by the entrepreneur) and results in a context-specific outcome.

Future research on gender and entrepreneurship can gain ground by following calls to contextualise entrepreneurship (cf. Steyaert and Katz, 2004; Zahra, 2007; Welter 2010). For example, Zahra (2007) stated that contextualising research effectively means linking theory, research objectives and sites. Welter (2010) classified the dimensions of context as business (industry, markets), social (networks), spatial (geographic environments) and institutional (culture, society, political and economic systems). In recognising context, future network studies can overcome the shortcomings attributed to women that a GAV approach may perpetuate. Differences in contextual factors such as legislative and cultural restrictions, welfare state systems and family policies, regional environment, industrial context and access to capital etc. are likely to affect how entrepreneurial networks are initiated, maintained and developed by women. A focus on contextualising networks leaves future scholars an opportunity to use contingency studies, comparative studies and studies of how networks are gendered within social orders and structures.

In moving more specifically to institutions, Tolbert et al. (2011) claimed that the mutual neglect of entrepreneurship research and institutional theory has limited the development of both traditions. I therefore make a call for future scholars to address the formation of entrepreneurial networks across the regulative, normative and cultural-cognitive pillar (Scott, 2014). The *regulative pillar* concerns specifications including laws, governance and monitoring systems. This pillar, derived from economics, represents a rational actor model of behaviour including rules, sanctions and conformity. Possible 'take-aways' for future research may include how entrepreneurship is regulated in different countries and which incentive mechanisms operate for entrepreneurial initiatives. Nations have different regulative systems, and networks form between actors who need to obey the rules of entrepreneurship regulation (cf. Welter and Smallbone, 2011).

The *normative pillar* incorporates values, expectations and standards, including roles, repertoires of action and conventions. In applying this pillar to analysing gender and entrepreneurial networks, future research may encompass much of the intersectional focus that characterises gender and entrepreneurship literature (cf. Ahl and Nelson, 2015). How entrepreneurial networks form within different cultures, and how they connect to the values and expectations of entrepreneurship, is also important in order to gain new knowledge.

The *cultural-cognitive pillar* encompasses predispositions and symbolic value as models for individual behaviour regarding an individual's engagement with entrepreneurship. This is particularly important as individual behaviour and engagement clearly form relationships. Networks are inherently relational – they build on trust, which again is culturally conditioned. Following Scott (2014), an individual's interests are also culturally constructed. For diffusion of network processes to occur, actors must regard themselves as similar in some respects. This is an under-researched area in gender and entrepreneurship research.

A research framework where gender and entrepreneurial networks are studied within a broader institutional context will also acknowledge advice from researchers who publish entrepreneurship research in well-recognised journals outside of the entrepreneurship field. An early contribution of Mirchandani (1999), for example, suggested that existing knowledge on women and entrepreneurship may be enhanced by reflecting on the essentialism in the very construction of the category "the female entrepreneur", and the different ways in which the connections among gender, occupation and organisational structure affect female and male business owners (p. 225). Hanson (2009) concluded that the key to transformative processes in changing contexts through women's entrepreneurship is beyond access to microcredit alone.

> The keys to this transformative process are governmental and nongovernmental organizations and women's grassroots actions that are aimed at building women's skills, confidence and business network.
>
> *(p. 245)*

In another study, Hanson and Blake (2009) concluded:

> The literature on entrepreneurial networks and gender is so poorly developed that the main take-away message is simply how little is known. Yet the larger body of research

on gender and networks in general suggests that exploring the intersection of gender and entrepreneurs' networks should prove extremely fruitful. Such research needs to go beyond asking who networks with whom to look carefully at how networks are embedded in larger cultural discourses and structures and how networks actually work within these structures.

(p. 146)

These suggestions fit well with a future focus on integrating entrepreneurial networks within a larger institutional framework. Scott's (2014) three institutional pillars may offer a way to connect gender and networks in entrepreneurship research. Ahl and Nelson (2015) studied the positioning of women's entrepreneurship through entrepreneurship policy in Sweden and the US. Their main finding demonstrates how policy specifically aimed at supporting women's entrepreneurship did not actually amend the subordinated position women have in society. Thus, future research may gain from targeting analysis of the regulative pillar through governmental and non-governmental bodies – formal policy and codified rules for behaviour at national, regional and institutional levels of analysis. One may then analyse the network links at the normative level. Finally, through the cognitive pillar, individuals' perceptions, motives and beliefs about entrepreneurship can be analysed. Thus, structuration processes are both top-down and bottom-up. This suggests the need to study the embeddedness of gendered networks in a larger cultural and structural system, cf. Ahl and Nelson (2010). The study of the intersection of institutions and entrepreneurship is rich and important and should be extended. The nation, the state, religion, welfare and other regulatory systems, as well as language, data and statistics as means of research are all examples of institutions that intersect with entrepreneurship with consequences for male and female entrepreneurs and thus society.

Conclusions

This chapter has revealed that the discourse on networks and gender in entrepreneurship research has not changed much in recent years in articles published in the field. Hegemonic statements that: women network "poorly", are inherently relational in their networking and that weak ties are the clue to economic performance remain as published knowledge or "truth". By drawing on essential work from feminist theory, as well as recent calls for contextualising research (Welter, 2011), gender and network research needs to take new directions in order to create new knowledge. Studies of the role of gender in network research still utilise the same theories, employ the same methods and produce the same findings. We do not need more studies of biological sex and networks. Work examining how entrepreneurial networks are built, developed, maintained and changed within different levels of institutional layers (Scott, 2014) is needed in order to change a discourse that merely seems to repeat itself. Future entrepreneurship scholars interested in developing new discourses and exploring innovative research avenues within gender and network studies should seek to investigate the rich theoretical and empirical opportunities available instead of repeating old and tired rhetoric.

Note

1 The selection criteria were that the articles dealt with all three categories: gender, networks and entrepreneurship.

References

Ahl, H. (2007) A Foucauldian framework for discourse analysis. In Neergard, H. Ulhoj, J.P. (eds), *Handbook of Qualitative Research Methods in Entrepreneurship*. Cheltenham: Edward Elgar, 216–250.

Ahl, H. & Nelson, T. (2010) Moving forward: Institutional perspectives on gender and entrepreneurship. *International Journal of Gender and Entrepreneurship, 2*(1), 5–9.

Ahl, H., & Nelson, T. (2015) How policy positions women entrepreneurs: A comparative. analysis of state discourse in Sweden and the United States. *Journal of Business Venturing, 30*(2), 273–291.

Aldrich, H., Rosen, H., and Woodward, W. (1987) The impact of social networks on business foundings and profit: A longitudinal study. In N.C. Churchill et al., eds, *Frontiers of Entrepreneurship Research*. Wellesley, MA: Babson College, 154–168.

Alvesson, M. & Due Billing, Y. (1999) Kön och organisation. Studentlitteratur: Lund.

Birley, S. (1985) The role of networks in the entrepreneurial process. *Journal of Business Venturing, 1*(1), 107–117.

Brush, C. G., De Bruin, A., & Welter, F. (2009) A gender-aware framework for women's entrepreneurship. *International Journal of Gender and Entrepreneurship, 1*(1), 8–24.

Calás, M.B. & Smircich, L. (1996) From the woman's' point of view: Feminist approaches to organization studies. In Clegg, S. Hardy, C. and Nord, W. (eds) *Handbook of Organization Studies*. London: Sage, 218–257.

Fernández-Pérez, V., Alonso-Galicia, P. E., Fuentes-Fuentes, M. del Mar, & Rodriguez-Ariza, L. (2014). Business social networks and academics' entrepreneurial intentions. *Industrial Management & Data Systems, 114*(2), 292–320.

Foss, L. (1994) Entrepreneurship: the impact of human capital, a social network and business resources on start-up. Phd thesis, Norwegian School of Economics, Norway.

Foss, L. (2010) Research on entrepreneur networks: The case for a constructionist feminist theory perspective. *International Journal of Gender and Entrepreneurship, 2*(1), 82–101.

Foucault, M. (1972) *The Archeology of Knowledge*. Tavistock, London.

Greve, A., & Salaff, J. W. (2003) Social networks and entrepreneurship. *Entrepreneurship Theory and Practice, 28*, 1–22.

Grossman, E. B., Yli-Renko, H., & Janakiraman, R. (2012) Resource search, interpersonal similarity, and network tie valuation in nascent entrepreneurs' emerging networks. *Journal of Management, 38*(6), 1760–1787.

Gulati, R., Nohria, N. and Zaheer, A. (2000) Strategic networks. *Strategic Management Journal*, 21, 203–215.

Haddad, G. & Loarne, S. L. (2015) Social networking and gender effects in opportunity identification. *International Journal of Entrepreneurship and Small Business, 24*(1), 23–40.

Hampton, A., Cooper, S., & McGowan, P. (2009) Female entrepreneurial networks and networking activity in technology-based ventures: An exploratory study. *International Small Business Journal, 27*(2), 193–214.

Hampton, A., McGowan, P. & Cooper, S. (2011) Developing quality in female high-technology entrepreneurs' networks. *International Journal of Entrepreneurial Behavior & Research, 17*(6), 588–606.

Hanson, S. (2009) Changing places through women's entrepreneurship. *Economic Geography, 85*(3), 245–267.

Hanson, S. & Blake, M. (2009) Gender and entrepreneurial networks. *Regional Studies, 43*(1), 135–149.

Harding, S. (1987). Introduction: Is there a feminist method? In Harding, S. (ed.) *Feminism and Methodology*. Bloomington, IN: Indiana University Press, 1–14.

Henry, C., Foss, L. & Ahl, H. (2015) Gender and entrepreneurship: A review of methodological approaches. *International Small Business Journal*, 1–25.

Hoang, H. and Antoncic, B. (2003) Network-based research in entrepreneurship: A critical review. *Journal of Business Venturing, 18*(2), 165.

Jack, S.L., Drakopoulou Dodd, S., & Anderson, A.R. (2004) Social structures and entrepreneurial networks: The strength of strong ties. *International Journal of Entrepreneurship and Innovation, 5*(2), 107–120.

Jennings, J. E. & Brush, C. G. (2013) Research on women entrepreneurs: Challenges to (and from) the broader entrepreneurship literature? *Academy of Management Annals*, 7, 663–715.

Johannisson, B. (2000) Networking and entrepreneurial growth, in Sexton, D. L. and Landström, H. (eds). *The Blackwell Handbook of Entrepreneurship*. Oxford: Blackwell, 368–386.

Klyver, K. (2011) Gender differences in entrepreneurial networks: adding an alter perspective. *Gender in Management: An International Journal, 26*(5), 332–350.

Klyver, K. & Grant, S. (2010) Gender differences in entrepreneurial networking and participation. *International Journal of Gender and Entrepreneurship, 2*(3), 213–227.

Kwon, S. W. & Arenius, P. (2010) Nations of entrepreneurs: A social capital perspective. *Journal of Business Venturing, 25*(3), 315–330.

Maas, J., Seferiadis, A. A., Bunders, J. F. G. & Zweekhorst, M. B. M. (2014) Bridging the disconnect: How network creation facilitates female Bangladeshi entrepreneurship. *International Entrepreneurship and Management Journal*, 1–14.

Marlow, S. & McAdam, M. (2012) Analyzing the influence of gender upon high-technology venturing within the context of business incubation. *Entrepreneurship Theory & Practice*, 36; 655–676.

Miller, G.E. (Ed.) *Explorations in interpersonal communication.* Oxford, England: Sage Explorations in interpersonal communication.

Mirchandani, K. (1999) Feminist insight on gendered work: New directions in research on women and entrepreneurship. *Gender, Work & Organization, 6*(4), 224–235.

Nahapiet, J. & Ghosal, S. (1998) Entrepreneurs' networks and the success of start-ups. Social Capital, Intellectual Capital, and the Organizational Advantage, *Academy of Management Review, 23*(2) 242–266.

Neergaard, H., Fredriksen, S. & Marlow, S. (2011) The emperor's new clothes: Rendering a feminist theory of entrepreneurship visible, in *The 56th ICSB Conference, Stockholm*, 15–18 June.

Renzulli, L.A. & Aldrich, H.E. (2005) Who can you turn to? Tie activation within core business discussion networks, *Social Forces, 84*(1), 323–341.

Robinson, S., & Stubberud, H. A. (2009) Sources of advice in entrepreneurship: Gender differences in business owners' social networks. *International Journal of Entrepreneurship, 13*, 83.

Scott, W. R. (2014) *Institutions and organizations: Ideas, interests, and identities,* 4th edition. Thousand Oaks, CA: Sage.

Steyaert, C. & Katz, J. (2004) Reclaiming the space of entrepreneurship in society: geographical, discursive and social dimensions. *Entrepreneurship & Regional development, 16*(3), 179–196.

Tolbert, P.S., David, R.J. & Sine, W. D (2011) Studying choice and change: The intersection of institutional theory and entrepreneurship research. *Organization Science, 22*(5), 1332–1344.

Tsuchiya, R. (2010) Neighbourhood social networks and female self-employment earnings in Taiwan. *International Entrepreneurship and Management Journal, 6*(2), 143–161.

Watson, J. (2011) Networking: Gender differences and the association with firm performance. *International Small Business Journal, 30*(5), 536–558.

Welter, F. (2011) Contextualizing entrepreneurship: Conceptual challenges and ways forward. *Entrepreneurship Theory and Practice, 35*(1), 165–184.

Welter, F. and Smallbone, D. (2011) Institutional perspectives on entrepreneurial behavior in challenging environments, *Journal of Small Business Management, 49*(1), 107–125.

Witt, P. (2004) Entrepreneurs' networks and the success of start-ups, *Entrepreneurship & Regional Development, 16*(5), 391–412.

Zahra, S. A. (2007) Contextualizing theory building in entrepreneurship research. *Journal of Business Venturing, 22*(3), 443–452.

PART IV

Identity

14

IDENTITY WORK, SWIFT TRUST AND GENDER

The role of women-only leadership development programmes

Claire Leitch, Richard Harrison and Maura McAdam

Introduction

This chapter explores the role of women-only leadership development programmes in shaping women's entrepreneurial leader identity. We conceptualise entrepreneurial leadership as the leadership role performed in entrepreneurial ventures, rather than in the more general sense of an entrepreneurial style of leadership (Leitch, McMullan and Harrison, 2012). The enactment of entrepreneurial leadership is a complex process of identity work (Watson, 2009). In essence, identity, which is concerned with an individual's attitudes, beliefs and behaviours, provides entrepreneurial leaders with a source of meaning from which to operate (Day and Harrison, 2007). However, many leaders of entrepreneurial ventures fail to see themselves as leaders (Anderson and Gold, 2009). This can be exacerbated for women, as the gendering of the dominant entrepreneurship discourse assumes a male entrepreneurial identity (Bruni, Gherardi and Poggio, 2004: Hamilton, 2013).

Acquiring and maintaining an identity is not a one-off event but instead can be learnt and practiced over the course of an individual's career and lifetime (O'Connell, 2014), through the process of identity work. Reflexive subjects undertake identity work in an attempt to be deemed legitimate within the various environments they encounter (Marlow and McAdam, 2012). This dynamic and iterative process is enacted within situated contexts and shaped by the characteristics of those involved (Sveningsson and Alvesson, 2003). Seeking and claiming legitimacy pivots upon successful identity work, as only by convincing the dominant referent group of one's 'fit' can an individual be deemed credible. As part of achieving credibility as an entrepreneurial leader, individuals can take actions to inform their sense of self as a leader, including participation in leadership development programmes (Carroll and Levy, 2010). However, while increasing attention has been paid to the construct of identity in entrepreneurship (Navis and Glynn, 2011), very few studies have investigated the process of identity work (see Watson, 2009; Philips, Tracey and Karra, 2013 for exceptions), even though the entrepreneurial context provides a rich opportunity for identity creation and interpretation.

Despite increasing policy initiatives and interventions, a shortage of women entrepreneurs in general and women entrepreneurial leaders in particular remains (Brush, Balachandra, Davis and Greene, 2014). More recently, economic and related leadership crises have led to calls for radically new approaches to gender in business (Wittenberg-Cox, 2013). The gender gap at senior levels tends to be attributed to structural and attitudinal barriers (Ely and Rhode, 2010; Ely, Ibarra and Kolb, 2011). Referred to as second-generation gender biases, these are so subtle, deep-rooted and covert that we are unconscious of their pervasiveness and influence on beliefs and behaviours (Kandola, 2009). Furthermore, these are often perpetuated as men continue to dominate leadership positions, ensuring that organizational structures, processes and practices are biased towards assumptions and behaviours potentially more suited to men. Structural barriers women face in organizations include under-representation in traditional structures of organizational power (Ely, 1995; Ridgeway, 1993), which can lead to limited access to informational networks (Ibarra, 1992). Furthermore, women tend to face the incompatibility of caring and domestic responsibilities with dominant forms of working including inflexible working hours, often associated with career progression (Ely and Rhode, 2010). Women's perceptions of themselves, rooted in traditional gender expectations and practices, also contribute to the gender gap (Ely and Rhode, 2010). One means of overcoming these invisible but pervasive forms of gender bias is through building and enhancing women leaders' identity and subsequent leadership capability. Recently, Ely et al. (2011) have called for a new leadership development agenda for women-only, with a specific focus on identity work, in an attempt to overcome the biases women experience that can impede the development of their leader identity. This is a timely call for women leaders in entrepreneurial businesses, who are generally underrepresented, marginalised and often isolated, lacking role models and having little opportunity to share their experiences (Fielden and Dawe, 2004; Hamilton, 2006; Stead, 2014). Women entrepreneurial leadership development programmes, thus, can provide women with an environment within which to explore the issues they potentially face. There is, however, very little research specifically on identity formation in the context of women-only leadership development programmes (Harrison, Leitch and McAdam, 2015).

While there has been a mixed response to women-only leadership development programmes (Devillard, Graven, Lawson, Paradise and Sancier-Sultan, 2012), such courses have endured and evolved over the last 35 years (Vinnicombe, Moore and Anderson, 2013). Indeed, in response to the leadership talent crisis and the diversity agenda, an increasing number of well-known and highly regarded US and European institutions now offer women-only leadership development (Ely et al., 2011). Although leadership development is a costly and high-profile human resources activity (Mabey and Finch-Lees, 2008: 3) there remain a number of unanswered questions (Mabey, 2013; Day, Fleenor, Atwater, Sturm and McKee, 2014). In particular, coherent and theoretically informed approaches shaping the development, operation and impact of women leadership are lacking (Ely et al., 2011). This chapter addresses these limitations and offers a deeper theoretical understanding and more reflective consideration of entrepreneurial leadership development. We do this by exploring the factors that influence women in the shaping, developing and revising of their entrepreneurial leader identity through participation in a women's leadership programme.

The chapter is structured as follows. In the next section, we review the nature and impact of women's leadership development programmes on identity development. We then outline the research design and approach adopted in this exploratory study. The presentation of the analysis and results is in two stages: first, we identify a number of themes associated with the design of and participation in women-only leadership development programmes, including building confidence (Coffman and Neuenfeldt, 2014), the approach to programme design and leadership skills development, and second, we identify a number of new themes emerging from the reflexive experience of participants, notably the role of the programme as an arena for identity work through leadership development and the creation of a shared safe space in which self-reflection and personal development can occur. In the final section of the chapter, we draw on the literature on swift trust to provide a theoretical grounding for our analysis and identify implications for practice in the design and delivery of women's leadership development programmes in an entrepreneurial context.

The contributions of the chapter are threefold. First, we provide insights into how entrepreneurial leadership identity is formed, shaped and maintained. Second, we advance gender theorising by exploring the role of gender in the design, delivery and impact of leadership development. Specifically, we employ the concept of swift trust (Meyerson, Weick and Kramer, 1996) to explain the emergence of a shared safe space in an entrepreneurial leadership development setting. Finally, from a practitioner viewpoint, we inform the design and development of future leadership development programmes for entrepreneurial leaders.

Leadership development programmes

Perspectives on addressing women's leadership development tend to take three main approaches (Ely et al., 2011). First, there is what Martin and Meyerson (1998, p. 312) have termed the "add-women-and-stir" approach, where women and men attend the same courses because it is assumed that gender does not impact leadership development. However, this does not take in to consideration the gendering of leadership development. For instance, Sinclair (1995, 1997) has argued that MBA courses are based on a masculinised set of practices that reinforce male dominance. This is manifested in the centralisation of authority and power in the educational space, the refusal to admit uncertainty, the focus on best practice instead of personal experience and the emphasis on analytical techniques at the expense of intuition and emotion. Ignoring the importance of socially aware learning in leadership learning and development activities can be problematic as it assumes that leadership, management and learning are neutral processes (Ramsey, 2005, p. 223). Such an assumption downplays the role that social context and social conditions play in the learning environment including the impact of gender, race and class (Brook, Pedler and Burgoyne, 2012; Ram and Trehan, 2010). Even if differences are acknowledged, attempting to neutralise them is unrealistic and counterproductive as it serves only to reinforce the dominant group (Reynolds and Trehan, 2003).

Second, there is the "fix-the-women" approach, which while acknowledging that gender is an issue adopts the view that women have not been socialised appropriately to compete in a man's world and thus need to be provided with the tools and skills to better equip them to do so (Ely and Meyerson, 2000). Third, there is what we call the "ourselves-alone" mind set that acknowledges that there are a number of issues in the workplace, such as power and politics, sexuality, sex differences in working approaches, stress and the nature of career development, that specifically concern women and are, therefore, best addressed in a women–only environment (Vinnicombe and Colwill, 1995). As such, Vinnicombe et al. (2013) advocate that any women's development programme must take into account both sex-related differences found in relation to leadership and the gender dynamics that, irrespective of size, shape most organizations' culture and the subsequent impact this can have on how women feel valued. Such courses provide women with an opportunity to reflect on and reinterpret their managerial experiences with other women in similar positions and to celebrate differences rather than being defensive about them (Vinnicombe and Singh, 2003). In particular, they help women leaders make sense of how gender operates in everyday business practice (Stead and Elliot, 2009). Nevertheless, a tension exists here in that while many women feel positive after attending a women-only programme, others (especially younger women) shun them for fear of being stigmatised (Vinnicombe et al., 2013, p. 408).

Given this, entrepreneurial leadership development has to take into consideration the immediate local context in which women leaders find themselves and "the broad social context that dictates gender roles, cultural norms and expected behaviours" (Bierema, 2001, p. 56). In the remainder of this chapter, we examine what resources and capabilities may be impacted by the single-sex environment in terms of programme design and participants' networking behaviours within that. We also consider from whom women seek legitimacy, explore the extent to which segregation can create challenges and consider the manner in which single-sex development can facilitate or hinder women's identity work and draw out the implications for research and practice. To illustrate this we draw on the experiences of both facilitators and participants of a women-only programme.

Research context and approach

In framing this chapter, we have argued that as reflexive individuals, people draw upon available discourses to make sense of and enact with reality (Watson, 2011). When referring to discourses, we follow Kelan (2009, p. 68) who argues that these are not comprised of just linguistic narratives but include, "spoken, written and acted texts". As such, discourses are diverse frames of reference that inform, constrain and/or enable our enactments of culturally and contextually appropriate behaviours. Accordingly, we consider entrepreneurial leadership to be a process and performance that has cognitive and physical components entrepreneurial leaders will encounter, negotiate and reproduce.

Given the exploratory nature of this pilot study, we adopted an interpretivist stance in order to gain understanding of the nuances of how identity is shaped, formed and maintained (Case, 2003; Weick, 2007). As a consequence, we acknowledge the importance of issues such as those of social construction, researcher interpretation and narrative/discursive framing without denying that there are realities that exist in the social world (Watson, 2011). By making use of a social constructivist perspective, this study is distanced from any ambition to create a grand narrative that suggests universal dimensions of order, but rather aims to explore the multiplicity of complexities and contradictions that shapes situated experience and activity (Boyce, 1996).

Our sample was drawn from the first cohort of participants in a women-only leadership development programme, and its designers and deliverers/facilitators (Ruth and Bonnie). All participants of the programme were employed at middle- or senior-manager level in their organisations. Each was afforded a pseudonym to preserve anonymity. Of the four participants, two (Anita and June) agreed to contribute to the study and discuss their experiences of identity work and leadership development in an entrepreneurial context. This allowed us to obtain a holistic perspective of the programme from facilitators and participants. This led to the generation of a wealth of contextualised material that accords with the rationale of interpretive pilot research regarding theory development where thick description and contextualised scripts are conceptually embedded in analytical frames.

Detailed empirical material was generated from an exploration of the experiences and insights of participants via semi-structured interviews. The interviews, which lasted approximately two hours, were tape recorded and transcribed. The interviewing schedules framed guided conversations; the stories that emerged however, were freely narrated responses, the questions acting to direct recollections and explorations around the key themes of identity work and leadership development. Following Boje (1991), the researcher acted as an informed listener attempting to 'get the story straight' but at the same time encouraging the discussion towards the analytical underpinnings of the study. Whilst the point of detailed, interpretive enquiry is to elicit depth and detail, this presents challenges in drawing out salient issues and ordering the material generated. To address this issue, we began the analysis by reading through transcripts and identifying and comparing initial concepts and grouping them into provisional categories (Strauss and Corbin, 1998). We then sought to identify ways in which these categories related to each other and the key themes within our framing analysis (Locke, 1996; Strauss and Corbin, 1998). This process is not linear but rather develops through a dialogue between the researchers and the respondents. A "recursive, process-oriented, analytic procedure" emerges (Locke, 1996, p. 240), drawing out key theoretical relationships. This process resulted in the following stories, which are made up of the strands that emerged from the data and reflect the key themes in the literature. To present a coherent analysis of the findings as outlined below, each theme is explored in detail illustrated with fragments of the narrative (Pratt, 2009).

Programme origin and design

The original genesis for the development of the programme resulted from Ruth's role as the only female management consultant in a leadership and management development consultancy. During the 1990s, she designed and facilitated open-access, generic leadership courses and observed that women tended to be under-represented. As a result, she decided to develop a women-only course. Initial background research, conducted by her, revealed that while women were technically competent comparatively few advanced to senior management positions or established their own business due to a perceived lack of confidence on their part and self-selected non-mobility. The latter, Ruth attributed to women being promoted to middle-management levels in the organisation and deciding that the additional responsibilities and pressures that might result were incommensurate with any extra remuneration they might receive. This resonates with preference theory (Hakim, 2000, 2006), which was the first attempt to explain women's behaviour and choices among family, work and market work, especially for those living in progressive, affluent and liberal modern societies.

Developed in recognition of the male bias in existing economic and sociological theory of labour market participation, which primarily referenced male labour market participation and men's work-life histories, it predicts diversity in work-lifestyle choices for three groups of women: home-centred women, adaptive women who combine work and family and work-centred women. Recent research confirms that there are fewer women in senior leadership positions than men as a result of family commitments (Opportunity Now, 2014). Despite legislation and policy initiatives, traditional organisational structures and expectations evident in hegemonic or greedy careers (Hakim, 2006) can be all consuming, especially at senior levels.

Course development was also informed by Simmons' (1996) work on the benefits of building an inclusive organisation, which he believed was hindered by gender conditioning leading many managers to build barriers preventing all employees from being fully involved. One means to overcome this, he suggested, was by eliminating institutional discrimination and prejudice. The initial course was scoped in conjunction with Michael Simmons, and while it has subsequently evolved, its basic premises remain. Three main elements provided the foundations of the programme, building confidence, creating context and the development of leadership skills and behaviours, and these are interwoven throughout its structure. Such an approach addresses the "ourselves-alone" mind set by specifically acknowledging the challenges and obstacles facing women leaders.

Identity work

Fundamental to the programme's design was the desire to build participants' identity, based on exploring their leadership journeys to date. At the outset, the initial focus is at the individual level and aims to get women to connect with positive aspects about themselves, for example by asking them who their heroes/heroines have been and how they have been heroines. In so doing, the emphasis is on women accessing who they are and being encouraged to own their style and strengths: in other words, identity work. The initial session also addresses the ways in which women and men are socialised and the subsequent impact of this. The dominant messages explored in this particular programme for women include looking nice, taking a backseat, taking care of people, not putting themselves first and not being aggressive. On the other hand, men are taught from an early age not to show weakness or to cry and from adolescence not to be close to other men, which can result in their being disconnected from their feelings (Simmons, 1996). The premise of this is to highlight to the women that men's attitudes and behaviours to leadership can be also limited by stereotypical attitudes.

Creating context

While building identity is the micro-foundation of the programme design, establishing the business case for women's participation in senior leadership positions provided its macro-context. This is based on the recognition that the barriers to career progression that women face are systemic and are not to do with personal attributes or characteristics. In particular, Ruth advocates the value of the business case for increased involvement of women in senior leadership positions predicated on economic and social factors such as talent management, succession planning, competition for the best people and the need to address the skills shortage. She strongly believes that equality should exist for both men and women and that it is important to have men as allies,

> someone said to me one time, to break the glass ceiling it's better that somebody drops a brick on it from above. So that is why I think you need senior men and others who sponsor good talent to come through. Rather than women bouncing up and down, you know trying to hit with their heads.
>
> *(Ruth)*

Leadership skills and behaviours

A key element in programme design was the belief in the importance of women managing their careers (goals and expectations) and obtaining skills and experience across a range of functions. This in turn was based on the view that women stay in jobs as a result of loyalty compounded by the fact that their leader, frequently male, may be reluctant to promote them as they have come to rely on them. This is a key structural cause and consequence of the glass ceiling phenomenon:

You get women that settle in a job in middle-management in their mid-40s and they stay there and they block that job for 20 years. And younger people coming up can't get through, there's no mobility, there's no exit... .

(Ruth)

The alternative, central to the rationale for and positioning of the programme, is that

they need to be moving, you know, even if I'm happy that **XXX** has been in a job for ten years and she's great in that job, that's all the more reason to move her. It'll keep her fresh, keep her learning and actually keeps the energy in the organization going.

(Ruth)

All of this, of course, raises issues of agency through women lacking energy, time and focus, their ability to handle criticism, to grant permission to protect themselves, stand up for themselves and to take risks. These are universal, not ad personam issues:

I think, whenever women realize it's not about me, this is universal, this happens to everyone and now I realize actually I can take action. Whereas, where I think I'm the deficit, I have to fix me, then it's harder.

(Ruth)

An interactive and experiential format with a high commitment to peer-learning was adopted, and care was taken to create safe spaces for learning. The programme has been designed to be flexible, built around three one-day sessions with coaching slots in between. The one-on-one coaching sessions are based on the feedback and issues arising from the application of a 360-degree, feedback assessment using a specially designed instrument that attempts to obtain objective feedback and evidence of participants' abilities. Reflecting on participants' reactions to the programme design and structure, Bonnie highlighted three key issues. First, the rapport between participants occurred much more rapidly than she had previously experienced in either male-only or mixed programmes:

...it felt like the intimacy and the connection was there a lot faster for the women.... People were very, very open and obviously felt safe enough that they could expose [themselves].

Second, the engagement with the learning opportunities that the programme afforded:

And they come in and they're quickly into it. Men are different, you know, much [less engaged].

This, Bonnie attributed to the women being at a non-mobility career threshold and having selectively chosen to come on the programme; in other words, they were heavily invested emotionally and instrumentally in it and what it represents. Third, the role of networking on and through the programme, and in particular the importance of developing weak not strong ties with shallow wide relationships, in which issues of reciprocity (Leitch, Harrison and Hill, 2015) and determining one's business value play a central role (Cross and Parker, 2004). Despite the small numbers Bonnie considered the programme to have achieved, and potentially exceeded, its aims:

...in that if we were measuring impact it was very successful.

241

Participant leadership development and identity work

Using the leadership programme as a contextual backdrop to analyse the process of gendered identity work in the search for entrepreneurial leadership identity enables us draw these constructs together and to contribute to contemporary debates. To explore how the women entrepreneurial leaders arrived at the decision to enrol in the programme, we asked them initially to reflect upon their entrepreneurial journey to date and the factors that had fuelled their pursuit of leadership-development identity work. Having established their motivations, we then focused specifically upon their recent experience of this particular women-only programme to gain a sense of how this had influenced and shaped the enactment of their leadership identity and its effects on leadership legitimacy and credibility in an entrepreneurial context. From the analysis of the findings, three critical themes emerged with related sub-themes: first, identity and identity work enacted as a gendered performance; second, leadership development as a specific type of identity work and finally, enablers of the enactment of identity work, which included shared safe space, swift trust and self-reflection. To illustrate these themes, we now describe fragments of the narrative accounts shared by the respondents.

Identity and identity work (enacted as a gendered performance)

The programme provided the opportunity for the women to take time out and invest in their identity work. Indeed, enrolling in the leadership programme was the first time that the participants had consciously thought about working on their identity as leaders. Three specific issues emerged: time and space for reflection, the solitary nature of women in leadership positions including a lack of role models and issues of leadership style and gender.

First, Anita wanted to participate in the programme as "I very much work on my own". In addition to this, she wanted skills to help her to work with external stakeholders and to gain structure, guidance and reassurance in planning her career. "I wanted formal support and mechanisms to put together a plan to steer my future" (Anita). Indeed, taking time out (away from the normal working day and normal physical environs) was important for both women, with June referring to the leadership course as defining in the sense that "I started treating my leadership and my leadership role seriously". Second, the solitary nature of being a woman in a leadership position was emphasised, which was exacerbated by a lack of female role models "there are very, very few females who I have met throughout my career who became my role models" (June). Added to this was the women's awareness of the importance of network development in relation to their leadership development "developing networks on a really, really high level, and maintaining those networks is crucial" (June).

Third, the impact of different styles of leadership and the influence of gender on shaping, forming and maintaining leader identity were highlighted. The participants referred to the concept of servant leadership (Greenleaf, 2002), of "being the facilitator behind the scenes, not only doing the work but also influencing the decisions while, to some extent, men take the ownership" (June). This prompted a wider reflection on gender and leadership style, reflecting more general discussions of the so-called feminisation of leadership in the twenty-first century (Fletcher, 2004): "Definitely there are different styles. I think that there are gender differences and we are motivated and driven differently... [I'm] not pretending that it's all generic, so I think the first thing we have to do is acknowledge that there are gender differences" (June). In part, this is an outcome of a more self-effacing leadership style: "Women lead the way from behind the scenes" (Anita). However, there is a downside to this, as observed by June in that "women have to be more chameleon-like, in adjusting to the mood of the group, to facilitate".

Entrepreneurial leadership development
(as a specific type of identity work)

Given these observations, the programme participants reflected more specifically on the link between leadership development activities and their identities. This was the first time that either participant had opted for a women-only programme, but given where both were with regards their own leadership development journey they felt that it was essential: "other programmes would normally be dominated by males therefore if they're dominated by males there would be always be a certain take on things" (June). Reflecting concerns that mixed-sex programmes, especially those where men dominated, could be intimidating and competitive environments, our respondents expressed concerns about the extent to which they would be able to participate in, and benefit from, such a programme:

> Men can potentially be overpowering and can take over and I was concerned that I wouldn't get an opportunity to talk or participate about what I needed to.
>
> *(Anita)*

This in part reflected their experience-based beliefs about male participative styles:

> Men are better talking about what they have done even if they haven't done it. Women are more likely to ground their talk in experience.
>
> *(Anita)*

However, in a mixed group this grounded talk was less likely to be articulated, especially in circumstances where the participant felt unease or discomfort:

> Within the first hour we were propelled into something uncomfortable – I didn't know what to say. However, once the other participants started to talk about their experiences, I could see similarities and started to relax.
>
> *(Anita)*

There is, in other words, a very real sense of a women-only leadership programme being seen as a protected supportive arena in which issues of leader identity could be explored freely and openly.

Enablers of the enactment of identity work

Shared safe space and swift trust

The programme provided an environment away from the women's working day, and it became clear that this evolved into a shared safe space as the women started to exchange experiences. This sharing was aided by the structure of the programme:

> So I think it was nice to be in an environment or to network with other female leaders and to see what challenges other female leaders experience.
>
> *(June)*

243

The consequence of the programme design was that both participants "felt more at ease and relaxed than with mixed programmes" (Anita), with "good participation with all of the women, easy to relate to each other, good dynamics from the outset, sharing similar experiences" (Anita). This was notwithstanding the challenges of participation: "The first day I was out of my comfort zone, a very emotional day, though I felt reassured at the end of it" (Anita). As an opportunity to explore one's entrepreneurial leader identity three observations can be made. First, the women reported a very positive experience of the benefits of participating in a women-only leadership development programme in comparison with prior experience in mixed-sex ones. Second, the participants acknowledged that the programme provided an environment that was a shared safe space allowing them to be vulnerable and to explore issues of personal significance. Third, the rapid development of sharing relationships within the programme demonstrates many of the characteristics of swift trust (Meyerson et al., 1996), an issue we develop below.

Self-reflection

Given that the programme provided a shared safe space within which trustful relations could develop swiftly, it is unsurprising that the opportunity for self-reflection was a major benefit identified by participants:

> I think that is what we're all missing in life - self-reflection, which was the most defining thing for me, actually to stop and to think where I am, where I want to be. It's so simple but not always obvious.

> *(June)*

However, while it was recognised that the programme played a role in encouraging reflection, the common consensus amongst the women was that this reflection needed to be facilitated as:

> if I sat at home or went for a walk and started thinking, well that's one thing, but having a little bit of structure, a little framework, it's important. Yes, having the framework was probably the key thing for me.

> *(June)*

This is consistent with the findings of prior research into entrepreneurial leadership (Leitch, McMullan and Harrison, 2012) and investment decision-making (Harrison, Mason and Dibben, 1996), which identified that the coordinator or facilitator of a network, group or leadership development programme cohort plays a critical role in brokering the rapid development of trust relationships.

Personal development

One of the most evident outcomes of participation in the programme was the change in leadership style, moving away from the servant leadership expressed at the outset to a more assertive, less self-effacing style:

> I think this was one of the key things I took away, that it's no longer about serving and the idea of servant leadership and facilitating. No, now it's time for me to lead, it's time for me to take charge.

> *(June)*

In other words, "I'm moving now from being a facilitator and servant leader to being a leader" (June). This reflects increased confidence, in terms of both the participants' self-confidence and in the increased confidence placed in them by others:

> I have the confidence to say no now – interestingly people accept it, my boss has commented on this a couple of times recently.
>
> *(Anita)*

This confidence is reflected in a greater willingness to demonstrate leadership and to seek out further opportunities for leadership development:

> I now need recognition and to promote myself, step out from the shadows . .... The course provided me with evidence that I had some leadership skills and how to get to the next level. ....At meetings I now ask questions – I now want people to remember me so I ask questions. I always had something to say but was afraid to say it.
>
> *(Anita)*

For both women, the overarching benefit of participation in a women-only leadership development programme was the development of a stronger sense of leader identity: "Instead of seeking approval, I am much more direct and prepared to take the consequences afterwards which is a radical transformation" (Anita). "So I don't have to struggle anymore to prove myself" (June).

Discussion

This research confirms the findings of other studies of the importance of creating a shared safe space for women to work on their leadership (Vinnicombe et al., 2013), which is best achieved by helping women to make sense of their entrepreneurial experiences in a positive way (Ely et al., 2011). Our analysis demonstrates that creating this shared safe space and thereby enabling participants to feel comfortable enough to take psychological risks with one another by, for example, exposing vulnerabilities and frailties, seeking support and feedback and voicing problems, requires confidence to be built and trust to be established. Women's under-representation in organisational leadership positions reflects a domain-specific lack of confidence, attributable to a clash with the 'ideal worker' stereotype, a lack of supervisory support and too few role models (Coffman and Neuenfeldt, 2014). Trust has long been acknowledged as a critical component in entrepreneurial learning (Finnigan and Daly, 2012). Creating a trustful learning environment can reduce uncertainty and vulnerability and increase the depth of exchanges between participants. For Hosking (2014, pp. 2–3) when we talk about trust "we are talking of our feelings about the future ... [and] ... time, place, and social context are crucial to the trust assumptions on which we base all our thoughts and actions".

Trust is a complex construct, conceptualised in multiple ways in a variety of disciplines (Goel and Karri, 2006). Despite the multiplicity of definitions, it is generally associated with expectations of fair play, acceptance of the rights and interests of others, ideas of joint undertaking and a level of shared understanding of the rules of engagement and behaviour in a particular situation (Kasper-Fuehrer and Ashkanasy, 2001). Early studies of trust focused on long-term relationships, as it was believed that trust was built incrementally and accumulated over time. In other words, it was history dependent (Meyerson et al, 1996). An example of this tradition is Lewicki and Bunker's (1995, 1996) three-stage model in which they identify different types of trust emerging at different stages of group development.

In this perspective, trust is based on interpersonal relationships (Lewicki, Tomlinson and Gillespie, 2006). Calculus-based trust forms between individuals during the initial stage of a relationship and is based on the assessment of the outcomes of creating and sustaining the relationship vis-à-vis the costs of severing it. This tends to be the most common form of trust in a business relationship (Harrison et al., 1996). For groups that interact productively over a longer period of time, calculus-based trust is transformed into knowledge-based trust. This is grounded in individuals' knowledge of each other's behaviours, which permits them to make predictions about it, thus, reducing uncertainty. Identity-based trust is the final stage and occurs when individuals have a high degree of identification with each other's wishes and intentions, to such an extent that they are willing to act and substitute for each other. As Driver (2015, p. 2) points out, identity-based trust is considered to be the strongest form of trust on the basis that more identification leads to more trust (Terrion and Ashforth, 2002; Henderson and Gilding, 2004; Maguire and Phillips, 2008; Van der Zee et al., 2009; Zhang and Huxham, 2009).

In considering the relationship between trust and identity work, Driver (2015), building on Li (2011), argues that trust is a complex socially constructed, linguistic and ultimately elusive phenomenon. Identification, therefore, is never just an interpersonal phenomenon, concerning those persons involved in a trustful relationship; it is also a social, discursive linguistic construction. Specifically, people draw on trust discourse not only to validate their identities but also to feel validated. Thus, this trust discourse is necessarily integral to all attempts to narrate the self in an authentic and real manner. In short, the plurivocal narrative of identity construction and identity work (Hamilton, 2014) is, and has to be researched as, a narrative of the discourse of trust, which is a "fragile and temporary accomplishment aimed at stability but often under construction" (Driver 2015, p. 19).

However, this recent extension of trust theory to identity work, as with much of the existing corpus of work, does not have a well worked-out account of how trust develops in time-constrained circumstances. With increasing globalisation, changes in technology and the practice of using short-term and virtual project teams, attention has shifted to the development of high levels of initial trust in reduced time frames. Reflecting this, an alternative strand of research has developed in which interpersonal relations are given less prominence. Meyerson et al. (1996) proposed the term swift trust to explain the emergence of trust in situations where individuals have a limited history of working together and limited prospects of working together in the future – in this case a leadership development programme. Swift trust develops based on the knowledge and understanding of one's own capabilities (which of course might not be a realistic assessment) and the expected capabilities of others.

In entrepreneurship, the construct of trust has been explored primarily in the context of access to finance and lending decisions, including the relationships between entrepreneurs and banks (Howorth and Moro, 2006), entrepreneurs and business angel investors (Bammens and Collewaert, 2014; Mitteness, Baucus and Sudek, 2012; Ding, Au and Chiang, 2014; Harrison, et al., 1996), entrepreneurs and venture capitalists (Strätling, Wijbenga and Dietz, 2011) and in the processes of deal making (Scarborough, Swan and Amaeshi, 2013) and informal lending (Umoren, 2003). However, trust and in particular swift trust has not been used as a means of explaining the emergence of a non-competitive and supportive environment. Based on our research, we suggest that entrepreneurial leadership development programmes may be conceived as a temporary situation in which swift trust rather than time-dependent identification-based trust has to develop. Swift trust needs to be resilient enough to survive the life of a temporary group "there is quite literally, neither the time nor the opportunity in a temporary group for the sort of experience necessary for thicker [i.e. stronger] forms of trust to emerge" (Meyerson et al., 1996, p. 181). In such circumstances, a central indication of mutual trusting behaviour is seen in the willingness to cooperate or share personal information with a degree of vulnerability.

All leadership development programmes are essentially time constrained, characterised by a number of untested interpersonal relationships and by conditions of uncertainty. On commencing a programme, participants have to decide to what extent they wish to share insights and information about themselves and to which they can place their confidence and trust in others. They do so on the basis of an expectation that others will not take advantage of the situation and cause unnecessary harm, by entering "a state involving confident positive expectations about another's motives with respect to oneself in situations entailing risk" (Boon and Holmes, 1991, p. 194). This requires the establishment of a cooperative, non-competitive environment in which each individual's willingness to be vulnerable to another is based on the confidence that the latter party is benevolent, reliable, competent, honest and open (Cummings and Bromley, 1996; Hoy and Tschamen-Moran, 2003; Daly and Finningan, 2010). In this, and an extension of the original Meyerson et al. (1996) formulation, the role of the facilitator is important in creating an environment that allows trust to develop in relationships between others (Harrison et al., 1996; Leitch et al., 2012). This is typified by the creation of a temporary organisation as the basis for managing human social interaction through the establishment of clear expectations and responsibilities for all participants and the establishment of learning/psychological contract. In a time-constrained environment, it is the facilitation of a swift trust-based, shared safe space that results in a high-quality learning process, individual change and the generation of the desired outcomes for all.

Conclusions

The aim of this chapter was to explore the role of women-only leadership development programmes in shaping women's entrepreneurial leader identity. The leadership capability of an entrepreneurial leader can have a significant impact on the success or failure of their business. The higher likely impact of the entrepreneurial leader in her enactment of leadership is matched by the potentially greater challenges in developing appropriate and effective leadership capabilities and skills than would be the case in a corporate context. Entrepreneurial ventures are not simply scaled down versions of larger firms (Gibb, 2009) but are distinctive in terms of ambiguity, risk, uncertainty, innovation, organizational size and newness (Chen, 2007; Surie and Ashley, 2008; Autio, 2013) and are generally more sensitive to external contexts, especially environmental dynamism and volatility. Thus, the construction of an entrepreneurial leader identity is important in terms of developing insights into how to think and act like an entrepreneurial leader.

This research makes both a theoretical and a practical contribution to the field of entrepreneurial leadership development. First, we provide insights into how entrepreneurial leadership identity is formed, shaped and maintained through a leadership development programme. Second, we advance gender theorising by exploring the role of gender in the design, delivery and impact of leadership development activities, which differ to those on mixed programmes. Specifically, we employ the concept of swift trust (Meyerson et al., 1996) to explain the emergence of a shared safe space in an entrepreneurial leadership development setting. In this arena, from a practitioner viewpoint, we illustrate the need to understand and enhance developmental processes as opposed to concentrating on leadership per se (Day et al., 2014) and, in so doing, shed light on pedagogy and the role of the facilitator (Ely et al., 2011).

Therefore, future research into identity work and gender in entrepreneurial leadership development should be concerned more with investigating how entrepreneurs might be facilitated in constructing their leader identity and their subsequent enactment of entrepreneurial leadership. In other words, the focus should be on what entrepreneurial leaders do as opposed to who they are. As a result, ways in which gender bias may arise can be addressed. We have argued here that within the shared safe space of a women-only entrepreneurial leadership development programme, trust is necessarily implicated in all individual attempts to narrate the self through language. Trust, therefore, in this view, is intimately connected to identity work, which itself is the ongoing process of creating and recreating identity, that fragile and fleeting accomplishment that is an ongoing narrative construction that is plurivocal and co-performed (Sermijn, Devlieger and Loots, 2008; Driver, 2015). This is not to conclude that single-sex environments are the only ones in which this is achieved, rather, they form an appropriate, but not exclusive, part of a mix of experiences for the development of entrepreneurial leader identity. Our research participants, both programme designers/facilitators and programme participants, recognise that single-sex environments provide a necessary shared safe space in which to share and expose one's vulnerabilities and frailties in a way that would not happen in other, more masculinist, contexts. They also recognise that this provides a foundation from which an identity can be formed and/or developed, a narrative can be crafted around that identity and legitimacy sought from one another as self-confidence is developed, as the basis for the practice of entrepreneurial identity in other, non-single sex, situations.

References

Anderson, L. and Gold, J. (2009) Conversations outside the comfort zone: Identity formation in SME manager action learning, *Action Learning: Research and Practice* 6 (3), pp. 229–242.

Autio, E. (2013) *Promoting Leadership Development in High-Growth New Ventures*, Discussion Paper, Paris: OECD.

Bammens, Y. and Collewaert, V. (2014) Trust between entrepreneurs and angel investors: Exploring positive and negative implications for venture performance assessments, *Journal of Management* 40, pp. 1980–2008.

Bierema, L. L. (2001) Women, work and learning, *New Directions for Adult and Continuing Education* 2001, pp. 53–62, doi: 10.1002/ace.40.

Boje, D. (1991) The storytelling organization; a study of storytelling performance in an office supply firm, *Administrative Science Quarterly* 36 (1), pp. 106–126.

Boon, S. D. and Holmes, J. G. (1991) The dynamics of interpersonal trust: Resolving uncertainty in the face of risk. In R.A. Hindle and J. Groebel (eds) *Cooperation and Prosocial Behavior*, pp. 190–211. Oxford: Basil Blackwell.

Boyce, M. (1996) Organizational story and storytelling: A critical review, *Journal of Organizational Change Management* 9 (5), pp. 425–450.

Brook, C. M., Pedler, M. and Burgoyne, J. (2012) Brief thoughts on facilitating action learning, *Action Learning: Research and Practice* 10 (2), pp. 158–159.

Bruni, A., Gherardi, S. and Poggio, B. (2004) Doing gender, doing entrepreneurship: An ethnographic account of intertwined practices, *Gender, Work and Organization* 11 (4), pp. 406–429.

Bruni, A., Gherardi, S., and Poggio, B. (2004) Entrepreneur-mentality, gender and the study of women entrepreneurs, *Journal of Organizational Change Management* 17 (3) pp. 256–268.

Brush, C., Balachandra, L., Davis, A. and Greene, P. G. (2014) *Investing in the Power of Women. Progress Report on the Goldman Sachs 10,000 Women Initiative.* New York/Boston: Goldman Sachs/Babson College.

Carroll, B. and Levy, L. (2010) Leadership development as identity construction, *Management Communication Quarterly* 24 (2), pp. 211–231.

Case, P. (2003) From objectivity to subjectivity: Pursuing subjective authenticity in organizational research. In R. Westwood and S. Clegg (eds) *Debating Organization: Point–Counterpoint in Organization Studies*, pp. 35–49. Oxford: Blackwell.

Chen, M-H. (2007) Entrepreneurial leadership and new ventures: Creativity in entrepreneurial teams, *Creativity and Innovation Management* 6, pp. 239–249.

Coffman, J. and Neuenfeldt, B. (2014) *Everyday Moments of Truth: Frontline Managers Are Key to Women's Career Aspirations*. New York: Bain and Company.

Cross, R. and Parker, A. (2004) *The Hidden Power of Social Networks: Understanding how work really gets done in organizations*. Boston, MA: Harvard Business School Press.

Cummings, L. L. and Bromily, P. (1996) The organizational trust inventory (OTI): Development and validation. In R. M. Kramer & T. R. Tyler (Eds), *Trust in Organizations: Frontiers of theory and research*, pp, 261–287. Thousand Oaks, CA: Sage.

Daly, A. J., and Finnigan, K. S. (2010) A bridge between worlds: Understanding network structure to understand change strategy. *Journal of Educational Change* 11 (2), pp. 111–138.

Day, D. V., Fleenor, J. W., Atwater, L. E., Sturm, R. E. and McKee, R. A. (2014) Advances in leader and leadership development: A review of 25 years of research theory, *The Leadership Quarterly* 25, pp. 63–82.

Day, D. V. and Harrison, M. M. (2007) A multilevel, identity-based approach to leadership development, *Human Resources Management Review* 17, pp. 360–373.

Devillard, S., Graven, W., Lawson, E., Paradise, R. and Sancier-Sultan, S. (2012) *Women Matter 2012: Making the Breakthrough*. McKinsey and Company.

Ding, Z., Au, K. and Chiang, F. (2015) Social trust and angel investors' decisions: A multilevel analysis across nations, *Journal of Business Venturing* 30, pp. 307–321.

Driver, M. (2015) How trust functions in the context of identity work, *Human Relations* DOI: 10.1 1177/001872671-4548080.

Eagly, A. H. and Carli, L. L. (2007) *Through the Labyrinth; The Truth about How Women Become Leaders*, The Leadership for Common Good Series. Cambridge, MA: Harvard Business School Press and Center for Public Leadership.

Ely, R. J. (1995) The power in demography: Women's social constructions of gender identity at work, *Academy of Management Journal* 38, pp. 589–634.

Ely, R. J., Ibarra, H. and Kolb, D. M. (2011) Taking gender into account: Theory and design for women's leadership development programs, *Academy of Management & Education* 11 (3), pp. 474–493.

Ely, R. J. and Meyerson, D. E. (2000) Theories of gender: A new approach to organizational analysis and change, *Research in Organizational Behaviour* 22, pp. 103–153.

Ely, R. J. and Rhode, D. L. (2010) Women and leadership: Defining the challenges. In N. Nohira and R. Khurana (Eds), *Handbook of Leadership Theory and Practice*, pp. 377–410. Boston, MA: Harvard Business Publishing.

Fielden, S. L. and Dawe, A. (2004) Entrepreneurship and social inclusion, *Women in Management Review* 19 (3), pp. 139–142.

Finnigan, K. S. and Daly, A. J. (2012) Mind the gap: Organizational learning and improvement in an underperforming urban system, *American Journal of Education* 119 (1), pp. 41–71.

Fletcher, J. K. (2004) The paradox of postheroic leadership: An essay on gender, power, and transformational change, *Leadership Quarterly* 15 (5), pp. 647–661.

Gibb, A. (2009) Meeting the development needs of owner managed small enterprise: A discussion of the centrality of action learning, *Action Learning: Research and Practice* 6 (3), pp. 209–227.

Goel, S. and Karri, R. (2006) Entrepreneurs, effectual logic, and over-trust, *Entrepreneurship Theory and Practice* 30, pp. 477–493.

Greenberg, D., McKone-Sweet, K. and Wilson, H. J. (2011) *The New Entrepreneurial Leaders: Developing Leaders who Shape Social and Economic Opportunity*. San Francisco: Berrett Koehler.

Greenleaf, R. K. (2002) *Servant Leadership: A Journey into the Nature of Legitimate Power and Greatness*. Mahwah, NJ: Paulist Press.

Hakim, C. (2006) Women, careers and work-life preferences, *British Journal of Guidance and Counselling* 34 (2), pp. 279–294.

Hakim, C. (2000) *Work-Lifestyle Choices in the 21st Century*. Oxford: Oxford University Press.

Hamilton, E. (2013) The discourse of entrepreneurial masculinities (and femininities), *Entrepreneurship and Regional Development* 25 (1–2), pp. 90–99.

Hamilton, E. (2014) Entrepreneurial narrative identity and gender: A double epistemological shift, *Journal of Small Business Management* 52, pp. 703–712.

Hamilton, E. (2006) Whose story is it anyway? Narrative accounts of the role of women in founding and establishing family businesses, *International Small Business Journal* 24 (3), pp. 253–271.

Harrison, R. T., Leitch, C. M. and McAdam, M. (forthcoming) Breaking glass: Towards a gendered analysis of entrepreneurial leadership, *Journal of Small Business Management*.

Harrison, R. T., Mason, C. M. and Dibben, M. (1996) The role of trust in the informal investor's investment decision: An exploratory analysis, *Entrepreneurship Theory and Practice* 21 (Summer), pp. 63–81.

Henderson, S. and Gilding, M. (2004) I've never clicked this much with anyone in my life: Trust and hyperpersonal communication in online friendships, *New Media & Society* 6, pp. 487–506.

Hosking, G. (2014) *Trust: A history.* Oxford: Oxford University Press.

Howorth, C. and Moro, A (2006) Trust within entrepreneur-bank relationships: Insights from Italy, *Entrepreneurship Theory and Practice* 30, pp. 495–517.

Hoy, W. K. & Tschannen-Moran, M. (1999). The five faces of trust: An empirical confirmation in urban elementary schools, *Journal of School Leadership* 9, pp. 184–208.

Ibarra, H. (1992) Homophily and differential returns: Sex differences in network structure and access in an advertising firm, *Administrative Science Quarterly* 37, pp. 422–477.

Kandola, B. (2009) *The Value of Difference: Eliminating Bias in Organizations.* London: Pearn Kandola.

Kasper-Fuehrer, E. C. and Ashkanasy, N. M. (2001) Communicating trustworthiness and building rust in interorganizational virtual organizations, *Journal of Management* 27, pp. 235–254.

Kelan, E. K. (2009). Gender fatigue: The ideological dilemma of gender neutrality and discrimination in organizations, *Canadian Journal of Administrative Sciences* 26 (3), pp. 197–210.

Kuo, F. and Yu, C. (2006) An exploratory study of trust dynamics in work-oriented virtual teams, *Journal of Computer-Mediated Communication* 14, pp. 823–854.

Leitch, C. M., Harrison, R. T. and Hill, F. M., (2015) Women entrepreneurs and the process of networking as social exchange. In A. Fayolle, D. Chabaud, S. Jack and W. Lamine (Eds), *Entrepreneurial Process and Social Networks: A dynamic process.* Cheltenham: Edward Elgar Publishing.

Leitch, C. M., McMullan, C. and Harrison, R. T. (2012) The development of entrepreneurial leadership: The role of human, social and institutional capital, *British Journal of Management* 24 (3), pp. 347–366.

Lewicki, R. J. and Bunker, B. B. (1996) Developing and maintaining trust in work relationships. In R. M. Kramer and T. R. Tyler (Eds) *Trust in Organizations: Frontiers of theory and research*, pp. 357–389. Thousand Oaks, CA: Sage Publications.

Lewicki, R. J. and Bunker, B. B. (1995) Trust in relationships: A model of trust development and decline. In B. B. Bunker and J. Z. Rubin (Eds) *Conflict and Justice*, pp. 133–173. San Francisco: Jossey-Bass.

Lewicki, R. J., Tomlinson, E. C. and Gillespie, N. (2006) Models of interpersonal trust development: Theoretical approaches, empirical evidence, and future directions, *Journal of Management* 32, pp. 991–1022.

Li, P. P. (2011) The rigor-relevance balance for engaged scholarship: New frame and new agenda for trust research and beyond, *Journal of Trust Research* 1, pp. 1–21.

Locke, K. (1996) A funny thing Happened? The management of consumer emotions in service encounters, *Organization Science* 7 (1), pp. 40–59.

Mabey, C. (2013) Leadership development in organizations: Multiple discourses and diverse practice, *International Journal of Management Reviews* 15, pp. 359–380.

Mabey, C. and Finch-Lees, T. (2008) *Management and Leadership Development.* London: Sage Publications.

Maguire, S. and Phillips, N. (2008) 'Citibankers' at Citigroup: A study of the loss of trust after a merger, *Journal of Management Studies* 45, pp. 372–401.

Marlow, S. and McAdam, M. (2012) Analysing the influence of gender upon high technology venturing within the context of business incubation. *Entrepreneurship, Theory and Practice*, 36 (4), pp. 655–676.

Martin, J. and Meyerson, D. (1998) Women and power: Conformity, resistance and dis-organized coaction. In R. Kramer and M. Neale (Eds) *Power, Politics and Influence*, pp. 311–348. Newbury Park, CA: Sage Publications.

McKnight, D. H., Cummings, L. L. and Chervany, N. L. (1998) Initial trust formation in new organizational relationship, *Academy of Management Review* 23, pp. 473–490.

Meyerson, D., Weick, K. E. and Kramer, R. M. (1996) Swift trust and temporary groups. In R. M. Kramer and T. R. Tyler (Eds) *Trust in organizations: Frontiers of theory and research*, pp. 166–195. Thousand Oaks, CA: Sage Publications.

Mitteness, C. R., Baucus, M. S. and Sudek, R. (2012) Horse vs jockey? How stage of funding process and industry experience affect the evaluations of angel investors, *Venture Capital: An International Journal of Entrepreneurial Finance* 14, pp. 241–267.

Navis, C. and Glynn, M. A. (2011) Legitimate distinctiveness and the entrepreneurial identity: Influences on investor judgments of new venture plausibility, *Academy of Management Review* 36 (3), pp. 479–499.

O'Connell, P. (2014) A simplified framework for 21st century leader development, *The Leadership Quarterly* 25, pp. 183–203.

Opportunity Now (2014) *Project 28–40. The Report.* London: Business in the Community.

Philips, N., Tracey, P. and Karra, N. (2013) Building entrepreneurial tie portfolios through strategic homophily: The role of alternative identity work in venture creation and early growth, *Journal of Business Venturing* 28 (1), pp. 134–150.

Pratt, M. (2009). For the lack of a boilerplate: Tips on writing up (and reviewing) qualitative research, *Academy of Management Journal* 52 (5), pp. 856–862.

Ram, M. and Trehan, K. (2010) Critical action learning, policy learning and small firms: An inquiry, *Management Learning* 41 (4), pp. 415–428.

Ramsey, C. (2005) Narrative: From learning in reflection to learning in performance, *Management Learning* 36 (2), pp. 219–235.

Reynolds, M. and Trehan, K. (2003) Learning from difference? *Management Learning* 34 (2), pp. 163–180.

Ridgeway, C. L. (1993) Gender, status and the social psychology of expectations. In P. England (Ed.) *Theory on Gender/ Feminism on Theory*, pp. 175–197. New York: Aldine de Gruyter.

Scarborough, H., Swan, J. and Amaeshi, K. (2013) Exploring the role of trust in the deal-making process for early-stage technology ventures, *Entrepreneurship Theory and Practice* 37, pp. 1203–1228.

Sermijn, J., Devlieger, P. and Loots, G. (2008) The narrative construction of the self: Selfhood as a rhizomatic story, *Qualitative Inquiry* 14, pp. 632–650.

Simmons, M. (1996) *New Leadership from Women and Men: Building an inclusive organization.* Aldershot, Hampshire: Gower.

Sinclair, A. (1997) The MBA through women's eyes, *Management Learning* 28 (3), pp. 313–330.

Sinclair, A. (1995) Sex and the MBA, *Organization* 2 (2), pp. 295–317.

Stead, V. (2014) The gendered power relations of action learning: A critical analysis of women's reflections on a leadership development programme, *Human Resource Development International* doi 10.1080/13678868.2014.928137.

Stead, V. and Elliot, C. J. (2009) *Women's Leadership.* Basingstoke: Palgrave Macmillan.

Stead, V. and Elliot, C. (2013) Women's leadership learning; a reflexive review of representations and leadership teaching, *Management Learning* 44, pp. 373–394.

Strätling, R., Wijbenga, F. H. and Dietz, G. (2012) The impact of contracts on trust in entrepreneur-venture capitalist relationships, *International Small Business Journal* 30, pp. 811–831.

Strauss, A. and Corbin, J. (1998) *Basics of Qualitative Research.* Thousand Oaks, CA: Sage.

Surie, G. and Ashley, A. (2008) Integrating pragmatism and ethics in entrepreneurial leadership for sustainable value creation, *Journal of Business Ethics* 81 (1), pp. 235–246.

Sveningsson, S. and Alvesson, M. (2003) Managing managerial identities: Organizational fragmentation, discourse and identity struggle, *Human Relations* 56, pp. 1163–1193.

Terrion, J. L. and Ashforth, B. E. (2002) From 'I' to 'we': the role of putdown humor and identity in the development of a temporary group, *Human Relations* 55, pp. 55–88.

Umoren, N. J. (2003) Does trust influence the informal lending decision? An investigative analysis, *South African Journal of Economic and Management Sciences* 6, pp. 72–88.

Van der Zee, K. Vos, M. and Luijters, K. (2009) Social identity patterns and trust in demographically diverse work teams, *Social Science Information* 48, pp. 175–198.

Vinnicombe, S. V. and Colwill, N. L. (1995) *The Essence of Women in Management.* London: Prentice-Hall.

Vinnicombe, S. V., Moore, L. L. and Anderson, D. (2013) Women's leadership programmes are still important. In S. Vinnicombe, R. J. Burke, S. Blake Burke and L. L. Moore (Eds), *Handbook of Research Promoting Women's Careers*, pp. 406–419. Cheltenham: Edward Elgar.

Vinnicombe, S. V. and Singh, V. (2003) Women-only management training: An essential part of women's leadership development, *Journal of Change Management* 3 (4), pp. 294–306.

Watson, T. J. (2009) Entrepreneurial action identity work and the use of multiple discursive resources: The case of a rapidly changing family business, *International Small Business Journal* 27 (3), pp. 251–274.

Watson, T. J. (2011) Ethnography, reality and truth: The vital need for students of 'how things work' in organisations and management, *Journal of Management Studies* 8 (1), pp. 202–216.

Weick, K. (2007) The generative properties of richness, *Academy of Management Journal* 50 (1), pp. 14–19.

Wittenberg-Cox, A. (2013) Stop fixing women, start building management competences. In S. Vinnicombe, R. J. Burke, S. Blake Burke and L. L. Moore (Eds), *Handbook of Research Promoting Women's Careers*, pp. 106–116. Cheltenham: Edward Elgar.

Zhang, Y. and Huxham, C. (2009) Identity construction and trust building in developing international collaborations, *Journal of Applied Behavioral Science* 45, pp. 186–211.

15

POSTFEMINISM AND ENTREPRENEURSHIP

Exploring the identity of the mumpreneur

Patricia Lewis

Introduction

The field of entrepreneurship studies is characterised by theoretical variation, but research influenced by economic or psychological perspectives has dominated while the impact of social and cultural factors on enterprise development has been relatively neglected (Steyaert & Katz, 2004; Karatas-Ozkan et al., 2014; Tedmanson et al., 2012). Entrepreneurial studies are, however, evolving, and the notion that entrepreneurship is a social phenomenon and, therefore, should be investigated through a social lens is gaining ground (Tatli et al., 2014; Thornton et al., 2011). The claim that enterprise and entrepreneurial activity is a socio-cultural-economic phenomenon is based on the proposition that entrepreneurship is a collaborative social *achievement* with the 'social' playing a role in the entire business start-up and innovation process (Korsgaard & Anderson, 2011; Tatli et al., 2014). Studies of entrepreneurship that draw on the concept of identity as a way of exploring entrepreneurial experiences, organisation creation, and the business start-up process are part of this 'turn to the social'. This chapter contributes to the developing body of research that considers identity as an aspect of business ownership (e.g. Ainsworth & Hardy, 2008; Chasserio et al., 2014; Cohen & Musson, 2000; Down & Warren, 2008; Essers & Benschop, 2007; Foss, 2004; Jones et al., 2008; Mallett & Wapshott, 2015; Warren, 2004; Watson, 2009) by examining the emergence and representation of the mumpreneur as an entrepreneurial character, understood here as a woman who runs a business from home alongside the active parenting of children and the management of a household.

In exploring the surfacing of the mumpreneur as an entrepreneurial persona, the chapter draws mainly on discursive understandings of identity that highlight the fluctuating and fluid discourses that influence the formation of self, emphasising how phenomena such as 'woman' and 'entrepreneur' are socially constituted (Hekman, 2000). Research that investigates the notion of entrepreneurial identity tends to be informed by a social constructionist orientation that concentrates on the way individuals actively construct the world of entrepreneurship and its constituent elements through discourse (Ahl, 2012; Anderson et al., 2009; Hamilton, 2014). Thus, investigations of entrepreneurial identity demonstrate that entrepreneurship "arises from within the social" and that social context is not just a background factor

(Korsgaard & Anderson, 2011). Here, the individual entrepreneur can be viewed historically, the interactions that take place between the individual and the environment made visible and performances and enactments of entrepreneurial identity explored. In other words, studies of entrepreneurial identity demonstrate how being an entrepreneur is something that is *accomplished* within a particular social milieu. Attempts to isolate the traits or common thinking processes of entrepreneurs, or to specify differences between entrepreneurial and non-entrepreneurial people, are therefore set aside, in favour of an approach that considers how individuals draw on a discourse of enterprise to construct an entrepreneurial identity.

A discourse such as that of enterprise provides an understanding of what a character such as an 'entrepreneur' is like. However, cultural story lines about a persona such as the entrepreneur are not neutral, with many commentators arguing that entrepreneurship is the performance of a form of masculinity (Bruni et al., 2004a; Hamilton, 2013; Lewis, 2006). Asserting that the concept of entrepreneurship is gender biased and the discourse of enterprise is masculine means that individuals (male or female) who wish to shape and construct an entrepreneurial identity do so within a context characterised by masculine discursive practices (Ogbor, 2000). One key source of discursive representations of entrepreneurship is the media, particularly newspapers, that according to Achtenhagen & Welter (2011) disseminate public discourses on entrepreneurship. Research indicates that media representations of the entrepreneur depict entrepreneurship as dominated by male experience and masculine stereotypes (Bird & Brush, 2002), drawing "upon a narrow range of stereotypes, typically the heroic adventurer (who is) individualistic, ruthless and aggressive" (Hamilton, 2013: 91). Individuals who set up a business and lay claim to an entrepreneurial identity are judged against such discourses with the expectation that they resonate with wider societal beliefs about the masculinity attaching to the entrepreneur if their take-up of this persona is to be accepted as legitimate. In other words, an individual's entrepreneurial identity claim must mesh with the pre-existing, ongoing and encompassing cultural story lines encapsulated in the enterprise discourse and circulated via media, educational, business and popular culture channels (Aldrich & Fiol, 1994; Suchman, 1995).

Within such a discursive context individuals can either abide by the requirements of this masculine enterprise discourse or seek to shape an alternative entrepreneurial identity such as one that abides by the demands of femininity (Lewis, 2013). In the normal course of events an individual is likely to have more than one identity with these different identities impacting on each other. The multiple identities that one individual may possess should not be understood as something additive with several identities 'layered' on each other, rather different "...forms of identity should be seen as interactive and mutually constitutive..." (Lawler, 2008: 3). However, recognition of multiple identities does not always mean that together they make a coherent 'whole' as the co-existence of different selves can divide a person. As Hekman (2000: 296) drawing on Curry-Johnson (1995) suggests:

> Each identity defines me; each is responsible for elements of my character; from each I devise some sustenance for my soul. But these identities do not peacefully co-exist. The effort to blend them together harmoniously (can be) desperate.

Conventionally, the identities of 'entrepreneur' and 'mother' were perceived as being mutually exclusive and oppositional, with motherhood being understood as significantly problematic for entrepreneurship. However, the emergence of the new entrepreneurial identity of the mumpreneur appears to suggest that these identities are no longer in tension (Duberley & Carrigan, 2013).

As a means of exploring the new entrepreneurial identity of mumpreneur, the materialisation of which is based on contemporary women's willingness to be a subject of economic capacity while also taking up the traditionally marked out roles of mother and wife, attention will be directed at the issue of femininity in its changed postfeminist form and how this relates to entrepreneurship (Gill, 2007; Lewis, 2014a, 2014b; McRobbie, 2009). Following this, media representations of the mumpreneur will be briefly considered and data from an interview study drawn upon to facilitate examination of how women, who see themselves as simultaneously mothers and business owners, react to, construct and perform the identity of the mumpreneur. The chapter will conclude with a consideration of the issues raised.

Postfeminism and entrepreneurship

Reconfiguring femininity – the co-existence of the masculine and the feminine

Much of the research on female entrepreneurship has focused on the presence of women within the entrepreneurial field examining their 'unique' experience as business owners (Berg, 1997; Calas et al., 2007; Green & Cohen, 1995; Hamilton, 2013). In contrast, an alternative strand of feminist research asserts that gender in the entrepreneurial sphere is not simply something that attaches to women as business owners, rather it is a principle of the social organisation of entrepreneurship, being integral to the structures, institutional and cultural practices and discourses connected to entrepreneurial activity (Lewis, 2014a). What this approach highlights is that despite the novelty, risk-taking, innovation and dynamism attached to entrepreneurship as an economic activity, it has not historically been characterised by a corresponding normative freedom, encumbered as it is by a set of norms that produce "...the entrepreneurial subject through hegemonic masculinities in which women must recognize themselves" (Calas et al., 2007: 94). Feminist studies have made visible how masculinity is central to the enactment of successful entrepreneurship and the subjectivity of the entrepreneur (e.g. Ahl, 2006; Ahl & Marlowe, 2012; Bruni et al., 2004a; Lewis, 2006; Mirchandani, 1999; Ogbor, 2000; Simpson & Lewis, 2005). Thus, specified as a gendered activity entrepreneurship has been identified as an arena within which gender (masculinity) is 'done', with gender and entrepreneurial activity being mutually constitutive (Bruni et al., 2004a).

Alongside the significant attention directed at the in-built masculinity of entrepreneurship, a small number of studies have explored the relationship between femininity and entrepreneurship. From this perspective, there are studies (e.g. Buttner, 2001; Lee-Gosselin & Grise, 1990; Fenwick, 2002) that suggest that women business owners challenge the masculine emphasis on growth as the defining characteristic of entrepreneurship, by arguing for a feminine model of 'small and stable' business, connected to equal value being assigned to home and work. While Bruni et al. (2004b: 264) are critical of such research because of its essentialist assumptions, it has contributed to the notion of a masculine versus a feminine way of 'doing' business, an orientation that has been taken up by commentators such as Bird and Brush (2002). They argue that "it is reasonable to assume that masculine and feminine aspects will be incorporated into...new venture(s)" and that firms should aim for "gender balance" (2002: 43). In asserting this position they suggest that in contemporary accounts of entrepreneurship emphasis is placed on a masculine gender framework with a lot less attention directed at the feminine attributes and behaviours that contribute to successful business start-up. They argue that business owners who display 'gender maturity' defined as "…the conscious integration, acceptance, appreciation and enactment of qualities of both genders…" will establish gender-balanced organizations (Bird and Brush, 2002: 56).

The emergence of this strand of research, despite being a minority presence in the gender and entrepreneurship literature, is important for two reasons. First, it signals that the masculinity attached to entrepreneurship is no longer as exclusionary for women as it was in the past. Recent research (e.g. Hall & Donoghue, 2013; Katila & Eriksson, 2013) suggests that masculine characteristics in women are only viewed negatively if they are *not* combined with overt displays of feminine qualities. Second, consideration of women's inclusion in the world of entrepreneurship – as well as inclusion in the wider organisational field – appears to be shifting to a 'balancing' of masculinity and femininity. Thus, rather than women being required to sublimate their femininity and go through a process of masculinisation, they are expected to integrate feminine ideals with masculine-marked practices in organisational contexts (Hall & Donoghue, 2013; Kark et al., 2012). However, there is a problem with interpreting the co-existence of masculine and feminine behaviours in terms of 'balance' or 'androgyny' as this does not take into account the on-going socially marked tension between masculinity and femininity (Carlson, 2011). In other words, there is an enduring binary divide and associated hierarchical ordering of masculinity and femininity, with the former still being more highly valued than the latter, and this has significant implications for the inclusion of women in the organisational field in general and the entrepreneurship arena in particular. Thus the required 'balancing' of masculinity and femininity should not be understood in terms of women adopting an androgynous persona, constructed as "an integrated presentation of herself as both agentic (masculine) and communal (feminine)" (Hall & Donoghue, 2013: 635). Rather, the need to 'do' both masculinity and femininity should be understood as a dialectic negotiation that is constitutive of a *reconfigured femininity*. The suggestion here is that this reconfiguration of femininity, connected to the cultural logic of postfeminism, has given rise to the entrepreneurial identity of the mumpreneur (Carlson, 2011; Lewis, 2014b).

Postfeminism and the reconfiguration of femininity

Femininity as traditionally understood – passive, dependent, supportive of men, attractive to men, infantile – was something women were compelled to perform and acted to signal women's subordinate position in relation to men. However, according to McRobbie (1993: 409) "feminist ideas (e.g. equality of opportunity in education and the workplace) have slowly worked their way into the material and ideological structures of society, and have become part of the general culture of femininity". The cultural presence of feminism in contemporary femininity contributes to the celebration of qualities such as individuality, autonomy, dynamism, risk-taking, independence, self-reliance in women – characteristics and behaviours that are associated with (masculine) entrepreneurship (Lewis, 2014a). Nevertheless, the feminist egalitarianism, which is emblematic of contemporary femininity, has not entirely replaced traditional understandings and expectations of feminine behaviour. Instead, this new feminist egalitarianism co-exists with a reinstatement of traditional familialism (Cotter et al., 2011), which emerges through the "well-disguised re-articulation of traditional gender stereotypes" (Thornham & McFarland, 2011: 66).

Postfeminism is a useful frame for exploring this reconfiguration of femininity as it encapsulates the cultural logic and the various factors that contribute to the reshaping of the feminine in contemporary times (Lewis, 2014a, 2014b). While there is more than one interpretation of what postfeminism as a cultural phenomenon is, for our purposes the most useful understanding is provided by Gill (2007) and McRobbie (2009). Both of these commentators depict postfeminism as a cultural discursive entity, made up of interrelated themes, produced through the intersection of a group of hegemonic discourses around gender, feminism and femininity. As a discursive phenomenon postfeminism encapsulates the restabilisation of traditional gender norms alongside the acceptance of equality and the incorporation of selectively defined (liberal) feminist values into the mainstream (McRobbie, 2004, 2009). This concurrence of tradition and equality manifests in a range of stable features including femininity as a bodily property; a shift from objectification to subjectification; self-surveillance; individualism, choice and empowerment; make-over and reinvention; resexualisation of women's bodies and, finally, retreat to home as a matter of choice not obligation (Gill, 2007; Negra, 2009). In exploring the emergence of the entrepreneurial identity of the mumpreneur, three of these postfeminist elements are important – individualism, choice and empowerment, notions of 'natural' sexual difference and retreat to the home as a matter of choice not obligation. Together, these three elements represent the co-existence of tradition and equality and "capture the tension between feminism (understood in terms of achievement in the public, masculine world of work) and femininity (understood in terms of feminized behaviour and domestic responsibilities in the private, feminine world of home)" (Lewis, 2014b: 1851). Looking at female entrepreneurship through the lens of postfeminism and the development of the entrepreneurial identity of mumpreneur, we can see that as entrepreneurs, women now occupy the masculine realm of business and the feminine realm of home and are 'doing' both masculinity and femininity. This entails the performance and embodiment of the feminine characteristics of nurture, emotion, passivity and attractiveness in conjunction with the masculine (individualised) traits of economic and emotional independence, assertiveness, rationality and autonomy (Carlson, 2011; Lewis, 2014b).

The emergence of the mumpreneur as a new entrepreneurial identity

At first glance, the emergence of the mumpreneur can be connected to the long-standing view that a key reason women set up a business is to secure flexibility around the performance of domestic and childcare responsibilities. Conventionally, much research attention has been directed at the tension between achievement in the field of entrepreneurship and issues of family responsibility and domesticity. Paradoxically, while having children significantly increases the likelihood that women will embark on an entrepreneurial path, research continues to indicate that business ownership and family obligations are incompatible responsibilities (Hamilton, 2006; Loscocco & Bird, 2012). Hundley (2000, 2001) has demonstrated that marriage has a negative impact on the earnings of women business owners, and Jennings and McDougald (2007: 748) have highlighted how differences between men and women around work-family interface can account for "the smaller employment size, revenues and income level of female-headed firms". Furthermore, use of the home as a base for a business is perceived to have a particularly negative impact on female-owned firms with women's home-based businesses being more likely to suffer than those owned by their male colleagues (Rouse & Kitching, 2006). Thus, women are normally advised to establish a clear division between home and business, that is, to leave their 'home selves' behind so that they can be more ambitious, take risks and expand their entrepreneurial activities. Here, there is only space for one form of entrepreneurial subject "requiring of women that they pursue a fantasy of the (entrepreneurial) subject as fully unified and coherent, able to define herself and her world unambiguously" (Johnson & Lloyd, 2004: 17).

While the emergence of the mumpreneur may appear to 'fit' into this pre-existing research stream, it is important to note that within the context of a postfeminist gender regime, the relationship between home and work for women in general, and mumpreneurs in particular, has different cultural connotations attached to it. Specifically, the postfeminist reconfiguration of femininity requires that women demonstrate 'success' at work *and* at home simultaneously. Mumpreneurship is a clear manifestation of this contemporary demand given its rejection of a strict separation between home and entrepreneurial activity and its connection to the postfeminist emphasis on equality, inclusion and free choice alongside active motherhood. The mumpreneur first materialised in the media in the early 2000s with growing reference made to this entrepreneurial identity from then onwards. Defining a certain type of behaviour by associating it with a named social category is politically powerful and not only discovers and defines this category but also in some ways creates it (Hall & Rodriguez, 2003). As such, it can be argued that the mumpreneur is a media-created social category, particularly in terms of the media's early use of the label and the volume of references made to it. One of the early references to the mumpreneur in the British media occurred in 2001, in an article that made reference to an American text entitled *Mumpreneurs: A Mother's Practical Guide to Work-at-Home Success* by Ellen Parlapiano and Patricia Cobe (Lynn, 2001). Since then a significant number of other texts have been published (see Table 15.1) contributing to and reinforcing the materialisation of the mumpreneur entrepreneurial identity.

Depictions of business owners in the media, both male and female, provide us with access to the social norms and beliefs that surround entrepreneurial behaviour. As stated in the introduction, previous studies of representations of entrepreneurs in the media highlight the dominance of male experience and the categorisation of entrepreneurial activity into a restricted range of masculine stereotypes (Hamilton, 2013). Given this, the active promotion

Table 15.1 Mumpreneur texts

Title	Author	Year of Publication
Kitchen Table Tycoons	Anita Naik	2008
Boogles and the Mumpreneur	Lisa Newton & Pearl Clarke	2009
Supermummy: The Ultimate Mumpreneur Guide to Online Business Success	Mel McGee	2009
The Mumpreneur Diaries	Morag Cuddefore-Jones	2009
The Mumpreneur and the Bookkeeper	Lisa Newton & Pearl Clarke	2010
The Mumpreneur Guide	Antonia Chitty	2011
Mumpreneur Online Exposed	Fiona Lewis	2011
Mum to Mumpreneur	Jodi Gibson	2011
Mumpreneur Magic	Celina Lucas	2012
Essential Twitter Guide for Mumpreneurs	Suzannah Butcher & Laura E. James	2012
Realistic Ways to Become a Mumpreneur	Rebecca Plumridge	2013
Millionaire Mumpreneurs	Mel McGee	2013
Start Holidaying in Barbados: Sun-Kissed Success for Mumpreneurs	Anna Davidson Thawe	2013
How to Be a Mumpreneur	Annabel Karamel	2014

of mumpreneurship by the media and the materialization of its representation are quite significant. According to Achtenhagen & Welter (2011: 765):

> societal attitudes influence the extent to which female entrepreneurs are a tolerated, accepted or encouraged phenomenon. …In this context, public discourses as transmitted by mass media, and especially newspapers, play an important role. Newspapers are an especially powerful producer and reproducer as well as circulator of public discourse on entrepreneurship, as they persuade our consent to ways of talking about reality that are often regarded as normal and acceptable beyond the confines of media.

In recognition of this, Nexis UK, an online archive of printed sources, was accessed during the period July to September 2011, to examine English language publications using the keyword 'mumpreneur' from 2001 to 2011. This search yielded 416 articles from countries including New Zealand, Singapore, Republic of Ireland, Australia and the United Kingdom (UK). As over half of these articles appeared in the UK, the British context was the focus of analysis with 36 articles with the word 'mumpreneur' found in UK national newspapers, 17 appearing in UK Broadsheets and 185 articles located in UK regional newspapers. The vast majority of these articles adopted a positive tone towards the figure of the mumpreneur, commenting in a favourable way on the emergence of this entrepreneurial character. In addition, many of them provide details of mumpreneur networks, mumpreneur competitions, mumpreneur experiences and mumpreneur profiles.

Following Hall & Rodriguez (2003), a qualitative analysis of these articles, entailing a concentrated reading of their content and identification of the issues and themes embedded in them, was conducted. Four themes (see Table 15.2) associated with the 'mumpreneur' were identified including the primary theme of a positive association between motherhood and entrepreneurship, accentuating how compatible motherhood is with entrepreneurship. Also detected were three other secondary themes: benefits to the business of spending time with children; being in control of one's own time and effort and being able to create wealth through a successful business (Lewis, 2013).

These four themes contributed to two key characteristics of the media representation of the mumpreneur, both of which go against the research findings on the tension between entrepreneurial achievement and home responsibility, referred to earlier. First, the image of the mumpreneur presented in the media is one in which success is achieved not by disentanglement from the domestic sphere but rather by fully involving children and the household in the entrepreneurial activities. This is especially notable, as a long-standing premise of second-wave feminism, translated into ways of thinking about entrepreneurship, is that engagement in domestic and childcare responsibilities prevents women from achieving success and self-actualising in the public world (Johnson & Lloyd, 2004).

Second, the vast majority of media accounts reviewed presented mumpreneur businesses as having the potential to earn their founders multi-million pound fortunes. This impression is given in two ways: first, reference is made to the aggregate contribution such businesses make to the UK economy through statements that mumpreneur businesses are now generating 4.4 billion pounds annually for the UK economy (Dent, 2008). Second, a more significant manoeuvre in constructing the notion of significant riches deriving from mumpreneur businesses is the retrospective application of the label mumpreneur to well-established, already-successful businesses. In the context of discussing the potential of mumpreneurs, reference is made to J.K. Rowling, author of the Harry Potter novels, and her struggle as a single mum (Vickery, 2005); Annabel Karmel (who has recently

Table 15.2 Media review themes

Primary Theme	Secondary Themes
Compatibility of Motherhood & Entrepreneurship **Skills provided by the experience of motherhood are crucial to entrepreneurial success and more important than skills gained from work experience** *"We'd both gained skills from our previous jobs but to be honest the best transferable skill was from being a parent"* (Davies, 2009, *The Journal Newcastle*). *"These days I wouldn't consider employing anyone who wasn't a parent because they don't have the foresight"* (Slater, 2008, *The Sunday Times*). *"Running a business is a lot like raising a child"* (Lynn, 2001, *Evening News Edinburgh*). **Motherhood valorised as a key source of entrepreneurial creativity and capability** *"Mums have loads of brilliant ideas and the creativity and inventiveness we use every day with our children can be put to great use in the world of business too"* (*Nottingham Evening Post*, 2008). *"I'll be feeding Jacob and looking down and think this spoon could be designed better. ...When you're at home and it's just you and the baby you have the opportunity to analyse things more and think about how it could be improved. There is less stress and it gives you time to think things through"* (Watson, 2006, *Western Mail*). *"(Ideas move from) the kitchen table to the factory and from there to retailers around the world"*(McLellan, 2011, *The Independent*).	**Positive impact on children** *"With her iPhone strapped to a double buggy, the enterprising mother-of-two conducts virtual business deals all over the world while enjoying a leisurely stroll in an Edinburgh park with her children"* (McCann, 2010, *Evening News Edinburgh*). *"My children enjoy helping with tastings, coming up with ideas. ...It has been brilliant for me: I can invent mixes while we're all chatting in the kitchen"* (Slater, 2008, *The Sunday Times*). **Control of their world** *"You're also in the driving seat to tailor your working hours to suit yourself and your family"* (*Essex Chronicle*, 2007). *"I work long hours because I'm so driven but I'm very protective of my time with my husband and daughters – our family time doesn't suffer"* (Dodds, 2008, *Daily Express*). **Wealth Creation** *"I've never had a single loan or investor and the business is growing constantly"* (Dodds, 2008, *Daily Express*). *"Motherhood...is the spur she needs to dump her unfulfilling office job and set up her own business (giving her) flexible hours... and, oh yes, a multimillion-pound fortune"* (Slater, 2008, *The Sunday Times*). *"(Earning) money from the comfort of their home... being there...at the school gates and at the same time have the satisfaction of watching the business grow"* (*Daily Record*, 2010).

written a book on mumpreneurship), who started writing cookery books with the theme of healthy eating for children in the early 1990s followed by the Eat Fussy ready meal range, which has an annual turnover of 4 million pounds (Law, 2008); Laura Tenison, who set up the maternity and children's clothing company JoJo Maman Bebe in 1993 (Watson, 2006); Mandy Haberman, who set up her business in the 1980s and whose Anywayup Cup is sold worldwide and now makes more than £5million a year (Lynn, 2001); Sarah Tremellen, who set up lingerie store Bravissimo and is now worth £13 million (Rose, 2008a); Chrissie Rucker, founder of The White Company, who has over 20 stores (Rose, 2008b); and, Justine Roberts and Carrie Longton, who met at an antenatal class and set up Mumsnet.com, which has over one million visitors a month (Rose, 2008b). Though the mumpreneur experience is more likely to be presented from the perspective of younger or more modest businesses, the stratagem of applying the mumpreneur label retrospectively to well-known, successful businesses, established before the label mumpre-neur emerged, produces the impression of significant wealth creation being the norm for mumpreneur businesses (Lewis, 2013).

From this review of accounts of the mumpreneur in the media we can see how this entre-preneurial identity has been materialised through the cultural logic of postfeminism, which has contributed to a reconfiguration of femininity based around feminist egalitarianism and traditional familialism (Cotter et al., 2011; Lewis, 2014a, 2014b). The postfeminism, which is emblematic of media accounts of mumpreneurship, accentuates the liberating and empower-ing possibilities of the reconfigured femininity, which underpins the entrepreneurial identity of the mumpreneur. This celebration of the power attaching to this new femininity acts to obscure the ongoing social constraints experienced by girls and women. Thus, with only a tiny number of newspaper articles (five out of the 238 British articles reviewed) addressing the difficulties involved in running a business with small children around, the media focus is clearly on the empowering possibilities attached to mumpreneurship. It is, therefore, clear that the social constraints on women's entrepreneurship, well documented in the general entrepreneurship research, are deemed unimportant in media accounts of the mumpreneur, with more emphasis placed on free choices and the equality experienced by women who 'choose' active motherhood. In light of this media representation of the mumpreneur, we now turn to data drawn from a qualitative interview study, to explore how women who see themselves as simultaneously mothers and business owners react to, construct and perform the identity of mumpreneur.

Experiencing the entrepreneurial identity of mumpreneur

The research reported in this section of the paper is based on an inductive, interpretive research strategy that approaches issues of entrepreneurship and identity as being socially constructed within historical, societal and institutional constraints. Twenty-one in-depth interviews were conducted during a one-year period (2012–2013), with this data collection funded by a British Academy Small Grant. An iterative approach (Srivastava & Hopwood, 2009) to data analysis was adopted characterised by constant movement back and forth be-tween the data and critical use of the concept of postfeminism around the three elements of individualism, choice and empowerment, retreat to the home as a matter of choice not obligation and 'natural' sexual difference. This analysis (summarised in Table 15.3) is pre-sented as a means of making visible the impact of the postfeminist cultural logic that has given rise to the entrepreneurial identity of the mumpreneur and contributes to the small but developing body of research (e.g. Duberley & Carrigan, 2013; Ekinsmyth, 2011, 2014; Korsgaard, 2007; Lewis, 2010; Nel, Maritz & Thongprovati, 2010; Richomme-Huet et al., 2013), which explores the establishment of a specific link between motherhood and entre-preneurial activities.

All of the respondents placed an emphasis on their desire to be active mothers fully in-volved in the everyday life of their children as the following illustrates:

> My children are young and they need me and I think for their education and their personality, to raise them as good children, you know, children who respect the world, respect people, who care for others, I think it comes from the home, it's not the school who should be doing all the work, it comes from the heart and it's here, it's the parents and if you are not there to teach those values to your children at a young age, guide them through life then of course they're going to go pear shaped.

Table 15.3 Postfeminism and the mumpreneur

The Cultural Logic of Postfeminism	The Entrepreneurial Identity of the Mumpreneur
Reconfiguration of Femininity occurs through: Intersection of a group of hegemonic discourses around gender, feminism and femininity	**The Emergence of the Mumpreneur associated with three postfeminist elements: Retreat to home as a matter of choice not obligation** *"I wanted to have my life with a family, I wanted to be able to have children and to be able to spend a bit of time with them and to be a bit more flexible, I didn't want to go down that route of being a full-time (working) mum where my children were in nursery all the time... .I just didn't want that sort of life where I was that sort of full-time employee with...I just didn't think it was going to work"*
Restabilisation of traditional gender norms alongside the acceptance of equality and assimilation of (liberal) feminist values into the mainstream	
The 'reconciliation' of feminism and femininity is manifest in a range of stable features including:	**Individualism, choice and empowerment** *"I wanted to do something. Children are great but I mean to be honest with you once they go out to school how much cleaning can you do? I've never been one of those girls who want to go and have, you know, lunch and, once in a while yes, not every day of the week, no. Yeah, you know and a bit of my own income as well. It's all very nice having your husband's money to spend but it's not quite the same"*
Femininity as a bodily property	
Shift from objectification to subjectification	
Emphasis upon self-surveillance	
Prominence given to individualism, choice and empowerment	
Ascendancy of a make-over paradigm	**"Natural" sexual difference and co-existence of doing masculinity & doing femininity** *"Because they see me being a mum, they see me on the school run, they see me at every play so how can I be that busy? So I think people who know me like that – I can't possibly be doing very much because I'm with the children so much. But I just balance so then I'm either working in the day but then they don't see me working in the evening or working at the weekend...".*
"Natural" sexual difference	
Resexualization of women's bodies	
Retreat to home as a matter of choice not obligation	
(Gill, 2007; McRobbie, 2009; Negra, 2009)	

In addition to stressing the importance of being 'there' for their children, prominent in some accounts of why they set up the business was the additional claim that without the children the business would not be so successful, or possibly would never have been set up:

> Although at times you're tearing your hair out, I think you do anyway with children so you kind of use this but it gives you a new energy I think when you have children and it makes you start thinking out of the box a little more, it makes you start being, you're negotiating all of the time with children so that becomes an easier job. You're sort of making decisions quickly because you have to with children and it seems, one complements the other. ...I feel that if I didn't have one I certainly wouldn't have the other so they come together.

Alongside this sentiment, a number of respondents emphasised their own need for self-actualization, because though they wanted to be available to their children and involved in their day-to-day lives, further fulfilment was sought:

I was bored is what the problem was, that's why I set it up because I was just, it was boring and I knew I wasn't going back to work full-time, we'd already decided I wasn't going back to work.

(I) want to be the prime parent rather than … yeah that's your prime duty (but) I want something for me. …A lot of women are used to using their brains, not that you're not if you're a full-time mum, but in a work environment, and they don't want to lose that … you have got that significant work experience because of that so you, it was such a major part of your life before children you want to keep your hand in to do something.

These views are a manifestation of what McRobbie (2009) refers to as female individualisation where women want both a successful career and a family. While women are now able to develop their own biographies and create a life in similar ways to their male colleagues, they must do so while maintaining a foothold in the domestic realm. However, unlike in the past, this domestic positioning is not forced on them, rather in the contemporary era all aspects of individuals' lives are viewed through the prism of personal choice and self-determination (Gill, 2007). Observed through the lens of choice, these respondents understand themselves as autonomous agents who are no longer constrained by inequality. The sense of autonomy these women articulate is largely understood as being internally referential, down to their own motivation and 'can-do' attitudes, as opposed to being externally structured (Baker, 2010) as the following illustrates:

I'm constantly full on, you know, always pressed (for time) and I squeeze every single … I have 15 minutes, I have 10 minutes I will squeeze something. … I will not sit down and have a cup of tea ever! If I have a cup of tea its working you know, I would eat, sometimes I eat standing, well it's not, I always eat standing up for five minutes, do a sandwich, bang, finish and back to work.

In looking at the experience of these respondents, we can see that in terms of the postfeminist elements of retreat to the home as a matter of choice not obligation and individualism, choice and empowerment, there is an alignment with the representation of the mumpreneur constructed in the media. This manifests in terms of the stress placed on the importance of being an active mother, the claims that motherhood is compatible with business and their own accounts of the strength of their motivation displayed in their working practices. Nevertheless, it is in response to a question about the term 'mumpreneur' and whether they would apply it to themselves that movement away from media representations becomes visible. Specifically, a differentiation is made between those businesses perceived to be feminine in nature and therefore not 'serious' as the following illustrates:

You meet cottage industry businesses. I don't mean to be rude but it's all the women who do patchwork and bunting, I don't know how many bunting people you've met, colour me beautiful people, the people that do very chintz women's things, jewellery making.

Although I don't find it an offensive term in any way, it implies more of a sort of cottage industry like somebody doing quite a small thing from their house, selling little bits and pieces at a fair.

And that is frustrating for the rest of us who are not doing baby products … so with the mumpreneur that's what I probably don't like that much is that there is a certain connotation that it would be somehow related to a woman thing, you know a baby thing.

A clear differentiation is being made here between 'feminine' (chintz, homely, cottage) businesses and businesses that 'fit' with the (masculine) norm of conventional entrepreneurship. This distinction is not simply presented as a co-existence of feminine and masculine businesses or the 'doing' of masculinity and femininity characterised by equality and complementarity, rather there is an ongoing privileging of the masculinity associated with mainstream entrepreneurship and a downgrading of the 'feminine' (Lewis, 2014a). This is demonstrated in the use of adjectives such as 'chintz' and referral to the products and services of these businesses as 'women's things'. Thus unlike the dominant media representation of the mumpreneur, which associates this entrepreneurial identity with multi-million pound business opportunities connected to women's traditional caring responsibilities (Lewis, 2010), a number of the respondents in this study insinuate that these types of mumpreneur businesses are not 'proper', 'serious' entrepreneurial endeavours. This distinction between so-called 'cottage' businesses and the inferred 'proper' businesses is further elaborated by respondents who do not reject the mumpreneur label outright but instead place more emphasis on the entrepreneurial aspect of this identity as the following illustrates:

> So I think mumpreneur, for me, I think it is this variation of entrepreneur... I know lots of other mums who work at home, I would probably refer to them as "work-at-home" mums as opposed to mumpreneurs...If it's a woman on her own, if she's the one who's mainly doing it and she's done something successfully then I see her as a mumpreneur. But if it's someone who's just working at home and they've got young children and they're trying to juggle everything, I see them more as work-at-home mums.

> The mumpreneur (network) because it attracts the people who are actually entrepreneurial mums when you go down and meet them the women are actually, they face the same challenges as you, they've got the same issues as you, they've got the same business expansion problems. ...So when you're speaking to them it's not cottage industry people as a rule, I mean there are still, you know, we still met a few at mumpreneur but most of them are running a business as opposed to "I'm running something from home and I've got a candle making business or a soap maker or people that work with children..." I work with kids" – oh dear not another one.

This exploration of the emergence of the mumpreneur identity demonstrates its location between liberal (masculine) feminism and femininity linked to discourses of retreatism, individualisation and difference and constituted by qualities associated with them (Lewis, 2014b). Use of postfeminism as a critical concept makes visible the way in which the entrepreneurial identity of the mumpreneur incorporates both masculine and feminine elements. This is reflective of Carlson's (2011) suggestion that the successful execution of femininity today engages norms as well as social spheres marked by both masculinity and femininity. In addition, we have highlighted the ongoing socially marked tension between masculinity and femininity in the form of the negative contrast made between businesses designated as 'chintz' and businesses perceived as appropriately entrepreneurial.

Conclusions

This chapter has sought to explore the emergence of the mumpreneur and women's take-up and response to this entrepreneurial identity. While the latter aspect of the chapter concurs with previous research on mumpreneurs (e.g. Duberley & Carrigan, 2013) highlighting the entwined nature of mumpreneurs' entrepreneurship and motherhood activities, it also makes visible the tensions surrounding this entrepreneurial identity. In doing this it contributes to research on the mumpreneur in a number of ways. First, the chapter has demonstrated that the appearance of the mumpreneur is associated with the reconfiguration of contemporary femininity connected to the cultural phenomenon of postfeminism. Specifically, drawing on the postfeminist elements of retreatism, individualisation and difference, the analysis above has highlighted how take-up of the entrepreneurial identity of mumpreneur requires that women integrate the feminine ideals of motherhood with the masculine-marked practices of entrepreneurship. As such being a mumpreneur requires that the women who take up this identity must demonstrate that they are more than 'just' a woman or more than 'just' a mum. Rather mumpreneurs, like other feminine entrepreneurial identities, must occupy a multiplicitous subjectivity (Carlson, 2011; Lewis, 2014b). Second, the socially marked tension between the masculine and feminine elements of the mumpreneur identity means that as an entrepreneurial character, it is not a clear-cut category despite media representations. Analysis of the interview data above demonstrates that the lived experience and perception of this identity does not fully co-ordinate with its materialisation in the media. Finally, a hierarchy is clearly evident between those women who perceive themselves as running a 'proper', growth-focused business that embraces conventional (masculine) business practices alongside the doing of active (feminine) motherhood and those women who are perceived as being excessively feminine. Excessive femininity manifests as a cottage business producing 'women's things' alongside motherhood. Successful (recognisable) femininity today requires that women demonstrate an ability to engage with the conflicting norms of masculinity and femininity and women who are too 'mumsy' or conventionally feminine in their choice of business as well as how they run it are viewed negatively. As Carlson (2011: 80) argues, "while there are sanctions for women who exclusively perform masculinity, doing femininity without doing (or having done) masculinity seems increasingly less tenable, less desirable and less (economically) liveable; rather an 'independent' woman who can balance masculinity with femininity seems increasingly culturally validated…".

Acknowledgement

The interview data drawn upon in this chapter were collected as part of a project entitled Mumpreneurs: Reframing Women's Entrepreneurial Activity? sponsored by the British Academy, grant reference SG112159.

References

Achtenhagen, L. & Welter, F. 2011: Surfing on the ironing board – the representation of women's entrepreneurship in German newspapers. *Entrepreneurship & Regional Development*, 23(9–10): 763–786.

Ahl, H. 2006: Why research on women entrepreneurs needs new directions. *Entrepreneurship, Theory and Practice*, 30(5): 595–621.

Ahl, H. 2012: Gender, organizations and entrepreneurship. In Hjorth, D. (ed.) *Handbook on Organizational Entrepreneurship*, pp. 134–150. Cheltenham: Edward Elgar.

Ahl, H. & Marlow, S. 2012: Exploring the dynamics of gender, feminism and entrepreneurship: Advancing debates to escape a dead end. *Organization*, 19(5): 543–562.

Ainsworth, S. & Hardy, C. 2008: The enterprising self: an unsuitable job for an older worker. *Organization*, 15(3): 389–405.

Aldrich, H.E. & Fiol, C.M. 1994: Fools rush in? The institutional context of industry creation. *Academy of Management Review*, 19(4): 645–670.

Anderson, A., Dodds, S. & Jack, S. 2009: Aggressors, winners, victims & outsiders: European schools' social construction of the entrepreneur. *International Small Business Journal*, 27(1): 126–136.

Baker, J. 2010: Claiming volition and evading victimhood: Postfeminist obligations for young women. *Feminism & Psychology*, 20(2): 186–204.

Berg, N. 1997: Gender, place and entrepreneurship. *Entrepreneurship and Regional Development*, 9(4): 259–268.

Bird, B. & Brush, C. 2002: A gendered perspective on organizational creation. *Entrepreneurship, Theory and Practice*, 26(3): 41–65.

Bruni, A., Gherardi, G. & Poggio, B. 2004a: Doing gender, doing entrepreneurship: An ethnographic account of intertwined practices. *Gender, Work and Organization*, 11(4): 406–429.

Bruni, A., Gherardi, G. & Poggio, B. 2004b: Entrepreneurship-mentality, gender and the study of women entrepreneurs. *Journal of Organizational Change Management*, 17(3): 256–269.

Buttner, E.H. 2001: Examining female entrepreneurs management style: An application of a relational frame. *Journal of Business Ethics*, 29(3): 253–269.

Calas, M., Smircich, L. & Bourne, K. A. 2007: Knowing Lisa? Feminist analyses of gender and entrepreneurship. In Bilimoria, D. & Piderit, S.K. (eds) *Handbook on Women in Business & Management*, pp. 78–108. Cheltenham: Edward Elgar.

Carlson, J. 2011: Subjects of stalled revolution: A theoretical consideration of contemporary American femininity. *Feminist Theory*, 12(1): 75–91.

Chasserio, S., Philippe, P. & Poroli, C. 2014: When entrepreneurial identity meets multiple social identities: Interplays and identity work of women entrepreneurs. *International Journal of Entrepreneurial Behaviour & Research*, 20(2): 128–154.

Cohen, L. & Musson, G. 2000: Entrepreneurial identities: Reflections from two case studies. *Organization*, 7(1): 31–48.

Cotter, D., Hermsen, J. M. & Vanneman, R. 2011: The end of the gender revolution? Gender role attitudes from 1977 to 2008. *American Journal of Sociology*, 117(1): 259–289.

Daily Record 2010: We're the mothers who want it all: Mumpreneurs are setting up businesses to suit their lifestyles, 17 August.

Davies, H. 2009: Baby bargains. *The Journal (Newcastle)*, 1 December.

Dean, J. 2010: *Rethinking Contemporary Feminist Politics*. Basingstoke: Palgrave Macmillan.

Dent, K. 2008: Mum's the buzz word on going it alone from home. *The Journal (Newcastle)*, 5 March.

Dodds, S. 2008: Women who mean business. *Daily Express*, 4 October.

Down, S. & Warren, L. 2008: Constructing narratives of enterprise: Clichés and entrepreneurial self-identity. *International Journal of Entrepreneurial Behaviour and Research*, 14(1): 4–23.

Duberley, J. & Carrigan, M. 2013: The career identities of 'mumpreneurs': Women's experiences of combining enterprise and motherhood. *International Small Business Journal*, 31(3): 629–651.

Ekinsmyth, C. 2011: Challenging the boundaries of entrepreneurship: The spatialities and practices of UK mumpreneurs. *Geoforum*, 42(1): 104–114.

Ekinsmyth, C. 2014: Mothers' business, work/life and the politics of mumpreneurship. *Gender, Place & Culture*, 21(10): 1230–1248.

Essers, C. & Benschop, Y. 2007: Enterprising identities: female entrepreneurs of Moroccan or Turkish origin in the Netherlands. *Organization Studies*, 28(1): 49–69.

Essex Chronicle 2007: Housework that pays, 25 January.

Fenwick, T. 2002: Transgressive desires: New enterprising selves in the new capitalism. *Work, Employment and Society*, 16(4): 703–723.

Foss, L. 2004: Going against the grain... .Construction of entrepreneurial identity through narratives. In Hjorth, D. & Steyaert, C. (eds) *Narrative and Discursive Approaches in Entrepreneurship*. Cheltenham: Edward Elgar.

Gill, R. 2007: Postfeminist media culture: Elements of a sensibility. *European Journal of Cultural Studies*, 10(2): 147–166.

Green, E. & Cohen, L. 1995: Women's business: Are women entrepreneurs breaking new ground or simply balancing the demands of "women's work" in a new way? *Journal of Gender Studies*, 4(3): 297–314.

Hall, E. J. & Rodriguez, M.S. 2003: The myth of postfeminism. *Gender and Society*, 17(6): 878–902.

Hall, L. J. & Donoghue, N. 2013: Nice girls don't carry knives: Constructions of ambition in media coverage of Australia's first female prime minister. *British Journal of Social Psychology*, 52(3): 631–647.

Hamilton, E. 2006: Whose story is it anyway? Narrative accounts of the role of women in founding and establishing a family business. *International Small Business Journal*, 24(3): 253–271.

Hamilton, E. 2013: The discourse of entrepreneurial masculinities (and femininities). *Entrepreneurship & Regional Development*, 25(1-2): 90–99.

Hamilton, E. 2014: Entrepreneurial narrative, identity & gender: A double epistemological shift. *Journal of Small Business Management*, 52(4): 703–712.

Hekman, S. 2000: Beyond identity: Feminism, identity and identity politics. *Feminist Theory*, 1(3): 289–308.

Hundley, G. 2000: Male/female earning differences in self-employment: The effects of marriage, children and the household division of labour. *Industrial and Labour Relations Review*, 54(1): 95–114.

Hundley, G. 2001: Why women earn less than men in self-employment. *Journal of Labour Research*, 22(4): 817–829.

Jennings, J. E. & McDougald, M. S. 2007: Work-family interface experiences and coping strategies: Implications for entrepreneurship research and practice. *Academy of Management Review*, 32(3): 747–760.

Johnson, L. & Lloyd, J. 2004: *Sentenced to Everyday Life: Feminism and the Housewife*. Oxford: Berg Publishers.

Jones, R., Latham, J. & Betta, M. 2008: Narrative construction of the social entrepreneurial identity. *International Journal of Entrepreneurial Behaviour and Research*, 14(5): 330–345.

Karatas-Ozkan, M., Anderson, A. R., Fayolle, A., Howells, J. & Candor, R. 2014: Understanding entrepreneurship: Challenging dominant perspectives and theorising entrepreneurship through new postpostivist epistemologies. *Journal of Small Business Management*, 52(4): 703–712.

Kark, R., Waismel-Manor, R. & Shamir, B. 2012: Does valuing androgyny and femininity lead to a female advantage? The relationship between gender-role, transformational leadership and identification. *The Leadership Quarterly*, 23(3): 620–640.

Katila, S. & Eriksson, P. 2013: He is a firm, strong minded and empowering leader but is she? Gendered positioning of female and male CEOs. *Gender, Work and Organization*, 20(1): 71–84.

Korsgaard, S. 2007: Mumpreneurship as a challenge to the growth ideology of entrepreneurship. *Kontur*, 16(1): 42–45.

Korsgaard, S. & Anderson, A. R. 2011: Enacting entrepreneurship as social value creation. *International Small Business Journal*, 29(2): 135–151.

Law, C. 2008: Come on in, the kitchen's lovely. *The Sunday Times*, 13 July.

Lawler, S. 2008: *Identity: Sociological Perspectives*. Cambridge: Polity Press.

Lee-Gosselin, H. & Grise, J. 1990: Are women owner-managers challenging our definitions of entrepreneurship? An in-depth survey. *Journal of Business Ethics*, 9(4-5): 423–433.

Lewis, P. 2006: The quest for invisibility: Female entrepreneurs and the masculine norm of entrepreneurship. *Gender, Work and Organization*, 13(5): 453–469.

Lewis, P. 2010: Mumpreneurs: Revealing the post-feminist entrepreneur. In Lewis, P. & Simpson, R. (eds) *Revealing and Concealing Gender: Issues of Visibility in Organizations*, pp. 124–138. Basingstoke: Palgrave Macmillan.

Lewis, P. 2013: 'Mumpreneur': The emergence and implications of a postfeminist entrepreneurial identity. *British Academy of Management Conference*, Liverpool.

Lewis, P. 2014a: Feminism, post-feminism and emerging femininities in entrepreneurship. In Kumra, S., Simpson, R. & Burke, R. (eds) *The Oxford Handbook of Gender in Organizations*, pp. 107–129. Oxford: Oxford University Press.

Lewis, P. 2014b: Postfeminism, femininities and organization studies: Exploring a new agenda. *Organization Studies*, 35(12): 1845–1866.

Loscocco, K. & Bird, S.R. 2012: Gendered paths: Why women lag behind men in small business success. *Work and Occupations*, 39(2): 183–219.

Lynn, A. 2001: Life: Forward march of the mumpreneurs. *The Daily Express*, 28 June.

Mallett, O. & Wapshott, R. 2015: Making sense of self-employment in late career: Understanding the identity of olderpreneurs. *International Small Business Journal*, DOI: 10.1177/0950017014546666.

McCann, D. 2010: Busy mum who has time for tea. *Evening News (Edinburgh)*, 27 September.

McLellan, A. 2011: The mums who know what's best for business: Entrepreneurial mothers are starting companies while caring for their newborns. *The Independent*, 28 July.

McRobbie, A. 1993: Shut up and dance: Youth culture and changing modes of femininity. *Cultural Studies*, 7(3): 406–426.

McRobbie, A. 2004: Post-feminism and popular culture: Bridget Jones and the new gender regime. *Feminist Media Studies*, 4(3): 255–264.

McRobbie, A. 2009: *The Aftermath of Feminism*. London: Sage.

Mirchandani, K. 1999: Feminist insight on gendered work: New directions in research on women and entrepreneurship. *Gender, Work and Organization,* 6(4): 224–236.

Negra, D. 2009: *What a girl wants? Fantasizing the reclamation of self in postfeminism.* London: Routledge.

Nel, P., Maritz, A. & Thongprovati, O. 2010: Motherhood and entrepreneurship: The mumpreneur phenomenon. *International Journal of Organizational Innovation,* 3(1): 6–34.

Nottingham Evening Post 2008: Do you have a great home business idea? 3 October.

Ogbor, J. O. 2000: Mythicizing and reification in entrepreneurial discourse: Ideology-critique of entrepreneurial studies. *Journal of Management Studies,* 37(4): 605–635.

Richomme-Huet, K., Vial, V. & d'Andria, A. 2013: Mumpreneurship: a new concept for an old phenomenon? *International Journal of Entrepreneurship & Small Business,* 19(2): 251–275.

Rose, H. 2008a: Mothers of invention. *The Times,* 19 July.

Rose, H. 2008b: Million dollar mum. *The Times,* 19 July.

Rouse, J. & Kitchings, J. 2006: Do enterprise support programmes leave women holding the baby? *Environment and Planning C: Government and Policy,* 24(1): 5–19.

Simpson, R. & Lewis, P. 2005: An investigation of silence and a scrutiny of transparency: Re-examining gender in organization literature through the concepts of voice and visibility. *Human Relations,* 58(10): 1253–1275.

Slater, L. 2008: Enter the mumpreneurs. *The Sunday Times,* 30 March.

Srivastava, P. & Hopwood, N. 2009: A practical iterative framework for qualitative data analysis. *International Journal of Qualitative Methods,* 8(1): 76–84.

Steyaert, C. & Katz, J. 2004: Reclaiming the space of entrepreneurship in society: Geographical, discursive and social dimensions. *Entrepreneurship & Regional Development,* 16(3): 179–196.

Suchman, M. C. 1995: Managing legitimacy: Strategic and institutional approaches. *Academy of Management Review,* 20(3): 571–610.

Tatli, A., Vassilopoulou, J., Ozbilgin, M., Forsan, C. & Slutskaya, N. 2014: A Bourdieuan relational perspective for entrepreneurship research. *Journal of Small Business Management,* 52(4): 615–632.

Tedmanson, D., Verduyn, K., Essers, C. & Gartner, W. B. 2012: Critical perspectives in entrepreneurship research. *Organization,* 19(5): 531–541.

Thornham, H. & McFarland, A. 2011: Cross-generational gender constructions: Women, teenagers and technology. *Sociological Review,* 59(1): 64–85.

Thornton, P. H., Ribeiro-Soriano & Urbano, D. 2011: Socio-cultural factors and entrepreneurial activity: An overview. *International Small Business Journal,* 29(2): 105–118.

Vickery, L. 2005: Will having one of these make you rich and happy? *Daily Post (Liverpool),* 10 May.

Warren, L. 2004: Negotiating entrepreneurial identity: Communities of practice and changing discourses. *International Journal of Entrepreneurship and Innovation,* 5(1): 25–35.

Watson, M. 2006: Meet the mumpreneurs. *Western Mail,* 3 May.

Watson, T. J. 2009: Entrepreneurial action, identity work and the use of multiple discursive resources: The case of a rapidly changing family business. *International Small Business Journal,* 27(3): 251–274.

16

FEMALE LIFESTYLE ENTREPRENEURS AND THEIR BUSINESS MODELS

Helle Neergaard and Dorthe Refslund Christensen

Introduction

Traditionally, entrepreneurship has been associated with economic and business growth opportunities, economic motives and a profit-driven orientation (Ateljevic and Doorne, 2000; Cederholm and Hultman, 2008). Lifestyle entrepreneurship, on the other hand, has been equated with non-growth businesses and motives that involve balancing family and work obligations (Harris, 2007), as well as a need for flexibility in everyday life, greater personal freedom or the support of a particular lifestyle (Cederholm and Hultman, 2008), generating a family income without leaving the family (Dawson et al., 2011; Marcketti et al., 2006) or merely working with one's true passion. Thus, a clear orientation towards non-economic motives can be identified among lifestyle entrepreneurs (Morrison, 2006).

Lifestyle businesses are commonly found within the hospitality, tourism (particularly rural tourism), leisure and creative craft industries (Getz and Peterson, 2005) and are typically home based. In the past decade, a shift can be observed. First, although traditional industries still dominate, there has been a change in the demand for differentiated and tailor-crafted tourism products (Ateljevic and Doorne, 2000); second, even if lifestyle businesses are still found mainly in rural areas, they make avid use of the Internet to create reach; and third, some lifestyle businesses have taken on a new twist: even if they originally were oriented towards enhancing their own life quality, they may grow to become almost religious movements in that they attract customers who become 'disciples' and buy into the lifestyle because they hope it will bring them a new lease of life that will make them happier. Indeed, lifestyle is seemingly becoming transformed into a 'commodity' that can be sold in line with a physical product. This is both a new phenomenon and a new type of business model that is greatly assisted by the spread of the Internet. Thus, when viewing lifestyle entrepreneurship from this perspective it becomes pertinent to look to religious sociology for elucidation of the phenomenon.

This chapter, therefore, sets out to investigate and understand the current role and impact of the business model used by lifestyle entrepreneurs through the lens of soteriology. The remainder of the chapter is structured as follows: the next section introduces a brief review of the literature on lifestyle entrepreneurship, building a taxonomy of lifestyle entrepreneurs. We then proceed by introducing the theoretical framework of soteriology. The methodology section presents the sample and approach taken. This is followed by an introduction of four cases, which are discussed in relation to the soteriological framework in order to create a new understanding of the present importance of this particular type of lifestyle entrepreneurship. Finally, in conclusion, we suggest that the traditional lifestyle entrepreneur may have much to learn about the use of business models from soteriological lifestyle entrepreneurs.

Theoretical background

From a traditional economic perspective, the key aspiration for entrepreneurs is to generate employment and profit for themselves. Lifestyle entrepreneurs, on the other hand, are guided more by personal values than by profit (Dewhurst and Horobin, 1998). The motives are typically a mixture of life balance and autonomy, e.g. the need for independence and being your own boss (Peters et al., 2009), achieving quality of life through, for example, a slower pace of life (Ateljevic and Doorne, 2000) and a better work-life balance (Peters et al., 2009). Lifestyle entrepreneurs are typically sole proprietors whose businesses only need to support their chosen lifestyle in an enjoyable and satisfactory way to the extent that they are not particularly concerned with profit (Morrison et al., 1998). Moreover, lifestyle entrepreneurs tend to be situated outside cities and often in rural areas because this choice of location supports their view of life (Shaw and Williams, 1998).

Wagner and Ziltener (2008: 4) claim that lifestyle entrepreneurs "build and manage their business in a manner that reflects their particular personality traits, human capital resources and prior experience gained within a particular local environment". Indeed, in terms of human capital, lifestyle entrepreneurs are often associated with low education and poor management and marketing skills (Hollick and Braun, 2000); they fail to appreciate the advantages of ICT (which may enhance the economic sustainability that they otherwise may lack due to their peripheral location), and they do not focus on innovation (Peters et al., 2009). In addition, they tend to lack sufficient capital to grow their business; they share this characteristic with many other entrepreneurial minorities. Finally, some studies find that they are also lacking in social capital (Mottiar, 2007; Velasco and Saleilles, 2007), suggesting that lifestyle entrepreneurs have a low level of local embeddedness resulting from insufficient network engagement with other entrepreneurs; this in turn limits their local impact. Success, therefore, seems to be more dependent on serendipity than on the implementation of a focused strategy.

Shaw and Williams (1990, 1998, 2003, 2004) identify the tourism and hospitality sector as one area in which lifestyle entrepreneurs abound in the form of B&Bs, one- or two-star inns, guest houses, local restaurants offering locally produced food, farm shops and arts and crafts shops (pottery, glass and woodcraft). Certain types of experience-driven lifestyle entrepreneurship such as farm tourism, weekend workshops – where one can stay at an inn while learning to cook fine foods, or make jewellery or pottery – or wellness weekends have also mushroomed in recent years. Such businesses are typically located outside cities, often in the periphery and in rural areas. Hence, the dream about a certain lifestyle that lifestyle entrepreneurs create not only involves independence but also a different pace of life, a closer relationship with nature, less commuting and an awareness of our impact on nature. Thus, lifestyle entrepreneurship encompasses a certain set of personal socio-political values.

In the following sections we define a lifestyle entrepreneur as: 'an *individual who owns and operates a business closely aligned with his/her personal values, beliefs, interests and passions'*. Certain lifestyle entrepreneurs tend to be avid users of ICT, and engage with 'niche' market consumers informed by values similar to their own, and they are "often instrumental in the creation and introduction of innovative products to the wider industry" (Ateljevic and Doorne, 2000: 378). Further, Marchant and Mottiar (2011) examined the similarities of lifestyle entrepreneurs with regard to their skillset and concluded that being good communicators, enjoying interacting with people and being well educated were amongst the most prevalent skills; such findings would appear to be contradictory to the traditional perception of lifestyle entrepreneurs. In addition, Wagner and Ziltener (2008) found that self-actualisation has become an important factor for lifestyle entrepreneurs.

In a society where most of the population is affluent and well educated, new forms of entrepreneurship are emerging. Despite some critique (see e.g. Wahba and Bridwell, 1976), Maslow's framework (1971) represents a useful model for understanding how entrepreneurial initiatives are contextually conditioned. Once individuals have reached the highest level of the pyramid – the level of self-actualisation – they start looking for ways to help others fulfil their needs. In terms of entrepreneurship, there are two ways of doing this: first, through social entrepreneurship. A growing number of young people spend time helping the underprivileged, ill or deprived individuals or animals under threat. These youngsters have typically grown up having had all their needs covered; they have never gone hungry or feared for their safety; they have belonged socially, and they have achieved academically. It is only through helping others 'step up the ladder' that they can grow further themselves. These individuals Maslow (1971) describes as: those who "try to set things right, to clean up bad situations and those who are attracted to unsolved or difficult problems". The second way is through soteriological entrepreneurship. Soteriology as a theory represents a path to salvation or a doctrine of salvation. According to soteriology, human beings are trapped in some kind of non-ideal state from which they can only be delivered if they reach an ideal state, as illustrated in Figure 16.1.

The transformation can only be obtained through individual awareness creation and a ritualised lifestyle or through divine intervention. According to Heelas (1996), all spiritual awareness activities – referred to as New Age – that influenced Western culture heavily during the late '80s and '90s shared one basic characteristic, namely, that of being self-religious. In other words, the New Age movement reflected Western cultures' general and enormous need for self-improvement and development. This meant, among other things, that self-improvement strategies (traditionally belonging to the field of religion) became more psychological in nature and were transformed into hybrid cultural forms involving a varied field of bodily, ritualised and spiritual practices. Such practices challenged the traditional views of religion and spirituality, sharing a pursuit for transforming the individual's life from being in deficit to acquiring a surplus.

For entrepreneurship, soteriology has several implications: first, soteriological entrepreneurs have typically been men who have established a new 'church' or created a 'following' that would enable them to make a living; there are countless examples, particularly in the United States. However, traditionally, such individuals have not been categorised as entrepreneurs. Second, the spiritual sphere is more often associated with women who tend to

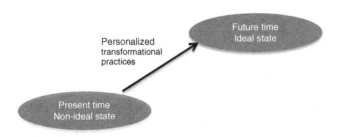

Figure 16.1 The soteriological process

Table 16.1 Taxonomy of modern lifestyle entrepreneurs

	Traditional lifestyle entrepreneurship 'Making a living'	Modern lifestyle entrepreneurship 'Making a profit'
Life quality for self	Work-life balance	
Life quality for others (consumers/community)	Social entrepreneurship	Soteriological entrepreneurship

be less objectively and more emotionally oriented than men and, therefore, more likely to believe in the intangible aspects of the universe. Hence, it is probably not surprising that a significant number of new age soteriological entrepreneurs are women. Further, since the '90s, religion has 'moved out of' religion, and so have soteriological practices. Even though classical soteriologies were always for sale and not offered for free, they have become more and more accepted and integrated into regular business strategies, both as part of the production of immaterial values in the experience economy and as an important part of the products sold by entrepreneurial businesses. Soteriology can, therefore, be said to constitute a new business model for female lifestyle entrepreneurs.

Soteriological lifestyle businesses typically originate from their founders' intention to transform their own lives into something qualitatively and profitably better. The motives of the lifestyle entrepreneur show a strong social orientation, thus, even if they start the business with the view that they need to enhance their own lifestyle, it can be assumed that they aim to create life quality and lifestyle both for themselves and for others. Cederholm (2008) discusses the producer and consumer dichotomy with regard to the intimacy level and producer experience. Soteriological lifestyle entrepreneurs minimise the gap between the producer and the consumer experience. Often, they consider their business as their home (Harris et al., 2007) and their customers as 'friends', which Cederholm (2008) describes as a commercial friendship. Thus, it can be implied that the business positively contributes to the life quality of both the customers and the community.

This review of extant literature thus permits the creation of a taxonomy, as illustrated in Table 16.1, which aims to explain the relationship between the motives for the entrepreneur and the impact for customers and society with regard to the traditional lifestyle entrepreneur and the modern lifestyle entrepreneur.

Thus, there seems to be growing acceptance that entrepreneurship is no longer only for high-growth, high-tech and high-risk businesses (Marcketti et al., 2006). In view of this, we need to gather knowledge on a new type of lifestyle entrepreneur in society. Who are these entrepreneurs, what do they do, and how do they contribute? We explore these questions in the following sections.

Methodology

We approach the empirical setting from a social constructivist perspective. Not only do the female soteriological entrepreneurs in our sample construct their own social world, they also influence how other women construct theirs. We proceed to investigate female entrepreneurs who have started a thriving business based on ideals of personal growth and self-transformation. We selected four purposefully sampled intensive cases representing successful female entrepreneurs who have become Danish lifestyle 'gurus' in the past 10 to 15 years. Intensity sampling seeks examples that are remarkable in some way. The choice

Table 16.2 Sample frame

	Team	Solo
Personal development	Giveyourself	Healthy2theCore Family
Personal development and home design	Millionairess Method	Ranvita

of an intensity case often requires considerable knowledge of the case up front in order to determine whether it manifests the phenomenon intensely. Thus, an intensity case manifests the phenomenon intensely but not extremely (Neergaard, 2007). We, therefore, gathered background data via the Internet before deciding which entrepreneurs to include in the sample. The chosen entrepreneurs are remarkable because they succeeded in: a) becoming very visible in the business landscape and (because of this), b) becoming very profitable. We also subscribed to some of their newsletters in order to gain access to those parts of their business that were not readily available to the casual browser. All material was retrieved during 2013.

The cases chosen include www.kernesundfamilie.dk, www.millionoesemetoden.dk, www.givdigselv.dk and www.ranvita.com. The cases were chosen to reflect a broad variety of product offerings. As illustrated in Table 16.2, two businesses focus on personal development only, the others combine personal development with home design. The choice of cases was also based on whether the businesses were individual or team. Two businesses were established by team formation; the other two are solo ventures. However, one of the entrepreneurs has a second business together with her husband. Three of them could be termed 'serial entrepreneurs', however, this dimension was not part of the sampling criteria.

We performed documentary analysis using discourse and semiotic techniques on information from the businesses' websites and newspaper articles in order to gain knowledge about the founders, their motives and aspirations as well as their products and strategy (see e.g. Smith and Anderson, 2007, for an account of semiotic techniques). All information in the case boxes has been obtained from the websites, which are publicly available, and translated verbatim by the authors of this paper. The authors have not attempted to refine or bolster the language used.

Case presentations

Case 1: www.kernesundfamilie.dk (Healthy2theCoreFamily)

Ninka, who is the founder or 'prophet' of Kernesund Familie, tells her story on the homepage of her website, through which she sells "joy, happiness and mental strength for women and children". Her story is presented in Box 16.1:

Box 16.1 Ninka's story

The anomaly

One summer six years ago became the "point of no return" for me. I was 20 kilos over weight. The whole family would get out of breath if we had to take the stairs to the second floor. I was stressed, irritated, depressed. My children and my husband had asthma, which required medical

---

treatment. My oldest son was autistic, and his aggressive behaviour controlled the whole family. We didn't get enough sleep, were stressed and scared. I worked too much and didn't have enough money. Nothing in my life was what I had dreamed about.

The solution

I have lost 20 kilos. I run 50 kilometres every week with my children. I love, respect and honour myself. I have time and peace with my children. I have the financial surplus to do the things I dreamed about. My family no longer has asthma. My son has lost his repetitive, angry behaviour and is living a good life; he has become emphatic, loving and lives a normal life attending normal school. So, now, I want to share my tools with the whole world via my blog, workshops, retreats, webinars, home-study kits and books.

http://www.kernesundfamilie.dk/om-kernesundfamilie/

Ninka has a degree in journalism and used to work as a journalist and PR expert. She started out by writing a book about how she transformed from her non-ideal state to her ideal state, and has sold over 200,000 copies – a large number in a small country such as Denmark. She offers a subscription to her homepage for €15 per year to which subscribers can add various extras (for an additional cost). Club Kernesund Familie has 20,000 regular subscribers. To illustrate how Ninka self-stages, and what she sells, one of her products is described in Box 16.2.

Box 16.2 World's best detox retreat (sold out)

Imagine hot sauna-rituals, intensive cleansing, the North Sea, tranquillity, enjoyment and peace. Imagine fat burning and detox without hunger, and relaxing coaching within an affectionate group of eight likeminded women.

Do you want to get rid of the toxic oestrogens that accumulate on your thighs as fat (which is why you cannot lose weight without help)?

Do you dream about getting rid of all the poisons that make you fat and old before your time, simultaneously getting rid of old patterns, barriers and habits?

Do you dream about detoxing and fasting on liquid 'superfood' without hunger, and the harmful side effects that fasting usually involves?

Do you dream about disappearing from your everyday life?

Do you dream about only paying attention to yourself, tranquillity, sea bathing and sauna rituals?

I am trained in the most up-to-date methods in detox and fat burning, and I have not been able to find a retreat that does this as perfectly and efficiently as I want. So, now I do it myself. Do you want to join?

http://www.kernesundfamilie.dk/lpnyretreat2/

Case 2: *www.millionoesemetoden.dk*
(the millionairess method)

The two founders of the 'millionairess method' were both educated within the humanities: one holds a master's degree in modern culture and cultural communication; the other has a language degree in Danish and English. The former was a journalist in New York where she lived and worked for 11 years doing local TV in Manhattan and working freelance for Danish TV, newspapers and magazines. She has written five books on innovative ways of living and working.

Both of the women are serial entrepreneurs and run other businesses. One has two 'side' businesses where she works with transformation, leadership and business; amongst these is the feminine Goddess School where she teaches what she calls 'feminine leadership'. The other woman runs a 'spiritual salon', where she teaches spirituality, energy work, sales and marketing, which she links with developmental tools to create 'growth, happiness and transformation'. Courses in the various businesses cost upwards of €2,000, the most expensive being €7,000. Box 16.3 presents a short, illustrative excerpt from the website:

The founders of the millionairess method further collaborate with Ninka from Healthy2theCoreFamily, having developed a course titled Healthy2theCoreMillionairess.

Box 16.3 The Millionairess Method

You too can achieve this life. As a millionairess, you become rich by enriching the world, you have an excess of everything because you are good at filling up your own cup before you pour for others. However, the millionairess method requires courage.

If you take this road, you have to be willing to forge new paths. You need the courage to raise yourself to new levels, taking leaps of faith, and perceive adversity as the key to your new life. If you do not want to show such courage, stop now. But then the world will never benefit from your abilities.

If instead you take responsibility for your position, using the spiritual, transforming and thoroughly tested millionaires' method step by step, you will change your convictions, change gear from middle class to millionairess, and earn millions on your unique starting point and experience happiness and joy. It is our experience that once you have acquired a taste for the millionairess road then it is an enjoyable path to take, and most do not want to leave it again.

Are you ready for a surplus in your bank account, in the calendar, in your body, in love and the life you only dreamt about minutes ago?

http://millionoesemetoden.dk/millionoesemetode

Case 3: *Ranvita.com – happy living.com*

Ranvita was originally educated as a TV presenter at the Danish School of Film; she has worked many years in the industry as both a host and presenter. Serendipity brought her into contact with an interior designer and philosopher in feng shui, and in 2000 she changed her career and opted to follow her passion for working with personal development and spirituality. This developed into an interest for the interaction between individuals and their homes and interior design and its influence on the way we lead our lives. She attended courses in feng shui and NLP and works in clairvoyance. In 2004, she participated in a Danish TV programme 'Living with Feng Shui'. This was the start of her business, which involved providing inspiration, talks and workshops. She has also written a book *Love your home from A-Z* and is co-author of the book *Simple Living: Educated in America.*

Today she works with the 'Love-your-home-method'®, which consists of a combination of the aesthetic, psychological and spiritual, according to which the home should be designed so that it will please the eye, the spirit and the soul. She also shares a spin-off from the business, HappyLiving.dk, with her partner. The entry page on the website (Box 16.4) tells the following story:

Box 16.4 Love your home, love your life

Did you know that your home is a mirror of your life? Receive tips and ideas about how you can change your home, so it supports your life in Ranvita's newsletter. When you become a member you will receive a free live-recording of the 'teleclass'. This is how you get more energy and a better love life by avoiding the three biggest mistakes in the bedroom."

My passion is to create a more beautiful world – inside ourselves and in our homes.

http://www.ranvita.dk

The webpage starts out with a section called 'about Ranvita', and her picture takes up the entire page. She then provides answers to a number of questions, such as, 'Which things would you not be without?' and what is 'Your best beauty tip?' A different page presents her products, which encompass eight different categories: i) courses and workshops, ii) baguacards,[1] iii) tantraphotos,[2] iv) feng shui crystals, v) word pictures, vi) beautiful things, vii) books and finally, viii) clothes. In most of these categories there is only one product. Courses and workshops are clearly her main focus, and the prices range from about €20 for an evening course lasting a couple of hours to longer lasting courses costing between €200 and €500.

Case 4: Givdigselv.dk

Giveyourself (*give yourself*) sells online self-development tools that provide the consumer with everyday mental fuel and surplus energy. The business arranges live events with special benefits for subscribers. All profits from subscriptions are given to charity. Membership costs €40 per year. The business is established as a formal society with Articles (§) and an Annual General Assembly. There is also a network, which members of 'giveyourself' can join. Here they give advice, run a blog, etc. Box 16.5 provides an example of the areas within which one of the founders gives advice/coaching. For each of the tools there is a separate page with a description of this tool.

Each of the two founders simultaneously runs her own business; one runs an online lifestyle 'mekka', started at the kitchen table in 2003. This business sells furniture, gifts and other home interiors (e.g. tablecloths, candles, etc.). The other is a life coach, who was educated in the U.S. and holds a Master's Degree in Psychology. She has worked for Danish TV,

---

Box 16.5 Tools for a better life

Relationships	Conflict solution	Career advice	Other
Your relational circle	Your reaction in conflicts	The heart as your career guide	Good questions
Give to all your relations	Stop personal intimidation	What is career?	
			www.givdigselv.dk
Safeguard your relations	Conflict fear		
	A good conflict		

---

participating in a programme entitled 'A better life', and in 2011 she had her own weekly radio programme. She also writes regularly for a Danish women's weekly magazine. She has written a book as well as chapters for other books on coaching and self-development. She is considered the most successful 'life coach' in Denmark. The combination of the two businesses illustrates how self-development and home/garden design go hand in hand.

Most importantly, however, they market their initiative as a not-for-profit social enterprise; all of the profits from the membership go to support a Kenyan initiative, 'Women gain influence'.

Findings

Four characteristics of the founders and their founding processes should be noted from the above cases. First, all of the women have an educational background from the humanities, being either journalists or communication specialists. Second, most have experience in journalism. Third, most have lived, worked and adopted the simple living and spiritual trend in the U.S. during the first decade of the new millennium. Only Healthy2theCoreFamily distinguishes herself, but then her business is more about food and less about spirituality than the other three. She is also the only one who is basing her business on a personal disharmony 'the opportunity within' – namely that of being overweight and having a dysfunctional family. The others seem to have picked an 'opportunity out there' and are the first movers of an American spirituality trend in Denmark. Fourth, all of the businesses started with the protagonist writing a book about her own experiences – a book, which was then sold in large numbers. Finally, although the personal disharmony aspect is not necessarily explicated, in order to start engaging with the new age movement there is typically an underlying dissatisfaction with one's existing life/lifestyle. For example, Ninka from Healthy2theCore Family clearly states that she was dissatisfied with her personal appearance and the way her family functioned. For some of the others, it was a less apparent dissonance with something else in their lives that made them seek out yoga, feng shui and coaching initially as a tool for their own self-development and then as a tool for other women's self-development. For example, one lost a child to an accident.

Only one of the businesses, Giveyourself, combines the soteriological business with a social enterprise. Here, customers contribute to helping set Kenya's women free by becoming members and paying a yearly fee. However, even if all the activities, advice and tools on this website are free, there are links to the two women's other businesses, which is where they earn their money. There is no doubt that their business model is a very lucrative one.

All of the homepages are awash with pictures of the women in '*look at me, I am so happy*' or '*I am so beautiful*' poses. Some even have sexual undertones. The website of Ranvita, for example, is very vocal about the importance she accords to sex. Although the millionairess method has no sexual undertones, the Goddess School, which is linked through the website, is full of them, for example, "Live like a goddess, and have other people worship you." Thus, the holistic message of the New Age movement that body, mind and spirit should be in balance with each other is also a focus here. It becomes a matter of meeting the challenges that life presents on all levels, with regard to relationships, work and career, family, finances, health and body, love and sex.

Furthermore, the soteriological entrepreneurs are eminent network users. An analysis of their reference patterns shows how they consistently refer to each other's websites when they write articles, thus making their own customers aware that other offerings exist. This shows how they see each other as potential partners rather than competitors.

Discussion

The case exemplars presented in this chapter are illustrative of several trends that are influential in today's society. First, all of these female entrepreneurs sell a product with soteriological perspectives, which include objects or practices aimed at the personal transformation of their clients or their material reality to reflect the desire for 'becoming' rather than 'being'. Thus, their websites sell tools for changing those who long to become extraordinary: as a wife, a lover, a mother or in any other area of life. Some even promise that a financial gain will (automatically) result from the spiritual gain. The change is all-encompassing – if you change one aspect of life – and, in particular, the way you think – the rest will automatically follow: as one of them states "*For many people it is a great pain and a problem that their life is not the way they want for it to be. My product is spiritual wisdom turned into an easy to follow recipe, which will give success if you follow it: The first step involves: send your wish to the universe. Second step sounds: let the universe fulfil your wish*". The entrepreneur, thus, becomes a role model per se, both as a source of identification in the soteriological before-stage, through imitations and citations that the selling of her practices makes possible for the customer to attain, and not least, the goals the customers are hoping to achieve.

Second, the soteriological entrepreneur also plays on the customer's wish to belong to a group – a successful group, which constitutes the second step in Maslow's needs hierarchy. Indeed, social belonging has become a very powerful requirement today, to the extent that we all belong to several groups on the Internet, Facebook and Linkedin, for example. Through these groups, we feel 'a belongingness' that today's family or workplace may not be able to supply.

Third, they follow the new trend in society among women who have reached high levels of education and the highest level of the needs' pyramid, namely 'self-actualization'. They start to look towards helping individuals (particularly other women) at the bottom of the pyramid climb further up. Women have the right to become successful both in their work and in their families. Workwise wealth comes in terms of money – and a lot of it. Familywise, the money helps, but here it is about becoming rich in yourself – moving from the soteriological 'minus' to the 'plus.'

Fourth, the case exemplars presented here share the strategy of turning their own personal anomaly into a business model and branding their product through a very personalised staging and framing, for example: "*I was fat and had no energy. Now I want what happened to me to happen to you, and so I share with you all the knowledge I strived to achieve and which helped me*". Thus, the personal disharmony is turned into a commodity of great value, and the entrepreneur is branded as the role model per se – as a source of identification in the soteriological before-stage. Further, through imitation, pursuit and introduction of the entrepreneur's practices in their own lives, the clients will be able to attain the lifestyle of the entrepreneur. This means that the female entrepreneur is more than merely a businesswoman; she is uniquely identified with the soteriological goals she sells. This seems to be a very interesting way of creating value.

Intrinsic motivations are very strengthening to these kinds of businesses; however, it might also make them vulnerable to what Weber (2015 a & b) calls the routinisation of charisma. This concept was introduced by Weber as a way of analysing what happened in a religion when the founding prophet, visionary or charismatic leader cannot keep up with the challenge of demands or dies. Typically, over time, the charisma that is vested exclusively in the leader will be transferred to specially designated 'officers' in charge of the religion's rituals, so that when a change of leader takes place, then the followers will follow the new leader(s). Translating this work into the world of female entrepreneurial businesses, these become vulnerable to success, especially in our mediatised culture where visibility, relations and direct communication remain very important. This, on the one hand, makes communication to larger groups very easy and cheap, but, on the other, the never-ending demand for personal presence is a huge challenge. Furthermore, succession in a soteriologically based business remains a challenge because goodwill hinges on the person and is usually not associated with the business as an entity.

Notwithstanding the above, two alternative interpretations of the business model exist. One is that these women are very successful entrepreneurs who just sell what the customer wants. The second is that they are actually making money out of other women's vulnerability, despair and craving for 'a better life'. As such, they are, perhaps, no better than those individuals in the Wild West who sold potions for all sorts of ailments. They sell 'make-belief'. Take your pick.

Conclusions and perspectives

Reflecting on the above discussion, it is clear that one can agree or disagree with the way that these women do business – i.e. whether it is strictly ethical, or whether the extent to which they profit from other women's hardship and existential problems is ethically wrong. However, one cannot deny that they are financially successful and have understood how to make a business out of the needs of others. They have also understood how to use websites as depositories for soteriological change.

The literature commonly laments lifestyle entrepreneurs. They are defined as the opposite of growth-oriented entrepreneurs, and their contribution to the economy is considered negligible, even though ten lifestyle entrepreneurs may equate to one small business with ten employees in terms of turnover. As we demonstrate in this chapter, there is no reason to lament. Lifestyle can definitely be used as a viable business proposition, often one where the initial investment does not need to be very high. These women sell advice, tools and courses over the Internet, and to the extent that a physical location is needed this can be obtained on a course-by-course basis, so that fixed costs are kept to a minimum. The fees charged for the various 'products' make these businesses very viable indeed, as long as other women are sufficiently dissatisfied and gullible to buy into the message.

Thus, what other lifestyle entrepreneurs can learn from soteriological entrepreneurs is that these businesses are: a) making and telling a good story not only about themselves but also about others; b) offering customers lifestyle components that they crave; c) making better use of the Internet, and d) using one business as the stepping stone for others, thus creating a basis for financial growth, without having to employ additional staff.

Finally, given the abundance of literature on business models it seems there is a gap in scholarship with regard to women's use of business models. Indeed, our findings suggest that: a) women may identify business opportunities in personal disharmonies, and b) they may find alternative low-cost ways of doing business. These may involve the use of e-business strategies and growing through networks. Thus, more research is needed into how women identify business opportunities and how they actually do business and circumvent the need for financing, which previous research has pointed out may be problematic (see e.g. Brush et al., 2006; Carter et al., 2003; Buttner and Rosen, 1988).

Acknowledgement

This project was sponsored by the Danish Business Authority in conjunction with the European Social Fund through the Danish Entrepreneurial University initiative. We would like to thank Kathleen Wagner and Sidsel Freja Trads Birk for their assistance with the research. The analysis and interpretation of the publicly accessible material used are exclusively the responsibility of the authors.

Notes

1 Baguacards help reveal what goes on with you at this moment based on your chakra, and helps transform your energy.
2 Tantra is an inner realisation that functions to prevent ordinary appearances and conceptions, and to accomplish the four complete purities of a Buddha (environment, body, enjoyments and deeds). Tantraphotos portray these purities.

References

Ateljevic, I. & Doorne, S (2000). 'Staying within the Fence': Lifestyle Entrepreneurship in Tourism. *Journal of Sustainable Tourism*, 8(5), 378–392.

Brush, C.G., Carter, N.M., Gatewood, E.J., Greene, P.G. & Hart, M.M. (2006). The Use of Bootstrapping by Women Entrepreneurs in Positioning for Growth. *Venture Capital*, 8(1), 15–31.

Buttner, E. H. & Rosen, B. (1988). Bank Loan Officers' Perceptions of the Characteristics of Men, Women, and Successful Entrepreneurs. *Journal of Business Venturing*, 3(3), 249–258.

Carter, N., Brush, C., Greene, P., Gatewood, E. & Hart, M. (2003). Women Entrepreneurs Who Break through to Equity Financing: The Influence of Human, Social and Financial Capital. *Venture Capital: An International Journal of Entrepreneurial Finance*, 5(1), 1–28.

Cederholm, E.A. & Hultman, J. (2008). Intimacy as a Producer Experience – The Boundary Work of Values among Lifestyle Entrepreneurs. *Conference Paper: 17th Nordic Symposium in Tourism and Hospitality Research*, (September 2008), 1–22.

Dawson, D., Fountain, J. & Cohen, D.A. (2011). Seasonality and the Lifestyle "Conundrum": An Exploratory Analysis of Lifestyle Entrepreneurship in Rural, Cool-Climate Wine Tourism Regions. *Asia Pacific Journal of Tourism Research*, 16(5), 1–32.

Dewhurst, P. & Horobin, H. (1998). Small Business Owners. In Thomas, R. (Ed.) *The Management of Small Tourism and Hospitality Firms*. (19–39) London: Cassell.

Harris, C., McIntosh, A. & Lewis, K. (2007). The Commercial Home Enterprise: Labour with Love. *TOURISM - An International Interdisciplinary Journal*, 55(4), 391–402.

Heelas, P. (1996). *The New Age Movement: The celebration of the self and the sacralisation of modernity.* Hoboken: Wiley-Blackwell.

Hollick, M. & Braun, P. (2005). Lifestyle Entrepreneurship: The unusual nature of the tourism entrepreneur. *Second Annual AGSE International Entrepreneurship Research Exchange,* 1–17.

Marchant, B. & Mottiar, Z. (2011). Understanding Lifestyle Tourism Entrepreneurs and Digging beneath the Issue of Profits: Profiling Surf Tourism Lifestyle Entrepreneurs in Ireland. *Tourism Planning & Development, 8*(2), 171–183.

Marcketti, S.B., Niehm, L.S. & Fuloria, R. (2006). An Exploratory Study of Lifestyle Entrepreneurship and Its Relationship to Life Quality. *Family and Consumer Sciences Research Journal, 34*(3), 241–259.

Maslow, A.H. (1971). *The Farther Reaches of Human Nature.* New York: Viking Press.

Morrison, A. (2006). A Contextualisation of Entrepreneurship. *International Journal of Entrepreneurial Behaviour and Research.* 12(4): 192–209.

Morrisson, A., Rimmington, M. & Williams, C. (1998). *Entrepreneurship in the Hospitality, Tourism and Leisure Industries.* Oxford: Butterworth-Heinemann.

Mottiar, Z. (2007). Lifestyle Entrepreneurs and Spheres of Inter-Firm Relations: The case of Westport, Co Mayo, Ireland. *The International Journal of Entrepreneurship and Innovation, 8*(1), 67–74.

Neergaard, H. (2007). Sampling in Entrepreneurial Settings. In Neergaard, H. and Ulhøi, J.P. (eds) *Handbook of Qualitative Research Methods in Entrepreneurship.* Cheltenham: Edward Elgar.

Peters, M., Frehse, J. & Buhalis, D. (2009). The Importance of Lifestyle Entrepreneurship: A Conceptual Study of the Tourism Industry. *PASOS. Revista de Turismo y Patrimonio Cultural, 7*(2), 393–405.

Shaw, G. & Williams, A.M. (1990). Tourism Economic Development and the Role of Entrepreneurial Activity. In Cooper, C.P. (Ed.) *Progress in Tourism, Recreation and Hospitality Management* (66–81) London: Bellhaven.

Shaw, G. & Williams, A.M. (1998). Entrepreneurship, Small Business Culture and Tourism Development. In Ioannides, D. and Debbnage, K.G. (Eds) *The Economic Geography of the Tourist Industry* (235–255) London: Routledge.

Shaw, G. & Williams, A.M. (2003). Entrepreneurial Cultures and Small Business Enterprises in Tourism. In Hall, M., Lwe, A. and Williams, A. (Eds) *Blackwell's Companion to Tourism Geography.* Oxford: Blackwell.

Shaw, G. & Williams, A.M. (2004). From Lifestyle Consumption to Lifestyle Production: Changing Patterns of Tourism Entrepreneurship. In Thomas, R. (Ed.) *Small Firms in Tourism: International Perspectives* (99–113) Amsterdam: Elsevier.

Smith, R. & Anderson, A. (2007). Recognising Meaning: Semiotics in Entrepreneurial Research. In Neergaard, H. and Ulhøi, J.P. (eds) *Handbook of Qualitative Research Methods in Entrepreneurship.* Cheltenham: Edward Elgar.

Velasco, M.G. & Saleilles, S. (2007). The Local Embeddedness of Lifestyle Entrepreneur: An explorative study. *Interdisciplinary European Conference on Entrepreneurship Research,* 1–4.

Wagner, K. & Ziltener, A. (2008). Discussion Papers on Entrepreneurship and Innovation. The Nascent Entrepreneur at the Crossroads: Entrepreneurial Motives as Determinants for Different Types of Entrepreneurs. *Swiss Institute for Entrepreneurship,* 2, 3–22.

Wahba, M.A. & Bridwell, L.G. (1976). Maslow Reconsidered: A Review of Research on the Need Hierarchy Theory. *Organizational Behavior and Human Performance,* 15: 2, 212–240.

Weber, M. (2015a) Politics as Vocation. In Waters, T. and Waters, D. *Weber's Rationalism and Modern Society* (129–198). New York: Palgrave MacMillan:.

Weber, M. (2015b) Discipline and Charisma. In Waters, T. and Waters, D. *Weber's Rationalism and Modern Society* (59–72). New York: Palgrave MacMillan.

Webpage

http://www.naturli.dk/naturli-viden/psykologi/2383-faa-det-som-du-vil-have-det. Retrieved 9th July 2012, 12.41.

17

TALES OF HEROINE ENTREPRENEURS

Karin Berglund, Helene Ahl and Katarina Pettersson

Introduction

Woman entrepreneurs are typically described as lacking, insufficient and 'less' in comparison to their male counterparts (Ahl & Marlow, 2012; Ahl, Berglund, Pettersson & Tillmar, 2016; Bruni, Gherardi & Poggio, 2004; Calás, Smircich & Bourne, 2009; Mirchandani, 1999; Ogbor, 2000). While individual male entrepreneurs are seen as 'generic', women entrepreneurs are positioned as less entrepreneurial, thus belonging to the group of non-entrepreneurs that are the antithesis of the entrepreneurial norm. Even if entrepreneurial traits are increasingly linked to everybody, underpinning the contemporaneous neoliberal subject, women are still positioned as needing help and support to be able to work on and release their entrepreneurial capability (Bröckling, 2005; Holmer Nadesan & Trethewey, 2000).

This has spurred a research interest in studying wo/men entrepreneurs from a feminist perspective (Achtenhagen & Tillmar, 2013; Ahl, 2006; Wee & Brooks, 2012). Studying entrepreneurship as a gendered phenomenon could avoid the unfortunate tendency to reproduce women entrepreneurs as 'others'. For this reason, suggestions have been made to expand the research focus of women's entrepreneurship and shift the perspective in terms of knowledge generation by moving from an objectivist to a constructionist epistemology (Ahl & Marlow, 2012). This implies studying how female and male entrepreneurs construct their lives and their businesses, which would lay the groundwork for creating new understandings about how social orders are gendered and about other mechanisms by which this gendering is reconstructed (Ahl, 2004).

In this chapter, we contribute to this knowledge by focusing on women entrepreneurs who are described as successful, presenting a contrast to the more usual depiction of entrepreneurial women in need of support. There are also studies that recognise woman entrepreneurs as active subjects. For example, Fournier (2002) shows how women generate confusion by positioning themselves in unexpected ways whereby they gain agency. Moving in and out of 'othered' positions that they found difficult to control gave them space to act. Likewise, Berglund (2006) shows how a woman entrepreneur acted as if she was a puzzle to be solved, not by herself but by those around her, which gave her the autonomy she needed to move on with her business. Essers and Benschop (2009) refer to this kind of identity pursuit as creative boundary work in their study of women entrepreneurs of Moroccan and Turkish origin in the Netherlands. In this process, boundaries defining "what is allowed for female entrepreneurs" were stretched (Ibid: 403). What all of these studies have in common is that they contribute to entrepreneurship studies by showing how women entrepreneurs gain agency in and through their entrepreneuring.

In their chapter "Knowing Lisa?" Calás, Smircich and Bourne (2007) rhetorically ask how we can get to know the entrepreneur Lisa in their elaboration of different feminist approaches to women's entrepreneurship. As they sum up their chapter they point to the advantage of using ethnographic approaches to follow the trajectories of Lisa's life, but they also acknowledge that many other sources of empirical material could be of interest. In this chapter, we will use three public speeches, broadcast on Swedish radio, by three celebrated women entrepreneurs: Amelia Adamo, who built a newspaper empire; Anna Carrfors Bråkenhielm, who made history with the reality show "Survivor"; and Clara Lidström, who has made a living blogging about her life as a rural housewife.

Adopting a narrative approach, we analyse their stories as presented on the radio show "Summer", where all three women speak openly about their lives and how they chose, struggled to achieve, developed and evaluated their entrepreneurship. In addition, these entrepreneurs talk about how they relate to, strive for and have struggled to gain and defend equal rights for themselves and for other women using various strategies that we interpret as feminist. This chapter can also be seen in itself as applying a feminist research strategy, representing women (as) entrepreneurs who are often made invisible in stories of entrepreneurship. Following a trajectory of feminist and narrative analyses (Davies, 1989; Smith, 2014, 2010; Smith & Anderson, 2004), we look at the kind of tales that successful women entrepreneurs tell about themselves and at what we can learn from how they address entrepreneurship and gender in their stories.

Methodology

Scholars have called for narrative approaches to study how individual and collective identity and organisations are coproduced over time (e.g. Downing, 2005; Steayert & Hjorth, 2004). It has been claimed that entrepreneurship is a grand narrative in society, which depicts human beings as heroes, invulnerable and free of defects (e.g. Berglund & Johansson, 2007; Dodd & Anderson, 2007; Jones & Spicer, 2009; Sörensen, 2008). This heroic, free-floating and a-contextual image of the entrepreneur is not only a popular media version, but has also been reproduced in, as well as through, entrepreneurship research. Gartner writes that, while he can name dozens of entrepreneurs, he doubts that he could tell many of their stories:

> I have logico-scientific descriptions, explanations, categories, concepts, and hypotheses about entrepreneurs, but, frankly, I don't have many stories to tell. Maybe you do.
>
> *(2007: 624)*

In response to Gartner, we suggest that we certainly do have stories to tell. In this chapter we will tell three stories of successful women entrepreneurs. We subscribe to the view that a narrative approach allows a study of the social construction of wo/men and fe/males. This means that the story makes up empirical material through which we can study how the gendered entrepreneur is produced. A story is nothing more, or less, than a 'personal myth', writes McAdams, who points out that "we do not discover ourselves in myth" (1993: 13), but we make ourselves through myth. He further argues that the sources we may use vary wildly. There are, thus, vast possibilities to construct ourselves in a number of ways. Surprisingly, however, the entrepreneurial heroic man is often represented as a yardstick, where the entrepreneurial woman falls short and is positioned to follow suit. In this chapter we will turn to three stories that are unusual in that they are told by three successful women entrepreneurs. Apart from representing the 'heroine entrepreneur', these three women have two things in common: all of them work in the media business, and all were invited to host the radio programme because they are seen as successful and, of course, because they have interesting stories to tell.

The three stories are analysed through the 'voice-centred relational method' elaborated by Mauther and Doucet (1998). This method is itself an attempt to problematise the idea of a separate, self-sufficient, independent, rational 'self' at the heart of the male-biased entrepreneurship discourse and to move towards a relational ontology that views humans as imbedded in a complex web of social relations (cf. Ahl, 2004; Calás, Smircich & Bourne, 2009; Davies, 1989; Lindgren & Packendorff, 2009). The methodological approach of listening to different voices is also deeply rooted within the broader tradition of feminist research practice. This method was originally developed for interpreting interviews, and it reflects the fact that an interview is a collective relational achievement. In this chapter, we have adapted it for our purpose, which is to analyse a monologue in the form of a radio talk. The three stories were read four times comprising a focusing on:

Reading 1: The overall plot and story. In this reading a 'reader-response' element is accounted for, which means paying attention to how the reader responds to the story emotionally as well as intellectually. As explained by Mauther and Doucet (1998), this means, for the researcher, reading "the narrative on her own terms" (p. 11). The point is that if we do not reflect on our assumptions they will express themselves in other ways in the text, for instance, through how we represent the person's story.

Reading 2: The voice of the 'I', focusing on how the person talks about her experiences and feelings. In this reading we paid attention to the active 'I' that tells the story and paid attention to the terms the speaker used to present herself. We also noticed if the storyteller struggled, emotionally or intellectually, to say something.

Reading 3: Relationships and how they were spoken of and how people were placed within broader cultural contexts and social structures in the stories. In this reading we were particularly interested in how and which interpersonal relationships were talked about, as well as how they were presented. In addition, we noted how the broader social networks that are/were part of the person's life were addressed.

Reading 4: How is gender addressed? In this part of the reading we looked into how the three women talked about themselves as women, but also how gender was woven into their stories in relation to others, their entrepreneurship and the wider societal context.

Each of the three stories was read by one of the co-authors respectively. Helene Ahl read the story of Amelia Adamo, Karin Berglund read the story of Anna Bråkenhielm and Katarina Pettersson read the story of Clara Lidström. The four readings (1–4) are presented below for each story separately. The first reading also includes a reader response by the reader of the story.

Stories by successful women entrepreneurs

Every summer day at 13.15, the song "summer, summer, summer" introduces the radio show "Summer" on Swedish radio's channel P1. P1 is the national radio channel that provides reflection and knowledge specialisation and is marketed as the channel to listen to if it is "science, documentaries, film, art, theatre, literature or philosophical questions that interest you". "Summer" is arguably the channel's biggest success in terms of audience size. It has been referred to as a 'radio heirloom'; first broadcast in 1959, it has presented 58 hosts every summer since then. For one and a half hours these summer hosts talk about their life experiences and play their favourite music. Currently "Summer" has an audience of millions with whom a mix of famous Swedes, including musicians, politicians, artists, businesspeople, writers, actors, scientists and entrepreneurs share their life stories. Lately, a great deal of attention has been paid to how these people challenge each other to tell even more personal and confessional tales. Thus, this radio show provides some insight into the lives of the famous, that moves beyond their motivations, goals, challenges and opportunities to also reflect upon their mistakes, losses, struggles, insights and changes in perspective.

The empire-building entrepreneur Amelia Adamo, a reading by Helene Ahl

Reading 1 – The plot and a general impression

Amelia Adamo, born in 1947, is a serial entrepreneur, or rather intrapreneur. She has started a number of successful women's magazines within the frame of her employment at Sweden's largest publishing house, Bonniers. The story of her career is well known to the Swedish audience – she has written an autobiography and is a frequent media guest. Indeed, she is on the cover of every single issue of her latest creation, the *M-magazine*, for women 50-plus. So, her summer talk is not so much about her business success as it is about her personal background and outlook on life.

Her opening line is that she should actually have been aborted. Her mother, a maid in a house in Rome, was seduced by the son of the household. He did not want the child. Amelia was born and lived her first nine months at a private birth clinic, where she and her mother stayed in return for her mother's cleaning and breast-feeding services to other people's children. She had an aunt, a father who denied her, and no grandparents. Her mother emigrated to Sweden with the baby, continuing to work as a live-in maid. When Amelia was six, she got an Italian-born stepfather, Oscar Adamo, and was sent to a Catholic convent school for five years. The family was so cramped for space that there was simply no room for her. She says the years with the nuns made her street smart and she grew a skin as thick as a hippopotamus's. At 11 she moved back home to a new one-bedroom flat, but so did Oscar's parents from Italy. There were constant Swedish/Italian cultural clashes and Amelia could not wait to get away. At 17 she moved out.

The 1960s was a time of unbounded optimism, when youth unemployment was unheard of. Amelia worked in offices, got her upper secondary degree through adult education, continued to work as a society columnist and went to university to get her BSc in behavioural sciences. She replaced one boyfriend with another in happy succession. She built a fabulous career at Bonniers and ended up marrying another editor-in-chief. This was the time when upward mobility was truly possible. In her forties she reconnected with her biological father, now divorced, and met two stepsisters. She was in touch with her father for five years before he died from cancer. She describes him as a funny but completely unreliable man. She was not allowed to attend his funeral – his ex-wife did not know of her existence.

This is the story of her life as told in the summer talk, but it actually covers less than half of the talk. The rest is devoted to reflections about men, sex, age, looks, clothes, money, the royal family, how to get ahead, our unfortunate fixation on youth and material success and modern

30-year-olds' unrealistic expectations from life and love – and also about the sexual abuse of women in Ethiopia and Catherine Hamlin's fistula hospital dedicated to helping them.

READER RESPONSE OF FIRST READING

I am not moved by Amelia's story as much as I thought I would, or should, be. I suppose most people would be devastated by such a start in life, but she talks in a way that you can almost feel the hippopotamus skin she grew as a child. Her tone is completely matter-of-fact. Nothing will hurt her. It creates a distance between her and the listener, perhaps augmented by the fact that she has led such a public life and is known as a tough publisher and editor-in-chief.

Somewhat surprised by my reaction of distance, I instead admire her rhetorical skills. For example, after Amelia discussed at length how it is lucky that Ethiopian women who had their savaged genitals repaired do not have to remarry, she drily observes that meanwhile, in Sweden, we buy dildos, go to sex parties and watch porn, all in an effort to use our genitals more.

Reading 2 – The voice of the 'I'

Being asked to give a summer talk is a great honour in Sweden. You are *Someone*. Amelia's opening line, "Here I am, this July day, I, who really should have been aborted", firmly positions her as a dandelion child,[1] a comer, and a success against all odds. She talks about her time at the convent school, where years of loneliness and longing for her mother made her street smart and tough, and the following years of conflict in the small apartment that made her determined to create a better future. She describes the following years as a time when "I travelled at turbo speed towards knowledge and new social classes".

She learnt that as an outsider, you have to make yourself visible – with clothes, demeanour, charm and voice. "I learnt how to get noticed; by making my way, by being heard, by wearing clothes that stood out". As an immigrant without networks and a social position one must trade on being different, she says, but not too different. And visible she is – on the cover of every magazine stand, every week. She says it is fun, but it has also created some anxiety about her body and her looks. "One should age with grace, but how can you do that in the most youth-fixated age ever – and we baby boomers have ourselves to blame – we invented the teens, and we want to stay there forever".

She talks about male singer-songwriters (like Leonard Cohen and Kris Kristofferson) as losers and drinkers that women, including herself, yearn to comfort, take care of and rescue, but, she adds, "…myself, I am far too materialistic to fall for that kind…I have chosen men with a future". Using the voice of others – perhaps to soften it – she says "You don't like weakness, my friends tell me – that's why you have always picked men with power".

She is very outspoken about her interest in sex, talking at length about study visits to sex shops, sex-toy home parties and the introduction of sex toys in pharmacies (obviously for profit reasons, she drily remarks). She attributes this interest to the nuns – forbidden fruit tastes best.

Amelia actually uses the word 'I' sparingly. More often she uses 'we', positioning herself firmly in the baby boomer generation, and contrasting the baby boomers' habits and outlook on life with those of today's 30-year-olds. She says she does not recognise herself in the immense ambitions for material and other success of today's youngsters. Today, well-chosen wines and a three-course dinner is the standard, she says. While "we drank wine without knowing anything about southern hillside slopes, tannins or terroir…we went to dinner parties bringing any bottle of wine and a pie…".

Reading 3 – Relationships

Amelia Adamo talks about her relationships with her parents, the men in her life, her children and grandchildren, the nuns at the convent school and about Kris Kristofferson, who once visited her home. She tells stories from her working life, about the royal family, which she followed as a society reporter, and she also mentions people who have helped her in her career – a boss, an older colleague and a consultant. She talks about herself as not a *real* entrepreneur by comparing herself to two other immigrant entrepreneurs who have built fully owned business empires in Sweden. And she talks about Catherine Hamlin in Ethiopia.

Amelia speaks with love and great admiration and respect for her mother. She is the heroine of the story. She had the guts to keep the baby, move to Sweden and start a new life. Amelia is forever grateful for her mother's support, and says that when she asks her mother where home is, the reply is, "Where you are". She ends the talk by giving her father an ironic tribute as well: "Had he not denied me, I would not be giving this talk today".

Her stepfather is mentioned as someone who tolerated her but was relieved when she moved out. The nuns are the ones who made her a toughie and immensely interested in sex. Her children and grandchildren are just mentioned in passing, but she says that becoming a grandmother made her start to think about her roots, the location of which is very uncertain since she has moved so many times and so far, both physically and socially.

Amelia uses her meeting with Kris Kristofferson to elaborate on men and on women's relationships with them, warning women about the desire to rescue seemingly needy men – "they will just dump you anyway". She also mentions this in contrast to her own, more productive, attraction to successful men. The royal family provides an interesting context for her to talk about her work as a society reporter and gives her the opportunity to offer some tantalising royal gossip. In addition, she says that the royals still greet her kindly, thus firmly positioning herself in Swedish high society.

Her mentors are experienced professionals, all men, giving her useful career and business advice, and the entrepreneurs she compares herself to are immigrant men, but she acknowledges that immigrant women entrepreneurs are beginning to enter the stage now, even if on a small scale so far. Catherine Hamlin's role in the story is as the person to be admired and respected, for her invaluable and heroic work for molested Ethiopian women. Apart from specific people, Amelia often situates herself in the context of her generation, firmly positioning it as very special and very different from today's youngsters.

Listeners to summer talks in Sweden have become accustomed to hearing moving, confessionary tales. Amelia's tale is definitely confessionary, but not emotionally moving. She is completely outspoken, but in no instance does she divulge any personal weakness or shortcoming. Yes – she did cry in Cannes as a young reporter when she did not get to interview the stars, but this only helped her get through the crowds. She talks about her relationships and her wider context in a manner that portrays a very strong, hard-working woman who has been rewarded by financial and social success.

Reading 4 – How gender is talked about

In a sense, the whole talk is about gender, sex and womanhood. In terms of gender and career, Amelia talks about being an outsider – as a woman, a member of the working class and an immigrant – and using it to her advantage.

> You get ahead, a boss once told me. I thought: advantage immigrant. Because we all need to be seen. I learnt how to get noticed: by getting ahead, being heard, wearing

eye-catching clothes – not that anxious black, I was more Christmas-tree-like. ...When you have no contacts...being an outsider can help. You become a bit different.

However, she does not acknowledge herself fully as an entrepreneur – the ones she compares herself to, the 'real' ones, are immigrant men who have risked their own money. Her recipe for how to get ahead is: "In management language: deliver".

There is unacknowledged ambiguity about gender in her talk, but this is our interpretation – her own words are not the least bit ambiguous. She regrets our obsession with looks, not least her own as a weekly cover-girl, but she makes no acknowledgement of the fact that her whole career as a publisher of women's magazines is built on women's relationship to their looks.

Likewise, she laments the obsession of today's 30-year-olds with perfection and with material and other success, but she does not mention the role of her own products, women's magazines, as part and parcel of the 'self-improvement industry' that needs an audience willing to be improved:

> Today's 30-year-olds have very many and very high demands on what to achieve and what to show off. It won't be long before they must be able to make a bird of paradise napkin fold. Where do all these ambitions about perfection come from? It can only end on the therapist's couch. They must cool down, life must be fun too.

Amelia's engagement with the fistula hospital in Ethiopia shows some serious engagement for women's rights and women's suffering, but apart from this, she has a totally pragmatic attitude towards any stereotypical gender constructions. They are there anyway, so why not make money from them?

The independent and rowdy entrepreneur Anna Carrfors Bråkenhielm, a reading by Karin Berglund

Reading 1 – The plot and a general impression

Anna Carrfors Bråkenhielm was born in 1966 and is the former president and development manager at Strix Television Production Company. She is the one who took the decision to buy the Nordic rights to "Survivor" (Robinson) in 1996 and made, not only Swedish, but international television history. She began her career as a journalist and PR consultant. After her time with Strix, she founded the production company Silverback, and became its CEO. The company was sold after five years for 6.6 million euros.[2] Today she is the owner of *Passion for Business*,[3] a business and career magazine for women aiming to empower women as both entrepreneurs and managers. Anna's summer show was broadcast on the 5th of July 2010. She opens the radio programme by saying, "I've done it again: resigned from a job I love. This is the second time in five years".

She tells the listeners that her programme will be about breaking up, the constant pursuit of freedom and autonomy of being an entrepreneur, the joy of starting anew again and again, and the security of having 'fuck-off money' or just the ability to say 'fuck off', regardless of economic security. During her one and a half hours she mixes her story with music, such as "Country Girls" by Primal Scream, "I feel you" by Depeche Mode and "(White Man) in Hammersmith Palais" by The Clash. She tells of the role models that have guided her, how she was surprised when she was asked, at the age of 29, to be CEO of Strix, a company that over the years grew from a turnover of 40 million to over half a billion SEK and employed 1,000 people. She also points to the benefits of being brought up in the countryside, and the advantage she has found in being a good salesperson; "because then they cannot get rid of you, even if they consider you to be a bitch".

When Anna talks about women entrepreneurs, she says she thinks it is a shame that there are so few women who have started, or who run, companies with a turnover of more than 100 million SEK in Sweden. She acknowledges that she has benefited greatly from being the only woman, or one of a few women, in different situations. "You are seen and heard in a different way when you are in the minority". This has made it possible for Anna to move in contexts where different prizes are awarded and to appear on talk shows, and thus to have a public voice when she is asked to comment on everything from the royal family to a new documentary and how it feels to be a woman who has a "rudely high salary". Her message for the audience of her radio show is to begin to set quotas for women on company boards in order to change the male-dominated business world.

READER RESPONSE OF FIRST READING

My immediate thought when listening to Anna's story is that this is a woman who not only knows what it means to go her own way, but who has learned to reflect upon her mistakes and turn them into advantages. What I think she stresses throughout her talk is how she is practising 'street smarts'. I felt that I could strongly relate to some parts of her story from my own experiences of working in a small male-dominated company and from starting up my own business. I also started to reflect upon how we as researchers are inclined to tell stories – similar to those of entrepreneurs – stressing the autonomy of the researcher, the will to change (unequal) conditions and the impetus to move forward by posing new research questions.

While Anna talks confidently about herself as an entrepreneur, she uses a different voice when she speaks about her female role models, such as her grandmother. Even if she is not expressing these emotions explicitly in her talk, her voice signals how she finds herself emotionally tied to her female ancestors, wanting to pursue their feminist mission in her way. This made me think about my own grandmother, who was a teacher, and how much she has meant to me, being the one who opened the door to curiosity, knowledge and a desire to make a difference for other people. She had the ability not only to talk the talk, but also to walk the walk. So perhaps it was her shift from a self-assured to an emotional voice when Anna talked about what her grandmother meant to her that made me connect to her story and remember my own grandmother. The fact that she let her voice tremble even as she was expressing her determination to transform unjust conditions touched me and also inspired me to recognise my own 'mission' in the life path I have chosen.

Reading 2 – The voice of the 'I'

Typically, Anna refers to herself in terms of an active subject – she presents herself as a doer who takes initiative and risks, challenges norms and calls for change. One example she gives is when she was called to the job interview at Strix Television in 1990 (which later paved the way for her first CEO position). To show off her research skills she had done some checking on the managers she would meet at the interview. By finding out a lot about these people – about their parking tickets, houses, boats, mistresses and teenage transgressions – she was able to demonstrate her skills, not just talk about them. "They were very impressed", she admits.

During her summer talk, broadcasting to millions of listeners, she takes the opportunity to invite all Swedish company boards to invest in women. She also talks about how she made long lists of women role models she would like to see interviewed on TV, at a time when TV talk shows were predominantly dominated by old men. She tells how she "like a gambler late at night in a casino", put a bid on a new business concept. So she views herself as an entrepreneur who likes to do things her way and longs for her freedom:

> I identify strongly with real entrepreneurs, because I have the habit – perhaps a bad habit – of running the companies where I am employed as if they were my own. [...] I think I have been and wanted to be a manager because I like to have freedom of action, to have the opportunity to implement my ideas or simply because I do not like having others decide over me.

Thus, Anna presents herself as a strong and active person – one who takes charge – which we are used to in stories of entrepreneurs. She not only positions herself as active but also avoids positioning herself as vulnerable and passive. When she suddenly talks about the checklist that she uses to reflect upon whether she would recognise that she is about to stagnate, a sense of sadness emerges. However, rather than talking about herself as a person who would feel sad and depressed – something that in our entrepreneurial culture would be perceived as a weakness – when she lists the items on her checklist (quoted below) she does not refer to herself in the first person:

> When you start to feel a little sad on Sunday evenings because the weekend is over, and when there is a rush of joy on Thursday afternoons because it's Friday the next day, and worst of all: when you do not learn something new, and lack those really big challenges.

Her response to this condition is to 'move on', to pack up and quit. She avoids presenting herself as insufficient, unsuccessful, passive and docile and thereby avoids being portrayed as 'weak'. Instead, she positions herself as active, risk taking, erratic and in need of her own freedom, affirming independence and being rowdy. She appears to be well aware of the braveness and noisiness she possesses. When she quit her job after a couple of fun years at one PR agency her boss told her to compose her own letter of recommendation, but in his name. Accordingly, she gladly wrote: "Should I get the chance in the future, I would employ Anna again at any time". Reflecting upon how she has excitedly asked her employees for 20 years to write their own letters of recommendation, she says she has never "encountered such audacity".

Reading 3 – Relationships

Anna's relationship with her family, and in particular with her children, reoccurs in the story and appears as a secure point in life that creates stability. She tells about how she, with her daughter, took a trip to Mallorca after quitting her job. Her daughter was also the one who noticed how tired Anna was and who asked the important and life-changing questions, such as "Mom, why do you want to be the boss?" Through her children she got the opportunity to create some distance and make time for personal reflection.

Anna acknowledges that it is a great asset to have many male friends whom she also has "a lot of fun with". One of the two male friends that appear in her story is Robban Aschberg, a high-profile media personality in Sweden who acted as her mentor and offered her protection, support and stability during her years as CEO at Strix Television. The other man is the billionaire John de Mol, whom she represents more as an entrepreneurial soul mate. Once he told her, "You must understand, Anna, that people like us are basically unemployable". Apart from these two friends, she explains her wish to work for the female CEO Dawn Arrey at ITV Productions. Here Anna admits that the very reason she dared to sell her business to ITV, the UK's largest commercial television channel, was that Dawn was the boss and that she was really fond of her. Dawn was nicknamed 'Scary Arrey' and is regarded by Anna as an "incredibly cool woman with huge experience, a sharp sense of humour and a big heart". She was also married to a woman and became a mother at the age of 46. Unfortunately, Dawn appeared to have a nomadic entrepreneurial spirit similar to Anna's, and she quit her job just after Anna was about to start working as CEO for Silverback, now owned by ITV.

Other women role models who appear in Anna's story are her mother, her grandmother and her grandmother's sisters. They are portrayed as people who "march to their own drum,[4] perfectly off-road-walking" persons. She describes her grandmother as someone who thought of others before herself, but who also showed an incredible ability to initiate projects and assumed that other people were just as willing to actively participate in the initiatives as she was. She remembers her as a 'juggernaut', but also as someone who was loving and caring. Her grandmother was the only woman in the city council at a time when not many women were engaged in politics. She also actively debated the then hot topic of women priests. In a letter to Anna's mother in 1958 she writes "It would be wonderful to understand the psychology behind their immense despair about the General Synod's decision. I wonder if they would be equally distraught over a decision that would not so thoroughly touch their male self-assertion". In her grandmother's footsteps, Anna is today actively pursuing the matter of quotas for women to company boards.

Reading 4 – How gender is talked about

Throughout the show Anna mentions women. She highlights the role models she had in her mother, grandmother, cousins, sisters and, not least, her two aunts. Her aunts never married but educated themselves and worked as principals; they taught her the importance of having "fuck-off money" in order to gain financial independence and not have to be provided for by someone else. In addition, she emphasises her efforts to make women visible in different contexts – not only as entrepreneurs, but as managers in general, and as any part of the TV shows during the early times when she worked for Strix and found that the sitcoms they produced were mainly populated by men:

> My first task was to try to fix the number of [too few] female guests to the programme. There are no worthwhile women to invite, Robert and the other guys in the newsroom whined. But how wrong they were. I made long lists and began to schedule all of my favourite female writers and other role models. Suddenly the couch was full of wonderful, charismatic, witty and eloquent guests. [...] The women made the programme better, and I had just navigated according to my own taste and chose those I found to be interesting. The guys in the newsroom had not seen them! They had other interests and their attention was directed elsewhere. Yes, women as well as men choose according to their own frames of reference. Just as it is in business. Men choose men, for they know no better and do not know where to find the women.

In her talk Anna mentions how she had recently been given the epithet 'entrepreneur', but often with 'female' as a prefix, after which she rhetorically asks, "Because there must be a difference between female and male entrepreneurs?" The gendered entrepreneur is thus problematized as something that she is trying to relate to by pointing out that she is more an entrepreneur than a woman. From my interpretation of Anna's talk, she stresses that men and women are more alike than they are different but that the way business, entrepreneurship and other societal phenomena are gendered may present huge obstacles to women. She was not always an advocate of quotas for women but became one after she was asked to write a column on the subject. At that point she decided to take action politically, as she had seen her grandmother do before her, and since then she has worked to change the male-dominated boards of listed companies.

She views her magazine *Passion for Business* as a platform for advocacy. Although she describes herself predominantly as an autonomous 'I', this changes when she talks about the magazine, where she instead constructs a 'we' who took the lead in the debate about the lack of competent women by providing a list of 549 women qualified to be on the listed companies' boards, "in the event that they would be hard to find".

Anna ends the programme stressing her unruly entrepreneurial identity, by thanking all of the people who have discouraged her, who failed to believe in her abilities and who did not think of her as the doer she really is. Because these people also spurred her to move forward:

> I must thank all the talented, experienced media people who strongly dissuaded me and predicted my downfall; your words have been one of my strongest motivations. And one thing is very sure: I will continue to fight for affirmative action and equality in business until something happens – with or without a magazine in my hand.

Living her dream – the blogging homemaker Clara Lidström, a reading by Katarina Pettersson

Reading 1 – The plot and a general impression

Clara Lidström is a 25-year-old woman living in a house in a rural area in northern Sweden writing a blog that, since 2006, has attracted one and a half million visits per month. She married at the age of 21 and has a child. Her story is centred on her realising her dreams. She explains that, because life is short, you should not wait to realise your dreams, because then it might be too late. When Clara was 21, she lost her mother, at only 52 years old, to breast cancer. She says, among other things, "I am living my dream, which is not always that practical".

Clara's story contains clear elements of equity and gender equality, and she explicitly calls herself a feminist – a feminist of the 1980s. Positioning herself as such implies placing her feminism in contrast to the feminism of women from her mother's generation. This still means realising herself and her dreams. But being a feminist of the 1980s, according to Clara, is not performed through having a successful career, making a lot of money, having a perfect garden, children and ambitious dinner parties, nor through partying and having a career built on full-time employment in the city. Instead, Clara explains that, for her, feminism of the 1980s includes having enough time to take it easy and to spend a lot of time at home, not being stressed-out.

> For me the biggest revolution that I could make, in opposition to all that was expected of me, was to be 'saved', a teetotaller, marry young and move to the countryside. To

wear old fashioned ruffled skirts instead of squeezing into awful jeans, which you cannot sit down in.

An element of Clara's story, and of her realising her dream, was moving to a rural area, and even though living in a house with a garden implies a lot of work – such as preparing firewood and making fires – and dealing with challenges such as poor access to the Internet (which is a virtual lifeline for a blogger), it also represents time, free exercise and a sense of belonging to a village community and not being lonely.

As a blogger, Clara can work from home. Furthermore, homemaking – interior design, child care, parenting, baking, preparing food (sometimes from vegetables grown in the garden), taking care of the hens and the dog – are also integral to her blogging. This appreciation of the home and homemaking is part and parcel of Clara's feminism and blogging, which also includes embracing older women's knowledge and inventions. Clara has, in addition to the blog, been the host of a radio show called "The Housewife School at Wonderful Clara's Home". Clara presents blogging as writing about and analysing oneself, which she points out as an activity at which women are experts, having been raised to constantly perform self-analyses.

Clara also tells the listeners about some of the criticisms she receives – regarding her appearance and her taste in music, for example – as well as her views about parenting and gender equality and her belief in God; on a more overarching level she talks about being questioned regarding 'who she thinks she is'. She presents a strategy of handling criticism by not caring, because you cannot be loved by everyone.

READER RESPONSE OF FIRST READING

My first reading of Clara's story makes me happy and leaves me with a feeling of being part of the same sisterhood with her. However, I realise that I am much older than she is, being born in the early 1970s, and that my feminism might be exactly the kind of feminism that she is critical towards. I think that I have realised myself through building an academic career, working more or less full time, and living in the city where I am raising children and own a nice (expensive) house. I also love wearing jeans, and I find myself asking: Am I persuaded by the feminism that Clara says is not for her? At the same time, listening to her story makes it sound so nice to have enough time and be at home taking care of your children and being a homemaker.

Reading Clara's story, I am also impressed by all that she has achieved in life at such an early age, and it makes me think that she is a very mature 25-year-old. This, however, also makes me wonder what this feeling of being impressed says about my view of young women – do I expect them to have achieved little and be immature?

Reading 2 – *The voice of the 'I'*

Clara represents herself as Wonderful Clara – which is the name of her blog. She clearly describes blogging as her work, which includes writing, photography and 'pottering'. She does not call herself an entrepreneur (even though she has published a book on digital entrepreneurship, together with Annakarin Nyberg).

Clara uses the word 'I' extensively and her story is focused on telling listeners the story of her life. Clara uses the first person throughout her talk, but I have interpreted her voice of the 'I' more specifically as the occasions where she expresses her feelings. Her feelings in the story move between the extremes of love and happiness – for her partner, home, home-making, writing and being read – and grief over the loss of her mother. She ends her talk by saying "I can feel happiness, at the same time as I always miss you", whereby she moves between these feelings or perhaps rather encompasses them at the same time. The grief is especially strong in the passage of her story where she talks about the morning when she was 16 years old and learnt that her mother had cancer.

> There and then time stops. I have heard that it can when you get a shock. Don't under-stand what she says: cancer, cancer. [...] And I do not yet know that this is the beginning of five hard years, which will end with me losing my mother.

A prominent feeling expressed in the story is related to the loss of her mother, which is a fear of daring – for example, to get married, get a house, a dog and a child at such a young age. But there is also an expression of a fear of not daring, because it might soon be too late:

> Perhaps children who lose their parents early are in a hurry, in a hurry to live and realize their dreams.

Clara also confesses that she is shy of people, and she says that this is the first time she has told anyone about this fear: "But now you know; I am afraid of you". She explains her move to the countryside as motivated by this shyness and that her work as a blogger allows her to control contact with other people (the readers, blog visitors) as she can cut the Internet con-nection when she wants to. However, living in a rural area, somewhat paradoxically, forces Clara to make contact with people in her village, as people in small communities need to help each other. She expects that she might have been more lonely living in a city.

Reading 3 – Relationships

The story Clara tells is centred on herself, and because she likes solitude, there are rather few passages in the story that focus on relationships with other people. However, a recurring theme regarding relationships is her being part of a 'heritage line of women', especially her relationship with her mother and grief over her loss. Other important women in her rela-tionships are her grandmothers. So even though she does not explicitly express a lot about her relationships, she places her story, herself and her work at the centre of these female relationships and relatives. Her work seems devoted to praising the deeds of her ancestral mothers:

> And I think of grandmother and grandmother: the generation of women who have borne and fed this country – often without receiving thanks or recognition.

Her grandmother and grandfather also provided a space where time, warmth and safety were provided, and at the same time they were an inspiration for Clara's feminism: centred on re-alising herself from home and having 'enough time'. We can clearly see here that an import-ant feature of Clara's story is the relationship – not only to other persons, but also to places and, in particular, to her country home, especially the kitchen. Utilising and underlining the home as a site for feminist action could be interpreted as paradoxical, as the home has been found to be a place of subordination of women, women's work and a place of (domestic) violence. In her story Clara seems conscious of this, and she reflects on the representation of the home as a haven in line with 1940s imagery, and on the how presenting home as a place for self-realisation and feminism is controversial:

> Some wonder why the hell I walk around in an apron like a housewife from the '40s. Others love the geraniums, the sheer curtains and the chipped coffee cups. The image of a young woman in a kitchen gives rise to strong feelings.

In her home Clara also has important relationships with her family, which consists of her husband and child.

Reading 4 – How gender is talked about

Being a feminist and discussing gender (in-)equality – in addition to desiring and discussing equity – is a prominent feature of Clara's story. In a sense, the whole talk is about feminism, gender equality and womanhood. Besides talking about her own feminism Clara reflects more generally on the situation of women, and especially young women. For example, she talks about how young women who are blogging are being patronised, because they are taking themselves too seriously and focusing on themselves. According to Clara, however, instead of putting energy into pleasing others, young women should direct it towards achieving great deeds.

Reflecting on older women Clara, in her work and talk, also seeks to spread their knowledge – which she appreciatively calls 'grandmother's knowledge' and 'housewife's advice':

> I want to pass on the inventions that older women have made, but which are sometimes despised [...]. Do not forget who invented it first. Do not forget the women who were the inventors.

Clara says that gender equality is good, but that it needs to be really gender equal, implying that women should not have to adapt to male traditions. It is clear from the above that Clara formulates gender equality as praise and appreciation for women (their deeds, work, inventions and knowledge). She also says:

> My experience of women is that they are loyal, honest and supportive. I have had so much incredible sisterly love as a blogger. There is a place in heaven for women helping each other.

The tale of the heroine entrepreneur

So far we have presented tales of three heroine entrepreneurs and, spurred by a feminist method, we have also reflected on how the three of us (researchers) reacted to them. We now ask ourselves what we have learned from adopting the voice-centred relational method and also what we have learned from the four readings of the three tales of successful entrepreneurship.

The method applied was developed to approach interviews (situations and material) from a relational perspective. The researchers made an effort to avoid positioning themselves as distant interpreters and interrogators, instead engaging with the talks as if they were interviewers, listening carefully, posing questions to themselves and following the trajectory of the conversation.

None of us was involved in producing the material that we have worked with in this chapter. The production of the texts was most likely a matter between each speaker and her producer. We have thus not been able to ask questions or follow how the story was shaped as a relational outcome between two people involved in a conversation. The interview is in the form of a dialogue, while the radio show takes the form of a monologue. This does not mean, however, that we did not respond to the stories told. We all responded – quite emotionally at times – and were, through this method, invited to reflect upon our responses to the stories.

Our reactions signalled that we felt either distant from or close to the stories. We also tended to moralise the stories, in that we viewed them as encompassing good or bad actions and reflections. For instance, one of us was inspired by Anna and her 'street smarts', which at first sight (or reading) was seen as something worth striving for, and thus as something 'good'. The reading of Amelia's story questioned the morality of making a profit by giving advice on how to address women's shortcomings – advice that ends up creating the idea of such alleged shortcomings. Reading Clara's tale alerts us to the moral dilemma of representing a feminist agenda and being focused on homemaking. Her praise of women and womanhood also risks creating a moral of women as good and men as bad, when feminism can be taken as questioning constructions of gender.

Reminding ourselves that entrepreneurial tales are structured according to the twin virtues of morality and success, this might not come as a surprise (Smith & Anderson, 2004: 126). The word 'moral' is derived from the Latin concept '*moralis*' and refers to the recurrent human tendency to make distinctions between good and bad behaviour. One could say that entrepreneurial tales prompt us to draw the line. Apparently, parts of our reflection involved making a judgemental (moralizing) comment on the tales.

The four readings also brought about new aspects of the narratives, which highlighted the tension between the heroines' emphasis on themselves and how this was (or was not) in tune with women's collective organising for liberation and gender equality. All of the stories are about successful entrepreneurs who, in various ways, have pioneered in the media industry. Interestingly, they all make money on women's 'feminine' interests and women's desire to become better, stronger, more beautiful and more successful. The discourse of 'self-help' is, according to Bröckling (2005), a vital part of women's magazines, with the effect of enticing women to self-realise, self-improve and self-discipline through meticulous rituals of activity. This constitutes a manual to a 'Me Inc.' rather than to Fem.Incism (cf. Ahl et al., 2016).

None of the tales of the heroine entrepreneurs mentions that they, in some respects, profit from exploiting femininity and a subordination of women. Rather, the tales focus on the entrepreneurs' contributions to something that is larger than themselves. In Amelia's case it is her commitment to the fistula hospital in Ethiopia. Her talk about the poor Ethiopian women somehow compensates for the fact that she earned money from women's vanity and insecurity, even though this is not explicitly addressed. Anna makes an effort to lift women in our part of the world through the business magazine, the yearly "Beautiful Business" award and advocacy for quotas for company boards. Clara praises older women and their inventions, yet at the same time her presentation of homemaking risks putting women who are not interested in homemaking in a position of 'the insufficient woman'.

Our readings of relationships show an interesting difference compared to the traditional male hagiography. It has been argued that (beautiful) women have historically been seen as symbols of male success (Smith, 2014). The tales of the heroines do not invoke the male as a symbol of the women's success. Men are indeed part of the three heroines' tales, and they are acknowledged as friends, lovers, fathers and husbands. They are not, however, described as a reason for success, and they occupy a place in the margins of the tales. In contrast, the relationships with other women, and especially their women ancestors, make up a key theme in the narratives: mothers, grandmothers, aunts and daughters are highlighted. The entrepreneurs thus position themselves in a historical lineage of women, giving voice to women and a justifiable place in their history.

To conclude, success through business seems to be a double-edged sword. Further, these moral tales also have two sides to them, be they dark or bright, good or bad. The women entrepreneurs in our stories speak for women, while simultaneously making a profit from reproducing women's subordination. But that may be the name of the game. If they put up too much resistance towards the 'rules of the game', they will probably go out of business, giving up a position where they can achieve something.

Conclusions

By adopting a voice-centred relational method, we have analysed the stories of three successful entrepreneurs. We have pointed to how women entrepreneurs are often described as lacking, inadequate or 'other', and highlighted the need for providing stories of 'successful women entrepreneurs', yet avoiding presenting them either as role models for other women or counterparts to the male norm. Through experimenting with a feminist narrative approach we have pointed to the morals of the stories as well as our own (moral) reactions, how the stories link to feminist action as well as exploitation of femininity and how men and male norms are talked about and also marginalised in the stories, while women ancestors are given a central position. From this chapter it can be concluded that heroines should be given more recognition in women's entrepreneurship studies. We also welcome further experimentation with feminist methodologies, such as the voice-centred relationship method adopted here.

Notes

1 A dandelion child is one who in spite of a difficult and troubled upbringing still does well in life, just as a dandelion has the strength to grow up through asphalt.
2 The amount was mentioned not in the TV programme, but in an interview in the digital magazine "Resumé". http://www.resume.se/nyheter/2008/05/15/jag-ar-valdigt-nojd-med-su/.
3 Anna Carrfors Bråkenhielm started the magazine *Passion for Business* (PFB) in 2008. Apart from highlighting ambition and expertise among women, the magazine seeks to inspire and coach women to achieve their career goals. In addition, PFB is a member of the network of women with 12 yearly events. PFB has also teamed up with the daily Swedish business paper "Dagens Industri", http://www.passionforbusiness.se/om-oss/.
4 Anna was using another Swedish expression here, but because that expression did not translate quite right, we choose a similar English expression. The point she makes is that her grandmother and her sisters are people who don't follow what everyone else is doing, but instead follow their own path and values.

References

Achtenhagen, L. & Tillmar, M. (2013) Studies on women's entrepreneurship from Nordic countries and beyond. *International Journal of Gender and Entrepreneurship*, 5(1), 4–16.
Ahl, H. (2006) Why research on women entrepreneurs needs new directions. *Entrepreneurship Theory and Practice*, 30(5), 595–621.
Ahl, H. J. (2004) *The Scientific Reproduction of Gender Inequality: A discourse analysis of research texts on women's entrepreneurship*. 1. [ed.] Stockholm: Liber.
Ahl, H., Berglund, K., Pettersson, K., & Tillmar, M. (2016) From feminism to FemInc.ism: On the uneasy relationship between feminism, entrepreneurship and the Nordic welfare state. *International Entrepreneurship and Management Journal*, 12(2), 369–392.

Ahl, H. & Marlow, S. (2012) Exploring the dynamics of gender, feminism and entrepreneurship: Advancing debate to escape a dead end? *Organization*, 19(5), 543–562.

Berglund, K. (2006) Discursive diversity in fashioning entrepreneurial identity. In Hjorth, D. & Steyaert, C. (Eds) *Entrepreneurship as Social Change – A Third Movements in Entrepreneurship Book*, Cheltenham, UK and Northampton, MA, USA: Edward Elgar, 231–250.

Berglund, K. & Johansson, A. W. (2007) The entrepreneurship discourse - outlined from diverse constructions of entrepreneurship on the academic scene. *Journal of Enterprising Communities: People and Places in the Global Economy*, 1(1), 77–102.

Bruni, A., Gherardi, S. & Poggio, B. (2004) Entrepreneur-mentality, gender and the study of women entrepreneurs, *Journal of Organizational Change Management*, 17(3), 256–268.

Bröckling, U. (2005) Gendering the enterprising self: Subjectification programs and gender differences in guides to success, *Distinktion*, 11, 7–23.

Calás, M. B., Smircich, L., & Bourne, K. A. (2009) Extending the boundaries: Reframing "entrepreneurship as social change" through feminist perspectives. *Academy of Management Review*, 34(3), 552–569.

Calás, M. B., Smircich, L. & Bourne, K. A. (2007) Knowing Lisa? Feminist analyses of 'gender and entrepreneurship'. *Handbook on Women in Business and Management*, 78–105.

Davies, B. (1989) *Frogs and Snails and Feminist Tales*. North Sydney: Allen & Unwin Australia.

Dodd, S. D. & Anderson, A. R. (2007) Mumpsimus and the mything of the individualistic entrepreneur. *International Small Business Journal*, 25(4), 341–360.

Downing, S. (2005) The social construction of entrepreneurship: Narrative and dramatic processes in the coproduction of organizations and identities. *Entrepreneurship Theory and Practice*, 29(2), 185–204.

Essers, C. & Benschop, Y. (2009) Muslim businesswomen doing boundary work: The negotiation of Islam, gender and ethnicity within entrepreneurial contexts. *Human Relations*, 62(3), 403–423.

Fournier, V. (2002) Keeping the veil of otherness. In Czarniawska, B. & Höpfl, H. (Eds), *Casting the Other: The production and maintenance of inequalities in work organizations*, 68–88.

Gartner, W. B. (2007) Entrepreneurial narrative and a science of the imagination. *Journal of Business Venturing*, 22(5), 613–627.

Hjorth, D. & Steyaert, C. (Eds) (2004) *Narrative and Discursive Approaches in Entrepreneurship: A Second Movements in Entrepreneurship Book*. Cheltenham: Edward Elgar.

Holmer Nadesan, M. & Trethewey, A. (2000) Performing the enterprising subject: Gendered strategies for success (?), *Text and Performance Quarterly*, 20(3): 223–250.

Jones, C. & Spicer, A. (2009) *Unmasking the Entrepreneur*. Cheltenham: Edward Elgar.

Lindgren, M. & Packendorff, J. (2009) Social constructionism and entrepreneurship: Basic assumptions and consequences for theory and research. *International Journal of Entrepreneurial Behaviour & Research*, 15(1), 25–47.

Mauthner, N.S. & Doucet, A. (1998) Reflections on a voice-centred relational method of data analysis: Analysing maternal and domestic voices. In Ribbens, J. & Edwards, R. (Eds), *Feminist Dilemmas in Qualitative Research: Private lives and public texts*. London: Sage, 119–144.

McAdams, D. P. (1993) *The stories we live by: Personal myths and the making of the self.* Guilford Press.

Mirchandani, K. (1999) Feminist insight on gendered work: new directions in research on women and entrepreneurship. *Gender, Work & Organization*, 6(4), 224–235.

Ogbor, J. O. (2000) Mythicizing and reification in entrepreneurial discourse: Ideology-critique of entrepreneurial studies. *Journal of Management Studies*, 37(5): 605–635.

Smith, R. (2010) Masculinity, doxa and the institutionalisation of entrepreneurial identity in the novel Cityboy. *International Journal of Gender and Entrepreneurship*, 2(1), 27–48.

Smith, R. (2014) Images, forms and presence outside and beyond the pink ghetto. *Gender in Management: An International Journal*, 29(8).

Smith, R. & Anderson, A. R. (2004) The devil is in the e-tail: Forms and structures in the entrepreneurial narratives. In D. Hjorth & C. Steyaert (Eds), *Narrative and Discursive Approaches in Entrepreneurship*. Cheltenham: Edward Elgar, 125–143.

Sørensen, B. M. (2008) 'Behold, I am making all things new': The entrepreneur as savior in the age of creativity. *Scandinavian Journal of Management*, 24(2), 85–93.

Wee, L. & Brooks, A. (2012) Negotiating gendered subjectivity in the enterprise culture: metaphor and entrepreneurial discourses. *Gender, Work & Organization*, 19(6), 573–591.

18

PERCEIVED LEGITIMACY OF WOMEN ENTREPRENEURS

Between identity legitimacy and entrepreneurial legitimacy

Philippe Pailot, Corinne Poroli and Stéphanie Chasserio

Introduction

The question of the legitimacy of women entrepreneurs is far from self-evident. Indeed, entrepreneurship and the characteristics traditionally associated with the entrepreneur (risk taker, results-oriented, professionally and/or personally deeply engaged, adventurous, appreciative of the norm of internality) appear to be largely tied to the traditional Western view of masculinity (Bird & Brush, 2002; Ahl, 2006; Calas, Smircich & Bourne, 2009). The work of historians shows that, apart from certain sectors (Feydeau, 2000), entrepreneurship has long been an exclusively male activity (Barjot, Anceau, Lescent-Gilles & Marnot, 2003; Marseille, 2000). This socio-historic reality is not neutral if we consider that "the male environment is often hostile to the arrival of women" (Guichard-Claudic, Kergoat & Vilbrod, 2008:17).

Academic Anglo-Saxon research reserves a special place for women's entrepreneurship. Institutional actors (international organizations, states, local authorities, consular bodies, etc.) increase incentives to develop such entrepreneurship. Yet, do women entrepreneurs see themselves as sufficiently legitimate to enter into this domain? Do they feel they are deemed legitimate by different internal and external stakeholders? In this chapter we investigate the legitimacy perceived (Major & Schmader, 2001; Costarelli, 2007) by women entrepreneurs in relation to themselves (what we term "identity legitimacy") and in their interactions with their stakeholders (termed, "entrepreneurial legitimacy"). Taking into account the institutional inclusion of legitimacy that acts as an implicit backdrop, we believe that legitimacy is constructed and expressed in interactions in line with certain developments in the theories of recognition (Guéguen & Malochet, 2012). Additionally, we believe that these two poles of legitimacy are closely linked because, as noted by Taboada-Leonetti (1990:44), "it is in relationship with the other that one develops the self."

In this research, we postulate that legitimacy and identity represent two facets of the same phenomenon. In effect, identity, seen as a representation and a definition of self, requires an additive to build and construct itself. This additive is legitimacy, which, in interactions, is the foundation of both others' recognition and of identity confirmation. However, in this theoretical framework we add a gendered lens. Our aim in this chapter is to underline those gendering processes in entrepreneurship that "produce and reproduce a culturally institutionalized system through relations of subordination and domination based on historical hierarchical differentiation by sex (and also by class and race)" (Calas, Smircich & Holvino, 2014:35). By focusing on sex (as a biological attribute) and sex categorisation as sources of differentiated treatments, we observe how interactions may produce specific outcomes for women, and how entrepreneurial processes and norms contribute to "the creation and recreation of the gendered substructures" of entrepreneurship (Calas, Smircich & Holvino, 2014:28). As underscored by West and Zimmerman (1987), gender is constantly "doing" through interactions. Therefore, in this chapter we will present how women entrepreneurs are doing gender (sometimes undoing gender - Deutsch, 2007) to construct their legitimacy as entrepreneurs. We contribute to extant literatures by: a) presenting a theoretical model regarding the process of entrepreneurial legitimacy construction in relation to identity legitimacy through the interactions of women entrepreneurs with their stakeholders; and b) showing how social interactions are strongly imbued with categorical gender judgments that women entrepreneurs must counter through the development and implementation of interesting strategies in order to acquire legitimacy. These analyses give rise to new theoretical avenues of research inquiry.

The remainder of this chapter is structured as follows. The first part presents the various principle theoretical definitions for the concept of legitimacy as dependent on disciplines. On this point, we articulate two theoretical corpuses—the theory of auto-categorization built in extension of social identity, and Goffman's interactionist paradigm. We thus develop identity legitimacy followed by entrepreneurial legitimacy. We then describe our research strategy and the approach used to analyze data based on the grounded theory method. The third part of the chapter deals with our main findings concerning legitimacy among the women entrepreneurs in our study. Finally, conclusions are presented, and avenues for further research are identified.

Literature review

The review of literature we present here shows vastly diverse interpretations of the term "legitimacy" in order to clarify the particular perspective we adopt in the chapter. Next, we detail the process of the construction of identity legitimacy and the principle of self-categorization, or how a woman entrepreneur recognizes herself to be legitimate in her role. Finally, we discuss entrepreneurial legitimacy as a result of recognition of the subject by "other" signifiers (i.e., the stakeholders who the woman entrepreneur faces).

Legitimacy: different perspectives

Situated in the heart of political thought for centuries (Dogan, 2010; Weber, 1995), legitimacy has been the subject of a plethora of social science works. In the organizational sciences, the subject of legitimacy has received special attention from researchers involved in sociological neo-institutional theory (Meyer & Rowan, 1977; Powell & DiMaggio, 1991; Scott, 2001), population ecology (Baum & Oliver, 1991; Hannan & Carroll, 1992) and, more recently, stakeholder theory (Bonnafous-Boucher & Pesqueux, 2006). In entrepreneurship, it is widely accepted that legitimacy plays a central role in the creation, the development, and the survival of an enterprise (Zimmerman & Zeitz, 2002), because legitimacy directly affects entrepreneurial success by influencing relationships with the stakeholders and the abilities of businesses to access multiple resources (Aldrich & Fiol, 1994; Lounsbury &

Glynn, 2001; Zimmerman & Zeitz, 2002; Drori, Honig & Sheaffer, 2009; Nagy, Pollack, Rutherford & Lorhke, 2012).

The very wide array of phenomena related to legitimacy feeds into a sense of confusion regarding this concept. Indeed, legitimacy is mobilized to understand various different social processes (e.g., practices, status, roles, identities, power, authority, rules, social control, social change, etc.) at three different levels of analysis (e.g., persons, groups, institutions) (Zelditch, 2001). In the management literature, the authors thus distinguish between external legitimacy and internal legitimacy (Drori & Honing, 2013), cognitive legitimacy (Sheperd & Zacharakis, 2003; Pérez Rodriguez & Basco, 2011; Pollack, Rutherford & Nagy, 2012), organizational legitimacy (Golant & Sillince, 2007; Vergne, 2011; Schröder, 2013), entrepreneurial legitimacy (De Clerq & Voronov, 2009), institutional legitimacy (Cho, Lee, Sung & Kim, 2011), cognitive and socio-political legitimacy (Aldrich & Fiol, 1994), and regulatory socio-political legitimacy, normative socio-political legitimacy, and cognitive legitimacy (Zimmerman & Zeltz, 2002).

In general, there is consensus amongst management definitions that legitimate order is produced according to a given social context's accepted norms (Weber, 1995). These norms highlight at least two fundamental dimensions of legitimacy: its prescriptive character concerning behavior and attitudes in relationship to norms; and its evaluative character, which permits the judgment of actions, acts, and behavior *vis-à-vis* a normative order that is perceived as legitimate. Legitimacy is not self-decreed and cannot be unilaterally self-proclaimed because it depends upon the opinions of those who are evaluating the subject (Zimmerman & Zeiltz, 2002).

Identity legitimacy can be defined as the perception, evaluation, and subjectively significant ownership that an individual has of his or her worth (L'Ecuyer, 1978; Pharo, 2007) in relation to his or her occupation and construed as a condition of his or her self-esteem. Self-esteem is also reinforced by experiences all along the professional life. Entrepreneurial legitimacy is a result of the recognition and social judgment that internal and external stakeholders bestow upon a subject (in our case, women entrepreneurs) according to the ways in which the subject respects the socially expected norms of the entrepreneurial role. In their dialogic relationship, these two legitimacies are the source of women entrepreneurs' identity construction. In order to analyze each of these two poles, we rely on different (but complementary) theoretical corpuses. We understand identity legitimacy by way of social identity theories, in particular, the notions of social categorization and self-categorization. Entrepreneurial legitimacy is built in the interaction space, with reference to Goffmanian microsociology.

Construction of identity legitimacy

To understand the construction of identity legitimacy, we rely on the concept of self-categorization proposed by Turner et al. (1987). This concept focuses on intergroup relations in order to understand the shaping of social identification and social identity. The basic idea of this theory "is that a social category in which one may be included [...] provides a categorical definition of self that may establish an element of self-concept" (Hogg, 1995:166). The social categorization process consequently acts as a cognitive simplification tool used to classify individuals on the basis of characteristics or attributes that are directly observable (skin color, sex, age, etc.) or are not directly observable (religion, political affiliation, etc.) (Tajfel, 1972; Hogg, 2001), thus playing a key role in self-definition. Tajfel (1981) defines social identity as being a part of self-concept that stems from the understanding that an individual feels a sense of belonging to a social group or groups, as well as from the value and the emotional significance the individual attaches to such membership. Social identity is thus inextricably linked to the components of self-image that originate from the categorical membership criteria[1] referred to and valorized by the individual. This interpretation—which is both cognitive (social categorization) and emotional (subjective importance of membership)—acknowledges social membership as a prominent element in the concept of self from which an individual defines him or herself in an interactive situation and when acting as a social player.

The theory of self-categorization (Turner et al., 1987; Turner, 1985, 1995, 1999) focuses on the processes of self-perception and others' perception according to the mechanisms of self-categorization in connection with abstract social categories. Perhaps related to the subject's personal or social identity, this theory emerges as a self-categorization process through which social categories are internalized as aspects of the self. In line with a categorical group interpretation, Turner et al. (1987) believe that identity construction stems from an auto-categorization process in which self-perception, self-definition, and self-organization are central. Self-concept is structured by two main classes corresponding to particular forms of auto-categorization (Turner et al., 1987)—social identity and personal identity.

Social identity derives from an auto-categorization process constructed in reference to out-groups and in-groups in terms of the similarities and differences with others. It refers to the socially observable and non-observable categories that structure the subject's sense of group membership and his or her definition of identity, notably in regards to gender, profession and ethnic group. This concept, therefore, highlights the central importance of social membership in the definition of the individual (Deschamps & Molinier, 2012). Personal identity, on the other hand, is formed by the differentiation between the self and the other members of the membership category or group. It thus derives from an auto-categorization founded on a form of social comparison at the heart of the in-group that allows for a subject to distinguish him or or herself from the other members of his or her membership category (Turner, 1995).

Social categorization is accompanied by a depersonalization phenomenon that derives from a cognitive redefinition of self in terms of shared group and category membership rather than idiosyncratic identity markers (Turner, 1999). This phenomenon does not imply a loss of individual identity. It simply indicates the social stratum to which the definition of self relates. For example, if the identity of "head of an enterprise" becomes prominent for a subject, this identity can cause him/her to set aside personal characteristics or attributes in order that he/she may define him/herself first and foremost as a member of this professional group and adopt behaviors that are congruent with the normative frameworks associated with that group.

But categories of self remain "fluid, variable, and dependent on context" (Turner, 1995: 212). They, therefore, vary in both their content and meanings. Thus, the relevant category from which an individual wishes to construct and define his/her *self* will depend on his/her various categorical memberships and his/her specific situation. The gender identity of a woman entrepreneur can, therefore, be activated if she finds herself in a situation involving comparisons with men; the same woman can categorize herself as an entrepreneur if the situation leads to a comparison with other professional occupations or with certain stakeholders involved in her business. Thus, a self-image, such as the choice of a categorization level, is the fruit "of an interaction between the characteristics of the individual and the characteristics of the situation in which he finds himself" (Licata, 2007:28). According to the person's past experiences, his/her current expectations and motivations, and his/her values, goals and needs, certain categories are more likely to become prominent in a given context (to be cognitively accessible to him/her), and others will be rejected for various reasons. Therefore, for example, certain women entrepreneurs can actively reject the gendered dimension of their professional identities, preferring to retain only the generic features of an occupation. Yet, in certain contexts, faced with what they interpret as being gender discrimination on the part of certain stakeholders (such as a vendor or a financier), these women are able to revisit this identity and define themselves as "women entrepreneurs."

Individuals are, therefore, actively involved in categorical choices that seem relevant and useful in a given situation. Thus, they build meaning into perceived situations. These choices are activated more easily than the subjects realize, and can vary according to context.

Construction of entrepreneurial legitimacy

That construction of social identity is the foundation of entrepreneurial legitimacy—carried out through and within interactions—is largely demonstrated in the social sciences (Beauvois, Dubois & Doise, 1999; Deschamps et al., 1999; Deschamps & Molinier, 2012; Lipiansky, 1992). This subjective perception of self, this image of self in the sight of the "other," makes recognition by the other central to identity building and the fulfillment of identity needs (existence, relatedness, valorization.) Goffman pushes this logic even further. As Quéré recalls (1987:57), Goffman deems:

> that the subjective identity of the individual is not a priori data once and for all, that it is not housed in the innermost being. Rather, it is the result of the confrontation of claimed and allocated definitions of self; it is constantly called into play; and it is established and maintained in an external place, an intermediary place, that of bodies in relationship.

Thus, identity schemas are developed and constructed in interactions. The subject is always confronted with the risk that he/she will not uphold the identity to which he/she lays claim (Lipiansky, 1990; Marc, 2005), which would cause him/her to lose face (Goffman, 1973) and feel stigmatized (Goffman, 1975), or even rejected.

In a similar vein, entrepreneurial legitimacy—seen as a symbolic and socio-cognitive construct widely "bestowed and managed by the stakeholders" (Buisson, 2005:154)—also calls for the recognition of internal and external stakeholders who are likely to confirm (or refute) the identity legitimacy of the subject in question (see above).

Certain contributions of Goffman's micro-sociology allow a deeper understanding of this singular dimension of legitimacy. For Goffman (1973, 1974, 1975, 1987, 1991), interaction is the level of social analysis where reciprocal actions are developed and subjective identities are constructed. In general, the actors do not invent the rules of the social framework in which they operate; rather, they must function within them (Goffman, 1989). Interactions emerge as interpretation and adjustment processes that are ordered, organized, and structured by a "scene" (Goffman, 1987) that regulates them (by an "expressive order"). Interactional sequences (reciprocal adjustments, management and scheduling of the physical or virtual co-presence, etc.) are, nevertheless, fundamentally unspecified in their development within circumstances that are real and relatively autonomous from the imposed structures. They unfold within social frameworks (Goffman, 1991) that guide the perceptions and representations of reality while influencing the commitment and conduct of the interactants.

Women entrepreneurs and the specific French context

To better understand these social interactions, we need to add some precisions on the specific French social and gendered context.

In France the traditional sex role division between men and women remains predominant (Crompton et al., 2007). Men are expected to partake in the public and professional arena. Women remain predominantly the custodians of the private, familial and domestic domains. However, the French situation also appears as paradoxical. If we focus on the age group ranging between 25 and 54 years, we see that 83.6% of French women work (DARES, 2012). French women are also distinguished in Europe by their fertility rate, a rate of 2.01 children per woman, when the average across the whole of the European Union was at 1.59 in 2009 (DARES, 2012). French women continue to work even with one or two children, and of those who have children who are three years of age or older, 80% work. Thus, they adapt and modify their professional activities upon the arrival of children, but the fathers do not (Moschion, 2009). In France, the working woman is highly valued (Cocandeau-Bellanger, 2011:93); but at the same time, in order to be considered a woman in the full sense of the word, she must become a mother. For a long time, this focus on motherhood found its institutional expression through pro-birth family politics that were centered exclusively on the mother. In France, even if women enter into new areas of work or entrepreneurship, male domains, the gendered subtext of social interactions remains the same with the support of institutional and organizational contexts (Crompton et al., 2007).

Let us consider French women who choose to be entrepreneurs. In 2014, 38.5% of new ventures (with a legal status of individual company) in France were created by women (29% in 1997) (Batto & Rousseau, 2015). Similar to their male counterparts, 75% of their businesses do not have employees. However, amongst those companies with more than 20 employees, only 15% of these are women (Morin and Penicaud, 2015). The Kauffmann Report (Mitchell, 2011) mentions that women represent 35% of startup business owners in the United States. Nonetheless, the French rate remains within the average for the European Union (Kelley et al., 2013).

By seizing on clues in the women entrepreneur's discourse, one further understands how they organize the experience of an interactional situation in reference to explicit and implicit rules. The different layers of meaning associated with the practical rules mobilized by the interactants (gender stereotypes, the institutional and social gendered subtext, and norms of entrepreneurship) create the structure of the set experience. They define the terms and the patterns of interactions. Any refusal of the rules by an interactant can lead to a breakdown in the framework, which involves "an interactional disruption or mode change" (Goffman, 1991:367). This rupture can lead to: a) disengagement, b) a redefinition of the situations and forms of engagement in the interactions, or c) the development of practical rules that interactants follow in order to regain bearings, get focused, and deal with the situation, thus continuing the relationship.

In their relationships with stakeholders, women entrepreneurs can claim or favor a certain lack of gender differentiation, i.e., neutrality regarding the genders of those involved (Théry, 2007, 2011; West & Zimmerman, 1987). In a given interactional context, gender division on the part of the other party can lead to the shaping of a "framework of participation"[2] that imposes on women entrepreneurs a definition of identity that they do not want or that could be risky. This framework could require them to inhabit the role of "woman" before they can step into the role of "entrepreneur," thus depriving them of resources needed to develop satisfying social identities and establish their legitimacy. So, interactional rules can be traversed through the prism of gender difference, which is accompanied by a singular modality of "male domination" (Bourdieu, 1998) or a "differential valence of the sexes"

(Héritier, 1996) in the professional arena. It is necessary to analyze the ways in which gender categories and gender relations organize a system of asymmetrical relations between inter-actants wherein those searching for recognition as a "businesswoman" encounter difficulties obtaining the sought after confirmation. This form of identity reversal is likely to take several forms (verbal or non-verbal, behavioral, attitudinal, etc.); it can address both the capacity and the right of the actor to claim her place (identity legitimacy of the businesswoman), and the content of her action (entrepreneurial and professional legitimacy).

These different elements illustrate that the study of legitimacy requires one to make choices, particularly concerning the scale of observation that is used. Consistent with our research strategy, the scope of our study lies at the level of the subjective experience of women entrepreneurs, whom we consider to be woven into a complex web of dispositional and contextual determinants. This angle of analysis leads us to take interest in the women entrepreneurs' perceived legitimacy (Major & Schmader, 2001; Costarelli, 2007), both in their relationships with themselves (what we call "identity legitimacy"), and in their interactions with their stakeholders (termed "entrepreneurial legitimacy"). Furthermore, in accordance with the vast literature on entrepreneurship, our interpretive assumptions that gender (through institutional structures, social norms, social patterns, social practices) influences the framing of interactional arrangements in which the women entrepreneurs deploy strategies of exchange with their stakeholders (ex. Baron, Markman & Hirsa, 2001; Watson & Newby, 2005; Ahl, 2006; Gupta & Turban, 2013; Williams, 2012).

Methodology

We approached our study through grounded theory (Glaser & Strauss, 1967), which is particularly suitable for understanding the processes by which actors construct meaning from their intersubjective experiences. Additionally, our work focuses on the emergence of conceptualizations and interpretive grids suggested by the data we collected during our interviews. The goal was to gain understanding of the data analysis with the fewest preconceived interpretation grids in order to reflect reality as it is perceived and built by the interviewees. We thus aim to better understand the gendered legitimacy-building process of women who have created or taken over businesses. We have chosen to interview only women to grasp, through their discourses and testimonies, their subjective experiences of entrepreneurship, their perception of interactions with different stakeholders and their perception of their gendered legitimacy building process.

Data collection

We conducted semi-structured interviews with 41 women entrepreneurs operating in diverse business sectors (retail; personal service providers; service providers to businesses in the field of communications, advertising, human resources and training; and industries such as textiles, thermoforming, and construction). As illustrated in Table 18.1, half of the women we interviewed are members of a network of businesswomen. Following progressive analysis, the other half of the sample was constructed in a more opportunistic manner that involved meetings and co-optation practices based on interpersonal relationships between the women entrepreneurs. We interviewed the women entrepreneurs to the point of empirical saturation, that is to say, until the data collection ceased to provide new elements that could enrich our interpretive schemes (Glaser & Strauss, 1967).

Table 18.1 Research sample characteristics

Socio-demographic characteristics	
Study size (number of WE)	41
Average age of respondents at time of interview	42 years old
Age of respondents (Min – Max)	27 to 59 years old
Average age at business creation/take over	35 years old

Women entrepreneurs' matrimonial situations	
In couple	75.6 % (n=31)
Divorced/separated	17.1 % (n=7)
Widowed	2.4 % (n=1)
Single	4.9 % (n=2)
Percentage of women entrepreneurs that are mothers	85 %
Average number of dependent children	2

Business characteristics	
Business origin: created by WE	85.4 % (35/41)
Business origin: takeover or family business	14.6 % (6/41)
Age of business at time of interview	median age: 16 years old
	26/41: fewer than 5 years old
	the newest: 7 months old
	the oldest: 179 years old
Revenue	22/41: < 250 000 € per year
Number of employees	6/41: 0 employees
	22/41: 1 to 10 employees
	7/41: 11 to 49 employees
	4/41: 50 to 99 employees
	2/41: more than 200 employees

The semi-structured interview guide addressed a large variety of topics, including: motivation to create a business; difficulties in the daily management of a business; business financing; training; networking; balancing life and work with the concept of what it means to be a successful woman entrepreneur; and the woman entrepreneur's feeling of recognition and legitimacy with regard to herself and her business. These in-depth interviews offered the respondents a great deal of freedom to discuss outstanding episodes in their entrepreneurial journeys, and many questions led the respondents to discuss how they built legitimacy. The interviews lasted between one and three hours; they were recorded, fully transcribed, and coded.

During the semi-structured interviews, the interviewer leads the interviewee to question and reflect upon what she says, giving rise to "a provoked and accompanied self-analysis" (Bourdieu, 1993:915). The structure of the interview invites the subject to recount her experiences or express her feelings, and to understand the ways that her internalized models, her actual valuations, her habits, her social rules, and her symbolic codes can play roles in the understanding of her social behavior. The interview gives rise to the subject's point of view, granting a crucial role to her perceptions, her subjective logic, and her identity narrative. It is for these reasons that this form of interview is an ideal tool for the exploration of systems of representation.

Data analysis

The general principle of the data analysis was to bring forth elements of the women entrepreneurs' discussions and bring the concepts together, iteratively, to generate interpretive schemes. Our methodology of qualitative data analysis is based on an iterative and abductive approach, in the sense that we continuously moved back and forth between theory and empirical evidence throughout the research process (Dubois & Gadde, 2002; Strauss & Corbin, 1990). We see here the essential inductive nature of grounded theory methodology characterized by a form "of alternation" and "of circular interaction" (Guillemette, 2006) between the collection of data and its analysis (Glaser & Strauss, 1967; Corbin & Strauss, 2008). The interpretation that we have proposed seeks to identify the organization of structural and functional relations that characterizes the logic of the construction and expression of women entrepreneurs' perceived legitimacy.

Findings

First, we will discuss the construction process of identity legitimacy that results from women entrepreneurs' self-perceptions and self-definitions, as well as their ability to auto-categorize in the corresponding social category, entrepreneur. This process is reinforced or threatened by the opinion of others who do or do not recognize the subject as one of their own; for us, this is a matter of entrepreneurial legitimacy.

Second, we will show how gender influences and frames the elements of interactional arrangements and, *in fine*, the recognition of entrepreneurial legitimacy of these women. Following West and Zimmerman (1987), gendering entrepreneurship is doing through interactions between women and their different stakeholders. The elements must be considered in order to understand deeply women entrepreneurs' interactions with their different stakeholders. Indeed, the stigmatization or recognition of these women in their standings as business women will be built within the context of their interactions with different actors. At the end of each part, we propose a figure to summarize the observed processes of legitimacy construction.

Contrasting situations with regards to the construction process of identity legitimacy for women entrepreneurs

Auto-categorization as a woman entrepreneur: recognizing oneself as an entrepreneur

Some women assume their identity as entrepreneurs. They clearly claim that they are entrepreneurs. They manage to recognize themselves as entrepreneurs, usually following their experiences along their entrepreneurial life. They need time and proof of their entrepreneurial abilities to integrate and assume their entrepreneurial identity.

> I think that my age helps me. I think that it has to be more difficult for the young people starting their own businesses. They have to get [the establishment] to take them seriously.
>
> *(Céline)*

But for other women entrepreneurs, the process of auto-categorization as an entrepreneur or business owner poses a problem. It is interesting to show how these women entrepreneurs have difficulties in considering themselves as entrepreneurs and to satisfy traditional norms of entrepreneurship. For instance, Linda's comment is particularly relevant:

INTERVIEWER: Do you feel you are recognized as a business owner?
INTERVIEWEE: No, but I think that's because right now I have very few employees and I think that in France you have to have at least ten employees to be considered a real business leader. Until you do, it's more like you're considered a craftsperson or a retailer, even if you are the head of a business. That's not what I want to say, but it's the popular opinion.

(Linda)

Linda's response reveals her complete integration of traditional criteria to assess an entrepreneur, in particular the size of business. From a social perspective, the figure of paying out ten salaries is recognized as a level which confers a recognized social status as "real" entrepreneur. Indeed, according to Linda, French business institutions use the criteria of "at least ten employees" when granting the status of entrepreneur, and do not take into consideration managerial and strategic activities and the creation of wealth. As her business does not correspond to the socially recognized criteria for entrepreneurial legitimacy, she hesitates to grant herself entrepreneurial identity. Thus, she hesitates to assume her identity legitimacy. Even if in France 80% of the companies have less than ten salaries. She does not contest this traditional norm even if she has actually set up a company.

Another example is that some of our respondents (such as Joan) refuse to use the word "entrepreneur" to describe themselves. It is interesting to observe that they are business owners and they manage their businesses, but yet they are unable to, or they do not wish to, refer to themselves as "entrepreneurs".

It is not on my business card [title of business owner], it is not indicated like that. In fact, my card says "training manager". It [owning a business] is neither for the title, nor to be recognized. No, it is for the satisfaction of doing what I want to do. Even if everything is planned, measured, and organized.

(Joan)

Similarly, this entrepreneur describes how she feels:

I don't feel myself as a boss, I don't have yet a « boss » way to think, I feel that I am out of step with others. [INT: Do you feel that you are not legitimate?] Not legitimate, but actually, I always depreciate myself. And sometimes I don't feel in my place whereas I am. But I don't feel comfortable in the discussions. To be comfortable, I should not be pushed forward. I am too close to my employees as they (others business owners) say. Today, it's hard for me only to be faced bosses who really feel as big bosses. However, today I am a boss with a real turnover!!

These excerpts illustrate the difficulty that some of these women entrepreneurs have to auto-categorize themselves as business owners and constructing their identity legitimacy as business leaders. They subordinate their identity legitimacy to social norms, institutional criteria concerning entrepreneurship, accepting that they have not achieved enough to "deserve" the status of entrepreneur. These respondents have partially internalized the social norms associated with entrepreneurship, while at the same time pushing back against them.

They consider themselves to be outside of this social category because they do not correspond to it, despite the fact that from a technical point of view, and when considering their business activities, they are at the head of a business. In fact, they do not consider themselves to be a full and legitimate member of the category of "entrepreneur."

The gendered assessment of the professional activity

The struggle to feel legitimate can also result from categorization and hierarchization in the professional sectors, particularly with regard to women's participation rate in these sectors—a rate that is inversely related to the professional status of the sector. These difficulties are directly linked to the labor market's horizontal and vertical gendered job segregation, which the feminist literature has largely shown "in itself constitutes a qualitative marking that qualifies or disqualifies an activity" (Guionnet & Neveu, 2009:193). These obstacles to the construction of entrepreneurial legitimacy can be found in some women entrepreneurs who operate in sectors classified as "feminine" (retail, personal services, tertiary consulting services) due to the high rate of female participation in these sectors. The perceptual, socio-cognitive and evaluative constructs serve as social measures to a woman entrepreneur to evaluate whether she can consider herself to be legitimate in the role of entrepreneur (self-perception, self-definition, and auto-categorization). But the internal and external stakeholders also use this baseline to grant or deny recognition of the woman entrepreneur as a business leader.

Certain women entrepreneurs in our sample mentioned how difficult it was for their businesses to be recognized as legitimate. They experience "depreciatory recognition," (Renaul, 2004) characterized by demeaning judgments made about people's activities, or even about the people themselves. The differential valence of the sectors is accompanied by a denial of recognition that is not neutral regarding the self-perception and self-definition narratives of the women entrepreneurs.

> [People ask me] what do you sell? I say I make and sell premium artisanal jams, so maybe the way I present my business is complicated. I don't say "head of a jam business." It's pretty derogatory because [you mention] a woman who makes jams and immediately you get a certain image in your head. So it's really complicated.
>
> *(Sonia)*

This excerpt indicates the extent to which the woman entrepreneur is aware that her profession is the subject of unfavorable social judgment because it is considered to traditionally dwell within the private sphere, graciously performed by homemakers. It is also complicated for her in such context to assume her status of entrepreneur.

> At the beginning you have a business. You train and teach people, and teaching is thought of as a feminine activity, so it's considered a minor endeavor. Overall, it's not really a "business." Now we're a little more well known, and when people dig a little bit and ask me, "What exactly do you do?" I can say "Distance education, 38 collaborators, 3000 students." There, right away, when I say we have €1.8 million in revenue—that gets professional recognition.
>
> *(Sophie)*

Once more, this example of this woman entrepreneur operating in the teaching and training sector (which is considered a "feminine" activity) shows her legitimation strategy, which consists of using conventional quantitative indicators to deconstruct certain stereotypes associated with the fact that she is a woman operating in a business sector considered to be "feminine." However, we can link this behavior with gendering entrepreneurship where quantitative tools are used to justify the legitimacy of her activity. But in fact she does not contest the traditional norms of entrepreneurship.

When the others' opinions limit the WE from taking on a certain categorical membership, thus limiting the construction of identity legitimacy

Certain women entrepreneurs do not always feel that their stakeholders categorize and recognize them as business leaders. Their identity legitimacy can be difficult to construct in reference to a social and professional category (associated with attributes, social characteristics and positive identifying resources) to which they do not recognize their right to belong, as mentioned above. This category is even less likely to become prominent in a given situation with interactions between several actors if it is not cognitively accessible to the women entrepreneurs, particularly due to problems of recognition by members of the in-groups and out-groups. This situation can create tension between "identity for others" (Dubar, 2010)—related to identifying labels attributed by others (here, entrepreneurial legitimacy as it relates to others' recognition of the woman entrepreneur as a business leader)—and "identity for oneself" (Dubar, 2010) (developed in reference to identifying labels claimed for the Self—here, identity legitimacy). This tension is due to the difficulties encountered by the woman entrepreneur when she wants to activate categorical choices that seem to her to be relevant and useful. Indeed, the degree of confidence that an individual has in the validity of his or her categorical membership depends on the degree of support that he or she receives from the members of his or her in-group (Butera & Pérez, 1995).

Thus, for certain women entrepreneurs doing business in traditionally "masculine" professional sectors (such as construction), we see de-activation of certain forms of categorization (personal identity, sexual identity, etc.) in order that these women can see themselves as members of the social category of 'bosses' in their particular professional sector (a point which is also consistent with the explanatory base of the auto-categorization model—see above). These women entrepreneurs have to adopt the professions' masculine behavioral norms and attitudes, which leads them to describe themselves as men, re-emphasizing the contradictions that may exist between femininity and entrepreneurship (Diaz-Garcia & Welter, 2011) or between the professional cultures of some industries and the norms of entrepreneurship (Nadin, 2007). There is an acceptance and internalization of the dominant norm that is reflected through the mobilization of masculine images and clichés.

> Like my son rightly told you, I'm "a guy." It's true that I know how to be feminine, for sure. But in my job, I'm on construction sites a lot, so I have to be in jeans, in boots. This masculine side shocks [people].
>
> *(Andrée)*

This process is illustrated with the example of Andrée (who runs an electrician business with ten employees, working in the construction industry), who brings up her son's view on the subject without contradicting him. She then adds how her work attire—seen as a symbolic component in legitimacy construction (Daloz, 2012)—highlights her masculinity. She thus separates the contexts and social roles, allowing herself to be feminine in some situations and accommodating different scripts and expectations in others: she is "a guy" in her role as entrepreneur. These women entrepreneurs will also spontaneously use conventional terms to describe the ideal and heroic (male) entrepreneur. They describe themselves as possessing the qualities required to be "good entrepreneurs." They model themselves according to these external expectations.

The auto-categorization process (and thus these women entrepreneurs' choices of membership groups) is carried out through comparison by studying whether their own standards and values match those of the observed (desired/expected) group. This is also done to avoid being rejected or stigmatized by a group if there is no match. Thus, this observation-based comparison will determine the appropriate categorization that will achieve a satisfying and self-defined identity that may be in conflict with feminine norms (Diaz-Garcia & Welter, 2011). This categorical anchoring seems to be an important condition of recognition and, therefore, legitimacy in "masculine" sectors.

This search for legitimacy is also reflected in an appropriation of language codes. In the discourse of some of the women entrepreneurs we interviewed, we observed recurrent expressions very similar to those reported by Orser, Elliot and Leck (2011). The respondents described themselves by using qualities widely recognized in the description of the ideal (male) entrepreneur (Ogbor, 2000). When speaking of themselves, they said things such as: "I'm forward moving," "I love being independent," "I deal with things alone," "I'm disciplined," "I'm driven," etc. Some of them refer to physical strength and the ability to work long and hard. We see, therefore, that certain women entrepreneurs utilize a vocabulary that is completely in line with that of conventional "masculine" entrepreneurship (Ahl, 2006; Ogbor, 2000). However, these linguistic expressions are not neutral. They also reflect the customary thoughts, beliefs and judgments that characterize a social group, as well as the norms that regulate relationships established between individuals (Charaudeau & Mainqueneau, 2002). In this way, the rituals and discursive codes reflect an expression of categorization wherein the symbolic identity is forged in line with masculine norms (Ogbor, 2000).

To summarize this first part of our findings, we propose a figure (18.1) that portrays the dynamic of the construction process of legitimacy.

On the left of the figure, identity legitimacy results from the process of auto-categorization by women entrepreneurs themselves. This process of auto-categorization depends on several factors. First, the level of self-confidence and the definition of self impact on the ability of these women to recognize themselves as legitimate entrepreneurs. Second, the institutional and cultural contexts provide social norms, socio-cognitive and evaluative constructs. At this level, one can find the gendered subtext of a given society; it constitutes the structural

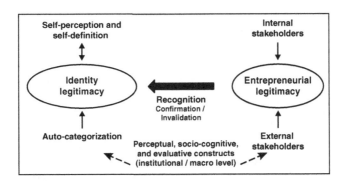

Figure 18.1 Identity legitimacy and entrepreneurial legitimacy

level where the interactions take place. This normative structure influences women themselves through, for example, gender stereotypes or expected behaviors according to sex categories. Obviously others actors in society such as their stakeholders (internal and external, detailed below) are also influenced by these social norms and socio-cognitive schemes. The construction of entrepreneurial legitimacy is therefore dependent on the recognition of the internal and external stakeholders, who could reinforce or refute the entrepreneur's identity legitimacy. However, their judgment—their recognition of women as "real" entrepreneurs (entrepreneurial legitimacy)—is the third fundamental element for women to build their identity legitimacy. We will now examine in more detail how to construct these discursive codes—these categorical judgments that are influenced by gender stereotypes and biases.

Framework elements of interactional arrangements and their effects on the construction of entrepreneurial legitimacy through the eyes of stakeholders

In keeping with the vast literature on entrepreneurship (Baron, Markman & Hirsa, 2001; Watson & Newby, 2005; Ahl, 2006; Gupta & Turban, 2013; Williams, 2012) and literature on gendering organizations (Acker, 1990; Calas, Smircich & Holvino, 2014; West & Zimmerman, 1987), our interpretative hypothesis is that gender is present in the framing of interactions wherein women entrepreneurs deploy strategies of exchange with their stakeholders. Our study reveals that this framing can lead women entrepreneurs to experience stigmatization (Goffman, 1975) in reference to the normative expectations of "ratified participants"[3] (Goffman, 1991). We will examine here how women entrepreneurs perceive their entrepreneurial legitimacy in their interactions with their different stakeholders.

During our interviews, the women entrepreneurs mentioned a lot of different stakeholders (internal and external). However, we will focus only on employees (internal), bankers and customers (external) who were, through testimonies, the most significant and, according to us, revealed gendering entrepreneurship through these women's experiences. They also mentioned—quite frequently—their interactions with their husbands. We do not present the details of this particular relationship, which has been already detailed in a previous paper (Chasserio, Lebègue & Poroli, 2014).

Employees: internal stakeholders among whom entrepreneurial legitimacy must be constructed

For women entrepreneurs, it is fundamental to be recognized by their employees as a boss and business leader. However, within the sample of respondents, we spotted some situations that brought to light the strength of gender stereotypes in some business circles, and the strategies that the women entrepreneurs used to counter these stereotypes.

As illustrated in Figure 18.1, entrepreneurial legitimacy must be acquired from stakeholders, including employees. The following example involves Sandra, a woman entrepreneur who took over her family business in the building industry, a very "masculine" sector (her company builds large community kitchens):

> Business only works if you're technically on top of it, so I deal with obtaining orders and then I deal with all of the technical parts, the construction site meetings. You have to establish yourself very quickly in a site meeting in front of 20 guys, saying "I want the kitchen there, the gas line there, that over there, and I want it there because that's

where I want it and nowhere else," because they can very easily try and run you over and discount you, thinking, "She's not going to get in our way, etc." I think that because I'm a woman, I've always done everything I could not to be faulted. I'm very demanding.

(Sandra)

This excerpt illustrates that the process of entrepreneurial legitimacy is marked over time between certain interrelated actors, and that it is punctuated with trials, tests and self-affirmation. This woman entrepreneur faces gendered categorical judgments on the part of her male employees. In this context, she works to influence the content of her interactions with them through attitude (by being demanding) and behavior (by being technically directive) in order to change the content of their judgments. In doing so, the woman entrepreneur can become an agent of social change; she can influence socially rooted representations and contribute to the revision of prejudices regarding women entrepreneurs and business leaders in the so-called "male" arenas by offering an example that is concretely different from the stereotype. To some extent, this situation refers to a strategy of "undoing gender" (Deutsch, 2007). However, some stakeholders may hold onto their sexist attitudes—despite examples that contradict them—because they prefer to think of these examples as the exceptions that confirm the rule. Thus, attachments to these characterizations may harm the social recognition of innovative individuals.

The following interview response also eloquently expresses how interactional arrangements work in a so-called "masculine" arena. This woman entrepreneur, Andrée (who leads a general electrical business specialized in construction and employs ten people), took over her boss's company upon his retirement; previously she was responsible for the administration and accounting.

INTERVIEWER: How was your taking over of the business perceived by the employees?
INTERVIEWEE: Very well. They were all long-standing employees and they all knew me well. But it was a bit weird that I was "above" them, and it made a few of them a little uncomfortable. But then we needed technical help, so I hired Mr. P. It comforted them.

(Andrée)

We see here certain elements highlighted by Bruni, Gherardi and Poggio (2004) in their case studies of Italian women. This woman entrepreneur displays confidence and affirms her status as an entrepreneur. In her relationships with her male personnel, she reported encountering no marked difficulties when establishing her authority. Yet, even if she had, by definition, statutory legitimacy, she acknowledges that hiring a male foreman helped to reassure her employees and to eliminate a certain emotional discomfort associated with a singular state of cognitive dissonance linked to the fact that the boss was a woman. This act of hiring was not a conscious strategy aimed at reducing the employees' cognitive dissonance regarding gender stereotypes of entrepreneurs, but it had that effect. The fact that a woman could be the head of a company in the construction sector could engender a certain amount of confusion or disturbance among male employees, generating a socially ambiguous situation incompatible with the norms and gender stereotypes that have been internalized in relation to, among other things, context. The arrival of a male middle manager to whom these male employees could relate reduced the cognitive dissonance.

This excerpt shows that even though the two parties had known each other previously and had worked together as colleagues, it was not sufficient to assuage the discomfort the male employees felt in the face of their colleague's new professional status when she became an entrepreneur, and thus their boss. This situation illustrates that the recognition of professional competencies acquired by women is contextual and scarcely transposable directly to the role of woman entrepreneur. The women entrepreneurs have to therefore rebuild, via interactions, the affirmation of their entrepreneurial legitimacy, even with stakeholders who knew them previously. Additionally, for the women who arrive in a new business sector and step into a new role (that of entrepreneur), strategic construction of interactions will be even more crucial with the various stakeholders in order to gain recognition of their entrepreneurial legitimacy as it extends above and beyond stereotypes and prejudice.

> The construction of entrepreneurial legitimacy also involves managing very symbolic elements, such as actual working hours and everyday presence in the company.
>
> You want to prove to the others that you're the boss, you want to justify your presence [...] You're always the last to go home, you're always the first there in the morning. For years, I got to work at 7 a.m. and I left at 7 p.m.
>
> *(Marion)*

Here, the symbolic elements of entrepreneurial legitimacy derive from a particular degree of proximity to which the employees are sensitive. Combining the expression of a value with the establishment of an ideology that is supportive of socially valued behaviors, these uses enable women entrepreneurs to build entrepreneurial legitimacy through their positions in relation to the social body (physical and psychological presence), their interactions (forms of relationships between the women entrepreneurs and their employees, accessibility, etc.) and the situations and circumstances (ability to intervene at any time).

We were also interested in external stakeholders (bankers, clients, etc.) and the ways in which they contribute to the construction of the women entrepreneurs' entrepreneurial legitimacy.

Women entrepreneurs' interactional arrangements vis-à-vis banks and financial institutions

Recognition on the part of stakeholders is essential to the acquisition of entrepreneurial legitimacy and the construction of identity legitimacy. However, these stakeholders build their judgments in a given social context, including perceptual, socio-cognitive and evaluative constructs that influence and affect the frameworks of the experience and interactions (see Figure 18.1). For instance, the case of bankers is instructive. Some women entrepreneurs faced a lack of entrepreneurial legitimacy in the eyes of their bankers:

> I went to the bank—I'll remember it until I die. I went into the banker's office; his desk was spotless. There wasn't a paper or a file in my name on its surface. I explained my project to him and give him my figures and he said, "I need your husband's guarantee." What?! [...] I told him that my husband had nothing to do with it. I was the one who asked for the loan and I had what was necessary to cover it! And that's where it ended. I told one of my clients about it, and he said, "Listen, call so-and-so and tell them I sent you." So I called so-and-so and I changed banks.
>
> *(Françoise)*

In this case, the denial of entrepreneurial legitimacy was the result of the stakeholder's refusal to accept the self-definition presented by the woman entrepreneur, that of entrepreneur. He (the banker) only recognized her in her role as a wife, not in the role of an autonomous and independent businesswoman. Gendered categorization thus appears as an implicit social marker that is simultaneously the fruit and the source of the rules that structure the social framework and the actor's engagement in the interaction. The woman entrepreneur's gender identity thus becomes a stigma, which is to say, "an unwelcome difference from that which was expected of a social subject" (Goffman, 1975:15).

In addition, the following excerpt illustrates the double evaluation that women seem to undergo in terms of their legitimacy in their roles as business leaders. The passage shows that the economic and financial performance of the business that these two women entrepreneurs head together seems to perfectly satisfy socially recognized criteria (sustained growth and progressive revenue). However, they face difficulties obtaining overdraft protection from their bank. It is remarkable to see that the explanations utilized by the bank include the number of children of one of the women, and the fact that the other woman is not in a romantic relationship.

> Even though we have €1 million in revenues, we still have problems. They want guarantees and assurances, and Christelle [her partner] having five children is a problem. It's never a sure bet. I'm a problem too—I'm single. I don't have millions of euros backing me up. So you see, those are the problems. ...
>
> *(Sophie)*

Thus, the arguments utilized by this woman entrepreneur establish a link between private and family life and business. For the bank, it seems that the company's financial success does not constitute a determining factor in credit risk assessment. The number of dependent children, however, makes the commercial relationship more fragile and risky in the eyes of the bankers. Sex thus fuels the socially rooted social sex categorization mechanisms that shape reality interpretation activities that are characterized by perceptual bias and differentiated assignments to various social roles. This leads to overestimating the differences between women and men and also to apportioning greater weight to the family roles of women than to those of men or indeed to assigning a level of risk to women's family roles.

Certain bank practices sometimes lead bankers to draw conclusions from their own gender stereotypes and/or discriminatory practices with regard to women entrepreneurs, appearing to have integrated the consequences of these stereotypes. We thus see at what point the framework of experience is marked by stigmas, and, at the same time, how this framework structures the interactions and their content. This framing of the situation has every chance of creating difficulties for the women entrepreneurs striving to establish their entrepreneurial identities, because this framing is based on the stigma attached to being a woman.

Clients' categorical judgments in the recognition of women entrepreneurs' entrepreneurial legitimacy

Women entrepreneurs are shaking up conventional representations prevalent in society. Additionally, several women entrepreneurs interviewed spoke of the difficulties they faced gaining their clients' recognition of them as business leaders. For example, in their first appointments, some clients thought the women entrepreneurs were secretaries or, at best, sales representatives. The following explicitly illustrates this:

> People see a woman, and women are either behind their desks or they're salespeople. For example, on the phone, people who don't know me automatically say, "Pass me the boss."
>
> *(Andrée)*

> Sure, they talked to my account manager and the client looked at me like I was the secretary. And the account manager said, "Excuse me, Mr. So-and-so, this is Mrs. B, the director." And I said, "Does that bother you?" The response? "Not at all."
>
> *(Clio)*

We can see that the resistance on the part of certain men (here, clients) can be strong with regard to the entrance of women into so-called "male" professions or business arenas. Here, the stereotypes associated with the social construction of gender differences and social division of social roles are producers of both categorization and social hierarchy. Interactions thus contribute to the production and reproduction of gender categories, such as structural and hierarchical elements of social organization and relational patterns. That which is perceived by some players to be a reversal of gender positions in the professional world again leads to a form of stigmatization of women entrepreneurs. Even if not all clients adopt this attitude, the woman entrepreneur has to prove her technical competence and the quality of her product or service. It is only following these demonstrations that she obtains client recognition and thus is seen to be a legitimate entrepreneur. But, as recalled by Goffman (1975:57) and illustrated in the case of Clio mentioned above:

> The most common approach is to not openly acknowledge that which discredits him (the discredited individual), in a careful effort of indifference that is often accompanied by feelings of tension, uncertainty, and ambiguousness felt by all parties, and certainly by the individual who is stigmatized. The stigmatized individual's cooperation with the "normal people" in order to pretend that any notable difference is insignificant and unworthy of attention represents one of the main events that can mark the existence of that person.

This type of situation was mentioned a few times by our respondents, particularly those who do business with foreign countries where the cultural differences regarding a woman's place and role may be more pronounced and restrictive:

> Yes, of course, in business competition and all that, there are people who only want to work with male bosses. But you don't always catch on to this right away.
>
> *(Manon)*

> I remember 15 years ago a Chinese man came [to France] and wanted to do business with us, and my husband met with him. My husband called me in to introduce me, and I gave him my business card for my other business that makes [hardware] nuts. He wanted to sell nuts. I gave him my card that said I was the company president. He didn't shake my hand. He looked at my husband and said, "Shall we continue?" So, there are still countries where it's not always easy.
>
> *(Agnès)*

The possibility for some women to circumvent conventions and impose themselves in particularly gendered occupations where the masculine principle is established as a measure of all things (Bird & Brush, 2002; Bruni, Gherardi & Poggio, 2004; Ahl, 2006; de Bruin, Brush & Welter, 2007; Calas, Smircich & Bourne, 2009; Gupta, Turban, Wasti & Sikdar, 2009) is still not enough to "undermine the accepted order of the foundations of hierarchical domination, of accepted rituals, and of the virility that it expresses" (Guichard-Claudic, Kergoat & Vilbrod, 2008:14). The involvement of women in entrepreneurship (particularly in the so-called "masculine" fields) may clash with social representations or be seen as transgressing social norms (Gallioz, 2008). We find here classic forms of "subtle stereotyping" (Fiske & Taylor, 2011) regarding the concepts of masculinity and femininity that are based on the processes of basic categorization and rapid association. These forms shape the order of integrations, the ways in which to coordinate within a situation, etc., in a vague connection with elements that do not entirely fall within the set interaction. In this case, questions of positive identity confirmation and of recognition (thus, legitimacy) arise by virtue of one's position.

As illustrated in above excerpts and in Figure 18.1, identity legitimacy and entrepreneurial legitimacy feed into each other. Therefore, identity legitimacy, with a corollary feeling of self-confidence, will be even stronger as the various stakeholders recognize the legitimacy of the businesswoman—that is to say, when they see her as being "in her rightful place" and belonging to the category of "entrepreneur." In the same way, situations of stigmatization (occurring in the lives of these women entrepreneurs) negatively impact their exchanges with their stakeholders and the recognition of their social identities as entrepreneurs. This phenomenon harms their process of auto-categorization and the construction of their identity legitimacy.

Therefore, the construction of entrepreneurial legitimacy is dependent on the recognition of the internal and external stakeholders, who could reinforce or refute the entrepreneur's identity legitimacy. In this regard, our findings suggest that both the construction of the women entrepreneurs' legitimacy and their identity confirmation can mean that certain attributes (sex) are weighed more heavily than others (status, occupation, professional experiences, etc.). Sex and sex category (West & Zimmerman, 1987) can prove to be more prominent in the stakeholders' cognitive representations, thus shaping the framework of their interactions with women entrepreneurs. In the eyes of the stakeholders, some women entrepreneurs do not appear to hold the prerequisite attributes compatible with the statutory and social positions they occupy and the professional roles they assume. In these cases, women entrepreneurs are very likely to be stigmatized (Goffman, 1975).

To summarize this second part of our findings, we propose a table (Table 18.2) that portrays the various strategies used by our respondents to build their legitimacy.

Conclusions

Through this paper, we have proposed an original theoretical reading of the construction of the legitimacy of women entrepreneurs. We have shown that this construction emerges at least partially from the interactional sequences inscribed in social scenes (conventional rules, reciprocal adjustments, situational skills, etc.) by means of invalidation or conformation games and from long-lasting recognition or refutation. In this respect, women entrepreneurs may encounter social stereotypes that are deeply buried in the individual and collective unconscious and that will shape the definitions of self and the dynamic

Table 18.2 Gendered challenges to build legitimacy and strategies adopted by women entrepreneurs

Challenges to feel oneself legitimate as entrepreneur	Adopted strategies	Concrete applications
Women entrepreneurs in general	Reconsidering the traditional "male" norms of entrepreneurship to adapt them to its situation	Questioning criteria to assess business, size, turnover, number of employees
Women in "masculine" sectors	Deactivation of certain forms of categorization (as women for instance) and focus on entrepreneurial identity and expected behaviors	Becoming a "male" entrepreneur by masking her female sex identity (adopting masculine clothes and discourses) (identificatory display – West and Zimmerman, 1987)
Women in "feminine" sectors	Presenting a traditional (and depreciated) feminine activity with traditional "male" criteria of entrepreneurship	Highlighting the financial and commercial features of the business, a hyper-professionalization of the discourse to be a "real" entrepreneur

Challenges to being recognized internally and externally as a legitimate entrepreneur (according to a masculine-gendered entrepreneurship)	Adopted strategies	Concrete applications
	Being an expert without any professional fault or mistake; being a perfect professional	Being present on the floor, by proving your knowledge in a complex technical situation
	Adopting specific attitudes and behaviors to act as a "male" entrepreneur	Being directive with employees
	Using a male intermediary with teams, not directly managing people	Employing a male supervisor
	Proving their ability and availability to be a "real" entrepreneur by adopting expected ("male") behaviors; organizing a gender display	Working long hours Being the first at job the morning, the last the evening; not mentioning family responsibility

ordering of interactions wherein areas of tension are built among different identities (the prescribed identity, the desired or claimed identity and the recognized identity). Our analysis and discussion also reflects a double process involved in the construction of identity legitimacy and entrepreneurial legitimacy, both of which are critical bases of identity construction.

From an academic point of view, this work contributes to the debate about the gender models that underlie the construction of the entrepreneurial legitimacy of women entrepreneurs. In the context of France (where this research was undertaken), we have observed that social representations of "the entrepreneur" are largely marked by masculine norms. Thus, many women entrepreneurs use conventional terms, associated with masculinity, to describe entrepreneurship. At times, some even adopt the masculine behavioral norms associated with the ideal heroic entrepreneur, as well as the stereotypes or even the prejudices linked with these norms. Furthermore, different stakeholders (such as bankers, clients and employees) hold traditional expectations of collaboration with a male head of business and not a woman. This study therefore shows that the French entrepreneurial environment is still deeply structured according to male-gendered norms, which impact the women who enter into these domains. Additionally, in this specific context, this work on women's entrepreneurial legitimacy is exploratory and may encourage further research in other cultural contexts.

From an empirical point of view, our findings show that the process of constructing one's self as a woman entrepreneur does not just occur; it poses challenges that the women entrepreneurs respond to through different strategies. Furthermore, in addition to obtaining legitimacy vis-à-vis themselves, the women entrepreneurs also have to gain legitimacy from their various shareholders. In this respect, financial institutions, as well as business support services and entrepreneur training organizations, would benefit from recognizing and calling into question gender stereotypes that contribute to the de-legitimization of women entrepreneurs. This work gives us the opportunity to reconsider the content of training and support programs for women entrepreneurs. These programs should give more consideration to the specific difficulties encountered by women entrepreneurs and help them better understand and deconstruct the masculine norms that are infused in the entrepreneurial process.

However, our research has a certain number of limitations. In terms of method, it would have been relevant to interview not just the women entrepreneurs, but also their various stakeholders in order to better understand the legitimacy of these women entrepreneurs' entrepreneurial identities. Indeed, our work depends entirely on the perception that the women entrepreneurs have of their legitimacy and of their interactions with their stakeholders. Concerning the cultural aspect of this study, it would be fruitful to conduct research and cross analyses in other cultural contexts. Indeed, in international contexts, the situation of women and social gender relations may differ considerably.

In this chapter, we focused on gendered features and gendered dynamics in entrepreneurship to understand the construction of women entrepreneurs' legitimacy. However, we did not mention some other aspects (such as age, cumulative experience seniority, ethnic origins, etc.), which are also relevant in terms of legitimacy. Our intuition is that it would be relevant to undertake a study on legitimacy with an intersectional theoretical framework. This study represents a first step that needs deeper analysis.

Finally, in studying women entrepreneurs, we are pointedly singling out interactions among different social gender roles. Women entrepreneurs develop and implement strategies that challenge certain conventional norms. Furthermore, it is perhaps time to consider that these practices of women entrepreneurs herald and shape social change in our societies. From this perspective, the work focusing on women entrepreneurs could lead to a reconsideration of the entrepreneurial norms, both for women and men, refuting the homogenous image of "the entrepreneur" and the indicators used in the establishment of such an image, such as a minimum number of employees required.

Notes

1 For Doise (1987: 24), these criteria "are often multiple, [they] don't necessarily function by way of resolved inclusions or exclusions, and there are degrees and levels of belonging to different categories."

2 Which regulates the subjects' mode of engagement in an interaction situation (Cefaï & Gardella, 2012).

3 The participants ratified by an interaction situation are those whose presence is "required by the participation framework" and whose "places and roles are predefined by the institutional guidelines and by the established customs, but are formed specifically in the course of a meeting" (Cefaï & Gardella, 2012: 245–246).

References

Ahl, H. 2006. Why research on women entrepreneurs needs new directions, *Entrepreneurship Theory and Practice*, 30(5): 595–621.

Aldrich, H. E. and Fiol, C. M. 1994. Fools rush in? The institutional context of industry creation, *Academy of Management Review*, 19(4): 645–670.

Barjot, D., Anceau, E., Lescent-Gilles, I. and Mamot, B. 2003. *Les Entrepreneurs du Second Empire*, Presses de l'Université Paris Sorbonne.

Baron, R. A., Markman, G. D. and Hirsa, A. 2001. Perceptions of women and men as entrepreneurs: Evidence for differential aspects of attributional augmenting, *The Journal of Applied Psychology*, 86(5): 923–929.

Batto, V. and Rousseau, S. 2015. Hausse des creations d'entreprises en 2014, notamment des sociétés. *INSEE Premières*, n° 1534.

Baum J. A. and Oliver, C. 1991. Institutional linkages and organizational mortality, *Administrative Science Quarterly*, 36(2): 187–218.

Beauvois, J.-L., Dubois, N. and Doise, W. 1999. *La Construction Sociale de la Personne*, Presses Universitaires Grenoble.

Bird, B. and Brush, C. G. 2002. A gendered perspective on organizational creation, *Entrepreneurship Theory and Practice*, 26(3): 41–65.

Bonnafous-Boucher, M. and Pesqueux, Y. (dir) 2006. *Décider avec les Parties Prenantes: Approches d'une Nouvelle Théorie de la Société Civile*, Editions La Découverte.

Bourdieu, P. 1998. *La Domination Masculine*, Editions du Seuil.

Bourdieu, P. (dir) 1993. *La Misère du Monde*, Editions du Seuil.

Bruni, A., Gherardi, S. and Poggio, B. 2004. Entrepreneur-mentality, gender and the study of women entrepreneurs, *Journal of Organizational Change Management*, 17(3): 256–268.

Buisson, M.-L. 2005. La gestion de légitimité organisationnelle: un outil pour faire face la complexi-fication de l'environnement? *Management & Avenir*, 4(6): 147–164.

Butera, F. and Perez, J. A. 1995. Les modèles explicatifs de l'influence sociale. In Mugny, G., Oberle, D. and Beauvois, J.-L. (dir.), *Relations Humaines, Groupes et Influence Sociale*, Presses Universitaires Grenoble. pp. 202–223.

Calás, M. B., Smircich, L. and Bourne, K. A. 2009. Extending the boundaries: Reframing 'entre-preneurship as social change' through feminist perspective. *Academy of Management Review*, 34(3): 552–569.

Calás, M. B., Smircich, L. and Holvino E. 2014. Theorizing gender-and-organization. Changing times…changing theories? In Kumra, S., Simpson, R. and Burke, R. (eds) *The Oxford Handbook of Gender in Organizations*. Oxford: Oxford University Press, 17–52.

Cefaï, D. and Gardella, E. 2012. Comment analyser une situation selon le dernier Goffman. In Cefaï, D. and Perreau L. (dir.) 2012. *Erving Goffman et l'Ordre de l'Interaction*, CURAPP-ESS/CEMS-IMM), 231–263.

Charaudeau, P. 2001. Langue, discours et identité culturelle. *Etudes de Linguistique Appliquée*, 3(123–124): 341–348.

Charaudeau, P. and Maingueneau, D. 2002. Dictionnaire d'analyse du discours. Paris: Seuil.

Chasserio, S., Lebègue T. and Poroli, C. 2014. Heterogeneity of spousal support for French women entrepreneurs. In Lewis, K. V., Henry, C., Gatewood, H. J., and Watson, J. (eds) *"Women's*

Entrepreneurship in the 21st Century: An International Multi-level Research Analysis". Cheltenham: Edward Elgar Publishing Inc., pp. 236–257.

Chasserio, S., Pailot, P. and Poroli, C. 2014. When entrepreneurial identity meets multiple social identities: Interplays and identity work of women entrepreneurs. *International Journal of Entrepreneurial Behavior & Research*, 20(2): 128–154.

Cho, H.-D., Lee, B.-H., Sung, T.-K. and Kim, S.-W. 2011. Assessing the institutional legitimacy of research and technology organizations in South Korea—A content analysis approach, *Science, Technology and Society*, 16(1): 53–73.

Cocandeau-Bellanger, L. 2011. *Les Femmes au Travail*. Paris: Armand Colin.

Corbin, J. M. and Strauss, A. 1990. Grounded theory research: Procedures, canons, and evaluative Criteria, *Qualitative Sociology*, 13(1): 3–21.

Corbin, J. M. and Strauss, A. 2008. *Basics of Qualitative Research: Techniques and Procedures for Developing Grounded Theory*. Sage Publications (3rd revised edition).

Costarelli, S. 2007. Intergroup threat and experimental affect: The distinct roles of causal attributions, ingroup identification, and perceived legitimacy of intergroup status, *Personality and Social Psychology Bulletin*, 33(11): 1481–1491.

Daloz, J.-P. 2012. Comment les représentants s'assurent la légitimité: Une approche symbolique, *Revue Internationale des Sciences Sociales*, 196/2: 127–140.

De Bruin, A., Brush, C. G. and Welter, F. 2007. Advancing a framework for coherent research on women's entrepreneurship, *Entrepreneurship Theory and Practice*, 31(3): 323–339.

De Clercq, D. and Voronov, M. 2009. Toward a practice perspective of entrepreneurship: Entrepreneurial legitimacy as habitus, *International Small Business Journal*, 27(4): 395–417.

Deschamps, J.-C. and Molinier, P. 2012. *L'Identité en Psychologie Sociale: Des Processus Identitaires aux Représentations Sociales*, Editions Dunod.

Deschamps, J.-C., Morales, J. F., Paez, D. and Worchel, S. 1999. *L'Identité Sociale: La Construction de l'Individu dans les Relations Entre Groupes*, Presses Universitaires Grenoble.

Deutsch, F.M. 2007. Undoing gender, *Gender and Society*, 21(1): 106–127.

Diaz Garcia, M.-C. and Welter, F. 2011. Gender identities and practices: Interpreting women entrepreneurs' narratives, *International Small Business Journal*, 31(4): 1–21.

Dogan, M. 2010. La légitimité politique: Nouveauté des critères, anachronisme des théories classiques, *Revue Internationale des Sciences Sociales*, 196/2: 21–39.

Doise, W. 1987. Identité, conversion et influence sociale. In Moscovici, S. and Mugny, G. (dir.), *Psychologie de la Conversion*, Editions Delval, pp. 23–33.

Drori, I. and Honig, B. 2013. A process model of internal and external legitimacy, *Organization Studies*, 34(3): 345–376.

Drori, I., Honig, B. and Sheaffer, Z. 2009. The life cycle of an internet firm: scripts, legitimacy, and identity, *Entrepreneurship Theory and Practice*, 33(3): 715–738.

Dubar, C. 2010. *La Crise des Identités: L'Interprétation d'une Mutation*. Presses Universitaires de France.

Dubois, A. and Gadde, L. E. 2002. Systematic combining: An abductive approach to case research, *Journal of Business Research*, 55(7): 553–560.

Duran, P. 2009. Légitimité, droit et action publique, *Année Sociologique*, 59(2): 303–344.

Feydeau, E. de. 2000. Les femmes créatrices d'entreprise dans la beauté. In Marseille, J. (dir.), *Créateurs et Créations d'Entreprises de la Révolution Industrielle à Bos Jours*. ADHE, pp. 213–228.

Fiske, S. T. and Taylor, S. E. 2011. *Cognition Sociale: Des Neurones à la Culture*, Editions Mardaga.

Gallioz, S. 2008. Etre une femme et entrer dans le secteur du bâtiment: Recherche de l'exception ou acte de folie. In Guichard-Claudic, Y., Kergoat, D., and Vilbrod, A. (dir.), *L'Inversion du Genre: Quand les Métiers Masculins Se Conjuguent au Féminin … et Réciproquement*. Presses Universitaires de Rennes, pp. 325–339.

Glaser, B. G. and Strauss, A. L. 1967. *The Discovery of Grounded Theory: Strategies for Qualitative Research*. Aldine de Gruyter.

Goffman, E. 1973. *La Mise en Scène de la Vie Quotidienne*, Editions de Minuit.

Goffman, E. 1974. *Les Rites d'Interaction*, Editions de Minuit.

Goffman, E. 1975. *Stigmates: Les Usages Sociaux des Handicaps*, Editions de Minuit.

Goffman, E. 1987. *Façons de Parler*, Editions de Minuit.

Goffman, E. 1989. Réplique à Denzin et Keller. In Joseph, I., Castel, R., and Cosnier, J. (eds) *Le Parler-frais d'Erwing Goffman*, Editions de Minuit.

Goffman, E. 1991. *Les Cadres de l'Expérience*, Editions de Minuit.

Golant, B. D. and Sillince, J. A. A. 2007. The constitution of organizational legitimacy: a narrative perspective, *Organization Studies*, 28(8): 1149–1167.

Guéguen, H. and Malochet, G. 2012. *Les Théories de la Reconnaissance*, Editions La Découverte.

Guichard-Claudic, Y., Kergoat, D. and Vilbrod, A. (dir.) 2008. *L'Inversion du Genre: Quand les Métiers Masculins Se Conjuguent au Féminin … et Réciproquement*, Presses Universitaires de Rennes.

Guillemette, F. 2006. L'approche de la Grounded Theory: Pour innover? *Recherches Qualitatives*, 61(1): 32–50.

Guionnet, C. and Neveu, E. 2004. *Féminins/Masculins: Sociologie du Genre*, Armand Colin.

Gupta, V. K. and Turban, D. B., 2013. Differences between men and women in opportunity evaluation as a function of gender stereotypes and stereotype activation, *Entrepreneurship Theory and Practice*, 37(4): 771–788.

Gupta, V. K., Turban, D. B., Wasti, S. A. and Sikdar, A. 2009. The role of gender stereotypes in perceptions of entrepreneurs and intentions to become an entrepreneur, *Entrepreneurship Theory and Practice*, 33(2): 397–417.

Hannan, M. T. and Carroll, G. 1992. *Dynamics of Organizational Populations: Density, Legitimation and Competition*. Oxford: Oxford University Press.

Héritier, F. 1996. *Masculin/Féminin: Penser la Différence*, Editions Odile Jacob.

Hogg, M. A. 1995. Le concept de soi reformulé: une approche en termes de catégorisation et d'identité sociale. In Mugny, G., Oberlé, D. and Beauvois, J.-L. (dir.), *Relations Humaines, Groupes et Influence Sociale*, Presses Universitaires Grenoble, pp. 161–174.

Hogg, M. A. 2002. Social categorization, depersonalization, and group behavior. In Hogg, M. A. and Tindale, S. (eds) *Blackwell Handbook of Social Psychology: Group Processes*, Blackwell Publishers Ltd., pp. 56–85.

Kelley, D. J., Brush, C. G., Greene, P. G., and Litovsky, Y. 2013. Global Entrepreneurship Monitor (GEM) 2012 Women's Report, available 12/24/16 at: www.babson.edu/Academics/centers/…/ GEM%202012%20Womens%20Report.pdf.

L'Ecuyer, R. 1978. *Le Développement du Concept de Soi de l'Enfance à la Vieillesse*, Presses Universitaires de France.

Lahire, B. 2005. *L'esprit sociologique*, Editions La Découverte.

Licata, L. 2007. La théorie de l'identité sociale et la théorie de l'auto-catégorisation: Le Soi, le groupe et le changement social. *Revue électronique de Psychologie Sociale*, 1: 19–33.

Lipiansky, E.-M. 1990. Identité subjective et interaction. In, *Stratégies Identitaires*, Presses Universitaires de France, pp. 173–211.

Lipiansky, E.-M. 1992. *Identité et Communication*, Presses Universitaires de France.

Lounsbury, M. and Glynn, M. A. 2001. Cultural entrepreneurship: Stories, legitimacy, and the acquisition of resources, *Strategic Management Journal*, 22(6–7): 545–564.

Major, B. and Schmader, T. 2001. Legitimacy and the construal of social disadvantage. In Jost, J. T., Major, B. (ed.) *The Psychology of Legitimacy: Emerging Perspective on Ideology, Justice, and Intergroup Relations*. Cambridge: Cambridge University Press, pp. 176–204.

Marc, E. 2005. *Psychologie de l'identité: Soi et le Groupe*, Editions Dunod.

Marseille, J. (dir.) 2000. *Créateurs et Créations d'Entreprises de la Révolution Industrielle à Nos Jours*, ADHE.

Meyer, J. W. and Rowan, B. 1977. Institutionalized organizations: Formal structure as myth and ceremony, *American Journal of Sociology*, 83(2): 340–363.

Morin, T. and Penicaud, E. 2015. Indépendants et dirigeants salariés d'entreprise: un tiers de femmes. *INSEE Premières*, n° 1563.

Moschion, J. 2009. Offre de travail des mères en France: l'effet causal du passage de deux à trois enfants, *Economie et Statistique*, 422(1): 51–78.

Nadin, S. 2007. Entrepreneurial identity in the care sector: Navigating the contradictions, *Women in Management Review*, 22(6): 456–467.

Nagy, B. G., Pollack, J. M., Rutherford, M. W. and Lohrke, F. T. 2012. The influence of entrepreneur's credentials and impression management behaviors on perceptions of new venture legitimacy, *Entrepreneurship Theory & Practice*, 36(5): 941–965.

Ogbor, J. O. 2000. Mythicizing and reification in entrepreneurial discourse: Ideology-critique of entrepreneurial studies, *Journal of Management Studies*, 37(5): 605–635.

Orser, B., Elliot, C. and Leck, J. 2011. Feminist attributes and entrepreneurial identity, *Gender in Management: An International Journal*, 26(8): pp. 561–589.

Paille, P. 1994. L'analyse par théorie ancrée. *Cahiers de Recherche Sociologique*, (23): 147–181.

Passeron, J.-C. 2006. *Le Raisonnement Sociologique*. Editions Albin Michel.

Peneff, J. 1997. *La Méthode Biographique: De l'École de Chicago à l'Histoire Orale*, Armand Colin.

Perez Rodriguez, M.-J. and Basco, R. 2011. The cognitive legitimacy of the family business field, *Family Business Review*, 24(4): 322–342.

Pharo, P. 2007. La valeur d'un homme. In Caille, A. (dir.), *La Quête de Reconnaissance: Nouveau Phénomène Social*, Editions La découverte, pp. 107–121.

Pollack, J. M., Rutherford, M. W. and Nagy, B. N. 2012. Preparedness and cognitive legitimacy as antecedents to new venture funding in televised business pitches. *Entrepreneurship Theory and Practice*, 36(5): 915–939.

Powell, W. W. and DiMaggio, P. J. (ed.) 1991. *The New Institutionalism in Organizational Analysis*. Chicago: University Chicago Press.

Quéré, L. 1987. "La vie sociale est une scène" Goffman revu et corrigé par Garfinkel, in *Le parler frais d'Erving Goffman*, Les Editions de Minuit, pp. 47–82.

Renault, E. 2004. *L'expérience de l'Injustice: Reconnaissance et Clinique de l'Injustice*, Editions La Découverte.

Rosanvallon, P. 2008. *La Légitimité Démocratique: Impartialité, Réflexivité, Proximité*, Editions du Seuil.

Schröder, M. 2013. How moral arguments influence economic decisions and organizational legitimacy—the case of offshoring production, *Organization*, 20(4): 551–576.

Scott, W. R. 2001. *Institutions and Organizations*. Sage Publications.

Sheperd, D. A. and Zacharakis, A. 2003. A new venture's cognitive legitimacy: An assessment by customers, *Journal of Small Business Management*, 41(2): 148–167.

Singly, F. de 2005. La place du genre dans l'identité personnelle. In Maruani, M. (dir). *Femmes, Genre et Sociétés: l'Etat des Savoirs*, Editions La Découverte, pp. 48–51.

Taboada-Leonetti, I. 1990. Stratégies identitaires et minorités: Le point de vue sociologique. In *Stratégies Identitaires*. Presses Universitaires De France, pp. 43–83.

Tajfel, H. 1972. La catégorisation sociale. In Moscovici, S. (ed) *Introduction à la Psychologie Sociale*, Editions Larousse, pp. 272–302.

Tajfel, H. 1981. *Human Groups and Social Categories*. Cambridge: Cambridge University Press.

Tajfel, H. and Turner, J. C. 1979. An integrative theory of intergroup conflict. In Worchel, S. and Austin, W. (eds) *The Social Psychology of Intergroup Relations*. CA/Brooks,/Cole, pp. 33–48.

Théry, I. 2007. *La distinction de Sexe: Une Nouvelle Approche de l'Egalité*. Editions Odile Jacob.

Théry, I. 2011. *Qu'est-ce la Distinction de Sexe?* Editions Fabert.

Turner, J. 1995. Autocatégorisation et influence sociale. In Mugny, G., Oberlé, D. and Beauvois, J.-L. (dir.), *Relations Humaines, Groupes et Influence Sociale*, Presses Universitaires Grenoble., pp. 210–213.

Turner, J. 1999. Some current issues in research on societal identity and self-categorization theories. In Ellemers, N., Spears, R., and Doosje, B. (eds), *Social Identity: Context, Commitment, Content*. Blackwell Publishers, pp. 6–34.

Turner, J., Hogg, M. A., Oakes, P. J., Reicher, S. and Wetherell, M. S. 1987. *Rediscovering the Social Group: A Self-Categorization Theory*. Oxford: Basil Blackwell.

Turner, J. C. 1985. Social categorization and the self-concept: A social-cognitive theory of group behavior. In Thye, S. R., and Lawler, E. J. (eds) *Advances in Group Processes: Theory and Research*, CT: JAI Press, pp. 77–122.

Vergne, J.-P. 2011. Toward a new measure of organizational legitimacy: Method, validation, and illustration, *Organizational Research Method*, 14(3): 484–502.

Watson, J. and Newby, R. 2005. Biological sex, stereotypical sex-roles, and SME owner characteristics, *International Journal of Entrepreneurial Behavior & Research*, 11(2): 129–143.

Weber, M. 1995. *Economie et Société*, Editions Agora.

West, C. and Zimmerman, D. 1987. Doing gender, *Gender and Society*, 1(2): 125–151.

Williams, D. R. 2012. Gender discrimination and self-employment dynamics in Europe, *The Journal of Socio-Economics*, 41(2): 153–158.

Zelditch, M. Jr. 2001. Theories of Legitimacy. In Jost, J. T. and Major, B. (ed.), *The Psychology of Legitimacy: Emerging Perspective on Ideology, Justice, and Intergroup Relations*, Cambridge University Press, pp. 33–53.

Zimmerman, M. and Zeitz, G. J. 2002. Beyond survival: Achieving new venture growth by building legitimacy. *Academy of Management Review*, 27(3): 414–431.

PART V

Demography

19

WOMEN, DISABILITY, AND ENTREPRENEURSHIP

Kate Caldwell, Sarah Parker Harris, and Maija Renko

Introduction

Within a global context, entrepreneurship for people with disabilities differs significantly among regions, depending upon international and national policy efforts. In the UK the advancement of the 'Learning Society' has led to the promotion of developing entrepreneurial skills in education, but not necessarily materially supporting small business development (Pavey, 2006). The history of disability and institutionalization is distinct in many European countries, where an entire generation was lost to the Eugenic influences of the second World War (Mitchell & Snyder, 2003). This has been reflected in their employment programs, which vary substantially: from truly innovative approaches to inclusion to regressive approaches that further segregate people with disabilities. While rates of people with disabilities in self-employment vary widely among Member States within the European Union, community integration has been a strong mandate in current policy that indirectly supports entrepreneurship as a strategy under the broader umbrella of participation in employment (Halabisky, 2014). In developing countries, entrepreneurship has been used as an anti-poverty strategy to help individuals with disabilities and communities in remote regions (van Niekerk, Lorenzo, & Mdlokolo, 2006). Given that Article 27 of the United Nations Convention on the Rights of Persons with Disabilities (UNCRPD) explicitly identifies self-employment and entrepreneurship as a right, it is expected that there will be continued growth in this area across the world. However, it is unclear how change might be implemented or evaluated on an international scale. For example, in India there has been some controversy surrounding the implementation of micro-enterprise programs that are intended to support entrepreneurship but instead promote a neoliberal agenda that further disadvantages people with disabilities (Chaudhry, 2012). However, such claims demand further research, especially as pertaining to gender.

There is a long history of entrepreneurship in the United States. It is ingrained in the very social fabric of the American Dream, epitomized through the work ethic in the classic Horatio Alger myth of 'rags to riches' that tells us hard work will lead to success (Sarachek, 1978). Indeed, entrepreneurship has been used as a strategy to help marginalized and disadvantaged populations, such as women, immigrants, and ethnic minorities, enter the labor market. However, entrepreneurship for people with disabilities is still a nascent topic in research, policy, and practice (Parker Harris, Caldwell, & Renko, 2014, 2013; Renko, Parker Harris, & Caldwell, 2015) – especially for women with disabilities. Women-owned firms represent an increasingly important segment of new businesses. In the United States, 40 percent of all privately held firms are owned by women at 50 percent or more (Center for Women's Business Research, 2009). Still, women-owned firms underperform firms owned by men in assets, revenue, income, and profits (Robb & Coleman, 2009). Women entrepreneurs are disadvantaged relative to men due to overt discrimination and to systemic factors that deprive them of vital resources, such as startup capital, relevant education and experience, or legal resources (Fischer, Reuber, & Dyke, 1993). This chapter will discuss similar barriers preventing people with disabilities from participating in entrepreneurship and additional barriers further compounded by the challenges faced when starting and running a business as a woman with a disability. Approximately 56.7 million people (18.7%) of the civilian non-institutionalized United States population age 16 to 64 have a disability (Brault, 2012). Yet we know little about the experience of entrepreneurship in this group of people and women specifically. We will also survey the literature and policy on disability and entrepreneurship; offering an overview of current debates, critiques, and controversies surrounding entrepreneurship for people with disabilities; and finally centering gender within the broader context of disability and business research.

Definitions of disability

There are many ways that 'disability' has been defined. Disability studies scholars have challenged reductionist approaches where disability has been defined using deficiency models, often referred to as the medical model. The medical model posits that disability is a deficit or problem within the individual that needs to either be fixed or eradicated (Oliver, 1990) and historically has been used as a rationale in segregating and disadvantaging people with disabilities (Carey, 2003; Llewellyn & Hogan, 2000; Longmore & Umansky, 2001). One of the most commonly used definitions is found in the Americans with Disabilities Act (ADA) that defines disability, with respect to an individual, as a physical or mental impairment that substantially limits one or more major life activities. In a parallel move away from deficit models of disability, the World Health Organization developed the International Classification of Functioning, Disability and Health (WHO-ICF). The WHO-ICF recognizes disability as a contextual variable that is affected by social and environmental factors. These definitions are informed by what is known as the social model of disability, which argues that disability is not inherent in the person, but rather it is society's inability to meet the individual's needs that is disabling. The social model focuses on the systemic, socially constructed barriers and restrictions that people with impairments face and thereby removes blame from the individual, transferring it to society (Oliver, 1996). The social model of disability has proven politically effective because it provides a material and concrete solution for addressing discrimination by removing barriers to social and economic participation. The politicization of people with disabilities in the U.S. has also contributed to the prominence of a minority model of disability; a rights-based approach recognizing people with disabilities as a minority group analogous to other disadvantaged populations (Hahn, 1985). Similar to other minorities, the cultural exclusion of people with disabilities has manifested through societal prejudice and discriminatory practices.

Within the context of entrepreneurship, it is important to recognize the extent of the marginalization and structural disadvantage currently facing people with disabilities

(Caldwell, Parker Harris, & Renko, 2012). On the one hand, the barriers facing people with disabilities' participation in the labor market often serve as powerful motivation for pursuing entrepreneurship, such as discrimination in hiring, salary, and promotion. On the other hand, people with disabilities continue to encounter considerable barriers as they pursue entrepreneurship (Parker Harris et al., 2013; Parker Harris, Renko, & Caldwell, 2014; Renko et al., 2015).

Understanding the context of disability

In the U.S., people with disabilities have a long history of oppression and segregation that continues today and is represented in their exclusion from employment on a structural and cultural level. Structurally, the category of disability has been defined, as modern industrialized society progressed, by excluding individuals seen as being limited in the kind or amount of work they did and thereby equating disability with unemployability itself (Hahn, 1985; Oliver, 1990). In this way, both the social organization of work and the economic operation of the labor market contribute to hegemonic conceptions of disability that marginalize and disadvantage people with impairments, impeding their ability to participate in the labor force, and having little to do with the functional limitations of the individuals themselves (Barnes, 2000). For example, following the two World Wars, Vocational Rehabilitation (VR) centers were created to provide a charitable service for veterans disabled during the wars as people with disabilities were commonly seen as incapable of entering the paid labor market (Scotch, 2001).

Within our contemporary political economy, people with disabilities have been included but as an excludable type (Titchkosky, 2003). The economic exclusion of people with disabilities is derived from having value attributed to an individual's productivity. Within an economic model, disability is defined by one's ability to work, and value is attributed to those individuals with disabilities who are 'able' to work and whose productivity is tied to their participation in society. Critique of an economic approach to disability, one that measures value in terms of participation in the workforce, permeates theoretical discourse on the political economy and the position of people with disabilities in it. However, such an approach does not appreciate mitigating factors affecting one's ability to participate and the barriers to participation (Parker Harris et al., 2013).

Much of the literature on employment and disability emphasizes the significance of social and attitudinal barriers (Blanck, 2000; Livermore & Goodman, 2009; Stapleton & Burkhauser, 2003; Wilson-Kovacs, Ryan, Haslam, & Rabinovich, 2008). In general, people with disabilities experience significant barriers in employment that include accessing employment training, finding employment that matches their skills and abilities, and maintaining employment in a difficult job market (Livermore & Goodman, 2009; National Council on Disability, 2011). Barriers affect not just being able to find or retain employment, but also job choice. Issues regarding transportation, health concerns, and financial disincentives limit one's options for productive engagement and may also limit the number of hours spent participating in work (Lysaght, Ouellette-Kuntz, & Morrison, 2009). The National Council on Disability (2007) highlighted several key barriers and challenges that range from the extra costs of work to the need for increased flexibility, the need for accommodations, the lack of information coupled with lower levels of education and training as well as concerns regarding disability income and healthcare, employer discrimination and reluctance to hire people with disabilities. The fear of loss of services that are provided through necessary benefit programs, such as Medicaid, Medicare, or veteran's disability payments, poses a significant disincentive to people with disabilities' participating in competitive or gainful employment (National Council on Disability, 2011). Entrepreneurship can offer a meaningful way for people with disabilities to participate in the labor market and complement existing strategies in competitive and customized employment to promote choice and self-determination.

Stigma and discrimination limit opportunities for workers with disabilities. In fact, disability discrimination claims filed with the Equal Employment Opportunity Commission (EEOC) increased by 17 percent in 2010, evidencing the highest volume of claims in its 45-year history (National Council on Disability, 2011). Indeed, hiring discrimination and other forms of job discrimination play a key role in the justification for pursuing self-employment and entrepreneurship. People with disabilities, and women in particular, encounter both a glass ceiling and a glass cliff effect (Braddock & Bachelder, 1994; Wilson-Kovacs et al., 2008). Due to discrimination in advancement and promotion, it can be difficult to attain leadership or management positions. Further, those that are successful in filling leadership roles find them to be precarious positions that are difficult to retain. Antidiscrimination legislation such as the Americans with Disabilities Act (ADA) and the ADA Amendments Act of 2008 have contributed to reducing some of the barriers impeding the participation in the labor force of people with disabilities. Since the passage of the ADA, more people with disabilities are choosing to pursue small business and self-employment opportunities (Blanck, Sandler, Schmeling, & Schartz, 2000). This makes sense given that for people with disabilities who want to work, but who cannot find full-time or part-time work that pays a living wage, entrepreneurship holds potential to create a customized job that meets not only their interests but also any need for accommodation they may have in terms of assistive technology, transportation, flexible work schedules, or personal assistance. Considerable efforts, in both programs and policy, have been spent on establishing that people with disabilities are interested in becoming entrepreneurs, and that it can be a viable employment strategy (please see Parker Harris, Caldwell, et al., 2014). However, little research has examined how people are actually participating in entrepreneurship, what barriers they experience, and what their current needs are.

Current debates, critiques, and controversies

Over the past two decades, entrepreneurship has been promoted as a strategy for addressing the prevalence of unemployment and underemployment among people with disabilities (Blanck et al., 2000; Lind, 2000; Office of Disability Employment Policy, 2005). However, it wasn't until the Choice Access Project that researchers and policymakers alike recognized that people with disabilities had an interest in entrepreneurship (Arnold & Ipsen, 2005; Callahan, Shumpert, & Mast, 2002). The Choice Access Project was a demonstration grant looking at consumer-driven employment services. Originally, self-employment and entrepreneurship were not included as possible options for people with disabilities using "choice" services because researchers did not anticipate there would be a demand. However, the researchers soon found that not only was there an interest in these services, but that it was surprisingly high at 21 percent of program participants who chose self-employment and entrepreneurship.

A systematic literature review and policy analysis revealed that there are seven main benefits and barriers specific to entrepreneurship for people with disabilities (Parker Harris, Caldwell, et al., 2014). It is interesting to note how the lists mirror each other, where each benefit correlates directly to a barrier that needs to be ameliorated. The stated benefits include: 1) participation in the mainstream economy; 2) promotion of economic growth; 3) promotion of attitudinal change; 4) improved quality of life; 5) independence, autonomy, and empowerment; 6) accommodations and flexibility; and 7) integration and social participation. It is important to note that this analysis reflects the 'stated benefits' one hopes to achieve through entrepreneurship, and not those found through empirical research. Rather, research, policy, and practice have focused instead on identifying the barriers. The main barriers to entrepreneurship include: 1) the lack of centrally reported data; 2) financial and economic barriers; 3) attitudinal barriers; 4) the traditional-expectations barrier; 5) the low-readiness barrier, which is affected by a) access to education, training, and technical assistance, b) access to business development services, and c) individual characteristics; 6) systemic barriers, which consists of a) programmatic barriers, b) public services and assistance, and c) technological barriers; and finally 7) social support barriers. Future research should focus on the extent to which entrepreneurship as an employment strategy for people with disabilities leads to achieving these benefits.

Similar to people with disabilities, women's less-frequent engagement in entrepreneurship has often been attributed to structural barriers (N. M. Carter & Williams, 2003; Fischer et al., 1993). Women may, for example, have access to fewer financial resources and less industry-specific work experience than men do (N. M. Carter, Williams, & Reynolds, 1997). In addition, women may face difficulties in finding business partners and accessing networks (Ruef, Aldrich, & Carter, 2003). Understanding this phenomenon is particularly important as, even when significant differences do not appear to manifest in the eventual, absolute start-up capital or mentoring resources available to male and female entrepreneurs, women continue to face more difficulties than men in gaining access to each of these resources.

There has yet to be a generative discussion about what additional, distinct barriers women entrepreneurs with disabilities may be facing, in particular, whether and to what extent they differ from the general population and from men with disabilities. Currently, it is unknown if women with disabilities are treated differently when seeking disability and/or business services. Further, it is unknown how normative, gendered expectations influence women with disabilities pursuing entrepreneurship. On the one hand, it likely poses a barrier in and of itself. On the other hand, it could likely serve as strong motivation for pursuing entrepreneurship as women with disabilities are often seen as deviating from or not conforming to ableist norms. If the latter were true, we would expect to see more women with disabilities engaged in entrepreneurship. However, it is important to unpack the ways in which the former constricts their participation both materially and structurally.

Material concerns and access to resources

Three main material concerns face policymakers, service providers, and entrepreneurs with disabilities themselves (Parker Harris et al., 2013):

1 Education, training, and informational needs
2 Finance, funding, and asset development needs
3 Networking and support needs

One of the largest barriers inhibiting both business start-up and growth is access to adequate and appropriate education, training, and information. Disability is an important aspect of the social environment. The very context of disability influences access to resources that nascent entrepreneurs invest in their businesses and the outcomes of the start-up process (Renko et al., 2015). The same barriers that people with disabilities encounter seeking salaried employment (Barnes & Mercer, 2005; Shier, Graham, & Jones, 2009) appear to be similarly inhibiting their start-up efforts, in particular, with regards to educational levels, financial resources, and social support structures (Renko et al., 2015). In general, there is need for better policy and benefits education for people with disabilities, but even more so in regards to how it interacts with entrepreneurship. Corresponding to barriers encountered in finance, funding, and asset development, there is a need for greater financial literacy and education. Existing programs in this area within the disability community are not specific to business development, and existing programs for entrepreneurs do not address the overwhelming need for benefits planning in managing both personal and business finances.

Networking and supports need to be addressed on two levels, both formal and informal networks and supports. Formal networks include agencies providing employment services to people with disabilities, such as VR, and providing services to entrepreneurs, such as small business development centers (SBDC). However, concern exists regarding VR's and SBDCs' ability to provide adequate and appropriate services where the two intersect – to support entrepreneurs with disabilities. Formal networks and supports also include programs and organizations operating in this disability and/or business sector at the national, state, and local levels. However, research has found that many entrepreneurs with disabilities and service providers are unaware that many of these formal resources exist (see Appendix 3 in Parker Harris et al., 2013). Informal networks, such as family and friends, can often help entrepreneurs with disabilities compensate for support needs that are not being met through formal networks. More research is needed to understand whether and to what extent the use of informal networks differs for individuals with disabilities compared to the general population, particularly in light of the finding that people with disabilities have restricted social networks (Lippold & Burns, 2009; Renko et al., 2015) and that restricted social networks have been identified as a challenge to women and minorities in entrepreneurship (Ibarra, 1993). For example, Godwin, Stevens, and Brenner (2006) posited that if women partner with men to found ventures in male-dominated contexts (such as construction and information technology) they can reduce gender-based stereotypes and overcome obstacles in accessing resources and building legitimacy as entrepreneurs. However, doing so runs the risk of women entrepreneurs continuing to be marginalized and further perpetuates gender stereotypes for women in business.

The questions of what material concerns affect women with disabilities differently from the general population and from men with disabilities in entrepreneurship bear consideration. Do women with disabilities have the same access to business education or opportunities offered to them by schools and disability service providers to gain skills and training that would benefit them in starting a business? In starting a business, are there any additional financial constraints that affect women with disabilities disproportionately? This includes material concerns such as the cost of childcare in terms of both time and expenses, the marriage penalty facing people receiving public benefits, and the expenses associated with presenting a professional appearance, which may require the use of personal assistance services.

For example, Maria Town is an entrepreneur whose blog, CP Shoes,[1] began as a way of chronicling her experience wearing shoes as a young working professional with cerebral palsy and the expense that they incur. It has since received significant attention from other women with various disabilities who encounter similar frustrations at the intersection of fashion and disability in the working world and has grown into part of a larger network of individuals and organizations that are advocating for and developing creative solutions to the problems posed through these discussions.

Structural concerns and the political economy

The majority of the structural concerns that entrepreneurs with disabilities encounter speak to the position of disability in the political economy. Accordingly, structural concerns occur on three levels (Parker Harris, Renko, et al., 2014):

1   The role of government
2   The role of funding
3   The role of culture

In a disability context, the role of government is often seen as providing for equal access and opportunity for individuals who are discriminated against when seeking employment. Conversely, in the context of entrepreneurship, often a free market ideology is espoused that seeks to limit the government's interference in business. The importance of disability-entrepreneurship lay in recognizing that while such ideologies are constructed in policy silos, in praxis disability and entrepreneurship do and must co-exist. To serve the needs of entrepreneurs with disabilities, they must be interdependent and complementary structures that allow for individuals who rely upon public benefits and services for equal access and opportunity to have the same chance of succeeding or failing in entrepreneurship on their own merits rather than due to the position disability holds in society and the stigma attendant.

One of the largest barriers to entrepreneurship is access to capital during start-up and growth. In the current market, loans have become more difficult to acquire across the board. However, marginalized groups, such as women and immigrants, can be highly disadvantaged in starting a business due to disparities in asset accumulation and access to capital. However, unlike other marginalized groups, entrepreneurs with disabilities have disability-specific concerns that constitute funding barriers (Parker Harris, Renko, et al., 2014). For instance, not only is there a high level of income poverty among people with disabilities, but there is also a high level of asset poverty. This is due primarily to the asset limitations and disincentives to saving imposed upon individuals receiving public benefits, such as social security and Medicaid (Parker Harris, Caldwell, et al., 2014). Subsequently, asset limitations and the absence of savings or a credit history make it nearly impossible for entrepreneurs with disabilities to apply for a loan or for micro-financing.

Negative cultural stereotypes have been a dominant theme running throughout the existing research on disability-entrepreneurship, contributing to attitudinal barriers that impact the motivations and expectations people have about their own capabilities as well as the expectations others have of them (Caldwell, Parker Harris, & Renko, under review; Parker Harris, Renko, et al., 2014). For example, entrepreneurs with disabilities have spoken about the difficulty with not being taken seriously as businesspeople. An intense need has been expressed for mentorship by entrepreneurs with disabilities. There is a need for sharing stories of people with disabilities who have succeeded in entrepreneurship as well as stories of those who may not have succeeded, but have learned from their ventures in entrepreneurship so that others might learn from their experiences as well.

What structural concerns may be affecting women entrepreneurs with disabilities differently, given their position in the political economy, bears consideration. Do women with disabilities see the role of government differently from women who do not have disabilities or from men with disabilities? Are they treated differently by investors and lending institutions? While many women in business are worried about being perceived as weak or somehow burdensome, this stigma is even more pervasive for women with disabilities. Women with disabilities become caught in an unenviable position between the dogma of independence and the stigma of dependence. In recent years, the field of disability studies has recognized the value of interdependence, which counter-poses the need/desire to be independent and self-sufficient with the reality of relying upon a network of services and supports in order to actualize one's independence (Caldwell, 2014; Morris, 2004; Reindal, 1999).

For example, Patricia Hardy is an entrepreneur who had successful businesses in the past. However, due to serious health concerns she ended up having to live in a nursing home. She encountered significant structural barriers that prevented her from leaving as her health improved and she wanted to live independently again. Through working with the local Center for Independent Living (CIL) she was able to move out of the nursing home and get a job working for the CIL.[2] She is now looking forward to starting her new entrepreneurial venture: Educated, Motivated & Empowered (EME). Similarly, we spoke with a young woman from Michigan during our recruitment for research who found herself living in a nursing home, despite being in her early 20s. Through the assistance of a disability community agency that had obtained a microenterprise grant, she was able to start a coffee business and eventually made enough profit that she was able to move into a small apartment and live independently with her friends. She is now thinking about starting a new entrepreneurial venture for this new phase of her life. In both of these instances, the opportunity provided through disability community organizations led to these women tackling the structural disadvantage that had been disabling them to pursue entrepreneurship.

Disability-entrepreneurship: bridging the fields

There is a critical need to bridge disability studies with entrepreneurship studies to provide foundational knowledge, understanding, and insights into the state of the field. Current gaps in both disability and business fields need to be addressed in order for effective policy supporting entrepreneurship by people with disabilities to be formulated. These problems can be viewed from two distinct but complementary perspectives: entrepreneurship research and disability employment research. The integration of disability into the study of entrepreneurship is at its infancy. While a number of other contexts and specific demographics— most notably women (e.g., N. Carter, Brush, Greene, Gatewood, & Hart, 2003; Manolova, Carter, Manev, & Gyoshev, 2007) and immigrants (e.g., Bates, 1994; Robb & Fairlie, 2009; Sanders & Nee, 1996)—have been widely discussed in entrepreneurship research, disability has been largely overlooked. This is surprising given that a larger proportion of workers with disabilities are self-employed in the U.S. than those with no disability, at 11 percent versus 6 percent (Bureau of Labor Statistics, 2014). Further, there are indications that these statistics are under-reported (Parker Harris, Caldwell et al., 2014). If we are to develop effective employment policies and practices that harness the power of entrepreneurship for people with disabilities, we need to start with a closer integration of approaches to entrepreneurship and disability employment.

The limited opportunities in traditional employment for people with disabilities and the promise of increased flexibility that entrepreneurship offers are themselves powerful incentives to business ownership (Blanck et al., 2000). Entrepreneurs with disabilities represent a source of innovation and productivity, as they draw upon their experience with disadvantage and unmet need in their community in developing business ideas. If people with disabilities are offered adequate resources, entrepreneurship is an employment strategy that can lead to economic self-sufficiency and empowerment (Bichard, 2008; Lind, 2004; Office of Disability Employment Policy, 2007). Yet the entrepreneurial potential of any individual is determined not solely by one's own self-contained characteristics, but also by the economic, cultural, and institutional frameworks within which organizational emergence takes place (Parker Harris, Renko et al., 2014). Accordingly, entrepreneurs with disabilities need access to resources that address the social and environmental barriers they encounter in education and information, in finance and funding, and in social networking and mentorship (Parker Harris et al., 2013). Such resources are necessary to ensure that people with disabilities have equal opportunity to succeed or fail in entrepreneurship based on their own merits, not on the socio-cultural or political-economic disadvantage they experience (Parker Harris, Renko et al., 2014).

Bringing together disability and entrepreneurship advances theory, research, and policy in two important ways. First, the introduction of theories of entrepreneurial opportunity recognition to the field of disability studies prompts new thinking around the potential of the disability experience as a source of creative solutions. Entrepreneurial opportunity recognition involves addressing 'what do entrepreneurs do?' types of questions (Shane & Venkataraman, 2000; Venkatraman, 1997). An 'entrepreneurial opportunity' is an opportunity to bring new goods, services, raw materials, and organizing methods into existence, a process that occurs when an entrepreneur is alert to a mismatch between the value of resources and their best use (Casson, 1982; Shane, 2000). A common theme in much research on entrepreneurial opportunity recognition has been the suggestion that entrepreneurs' previous experiences and knowledge play a crucial role in the process. Many different perspectives and theories converge on the view that in order to identify opportunities, entrepreneurs must somehow gather, interpret, and apply information about specific industries, markets, government policies, and social contexts (Ardichvili, Cardozo, & Ray, 2003; Ozgen & Baron, 2007; Shane, 2003). Previous life experiences help individuals to 'connect the dots' between seemingly independent pieces of information; perceiving patterns that can constitute the basis for identifying specific entrepreneurial opportunities (Ozgen & Baron, 2007).

The experience of disability is often a powerful part of an individual's identity and culture (Gill, 1997). Such unique experiences and perspectives can provide a basis for particularly creative idea generation and opportunity perception. Further, if the appropriate resources and incentives are in place, these can combine into successful entrepreneurship. Indeed, previous entrepreneurship research often emphasizes the subjective, perceived nature of insights behind opportunity recognition (Klein, 2008). For example, McMullen and Shepherd (2006) argue that entrepreneurial decisions are based on *a priori* beliefs. These beliefs are shaped via information, experience, and deeper values, and these elements are further mixed to generate opportunity beliefs (McMullen & Shepherd, 2006). In the disability context, the role of personal experience among women with disabilities may be particularly influential.

The second area where bringing disability and entrepreneurship together advances knowledge is through the introduction of disability to the domain of entrepreneurship research, prompting the field to consider the embeddedness and context specificity of entrepreneurship (Renko et al., 2015). Traditionally, disability as context has been lacking from entrepreneurship literature, likely because the foundation of entrepreneurial theory is deeply rooted in economics (Shane, 2003). Considering context specificity and societal dimensions, entrepreneurship among people with disabilities needs to be analyzed and understood in its social context. Existing theories in entrepreneurship need to be expanded to incorporate explanations for the distinctiveness of entrepreneurship among people with disabilities, and women with disabilities in particular. For example, while the experience of living with a disability is distinct, it is important to understand the ways in which ableism has shaped inequality on the basis of gender, race, and ethnicity. Historically, stigmatized beliefs about disability have been used as justification for discrimination against not only people with disabilities, but other minority groups as well. Eugenics have been used to limit the rights and freedoms of individuals seen as deviating from the hegemonic societal norm. For women, this meant calling upon disability to justify unequal treatment by calling into question their physical, intellectual, and psychological capabilities (Baynton, 2001). Accordingly, scholars in entrepreneurship research must take care not to inadvertently reinforce ableism by focusing on proving their physical, intellectual, and psychological capabilities and thereby excluding women with disabilities who have impairments that make it impossible to meet those ideals.

One example can be found in the study of women's entrepreneurship where social feminist theory has been used to illuminate how women and men have different experiential backgrounds and different—but equally valid—ways of thinking, resulting from variation in socialization patterns. Previous entrepreneurship studies that have compared men and women on socialized traits and values are consistent with such a social feminist perspective (Fischer et al., 1993; Wilson, Kickul, & Marlino, 2007). In an example of social feminist approach, DeTienne and Chandler (2007) find that women and men utilize their unique stocks of human capital to identify entrepreneurial opportunities and use fundamentally different processes of opportunity identification. Here the context of disability can be used to further historicize and interpret existing findings. Moreover, future findings should consider how the development of social and human capital differs for women with disabilities, who experience educational and informational barriers and tend to have smaller and more restricted social networks (Parker Harris et al., 2013; Renko et al., 2015).

Gender in disability-entrepreneurship

There is a paucity of research investigating the role of gender and race in disability employment, not having advanced much since the 1980s. What progress has been made in this area in practice is not reflected in the literature. For example, findings as recent as 2002 equate lower-quality case closures in employment among women, in comparison to men, with women *wanting* lower-quality VR case closures. The authors argue that this finding is not the result of discrimination or gender inequality if women want to become a homemaker versus finding a job placement in competitive employment (Capella, 2002). In the absence of data that indicate the actual motivations of female job seekers using VR services, this interpretation of the findings speaks instead to our severe lack of knowledge about the experiences of women with disabilities in the workforce and the specific barriers they experience. What we do know is that in addition to having lower-quality closures, the quality of employment outcomes in VR decreases significantly with age (Capella, 2002). Further, White and Hispanic women tend to earn lower wages and are less likely to receive medical coverage provided by their employer than their male counterparts (Martin, 2010). Gender differences have also been found in discrimination claims filed with the EEOC. While women are less likely to report employment discrimination, when they do file it is primarily due to constructive discharge (i.e., resigning due to a hostile work environment), lack of reasonable accommodation, or harassment. Employment discrimination claims for men typically were due to hiring discrimination, layoff, and discharge (Lewis, Hurley, Lewis, & McMahon, 2014). Women with disabilities are using entrepreneurship and social entrepreneurship as a vehicle for economic and social participation, resisting ableist and normative assumptions about the employment capacity of women with disabilities, the roles that they hold, and the fields within which they work. Nevertheless, women have been largely under-represented in research on self-employment and entrepreneurship among people with disabilities. This phenomenon is illustrated in the seminal Iowa Entrepreneurs with Disabilities (EWD) study, which described the typical participant as a married, white male in his mid-40s with at least a high-school education and primarily orthopedic disabilities or neurological disorders (Blanck et al., 2000).The participants interviewed for the EWD study were overwhelmingly white (92.6%) and male (83.3%). Conversely, our research on social entrepreneurs with disabilities showed a striking difference in the demographic composition of participants (Parker Harris, Renko et al., 2014). The majority of social entrepreneurs with disabilities were minorities, with white participants accounting for only 44 percent, and over half were female (52%). Moreover, while the majority of male participants in the research was white (33%), the majority of female participants actually identified as black or African American (33%).

Although women are less likely to engage in entrepreneurial activity (Robb & Coleman, 2009), when they do participate they are more likely to pursue social entrepreneurship (Hechavarría, Ingram, Justo, & Terjesen, 2012) The same holds true for marginalized groups that have been excluded from the labor market (Williams, 2007), such as people with disabilities. This may partially explain why the majority of participants in our research on social entrepreneurship were women and/or minorities when in prior research on self-employment and entrepreneurship the majority of respondents were white and male.

All of the available evidence indicates that women with disabilities are interested in entrepreneurship and social entrepreneurship, and that they likely experience distinct material and structural barriers to entrepreneurship due to the confluence of gender and disability, which are not being addressed in current research, policy, or practices at the intersection of disability employment and entrepreneurship—speaking to the need for bridging these fields and centering gender within emerging discourse on disability-entrepreneurship.

Conclusions

We have expanded the discussion on gender differences in entrepreneurship to include the experience of disability, which impacts about 20 percent of all women (Brault, 2012). Both people with disabilities and women, independently, face barriers in accessing important startup resources, which affects their involvement in entrepreneurship. These resource barriers may be further heightened when the entrepreneur is a woman with a disability, as they are more likely to experience additional barriers in areas such as access to education, training, and networking. Coupled with systemic discrimination (e.g., constraints on asset development) and cultural discrimination (e.g., negative stereotypes about disability), women entrepreneurs are often limited in their opportunities for business start-up.

Despite these barriers, entrepreneurship remains an appealing option for many women with disabilities as it can offer an alternate pathway to enter the labor market and increase economic self-sufficiency. For people with disabilities, entrepreneurship offers a greater degree of flexibility, accommodation, and autonomy than traditional work arrangements. Further, self-employment circumvents discrimination in hiring and promotion, which has contributed to the problem of unemployment and underemployment for people with disabilities. However, it is critical to take into account disability difference when assessing the viability of entrepreneurship as an employment strategy. By bridging entrepreneurship research with contemporary advances in disability employment we could better support and increase economic and social opportunities for women with disabilities.

Notes

1 http://cpshoes.tumblr.com/.
2 http://www.oakpark.com/News/Articles/9-13-2005/Fighting-for-equal-rights/.

References

Ardichvili, A., Cardozo, R., & Ray, S. (2003). A Theory of Entrepreneurial Opportunity Identification and Development. *Journal of Business Venturing, 18*, 105–123.

Arnold, N. L., & Ipsen, C. (2005). Self-Employment Policies: Changes through the Decade. *Journal of Disability Policy Studies, 16*(2), 115–122. doi:10.1177/10442073050160020201.

Barnes, C. (2000). A Working Social Model? Disability, Work and Disability Politics in the 21st Century. *Critical Social Policy, 20*(4), 441–457. doi:10.1177/026101830002000402.

Barnes, C., & Mercer, G. (2005). Disability, Work, and Welfare: Challenging the Social Exclusion of Disabled People. *Work, Employment & Society, 19*(3), 527–545. doi:10.1177/0950017005055669.

Bates, T. (1994). Social Resources Generated by Group Support Networks May Not Be Beneficial to Asian Immigrant-Owned Small Businesses. *Social Forces, 72*, 671–689.

Baynton, D. C. (2001). Disability and the Justification of Inequality in American History. In P. K. Longmore & L. Umansky (Eds), *The New Disability History: American Perspectives* (pp. 33–57). New York, NY: New York University Press.

Bichard, E. (2008). *Wealth Bringers - The Sustainable Value of Disabled Entrepreneurs in England's Northwest.*

Blanck, P. (2000). *Employment, Disability, and the Americans with Disabilities Act: Issues in Law, Public Policy, and Research.* Evanston, IL: Northwestern University Press.

Blanck, P., Sandler, L. A., Schmeling, J. L., & Schartz, H. A. (2000). The Emerging Workforce of Entrepreneurs with Disabilities: Preliminary Study of Entrepreneurship in Iowa. *Iowa Law Review, 85*(5), 1583–1661. Retrieved from http://disability.law.uiowa.edu/lhpdc/publications/moreinfo/entrepIA.html.

Braddock, D., & Bachelder, L. (1994). *The Glass Ceiling and Persons with Disabilities.* Retrieved from Ithaca, NY: http://digitalcommons.ilr.cornell.edu/key_workplace/114/.

Brault, M. (2012). *Americans with Disabilities: 2010 Household Economic Studies.*

Bureau of Labor Statistics. (2014). *Persons with a Disability: Labor Force Characteristics Summary.* Retrieved from Washington, DC: http://www.bls.gov/news.release/disabl.nr0.htm.

Caldwell, K. (2014). Dyadic Interviewing: A Technique Valuing Interdependence in Interviews with Individuals with Intellectual Disabilities. *Qualitative Research, 14*(4), 488–507. doi:10.1177/1468794113490718.

Caldwell, K., Parker Harris, S., & Renko, M. (2012). The Potential of Social Entrepreneurship: Conceptual Tools for Applying Citizenship Theory to Policy and Practice. *Intellectual & Developmental Disabilities, 50*(6), 505–518. Retrieved from http://aaiddjournals.org/doi/abs/10.1352/1934-9556-50.06.505.

Caldwell, K., Parker Harris, S., & Renko, M. (under review). Social Entrepreneurs with Disabilities: Exploring Motivational and Attitudinal Factors. *Journal withheld.*

Callahan, M., Shumpert, N., & Mast, M. (2002). Self-Employment, Choice and Self-Determination. *Journal of Vocational Rehabilitation, 17*(2), 75–85. Retrieved from http://search.ebscohost.com/login.aspx?direct=true&db=aph&AN=6969772&site=ehost-live.

Capella, M. E. (2002). Inequities in the VR System: Do They Still Exist? *Rehabilitation Counseling Bulletin, 45*(3), 143–153. doi:10.1177/003435520204500303.

Carey, A. C. (2003). Beyond the Medical Model: A Reconsideration of 'Feeblemindedness', Citizenship, and Eugenic Restrictions. *Disability & Society, 18*(4), 411–430. doi:10.1080/0968759032000080977.

Carter, N., Brush, C., Greene, P., Gatewood, E., & Hart, M. (2003). Women Entrepreneurs Who Break Through to Equity Financing: The Influence of Human, Social and Financial Capital. *Venture Capital, 5*(1), 1–28.

Carter, N. M., & Williams, M. (2003). Comparing Social Feminism and Liberal Feminism. In J. E. Butler (Ed.), *New Perspectives on Women Entrepreneurs* (pp. 25–50). Charlotte, NC: Information Age Pub.

Carter, N. M., Williams, M., & Reynolds, P. D. (1997). Discontinuance among New Firms in Retail: The Influence of Initial Resources, Strategy, and Gender. *Journal of Business Venturing, 12*(2), 125–145. doi:http://dx.doi.org/10.1016/S0883-9026(96)00033-X.

Casson, M. (1982). *The Entrepreneur: An Economic Theory.* Totowa, NJ: Rowman & Littlefield.

Center for Women's Business Research. (2009). *The Economic Impact of Women-Owned Businesses in the United States.* Retrieved from McLean, Virginia.

Chaudhry, V. (2012). *Disability and Participatory Development in South India: Perils of Neoliberal Governance.* University of Illinois at Chicago.

DeTienne, D. R., & Chandler, G. N. (2007). The Role of Gender in Opportunity Identification. *Entrepreneurship Theory and Practice, 31*(3), 365–386. doi:10.1111/j.1540-6520.2007.00178.x.

Fischer, E. M., Reuber, A. R., & Dyke, L. S. (1993). A Theoretical Overview and Extension of Research on Sex, Gender, and Entrepreneurship. *Journal of Business Venturing, 8*(2), 151–168. doi:http://dx.doi.org/10.1016/0883-9026(93)90017-Y.

Gill, C. J. (1997). Four Types of Integration in Disability Identity Development. *Journal of Vocational Rehabilitation, 9*(1), 39–46. doi:10.1016/S1052-2263(97)00020-2.

Godwin, L. N., Stevens, C. E., & Brenner, N. L. (2006). Forced to Play by the Rules? Theorizing How Mixed-Sex Founding Teams Benefit Women Entrepreneurs in Male-Dominated Contexts. *Entrepreneurship Theory and Practice, 30*(5), 623–642. doi:10.1111/j.1540-6520.2006.00139.x.

Hahn, H. (1985). Towards a Politics of Disability: Definitions, Disciplines and Policies. *The Social Science Journal, 22*(4), 87–105.

Halabisky, D. (2014). *Entrepreneurial Activities in Europe - Entrepreneurship for People with Disabilities* (Vol. 6). Paris, France: OECD Publishing.

Hechavarría, D. M., Ingram, A., Justo, R., & Terjesen, S. (2012). Are Women More Likely to Pursue Social and Environmental Entrepreneurship? In K. D. Hughes & J. E. Jennings (Eds), *Global Women's Entrepreneurship Research: Diverse Settings, Questions, and Approaches* (pp. 135–151). Northampton, MA: Edward Elgar Publishing Limited.

Ibarra, H. (1993). Personal Networks of Women and Minorities in Management: A Conceptual Framework. *The Academy of Management Review, 18*(1), 56–87. doi:10.2307/258823.

Klein, P. G. (2008). Opportunity Discovery, Entrepreneurial Action, and Economic Organization. *Strategic Entrepreneurship Journal, 2*, 175–190.

Lewis, A. N., Hurley, J. E., Lewis, P., & McMahon, B. T. (2014). Gender, Disability, and ADA Title I Employment Discrimination: A Comparison of Male and Female Charging Party Characteristics: The National EEOC ADA Research Project. *The Review of Disability Studies: An International Journal, 7*(1). Retrieved from http://www.rds.hawaii.edu/ojs/index.php/journal/article/view/141.

Lind, P. (2000). *Getting Down to Business: A Blueprint for Creating & Supporting Entrepreneurial Opportunities for Individuals with Disabilities.* Retrieved from Washington, DC.

Lind, P. (2004). Self-Employment: Another Road to Self-Sufficiency for People with Disabilities. *Equity e-Newsletter, May.* http://www.wid.org/programs/access-to-assets/equity/equity-e-newsletter-may-2004/self-employment-another-road-to-self-sufficiency-for-people-with-disabilities/?searchterm=entrepreneur Retrieved from http://www.wid.org/programs/access-to-assets/equity/equity-e-newsletter-may-2004/self-employment-another-road-to-self-sufficiency-for-people-with-disabilities/?searchterm=entrepreneur.

Lippold, T., & Burns, J. (2009). Social Support and Intellectual Disabilities: A Comparison between Social Networks of Adults with Intellectual Disability and Those with Physical Disability. *Journal of Intellectual Disability Research, 53*(5), 463–473. doi:10.1111/j.1365-2788.2009.01170.x.

Livermore, G. A., & Goodman, N. (2009). *A Review of Recent Evaluation Efforts Associated with Programs and Policies Designed to Promote the Employment of Adults with Disabilities.* Retrieved from Ithaca, NY.

Llewellyn, A., & Hogan, K. (2000). The Use and Abuse of Models of Disability. *Disability & Society, 15*(1), 157–165. Retrieved from http://www.informaworld.com/10.1080/09687590025829.

Longmore, P. K., & Umansky, L. (2001). *The New Disability History: American Perspectives.* New York, NY: New York University Press.

Lysaght, R., Ouellette-Kuntz, H., & Morrison, C. (2009). Meaning and Value of Productivity to Adults with Intellectual Disabilities. *Intellect Dev Disabil*, 47(6), 413–424.

Manolova, T. S., Carter, N. M., Manev, I. M., & Gyoshev, B. S. (2007). The Differential Effect of Men and Women Entrepreneurs' Human Capital and Networking on Growth Expectancies in Bulgaria. *Entrepreneurship Theory and Practice*, 31(3), 407.

Martin, F. H. (2010). Racial Variation in Vocational Rehabilitation Outcomes: A Structural Equation Modeling Approach. *Rehabilitation Counseling Bulletin*, 54(1), 26–35. doi:10.1177/0034355209360420.

McMullen, J. S., & Shepherd, D. A. (2006). Entrepreneurial Action and the Role of Uncertainty in the Theory of the Entrepreneur. *Academy of Management Review*, 31(1), 132–152.

Mitchell, D., & Snyder, S. (2003). The Eugenic Atlantic: Race, Disability, and the Making of an International Eugenic Science, 1800–1945. *Disability & Society*, 18(7), 843–864. doi:10.1080/0968759032000127281.

Morris, J. (2004). Independent Living and Community Care: A Disempowering Framework. *Disability & Society*, 19(5), 427–442. Retrieved from http://www.informaworld.com/10.1080/0968759042000235280.

National Council on Disability (2007). *Empowerment for Americans with Disabilities: Breaking Barriers to Careers and Full Employment*. Retrieved from Washington, DC.

National Council on Disability. (2011). *National Disability Policy: A Progress Report*. Retrieved from Washington, DC.

Office of Disability Employment Policy. (2005). Entrepreneurship: A Flexible Route to Economic Independence for People with Disabilities. Retrieved from http://www.dol.gov/odep/pubs/misc/entrepre.htm.

Office of Disability Employment Policy. (2007). Entrepreneurship for Youth with Disabilities. Retrieved from http://www.ldonline.org/article/Entrepreneurship_for_Youth_with_Disabilities.

Oliver, M. (1990). *The Politics of Disablement*. New York, NY: Macmillan Education.

Oliver, M. (1996). The Social Model in Context. In M. Oliver (Ed.), *Understanding Disability: From Theory to Practice* (pp. 30–41). New York, NY: St. Martin's Press.

Ozgen, E., & Baron, R. A. (2007). Social Sources of Information in Opportunity Recognition: Effects of Mentors, Industry Networks, and Professional Forums. *Journal of Business Venturing*, 22(2), 174–192. doi:10.1016/j.jbusvent.2005.12.001.

Parker Harris, S., Caldwell, K., & Renko, M. (2014). Entrepreneurship by Any Other Name: Self-Sufficiency versus Innovation. *Journal of Social Work in Disability & Rehabilitation*, 13(4), 1–33.

Parker Harris, S., Renko, M., & Caldwell, K. (2013). Accessing Social Entrepreneurship: Perspectives of People with Disabilities and Key Stakeholders. *Vocational Rehabilitation*, 38, 35–48.

Parker Harris, S., Renko, M., & Caldwell, K. (2014). Social Entrepreneurship as an Employment Pathway for People with Disabilities: Exploring Political-Economic and Socio-Cultural Factors. *Disability & Society*, 29(8), 1275–1290. doi:10.1080/09687599.2014.924904.

Pavey, B. (2006). Human Capital, Social Capital, Entrepreneurship and Disability: An Examination of Some Current Educational Trends in the UK. *Disability & Society*, 21(3), 217–229. doi:10.1080/09687590600617337.

Reindal, S. M. (1999). Independence, Dependence, Interdependence: Some Reflections on the Subject and Personal Autonomy. *Disability & Society*, 14(3), 353–367. Retrieved from http://www.informaworld.com/10.1080/09687599926190.

Renko, M., Parker Harris, S., & Caldwell, K. (2015). Entrepreneurial Entry by People with Disabilities. *International Small Business Journal*. doi:10.1177/0266242615579112.

Robb, A., & Coleman, S. (2009). *Characteristics of New Firms: A Comparison by Gender*. Retrieved from http://ssrn.com/abstract=1352601.

Robb, A., & Fairlie, R. (2009). Determinants of Business Success: An Examination of Asian-Owned Businesses in the USA. *Journal of Population Economics*, 22(4), 827–858. doi:10.1007/s00148-008-0193-8.

Ruef, M., Aldrich, H. E., & Carter, N. M. (2003). The Structure of Founding Teams: Homophily, Strong Ties, and Isolation among U.S. Entrepreneurs. *American Sociological Review*, 68(2), 195–222. doi:10.2307/1519766.

Sanders, J. M., & Nee, V. (1996). Immigrant Self-Employment: The Family As Social Capital and the Value of Human Capital. *American Sociological Review*, 61(2), 231–249.

Sarachek, B. (1978). American Entrepreneurs and the Horatio Alger Myth. *The Journal of Economic History*, 38(2), 439–456. Retrieved from http://www.jstor.org/stable/2119834.

Scotch, R. K. (2001). *From Good Will to Civil Rights: Transforming Federal Disability Policy* (2nd ed.). Philadelphia, PA: Temple University Press.

Shane, S. (2000). Prior Knowledge and the Discovery of Entrepreneurial Opportunities. *Organization Science, 11*(4), 448–469. Retrieved from http://www.jstor.org/stable/2640414.

Shane, S. (2003). *A General Theory of Entrepreneurship: The Individual-Opportunity Nexus.* Cheltenham, UK; Northampton, MA: Edward Elgar.

Shane, S., & Venkataraman, S. (2000). The Promise of Enterpreneurship as a Field of Research. *The Academy of Management Review, 25*(1), 217–226. Retrieved from http://www.jstor.org/stable/259271.

Shier, M., Graham, J. R., & Jones, M. E. (2009). Barriers to Employment as Experienced by Disabled People: A Qualitative Analysis in Calgary and Regina, Canada. *Disability & Society, 24*(1), 63–75. doi:10.1080/09687590802535485.

Stapleton, D. C., & Burkhauser, R. V. (2003). *The Decline in Employment of People with Disabilities: A Policy Puzzle.* Kalamazoo, MI: W.E. Upjohn Institute for Employment Research.

Titchkosky, T. (2003). Governing Embodiment: Technologies of Constituting Citizens with Disabilities. *The Canadian Journal of Sociology / Cahiers canadiens de sociologie, 28*(4), 517–542. Retrieved from http://www.jstor.org/stable/3341840.

van Niekerk, L., Lorenzo, T., & Mdlokolo, P. (2006). Understanding Partnerships in Developing Disabled Entrepreneurs through Participatory Action Research. *Disability & Rehabilitation, 28*(5), 323–331. doi:10.1080/09638280500166425.

Venkatraman, S. (1997). The Distinctive Domain of Entrepreneurship Research. *Advances in Entrepreneurship, Firm Emergence and Growth, 3*, 119–138.

Williams, C. C. (2007). Socio-Spatial Variations in the Nature of Entrepreneurship. *Journal of Enterprising Communities, 1*(1), 27–37. doi:10.1108/17506200710736249.

Wilson, F., Kickul, J., & Marlino, D. (2007). Gender, Entrepreneurial Self-Efficacy, and Entrepreneurial Career Intentions: Implications for Entrepreneurship Education. *Entrepreneurship Theory and Practice, 31*(3), 387–406. doi:10.1111/j.1540-6520.2007.00179.x.

Wilson-Kovacs, D., Ryan, M. K., Haslam, S. A., & Rabinovich, A. (2008). 'Just Because You Can Get a Wheelchair in the Building Doesn't Necessarily Mean that You Can Still Participate': Barriers to the Career Advancement of Disabled Professionals. *Disability & Society, 23*(7), 705–717. doi:10.1080/09687590802469198.

20

FEMALE IMMIGRANT GLOBAL ENTREPRENEURSHIP

From invisibility to empowerment?

María Villares-Varela, Monder Ram and Trevor Jones

Introduction

Contrary to the tide of popular anti-immigration sentiment currently washing over much of the destination countries in the global North (Lesińska, 2014) and global South (Banda and Mawadza, 2014; Whitaker and Giersch, 2015), a dispassionate consideration of the relevant evidence suggests that immigrants make a positive socio-economic contribution to their destination countries, not least by introducing demographic and cultural diversity (Sepulveda et al., 2011). As well as their vital contribution as workers in essential but often unpopular sectors of the economy (Virdee, 2014), such as cleaning, care work, catering or construction, they are also playing a growing role as business owners. In the UK it is estimated that one in seven new start-ups are owned by immigrants[1] (Duedil, 2014), part of a wider trend in which "entrepreneurship by immigrants is increasingly important to Western capitalist societies" (Low and Collins, 2007, 16). With regard to the gender distribution of these migrant entrepreneurs, this same report (Duedil, 2014) shows that a lower proportion of migrant women start businesses compared to British women (25.9% and 29.1% respectively); however, there are exceptional nationalities where migrant women entrepreneurs actually outnumber men (for example, Thai, Filipino and Vietnamese women entrepreneurs). Moreover, the proportion of female entrepreneurs is higher than that of the British-born among over 60 nationalities, including Zimbabwean, Singaporean, Chinese, Russian or Brazilian (ibid). This significant presence of migrant women entrepreneurs challenges the standard image of dependency on men and labour market subordination (Morokvasic, 1999).

While recognising the key role of migrant women in starting up new businesses, we also need to highlight their hitherto largely hidden role in supporting businesses formally owned by their husbands, fathers or brothers. We have argued elsewhere (Ram et al., 2001), that despite the lower acknowledged number of women migrants running businesses, in reality women tend to be a key part of the entrepreneurial projects owned by men. This is not a unique feature of immigrant entrepreneurship (for an extended review of role of women in family firms, see Martinez Jimenez, 2009). However, the reliance on family for the survival of the business is a more common strategy for migrant owners, given that the competitive advantage of these businesses is based on intensive use of workforce. These household-entrepreneurial strategies and negotiations involving women as key contributors to the business activity are shaped by gendered practices.[2]

Women represent almost half of the international migrants in the world (48%) (UN-OECD, 2013), and in the period 1960 to 2000 there has been a moderate shift in gender ratios from 46.6% to 48.8% (Zlotnik, 2005). This has been interpreted as the indicator of a growing feminisation of migration flows as part of a distinctive new age of migration (Castles and Miller, 1998). Early research tended to represent women as dependent on their husbands or parents (Morokvasic, 1984) thus underplaying their individual trajectories and significant contributions to the economic sphere. Research on female immigrant entrepreneurship has followed a similar path to that on women and migration (Hondagnou-Sotelo, 2003): from a first stage of invisibility, unduly emphasising the *culturalization* and victimisation of the business experience, to an eventual recognition of enterprise as a means of female empowerment (Apistzch and Kontos, 2003; Baycan et al., 2003; Morokvasic, 1999). We argue that the main theoretical approaches to immigrant entrepreneurship – middleman minorities (Bonacich, 1973), interactive models (Aldrich and Waldinger, 1990), mixed embeddedness (Kloosterman et al., 1999) – have overlooked the gendered social structures that constitute migrant entrepreneurial processes. Feminist scholarship has condemned the 'gender-blindness' of the field of immigrant entrepreneurship and its failure to explore the implications of patriarchy[3] (Phizacklea, 1998; Westwood, 1988; Morokvasic, 1991; Josephides, 1988; Dhaliwal, 1998; Hillman, 1999). Some of the most prominent entrepreneurial minorities in the advanced world (such as South Asian, Korean or Hispanic immigrants) are rooted in traditionalist societies where patriarchy holds sway. Here we note that from the very outset of research on South Asian businesses in Britain, researchers were struck by the near absence of officially recognised female owners (Aldrich et al., 1981).

Questioning this 'gender-blindness', subsequent exploration of the distinctive roles of immigrant men and women in self-employment has noted the blurring of divisions between the productive and reproductive spheres as well as a widespread lack of recognition of women's entrepreneurial contribution to immigrant businesses (Anthias and Mehta, 2003; Baycan et al., 2003; Hillman, 1999; Westwood, 1988). Progressive though they may be, these moves to bring women to the research agenda run the risk of constructing women as passive rather than active agents (Song, 1995; Morokvasic, 1999). Aware of this danger, other accounts have highlighted the nuanced nature of women's ostensible compliance in subordinate business roles (Anthias, 1992; Essers et al., 2013). There is also a growing strand of research on business ownership as a means of female empowerment, in which social mobility can be achieved on women's own terms (Morokvasic, 1999).

In this chapter, we also aim to broaden the geographical scope of a literature overwhelmingly located within the advanced urban realm of North America and North-Western Europe. Accordingly, we consider female immigrant enterprise in the Mediterranean (Lazaridis, 2003; Oso et al., 2004; Ribas and Villares-Varela, 2012), South Africa (Halkias and Anakst, 2004), India (Goel et al., 2010) and Argentina (Cha et al., 2010), spreading our gaze to fresh contributions and themes from emerging migrant destinations.

Thus, this chapter reviews the extant discourse on female immigrant entrepreneurship, as well as highlighting the approaches in the field from a global perspective. By doing so, it discusses the invisibility of gender in the main theoretical approaches to explain immigrant entrepreneurship and the evolution of the female immigrant entrepreneurship sub-field since the mid-'80s up to the present, paying particular attention to how the role of women in the immigrant enterprise has been conceptualised. Organising this extensive field into sections, we deal first with the longstanding gender blindness of immigrant entrepreneurship theory, noting its lack of attention to the structural impact of gendered modes of migration, globalisation, labour market incorporation, ethnic relations and the configuration of family systems. We then review the recent efforts made to address these deficiencies, through studies explicitly designed to: a) explain differences between men/women immigrant business owners regarding motivations, barriers and opportunities for business entry; b) unpack the role of women in immigrant family businesses; and c) explore business as a means of empowerment and independence. Key examples from research carried out beyond the global core regions are then presented. Finally, we propose new paths for future research.

Theorising immigrant entrepreneurship: the invisibility of gender

Since its entry on to the research agenda, the study of immigrant entrepreneurship has made continual theoretical strides (Ram and Jones, 2008). Especially important since the 1980s has been the switch away from supply-side accounts of the rise of immigrant firms in terms of ethnic resources (Light, 1972; Ward, 1987) to a more realistic emphasis on the demand for them (Kloosterman et al., 1999). Even so there are plausible claims that, despite its progressive momentum, this literature has continued to downplay the gendered aspects of this, with Brettell (2007, 84) expressing perplexed frustration: "curiously in this vast corpus of scholarship, very little attention has been paid to women entrepreneurs". Notable here is the neglect of the impact of patriarchy on social relations between migrant owners and their workers and family members (Phizacklea, 1988; Collins and Low, 2010; Halkias, Harkiolakis, Caracatsanis, 2012).

Given the labour-intensive nature of so many migrant firms, this 'inadequate theorising' in relation to gender dynamics (Phizacklea, 1988, 16) results in the neglect of a key characteristic of migrant entrepreneurship. Scholarship struggles to confront sexism and racism together as part of an inter-related exclusionary process, tending rather to address "either gender or ethnicity in relation to entrepreneurship, but ... [not] ... both of them simultaneously" (Essers, Benschop and Doorewaard, 2010, 323). Lacking is the understanding of the *interaction* between gender and ethnicity, where for example the disadvantages of a racialised identity have different outcomes and lived experiences for men and women. For example, immigrant men might overcome their disadvantaged position in the labour market due to discrimination by means of utilising the cheap and flexible labour force of women in their families.

When the research emphasis began to turn towards the opportunity structure as a shaper of immigrant entrepreneurship, a welcome emphasis emerged on structural factors like the availability of market space in certain sectors and activities and the negative labour market deterrent of low pay and discrimination (Portes and Rumbaut, 1990). Attempting to bridge the gap between cultural and structural elements, Aldrich and Waldinger (1990) examine the interplay between opportunity structure on the one hand and the resources of ethnic networks (defined as social ties with co-ethnics) on the other. Despite the importance of this exercise, there was little consideration of gendered patterns of migration, labour incorporation or family relationships within the household.

This gender lacuna largely persists in the most recent and influential *mixed embeddedness* model advanced by Kloosterman et al. (1999; see also Kloosterman, 1996, 2000; Rath, 2002). This perspective argues that, for all its entrepreneurial importance, the ethnic resources network of immigrant entrepreneurs should be seen in the context of the larger business environment, including politico-legal regulations as well as market opportunities. Yet even while challenging the imbalance of previous culturalist approaches, it nonetheless fails to incorporate gender dynamics or to provide any insight on how the institutional framework influences migrant men and women differently.

Borrowing from the broad female entrepreneurship literature, themes explored in debates on female immigrant business-owners include motivations, performance, opportunities, barriers, access to finance and use of networks (Smallbone et al., 2003; Baycan et al., 2003; Abbasian and Yazdanfar, 2013; Carter et al., 2015). From this we now know something of the role of women in the family firm and how the use of family ties varies between women and men. Also emerging is critical analysis of the complexities of compliance with patriarchal norms and of identity as migrant women, a multi-layered negotiated condition.

Differences between immigrant men, native women and immigrant women

Scholarship is beginning to highlight the sometimes sharp differences in the entrepreneurship profiles of immigrant men and women, with women less likely to be business owners and, when they are, more likely to be running under-funded enterprises (Smallbone et al., 2003; Abbasian and Yazdanfar, 2013). In a case study of Turkish women in Amsterdam, Baycan et al. (2003) explore the intersection of motivations, goals, characteristics and barriers and show that women tend to have higher levels of education and professional experience than men. Yet, despite this human capital advantage, female business start-up is still motivated mainly by unemployment and is even more dependent than its male counterpart on co-ethnic custom in the service sector (ibid).

Essentially, the intersection of gender and ethnicity shapes the opportunities and barriers facing migrant women in business. Female-headed firms are often under-capitalised, frequently more so than migrant enterprises because of their small sizes and over-concentration in the service sector (Carter et al., 2013). UK-based research finds that, while immigrants as a whole suffer restricted access to finance, there are specific limitations for ethnic minority women, with ethnic minority men significantly more likely than women to access capital from formal sources (Smallbone et al., 2003). By no means UK-specific, this male-female finance gap has been identified elsewhere, as for example by Abbasian and Yazdanfar (2013), who conclude that immigrant women in Sweden are more likely to rely on loans from family members than on formal credit from the banking sector, a shortfall more common among younger women. Unhappily for hopes that superior human capital can overcome such bounds, this study finds that levels of education and experience had no significant effect on the ability to secure access to finance.

Gender and family relations: the role of women in family businesses

Among the many explanatory narratives on migrant women in business, one of the most enlightening is the exploration of their role in the family business, that backbone of the labour-intensive sectors characteristic of migrant entrepreneurship (Kloosterman, 2010). The centrality of family as a unit of analysis to understand entrepreneurship strategies has been addressed by Aldrich and Cliff's (2003) paper on revisiting the 'family embeddedness perspective', in which they argue that family dynamics and transformations influence entrepreneurship, particularly in understanding the venture-creation decision as well as the resources to be mobilised to support the business. Relations among family members, new forms of family and the role of children are key themes to be integrated in this perspective, in order to have a better understanding of the overall dynamics of entrepreneurial activities (*ibid.*).

The embeddedness of the family has been examined by analysing the impact of household composition and dynamics (Alsos, Carter and Ljunggren, 2014) on business set up and growth strategies. Understanding these family dynamics requires an assessment of gendered distributions of resources and work within the household-business unit. When exploring the contributions of women to family firms, some of the aspects explored are: the general invisibility of the key contributions women make to family firms, the important role they play in the sustainability and growth of family businesses (Cole, 1997), as well as the drivers to achieve positions of leadership (Martinez Jimenez, 2009).

However, the specific role of minority women in family firms remains underdeveloped despite its potential to cast light on patriarchal relations in the ethnic economy and the blurred boundaries between work and household (Ram, 1994). Migrant enterprises often survive hostile market environments by the intensive utilization of family and ethnic labour (Sanders and Nee, 1996; Ram, 1994). Research in this sphere has pointed to the need to understand how family relationships are structured, especially regarding the negotiation of individual roles in the reproductive and productive spheres (Ram et al., 2001; Raijman and Tienda, 2000; Cobas and De Ollos, 1989). In line with this shifting focus from firm to household, Ram et al. (2001) argued that relationships of mutual obligation and trust can translate into higher involvement in the business activity. Beyond this the family can also provide income from paid employment, contribute to reproductive tasks, or build social ties and networks supportive of its economic activities (ibid).

At first sight, all this creates an impression of harmonious co-operation within a collective of equals, but closer scrutiny often shows the immigrant family business as an outfit run by a man and deriving competitive advantage from the cheap labour of his wife and children (Phizacklea, 1988; Hillman, 1999; Pearce, 2005). Such a depiction reflects the way in which the real contribution of women is generally unacknowledged, a consequence of patriarchal household employment relations and a classic case of scholastic 'gender-blindness' (Phizacklea, 1988; Westwood, 1988; Josephides, 1988; Dhaliwal, 1998; Hillman, 1999). Homing in on the realities of the female role, Phizacklea (1988, 18) narrates how "ethnic business is predominantly male-controlled and labour intensive. Men are bosses and women are either workers or can expect to control or give orders only to other women". In a passage that could well apply to South Asian family firms in Britain, Phizacklea goes on to argue that "those ethnic groups deemed to be more 'successful' in the business world than others, are characterised by social structures which give easier access to female labour subordinated to patriarchal control mechanisms" (1988, 18). Extending this theme, Hillman's (1999) work on Turkish firms in Berlin shows that the survival of male-headed ventures depends upon the unrewarded effort of 'family work' or, more accurately, the hidden female input, which in effect enables fathers and brothers to collect the earnings of daughters and sisters. For Hillman (1999), the only escape for Turkish women from this subordination is to set up their own businesses outside the ethnic economy. Graphically illustrated here is the blurring of the production/reproduction divide, where women's work is seen simply as an extension of their family role rather than a source of economic independence (Westwood, 1988). This applies even though their work is often indispensable to the start-up and consolidation of the business (ibid).

Alive to the exploitative effects of this, Anthias and Mehta (2003) expressly state that male owners use patriarchal power as a means of compensation for their ethnic disadvantage. Certainly there can be little doubt that the ethnic family business offers an ideal enclosed space within which control over women members can be readily exercised, with working at home presented as offering a 'safer' environment than outside employment. Readily illustrating this is a study of Cypriot firms in the UK showing that the protection of the community's women from exposure to outsiders is a key motive to keeping them in the ethnic economy. For the women themselves the dubious benefits of 'protection' are gained in return for a complete loss of economic independence (Josephides, 1988).

At this point it is worth noting that not all immigrant communities do in fact conform to the patriarchal model of relations within the business and household. In Britain, studies have pointed to African-Caribbean women entrepreneurs as operating independently often in the absence of any male family assistance and frequently in market sectors far removed from the low-value markets in which South Asians and other immigrant-origin entrepreneurs are ghettoised (Alexander-Moore, 1991). Perhaps the inconveniently exceptional nature of these cases has prevented them from being picked up as an integral part of the discourse on gendered paths to immigrant entrepreneurship. Even so, as we shall see in a later section, the incidence of female-headed ventures operating completely free of male inputs seems to be increasing to the point where it can no longer be ignored.

Returning to the standard narrative on traditionalist patriarchal firms, research needs to take scrupulous care to avoid the depiction of women as passive victims compelled simply to react to what is being done to them (Morokvasic, 1991). Attempts have been made to chart a more nuanced path between the two extremes of 'exploited' and 'empowered', as with Bhachu's (1987) study arguing that women can sometimes find autonomous space within the overall patriarchy of the family firm, particularly when they have previously held paid employment outside of the family business. Here it seems that attitudes gained from their previous experience in paid employment have supported them in negotiating their roles within the family firm.

Further developing this nuanced perspective is Anthias (1992), whose work on Cypriot women in co-ethnic businesses in the UK examines how the standard class antagonisms of the workplace are over-ridden by a combination of ethnic and kinship loyalties: women can hardly identify their employer as their exploiter when he is a blood relative. Kinship and group loyalty prevent women organising for their working rights, an imperative reinforced by the urgent need to hold onto their jobs in the ethnic economy, a necessary insurance against the limited alternative options in the mainstream economy (ibid).

Immigrant entrepreneurship as means of empowerment

Going beyond these notions of islands of autonomy in a sea of exploitation, a growing number of recent writers have begun to examine the self-empowerment potential of business ownership in its own right (Gill and Ganesh, 2007). This area has also developed within the study of female immigrant entrepreneurship (Apistzch and Kontos, 2003; Baycan et al. 2003; Morokvasic, 1999; Lazaridis, 2003; Pio, 2007). Migration scholarship (Pessar, 2005; Hondagnou-Sotelo, 2003) has pointed to how the migration experience can transform gender ideologies, power relations and aspirations, both in the countries of destination (e.g. women engaging in paid employment in contrast with lower labour incorporation in the country of origin) and the countries of origin (the impacts of migration on power relations for men and children left behind, when women become heads of households through migration) (see Pessar (2005) for a review on the outcomes of migration for women's empowerment, and its criticisms).

Laying down some conditions for understanding entrepreneurship as a means of empowerment, Morokvasic (1999) argues that we should focus upon women who, motivated by personal independence, lead businesses geared to mainstream customers outside the traditional segregated migrant niches. Exemplifying this principle of female entrepreneurial autonomy, Lazaridis (2003) cites immigrant women in Greece who, in the face of the severely limited job opportunities available in domestic and care work, open up their own ventures as virtually the only means of socio-economic mobility on their own terms. Further light on this question of independent female motivation is cast by Anthias and Mehta's (2003) comparison of gender relations within the ethnic economy for migrant women, migrant men and native women. In this complex intersection of gender, ethnicity and family, reliance on family ties is indispensable for male owners while migrant women tend to draw a line between business and family relationships, particularly those with their husbands. Accordingly, women owners are much less reliant on family members to help out in the business, tending only to receive family financial support in the first stages of the business activity. This is consistent with a desire for independence and personal achievement in the complete absence of any spousal intervention (ibid).

Evaluating gender and ethnicity simultaneously has not been common within ethnic entrepreneurship studies, and a growing number of publications are taking into account the implications of the different meanings of becoming an entrepreneur (Katila, 2008; Essers, Benshop and Doorewaard, 2010; Billlore, 2011). Working in the family firm can reflect strategies of commitment and resistance to the familial orders, which are fluid and respond to broader processes of gender identification (Katila, 2008). Religion, culture, construction of femininity and professional identities can be explored in a setting where entrepreneurship is generally associated with white male middle class identity. Essers, Benshop and Doorewaard (2010) analyse the notion of female ethnicity through the narratives of women of Muslim background in the Netherlands overcoming the binaries between Western and non-Western, modern and traditional. In order to do so, they use an *intersectional* approach. *Intersectionality* is a theoretical and analytical approach, which refers to how variables such as gender, class, religion and ethnicity need to be considered simultaneously, rather than in isolation. This helps to reflect the way social divisions and categories are understood, where for example gender is always structured by one's ethnicity and class (Anthias and Yuval Davis, 1989). The analysis of four life stories of Muslim women entrepreneurs in the Netherlands (Essers and Benschop, 2009) shows that female ethnicity is negotiated with different groups in their social interactions, allowing them to develop coping strategies through hybrid identities moving beyond the image of women as passive and dependent. The authors argue that research needs to take into account gender and ethnicity at the same time, in order to capture the realities of migrant entrepreneurs. Essers and Benschop (2009) take the intersection of gender and ethnicity in entrepreneurial context further, looking at the interaction with Islam for women entrepreneurs; intersectionality is used as an analytical tool to understand conflicting identity regulations and the role of Islam in the emergence of differentiation strategies to enable entrepreneurship. Billore (2011) also explores the construction of multiple identities in a study on Indian immigrant women entrepreneurs in Japan; she reveals how entrepreneurial strategies shape their self-image throughout time, moving from activities relegated to the domestic sphere without compromising their expected family moral duties.

Insights from studies such as Bhachu (1987), Phizacklea (1988), Hillman (1999), Ram et al. (2001) and Baycan et al. (2003) allow us to develop a typology of the role of women in immigrant family firms. There are businesses run by a couple, where both spouses work together as 'copreneurs' (Fitzgerald and Muske, 2002). This form can also include income obtained in paid employment by one member of the family as part of a *patchworking* strategy (Ram et al., 2001). The notion of copreneurs, where both members of the couple work together, does not preclude power imbalances. Second, we can differentiate businesses where other family members also take part in the enterprise. These strategies generally refer to the participation of children of migrants in the business activity, to help out as a flexible and cheap labour resource, or as full-time workers (Song, 1999; Ram et al., 2001). The

Table 20.1 Type of immigrant family business according to the involvement of women

Involvement of women	Characteristics
1 Businesses run by a couple	'Copreneurs', where the spouses share the productive work, as well as *patchworking* strategies with part-time paid employment to complement the household income (Ram et al., 2001; Phizacklea, 1988; Westwood, 1988; Josephides, 1988) The business is considered an extension of the domestic space. Women are in charge of reproductive and productive work (Dhaliwal, 1998; Hillman, 1999)
2 Businesses relying on other family members	Children are involved in the business activity as flexible labour force (Song, 1997) Other members of the extended family can also be employed to cushion the barriers of labour incorporation but also help out with cheap and flexible labour force (Ram et al., 2001)
3 Women entrepreneurs	The support of the husbands is not common (Anthias and Mehta, 2003; Pearce, 2005) Women lead the business individually as a means of independence and empowerment (Lazaridis, 2003; Morokvasic, 1999; Baycan et al., 2003)
4 Business with 'hidden/ invisible women'	Women do not necessarily run the business or take part in major productive tasks, but they are the key support in other activities vital for the business survival: support in reproductive tasks, keeping kinship and solidarity ties, strengthening supply chains, etc., strengthening the entrepreneurial strategies of the family/husbands (Josephides, 1988; Song, 1997; Ram et al., 2001)

Source: Own elaboration based on the cited authors.

participation of children is highly dependent on variables such as age, but also gender: boys and girls will assume different tasks depending on the age and the type of business (Song, 1999). The third category that we can distinguish is that of the 'hidden' or 'invisible' women, where women do not appear as copreneurs, and are not presented as having an active and visible role in the productive activity, but they do have key tasks such as assuming the reproductive tasks and keeping kinship and solidarity ties that strengthen the entrepreneurial strategies (Phizacklea, 1988; Hillman, 1999; Ram et al., 2001). The fourth category is that of women running the business as sole entrepreneurs. Generally, migrant women running enterprises do not rely on their spouses to support the business activity to the same extent as immigrant men (Morokvasic, 1999; Anthias and Mehta, 2003).

Broadening the geographical perspective

Most studies set in this field draw on the experiences of immigrants in the urban-industrial core of North America and North-West Europe. Yet, as the geographical spread of migration broadens in the 21st century, new research contexts open up, revealing myriad new ways in which female immigrant enterprise is shaped by different political, social and institutional settings. At the same time, the nature of the migrant women themselves is different, revealing novel angles for research.

Since the 1990s, a refreshing development for researchers in this field has been the late capitalist flowering of the Mediterranean countries: Spain, Greece, Morocco, Turkey, characterised as they are by 'familistic' welfare state systems, increasingly feminised flows of inward migration and high labour demand in the service, domestic and care work sectors. Together with a substantial informal economy, these factors shape occupational paths for immigrant women, which contrast sharply with the nuclear family enterprise of research in North-West Europe (Ribas and Villares-Varela, 2013). In this context, much research on female immigrant business tends to focus on self-employment as the only possible means of escaping domestic and care work, whether in Greece (Lazaridis, 2003; Lazaridis and Koumandraki, 2003), Spain (Oso et al., 2004) or Portugal (Padilla, 2008). Migration flows to some Mediterranean countries are so feminised that much migrant business formation is occurring in the complete absence of husbands. These new models of family, with mothers and children only, cast new light on gender relations within the household, as in the cases of Dominican (Oso, 2004) and Brazilian women in Spain (Villares-Varela, 2008), where the gender and the position of children in the family shape the involvement and negotiation of tasks. The strategies of female immigrant entrepreneurs engaging in informal activities in urban markets have been researched across the Mediterranean, for Algerian women in Turkey (Peraldi et al., 2001), Tunisian in Italy (Schmoll, 2003) or Moroccan in Spain (Ribas, 2004), showing how these strategies are conditioned by the large size of the informal sector, sometimes by circular migration and the need for *patchworking* strategies (Oso and Ribas, 2006).

In perhaps the most novel twist of all, the location of many new studies has begun to move to the global South, the former 'Third World', once portrayed as trapped in poverty and an exporter of a low-skilled labour force. Since the 1990s, strong economic growth in countries like India has led to a reversal in the direction of migration, with inward migration setting the scene for new studies of female self-employment in India itself (Singh et al., 2012), Argentina (Cha et al., 2012), Nigeria (Nwajiuba et al., 2012) and South Africa (Thurman et al., 2012). In India, where the spread of the informal sector in New Delhi and other major cities has created business opportunities for women migrants from neighbouring countries, Singh et al. (2012) identify the random enforcement of migration policies in India as the main barrier for migrant entrepreneurs. In complete contrast, migration policy is seen as advantageous for migrant women entrepreneurs in Argentina, an open-doors approach deriving historically from the age of great migrations from Europe. Less happily, these low migration barriers do nothing to ease the lack of financial and social capital, the two endemic problems for female firms in this country (Cha et al., 2012). Indeed, experience suggests that this kind of deregulated environment actually aggravates such problems (Barrett et al., 2003). Very much in its infancy, this work on Africa, Asia and Latin America has far to go and is part of the future discourse discussed in the following section.

Paths to further advance research on female immigrant entrepreneurship

We have reviewed so far the evolution of the field of female immigrant enterprise and how it has been investigated from different disciplines and regions. In this section, we offer some suggestions for female immigrant entrepreneurship in the future.

Embedding gender in immigrant entrepreneurship: enhancing 'mixed embeddedness'

'Mixed embeddedness' is one of the most widely used frameworks to study immigrant entrepreneurship and is noted for its insistence on explaining migrant entrepreneurship in relation to broader social structures. Kloosterman (2010) identifies a specific space in the market for low-value activities that require intensive labour that are reserved for migrants. Social structures (market regulations, migration policies, welfare state system, local/regional/state institutional framework, etc.) shape migrants' entrepreneurial choices. However, mixed embeddedness overlooks how these spaces of the market available to migrants are also conditioned by gendered social structures, gendered nature of migration processes and work and employment. The underlying conditions that facilitate the origin and configuration of immigrant entrepreneurship are gendered: welfare state provision, labour market opportunities or migration policies impact men and women differently. Hence, these dimensions will also affect the spaces available in the market for migrants to become entrepreneurs.

For example, the weaker welfare state provision of Southern European countries, together with the higher access to education of women, and the weight of informal economies have created a demand for private care for the elderly and children, which has been filled by immigrant women (King and Zontini, 2000; Martinez, 2011). This is reflected in the feminisation of migration flows and labour market participation for migrant women. This specific outcome has facilitated the setting up of agencies by migrants catering to domestic and care work for the local population, being women particularly relevant in this sector. Hence, the appearance and continuation of this niche, has been shaped by gendered policies in the realm of a familistic Mediterranean system of welfare provision and its interaction with gendered migration policies that facilitated the migration of women into domestic and care work. Therefore, implementing a mixed embeddedness approach to analyse immigrant entrepreneurship requires sensitivity to the way in which gendered social systems contribute to the spaces available in the market for migrant entrepreneurs.

Intersectionality as a tool to explore gendered experiences of work

The approaches aimed at understanding the differential motivations and performances of entrepreneurship for migrant women have proved useful in mapping the overall characteristics of female immigrant enterprise in different contexts. However, we have seen the limitations of collecting data to produce portraits of immigrant women entrepreneurs in comparison with immigrant men entrepreneurs: they tend to use as a baseline the experiences and outcomes of the native male entrepreneur and advance knowledge regarding why (immigrant) women are deviant from the mainstream entrepreneurial trajectory of (native) men. As Marlow (2010) argues,

> reflecting this ontology, epistemological framing uncritically used gender as a variable whereby the entrepreneurial activities of men and women were compared across a range of performance indicators with women inevitably positioned in deficit such that their enterprises were condemned as smaller than, weaker than, lacking growth orientation or pejoratively dismissed as home-based, part time, life style - indeed, almost every detrimental business term possible has visited upon the hapless female entrepreneur […]. This in turn promoted a range of policy interventions across developed economies which reflected a similar message; namely, how to 'fix' the problem of the female entrepreneur". (2010, 103)

In the case of female immigrant entrepreneurship, we observe that the focus on the experiences of women is deviant from that on immigrant men, but also that native women militate against nuanced analyses of the implications of the *meaning* of paths to self-employment and gender relations within the immigrant firm. On the other hand, in-depth portraits of migrant women entrepreneurs run the risk of detaching women from their context, as victimised and without agency to mobilise resources. We suggest that, in order to advance the knowledge on the experiences of migrant women entrepreneurs, we should also focus on how 'being an entrepreneur' is experienced by men in relation to the construction of their ethnicity and ideas of masculinity. For example, we reviewed how, when looking at issues of access to finance in the UK (Smallbone et al., 2003) female participants in the study narrated that African-Caribbean men are more likely to suffer negative stereotyping when accessing formal sources of finance. This negative construction of masculinity and access to credit would be an interesting point to advance the analysis of racialised access to finance and experiences of masculine identities for ethnic minorities.

Given that these broad theoretical frameworks have not included the gender dimension systematically, understanding the experiences of work within entrepreneurship requires alternative analytical tools that capture the interactions among gender, ethnicity, class, religion, etc. Intersectionality has proven a very valuable tool to understanding these processes. Postmodern standpoint theory has contributed a range of important critiques as well as reflections from a Black Feminism perspective, which proposes an analysis of the intersection of these categories. This postmodern frame has particular implications for social identity and social axis of difference, because it prevents reifying groups together. As part of the postmodern critique of theoretical foundations, feminism has made an invaluable contribution to the way in which we understand social divisions and categories. It has been acknowledged that categories of 'race' and ethnicity do not work in isolation, but they are shaped by 'class' and 'gender' (Anthias and Yuval Davis, 1989). These theorists argue that one's gender and social class always structure the experience of being an ethnic minority. Intersectionality scholars such as Anthias and Yuval Davis (1992) and Brah and Phoenix (2004) have emphasised how particular identities are lived in the modalities of other categories of identity. For example, gender is always lived in the modalities of ethnicity and class, nationality in the modalities of gender and 'race' and class in the modalities of gender and nationality. We have seen how this tool brings nuances to the experiences of work and identity in the work of, for example, Essers, Benschop and Doorewaard (2010).

Gender relations within family business: exploring new theoretical approaches

When reviewing scholarship accounting for the role of immigrant women in family businesses, we have seen how most of these perspectives analysed these strategies as either exploitation of women by their husbands, brothers or fathers or conception of the business as a space of empowerment. We propose that immigrant entrepreneurship theories and empirical design should explore theoretical perspectives that take into account the complexities of the negotiations within households. Theoretical perspectives such as that developed by the economist Amartya Sen on gender and 'cooperative conflicts' might prove a useful tool to unpack the complexities of household-business dynamics for two main reasons: (1) it deconstructs the concept of 'productive' activities, giving a prominent role to those 'within the household' activities, that are necessary for the 'productive' activities to happen. Sen (1987) argues that

> The so-called 'productive' activities may be parasitic on other work being done, e.g. housework and food preparation, the looking after of children, bringing food to the

field where cultivators are working. (...) The prosperity of the household depends on the totality of various activities – getting money incomes, purchasing or directly producing (in the case of, say, peasants) food materials and other goods, producing eatable food out of food materials, and so on. But in addition to aggregate prosperity, even the divisions between sexes in general, and specifically those within the household, may also be deeply influenced by the pattern of gender division of work.

(Sen, 1987, 11)

In respect to immigrant entrepreneurship, this perspective would broaden the analysis of household-business dynamics and would help us to use the household-business as the unit of analysis and overcome the production/reproduction divide. (2) The use of the concept of 'cooperative conflicts' (Sen, 1989) allows us to analyse how domestic units work and argues that households can be harmonious and divergent simultaneously, where situations of cooperation and conflict happen at the same time:

Family relations similarly involve a combination of congruence and conflict. Obvious benefits accrue to all parties as a result of family arrangements, but the nature of the division of work and goods determines specific distributions and disadvantages and particular patterns of inequalities. It is important not to lose the sight of either these functions that families fill, since a model of pure conflict or pure congruence would undoubtedly miss something of substance in family relations.

(Sen, 1989, 61)

The *concept of cooperative* conflicts would help us resolve the compliance with gender systems for women in family businesses: "The choice among cooperative solutions, may be distinctively unfavourable to a group – women, for example-, (...), without any perceived sense of 'exploitation', given the nature of perceptions of self-interest and conceptions of what is legitimate and what is not" (Sen, 1989, 68). Hence, unpacking the household-business dynamics through the lens of cooperative conflicts would facilitate a nuanced analysis of the division of work and the negotiations of roles and tasks within the business.

Conclusions

This chapter has reviewed the main contributions to the scarcely developed field of female immigrant entrepreneurship. The perspectives theorising immigrant entrepreneurship have tended to neglect the importance of gendered processes of migration, labour market incorporation or household-business dynamics. Early research represented women as dependent on their parents or husbands and did not focus on how migrant women contributed to the production and reproduction of the family and business. Initial studies in the field relied on other theoretical tools, such as feminist perspectives to understand the role of women in immigrant enterprises. These studies successfully exposed the hidden nature of women's contribution, shedding light on the impact of patriarchal relations in the work and employment relations within the business and the household. Of great importance are those contributions focusing on the 'non-productive' aspects of how women contribute to the family firm, such as care activities or keeping fluid relationships through maintaining kinship and community ties that might be activated when needed for the business activity.

Emphasising the relevance of patriarchal relations to understand how immigrant men use the work of women within the family firm allows us to uncover how the division of labour, power and resources is neither random nor harmonious in a family business. However, these portrayals of women in family business have also left us with very little understanding of the way women bargain and negotiate their involvement in the household and business, revealing the need for more nuanced approaches to understanding the processes behind these negotiations, but also how the business might result in a means of independence and autonomy from the family.

In order to address the gendered nature of migration, work and enterprise, we propose using alternative theoretical perspectives that might help us enhance existing tested approaches in solving these shortcomings (i.e. intersectionality), which could help us to deconstruct the different experiences, processes and meanings of work and employment for immigrant men and women. Understanding power relations, division of labour and tasks within the business-household also requires unpacking how the household-business is organised, deconstructing the binary productive vs reproductive activities and understanding how family arrangements within the businesses can be harmonious and conflictive simultaneously.

Notes

1 We use the term immigrants to refer to those foreign born.
2 Gendered practices and experiences refer to the social structures underlying power relations between men and women in a given context. Using a gender approach allows us to move beyond the biological differentiations between men and women and understanding 'gender' as an acquired identity through socialization and division of labour in a given society (for an extended discussion of the relation between gender and biological differentiation between men and women see Delphy 1993).
3 Patriarchy refers to the social system of male dominance over women, through their position as heads of households, which has been used to explain the expropriation by men of the resources generated by women from their income and their work in the household (for an extended review of the theorizing of patriarchy, its different types and criticisms see Kandiyoti (1988) and Walby (1989)).

References

Abbasian, S. and Yazdanfar, D., 2013. Exploring the financing gap between native born women-and immigrant women-owned firms at the start-up stage: Empirical evidence from Swedish data. *International Journal of Gender and Entrepreneurship*, 5 (22), 157–173.

Aldrich, H., Carter, J., Jones, T. and McEvoy, D. 1981. Business development and self segregation: Asian enterprise in three British cities. In Peach, C., Robinson, V. and Smith, S. (eds), *Ethnic Segregation in Cities*. London, Croom Helm.

Aldrich, H.E. and Cliff, J.E. 2003. The pervasive effects of family on entrepreneurship: Toward a family embeddedness perspective. *Journal of Business Venturing*, 18 (5), 573–596.

Aldrich, H.E. and Waldinger, R. 1990. Ethnicity and entrepreneurship. *Annual Review of Sociology*, 16, 111–135.

Alexander-Moore, D. 1991. *The Black Cinderella*. London, Unity Books.

Alsos, G.A., Carter, S., & Ljunggren, E. 2014. Kinship and business: how entrepreneurial households facilitate business growth, *Entrepreneurship & Regional Development*, 26 (1–2), 97–122.

Anthias, F. 1992. *Ethnicity, Class, Gender and Migration: Greek Cypriots in Britain*. Aldershot: Avebury.

Anthias, F. and Mehta, N. 2003. The intersection between gender, the family and self-employment: The family as a resource. *International Review of Sociology*, 13 (1), 112–135.

Anthias, F. and Yuval Davis, N. 1989. *Woman-Nation-State*. New York: St. Martin's Press.

Apitzsch, U. and Kontos, M. 2003. Self-employment, gender and migration. *International Review of Sociology*, 13 (1), 201–214.

Banda, F. and Mawadza, A. 2014. 'Foreigners are stealing our birth right': Moral panics and the discursive construction of Zimbabwean immigrants in South African media. *Discourse & Communication*, 1750481314555263.

Barrett, G., Jones, T. and McEvoy. 2003. United Kingdom: Severely constrained entrepreneurialism. In Kloosterman, R. and Rath, J. (eds), *Immigrant Entrepreneurs: Venturing Abroad in the Age of Globalisation*. Oxford: Berg.

Baycan, T., Masurel, E., Nijkamp, P. 2003. Gender differences in ethnic entrepreneurship, *43rd European Congress, European Regional Science Association*, Jyväskylä, Finland, August 27–30.

Bhachu, P. 1987. Apni Marzi Kardhi. Home and work: Sikh women in Britain, In Westwood, S., and Bhachu, P. (eds), *Enterprising Women. Ethnicity, Economy, and Gender Relations*. London: Routledge.

Billore, S. 2011. Female immigrant entrepreneurship: Exploring international entrepreneurship through the status of Indian women entrepreneurs in Japan. *International Journal of Gender and Entrepreneurship*, 3 (1), 38–55.

Bonacich, E. 1973. A theory of middleman minorities. *American Sociological Review*, 583–594.

Bonacich, E. and Modell, J. 1980. *The Economic Basis of Ethnic Solidarity in the Japanese American Community*. Berkeley: University of California Press.

Brah, A. and Phoenix, A. 2004. Ain't I a Woman? Revisiting Intersectionality, *Journal of International Women's Studies* [1539–8706] 5 (3), 75.

Carter, S., Mwaura, S., Ram, M. Trehan. K. and Jones, T. 2015. Barriers to ethnic minority and women's enterprise: Existing evidence, policy tensions and unsettled questions. *International Small Business Journal*, 33 (1): 49–69.

Cha, N., Caracatsanis, S., and Polideras, K. 2012. Life chronicles of female immigrant entrepreneurs in Argentina. In Halkias, D., Thurman, P., Harkiolakis, N. and Caracatsanis, S. (eds) *Female Immigrant Entrepreneurs. The Economic and Social Impact of a Global Phenomenon*. Ashgate.

Cobas, J. and De Ollos, I. 1989. Family ties, co-ethnic bonds and ethnic entrepreneurship. *Sociological Perspectives*, 32, 403–411.

Cole, P. 1997. Women in family business. *Family Business Review*. December 10 (4), 353–371.

Collins, J. and Low, A., 2010. Asian female immigrant entrepreneurs in small and medium-sized businesses in Australia. *Entrepreneurship and Regional Development*, 22 (1), 97–111.

Delphy, C. 1993. Rethinking sex and gender, *Women's Studies Int Forum*, 16 (1), 1–9.

Dhaliwal, S. 1998. Silent contributors: Asian female entrepreneurs and women in business. *Women's Studies International Forum*, 21 (5), 463–474.

Duedil. 2014 *Migrant Entrepreneurs: Building Our Businesses, Creating Our Jobs*. Report.

Essers, C. and Benschop, Y. 2009. Muslim businesswomen doing boundary work: The negotiation of Islam, gender and ethnicity within entrepreneurial contexts. *Human Relations*, 62 (3), 403–424.

Essers, C., Benschop, Y. and Doorewaard, H. (2010). Female ethnicity: Understanding Muslim migrant businesswomen in the Netherlands. *Gender, Work and Organization*, 17 (3), 320–340.

Essers, C., Doorewaard, H., Benschop, Y. 2013. Family ties: Migrant female business owners doing identity work on the public-private divide. *Human Relations*, 66: 1645–1665.

Fitzgerald, M. A., & Muske, G. 2002. Copreneurs: An exploration and comparison to other family businesses. *Family Business Review*, 15 (1), 1–16.

Gill, R., & Ganesh, S. 2007. Empowerment, constraint, and the entrepreneurial self: A study of white women entrepreneurs. *Journal of Applied Communication Research*, 35 (3), 268–293.

Gillis-Donovan, J. and Moynihan-Bradt, C. 1990. The power of invisible women in the family business. *Family Business Review* June 3 (2), 153–167.

Halkias, D., Thurman, P., Harkiolakis, N. and Caracatsanis, S. 2012. *Female Immigrant Entrepreneurs. The Economic and Social Impact of a Global Phenomenon*. Ashgate.

Hillman, F. 1999. *A Look at the "Hidden Side": Turkish Women in Berlin's Ethnic Labour Market*. Blackwell Publishers.

Hondagneu-Sotelo, P. 2003. (Eds) Gender and US immigration. *Contemporary Trends*. University of California Publishers.

Jones, T., Ram, M., Villares-Varela, M., Edwards, P. and Doldor, S. 2014. New migrant businesses in the West Midlands: Beyond the economic dividend, paper presented at the RENT conference.

Josephides, S. 1988. Enterprising women. In Westwood, S. Bhachu, P. *Enterprising Women. Ethnicity, Economy and Gender Relations*. London: Routledge.

Kandiyoti, D. 1988. Bargaining with patriarchy. *Gender and Society*, 2 (3), 274–290.

Katila, S. 2008. Negotiating moral orders in Chinese business families in Finland: Constructing family, gender and ethnicity in a research situation. *Gender, Work and Organization*, 17 (3), 298–310.

King, R. and Zontini, E. 2000. The role of gender in the South European immigration model. *Papers: revista de sociologia*, (60), 35–52.

Kloosterman, R. 2010. Matching opportunities with resources: A framework for analysing (migrant) entrepreneurship from a mixed embeddedness perspective. *Entrepreneurship and Regional Development*, 22 (1), 25–45.

Kloosterman, R., Van der Leun, J. and Rath, J. 1999. Mixed embeddedness: (In)formal economic activities and immigrant businesses in the Netherlands. *International Journal of Urban and Regional Research*, 23, 252–266.

Lazaridis, G. 2003. From maids to entrepreneurs: Immigrant women in Greece. In Freedman, J. *Gender and Insecurity: Migrant women in Europe*. Ashgate.

Lazaridis, G. and Koumandraki, M. 2003. Ethnic entrepreneurship in Greece: A mosaic of informal and formal business activities. *Sociological Research on Line*, 8 (2), http://www.socresonline.org.uk/8/2/lazaridis.html.

Lesińska, M. 2014. The European backlash against immigration and multiculturalism. *Journal of Sociology*, 50 (1), 37–50.

Low, J. and Collins, A. 2007. Embedded intersections of ethnicity, class, gender and entrepreneurship. In Hafeez K., McEvoy D. and Keoy K. (eds), *Changing Faces of Ethnic Entrepreneurship*. University of Bradford.

Manry, V. 2005. Quand Fatima, Assia, Meryem et les autres prennent la route. Les mobilités féminines maghrébines comme analyseur des nouvelles formes de circulations dans l'espace euroméditerranéen. *Migrations Société*, 99–100, junio.

Martinez, R., 2011. La reorganización de los cuidados familiares en un contexto de migración internacional/The re-organization of the family care in an international migration context. *Cuadernos de relaciones laborales*, 29 (1), 93.

Martinez Jimenez, R. 2009. Research on women in family firms. Current status and Future Directions. *Family Business Review*, March 2009 22 (1), 53–64.

Morokvasic, M. 1984. Birds of passage are also women. *International Migration Review*, 18 (4) Special Issue: Women in Migration (Winter), 886–907.

Morokvasic, M. 1999. Beyond the hidden side: Immigrant and minority women in self-employment and business in Europe. Paper Presented at the IOM Workshop on Women in Migration, 1999.

Nwajiuba, C., Harkiolakis, N., Thurman, P., Halkias, D. and Caracatsani, S. 2012. Nigeria: Female immigrant entrepreneurship in Western Africa. In Halkias, D., Thurman, P., Harkiolakis, N. and Caracatsanis, S. (eds) *Female Immigrant Entrepreneurs. The Economic and Social Impact of a Global Phenomenon*. Ashgate.

OECD 2010. Entrepreneurship and migrants. Report by the OECD Working Party on SMEs and Entrepreneurship, OECD.

Oso, L. (dir.) 2004. *El empresariado étnico como estrategia de movilidad social para las mujeres inmigrantes*. Instituto de la Mujer (Unplished report).

Oso, L. (dir.), Carballo, M., López, I., Ramírez, A., Ribas, N., Sáiz, A. and Villares-Varela, M. 2008. Final Report from the Spanish Cooperating Project *The Chances of the Second Generation in Families of Ethnic Entrepreneurs: Intergenerational and Gender Aspects of Quality of Life Processes* (SERD-2002-00119-Etnogeneration).

Padilla, B., 2008. O empreendedorismo na perspectiva de género: uma primeira aproximação ao caso das brasileiras em Portugal. *Revista Migrações*, 3, 191–215.

Pearce, S. 2005. Today's immigrant woman entrepreneur. *Immigration Policy Center. A division of the American Immigration Law Foundation*.

Peraldi. M., A. Bettaieb y V. Manry. 2001. L'esprit de bazar. Mobilités transnationales maghrébines et sociétés métropolitaines: Les routes d'Istambul. In M. Peraldi (dir) *Cabas et containers. Activités marchandes informelles et réseaux migrants transfrontaliers*. Paris: Maisonneuve et Larose, 329–381.

Pessar, P. 2005. Women, gender, and international migration across and beyond the Americas: inequalities and limited empowerment. *Expert Group Meeting on International Migration and Development in Latin America and the Caribbean, Mexico City* (Vol. 30).

Phizacklea, A. 1988. Entrepreneurship, ethnicity and gender. In Westwood, S. (ed.), *Enterprising Women: Ethnicity, Economy, and Gender Relations*, 20–33. London: Routledge.

Pio, E. 2007. Ethnic entrepreneurship among Indian women in New Zealand: A bittersweet process. *Gender, Work and Organization*, 14 (5), 409–432.

Raijman, R. and Tienda, M., 2000. Immigrants' pathways to business ownership: A comparative ethnic perspective. *International Migration Review*, 682–706.

Raijman, R. and Tienda, M. 2003. Ethnic foundations of economic transactions. Mexican and Korean immigrant entrepreneurs in Chicago. *Ethnic and Racial Studies*, 26 (5), 783–801.

Ram, M. 1994. *Managing to Survive: Working Lives in Small Firms*. Blackwell Business.

Ram, M. and Jones, T. 2001. Making the link: Households and small business activity in a multi-ethnic context. *Community, Work and Family*, 4 (3), 327–348.

Ram, M. & Jones, T. 2007. Re-embedding the ethnic business agenda. *Work, Employment & Society*, 21 (3), 439–457.

Ram, M., Jones, T., Abbas, T., Sanghera, B. 2002. Ethnic minority enterprise in its urban context: South Asian restaurants in Birmingham. *International Journal of Urban and Regional Research*, 26 (1).

Rath, J. C. 2002. *Unravelling the Rag Trade. Immigrant Entrepreneurship in Seven World Cities*. New York: Berg.

Ribas, N. and Villares-Varela, M. 2012. Aproximación al empresariado de origen inmigrante desde una perspectiva europea y de género. In López, F. (coord.), *Empresariado Inmigrante, Instituciones y Desarrollo*. Ed. Comares. Granada.

Sanders, J. M., & Nee, V. 1996. Immigrant self-employment: The family as social capital and the value of human capital. *American Sociological Review*, 231–249.

Sanghera, B. 2002. Microbusiness, household and class dynamics: The embedding of minority ethnic petit commerce. *The Sociological Review*, 241–257.

Schmoll, C. 2003. Mobilità e organizzazione delle commercianti tunisine. En G. Sciortino y. A. Colombo (dir) Stanieri in Italia. Un'immigrazione normale. Bologna: Il Mulino, 195–211.

Sen, A. 1987. Gender and cooperative conflicts, *WIDER Working Papers, W18*.

Sen, A. 1989. Cooperation, inequality, and the family. *Population and Development Review*, Vol. 15, Supplement: Rural Development and Population: Institutions and Policy, 61–76.

Sepulveda, L. Syrett, S. and Lyon, F. 2011. Population super-diversity and new migrant enterprise: the case of London. *Entrepreneurship and Regional Development*, 23 (7/8), 469–497.

Singh, A., Rish, M., Harkiolakis, N. and Caracatsani, S. 2012. India: Female immigrant entrepreneurship in New Delhi. In Halkias, D., Thurman, P., Harkiolakis, N. and Caracatsanis, S. (eds), *Female Immigrant Entrepreneurs. The Economic and Social Impact of a Global Phenomenon*. Ashgate.

Smallbone, D., Ram, M., Deakins, D., & Aldock, R. B. 2003. Access to finance by ethnic minority businesses in the UK. *International Small Business Journal*, 21 (3), 291–314.

Song, M. 1995. Between 'the front' and 'the back'. Chinese women's work in family business. *Women's Studies International Forum*, 18 (2), 285–298.

Song, M. 1999. *Helping Out. Children's Labour in Ethnic Businesses*. Philadelphia: Temple University Press.

Thurman, P., Botha, M, Anast, J. and Halkia, D. 2012. Mediterranean female immigrants in South Africa: A case study on love of adopted country and longevity in entrepreneurship. In Halkias, D., Thurman, P., Harkiolakis, N. and Caracatsanis, S. (eds), *Female Immigrant Entrepreneurs. The Economic and Social Impact of a Global Phenomenon*. Ashgate.

UN-OECD. 2013. *A Joint Contribution by UN-DESA and the OECD to the United Nations High-Level Dialogue on Migration and Development*, 3–4 October 2013, United Nations.

Virdee, S. 2014. *Racism, Class and the Racialized Outsider*. Basingstoke: Palgrave Macmillan.

Walby, S. 1989. Theorising patriarchy. *Sociology*, 23 (2), 213–234.

Westwood, S. 1988. *Enterprising Women. Ethnicity, Economy and Gender Relations*. London: Routledge.

Whitaker, B. E. and Giersch, J. 2015. Political competition and attitudes towards immigration in Africa. *Journal of Ethnic and Migration Studies* (ahead-of-print), 1–22.

Zlotnik, H. 2005. International migration trends since 1980. In UNFPA (coord.), *International Migration and the Millennium Development Goals*. New York.

21

ENTREPRENEURIAL ACTIVITY AMONG IRISH TRAVELLER WOMEN

An insight into the complexity of survival

Thomas M. Cooney and Dennis Foley

Introduction

Since the 1960s, Ireland has experienced massive economic and social upheaval as it distanced itself from what was previously an agrarian economy. Nevertheless, the agri-food sector remains one of Ireland's most important industries representing 7.1% of the country's economy and 11% of its exports, while supporting approximately 170,000 jobs, which amount to 8.6% of the country's total employment (European Commission, 2013). Despite the continued strength of the agri-food industry, centuries of seasonal employment for itinerant unskilled agrarian labourers (predominantly male) are now a historical memory due to increased mechanisation and labour efficiencies. Ireland's transition to a modern digital economy has resulted in Traveller / Gypsy / Roma employment predominantly located within the 'settled', urban communities where job opportunities are much more limited (in Irish discourse 'settled' refers to a person who no longer follows a nomadic lifestyle). The traditional Irish Traveller community (which has a strong patriarchal system) has endured an increasingly marginalised role within Ireland's economic and social environment, which in turn has led to lower levels of waged-employment amongst Traveller men. This development has placed increased pressure on Traveller women since they are essentially responsible for looking after the needs of their nuclear family (which frequently is quite large). Although women traditionally played a subservient role within the Traveller community (unless they are a rare matriarch outliving their partner and/or his brothers), they are required to manage the home and family commitments. Typically, Traveller women were uneducated and illiterate and married very young into arranged marriages involving dowries. They usually led a life of hardship, continually on the move while raising a large family based on an economy of begging or hawking. According to Pavee Point (2008), Traveller women experience triple discrimination – discrimination as women, discrimination as Travellers, and discrimination as Traveller women. Pavee Point further argued that like women from other minority ethnic groups, Traveller women experience an intersection of oppressions through racism and sexism. However, for Traveller women in Ireland today, there are signs that life is changing for the better (Galway Traveller Movement, 2012; Nelson & Silva, 2010) and entrepreneurial activity has been identified as one of the avenues through which such change

358

can be engendered. However, there are many demanding complexities when seeking to enable entrepreneurial activity amongst Traveller women, since they face substantial challenges both inside and outside of their community. This chapter explores the environment in which Traveller women pursue their entrepreneurial activities, the challenges that they face and their ambitions for the future.

Background

Travellers are native to Ireland and have much in common with the European Roma, Sinti and Gypsy[1] communities, particularly in a desire to live a roving lifestyle and their general resistance to being assimilated into the majority population. The Irish Traveller community has been described as:

> A small indigenous minority group that has been part of Irish society for centuries. They have a value system, language, customs and traditions, which make them an identifiable group both to themselves and to others. Their distinctive lifestyle and culture, based on a nomadic tradition, sets them apart from the general population.
>
> *(University College Dublin, 2010: 6)*

Mistrusted by the broader population for the most part, their traditions and lifestyles have generally not been understood by the dominant society. Historically they were nomads who moved in caravans and lived in encampments on the side of the road.

The 2006 Irish Census (CSO, 2007) revealed a Traveller population of just over 22,000 in Ireland, but Martin Collins suggests 30,000 as a more accurate number (Fay, 2011). The University College Dublin report '*Our Geels: All Ireland Traveller Health Study Technical Report*' (2010) estimated the Traveller population at 40,129, almost double the 2006 census figure. If one considers females between 15 and 64 years old (which is deemed the potential entrepreneurial age), then approximately 11,638 women are of potential entrepreneurial or self-employment age (29% of the total Traveller population). Travellers endure widespread racism within Irish society both in public and private institutions and suffer from a lack of health, housing, education and employment programs. Despite such discrimination, successive governments have denied them basic human rights, with women and children suffering the most (Cavaliero, 2011; Cavaliero & McGinley, 2012; Fay, 2011; Foley, 2012a; Gmelch, 1991; Helleiner, 1999; Hodgins, Millar & Barry, 2006; Houses of the Oireachtas Joint Committee on Justice, Defence and Equality, 2014; Pavee Point, 2000; O'Brien, 2014).

The increasing criminalisation of 'halting sites' (locations where Travellers temporarily base their mobile homes) and Travellers' inability to camp on the same lands as previous generations had for hundreds of years have forced Irish Travellers off the road into alternative ways of living, which are alien to their traditional culture. Subsequently, a considerable percentage of the Traveller population is now largely dependent on welfare payments and/or a scavenging economy, their traditional way of life having been criminalised. Some writers (McVeigh, 2008; Power, 2003) have described this situation as an application of Foucauldian discourse indicative of a cultural genocide displayed by Irish LGAs. According to O'Shea and Daly:

> The Traveller community is widely documented as suffering severe social exclusion … and lack access to and participation in the systems which exist to benefit all Irish citizens. (2005: 5)

The exclusion or separateness of Travellers is partly by choice, possibly a survival preference, as this enables them to retain their identity as a distinct ethnic group, usually in the face of opposition and pressure to conform to general societal norms (Ní Shuinear, 1994). Their subsequent exclusion and low socio-social, socio-cultural and socio-economic status can prevent Traveller women from participating as equals in society, often aggravated by the hostility and misconceptions that 'settled' people show towards them (Helleiner, 1999, 2000; University College Dublin, 2010). Yet, there are also many positive aspects to Traveller life that are not generally appreciated by the wider population, and some of these characteristics align with findings in the social capital literature that advocate the positive benefits of social supports and networks, family ties and kinship, community participation and cross-generational respect, all hallmarks of traditional Traveller communities (Gmelch & Gmelch, 1976; University College Dublin, 2010).

Female Travellers and entrepreneurship

It is increasingly recognised that women-owned businesses are critical to economic prosperity, as recent research has found that economies that have more women entrepreneurs have higher standards of living (Barr, 2015; GEM, 2012; Ramaswami & Mackiewicz, 2009). Over the past two decades, it has been recognised that women's entrepreneurship contributes substantially to economic growth, employment, innovation and all other areas of a nation's commercial activity (GEM, 2012). Despite the development of literature on women entrepreneurs, there remains very little literature available on Traveller women entrepreneurs (see Cooney, 2009). McDonagh (1994) argued that Traveller women (as mothers, home-makers and carers) have to make do with low incomes, generally in poor living circumstances, and possibly without basic facilities such as running water and sanitation. Data from the Central Statistics Office (CSO, 2004) show that female Travellers will live 11.9 years less than settled women,[2] and (on average) will die at 55 years of age, *'the age it was for settled women in the 1940s'* (Redmond, 2009: 14). Traveller women's health and mental state of mind must also deal with life experiences such as:

- Cot deaths at 10–12 times higher than the national average
- Still-births 3 times higher than the national average
- Prenatal mortality rates 3 times higher than the national average
- Infant mortality rates 2.5 times higher than the national average
- High rates of metabolic and congenital disorders
- 1 in 4 families living in third-world conditions without access to water, toilets or refuse collection (Redmond, 2009; Western Heath Board, 2003).

Add to these statistics the low life expectancy of their menfolk in comparison to the mainstream 'settled' population, strong evidence of abuse and domestic violence, increasing rates of divorce and high levels of racial abuse, and the composite result is a high rate of depression and other related medical issues (Pavee Point, 2000; Redmond, 2009; University College Dublin, 2010).

Within the context of the social environment in which this chapter explores, there are inextricable linkages between the ideology of particular historical moments in Irish cultural evolution and the identity from which Traveller women practice entrepreneurship. The theoretical framework employed is that of social marginality, in which such marginality is viewed as socially constructed, and marginal regions where Traveller women are entrepreneurial are seen as sites of resistance against the status quo of their culture and also mainstream culture, offering new vantage points for social critique (Cullen & Pretes, 2000). To the casual observer, a Traveller woman's participation in entrepreneurship is often seen as simply a survival mechanism that many would classify as 'necessity' entrepreneurship (Brewer & Gibson, 2014) within a relatively small minority sample (Langowitz and Minniti, 2007). However, the casual observer possibly would not know, understand or be able to interpret the deeper connections of Traveller cultural practice (Cossée, 2005) and how they interrelate with entrepreneurial activity within the Traveller community to create a distinctive experience.

So who is a 'Traveller woman entrepreneur'? An entrepreneur generally means someone who starts and runs a small business as an individual, in partnership or as a family enterprise with the goal of producing a profit, recognizing that profit may be only one of several goals. Cooney (2009) and Foley (2012a) both found that Traveller women entrepreneurs start small businesses with the primary intention of supporting their nuclear families as necessity entrepreneurs (Langowitz & Minniti, 2007). As a secondary goal, they may also indirectly service their local communities, Traveller and non-Traveller, in trade or service related industries, including but not restricted to fast foods, clothing design and retail, grocery stores, hair salons, consultancies, computer repair services and restaurants. The process of starting and running a business as entrepreneurs involves leveraging who one is, what one knows and who one knows, in order to discover or create entrepreneurial opportunities, an approach that very much echoes the work of Sarasvathy (2001) on effectuation. In general, male and female Irish Traveller entrepreneurs manage without formal training or access to government-sponsored support systems, but instead utilise their unique cultural motivations, attributes, identity, skills and knowledge, as well as their existing and adopted social networks to provide business support and advice. In settled society (mainstream, non-Traveller) there are expectations about what it means to be an entrepreneur, but in Traveller societies, men rarely see women as entrepreneurial, even though *"women bear a considerable role in the preservation of identity and culture"* (Redmond, 2009: 15), which arguably is based on the entrepreneurial attitude of making something out of nothing, of '*doing a deal*'. This is the necessity entrepreneur in action, and Traveller women are often expected to provide food, shelter and warmth for the nuclear family (frequently independently of the male partner).

The amalgamation of the Traveller living space (be it sedentary or mobile) with its economic environment illustrates the complexity of the cultural history of enterprise and existence, since the two are usually combined into one within the Traveller community. Related to this co-existence of enterprise and living space, a Traveller's choice of economic independence and flexible economic organisation is usually located within the family unit. The extended family is the basic unit, in a lifestyle where older men work alongside their sons or other younger male relatives, and women and younger girls learn from the older women, in a pattern that resembles an apprenticeship that has both cultural and economic functionality. The living space is also the workspace, as it is rare that Travellers will actually own (or rent) a specific warehouse or workplace, due to their lifestyle (moving from place to place) and the difficulty that they experience in gaining access to property because of landlords' typical racism (Cossée, 2005).

Entrepreneurs normally set up their businesses according to some government standards, pay taxes and comply with local by-laws, but in many cases Travellers will ignore such regulations and operate within a 'black economy'. Generally only long-term sedentary Travellers recognise these legal requirements, and indeed one of the common criticisms levied at Traveller businesspeople by mainstream society is that they do not pay taxes. The Traveller economy is complex, moulded by centuries of negative mainstream governance. This is not raised as an excuse of some Travellers' behaviour but rather highlights that one should not always judge another society based on the stereotypes of his/her own society. One of the key issues settled society fails to understand is that Travellers in general do not trust banks or mainstream institutions, a belief-system based on countless generations of oppression, dominance and poor relationships. This has had an extensive impact on how Travellers manage their financial affairs. Travellers tend to carry their family wealth in their wallets or purses. Male or female, they generally live in a cash economy, ensuring what wealth they have is on their person and/or invested in their mobile homes or vehicles (Cossée, 2005). This practice can give mainstream observers a false impression of Travellers' true net worth, as they will judge them based on mainstream value systems.

The traditional cash economy utilised by Travellers is coming under increasing pressure to become more formalised, particularly given recent legislation relating to sole traders. What is lacking in Ireland is a two-tier system that progressively brings Travellers out of the cash economy, while simultaneously providing guaranteed support in business mentoring and access to start-up capital, procurement opportunities and supply networks *and* sets a moratorium on taxation requirements to encourage small business enterprise engagement. However Traveller women are increasingly engaging in formal social, economic and community development activities, while the Traveller men are more often entrenched in the cash economy of old (Cossée, 2005). Thus, as economic activity becomes more regulated, Traveller men are in an increasingly precarious position, whereas female Travellers are becoming more successful within the formal economy, and this is also being reflected in their increased educational attainments that – as has been shown in studies in other countries (Foley, 2012b) – is one of the foundation stones for economic growth within minority communities.

Building a conceptual framework

Gaining an accurate understanding of the challenges faced by Traveller women in developing their entrepreneurial activities is quite difficult, given the dearth of research undertaken in this area. Indeed, as Redmond (2009: 15) noted, *"the picture of the current lives of women Travellers is incomplete. They are often invisible"*. Developmental work by people such as Tamsin Cavaliero (2011, 2012, 2013), Cavaliero and McGinley (2012) and Tanya Lalor (Doyle & Lalor, 2012) is contributing to the greater understanding of women Travellers engaging in entrepreneurial activity in Ireland, which is slowly helping to build a clearer picture of female entrepreneurship within this specific population. However, more developed background literature can be found in Canadian government publications and in Canadian academic research, as such work has dominated the literature on the study of female entrepreneurship amongst Indigenous people over the past decade (Barker, 1998; Carrington, 2006; Fenwick, 2002; Heidrick & Nicol, 2002; Howe, 2006; Ibrahim & Soufani, 2002; Orser, 2008; Still & Timms, 2000; Todd, 2012; Williams & Guilmette, 2001). Irish Travellers, whilst not accepted as an ethnic minority by the Irish government, in respect of this research are identified as an Indigenous people of Ireland.

The research methodology adopted for the fieldwork that underpins this chapter is embedded within the broad domain of qualitative inquiry, which emanates from the interpretive and post-positivist genres, in order to seek deeper engagement with a specific research area. The primary research consisted of face-to-face semi-structured interviews with 35 Traveller women entrepreneurs in Ireland (predominantly from the Dublin, Galway and Sligo regions) in order to explore the lived-in and lived-through practice of entrepreneurship in the context of the Travellers' identity and the historical legacy. To define the ethnically unique Irish Traveller, the internationally accepted three part 'common law' definition of an Australian Aboriginal (AIATSIS, 2014) was applied to selecting the Traveller participants – that is, they were of Traveller *descent*, they *self-identified* as Travellers and they were *accepted* as Travellers *by the Traveller community*.[3] The research concerns Irish Traveller women entrepreneurs, so it is pertinent to note that, while both researchers were male (one is an Australian Aboriginal), the authors sought to write from a feminist Indigenous standpoint perspective based on their own previous publications and research history. Given the participant sample, the main propositions of the interviews were as follows:

1 How did Traveller women entrepreneurs practice their entrepreneurship?
2 What were the entrepreneurs' perceptions of the facilitating aspects of their practice?
3 What were the entrepreneurs' perceptions of the challenging aspects of their practice?

An overarching theme that appeared constantly within this research was the gaze of '*the other*' – the subjugating and overt racism displayed by a substantial proportion of Irish people towards Irish Travellers – and the gazing back at oneself in the context of this study to ensure objectivity by the researcher (Said, 1994). The time and space available to the authors prohibited comparative studies with non-Traveller women, but instead relative works by two Aboriginal feminist writers Huggins (1998) and Moreton-Robinson (2000) were investigated for additional insight. The writings of Bell Hooks (1988) were also used since the authors were writing as males on feminist issues, which is one of the reasons standpoint theory[4] was adopted. Having obtained initial introductions to some participants from professional women working in Traveller community support agencies, a snowball sampling approach (Morgan, 2008) was then used to gain further introductions. The research methodology employed sought to ensure that the sample base was eclectic and diversified in terms of industry, location and family representations. The names and geographic locations of the participants were omitted from the analysis to ensure privacy and instead codes were applied to participants such as A1 or C3. The research methodology uses a multiple case study approach applied within independent studies (Yin, 2002; Eisenhardt, 1989) along with a systematic literature review of Travellers in general (Tranfield et al., 2003; Pittaway et al., 2004). A thematic approach was applied to the empirical evidence to provide focus and unity (Thorpe et al., 2006), and the output of this approach is discussed in detail later in the chapter.

Developing a deeper understanding

When analysing the data from the primary research, a number of background characteristics were commonly found amongst the interviewees. Most of the participants fitted the stereotypical Traveller description that is the context of a Catholic wife, married as a child bride (often in an arranged marriage), existing mainly to provide a home for her husband and to care for her children in a tight cultural bond. The group of 10 participants located in a coastal town exhibited extreme shyness, and they only spoke to the researchers through an intermediary. Their children exhibited signs of poor diet, as did the interviewees themselves, and they acknowledged that they ate takeaway food most nights (sharing fried food), and were concerned at their welfare, openly stating that they were worried for their children's future. In terms of the participants' entrepreneurial behaviour, the research determined that many different approaches were adopted, and Schumpeter's (1967) notion of creative destruction (a process he termed 'bahnbrechen' – literally a break in a train track that forces progress into new directions) can be applied to the participants who positively created wealth when situations arose that required initiative and income-earning responses. Based on the research questions previously highlighted, the three key outcomes from the interviews were as follows:

1   *How did Traveller women entrepreneurs practice their entrepreneurship?*

Of the 35 independent female entrepreneurs interviewed, all initially began their entrepreneurial activity as an extension of their household, echoing the findings of Cossée (2005). In terms of marriage, 16 of them were divorced and were now acting without wider family support networks; of these, half operated from independent premises, while the rest remained in the home with children and other female family members (aged mothers and aunts). Of the remaining participants, 4 of them were unmarried, with their families generally unsupportive of their actions. In one case (D12) this led to a family feud after an aunt by marriage accused the entrepreneur of being promiscuous because of her 'un-Traveller' ways of living by herself, owning/driving a current model car and wearing stockings, high heels and business suits as she followed her commercial professional practice. She was also the only participant studied who had a tertiary qualification. The family dispute was settled by the entrepreneur's athletic younger brother hospitalising the aunt's eldest son (the entrepreneur's cousin) in a bareknuckle fistfight, thus maintaining an age-old Traveller tradition and upholding her honour, at least in the short term. This woman has refused her father's attempts to marry her off since she was 14 years of age (she intends to marry for love), which has caused further division within her immediate family. So the cost of following the path of financial independence has been considerable for this young woman in the loss of contact with her father, although two of her sisters are enrolled in college hoping to duplicate their sister's success and a male first cousin is also now at university. None of them (including the entrepreneur) had continued at high school past the age of 14, due to the racism and irrelevance of the education they were offered within the Irish school system.

Overall, the business practices encountered were diverse and complicated as the majority of the women were still living within a patriarchal society. For many their entrepreneurial activity was almost a subsistence existence where they had to earn income to provide for food, clothing and bare essentials such as heating and lighting by begging, hawking, sewing, dealing in second-hand clothing and doing small jobs. The economic position of the remaining entrepreneurs was much more positive, and they openly talked about product diversification, learning new techniques or undertaking business skill training. They had to succeed as they were targeting progressive improvement, whereas the control group were prepared to accept what society dealt them without any strategic planning other than succeeding in their day-to-day existence. Many of the entrepreneurs were considering the seasonal impact of products (e.g. Christmas, Easter, spring-winter, etc.), what they could produce, acquire or market at social functions and shows and how they might build on other successful entrepreneurs, Travellers and non-Travellers. In many ways, the approach of the Traveller women entrepreneurs to business opportunities followed the principles of effectuation (Sarasvathy, 2001), without ever realising that they were adopting known business practices.

2   *What were the entrepreneurs' perceptions of the facilitating aspects of their practice?*

The facilitating practice observed in both the control study group and the independent entrepreneurs' activities was the heavy reliance on networks, albeit initially limited and underdeveloped in the early stages of the business lifecycle and restricted to family associations.

The 10 women located in the same seaside tourist town did not change their business approach; they stuck to tried and trusted ways even though their income had steadily diminished over many years and in many cases their network circles had shrunk. In comparison, as the other 25 entrepreneurs gained experience and success, they soon developed stronger networks, seeking industry non-Traveller partners, business consultants and even in one case The Small Business Advice Programme. Vertical integration into complex supply lines and marketing opportunities resulted in increased bridging capital opportunity and much stronger bonding capital that linked into the dominant settled society. As one participant stated:

> I have never and will never forget that I am a Traveller and I have one foot firmly stuck in this culture. However to succeed in business I also have another foot running within the settler business world, learning and buying, but above all selling to them. The colour of their Euro is important as the notes are larger and more of them. I now earn an income in one month that my father in his prime would not earn in a year.
>
> *(Participant D 12)*

Increased wealth allowed this Traveller woman to ensure that her mother now had a permanent place to live, could afford the medicines she needed and was warm and secure in winter, thereby alleviating the mother's mental stress. Her mother was also there to help in the business, receiving and delivering goods, the entrepreneur's children were able to go to a school of their choice and no longer suffered as much taunts and racism and they had a positive future as they were in senior high school and thinking of going to university. Her sister was also working in the business, safe, not on the street, eating well and free from the mental trauma of a drug addiction and a spiral of hopelessness. The positive domino impact of the successful entrepreneur also had a positive impact on several other Traveller women, and indeed it was found she also positively influenced their male dependants both within and external to their family. To some extent, this was repeated in the cases of all 35 participants. However, the research found no positive examples of escaping the welfare 'rut', as poor education levels, limited skillsets and the lack of financial capital reserves offered them little hope, as in general they continued to suffer from poor physical and mental health due to the obvious socio-economic strains evident within their lifestyles (Hodgins et al., 2006).

3   What were the entrepreneurs' perceptions of the challenging aspects of their practice?

On-going racism (external and internal within their cultural circles) and the lack of start-up and working capital to fund business growth were the major recurrent issues that plagued the entrepreneurs (Helleiner, 1999). The issue of limited capital was met by innovative attempts to generate funding, but most started their businesses with savings and/or monies borrowed from close family members. Some sold heirloom jewellery, while one went to the UK, managed to get a small start-up business loan under an alias and then commenced the business in Ireland. It was common for the entrepreneurs to start business enterprises whilst drawing welfare, with all profits being put back into the enterprise, using standard bootstrapping methods to fund increased stock or the employment of others. With business success, several were able to obtain credit cards or credit facilities that enabled them to fund working capital. Almost 20% obtained small business grant funding through their local Traveller network and were very supportive of the larger and more proactive Traveller community organisations. However, several entrepreneurs were very critical of those same organisations, and there seemed to be some geographic rivalries, with some entrepreneurs being very critical of one organisation whilst others commended it and vice versa. Similar to many Indigenous cultures, harmony between people from clans is rare, although feedback can be positive if representative organisations listen to it and use it to improve their services.

The coastal town group of entrepreneurs experienced ongoing racism, not only from the settled community, but they also suffered exclusion from their former spouses, their own menfolk such as fathers and uncles, and occasionally even their mothers, sisters and aunts. In one case, an entrepreneur was even excluded by her own sons, who had turned against her and sided with their father based on misguided and antiquated 'cultural' beliefs. They also suffered racial abuse, exclusion from retail outlets (who generally believed they were there to shoplift) and in some cases physical and verbal abuse from both shop-keepers and police. They also told stories of harsh landlords and difficulties with settled neighbours in council housing and of negative attitudes from police, media and mainstream society's general attitude towards Traveller people.

Overall the results of the research revealed several key common traits, characteristics and general themes that interested the researchers, and these included the Traveller women's motivations, attributes, identity, skills and knowledge.

(1) Motivations

The primary motivations highlighted by the participants were the desire to succeed, to provide for their families and to improve themselves, while their long-term aspirations were to see their grandchildren grow up healthy and happy without hunger, and not to die in poverty or sickness, *'worn out like an overworked mule like my poor Gran'* (Participant 5 De). They also wanted to see Travellers accepted and to attain some 'basic human rights' (Participants 1C, 3WC, 4 De 5 De, 1TB, 10D, 11D, 12D & 13D) and to achieve a level of parity in what most people take for granted (employment/housing/education/access to health), as they viewed Travellers as being denied these basic human rights. Many of these motivations were broadly similar to the lower levels of Maslow's hierarchy of needs (1943). As women, many also wanted to be able to dress nicely, *'to wear expensive underwear, shop where I want to shop, wear makeup if I want, to feel like a woman'* (Participant 25 G). This could be interpreted as moving from Maslow's basic physiological needs and jumping to the needs of self-esteem and self-respect (Maslow, 1943).

(2) Attributes

The analysis found that Irish Traveller women entrepreneurs in general displayed intelligence and enhanced skills in opportunity recognition, together with business experience (which most unashamedly attributed to their mothers' cunning and their fathers' skills in seeing and making 'a deal'). Most also had good track records in money management, although three participants had failed in previous ventures and had moved on to their second or third enterprise. None of this group trusted banks, and they were all sceptical of having bank accounts or being a registered business (seeing these as necessary evils), while 12 proudly announced that they were taxpayers. When challenged on this by family members, they usually responded that they were working hard to create the wealth that paid for the welfare system that many unemployed Irish Travellers relied on. One attribute that was strongly evident in all of the women was pride. The women have a strength that is intergenerational, a belief that without their enterprise and industrious support, and their mothers and grandmothers, men would be without a resource and foundational support base that enabled the males to engage successfully in their own gender-based enterprise activities. Interestingly, Foley (2012b) found that some Aboriginal men have difficulty understanding or accepting the changed role of women in their communities in modernity, as 'colonisation' has in general destroyed their ability to comprehend traditional gender interaction in their adoption of perceived western male role functions. Prior to colonisation Aboriginal men and women both interacted separately and together, invariably relying on the other in a communal supportive existence. Likewise, Traveller men have difficulty understanding the female desire to be independent and pursue vocational aspirations, yet in more traditional circumstances they would support and follow separate, interactive yet communal, roles that ultimately ensure the continuation of the nuclear family and kinship relations (just like the Aboriginal male).

In general, the Traveller businesswomen displayed a strong conviction in their culture and beliefs and a longing for the up-skilling of old ways. However, two participants (D12 & G5) did not show this attribute and arguably risked further criticism by their community as they openly sought riches of the dominant society. Both women had already been cut off from their families and disparaged as promiscuous, soiled women for desiring what mainstream society would see as normal independent lives. They were outgoing and socially active and there was no evidence that they were any more sexually active than married or un-married Traveller women, so any accusation of promiscuity was based on ancient terminology and outdated beliefs. Interestingly, the women in question saw themselves as practising Catholics and attended mass regularly, although 'traditional' Traveller women attended church only for funerals, weddings, confirmations and baptisms (Redmond, 2009). However, the coastal town group's attributes were very different, as they were nervous, unsure, not proud of who they were and seemed to be living on the edge, suffering from fatigue and mental stress. It was difficult to unearth the reasoning behind the significant differences displayed by this group as they were reluctant to talk with the researchers and offered little information beyond answering the questions in a brief fashion.

(3) Identity

As noted in the previous section, the Traveller businesswomen were proud of their identities. However, until mainstream settler society accepts them as themselves, it has been substantiated by their common experience that it may not be in their best interests to display or identify their minority background publicly, because when they do they invariably suffer racial discrimination from potential purchasers or creditors. This discrimination includes people questioning the quality of the goods (as some Travellers are known to sell inferior goods) with resultant continuous negative outcomes for the women studied. Creditors decline credit facilities and demand cash only, which is difficult in growing businesses as trade credit is well recognised as a form of business 'growth' finance. Only a few of the entrepreneurs had received financial support from mainstream lending institutions (banks), while others had sought funds elsewhere, hiding their Traveller identity where credit is concerned. None of the women studied sold cultural Traveller products in a tourism context (or similar product/service based on cultural identity), so there was no need to market their identities to gain entry into a niche market, although they all strongly self-identified as Travellers in certain circumstances (especially in defence of their family and children). The coastal town group openly admitted that they tried to hide their identities when selling, scavenging and begging as they felt that it led to fairer treatment by mainstream society. However, many admitted that their dress sense and their accents made them instantly recognisable, frequently making hiding their identity quite difficult.

(4) Skills

The entrepreneurs continually displayed ever-increasing skill bases by engaging in training, industry exposure and/or formal education. Perhaps their greatest skill was the ability to move within the dominant society, being accepted as women in business first rather than being seen as Irish Travellers. They have also gained skills in talking to their business partners in the mainstream culture, whether purchasers or creditors. They were also developing their business models, borrowing initially from the settler model, but in time this could change to a Traveller business model (until broader success is achieved, the dominant society business model must be accepted). Due to their limited exposure to dominant society business acumen, many had suffered short-term financial losses by people such as associates and landlords, a normal business experience that many naïve, nascent Indigenous entrepreneurs might experience (Foley & Hunter, 2013).

(5) Knowledge

In general, the participant entrepreneurs had received more formal education than was generally found within the Traveller community, although the coastal town group mostly had only fractured engagement with schools up to the ages of 14 or less. The entrepreneurs generally had the same early experience growing up in the Traveller community, but later in life, on separation from their marriages or in their late teens, inspired mostly by Traveller self-help groups (such as Pavee Point, the Galway Association and the Irish Traveller Network), they had sought college entry, learnt new skills and worked to follow their dreams. Unlike the stereotypical mainstream perceptions of Irish Travellers, they are for the most part intelligent, bright and academically successful when given the opportunity and positive support networks. One entrepreneur (D5) has since gained a University qualification as she aims to establish a professional career. What Traveller women do lack initially is self-confidence, the product of generations of dominance by a patriarchal system and a racist dominant society. Education has proven to be the catalyst for success for all Traveller women interviewed, although not so much in the attainment of basic business skills, which they subsequently agreed was extremely important. Formal education pedagogy has assisted interpersonal skill development in the areas of how to talk, how to respond and how to think and interact in business, in other words how to interact within the dominant non-Traveller society of capitalistic endeavour. Human Capital attainment was minimal prior to the women's formal education, and in general they saw their participation in business training courses or college as a way of developing a broader knowledge skill base. The coastal town group had no college education and very low human capital attributes, having left school at an early age, predominantly because of bullying and racism. Additionally a lifestyle of changing schools on a regular basis did not allow them to gain any academic skills. They often faced hostile teachers, themselves racist towards Traveller children; many of the women could barely read, and some could not write more than their names, basic skills that they wished they possessed. Unfortunately, recent financial cutbacks to the Traveller special education provision will no doubt create another generation of uneducated Travellers. Possessing limited human capital creates a generation of labourers, and in a country with limited unskilled labouring work now available, it is arguable that the government has indirectly created increased welfare dependency for generations of Travellers to come. However, the educated women entrepreneurs have managed to break this cycle, adding weight to the positive potential of programs run by Traveller groups highlighted previously that include organisations such as Pavee Point, the Irish Traveller Network and the Galway Traveller Network.

Conclusions

The research contained within this chapter has revealed that, while Traveller women entrepreneurs have been able to maintain their strong cultural (kinship) networks (which are exceedingly important in their business pursuits), the lack of racial acceptance within the multiculturalism of the wider Irish community still appears to be an inhibiting factor to business growth. The well-being and care of their families were seen as primary motivators, along with a pooling of emotional, psychological and spiritual strengths for a shared purpose. Indeed, they reported this as their primary driving force to succeed in business and to overcome poverty. Perhaps the most sobering aspect of this research centres on the topic of discrimination within the business environment, as the experience of negative discrimination (racism) is so common that it is only acknowledged when it is physical or exclusionary. They also experienced the geographic isolation of residing in neighbourhoods with high unemployment and a lack of essential contact networks with the broader business community. The participants all faced cultural challenges that hindered self-employment and business success. These findings imply the need for enhanced political and structural changes to ensure that there are adequate policies and cohesive approaches to capital networks, training and employment opportunities for Traveller women. Longitudinal studies and linkages with policy development and deployment are also needed to further highlight the inextricable links between the ideology and identity of Indigenous women entrepreneurs.

There has been almost little credible research-based literature available on Traveller women in business in Ireland, and overall only a few publications exist in the specialist field of 'Traveller Women Entrepreneurs' and few in quality academic journals (with the majority of publications written by non-Traveller authors). This study will help create greater understanding of the challenges faced by the Traveller community, so that policy makers, financiers and industry groups may better understand the plight of Irish Traveller women entrepreneurs and small business owner-managers. Traveller women entrepreneurs and SME owners are generally suffering from lower levels of Human and Social Capital, which lead to lower Bridging and Bonding Capital, which means that they start businesses with smaller amounts of capital, as well as suffering from a lack of resources in terms of working capital and business connections. In general, they have poor education and low industry experience, are burdened by childrearing and are responsible for their nuclear families (often including siblings, wider family and parents). They are also likely to suffer from poor choices of partners, and to be exposed to sexual discrimination, harassment and/or 'physical' abuse, as well as enduring the trauma of high infant mortality and the other health issues that plague their society (Pavee Point, 2000). If such challenges are not enough to endure, the identity of Traveller women also invokes discrimination, which means that Traveller women in business have to be tough to survive, as they endure the negativity of Irish and their own patrilineal society expressed through bigotry and sexism. Indeed, some male bankers, financiers, real estate agents and trade creditors still ask female Travellers if they can speak to their husbands before making a decision on business applications. Traveller women entrepreneurs are discriminated against within their own society and within mainstream society, both as Irish Travellers and as female entrepreneurs, so they face triple sets of challenges when establishing and running a business. Much more needs to be understood about these barriers and how they might be overcome, but it is the ambition of this chapter to generate further interest in the topic and that colleagues will produce more literature to contribute to a research area that deserves further investigation and intervention.

Notes

1 Roma (or Romani) people have a long history of living in Europe with a presence recorded from the 13th Century. They are now widely recognized as one of the EU's largest minority groups with an estimate of more than 10 million Roma living in Europe.

    The Sinti (also *Sinta* or *Sinte*) are a Romani people of Central Europe, traditionally itinerant; today only a small percentage of the group remains unsettled. In earlier times, they frequently lived on the outskirts of communities. The Sinti of Central Europe are closely related to the group known as Manouche in France. They speak the Sinti-Manouche variety of Romani, which exhibits strong German influence.

    Gypsy (or Gipsy) is an English term; it originates from the Middle English gypcian, short for Egipcien. It is ultimately derived from the Greek Αἰγύπτιοι (Aigyptioi), meaning Egyptian, via Middle French and Latin. This designation owes its existence to the belief, common in the Middle Ages, that the Romani, or some related group (such as the middle eastern Dom people), were itinerant Egyptians. According to one narrative they were exiled from Egypt as punishment for allegedly harbouring the infant Jesus. As described in Victor Hugo's novel *The Hunchback of Notre Dame*, the medieval French referred to the Romanies as Egyptiens. The word Gypsy in English has become so pervasive that many Romani organizations use it in their own organizational names.

2 Interestingly, the life expectancy of a Traveller male is 61.7 years, 15.1 years less than men in the general population, also the comparative age of a non-Traveller in the 1940s (University College Dublin, 2010).

3 The utilization of the Australian Aboriginal definition provides a basis that ensures the research subject is qualified beyond doubt. The same definition is used by ethnographers and other researchers widely to determine a distinct ethnic minority member, that is descent, self-identification and acceptance by their community.

4 Standpoint theory is a postmodern method for analysing inter-subjective discourses. This body of work concerns the ways that authority (or agency) is rooted in individuals' knowledge (their perspectives – their culture), and the power that such authority/agency exerts.

References

AIATSIS, 2014, Australian Institute Aboriginal and Torres Strait Islander Studies, Confirmation of Aboriginality. Canberra ACT. http://www.aiatsis.gov.au/fhu/aboriginality.html. Accessed 25 September.

Appelton, L., Hagan, T., Goward, P., Repper, J. and Wilson, R. 2003, Smail's contribution to understanding the needs of the socially excluded: the case of gypsy and traveller women. *Clinical Psychology*, 24: 40–46.

Barker, K. 1998, Gender and lifelong learning: enhancing the contributions of women to small and medium sized enterprises in Canada for the 21st century. Canadian Case Study. APEC HRD Project. *Gender and Lifelong Learning: Enhancing the Contributions of Women to SME's in the Asia Pacific Region for the 21st Century. FutureEd*: Vancouver, BC., Canada.

Barr, M. S. 2015, *Minority and Women Entrepreneurs: Building Capital, Networking & Skills. The Hamilton Project. Discussion Paper 2015–03*. Washington, D.C.: University of Michigan.

Brewer, J. & Gibson, S. W. (Eds) 2014, *Necessity Entrepreneurs Microenterprise Education and Economic Development*. Cheltenham, UK: Edgar Elgar Publishing Ltd.

Carrington, C. 2006, Women entrepreneurs. *Journal of Small Business and Entrepreneurship*, 19 (2): 83–94.

Cavaliero, T. 2011, Travellers' experiences of education in County Sligo. *Research West Review* 1 (2).

Cavaliero, T. 2012, R.E.C.A.L.L – exploring the history of the traveller settled relationship in County Sligo. In White, K. and Costello, J. (eds) *The Imaginary of the Stranger: Encountering the Other. Port Na Fáilte< Donegal County Council.*

Cavaliero, T. 2013, 'How was your day?': Supporting travellers at primary level. In McTaggart, B. and Share, P. (eds) *Our Children-Our Future Conference Proceedings*. Big Fish Press.

Cavaliero, T. and McGinley, M. 2012, Travellers in Ireland and issues of social care. In Lalor, K. and Share, P. (eds) *Social Care in Ireland: Theory, Policy and Practice* 2nd edition forthcoming.

Cooney, T. M. 2009, Developing entrepreneurship programmes for female members of the Irish traveller community. *International Journal of Gender and Entrepreneurship*, 1 (2): 134–147.

Cossée, C. 2005, Travellers' economy in Europe: What recognition? Study for the ETAP transnational project (EQUAL European programme). With the participation of: Bríd O'Brien Pavee Point, Stéphanie Legoff FNASAT/CODIPE, Didier Botton FNASAT, Christophe Robert FORS – Social Research. FORS-Social Research. Union Nationale des Institutions Sociales d'Actions avec les Tsiganes.

CSO, 2004, Census 2002. Irish Traveller Community, Central Statistics Office, Dublin.

CSO, 2007, Census 2006. Dublin: Central Statistics Office, Dublin.

CSO, 2014. CD713: Irish Travellers by Age Group, Sex, Detailed Marital Status and Census Year, Central Statistics Office, Dublin http://www.cso.ie/px/pxeirestat/Statire/SelectVarVal/saveselections.asp accessed 23 June 2014.

Cullen, B. and Pretes, M. 2000, The meaning of marginality: Interpretations and perceptions in Social Science. *The Social Science Journal*, 37 (2): 215–229.

Doyle, G. & Tanya Lalor (eds) 2012, *Social Enterprise in Ireland: A People's Economy?* Cork: Oak Tree Press.

Eisenhardt, K. 1989, Building theories from case study research. *Academy of Management. The Academy of Management Review;* Oct., 14 (4): 532–550.

European Commission. 2013, Representation in Ireland, Benefits of the CAP: Economy. http://ec.europa.eu/ireland/key-eu-policy-areas/agriculture/benefits-of-the-cap/index_en.htm accessed 23 June, 2014.

Fay, R. 2011, Irish Travellers Shadow Report, Dublin: Pavee Point Travellers.

Fenwick, T. 2002, Canadian Women Negotiating Working Knowledge in Enterprise: Interpretative and Critical Readings of a National Study. CISAE/RCEEA 16 (2): 1–29.

Foley, D. 2012a, *Gulanyunung Pialla* ('Our talk'). An Australian Aboriginal review of Irish Travellers. In Heneghan, J., Moriarty, M. (Warde) and OhAodha, M. (eds), *Travellers and the Settled Community: A Shared Future*. Raheny, Dublin 5, Ireland: The Liffey Press.

Foley, D. 2012b, Teaching entrepreneurship to indigenous and other minorities: Towards a strong sense of self, tangible skills and active participation within society. *Journal of Business Diversity*, 12 (2): 59–74.

Foley, D. & Hunter, B. 2013, What is an Indigenous Australian business? *Journal of Australian Indigenous Issues*, 16 (3): 66–74.

Galway Traveller Movement, 2012, Enterprising Traveller women: A toolkit to inform enterprise programs. Empowering Traveller Women Enterprise Project. Galway Traveller Movement: Galway, Ireland.

GEM, 2012, Women's Report, GEM, Donna J. Kelley, Candida G. Brush, Patricia G. Greene and Yana Litovsky, Global Entrepreneurship Research Association. The Centre for Womens Leadership, Babson: Babson College.

Gmelch, S. 1991, *Nan: The Life of an Irish Travelling Woman*. Long Grove, IL: Waveland Press.

Gmelch, G. & S. Gmelch. 1976, The emergence of an ethnic group: The Irish Tinkers. *Anthropological Quarterly*, 49 (4): 225–238.

Government of Ireland, 2002, The Equal Status Act. Dublin: The Stationery Office.

Heidrick, T. & Nicol, T. 2002, Financing SME'S in Canada: Barriers faced by women, youth, aboriginal and minority entrepreneurs in accessing capital. Research Paper for Small Business Policy Branch, Government of Canada: Ottawa, On.

Helleiner, J. 1999, Women of the itinerant class: Gender and anti-traveller racism in Ireland, *Women's Studies International Forum*, 20 (2, March–April): 275–287.

Helleiner, J. 2000, *Irish Travellers: Racism and the Politics of Culture*. Toronto: University of Toronto Press.

Helleiner, J. 2003, *Irish Travellers: Racism and the Politics of Culture*. Toronto, Ont. Canada: University of Toronto Press.

Hodgins, M., Millar, M. & Barry, M. M. 2006, "...it's all the same no matter how much fruit or vegetables or fresh air we get": Traveller women's perceptions of illness causation and health inequalities. *Social Science & Medicine*, 62 (8): 1978–1990.

hooks, b. 1988, Talking back: Thinking feminist, thinking black. *Between the Lines*. Toronto, Ont. Canada.

Houses of the Oireachtas Joint Committee on Justice, Defence and Equality, 2014, Report on the Recognition of Traveller Ethnicity, Department of Justice and Equality, Dublin.

Howe, E. 2006, Saskatchewan with an Aboriginal majority: Education and entrepreneurship. Department of Economics Discussion Paper, Department of Economics: University of Saskatchewan, Saskatoon, Saskatchewan.

Huggins, J. 1998, Sister girl: The writings of Aboriginal activist and historian Jackie Huggins. St. Lucia Qld. Australia: University of Qld. Press.

Ibrahim, A. B. and Soufani, K. 2002, Entrepreneurship education and training in Canada: A critical assessment. *Education + Training*, 44 (8/9): 421–430.

Keane, D. 2005, International law and the ethnicity of Irish travellers. *Wash. & Lee Race & Ethnic Anc.* 11: 43.

Langowitz, N. and Minniti, M. 2007, The entrepreneurial propensity of women. *Entrepreneurship Theory and Practice* 31 (3): 341–364.

Maslow, A. H. 1943, A theory of human motivation. *Psychological Review*, 50 (4): 370–396.

McDonagh, R. 1994, Travellers with a disability: A submission to the Commission on the Status of People with Disabilities, Pavee Point, Dublin.

McVeigh, R. 2008, The 'final solution': Reformism, ethnicity denial and the politics of anti-Travellerism in Ireland. *Social Policy and Society*, 7: 91–102.

Meyer, K. 1909, The secret languages of Ireland. *Journal of the Gypsy Lore Society*, New Series, 2: 241–246.

Moreton-Robinson, A. 2000, Talkin' up to the white women: Indigenous women and feminism. St. Lucia Qld. Australia: University of Qld. Press.

Morgan, D. L. 2008, The SAGE Encyclopaedia of Qualitative Research Methods. SAGE Publications, Inc. pp. 816–817.

Murphy, M., McHugh, B., Tighe, O., Mayne, P., O'Neill, C., Naughten, E. and Croke, D. T. 1999, Genetic basis of transferase-deficient galactosaemia in Ireland and the population history of the Irish Travellers, *European Journal of Human Genetics*, 7 (5): 549–554.

Nelson, D. & Silva, N. 2010, For Traveller Women In Ireland, Life Is Changing. Hidden World of Girls, producer Steve Inskeep, April 29. National Public Radio. http://www.npr.org/templates/transcript/transcript.php?storyId=125907642 accessed 25 May 2015.

Ní Shuinear, S. 1994, Irish Travellers, ethnicity and the origins question. In MacCann, M., Síocháin, S. Ó. and Ruane, J. (eds), *Irish Travellers: Culture and Ethnicity*. Belfast: Institute of Irish Studies, Queens University.

O'Brien, C. 2014, Oireachtas group calls on State to recognize Traveller ethnicity. Irish Times, April 17. http://www.irishtimes.com/news/social-affairs/oireachtas-group-calls-on-state-to-reco... Accessed 24 April, 2014.

O'Shea, K. and Daly, M. 2005, Moving forward from here: Post-primary outcomes for young Travellers in County Longford. Longford Traveller Movement, Longford.

Orser, B. 2008, *Canadian Women Entrepreneurs, Research and Public Policy: A Review of Literature*. Foreign Affairs and International Trade Canada: University of Ottawa, On.

Pavee Point, 2000, *Pavee Beoirs: Breaking the Silence. Traveller Women and Male Domestic Violence*. Dublin, Ireland: Pavee Point.

Pavee Point, 2008, *Factsheets - Traveller Women*, Pavee Point, Dublin.

Pittaway, L., Robertson, M., Munir, K., Denyer, D. and Neeley, A. 2004, Networking and innovation: A systematic review of the evidence. *International Journal of Management Reviews* 5/6 (3/4): 137–168.

Power, C. 2003, Irish travellers: Ethnicity, racism, and pre-sentence reports. *Probation Journal*, 50 (3): 252–266.

Ramaswami, R. & Mackiewicz, A. 2009, *Scaling Up: Why Women Owned Businesses Can Recharge the Global Economy*, The Ground Breaks Series: Driving Business through Diversity. UK: Ernst & Young.

Redmond, A. 2009, *Irish Traveller Women: At the Brutal Intersections of Hate*. VDM Verlag Dr Muller Aktiengesellschaft & Co. KG Saarbrucken, Germany.

Said, E. W. 1994, *Orientalism*. New York: Vintage Books.

Sampson, J. 1926, *The Dialect of the Gypsies of Wales, Being the Older Form of British Romani Preserved in the Speech of the Clan of Abram Wood*. London: Oxford University Press.

Sarasvathy, S. D. 2001, Causation and effectuation: Toward a theoretical shift from economic inevitability to entrepreneurial contingency. *The Academy of Management Review*, 26 (2): 243–263.

Schumpeter, J. A. 1967, Capitalisme Socialisme et Democratie. Petite Bibliotheque Payot.

Still, L. & Timms, W. 2000, Women's business: The flexible alternative workstyle for women. *Women in Management Review Journal*. 15 (5/6): 272–283.

Thorpe, Holt, Pittaway and Macpherson. 2006, Using knowledge within small and medium-sized firms: A systematic review of the evidence. *International Journal of Management Reviews*. 7 (4): 257–281.

Todd, R. 2012, Young urban Aboriginal women entrepreneurs: Social capital, complex transactions and community support. *British Journal of Canadian Studies*, 25 (1): 1–19.

Tranfield, D. R., Denver, D. & Smart, P. 2003, Towards a methodology for developing evidence-informed management knowledge by means of systematic review. *British Journal of Management* 14: 207–222.

University College Dublin. 2010, Our Geels: All Ireland Traveller Health Study technical report 1 health survey findings, All Ireland Traveller Health Study Team, School of Public Health, Physiotherapy and Population Science, University College Dublin.

Western Heath Board, 2003, Bord Slainte an larthair 2003–2005, Why we are called Travellers. http://www.bundodyns.com accessed 14 June 2014.

Williams, A. & Guilmette, A. M. 2001, A place for healing: Achieving hwalth for Aboriginal Women in an urban context. *The Canadian Journal of Native Studies*, 11 (1): 1–25.

Yin, R. K. 2002, *Case Study Research, Design and Methods*. Newbury Park: Sage Publication, 3rd edition.

22

ENTREPRENEURSHIP, AGE AND GENDER

The Swedish case

Carin Holmquist and Elisabeth Sundin

Introduction

Research has shown that age and gender are closely connected and cannot be separated from each other (Fineman, 2011; Halford et al., 2015; Krekula, 2007; Lykke, 2010; Krekula et al., 2013; Riach et al., 2015). Neither age nor gender is a fixed category but is constructed in complex circuits of societal and organizational action (Pritchard & Whiting, 2015). These actions can be of different types, both material and economic, such as a retirement pension system constructed on biological age and sex, or non-material and non-economic, for example, expectations and identity of an individual (Kautonen et al., 2010, 2011). These material and non-material dimensions are connected, but the categories, subcategories and boundaries are not fixed, and their social and political meanings can vary and be continually challenged and restructured (Yuval-Davis, 2006).

Although in this chapter we embrace these perspectives and standpoints, we will approach the topic gradually starting with the key concepts—entrepreneurship, age and gender—one at a time. The concepts are elaborated, in different constellations, and finally discussed as a whole—entrepreneurship-age-gender. We will also present statistics relating to entrepreneurship divided by gender and age group. When presenting these facts and figures we adopt, and hence accept, the definitions and delimitations used by the organizations responsible for the statistics. These are, of course, socially constructed from a dominating understanding of both age and gender in the economic and social context where they are produced. We also present the Swedish case with some facts and figures (produced in the Swedish system) and use these to discuss and analyze the concepts from a Scandinavian welfare perspective. In the Swedish case a database, produced by Statistics Sweden, is used to describe older entrepreneurs. This means that we accept that an entrepreneur is an individual who establishes and/or runs his/her own business as self-employed or as owner-manager.

Entrepreneurship, age and gender—value-laden concepts of theoretical and political importance

Entrepreneurship is on the top of political agendas all over the world and has been for several decades. We might even talk of our time as 'the age of entrepreneurship' (Audretch, 2009). The explanations for this are many. The connection between entrepreneurship and unemployment and the political failure to solve the problem is one such explanation; a reference to the restructuring of welfare states along the lines of New Public Management is another (Kovalainen & Sundin, 2012). Both these lines of argument are evident in some of the research reports we use.

Entrepreneurship is presented as a solution for contemporary societies, while *age* (old age) is presented as a problem and has many negative connotations. Descriptions of the problem have many dimensions: demographic aging, non-sustainable pension systems, and increasing costs for health and care. Both nations and international organizations emphasize extending working lives and more effective care and health systems as a necessity. Connected to these lines of arguments are conclusions presenting life after 50 as a 'golden age' for individuals (Sawchuk, 1995; Kautonen & Minniti, 2014). These societal demands are seldom followed and connected to demands on the organizational level, to which we will come back.

Age is a key characteristic in society; the extent of age and how it varies is important. In western societies a human being's age counts from birth, and biology continues to play a role over one's lifetime. Biological characteristics are tied to a clock, and the most important and socially relevant changes are made visible through rites of passage. Laws, regulations and also more informal institutions consider (and also form) age: biological classifications can only be understood in their cultural and social context (Hareven, 1995).

Both in politics and research human beings are often divided into three groups: children, adults and old people—i.e., childhood, adulthood and old age. The construction of welfare states relates to age, with society taking responsibilities mainly for the young and the old. Age is a key characteristic in laws and regulations but is also often used as a characteristic in the marketplace. Older citizens—both when age is a stigma and when it is something positive—are often presented in one 'big lump', although the time span for being old lasts over decades for the individual, which means that the group 'old' is constructed of individuals with different experiences depending on when they were born, when they were young, and when they entered the labor market etc. (Pritchard & Whiting, 2014). Some distinction among the old is now made based on mental status and need for help and assistance. Hence the 'elderly' group is divided into the younger-old and the older-old or the third and fourth age (Tudor-Sandahl, 2009). Further, in some markets—for example, the labor market—one can be (too) old even before one reaches the elderly status of the younger-old. In summary, age, to be old and young, is socially constructed from different standpoints varying in many dimensions. This will be illustrated later in the chapter.

Having started the discussion on age and the importance and priority of youth, we will now do the same with *gender*, establishing the priority of men, masculinity and maleness. This is a truly global phenomenon described and analyzed by organizations internationally (e.g., United Nations and OECD), regionally (e.g., the European Union), and nationally (e.g., Statistics Sweden).

The expressions of masculinity differ for many reasons, such as history, tradition and economic development. Similarities exist across nations related to these reasons, for instance, in terms of different types of economies: innovation-driven, efficiency-driven or factor-driven. Nations also form groups or clusters based on how they handle challenges, problems and possibilities in different ways. The distinction made by Esping-Andersen (1990) in categorizing welfare states is still valid, although the social democratic welfare states have been challenged by changes inspired by New Public Management. Some political scientists find that Esping-Andersen's distinctions are male biased (although one of his main typologies is built on how traditional 'female' obligations are handled) and are also elaborated from a woman's perspective. Esping-Andersen himself discusses this critique in later works (2009).

Similar to age, sex and gender are key characteristics in all societies, and there is a constant gender-labeling process. The meaning and content of gender, i.e., what is female and what is male varies over time, space and other variables. As has been demonstrated, entrepreneurship in contemporary societies carries a male label (Holmquist & Sundin, 2015; Ahl, 2002; Bruni et al., 2004.)

Age, gender and entrepreneurship

As already discussed, both age and gender are constructed and unstable concepts connected in a complex contexture. We therefore consider these concepts now using important dimensions and taking as our starting point 'work and entrepreneurship.'

Work and entrepreneurship

In entrepreneurship research the labor market is often surprisingly absent. But there are exceptions, such as the work of German sociologist Dieter Bögenhold. In his publications (Bögenhold, 2004; Bögenhold & Fachinger, 2007) he emphasizes the importance of the labor market position both for individuals and groups so as to understand changes such as entry to self-employment. These individual and group changes create structural changes in the economy. In complementary research, Holmquist and Sundin (2002) interviewed women to discuss their decision to launch a firm as a personal labor market strategy and as a strategy to solve other (family) obligations. The authors named this strategy 'adaptation.' Family businesses as employment options are especially interesting since succession and the appropriate ways of dealing with them has been a topic of focus in entrepreneurship research for decades (Davis & Harveston, 1998). This research takes an interest in the age of the entrepreneur and how age is handled within the family. Other researchers examine the relationship between age and entrepreneurship directly, and the labor market concept is integrated. This acknowledges the political problem of employment for older individuals as owner-managers and as self-employed, and their labor market history, as well as its impact on decisions to start, to exit and to manage the progress of the enterprise.

Work and age

Health and working conditions are important as individuals make their decision whether to stay or leave the labor market. When older individuals are interviewed about their decisions to continue working, they emphasize the importance of the attitudes and actions taken by their work-mates and managers (Nilsson, 2013) as well as their own health status and that of their family members. Another factor is what their partners are doing. A retired partner makes the individual more inclined to leave work, while a partner still working makes them more willing to continue. In a study of 70-year-old men in the labor market in the US, Ozawa and Terry (2009) found that the men worked because they wanted to: they were committed to work, and they could work. Many of them, however, did not want to go on as they used to—they wanted to be more flexible and perhaps work part-time. These modifications are sometimes classified as 'bridge-employment' (Kerr & Armstrong-Stassen, 2011).

Much of the research on old individuals in the labor market describes and analyses problems—most often from the individual's perspective but also from the organization's perspective. Employers are sometimes motivated to keep old employees and to combat negative attitudes towards these individuals. Studies show that the problems of the old at work are not, as a rule, related to low competence, but rather to negative attitudes towards them—ageism in practice (Solem & Mykletun, 2014). The consequences could be that the seniors choose to leave organizations and take their competence with them. These negative attitudes, of course, make it especially hard for unemployed old individuals to get new jobs (Kadefors & Johansson, 2012). Working with these age-specific attitudes is now a human resources field as well as a research field labeled 'age management' (Fabisiak & Prokurat, 2011). The aim is to create 'harmonious aging' (Liang & Luo, 2012). Authorities, both national and international, are exploring how to increase the labor market activities of old citizens. An example is EU research and policy work delivering statistics and 'best practices' across Europe on how to work with old individuals and how to develop positive attitudes about them (Eurofund, 2012).

Explicit comparisons between self-employment and employment for old individuals are sometimes made. Kautonen et al. (2012) present a study of highly educated individuals and compare the self-employed with the employed. Both groups were very satisfied with their life and their work, but the self-employed were more so. The explanations were the 'classical' advantages following from entrepreneurship—self-direction and self-control, for instance. In the employed case, the researchers found that old individuals are very valuable to their employers and that more could be done to create working conditions that are attractive for these individuals.

Age and gender

Research on age does not always consider gender, although it is an important characteristic as observed by Liang & Luo (2012). As lived, age does not have the same meaning for women as for men. Age can create positive associations indicating experience and competence—these ideas are linked to maleness (Pritchard & Whiting, 2015). For women, the age experience is attached to an implicit negative image of advancing years (Krekula et al., 2013). Duberley et al. (2014) explain the different ways individuals leave the labor market, noting women's weaker position in the labor market and their lower salaries leading to lower pensions. Activities after retirement have a connection to past experiences: either they are a continuation of what was done before or, as they are now organized, represent a change. The importance of the position before retirement, as well as the social embeddedness, is also emphasized by Szinovacz and DeViney (2000). The decisions taken by women have reference to the economy of the family, while men consider their retirement in relation to the retirement status of their partners. This study was conducted in the U.S. while the empirical studies of Duberley et al. (2014) were conducted in the UK (Pleau & Shauman, 2013). The relevance of social and economic conditions is also stressed in the introduction to a special issue on "Gendered Aging in the New Economy" (Riach et al., 2015).

Age and entrepreneurship

Official ages for retirement often mark an end-point for discussions on age and the labor market: pre-retirement situations are currently the focus of much research and statistics. As for self-employment, official ages for retirement are important, but rather as a division line than as an end-point. In terms of the younger-old, incentives for establishing or running an enterprise are discussed as an alternative to being employed, whereas for the older group, interest lies in being self-employed versus just being retired. In their study, Curran & Blackburn (2001) asked retired people why they were not seeking employment and asked employed individuals why they were not self-employed. Among those not seeking employment, health problems and an adequate income were the main reasons given. Among those not seeking to be self-employed, income was also referred to, as was job-security and risk-awareness, followed by the question "it is too late?" In their conclusions, the authors state that starting a firm may not be the dream of so many: the most fulfilling alternatives "might not be connected to the formal economy at all" (p. 898). They also report that access to equity capital for older individuals, often stated as a comparative advantage, is available only for a minority.

In addition to research attention to incentives for choosing entrepreneurship, the alternative motives (push and pull) are often investigated (van Gelderen et al., 2015). These are also age dependent and related to ageism in markets, mainly the labor market. Push factors are more relevant under the age of retirement but not entirely so. Push turns out to be explicit for the elderly who experience negative attitudes and discrimination in the labor market. They are pushed into entrepreneurship as other alternatives are locked. The push dimension becomes more relevant if individuals have an economically problematic situation. Entrepreneurship is, however, not a guaranteed means of avoiding such problems (Weber & Schaper, 2004).

In their study, Annichiarico and Grasso (2011) discuss the OWLE-project (Older Women Learning) in relation to the problems associated with getting a job when one is classified as old and with regard to discrimination following employment (Kibler & Wainwright, 2011). In those cases leading to forced self-employment, it is acknowledged that there is a distinction between those who are self-employed with no ambition to expand or even to stay in the market and those who really want to be managers or owner-managers. Age could be of importance with regard to these different standpoints.

Singh and De Noble (2003) introduced the label 'bridge-employment' for retired individuals returning to the job market. The researchers state that the older bridge-entrepreneurs are of different types depending on what they did in their younger days and their motivation for starting a business. Entrepreneurship that is for the most part a continuation of pre-retirement work is labeled 'incremental,' and entrepreneurship in occupations different from work before retirement is defined as 'punctuated.' 'Punctuated' entrepreneurs also include individuals who realize a dream they have had for many years that could at last come true; this group is labeled the 'constrained.' Finally, there are also individuals starting a business for economic reasons. They think they must become entrepreneurs because they have found that they do not have a sufficient income post-retirement. These individuals are labeled 'reluctant.' The researchers found very entrepreneurial attitudes in the 'constrained' group, while those labeled 'incremental' were seen as being 'rational,' mainly in economic dimensions. They utilize their skills and contacts, which makes things relatively uncomplicated, as both the situation and occupation are familiar. The bridge-concept is used also by Kerr and Armstrong-Stassen (2011) in an article formulating the main question as: "Do individuals want to work after the official age of retirement?"

Weber and Schaper (2004) argue that two more groups should be added to Singh and DeNoble's groups: the 'life-style-entrepreneurs' and the 'seniorpreneur.' A different position is taken by Alsos and Kolvereid (1998) and by DeBruin & Firkin (2001), suggesting that the experience of being self-employed in younger days is positive even if it was in another line of business. For these groups they suggest the label 'serial' entrepreneurs. The small-firm owners who start one more organization and continue with both (it could of course be more than two) are called 'parallel' founders and the third group—the genuine new entrepreneurs—are given the label 'novice' entrepreneurs.

The bridge-concept indicates a start and an end, moving from one position to another. We have not found any studies focusing on why older entrepreneurs leave the marketplace and what happens to the individuals or to the firm. The question concerning staying or leaving is relevant also for entrepreneurs, and this is a main theme for the following empirical sections. The situation is often different for the self-employed and for employees. The decision is completely up to the self-employed, despite the fact that it is not easy or without restrictions. Studies by Kautonen et al. (2011 and 2010) found that the entrepreneurs often wanted to leave if they could find someone to take over the enterprise. They felt deeply for the enterprise and sometimes also for their employees, the customers or the location. Most of these reasons are social rather than economic. The economic position of the elderly going into self-employment differs not just at the individual level, but also at the national and regional levels. Senior entrepreneurship, therefore, has national characteristics, an aspect underlined by Kautonen et al. (2008). Weber and Schaper (2004) compare younger and older entrepreneurs. The dimensions of the comparison are: incentives, criteria for success, dependence of different resources and construction of policy for support of entrepreneurs and small and medium-sized firms. One important finding is that there are differences between older entrepreneurs who have been entrepreneurs all their lives and new entrepreneurs.

Age, entrepreneurship and gender

Entrepreneurship has a male label, and many of the characteristics connected to old age are opposite those connected to entrepreneurship. Older women have a double disadvantage relating to the image of entrepreneurship. Few studies focus on old women as entrepreneurs, but many researchers studying old owner-managers and the self-employed find and report differences between men and women without analyzing them (Kerr & Armstrong-Stassen, 2011; Kautonen, 2008; Kautonen et al., 2008).

Some studies focusing on incentives register differences between women and men. That women may have more economic incentives than men is also stated in official reports (OECD). In their report from the OWLE program, Roberts and Reynard (2011) tell us "many women desperately need an additional income." Other women-specific reasons are connected to family obligations that increase or decrease over time (Weber & Schaper, 2004).

The studies presented do not give an unambiguous picture; some show that old women are more interested in self-employment as a bridge-alternative than men (Kerr & Armstrong-Stassen, 2011; Quinn & Kozy, 1996). This indicates that the models of incentives for entrepreneurs are hard to apply to old entrepreneurs and that the age-specific models and concepts are hard to apply to old women. In this regard, research seems to be in an early stage, or could it be that the mixtures of pull and push are so individual, and the relevant circumstances so many, that the possibilities of building models and concepts are hard to achieve?

The Swedish case

The findings and discussions that were introduced in relation to the international debate on age, gender and entrepreneurship are relevant also in the Swedish case. As discussed, national contexts are important for understanding entrepreneurial behavior. This means that we have to consider how age, gender and entrepreneurship are handled and elaborated in a Scandinavian welfare state. Sweden scores high on international rankings on equality between women and men (United Nations). Labor market position is one of the dimensions used in the index. Swedish women participate in the labor market to a considerable extent—almost as much as Swedish men do. High levels of participation in the labor market are to a great extent enabled by a public childcare system available to all—an important part of the social democratic welfare state (Esping-Andersen & Korpi, 1987), accordingly labeling Sweden the women-friendly-welfare state (Hernes, 1987). Both the label and the statement 'women-friendly' have been debated in research and politics. One of the main discussions concerns the inequalities that still persist. Women, as a group, earn less than men, and occupations dominated by women have lower salaries than occupations dominated by men. Men are over-represented as managers despite the fact that women outnumber men as students at university (Statistics Sweden). Does this challenge the traditional gender segregation over the long term?

As a consequence of lower wages, women get lower pensions when they retire, as the Swedish system is connected to work in the market. Many women have been working part-time at least when their children were young. The expression 'the poor elderly' defined from EU standards concerns almost only women (*Pensionsmyndigheten*). These old women get public support to make it possible for them to have a home of their own. The retirement age is 65 to 67 years. In practice, the average age of retirement is lower, around 58 years. The reasons for leaving the labor market are often health-related.

The Swedish labor market is gender-segregated with regard to both occupations and employers. The expression 'the women-friendly-welfare state' was also justified by the fact that women are largely employed by public sector organizations—most often municipalities responsible for the care of the elderly and children. Also, New Public Management has been introduced and adapted in Sweden in the last decades, changing the labor market especially for women. The aim is to create a market of private suppliers to replace government action (Sundin & Tillmar, 2010; Sundin, 2011).

Entrepreneurship and self-employment among women have been on the political agenda for some decades (Holmquist & Sundin, 2015). The expansion of these programs has been described as an expression of the age of entrepreneurship (Global Entrepreneurship Monitor) and also connected to the New Public Management in its national and local interpretations. Around 30 percent of the self-employed and owner managers are women. The gender-segregation of the labor market in employment is not unique to Sweden: women working as owners and owner-managers are also working in different positions from their male colleagues. The Swedish position on the entrepreneurship score is seen in Figure 22.1, which shows a general pattern that men are more involved in entrepreneurship than women, regardless of the overall rate of entrepreneurship in a country. Figure 22.1 also shows that Sweden is at the lower end regarding engagement in entrepreneurship.

Age and ageism

The international glorification of youth is also evident in Sweden (Krekula, 2009). Individuals with disadvantaging characteristics such as the 'wrong sex,' 'wrong ethnicity,' 'wrong class' and 'wrong age' perceive age as the most negative and repressive aspect, a practice that has been labeled '*ålderism*,' the Swedish translation of ageism, by leading Swedish scholars in the field (Andersson, 2012). Ageism as manifested in organizational practice is essential to decisions made about staying in working life (Nilsson, 2013).

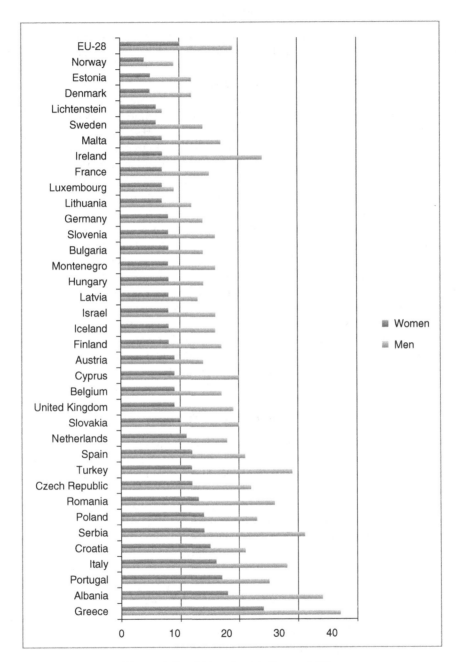

Figure 22.1 Entrepreneurship rate (of total labor force) in Europe 2012

Source: EU—Statistical Data on Women Entrepreneurs in Europe.

Age and entrepreneurship in Sweden

Method

In this chapter we study age and entrepreneurship in Sweden.[1] The statistics in this chapter have been derived from the large database, LISA, updated yearly with demographic data. We consider data up to 2010. In addition, a number of interviews were conducted with entrepreneurs and experts on entrepreneurship, age and the labor market. These interviews are mainly used for discussion and interpretation, as well as in the formulation of questions for further study and analysis.

Using the database as a primary source means that the definitions of 'entrepreneurship' and 'age' are a given. Establishing an organization that works in a market is the inclusion criteria used in the international GEM studies (Global Entrepreneurship Monitor) and also in the LISA database. Whether these individuals are entrepreneurial in other more action-oriented meanings of the word has to be considered alongside other methods, such as interviews. In LISA, the classification of individuals is made with reference to the main source of income coming from the market, which means that many part-time entrepreneurs will be excluded. It also means that a change in one dimension could follow from changes in another. As an example: an individual is employed and runs a firm of her own for a few hours a week. Before retirement this individual is classified as employed, and after retiring, as self-employed because the salary no longer exists. As a consequence, the individual is classified as an owner-manager in the statistics although nothing has changed in her enterprise activities, even if her pension is higher than the income from the enterprise.

Age (year of birth) is what the database gives us. Definitions of old age are, in the labor market as well as other markets, under constant negotiation and contextualized. After discussions with both researchers and key informants in different organizations, we have chosen to use 50 years of age as a starting point for our empirical study.

How many and at what age

The findings presented in the international literature on age, entrepreneurship and gender are interesting and often contradictory as they have different empirical bases as well as different theoretical perspectives. Here we will present findings from Sweden where the database used gives us the possibility to investigate over time, for age cohorts and for industry. Before presenting our own findings, we will present an international overview of entrepreneurs by age and gender in Europe by way of reference to the Swedish case.

As can be seen in Figure 22.2, when we look at age distributions for men and women, there are considerable similarities between self-employed men and women in Europe. Only a few percent of the self-employed are really young—in fact the oldest group (65+ years) is more than double the youngest. However, what is really interesting in these figures is the high proportion of men and women older than 50 years among the self-employed; close to 40 percent of the self-employed are in this age bracket. This means that the group we are discussing in this chapter, old entrepreneurs, actually constitutes almost half of all entrepreneurs, and we stress that this applies to women as well as men.

There is a clear similarity between the old self-employed women and men in Sweden: there is an increase in entrepreneurship around the age of retirement (in Sweden 65–67 years) as seen in Figure 22.3. The peak in the rate of entrepreneurship starts after 60, returning to pre-retirement levels around age 75, with a maximum at age 67. The self-employed also stay longer in the labor market than the employed do.

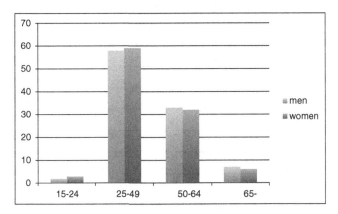

Figure 22.2 Entrepreneurship by age and gender in Europe, 2012
Source: EU—Statistical Data on Women Entrepreneurs in Europe.

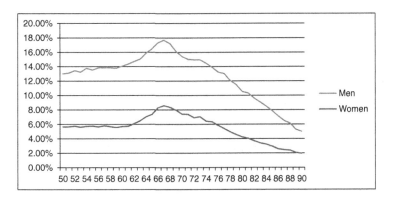

Figure 22.3 Proportion of entrepreneurs, by age and gender
Source: Statistics Sweden.

Although there is a reduction in the number of self-employed with age, the relative importance of self-employment increases. The increase in numbers and percentages from the age of 60 can be interpreted with concepts and findings from the international literature but must also be understood based on the Swedish context. The economic situation for a retired person often makes it important to work until the official age of retirement. For the unemployed, with little hope of finding a new employer, to establish an enterprise could be a way to stay in the market. To establish an enterprise could also be a way to prepare for an active working life after the official age of retirement. This decision could also be accelerated by age discrimination in organizations. These two alternatives are followed by different actions after retirement. The ones aiming at constructing a temporary solution will leave, similar to the employees, after the official age of retirement, while the second group can 'take it easy.' As seen from the diagram, these alternatives are, on a group level, similar for women and men.

From our data we also find that both women and men who are self-employed leave industries where physical strength is needed relatively early, as illustrated in Figures 22.4 and 22.5.

These industries are dominated by one gender at all ages, and work in such industries is physically demanding. As illustrated, the ones leaving self-employment with increasing age

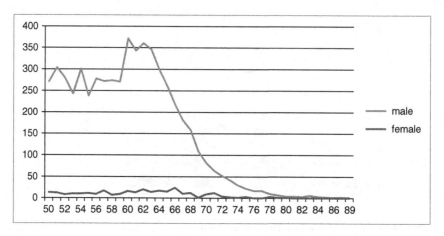

Figure 22.4   Number of entrepreneurs in building, by age and gender
Source: Statistics Sweden.

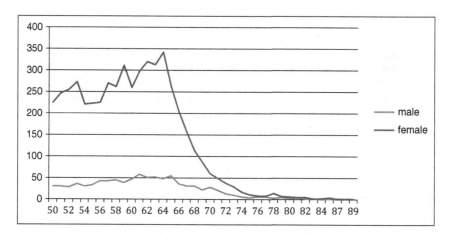

Figure 22.5   Number of entrepreneurs in hairdressing, by age and gender
Source: Statistics Sweden.

belong to the dominant sex, while the minority sex, the women in the building and construction sector and the men in hairdressing, stay on to a greater extent. It can also be noted that the decrease seems to start at the lower end of the retirement-age group (60+) in both these sectors. It is the same in other physically demanding sectors like restaurant work where both men and women leave from age 50 onwards.

From this perspective we see no difference between men and women. Older women, both under and over retirement age, are under-represented as owner-managers. Women seem to continue working longer than men as their rate increases from 30% among the 50-year-olds to 35 percent among the 80-year-olds. This could be seen as a sign that women as owner-managers are just as dedicated to their enterprise as men.

As Table 22.1 and Figure 22.6 show, the percentage of women is lower than that of men across age groups and across industries. The gender segregation on the labor market is similar to that of entrepreneurs and the self-employed. The distribution in the sectors is as expected.

Table 22.1 Share of women and men as self-employed in seven age-cohorts

Age	Share of women	Share of men
50	30	70
55	30	70
60	29	71
65	31	69
70	33	67
75	34	66
80	35	65

Source: Statistics Sweden.

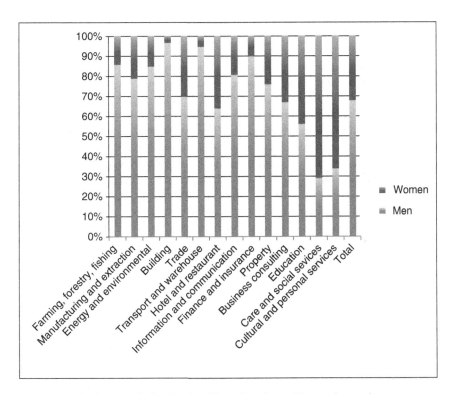

Figure 22.6 Distribution over industries for self-employed over 50 years by gender
Source: Statistics Sweden.

The level of gender segregation on the labor market, including entrepreneurs, changes little as people age. For both men and women, farming and forestry are the industries with the strongest increase over age, from 3.4% for the youngest women (20–34 years) to 16.8% for 65+ years, and for men from 6.5% to 24.6% from 20 to 34 years to 65+ years. For women, personal and cultural services are dominating in the younger age groups, up to age 54. The care industry is also expanding with age. Services to business (consultants) also increase with age for men, while in all other industries, especially in the construction of houses, it decreases. Partly, these changes depend on the registration of activities rather than on genuine changes in activities. The transformation from being an employee to being self-employed could be registered as a change from a specific occupation to a consultancy.

On the group level, it is clear that entrepreneurship and self-employment are not challenging the gender segregation of the labor market. It could even be argued that it seems to be the other way around. Our studies of employment agencies offering seniors for work show that gender stereotypes are strong arguments used in marketing (Cedersund et al., 2014).

One of the criteria for professions is that individuals can be self-employed as well as employed in the Swedish system (as is the case in most other countries). For quite some time, many of the professions have held a substantial share of women, and women are dominating amongst the student population. However, men are dominating among the total number of individuals with enterprises and working in the private market (although publicly funded). Men also move from public sector employees to owner-managers at a younger age.

Age, gender and entrepreneurship—Swedish women and men being older entrepreneurs

We conclude this chapter with a discussion on the Swedish findings, based on concepts and theories from the international literature and on our studies of older entrepreneurs. 'Push' and 'pull' are two of the main concepts used. From the aggregate figures we see that Swedish women (and men) are entrepreneurs and self-employed to a lesser extent, although they are in the labor market to a greater extent. The reasons for this are under debate; GEM data partly show that countries such as Sweden have lower levels of entrepreneurship than less-developed regions, with some attributing the lower entrepreneurship rate to the construction of the welfare state. Whether this is interpreted as good or bad is connected to political priorities. The age distribution of Swedish entrepreneurs seems to be similar to the rest of Europe—albeit slightly skewed towards the older age groups.

Push and pull are expressions used to represent the reasons for moving towards entrepreneurship for individuals of all ages. In the Scandinavian welfare system, the economic benefits and the pension system for retired persons mean that economic push seems to disappear with the age of retirement. There are old people, mainly women, with economic problems, but these problems are not typically solved by self-employment in the marketplace. The social security system and recruitment companies seem to be more common solutions. With the double burden of age and gender, this may be a rational conclusion.

For those under the age of 67, the situation is different. The priority for work, both from politics and culture, puts pressure on individuals—both women and men. Push and necessity are found in our interviews, as in the example of women cleaners who banded together when their unit closed down after contracting with a private cleaning supplier for the municipality. "I should not employ myself," said one of the unwilling entrepreneurs. For these women, the years as owner-managers are a bridge to retirement. In our interviews, we also found men who were pushed into retirement by younger colleagues who made them feel too old and uncomfortable in the organization. "I refuse to be managed by these juniors," says a 60-year-old IT consultant who found he was no longer asked to serve as project-leader.

The pushed men we interviewed continued as self-employed after retirement. In these cases, it is a mixture of push and pull, as is the case for some of our interviewed women. Let us cite just one woman who was asked to leave her employment due to reorganization. She described how she immediately said, "Sure—give me the papers—I will sign!" She received some severance pay and also was given advice by an organization owned by her union: her decision and position were economically safe. This woman then went on to found a business that was something completely new. From being an administrator at an industrial company, she moved to working with horses. She planned to do that "for the rest of her life"—a phrase associated with others who had been self-employed before retirement age.

For the individuals older than 67, push reasons seem to be non-existent in Sweden. We have, however, found entrepreneurs who feel obliged—if not pushed—to be entrepreneurs by their obligation 'to society.' For example, one woman stated that her way of teaching language is unique. Therefore, given the immigrant situation, she unfortunately must continue to teach other teachers. We also interviewed a man, a reformer, who is continuing his work with wind-power. He was formerly a teacher in technology—now after retirement he works at what he previously did but on a part-time basis. He was not constrained before, but he states that the knowledge needed to do the work he does "takes a life-time to obtain." These are examples of individuals with long-term perspectives on knowledge and competence.

In other papers (Sundin, 2015) we have focused on capital, as this seems to be of great importance in many sectors. To buy equipment and real estate is often the starting point for self-employment. Derogatorily expressed, it could be described as a way 'to buy a job'—but positively expressed, it could be described both as a good investment and as an activity making use of competence and knowledge-demanding experience. As men have more capital, they are dominating this group. Many of these interviewed persons could be labeled punctuated and constrained at first glance, but with a closer look, the punctuated label persists while the lifestyle concept also seems to be adequate. Perhaps we need a new concept emphasizing competence, knowledge and experience that are a part of the mature entrepreneur experience.

Not all of our interviewed persons are reformers. Some just want to go on working as long as they feel healthy, and they "do not want to take care of my grandchildren." The easiest way to accomplish this seems to be to go on with their work tasks for their former employer or find new work. They are incremental entrepreneurs who use an enterprise as a bridge to a new life as retired individuals. We also have found indications of family businesses newly created by seniors. The examples we have come across are innovative in many respects.

A conclusion is that the construction of the welfare state is of great importance for all citizens and may be more so for women than for men—and more so for elderly than for the middle aged. We have discussed this from an entrepreneurial perspective. Heterogeneity is a key impression and is made possible by collective solutions as often discussed by feminist researchers. Moreover, old entrepreneurs, both individuals and groups, challenge many of the negative assumptions about age—but not, it seems, gender labels.

Research directions

While the intersection of gender and entrepreneurship is an expanding research field, research on age, gender and entrepreneurship is modest, and so is research on age and entrepreneurship. The fact that it is modest is, as such, not an argument for an increase—but our findings indicate that there is much to learn from older entrepreneurs, especially if studies are conducted with a gender perspective. The studies so far also indicate that the ideas of 'older' and 'old' are constantly negotiated. As a starting point, we should distinguish between categories of older entrepreneurs. The official age of retirement is an important line of demarcation, but our research findings suggest additional categorization is valuable. Although the official age of retirement varies between nations, we are convinced that comparisons from an age, gender and entrepreneurship perspective will give great contribution to our understanding of comparative welfare regimes.

So far, studies on older individuals in the labor market, including entrepreneurship, have mainly been conducted using quantitative methods. To really determine the incentives, images, identities, etc. involved, we recommend qualitative methods, such as interviews and interactive discussion groups. Through qualitative methods, and open minds, we may also cross over sector demarcation lines challenging labels of innovations, in both concepts and practice. For example, we think that despite the presentation of social enterprises and social entrepreneurship as something new, they may actually be practices that have been in existence for a long time—just now including consideration of age groups, a concept often excluded.

Our studies and others make a contribution to the research fields of entrepreneurship, age and gender. This contribution represents a challenge to current understanding in these research fields and therefore creates a path to political conclusions. Through our studies, we have already found several interesting things. First, what is presented as general truths on entrepreneurship are restricted to only some age groups. Second, entrepreneurship is not a way to escape hierarchies, and power systems like class and gender seem to harden over the age of those involved. Third, old/older is a designation that needs to be divided into subgroups since there is a large heterogeneity in this group. Fourth, age and entrepreneurship are gendered concepts. In conclusion, it is our ambition to further study how age, gender and entrepreneurship are realized, separately and in interaction, as well as in processes over time.

Note

1 The authors are members of a research group studying older entrepreneurs. The research group also consists of Professor Elisabeth Cedersund, NISAL (National Institute for the Study of Ageing and Later Life); Associate Professor Martin Klinthäll and ec.mag. Gunilla Rapp, all at Linköping University. The research group leader is Professor Elisabeth Sundin. The project is financed by grants from the Jan Wallander and Tom Hedelius Foundation, and from the Tore Browaldhs Foundation.

References

Ahl H.J. (2002) *The making of the female entrepreneur: A discourse analysis of research texts on women's entrepreneurship.* PhD thesis, JIBS.

Alsos G.A. & Kolvereid L. (1998) The business gestation process of novice, serial, and parallel business founders. *Entrepreneurship Theory and Practice, 22*(4): 101–114.

Andersson L. (2012) *Ålderism.* Studentlitteratur.

Annichiarico A. & Grasso G. (2011) *OWLE 50+. Final Evaluation Review. An exploitation paper to illustrate the main findings and to suggest possible course for future action. Long Life Learning Programme.* London Metropolitan University.

Audretsch D.B. (2009) The entrepreneurial society. *The Journal of Technology Transfer, 34*(3), 245–254.

Bögenhold D. (2004) Creative destruction and human resources. *Small Business Economics, 22*(4): 167–177.

Bögenhold D. & Fachinger U. (2007) Micro-firms and the margin of entrepreneurship: The restructuring of the labour market. *Entrepreneurship and Innovation, 8*(4): 281–292.

Bruni A., Gherardi S. & Poggio B. (2004) Doing gender, doing entrepreneurship: An ethnographic account of intertwined practices. *Gender, Work & Organization, 11*(4): 406–429.

Cedersund E., Holmquist C., Klinthäll M., Rapp E. & Sundin E. (2014) *Staffing Agencies in Later Working Life.* Gender, Work and Organization 8th Biennial International Interdisciplinary Conference.

Curran J. & Blackburn R.A. (2001) Older People and the Enterprise Society: Age and Self-Employment Propensities. *Work, Employment Society, 15*(4): 889–902.

Davis P.S. & Harveston P.D. (1998) The influence of family on the family business succession process: A multi-generational perspective. *Entrepreneurship theory and practice, 22*(1): 31–54.

De Bruin A. & Firkin P. (2001) *Self-employment of the older worker.* Labour Market Dynamics Research Programme, Massey University.

Duberley J., Carmichael F. & Szmigin I. (2014) Exploring women´s retirement: Continuity, context and career transition. *Gender, Work & Organization, 21*(1): 71–90.

Duncan C. & Loretta W. (2004) Never the right age? Gender and age-based discrimination in employment. *Gender, Work and Organization, 11*(1): 95–115.

Esping-Andersen G. (1990) *The Three Worlds of Welfare Capitalism.* Cambridge, Polity Press.

Esping-Andersen G. (2009) *The Incomplete Revolution. Adapting to Women's New Roles.* Oxford, Blackwell Publishers.

Esping-Andersen G. & Korpi W (1987) From poor relief to institutional welfare states: the development of scandinavian social policy. In Erikson R. et al. (eds) *The Scandinavian Model, Welfare State and Welfare Research.* New York: Sharpe.

EU (2014) Statistical Data on Women Entrepreneurs in Europe.

Eurofund (2012) *Income from Work after Retirement in the EU.* Publications Office of the European Union, Luxembourg.

Eurostat: http://ec.europa.eu/eurostat.

Fabisiak J. & Prokurat S. (2011) Age management as a tool for the demographic decline in the 21st century: an overview of its characteristics. *Journal of Entrepreneurship, Management and Innovation, 8*(4): 83–96.

Fineman S. (2011) *Organizing Age.* Oxford University Press.

Global Entrepreneurship Monitor (GEM) www.gemconsortium.org.

Halford S., Kukarenko N., Lotheringen A.T. & Obstfelder A. (2015) Technical change and the un/troubling of gendered ageing in healthcare work. *Gender, Work & Organization, 22*(5): 495–509.

Hareven T.K. (1995) Changing images of aging and the social construction of the life course. In Featherstone A. (ed) *Images of Aging Cultural Representation of Later Life.* Routledge.

Hernes H. (1987) *Welfare State and Women Power. Essays in State Feminism.* Norwegian University Press.

Holmquist C. & Sundin E. (2002) *Företagerskan: Om kvinnor och entreprenörskap.* SNS förlag.

Holmquist C. & Sundin E. (2015) *25 år med kvinnors företagande. Från osynligt till drivkraft för tillväxt.* Tillväxtverket, Stockholm.

Kadefors R. & Johansson H. (2012) Employers attitudes towards older workers and obstacles and opportunities for the older unemployed to reenter working life. *Nordic Journal of Working Life Studies, 2*(3): 29–47.

Kautonen T. (2008) Understanding the older entrepreneur. Comparing third age and prime age entrepreneurs in Finland. *International Journal of Business Science and Applied Management, 3*(3): 3–13.

Kautonen T. (2012) Do age-related social expectations influence entrepreneurial activity in later life? *The International Journal of Entrepreneurship and Innovation, 3*(3): 179–187.

Kautonen T., Down S. & South L. (2008) Enterprise support for older entrepreneurs: The case of PRIME in the UK. *International Journal of Entrepreneurial Behavior & Research, 14*(2): 85–101.

Kautonen T., Down S., Welter F., Vainio P., Palmroos J., Althoff K. & Kolb S. (2010) "Involuntary self-employment" as a public policy issue: a cross-country European review. *International Journal of Entrepreneurial Behavior & Research, 16*(2): 112–129.

Kautonen T., Hytti U., Bögenhold D. & Heinonen J. (2012) Job satisfaction and retirement age intentions in Finland. Self-employed versus salary earners. *International Journal of Manpower, 33*(4): 424–440.

Kautonen T. & Minniti M. (2014) 'Fifty is the new thirty': ageing well and start-up activities. *Applied Economics Letters, 21*(16): 1161–1164.

Kautonen T., Tornikoski E.T. & Kibler E. (2011) Entrepreneurial intentions in the third age: the impact of perceived age norms. *Small Business Economics, 31*(2): 219–234.

Kerr G. & Armstrong-Stassen M. (2011) The bridge to retirement, older workers' engagement in post-career entrepreneurship and wage-and-salary employment. *Journal of Entrepreneurship, 20*(1): 55–76.

Kibler E.T. & Wainwright T. (2011) *Who are you calling old? Negotiating the 'deviant' levels of older self-employed workers.* Paper presented at the RENT-Conference.

Kovalainen A. & Sundin E. (2012) Entrepreneurship in public organizations. In Hjorth D. (ed.) *Handbook on Organizational Entrepreneurship.* Edward Elgar.

Krekula C. (2007) The intersection of age and gender: Reworking gender theory and social gereontology. *Current Sociology, 55*(2): 155–171.

Krekula C. (2009) Age-coding. On age based practices and distinction. *International Journal of Ageing and Later Life, 4*(2): 7–31.

Krekula C., Riach K., & Loretto W. (2013) Call for papers: Problematizing gendered ageing in the new economy. *Gender, Work and Organization, 20*(2): 216–217.

Liang J. & Luo B. (2012) Towards a discourse shift in social gereontology. From successful aging to harmonious aging. *Journal of Aging Studies, 26*(3): 327–334.

Lykke N. (2010) *Feminist Studies: A Guide to Intersectional Theory, Methodology and Writing.* London: Routledge.

Nilsson K. (2013) *To work or not to work in an extended working life? Factors in working and retirement decisions.* Lund University, Faculty of Medicine Doctoral Dissertation Series.

Ozawa M.L. & Terry Y. (2009) Men who work at age 70 or older. *Journal of Gerontological Social Work, 45*(4): 41–63.

Pleau R. & Shauman K. (2013) Trends and correlates of post-retirement employment, 1977–2009. *Human Relations, 66*(1): 113–141.

Pritchard K. & Whiting R. (2014) Baby boomers and the lost generation: on the discursive construction of generations at work. *Organization Studies, 35*(11): 1605–1626.

Pritchard K. & Whiting R. (2015) Taking stock: a visual analysis of gendered aging. *Gender, Work & Organization, 22*(5): 510–528.

Quinn J.F. & Kozy M. (1996) The role of bridge jobs in the retirement transition: Gender, race, and ethnicity. *The Gerontologist, 36*(3): 363–372.

Riach K., Loretto W., & Krekula C. (2015) Gendered ageing in the new economy: Introduction to special issue. *Gender, Work & Organization, 22*(5): 437–444.

Roberts K. & Reynard A. (2011) *The OWLE50+ TOOL KIT.* London Metropolitan University. www.owle50plus.eu.

Sawchuk K.A. (1995) From gloomy to boom age identity and target marketing. In Featherstone A. (ed) *Images of Aging Cultural Representation of Later Life.* New York: Routledge.

Singh G. & De Noble A. (2003) Early retirees as the next generation of entrepreneurs. *Entrepreneurship Theory and Practice, 27*(3): 207–226.

Solem P.E. & Mykletun R. (2014) Ageism: a barrier to employment among older adults. Paper presented and the NWLC (Nordic Working Life Conference).

Sundin E. (2011) Entrepreneurship and the reorganization of the public sector: A gendered story. *Economic and Industrial Democracy, 32*(4): 631–653.

Sundin E. (2015) *Older as Entrepreneurs – Diversified group.* Paper presented at the Work-conference in Turku 2015.

Sundin E. & Tillmar M. (2010) Masculinization of the public sector. Local-level studies of public sector outsourcing in elder care. *International Journal of Gender and Entrepreneurship, 2*(1): 49–67.

Szinovacz M.E. & DeViney S. (2000) Marital characteristics and retirement decisions. *Research on Aging, 22*(5): 470–498.

Tudor-Sandahl P. (2009) *Den fjärde åldern.* Brombergs, Stockholm.

United Nations Human Development Reports: www.hdr.undp.org.

Van Gelderen M., Kautonen T. & Fink M. (2015) From entrepreneurial intentions to actions: Self-control and action-related doubt, fear, and aversion. *Journal of Business Venturing, 30*(5): 655–673.

Weber P. & Schaper M. (2004) Understanding the grey entrepreneur. *Journal of Enterprising Culture, 12*(2): 147–164.

Yuval-Davis N. (2006) Intersectionality and feminist politics: *European Journal of Women's Studies, 13*(3): 193–209.

INDEX

Printed in the United States
by Baker & Taylor Publisher Services